W9-CQM-617

What Is monk?

Monk is the saga of two men, James Crotty and Michael Lane (The Monks), who quit their jobs, sold everything they owned, hit the road with their cats Nurse, Nurse's Aide, and Dolly Lama, and for twelve years gallivanted across America, publishing *Monk,* the world's only mobile magazine. They traveled first in a '72 Ford Econoline van and then a 26-foot Fleetwood Bounder motor home ("the Monkmobile"), reporting on the incredible people, places, and phone booths they encountered along the way, until they drove each other crazy living in such cramped quarters, especially after New York, where one too many breakdowns wiped them clean, sending the Monks on a long backwards spin to Arkansas, where yellowing back issues of *Monk* were held captive, awaiting a quantum shift in world consciousness.

Then, suddenly, from out of the deepest darkness, came the vision of a unique guidebook series spreading like a laser beam of light across the mallified American landscape, beckoning the Monks to pick themselves up by their hoods and trust that by spreading a message of peace, love, and excellence, while continuing to live their motto of "simple, mobile, and true," all their needs would be taken care of right down to their very next carton of soy milk.

So, the journey continues. . . .

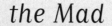

the Mad
M●NKS'
guide to
›california

by James Crotty and Michael Lane
(The Monks)

MACMILLAN • USA

MACMILLAN TRAVEL

Macmillan General Reference USA, Inc.
1633 Broadway
New York, NY 10019

ISBN 0-02-861666-9
ISSN 1520-5576

Editor: Matt Hannafin
Production Editor: Carol Sheehan
Photo Editor: Richard Fox
Design by Michele Laseau
Digital Cartography by Hans Andersson,
John Decamillis, and Roberta Stockwell
Front cover photo by Aaron Lauer

Manufactured in the United States of America

5   4   3   2   1

Note

Travel information is subject to change at any
time—and this is especially true of prices. We
therefore suggest you write or call ahead for
confirmation before making your travel plans.
The authors, editors, and publisher cannot be
held responsible for the experiences of readers
while traveling.

Preemptive Strike

Unlike guidebooks that simply recycle predictable
tourist attractions, with predictable middle-of-the-
road cultural assumptions (Fun! Kids! More Fun!),
and as opposed to the painfully lengthy, obtuse,
unwieldy if informative guides done by your average
local weekly, the *Mad Monks' Guide to California*
eschews the predictably mainstream and "alternative" to
uncover the most extraordinary travel experiences in the
Golden State.

Just because one of your favorite California haunts
doesn't appear here does not mean we haven't checked it
out. The strength of any guidebook is as much in what
is omitted as in what is included. If you feel something
is unjustly overlooked, write us at **monk@monk.com**.
Chances are, however, we've mentioned your haunt in
here somewhere, with candor, though not necessarily
with kindness.

>contents

6 ROAD TRIP: THE NORTH COAST   451

>contents

>Map List

>Map List

Credits

All intros, insets, and essays by Jim Crotty, except Mountains and Desert intros, which are by the Monks. All guide entries are by James Crotty and Michael Lane, unless otherwise indicated. "On the Road" by Michael Lane, except "On the Road with Jerry Maguire," by Jim Crotty. All interview intros by James Crotty, except "Elmer Zimmerman," "Leonard Knight," and "Border Patrol Agent K. W. Thomas," which are by Michael Lane. All interviews by the Monks. Portions of this guide have been adapted from editorial which has previously appeared in *Monk* magazine, on Monk.com, in the *USA Phrasebook* or *How to Talk American,* and on Playboy.com.

As you can imagine, a book of this magnitude requires an enormous quantity of research. While we did the bulk of the digging, we could not have been nearly as successful without the enthusiastic contributions of dozens of friends and followers. In particular, we'd like to acknowledge the extraordinary assistance provided by the following Monks and Monkettes. **General California:** the invaluable Jon "My Nephew Is On Road Rules" Burdick; Scott Egide; Don "Sasquatch" Francis; Trebor Healy; Daniel "Claypatch" Johnson; Michael Kassner; Kido the Monk; Laurel Pierce; Karen Steen; and Shira Tarrant. **Central Coast:** Victoria Lisowski and Vinny Pinto. **Central Valley:** Danny "Cuz" Crotty; Nancy "Thigpen" Glassberg; and Bob "Wolf" Quesada. **Desert:** the Center for Land Use Interpretation, one of the finest resources for Monk-worthy attractions in the world; and Scott Thomas. **Los Angeles:** Grover Babcock of Mark Lewis Radio Pictures; Adam Bregman, who deserves his own guide to L.A.; Lisa Fancher, AKA "Rhoda Penmark" (one day we'll go to San Pedro!); John Feins, for his uncanny contributions to the L.A. Road Mix; and Mark Kates, the Mack Daddy of Los Feliz and Grand Royale. **San Diego:** James "Sparkle Factor" Hebert and Ron McFee. **San Francisco:** Dak Abbe; Chris Keegan; and Sandra Watkins.

Photo Credits

All photos by the Monks or Monk Media, except as follows: Photos on pages ii, 1, 231, 309, 345, 371, 437, 442, and 560 by Aaron Lauer; page 11 courtesy of the LAPD; page 71 courtesy of the Yellin Company; pages 507 and 524 from the Wayne State University Labor Archives/Courtesy of Cesar E. Chavez Foundation; pages 23 and 44 by Mark Lewis.

Acknowledgments

Special thanks to our devoted agent, Jane Dystel; the heroic Matt Hannafin, the editor of all editors; and Doris and Jay Bouma, who gave us vital refuge during the final days of this project.

Dedication

The Monks met in California, traveled first in California, and invariably return to California. This state is the very symbol and substance of who we are. For anyone deeply interested in running with their own American Dream, California is the essential rite of passage. This book is dedicated to all those dreamers out there, young and old, who carry a little bit of California with them wherever they go. And to Jerry Maguire, the blessed child of the Golden State. We'll continue to pray for your safe journey, Jerry, if you continue to pray for our salvation.

The MONK Way:

A Preface

Indigenous peoples around the world, from Iceland to Australia, have a custom of revering specific features of the local landscape in myth and art. Though the spiritual aspect of this sanctifying process may have been lost, or at least is unconscious to locals today, the practice continues in many cities and towns across America. In fact, a key criteria in determining whether the Monks visit a locale is whether it has a vibrant mythology about itself.

While visiting local "sacred sites" may not put you in touch with the divine, as maybe the Navajo understand the term, it will put you in touch with the spirit of a place. By participating in the spirit of a place you cease to be a mere tourist, a gauche and bothersome "outsider," but, instead, make the leap to insider status, even just for a day.

Bringing to your attention these sacred, honored, and just plain representative places is what we do as Monks. We listen to the locals, we visit their favorite spots, we visit others we discover on our own, and we select those that we consider the most significant.

Of course, the notion of sacred has changed over time. We are not talking about Native American caves, hills, and buffalo here. What we are talking about are often popular icons, compelling structures or businesses that have magically survived the wrecking ball, whether because of their intrinsic aesthetic or historical value, because of their enduring commercial viability, or because of the unconditional love of the people. The state of California is filled with many examples of the latter.

You may have come to California for "entertainment." To "see the sights." After you are done reading this book, you will not see these "sights" in quite the same light. To us, travel should be transformative. When you travel with what Suzuki Roshi called "beginner's mind"—with what we call "Monk mind"—you are open to new ideas, you are vulnerable, you are committed to probing the depths of your experience, and you are willing to participate rather than just passively view. Many items chosen for this guidebook will show you something about California you may have never considered before, opening your eyes and possibly your heart. It's a sanctifying process as old as human civilization.

Serving the highest and deepest needs of your travel experience, we remain, your allies, The Monks.

>killa cali

There's california. And then there's the rest of America. Dubbed "the great exception," "an island upon the land," and "a land apart," california does appear to americans and the rest of the world as a separate nation . . .

Not only the most populous American state, with close to 35 million legal, and illegal, inhabitants (one out of every eight U.S. residents), California is also the richest, with more millionaires than any other state, and, according to the January 25, 1999, *Wall Street Journal,* a gross domestic product of $1 trillion. If California were indeed a country, its economy would rank as the eighth largest in the world. Only China, France, Germany, Italy, Japan, the U.K., and a non-California United States have larger GNPs. Strip California away from America, and the ensuing "Group of Eight" would have to include the Golden State.

According to Department of Defense records, so powerful is this state that California was awarded $18 billion in weapons contracts in 1997, more than twice that of runner-up Virginia. In addition, 40% of world Internet traffic is generated from California. In fact, California-based technology companies are a big part of the engine driving the largest peacetime U.S. economic boom in thirty years.

Of 1998's twenty top-grossing films, ALL were produced by California production companies. And all but five of the twenty top-rated TV shows for 1997/98 were produced and recorded in California, even though "E.R." was set in Chicago, and *Seinfeld, Friends,* and *NYPD Blue* were all set in New York (proving that while actors appear to live in other cities, almost every major television and film actor spends significant time working here). The five top shows that were not produced in California were CBS's *60 Minutes,* ABC's *20/20,* and three nights a week of *Dateline NBC,* prompting one California wag to state, "They ought to give Monica Lewinsky a lifetime pension."

And don't think because entertainment conglomerates like Viacom are based in New York that networks like Viacom-owned MTV do most of their work there too. The entire production staff of a show like MTV's *Road Rules* is based in L.A.

In terms of agriculture, others states can just fehgeddaboutit. Not only does California produce 87% of the nation's raisins and 94% of its almonds, but it's by far the largest state in all farm marketings—number one in crops by $10 billion over Iowa, and number two in livestock, behind only Texas. This despite the fact that the vast majority of Californians have never set foot on a farm or ranch.

California is number one in other areas too. The state has the highest point in the forty-eight states, Mount Whitney, and the lowest point on the North American continent, Death Valley, which is also the spot of the highest recorded temperature in the western hemisphere (134°). California is also number one in strawberries, lemons, national-park visitors, miles of highway, dollars spent on public education, immigrants, multiple birthings, civic orchestras, professional sports teams, roses, endangered ocean species,

Impression

"*California is America only more so.*"

—Wallace Stegner

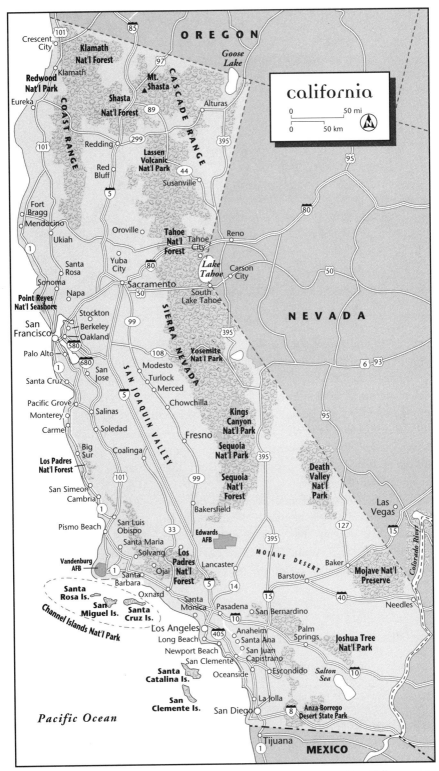

personal-injury lawyers, cat owners, convertibles, public fountains, bankruptcy filings, motor-vehicle registrations, and the consumption of Snickers bars.

While, technically, the number-one tourist destination in the world is Paris (no doubt because all those Brits can Chunnel over and back in a day) and number one in the United States is Disney World (because visitors come in packs of four or five instead of just one or two), San Francisco is a strong number two, and the L.A. region is a respectable number six. However, if you stipulate that people have to fly instead of drive, L.A. is the number one domestic flight destination in America. San Francisco is number three.

California is a state of mind. The mind that goes into fashioning most digital products, better nuclear bombs, ecological preservation, high-tech movie effects, extraordinary showmanship, pioneering cuisine, experimental music, fine wine, organic foods, deep spiritual consciousness, and the hula hoop. California not only represents the apotheosis of the American dream, it is the quintessential state of dreamers. And if America is the melting pot of the world, then California is the melting pot of America.

Trivia

The California Department of Finance projects that by the year 2040, sixty-three million people will live in California.

You will find everything that is America, for better and for worse, in California: unfathomable wealth and excess, criminal destitutes; unbridled hope and determination, profound alienation; brilliant, beautiful, and ethnically diverse communities, pathetic ignorance, degradation, and racism; an extraordinarily wide variety of rivers, mountains, coastline, valleys, and climates; plus frequent and severe droughts, fires, floods, and earthquakes. For all these reasons and more, right now, at this time in the planet's history, California is quite frankly the epicenter of creative human existence.

We Are the World, We Are the Content Providers

You can claim New York is the epicenter, but most creative New Yorkers have either moved here or are at least thinking about it. You can say Washington, D.C. is the epicenter, yet every national politician knows that not only does California have more congressional delegates than any other state (52 out of a total of 435) but many of the big-time campaign donors come out of here as well—names like Lew Wasserman (retired chairman of MCA), Gail Zappa (dental floss tycoon), Anna M. Murdoch (novelist wife of Fox Network owner Rupert Murdoch), Steven P. Jobs ("Interim CEO" of Apple Computer), Ron Burkle (Food 4 Less supermarket mogul), and Alfred Checchi (cochairman of Northwest Airlines and former gubernatorial hopeful). In addition, a disproportionately huge amount of campaign money is spent here. And now that the California primary has been moved up to early March, no presidential hopeful can hope to be successful without significantly courting the Bear Republic.

You could say London, Paris, or even Berlin is the epicenter, but most Brits, French, or Germans of talent seek to come here or are here already, mainly because of the immense California entertainment industry.

The American motion-picture services industry is an $11 billion annual business, most of it coming from California. California's "dream factories" also account for huge disproportionate shares of the $25 billion recreation and amusement services industries, the $108 billion engineering and management services industries, and the $53 billion electronic equipment industries, in which entertainment plays such a huge role. In fact, if you factor in software, the Internet, and games, entertainment

Trivia

As recently as 1970, almost 80% of California residents were non-Hispanic white. By 1990 only 57% of the state's residents were non-Hispanic white.

According to the Department of Finance, just after the turn of the century, no race or ethnic group will constitute a majority of the state's population.

Though California is probably too young to nurture much in the way of deep-seated urban antagonisms, and though the constant influx and outflow of people makes a solidified identity hard to develop, there is still a rivalry in this state between the north and the south, between No-Cal and Lo-Cal. Both Los Angeles and San Francisco claim to have pioneered "California Cuisine," claim to be the present and future of the digital revolution, and claim to have invented motion pictures. Here are these and other bones of contention between the two vortexes of California life. You will find, as a rule, that the L.A. version is slightly tackier, not as precisely elegant. However, it might have been first.

S.F. Bay Area	Los Angeles Metro
Haight Street	Venice
Fog	Smog
Acid	Cocaine
St. John Coltrane	Universal Church
Emperor Norton	Peter the Hermit
The Castro	West Hollywood
Jerry Brown	Tom Hayden
Jim Jones	Charles Manson
Jerry Garcia	Jim Morrison
Jello Biafra	Exene Cervenka
Manny the Hippie	Kato Kaelin
Murder Can Be Fun	Ben Is Dead
Mitchell Brothers	Menendez Brothers
O.J. (the early years)	O.J. (the Hertz years)
Skywalker Studios	Disney Imagineering
Robin Williams	Billy Crystal
Bobby Seale	Geronimo Pratt
The Gold Rush	*The Gold Rush*
Parking is HELL	Parking
left-turn signals	traffic flow
Al Davis	Al Davis
dehumidifier	air conditioner
Grace Slick	Courtney Love
Moonies	Scientologists
Herb Caen	Steve Harvey
Frisco	La La Land
Colma	Forest Lawn
The Mission	Los Feliz
Jack Boulware	Johnny Angel

S.F. Bay Area	Los Angeles Metro
The Alioto Family	The Chandler Family
Willigan's Island	Gilligan's Island
Portals	Studios
IPO's	Screenplays
Melvin Belli	Johnny Cochran
Harvey Milk	Rodney King
White Night	The Riots
Free Love	Free Parking
Snobbery	Flattery
Chinese	Koreans
Zen Center	Yoga centers
Werner Ehrhard	L. Ron Hubbard
Culture	Climate
Loma Prieta	Northridge
Niners	Lakers
Tahoe	Mammoth
Coit Tower	Capitol Records
Lucas	Spielberg
Vineyards	Orchards
Chez Panisse	Michael's
Fisherman's Wharf	Fisherman's Village
Silicon Alley	Silicone breasts
North Beach	Sunset Strip
SLA	NWA
Oakland	Long Beach
Fifth Generation Chinese	Fifth Generation Hispanics
Irish whiskey	Sex on the Beach
smoke-free bars	ostensibly smoke-free bars
Pretty, pale	Surgically enhanced, tan
Cable cars	Convertibles
Sharks	Ducks
sequoia trees	Joshua trees
Mount Tamalpais	Mount Baldy
Kerouac	Bukowski
Alternative Tentacles Records	SST Records
SUV Overkill	SUV OVERKILL!!
1906 Earthquake and fire	Stealing Owens Valley water
Jumping off Golden Gate Bridge	Overdosing at Marmont
Nob Hill	Hancock Park
Excessive smugness	Excessive self-loathing
The good life	The car

"The American people have assigned California a special role: to seek out the American future, to test it, to try its options, rejecting what doesn't work and building upon what does."

—Dr. Kevin Starr, State Librarian of California

products have surpassed food and aircraft as America's most lucrative export. A good majority of those entertainment products are generated right here in California, the Entertainment Supermarket to the World.

In addition, California ranks second in Fortune 500 companies, just a few behind New York, but includes Hewlett-Packard, Intel, Disney, Ingram Micro, Apple Computer, Sun Microsystems, Gap, Mattel, and Times Mirror, which shows how well the California economy is likely to do in the new millennium. In fact, at this point, California is so self-sufficient it really could secede, except for one thorny problem: water. But let's not talk about that.

As long as the water holds out (that is, as long as the state can beg, borrow, or steal the water from other states), and as long as the earthquake faults that line the state remain relatively quiescent, California will rule America, both culturally and economically.

>>>•<<<

The problem for the visitor to this large and dense place is that he or she usually comes armed with a bushel full of clichés, and a rather foggy set of expectations. As a result, the fruit of his or her visit is often bottomless disappointment. While California is truly the land of promise, it is also the ruthless destroyer of dreams. Or at least it appears to be ruthless. That actually is another cliché. California doesn't so much crush dreams, it just forgets about them, or moves on to the next dream. Continuity and solidity are not the strong suits of a place built on such a shaky physical foundation.

But if we buy the argument that reality is a shaky proposition to begin with, then we can forgive California. And, instead of clinging to our old worn dream, invent a new one. That's the California way.

If you go with that sort of open and adventurous attitude, that Monkish "beginner's mind," then you will already have attained the very spirit of this state. And you will then begin to appreciate what this guidebook is all about: bringing forth from the nooks and crannies the extraordinary treasures waiting to be discovered beneath all the speed, hype, and density. Follow the carefully conceived path we have laid before you, and you will be led into the true ephemeral beauty of this Golden State of dreamers.

Have a nice stay.

Modus **Monkerandi:**

A Subaru, a Dream, and a Headless Doll

We broke this book into eight regions because, well, like, you know. We really wanted to break it into seven, our favorite number, esoteric mystics' favorite number, probably Heaven's Gate's favorite number, but seven was too small for our purposes, and logic and topography dictated about twelve regions, and we weren't paid enough to write scintillating prose about twelve regions of California. In that fantasy commencement address that made the urban legend circuit a few years ago, the faux Vonnegut (*Chicago Tribune* columnist Mary Schmich) warned students to "Live in New York City once, but leave before it makes you hard . . . Live in Northern California once, but leave before it makes you soft." We'd grown soft. So, we settled on eight. Definitely not our favorite number, and not as ambitious as twelve, but, hey, you learn early on in this game.

We forgot *what* you learn early on in this game. It's too sunny out here.

>>>•<<<

The eight regions of *The Mad Monks' Guide to California* are **San Francisco** (including the East Bay), **the North Coast** (including Marin), **the Mountains** (including all of the Shasta Cascades, the Gold Country, and the High Sierras), **the Deserts, the Central Valley** (a big stretch of real estate we don't expect many of

The Monkmobile

The Subaru

you to visit, though you should), **the Central Coast** (including most of Silicon Valley), **Los Angeles** (including Orange County and the Inland Empire), and **San Diego.**

We drove the state primarily in one vehicle, our 1989 red Subaru Legacy, bought—yes, bought—from Scott Thomason Ford in Gladstone, Oregon. Our Subaru had this colorful doll tied to the front grill, which always caught the eye of passing pedestrians. This was because the doll had this insanely goofy grin, a long pencil thin neck, a gangly body, and a tuft of pointy hair sticking out the top. Plus, it made this hilarious quacking sound when you squeezed it. The Doll was given to us by Don "the Riverkeeper" Francis of Portland, Oregon, who was originally given the doll by a former girlfriend, who said, and we quote, "Whenever you get mad at me, hit the doll." Well, Don the Riverkeeper is not a violent man. He's a Sensitive New Age Guy (a SNAG), which means he takes out his anger in more indirect ways. So, one day, while very perturbed with his former girlfriend, Don decided he should wire the doll to our front grill. This gave us a wacky little hood ornament, which, in the absence of the broken down Monkmobile, would grab the attention of passers-by while slowly exorcising the demons of Don the Riverkeeper's former relationship.

However, from the very start, the Doll was a source of cognitive dissonance. For without the garish Monkmobile we were enjoying our newfound anonymity. The Doll invariably elicited big yuks from the passing multitudes, who expected the occupants of said vehicle to be as wacky as their wacky hood ornament. In order to snuff out the expectations of the passing throng, we would routinely give glum homicidal looks as a show of defiance.

No doubt mirroring our internal conflict about having a gangly pencil-necked doll wired to our grill, the elements conspired with California's spaced out drivers to cause the Doll to literally lose his head, and thus his quack, in a series of front-end collisions. However, the rest of the Doll never dislodged from the grill (ole Don the SNAG wired him *tight*).

True to Monk form, we've now grown used to our ugly, headless, silent hood ornament and are proud to introduce him as the tattered mascot of this guidebook.

When you think you can't go on, when you can't visit one more attraction, think of that Monk doll. That headless Monk doll, who to this day is still attached to the front bumper of our red Subaru, looking weirder than ever, beat to heck too, but still gaining the attention of passing pedestrians, and, most importantly, still at it, still ambling down the road, leading the way to our next destination, a martyr to broken hearts everywhere.

Like the Monks, the Doll endures.

LONG LIVE THE DOLL!!

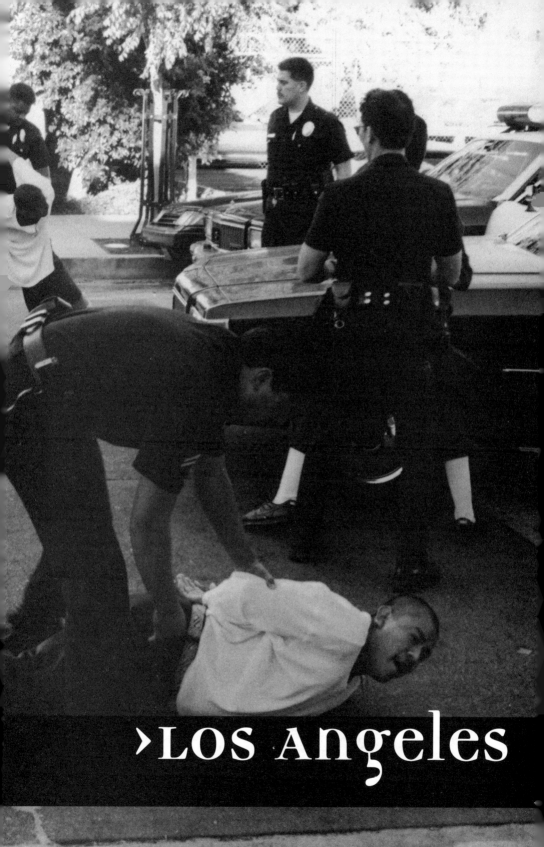

›LOS Angeles

Los Angeles: A Schizophrenic View

Despite its current cachet, Los Angeles still remains the evil urban empire in our collective national psyche. The land of riots, smog, gangs, congestion, ethnic rivalry, poor urban planning, tabloid murder, surgically enhanced (or disfigured) celebrities, and, of course, police brutality. L.A. is America's demon nightmare city because of the temporary triumph of the anti-L.A. mythos. Temporary because, as we show here, L.A. is on the rebound. And in time the L.A. anti-myth will once again give way to its more optimistic and enduring counterpart.

Until the last decade or two, the prevailing myth was that L.A. was the golden sunbaked land of opportunity. Paradise. The American Dream. Even though Nathanael West, Raymond Chandler, James Cain, Joan Didion, and other writers from the 1930s through the 1980s tried hard to debunk this myth, the legend proved quite resilient—withstanding irrefutable facts about urban decay and tragic ill-fated dreams of stardom. Even the Watts riots of 1965 didn't radically alter this perception. There were always people willing to see L.A. as the promised land of economic and spiritual salvation.

But the 1991 taped beating of "motorist" Rodney King changed all that, and in the ensuing riots the utopia myth finally gave way to its dark shadowy alter ego: the "L.A. as Hell" myth. According to this myth, L.A. is a series of long distractions that never return to a central argument, spreading out like a bad cancer, leaving exhaust, tract homes, and collective anomie in its wake. This myth contends that Los

Angelenos are escapists, insulated within the confines of their pricey automobiles and gated villas, hiding behind tinted glass and dark shades, unwilling to face the difficult problems of their city. This myth posits that behind the smiles, tans, and casual friendliness is a naked cruelty, a place and a people so devoid of heart, so unabashedly selfish, it defies belief. This myth sees Angelenos as shockingly shallow, consumed with image more than substance, where every seemingly authentic feeling is just another statement, another pose, another "take." In little ways, from *L.A. Story* to *Falling Down* to *The Player*, films have helped to give credence to this L.A. as Hell myth.

But as Monks we've had trouble swallowing this anti-L.A. myth from the very start. Every day we've found evidence that refutes the popular sentiment—examples of goodness, originality, and mindfulness that appear just as we're about to swallow the party-line pessimism. We've found a city blessed with surprisingly varied weather; invigorating and eclectic nature; decent, kind, and often intelligent people; negotiable traffic; increasing environmental awareness; and fantastic economic opportunity. Yes, L.A. has its hellholes, potholes, and assholes, but nothing worse than almost any other city of comparable size in the world. A far cry from its nightmare image.

So before you go dissin' The Big Nipple, listen to the Monk men and some very cogent reasons why the City of Angels scores big in our book.

Thirty-Three Reasons Why We Love L.A., 1999

1. **L.A. is the world's great melting pot.** New York is a distant second. At any time in this city there are dozens of radically different cultures and subcultures completely immersed in their own orbits. Rich to poor, Zulu to Kampuchean, Christian fundamentalist to Satanic cultist, straight to gay, L.A. is an 80-theater multiplex where a whole new culture awaits just a door away. If you get bored with one, just drive to another; it all comes with a single admission. Of course, each enclave doesn't have a clue as to what makes the other tick, which makes centralized control monstrously difficult. But that's all the better for personal freedom of movement and expression, though problematic in terms of creating a "common culture."

2. **Contrary to Marxist myth, L.A. is *not* a police state.** Though the number of officers on duty has increased 26% in the last few years, L.A. still has the lowest police officer per resident ratio of the six largest U.S. cities. The standard argument is that Los Angeles police are Gestapo-like bullies bent on pummeling average citizens into submission. Unquestionably, former police chief Darryl Gates was wholly insensitive to the needs of minorities. However, reforms instituted since the Riots, and since the departure of Gates, have dramatically improved relations between the police and the community. As a result, claims of police brutality have decreased substantially in recent years. It's easy to be cynical about law enforcement. It's far more difficult to see that police officers are primarily good people trying to do a difficult job in a difficult situation. After months of watching the LAPD in action, it is clear to us that Koon, Gates, and Powell are now the exception, not the rule.

3. **There is no one center.** There are centers. And at least one great place to hang out in every section of town. L.A. is probably the most decentralized city on the planet. And in that sense, more than any other, it is truly a harbinger of things to come.

4. **Because the city is so decentralized, you can carve out your own niche and extraneous people will leave you alone.** Unlike dense creative centers like Manhattan, there's room to free-associate here, both physically and mentally. We are happy to see the corporate—if not citizen—commitment to making downtown L.A. a viable cultural center, but L.A.'s hallmark will always be that there is no one center. Only in L.A. can you not predict the direction of traffic jams. This is because people are traveling, working, and living in all directions. Our advice? Embrace the anarchy, while pushing for strict boundaries on growth.

5. **If you can embrace the smog, you can thrive.** Seattle has its rain. New York has its dirt and density. San Francisco has its fog. And L.A. has its smog. L.A. isn't perfect—learn to live with it, while working to change it. Besides, the air is getting better every year, and there's always oxygen masks.

6. **And maybe it's not even smog.** We've learned that even without all the cars, the air and horizon would always be somewhat brown because of the rising dust and haze. Old photos of L.A. from 1910 prove the point—it looked as brown then as it does now.

7. **L.A. wins the international popularity contest hands down.** Tourists from all over the globe thrill to the prospect of coming here. And keep in mind that—riots, smog, congestion, floods, and all—L.A.–Long Beach is number one among the top 10 metropolitan areas of intended residence for admitted immigrants—double the number choosing New York City. More than any place in the world, L.A. remains the place where people believe they can come and re-create their lives in a way not possible "back home." Along with Las Vegas, it is the tabula rasa upon which are placed the dreams and fantasies of people around the world.

8. **Contrary to rumor, people aren't leaving.** Los Angeles was not even among the 30 cities with the largest percentage of population loss from 1980 to 1990. By contrast, *85 New Yorkers move to the greater L.A. area every day*— one every 17 minutes.

9. **Once you learn the ropes, you can get around quicker in L.A. than in several East Coast cities.** It's true, the freeways and major streets get congested several hours every day. However, even at the height of rush hour, there are other less trafficked escape routes that can get you quickly to your destination. Try Fountain in lieu of Hollywood. Wilton in lieu of Western. Sixth Street for getting from Downtown to Fairfax.

10. **Parking is rarely, if ever, a problem.** With the exception of West Hollywood and Beverly Hills, population density in any one area is so reasonable that there's plenty of spaces to go around. In L.A. population density is 6,830 people per square mile; in New York City, it's 23,494. This can actually be advantageous. We find it far easier to "get things done" in L.A. than in New York.

11. **Nonurban recreation is close by.** Where else in America do you have skiing, surfing, mountain biking, and desert trekking all within 45 minutes of the city? Think about it.

12. **L.A. is wacky.** There are simply far more wigged-out, goofy emporiums and museums here than anywhere else in America—museums devoted to golf, wedding cakes, and bananas, to name just a few. (All of which are, of course, covered in this book.) And in terms of colorful architecture, only Vegas, which is an extension of L.A., comes close to the fantastic structures found here. Check out the Bradbury Building, the Chemosphere House, and the Capitol Records Building to get a small idea of what we mean.

13. **L.A. is frivolous.** Which, after awhile, can make you feel at ease. Don't take this town too seriously. You have to drop your high-brow cultural standards,

your need for peppy, witty, culturally cross-referenced repartee, your undying faith in the Western Canon. Give in to the sunshine. Give in to the "mixturesque beauty." Give in to the mediocrity. Praise Ron.

14. **Yet, L.A. knows how to really work hard.** You can count on things being done right. As a rule, people are very ambitious, conscientious, and efficient. It's just that, with their laid-back attitude, Los Angelenos don't appear very ambitious, conscientious, or efficient. At first, a chatty hyperactive Easterner has a hard time grasping this fact.

15. **L.A. is not New York.** Get it out of your mind right now. New York is the ultimate vertical city. It looks and feels urban. L.A. is the ultimate horizontal city. It looks and feels suburban. New York has no space to expand. It's an island. L.A. has all the space in the world (well, figuratively speaking). Over time you start to appreciate that in L.A. you can see the sun and horizon (on a clear day) and that panhandlers aren't confronting you on every corner (except in downtown and Santa Monica). Bicoastal artists say they prefer the density and intensity of New York because it gives them a "push": It *forces* them to do something. But after 12 years of sampling both coasts, we no longer rely on such externals. Many great artists throughout this century have made their homes in L.A. As you get older, you realize that the vaunted New York pressure can actually wear out your creative juices. In L.A. you can discover your own natural rhythm, which, in the end, proves to not only be more healthy, but actually makes you more productive. And that's what we want, isn't it? To be PRODUCTIVE?!!

16. **There is far less palpable racism here than in any other city we've visited.** While a few Caucasians in outlying L.A. misjudge South Central as some God-forsaken blight where gangs run rampant through the streets, on the whole, the myriad of ethnic groups coexist amazingly well here. The Riots seemed like an aberration, and efforts to end bilingual education will in actuality bring people closer together. As it stands now, the lack of an enforced common tongue allows too many ethnic Los Angelenos to ghettoize themselves from the mainstream culture.

17. **Even in the so-called ghetto, the standard of living in L.A. is higher than in almost any other American city.** And the rents are far cheaper (60% less than for comparable rentals in San Francisco or New York).

18. **Celebrity attitude is way overrated.** It's far, far worse in New York and Europe. With few exceptions, so-called stars and their agents are very agreeable and down-to-earth. In addition, the image of a ruthless, power-lunching cabal of entertainment insiders is grossly inflated. Luck, talent, and timing seem as important here as Machiavellian machinations.

19. **With few exceptions, Angelenos are genuinely friendly.**

20. **Contrary to stereotype, a few people have actually returned our calls.**

21. **The Riots changed everything. There's more humility here now, less attitude.** More compassion, less cruelty. Sure, there's that on-going attempt to extol and document a rich, dark, and cynical L.A., but it seems like a retro pose, kept alive by a small cabal of Sky Bar habitués and young industry knuckleheads. Mature Angelenos have moved on.

22. **The Brits are drawn here.** And after a few years in the sun they become quite palatable.

23. **L.A. has the most beautiful ocean sunsets anywhere in America.**

24. **L.A. is the headquarters of the finest in American pop-culture artifacts.** Huge donuts, giant hot dogs, and 1950s-style eateries abound. This place is roadside vernacular heaven, with a vibrant and strong conservation community.

25. **L.A. has stars.** Oodles of them. And not just the *People* magazine pantheon either. In addition to the Bruce, Sly, and Arnold coterie, there's also the far more compelling Monk Trinity of Mark (Mothersbaugh), Ray (Bradbury), and Jim (Rome). As well as the Del Rubios, Vaginal Cream Davis, Miss Velma, the Irascible Make My Movie Guy, Angelyne, Long Gone John, Brendan Mullen, Kenneth Turan, Robert Altman, Billy Barty, Russ Meyer, and assorted others you will meet in this book.

26. **L.A. has brains.** We found just as many intellectually alive people here as in, say, New York, which prides itself on its intellectual superiority. In fact, a higher percentage of Nobel Laureates in the fields of math, science, and engineering come from L.A. than from any other city in the world. In addition, the Internet, hula hoops, and fast-food hamburgers all were invented in Los Angeles.

27. **L.A. streets are surprisingly clean.** Well, pretty clean. Okay, excepting Hollywood, Koreatown, Downtown, and most of South Central. Hey, Culver City's streets seem kinda clean.

28. **L.A. is heat.** It wears down resistance. Wears down acerbic irony too, but that's a small price to pay.

29. **L.A. is ocean.** Which cleans your aura and maintains your sanity amidst all the urban chaos.

30. **L.A. is palpably safer than many cities we've visited.** There is a felt sense of security here, now buttressed by a significant decrease in crime.

31. **Film, film, film.** It's the chief drawing card, lending an air of excitement to all aspects of the city. When you see film crews everywhere you turn, you really feel you are in the most happening place on the planet. Now if we could just get a few of those film people to lose their obnoxious SUV's.

32. **You can make a very good living as a writer here.** While it is true that film directors, producers, and actors are far higher on the totem pole, a well-written script is still the basis of almost every action taken in Hollywood. You may not like what they do with your masterpiece, but you will be paid handsomely to keep your opinions to yourself.

33. **Though a recent *Los Angeles Magazine* study found that 50% of Angelenos want to leave the city, it is also becoming clear that Angelenos are increasingly making a commitment to the place.** This is a huge point, and probably the one that bodes best for the city's future. For without significant citizen involvement, the problems of L.A. are indeed intractable. No city in America makes it easier to hide, to be a passive spectator. No city demands so little involvement from its citizens. But, trust us, the only way to feel fully alive here is to get proactive. Fortunately, because entertainment industry professionals have finally realized this basic point—"gosh, it looks like we're going to be here awhile"—Los Angeles is starting to witness huge investments in its future. From the renowned Getty Center, to the Disney Symphony Hall, to the redeveloped Walk of Fame, to more essential organizations like the David Geffen Center/AIDS Project Los Angeles, the Entertainment Industry Foundation, the Los Angeles Mission, Beyond Baroque, Friends of the Los Angeles River, One Voice (☎ 310/458-9961), which provides food for L.A.'s hungry around the holidays, and the Surfrider Foundation (www.surfrider.org), a most excellent nonprofit dedicated to the preservation and enhancement of the world's waves and beaches, the watchwords of post-Riots L.A. are "service to community." Citizens of less troubled, and possibly more idyllic, locales may not find this very special. But, given the ephemeral assumptions on which L.A. was built, it is nothing short of miraculous.

Because of these reasons and many more, it is our humble contention after two years in the Southland, that the worst days are over. The 1991–92 period was L.A.'s dark night of the desert. In 1999 and heading into the millennium, the City of Angels is poised for a major-league comeback, assuming L.A.'s cyclical penchant for decadent excess doesn't sap the piety and industry that have been so critical in creating the city's new-found prosperity.

When we look at L.A. we see a tremendous future. Opportunities aplenty. A city ready to break out and seize its true potential as the capital of the Pacific Rim.

Downtown at the corner of 3rd and Broadway sits perhaps the greatest indoor architectural gem in the West, the Bradbury Building. It could form one of the core architectural centerpieces of a plan to redevelop the *entire* Downtown, and not just the "Figueroa Corridor" (MOCA, the Colburn School of Performing Arts, the new Cathedral). As Los Angelenos seize upon this idea, they will have not only the best in weather and nature, but the best of what the East has to offer: vibrant, culturally diverse, and environmentally sophisticated high-use downtowns. In a city that has always cried out for a center, downtown L.A. is the one great hope. The generosity of Eli Broad (CEO of SunAmerica), Ron Burkle (Ralph's/Food 4 Less), Mike Bowlin (CEO of ARCO), Mark Willes (publisher of the *LA Times*), and even Mayor Riordan (who gave $5 million of his own money to help save Disney Hall) indicates that the corporate will is there. But to achieve a *completely* revitalized Downtown (and that includes the embarrassing squalor well below the appropriately named Bunker Hill) requires more than expensive restaurants, art galleries, and giant civic structures. It requires active citizen involvement from across the political and economic spectrum. Downtown is crying out for a master visionary to bring the city together and shape this area into something truly extraordinary.

Which is why we say, instead of the *Blade Runner* vision of L.A.'s future, Angelenos have the opportunity to create an ecologically blazing and economically sophisticated vision. Los Angeles is prepared to seize the future in a variety of industries, from electric cars and related recharging stations (pioneered right now by the Hughes Corporation) to exciting new interactive entertainment technologies (there are more Internet-related businesses in Los Angeles than in all of Silicon Valley). If politicians could let go of bailing out the outmoded defense industry, a new economically progressive L.A. would have a chance to emerge.

By the year 2010, the city of Los Angeles will have the finest, most elaborate mass transit in America (that is, if short-sighted politicos more concerned with short-term bottom line than long-term economic impact don't sabotage it once and for all). And if current environmental law is not scuttled for short-term economic gain, Los Angeles will, by the year 2010, have more electric and mixed-fuel vehicles on its streets and highways than any city in the world.

With a law on the books mandating an increasing number of zero-emission vehicles, we will go out on a limb and project that by the year 2010 Los Angeles will no longer be the most polluted city in America and won't even be among the top 10 in the world.

And as L.A. cleans up its air and water, it will become a far more livable place. Combined with fantastic year-round weather, a robust economy, and a revitalized downtown, this could make for a golden 21st century in "the City of Quartz."

L.A., it's your call, babe.

›I'm suing!
You're Ruining My Day!
(On the Road in L.A.)

The God of Freeways snakes through L.A. like a movie set, with a teasing promise to deliver us to Hollywood. It's perpetual summer and you can feel it—the apocalyptic roar of a thousand cars idling on the asphalt under an orgy of sunshine and haze. Mike fingers the map like a hungry junkie, high on exhaust, looking for a way out of the maze. But the radio crackles "Westbound *SIG ALERT!*"

The Monks take a quick exit, heading down Vine through the heart of Hollywood. Mike is driving the speed limit past the string of seat-upholstery shops, 7-11s, innocuous strip malls, markets, and electronics stores into the stretch where seedy, wino-laden Vine becomes elegant Rossmore, with its 80-year-old apartment buildings that suddenly loom seven stories tall. It's a stretch of classy buildings, with grand lobbies and doormen, parking garages, and ornate facades; where traffic moves along a narrow, winding, tree-lined street with sidewalks where people actually walk. Very un-L.A. Mike follows the traffic, playing dodge-the-parked-car as the right lane gets cut in half by a parking zone, leaving only inches to spare. Mike pushes the throttle to get through the intersection of Rossmore and Rosewood as a woman in a black Mercedes hangs a quirky left in the path of the Subaru. . . . *Kaboom. Crash.* And, like, *Screeeeeech!*

Twenty odd geriatrics in the retirement village on the corner, some wearing dusty bluish overcoats that are decades old, are interrupted amidst their card games. Michael Monk, caught in his seat belt by the sudden jolt, is stunned. As the car sits idling, the antlike passing motorists, not a one interested in asking if everything's okay, speed by in obvious irritation at the obstacle now interrupting their otherwise perfect, sunny California day.

It's not a pretty sight. There's broken headlight glass on the asphalt, a hissing sound coming out of the engine, and the black Mercedes is smashed accordionlike across its passenger-side rear trunk. The driver coasts out of the intersection dragging a fender, parks on the curb, and leaps out of the car. She is flashing gold jewelry, porcelain teeth, and a killer death stare in the direction of the Wal Mart–clad Monk. Her 12-year-old kid's in the back screaming bloody murder. Mike pulls behind her, completely panicked that the child has been hurt.

A long tall yuppie goddess with coifed hair, full makeup, nylons on a hot day, and a golden tanning salon hue is out walking her Labrador. She runs over, all good-Samaritan-like, with liberal concern written all over her tweezed and laser-dermed brows. Somewhere between a grimace, a smirk, and a compassionate smile she volunteers herself as a witness while proffering a business card.

Mike shrugs, "Like, sure, why not," and as he reaches to take the card the woman literally hisses at him, "I was talking to her!! You *are* at fault, you know!"

"What? She turned in front of me."

"If a left-turning car is more than one-third into the intersection they have right of way over oncoming traffic. Look it up!" she says while consoling the other woman, who is now holding the crying 12-year-old spoiled rotten BRAT.

Mike's never, in 30 years of driving, heard of that rule. Torn between sympathy and outrage, the Monk isn't sure of protocol, especially when the lady driver doesn't speak English and hasn't a clue to the "insurance, driver's license swap" ritual common to all collision participants on the streets of L.A. But she does have a cell phone, which she promptly uses to call her husband.

The "witness" presses on, now offering not only her support but jotting down the number of a personal friend, "the attorney." Well, that does it. Mike marches over to the corner senior's home and asks if anyone saw the accident from their big lobby windows overlooking the street. Bad luck: It's an Alzheimer's treatment center and none of the residents, not a one of them, recalls a thing.

"Hello, LAPD? I want to report an accident."

"What's your precinct?"

"I don't know, I'm just traveling through . . ."

"You'll have to call your precinct." *Click. Buzz.*

Two calls later Mike learns that in any accident that doesn't result in death or near fatal injury, and in which the cars can still move, it's the responsibility of the motorists to make their own police report.

The "witness" takes leave, promising to make it to court if needed, but the driver doesn't seem to understand a word. Finally, the "husband" arrives. He's in a maximum-child-carrying van with four kids onboard, all of whom bound out, dressed in tennis whites, speaking Spanish to the mom. She looks fortified as her family takes up position. The husband approaches with a notepad in hand. The two oldest sons adopt an offensive strategy, flanking Michael Monk.

The wife frantically recounts *her* version of the story to the husband, in Spanish, complete with sweeping arm gestures, hysterical shaking, and big pouty lips that curl in contempt at the allegedly reckless Monk and the featherweight red Subaru. The previously disturbed 12-year-old is now bored and wants to go home.

"Looks like you did about a thousand dollars damage on our car. So, we just settle now. Otherwise we take to insurance and your rates go up."

"You're out of your mind. She turned in front of me!" Mike exclaims.

"But look at your car. There's no damage. We have witness who says it's your fault."

Apparently the wife could understand a lot more English than she was willing to let on. Soon things escalate as the husband, claiming to be a low-income employed delivery driver barely making ends meet, has scribbled on a notepad the words *I accept personal liability for the accident between our two cars and agree to pay one-half damages for all repairs.* He thrust the note in front of Mike to sign.

"No fucking way! I'm calling the police, an attorney, and my insurance. May I please see her driver's license!"

Suddenly things get quiet. Without a single word, the low-income employed delivery driver, his gold-wearing, cell-phone–toting wife, and their four kids pile into the crippled black Mercedes and white, fully equipped minivan to drive off and continue their sunny Californian day.

While Michael Monk makes a mental note to install a 24-hour camcorder over the hood for future excursions on the streets of L.A., a crazy young woman pushing a shopping cart across the street screams at the top of her lungs, "I'm suing! You're ruining my day!"

›MONKS' L.A.,
A to Z

While we are fairly proficient at excavating the cultural gems buried beneath monochromatic topsoil, nowhere has our skills of discovery been put to a greater test than in Los Angeles. The eternally warm and sunny L.A. climate flattens out the senses. A Monk requires contrasts and extremes in order to highlight what is not readily apparent. Los Angeles rarely supplies that. It is easy to coast here, glossing over entire histories of cultural achievement. To stay alert to what is hidden is a daily challenge, necessitating every trick in the Monk arsenal. What we've come up with is a snapshot of this deceptively rich metropolis. The treasures of Los Angeles are encrypted in a secret code. It takes months of trial, error, and patience to break the code and enter the heart of the city. It takes some environmental compromise too. But you will be rewarded for your efforts. We feel we've started to get a handle on this city, yet we also have much more work to do, no doubt requiring yet another guidebook devoted exclusively to this complex and highly underrated place.

But, for now, here's L.A., A to Z. It won't park your car. It can't get your screenplay produced. But it will tell you the best of the city. It will also tell you what to avoid.

The Top Ten Distractions in L.A.

(Or, What You Should Definitely See if You Have Just Two Days in the City)

Because some of you have short attention spans, or are undecided whether you should purchase this book, or because you are sitting at Barnes & Noble or Borders looking to get the gist of the book without having to buy anything more than a cup of joe, or, more gently, because you only have two days in L.A., we've created this definitive list. These are the 10 things you absolutely *must* see to get a Mad Monk sense of the city. Each one is an unqualified gem of originality. Each one will reward you on subsequent return visits. They are sacred. They are true. They represent the very finest Los Angeles has to offer.

In alphabetical order they are:

1. **The Banana Museum** (Altadena). Where photographer Ken Bananaster displays his collection of banana-shaped treasures, including banana pillows and the world's oldest petrified banana. See "Museums" section and Banana Man interview.

2. **The Bradbury Building** (Los Angeles). Setting for the finale of L.A. futurist film fantasy *Blade Runner,* the Bradbury is the most amazing work of indoor architecture we've ever seen. A place so filled with surreal magic and mechanical surprise it left us gaping in awe. See "Buildings, Bridges, and Other Visual Landmarks."

3. **Dockweiler State Beach** (Playa del Rey). A beautiful sandy beach, with campground, situated adjacent to the LAX runway, right below the Hyperion sewage treatment plant, and next door to an oil refinery. The quintessential L.A. tableau of nature, oil, sewage, and NOISE. For the toxic tourist, this is the Unholy Grail. See "Accommodations."

4. **Elysium Fields** (Topanga Canyon). The only clothing-optional park in a metropolitan area anywhere in the United States. A rare and beautiful oasis in the heart and haze of Topanga Canyon. See "Parks."

5. **Forest Lawn Memorial Park Glendale** (Glendale). A country club for the dead, featuring talking statuary and other kitschy funeral art. Celebrities buried here include Clark Cable, Sammy Davis Jr., Jean Harlow, Walt Disney, Humphrey Bogart, W. C. Fields, Gracie Allen, Errol Flynn, and Chico Marx. Internment options include "Vesperland" and "Lullabyeland."

See "Buildings, Bridges, and Other Visual Landmarks" section (and read Evelyn Waugh's *The Loved One*).

6. **L. Ron Hubbard Life Exhibition** (Los Angeles). Shrine to the life and teachings of the great L. Ron—sci-fi author, L.A. patron saint, and inventor of the science-of-mind "religion" known as Scientology. It's full of Hubbard innovations like the E-Meter, which measures thought forms; the "20 Steps to Happiness" (which include "Set a good example" and "Do not steal"); and the sliding wall of proclamations received by L. Ron the eagle scout. See "Museums."

7. **L.A. Police Academy / L.A. Police Revolver and Athletic Club Cafe & Gift Shop** (Los Angeles). Dine with cops, view the Jack Webb Memorial Showcase and the Academy brass-knuckle collection, meditate in the Academy Chapel (adjoining the Academy shooting range), then drop in to the gift shop and buy some LAPD kitsch to commemorate your visit. Unfortunately, they've run out of Riot Commemorative Mugs. See "Stores/Shopping."

8. **Los Feliz Neighborhood** (Los Angeles). One whacked neighborhood, with fabled establishments like Koma (formerly Amok) bookstore, Mondo Video A-Go-Go, camp-lite emporium Y-Que, the unmarked Mako restaurant at 1802 Vermont, and Soap Plant/Wacko, which has the finest selection of counterculture/pop-culture books, cards, and artifacts in America. The people who run these places are living proof that L.A. still has a long way to go before it's mainstreamed all to hell. See "Neighborhoods."

9. **Museum of Jurassic Technology** (Culver City). Unquestionably the finest, most disturbing museum-going experience in all of California, its collection

of esoterica includes a history of motor homes and Hagop Sandaldjian's world of microminiatures (seen only through the aid of a magnifying glass). See "Museums."

10. **The Venice Beach Boardwalk, especially on a Saturday or Sunday Afternoon** (Venice). Testosterone central, populated by steroid-enhanced bodybuilders, gangbanging b-ballers, surfers, buzz-saw jugglers, and drum circle freaks, plus everything ugly, tacky, unwieldy, grotesque, and sketchy that can't breathe freely anywhere else. Predictable, but essential. See "Neighborhoods."

If You Have Four Days, Add These to Your List

11. **The Ackermansion** (Hollywood). Home of literary agent, actor, magazine creator, and all-around sci-fi pioneer Forrest "Forry" Ackerman and his extensive collection of sci-fi/horror props and memorabilia. See "Museums" section and Ackerman interview.

12. **Bischoff's Taxidermy** (Burbank). Though the heyday of the big-game hunter has long passed, their trophies have found a permanent home at Bischoff's. Like a frightening "Twilight Zone" episode, you walk the floors surrounded by tigers, leopards, moose, wolves, boar, fox, kangaroo, elk, sheep, buffalo, and even a brood of chickens. Hundreds of species stand with open eyes, ready to pounce. Upstairs, a corner of discarded body parts, including a snout-torn coyote, seems eerily feral. Packs of wolves lunge near a banister. See "Animals."

13. **El Floridita** (Hollywood). If you're in L.A. on a Monday night and want to dance salsa, you can do no better than this small Cuban restaurant, which sits nestled into a nondecrepit mini-mall. El Floridita has dancing Thursday, Saturday, and Sunday, but none of these nights compare to Monday. Make reservations at least 2 weeks in advance. See "Music Venues."

14. **5th Street Dick's** (Los Angeles). Seven nights a week this place serves up sweet-potato cobbler, tramp pot pies, and some of the best jazz in town. Friday and Saturday the place is smokin', with a house band till 1am followed by a jam session that goes till around 4:30am. This is the sort of small, packed, intimate place where jazz began. There's a great neighborhood street scene outside. See "Music Venues."

15. **Grand Central Public Market** (Los Angeles). A 75-year-old food bazaar populated by real ethnic Angelenos, it puts all other public markets to shame. The place is a model of what can happen when people decide in earnest to rebuild L.A. (see "Food" section). While in the neighborhood, check out Angels Flight (see "Transportation") and funky funky Broadway.

16. **Griffith Park Observatory** (Los Angeles). Yes, it is listed in every single guidebook to the city. But, when we tire of L.A., it is the first place we go to restore the faith. Go by day for a fantastic hike. Go again at night for the most amazing urban panorama on the West Coast. See "Views."

17. **The Hollywood Reservoir** (Los Angeles). This reservoir holds much of the imported water that keeps L.A. from drying up and blowing away the way nature intended. It's a true blue oasis, surrounded by pine and sycamore, where an eclectic community encompassing all races, sizes, and types comes for a little peace, cleanliness, and beauty. See "Parks and Nature."

18. **Löwenbräu Keller** (Los Angeles). German bar/restaurant with enough tacky chintzy schmaltzy kitsch to keep any ironic hipster in Smirk Heaven. One of the great gaudy highlights of one of the most gaudy cities on earth. See "Bars."

19. **Mulholland Drive** (Los Angeles). Great views, big stars, roadside fruit vendors, and vast tracts of undeveloped land. Here it is, drive it. See "Streets, Corners, and Highways."

20. **Watts Towers** (Los Angeles). The Coral Castle of the West. Simon Rodia's dreamlike masterwork is an odd shrine in an even odder location. The cement-and-steel towers stand nearly 100 feet tall and are imbedded with mosaics of seashells, bottles, and tiles. See "Buildings, Bridges, and Other Visual Landmarks."

And, if You STILL Have Time, Try . . .

21. **The Donut Hole** (La Puente). The most delicious work of roadside art in L.A. Portly patrons make their way through the sacred donut center and purchase a variety of sugar-rich treats from a drive-up window. See "Buildings, Bridges, and Other Visual Landmarks."

22. **Giovanni's Salerno Beach Restaurant** (Playa del Rey). If you have an itch to drive through the foul wetlands of Playa del Rey out to Dockweiler State Beach to catch the thunderous roar of departing jets from LAX, then you must at least make a stop at Giovanni's. An otherwise unimposing, old-signage Italian food joint, upon entering it begs the question, *What sort of LSD-inspired nightmare were these people on?* It's the Christmas that never sleeps. See "Food."

23. **Universal World Church** (Los Angeles). Don't be fooled: The drab exterior holds the doorway to another world. Inside, a deeply vaulted ceiling aims all eyes towards an altar overflowing with psychedelic Christian kitsch—it's one part medieval iconography, and two parts down-market mall decoration. Queen of all she surveys, Miss Velma sports an angelic silver coiffure and earnestly preaches arcane revelations to a diverse and slightly threadbare congregation. See "Spirituality."

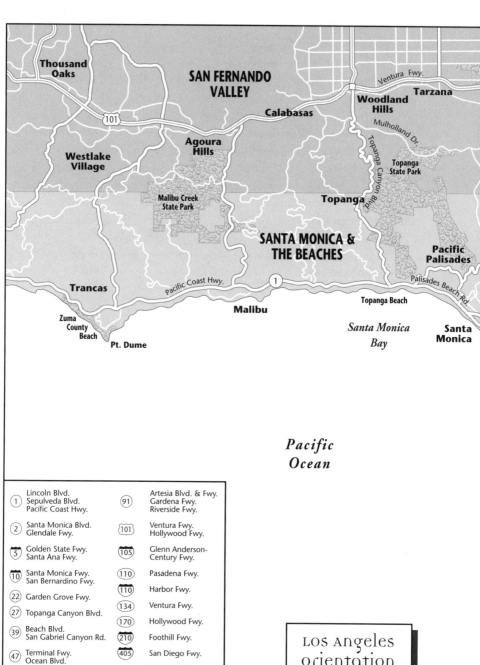

Thousand Oaks

SAN FERNANDO VALLEY

Ventura Fwy.

Tarzana

Woodland Hills

Calabasas

Mulholland Dr.

Agoura Hills

Westlake Village

Topanga State Park

Malibu Creek State Park

Topanga Canyon Blvd.

Topanga

SANTA MONICA & THE BEACHES

Pacific Palisades

Trancas

Pacific Coast Hwy.

1

Palisades Beach Rd.

Topanga Beach

Malibu

Santa Monica Bay

Santa Monica

Zuma County Beach

Pt. Dume

Pacific Ocean

Lincoln Blvd.
1 Sepulveda Blvd.
   Pacific Coast Hwy.

2 Santa Monica Blvd.
   Glendale Fwy.

5 Golden State Fwy.
   Santa Ana Fwy.

10 Santa Monica Fwy.
    San Bernardino Fwy.

22 Garden Grove Fwy.

27 Topanga Canyon Blvd.

39 Beach Blvd.
    San Gabriel Canyon Rd.

47 Terminal Fwy.
    Ocean Blvd.

55 Newport Fwy. and Blvd.

57 Orange Fwy.

60 Pomona Fwy.

90 Marina Fwy.

Artesia Blvd. & Fwy.
91 Gardena Fwy.
    Riverside Fwy.

101 Ventura Fwy.
     Hollywood Fwy.

105 Glenn Anderson-
     Century Fwy.

110 Pasadena Fwy.

110 Harbor Fwy.

134 Ventura Fwy.

170 Hollywood Fwy.

210 Foothill Fwy.

405 San Diego Fwy.

605 San Gabriel
     River Fwy.

710 Long Beach Fwy.

LEGEND

22 **State Highway**

101 **U.S. Highway**

210 **Interstate Highway**

Los Angeles orientation

0   2.5 mi

0   2.5 km

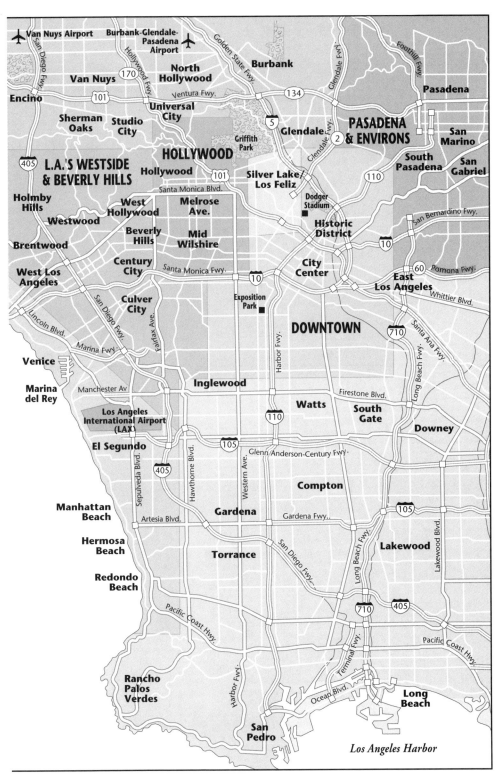

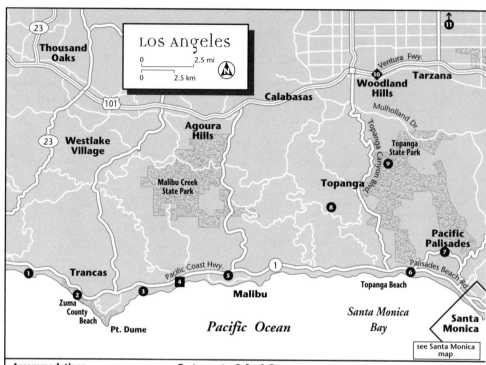

LOS ANGELES

0   2.5 mi

0   2.5 km

Thousand Oaks

Tarzana

Woodland Hills

Calabasas

Agoura Hills

Westlake Village

Topanga State Park

Malibu Creek State Park

Topanga

Pacific Palisades

Trancas

Pacific Coast Hwy.

Topanga Beach

Malibu

Zuma County Beach

Pt. Dume

Pacific Ocean

Santa Monica Bay

Santa Monica

see Santa Monica map

Accommodations

Ambassador Hotel **27**
Banana Bungalow **19**
Dockweiler State Beach **36**
The Mission Inn **44**
Malibu Beach RV Park **4**
Ritz-Carlton Huntington Hotel **25**

Restaurants, Cafes & Bars

Bahooka Ribs and Grog **28**
Barbata's **10**
China Inn Restaurant **22**
Dunbar Hotel **31**
Encounter Restaurant **36**
Kindle's Donuts **38**

Löwenbräu Keller **27**
Malibu Seafood **5**
Original Tommy's **27**
Pann's Restaurant **35**
Re$iduals **16**
The Village Coffee Shop **19**

All the Rest

1st A.M.E. **30**
5th Street Dick's **34**
Ackermansion **23**
American Military Museum/ Heritage Park **28**
Atlantis Books **18**
Banana Museum **24**
Batman Cave **17**
Beverly Hills Rent-a-Car **36**
Bischoff's Taxidermy **18**
Bob's Big Boy **15**
Bungalow Heaven **24**
Castaic Lake **11**
Charmlee Park **1**
City on a Hill **26**
Demille and Lasky Barn **19**
Disneyland **45**
Do-nut Hole **29**
Elysium Fields **9**
Elysium Nudist and Naturist Archives **8**
Farmer John's Mural **32**
Forest Lawn Memorial Park Glendale **22**

Garden of Oz **19**
Gelson's Market **7**
Glendale Central Library Cat Collection **22**
Golf Man **44**
Gondola Getaway **46**
Great Wall of Los Angeles **14**
Griffith Park Observatory **17**
Griffith Park Run **20**
Hawthorne High School **43**
Highway 105 heading West of 110 **39**
Hollywood Reservoir **19**
Hughes Market **5**
Huntington Library, Art Collection and Botanical Gardens **25**
The Ice House **24**
L.A. Police Academy **26**
L.A. Riot Flashpoint **37**
LAX **36**
Madonna's House **19**
Manhattan Beach Volleyball **42**
Montrose Bowl **21**
Old Town Music Hall **42**

Panoptikum **14**
Paul Ziffren Sports Resource Center Library **30**
Pyramid Lake Recreation Area **11**
Queen Mary **47**
Quick Rent A Car **41**
Raging Waters **28**
Ralph W. Miller Golf Library and Museum **33**
Rinzai-Ji Zen Center **30**
Robert H. Meyer Memorial Beach **1**
Rodney King, the Human Piñata **12**
Self-Realization Fellowship Lake Shrine **6**
Solstice State Park **3**
Tower of Wooden Pallets **13**
Tri-Ess Sciences **15**
Universal City Walk **17**
Universal World Church **27**
Watts Towers **40**
Welded Scary Monster **14**
Zuma Beach **2**

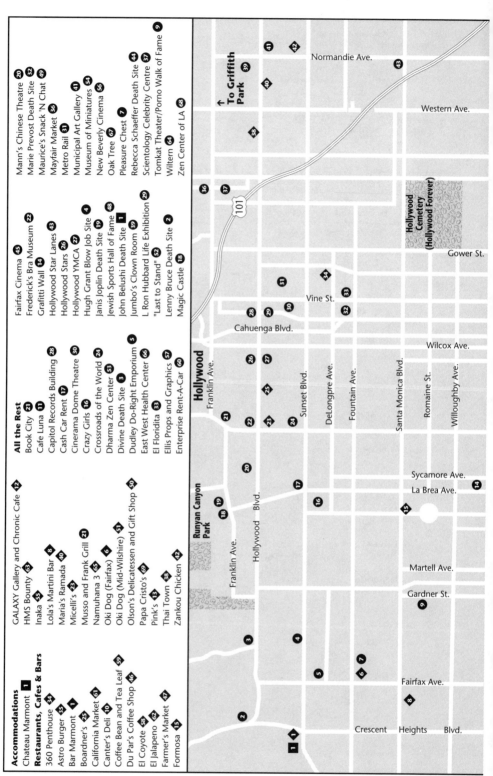

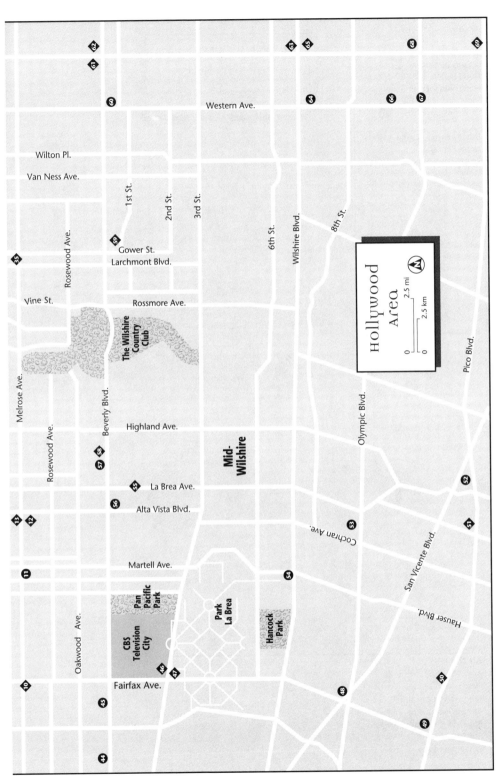

Hollywood Area

2.5 mi

2.5 km

Western Ave.

Wilton Pl.

Van Ness Ave.

1st St.

2nd St.

3rd St.

6th St.

Wilshire Blvd.

8th St.

Rosewood Ave.

Gower St.

Larchmont Blvd.

Vine St.

Rossmore Ave.

The Wilshire Country Club

Melrose Ave.

Beverly Blvd.

Rosewood Ave.

Highland Ave.

Mid-Wilshire

La Brea Ave.

Alta Vista Blvd.

Martell Ave.

Pan Pacific Park

Park La Brea

Hancock Park

CBS Television City

Oakwood Ave.

Fairfax Ave.

Cochran Ave.

San Vicente Blvd.

Hauser Blvd.

Olympic Blvd.

Pico Blvd.

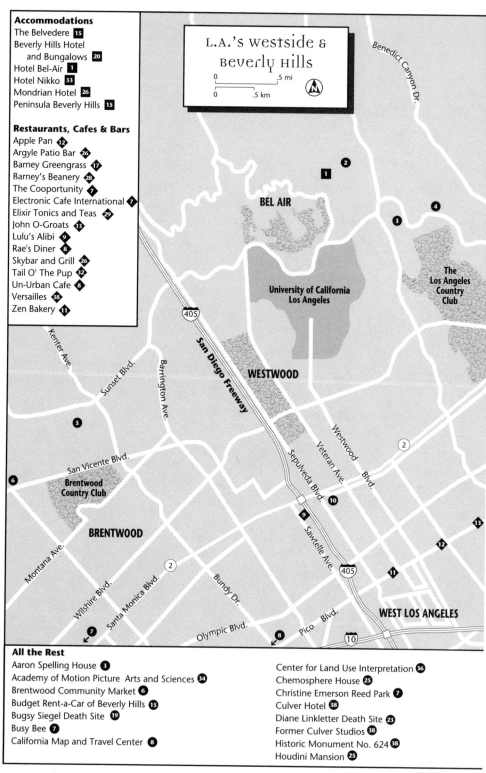

Accommodations
The Belvedere 15
Beverly Hills Hotel
  and Bungalows 20
Hotel Bel-Air 1
Hotel Nikko 33
Mondrian Hotel 26
Peninsula Beverly Hills 15

Restaurants, Cafes & Bars
Apple Pan 12
Argyle Patio Bar 26
Barney Greengrass 17
Barney's Beanery 28
The Cooportunity 7
Electronic Cafe International 7
Elixir Tonics and Teas 29
John O-Groats 13
Lulu's Alibi 9
Rae's Diner 8
Skybar and Grill 26
Tail O' The Pup 32
Un-Urban Cafe 8
Versailles 38
Zen Bakery 11

L.A.'s westside &
Beverly Hills

0   .5 mi

0   .5 km

BEL AIR

**University of California
Los Angeles**

**The
Los Angeles
Country
Club**

WESTWOOD

San Diego Freeway

Kenter Ave.

Sunset Blvd.

Barrington Ave.

Sepulveda Blvd.

Veteran Ave.

Westwood Blvd.

San Vicente Blvd.

**Brentwood
Country Club**

Montana Ave.

BRENTWOOD

Sawtelle Ave.

Wilshire Blvd.

Santa Monica Blvd.

Bundy Dr.

Olympic Blvd.

Pico Blvd.

WEST LOS ANGELES

All the Rest
Aaron Spelling House 3
Academy of Motion Picture Arts and Sciences 34
Brentwood Community Market 6
Budget Rent-a-Car of Beverly Hills 15
Bugsy Siegel Death Site 19
Busy Bee 7
California Map and Travel Center 8

Center for Land Use Interpretation 36
Chemosphere House 25
Christine Emerson Reed Park 7
Culver Hotel 38
Diane Linkletter Death Site 23
Former Culver Studios 38
Historic Monument No. 624 38
Houdini Mansion 25

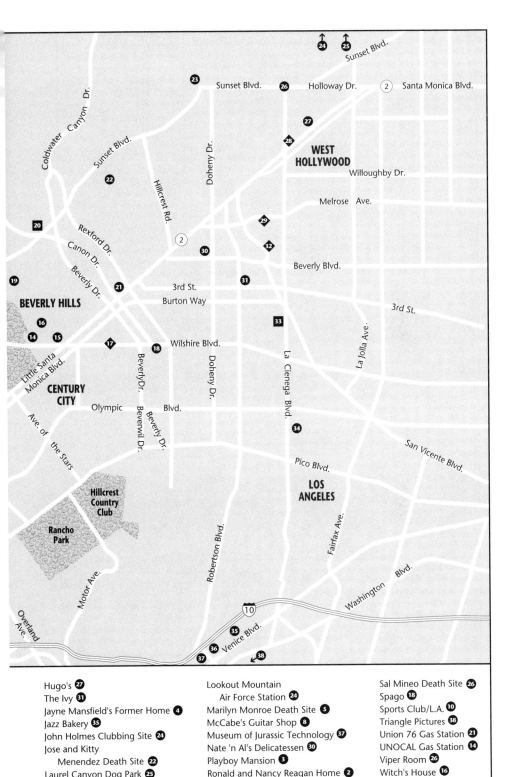

Hugo's **27**
The Ivy **31**
Jayne Mansfield's Former Home **4**
Jazz Bakery **35**
John Holmes Clubbing Site **24**
Jose and Kitty
   Menendez Death Site **22**
Laurel Canyon Dog Park **25**

Lookout Mountain
   Air Force Station **24**
Marilyn Monroe Death Site **5**
McCabe's Guitar Shop **8**
Museum of Jurassic Technology **37**
Nate 'n Al's Delicatessen **30**
Playboy Mansion **3**
Ronald and Nancy Reagan Home **2**

Sal Mineo Death Site **26**
Spago **18**
Sports Club/L.A. **10**
Triangle Pictures **38**
Union 76 Gas Station **21**
UNOCAL Gas Station **14**
Viper Room **26**
Witch's House **16**

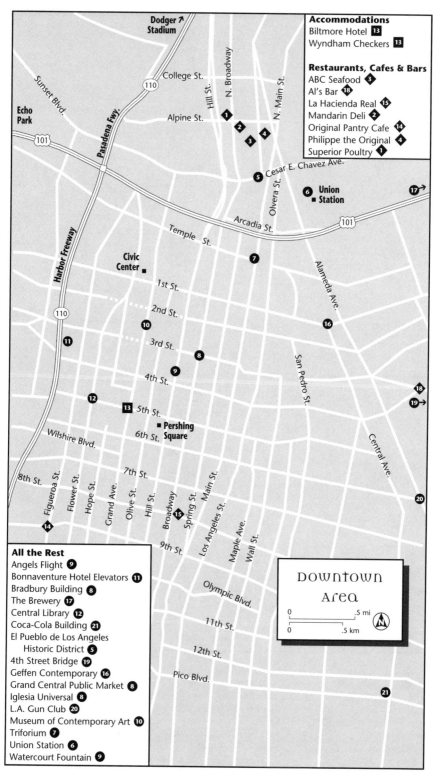

Dodger ↗
Stadium

College St.

Hill St.

N. Broadway

N. Main St.

110

Alpine St. **1**

2

4

Sunset Blvd.

Echo
Park

101

Pasadena Fwy.

3

Olvera St.

Cesar E. Chavez Ave.

5

6 ■ **Union**
Station

17 →

Arcadia St.

101

Temple St.

Harbor Freeway

Civic
Center ■

7

Alameda Ave.

1st St.

2nd St.

110

10

11

3rd St.

8

16

San Pedro St.

9

4th St.

12

13 5th St.

Wilshire Blvd.

6th St. ■ **Pershing**
Square

18

19 →

Central Ave.

7th St.

8th St.

Figueroa St.

Flower St.

Hope St.

Grand Ave.

Olive St.

Hill St.

Broadway

Spring St.

Main St.

Los Angeles St.

Maple Ave.

Wall St.

20

14

15

9th St.

Olympic Blvd.

11th St.

12th St.

Pico Blvd.

21

Downtown
Area

0   .5 mi

0   .5 km

N

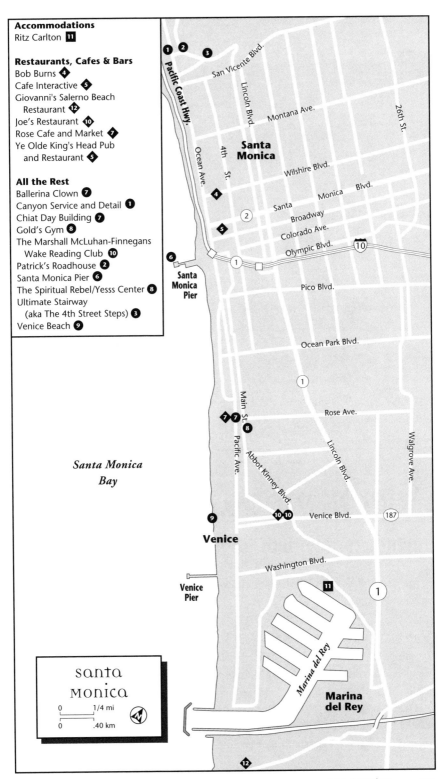

Accommodations
Ritz Carlton **11**

Restaurants, Cafes & Bars
Bob Burns **4**
Cafe Interactive **5**
Giovanni's Salerno Beach
  Restaurant **12**
Joe's Restaurant **10**
Rose Cafe and Market **7**
Ye Olde King's Head Pub
  and Restaurant **5**

All the Rest
Ballerina Clown **7**
Canyon Service and Detail **1**
Chiat Day Building **7**
Gold's Gym **8**
The Marshall McLuhan-Finnegans
  Wake Reading Club **10**
Patrick's Roadhouse **2**
Santa Monica Pier **6**
The Spiritual Rebel/Yesss Center **8**
Ultimate Stairway
  (aka The 4th Street Steps) **3**
Venice Beach **9**

Pacific Coast Hwy.

San Vicente Blvd.

Lincoln Blvd.

Montana Ave.

26th St.

Ocean Ave.

4th St.

Santa Monica

Wilshire Blvd.

Santa Monica Blvd.

Broadway

Colorado Ave.

Olympic Blvd.

Santa Monica Pier

Pico Blvd.

Ocean Park Blvd.

Main St.

Rose Ave.

Pacific Ave.

Abbot Kinney Blvd.

Lincoln Blvd.

Walgrove Ave.

Venice Blvd.

Santa Monica Bay

Venice

Washington Blvd.

Venice Pier

Marina del Rey

Marina del Rey

santa monica

0   1/4 mi
0   .40 km

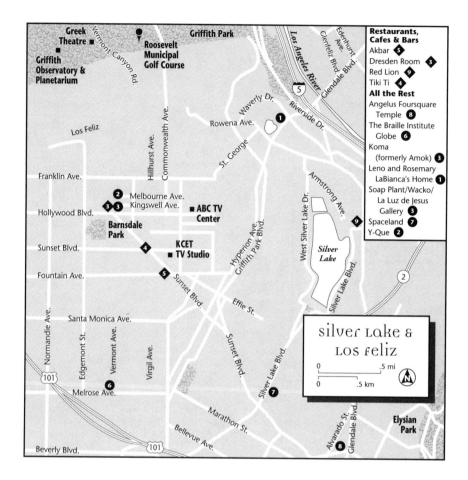

Silver Lake & Los Feliz

Restaurants, Cafes & Bars
Akbar **5**
Dresden Room **3**
Red Lion **9**
Tiki Ti **4**
All the Rest
Angelus Foursquare
    Temple **8**
The Braille Institute
    Globe **6**
Koma
    (formerly Amok) **3**
Leno and Rosemary
    LaBianca's Home **1**
Soap Plant/Wacko/
    La Luz de Jesus
    Gallery **3**
Spaceland **7**
Y-Que **2**

Accommodations

Architecturally, like, Significant

> **The California Club.** 538 S. Flower, between 5th and 6th (Downtown).
☎ 213/622-1391.

The exterior of this 1927 landmark looks like a five-story fortress. On the north side is the handsomely landscaped courtyard of the Downtown Library, a smaller but still tasteful version of New York's Bryant Park. And all around are the sleek angular skyscrapers of Bunker Hill. Though unquestionably grand and stately, the California Club is one of those funny L.A. contradictions. A place which requires men to wear a suit and tie AT ALL TIMES. Such rigid formality is quite surprising in a city that exudes such deliberate informality. A stricture that could only happen in L.A., which so desperately craves class, but ain't got it.

Note: security here is TIGHT. And the attitude is heavy. But, if accompanied by a member, one can dine, work out, and sleep at this ultimate club for downtown power players. Or just do as the Monks do, and act like you belong.

> **The Regal Biltmore Hotel.** 506 S. Grand Ave., at 5th St. (Downtown).
☎ **213/624-1011.**

A 1923 beaux arts masterpiece, from the low-lit Gallery Bar, to the deco-tiled pool, to the breathtaking lobby. Have tea and remember: There was a time when L.A. did have class.

Cheap, but Not Grody

As the adage goes, new money goes to the Peninsula, old money goes to the Bel-Air, and the Monks go wherever they can plug in a pressure cooker. The following are the best cheap accommodations in the city—and all of them will allow you to plug in a pressure cooker.

> **Banana Bungalow.** 2775 Cahuenga Blvd., at Mulholland Dr. (West Hollywood).
☎ **323/851-1129.** www.bananabungalow.com.

We're not big on hostels. We're not real big on the party-hardy Euro contingent that stay in them, either. But if you're a Euro tourist with not a whole lot of cultural ambition, and are very content to get sloshed with your fellow backpack-toting, sandal-wearing, looped and loopy Euro traveling compatriots, this place is for you. The hillside bungalows are far superior to your average hostel, with free movies, free breakfast, and free transportation to standard tourist attractions, as well as a tour of

---

L.A. Trivia

- Indians inhabited the L.A. basin for over 1,000 years before Spanish explorers arrived.
- The Spanish Land Grant of 1781 included 28 square miles. By 1980, Los Angeles city limits covered an area of 463.7 square miles. Today, in terms of area, L.A. is the largest urban metropolis in the world—well over 1,000 square miles, with a population over 13 million. Excluding California, L.A.'s population is exceeded by only four other states.
- The 1990 census recorded the city's population as 39.9% Latino, 37.3% white, 14% black, and 9.8% Asian. Between 1980 and 1990, L.A.'s total population increased by more than 10%, but the white and black population shares both declined.

gangland L.A. (for all the nouveau wiggers onboard). If you go in for this sort of thing, and can stomach the silly McSwedes and surly McBrits, Banana Bungalow has locations in several other cities. Check out their Web site for details.

> Park Plaza Hotel. 607 S. Park View St., at 6th St. (Downtown).
z☎ **213/384-5281.**

Wow! Like, what a bargain. $68.40 a night for a single in a gorgeous deco building that is the occasional set for great parties and film shoots.

Runner-up in the cheap but attractive department is the more strategically located **Magic Hotel,** 7025 Franklin Ave. (☎ **213/851-0800**).

Celebrity Ga-Ga

> Beverly Hills Hotel and Bungalows. 9641 Sunset Blvd., at Rodeo Dr. (Beverly Hills). ☎ **800/283-8885** or 310/276-2251.

There never has been and there never will be a Beverly Hills accommodation quite like the Beverly Hills Hotel. The tony Peninsula may have current star status (that is, if you consider homunculi like Sly Stallone a "star") but it can't hold a candle to this formerly "Pink" (now salmon) Mission Revival Palace. It is lush. It is pricey. And, yes, many celebrities have stayed here, including Howard Hughes (who had a separate room for his food taster), Clark Gable, and Carole Lombard (or, rather, Clark Gable *and* Carole Lombard, in bungalow number 4, to be precise), though today you are far more likely to find Midwestern doctors' wives than any so-called "celebrity." Everyone raves about the handsome Polo Lounge, but the highlight for us—and for très gaudy Jackie Collins, we hear—is the Beverly Hills Coffee Shop. This cute downstairs breakfast place is so PINK it looks like a powder room.

More Ga-Ga

Chateau Marmont (see below under "Historic") and the Peninsula Beverly Hills (see "Overrated, Overpriced, or Just Flat-Out Overdone") also count in the ga-ga category.

Historic

> Ambassador Hotel. 3400 Wilshire Blvd., at Vermont (Downtown).
☎ **213/387-7011.**

RFK was assassinated here while celebrating his victory in the 1968 California primary. Former home of the

Coconut Grove nightclub, the Ambassador was L.A.'s grand and celebrated answer to New York City's opulent Plaza. Currently operated as Wilshire Center Marketing Corp., it is used by the film industry for commercials, films, and special events.

› **Chateau Marmont.** 8221 Sunset Blvd., at Crescent Heights (Hollywood).
☎ **213/656-1010.**

If you're going to stay on the Sunset Strip (not what we would consider a bucolic hotel environment), you might as well stay at the best. While the neo-Gothic Marmont would never win awards for high-tech amenities, cutting-edge design, or engaging service (though where else in the city can you push a button in a lobby lounge and have a bartender suddenly appear), it is clearly the most relaxing oasis in the area, and a complete and total departure from the garish, loud environs of the Sunset Strip running right below. Most importantly, it exudes a kind of old-school class most hotels in the city simply lack. And while we were not particularly wowed by its celebrity pedigree (Wilder, Holden, Karloff, Harlow, Shepard, Newman, De Niro, et. al.), we were impressed by the discreet bungalows that wind up the hill and around the pool. Bungalow numbers 4 and 83 are our favorites, but any one of them are perfect for the rocker dude, indie filmmaker, or smack-addicted young star looking for a bit of country-club coziness amidst the cheese and sleaze of the 'hood. *Added bonus:* late night Ping-Pong under the stars.

Seattle's Ruby Montana on the Chateau Marmont

Ruby: Chateau Marmont. I just love that hotel.

Monk: What do you love about it?

Ruby: It's not fancy at all, but it's about the easiest hotel in the world. For instance, I was staying there by myself. Just an evening. And they have a CD library of everything Eartha Kitt's ever done, everything just about anybody kind of remotely obscure, way on beyond her. And they don't cost anything. So you can rent great music, you have a CD player in your room, and you just have such an easy time hanging out there. And, you know, we had Louis come. Our Chihuahua, Louis Lamour. And, you know, I thought it might be hard to have Lou, but it [became] clear to me that this was a first-rate hotel because they did not have a problem with having a dog there. Right off the bat, they said, *oh yeah, not a problem.* Well, I went out to the pool, there were dogs swimming in the pool. I mean, with these blue-haired rockers. Anything you did was more or less OK, but it was clear that you didn't go over a certain line, because people liked the freedom they gave you, so you didn't abuse anything. I just love that place.

Notable Feature

> **Hotel Nikko.** 465 S. La Cienega Blvd., at Wilshire (Beverly Hills).
☎ **310/247-0400.**

Turning Japanese, you really think so? Then stay here. It's very Japanese. We really think so.

> **The Mission Inn.** 3649 7th St., between Orange St. and the Main St. Mall
(Riverside). ☎ **909/781-8241.**

On the outer fringes of the L.A. sprawl is a kingdom known as the Inland Empire. On the surface it appears to be just a series of exits off major freeways. But as you meander off those exits, past the warehouses and truck stops and malls, you come across a less dense, though still urban, version of L.A. The last vestige of city, before space, not commerce, becomes the star attraction.

While Glen Ivy Hot Springs (25000 Glen Ivy Rd. in Corona) and Naked City L.A. (in Homeland) offer more sensual experiences of the Inland Empire, in the heart of this area is the most astounding architectural wonder in Southern California: the completely over-the-top Mission Inn. You won't find such rich Mission or Spanish Revival architectural detail until you reach Santa Fe. And even the best accommodations in that city cannot match the extremes of this 1-block hotel complex, featuring two restaurants, a coffee shop, bars, and lots of Christian kitsch. As you walk around the four-story building you will discover several architectural surprises, including saints, dragons, eight Tiffany windows, as well as the beautifully reverent Saint Francis chapel. Built at the turn of the century by eccentric millionaire Frank Miller, the Mission Inn has been a favorite of Republican celebrities for decades. In fact, both Richard Nixon and Ronald Reagan were married here, though, naturally, not to each other.

After Miller's death in 1931, the Mission Inn went through some difficult times. The Great Depression and the popularity of desert oases like Palm Springs sucked away the tourist trade. However, in 1992, Riverside resident Duane R. Roberts, whose father is known as the manufacturer of the first frozen burrito, took control of the then shuttered inn. While the rooms are not four-star, they are pleasant. And the vast labyrinthine complex is kept remarkably clean. The highlight of the hotel's year is its annual **Festival of Lights.** On the day after Thanksgiving, thousands of locals and tourists turn out for the "Switch-On Ceremony," when Riverside's premier architectural landmark is lit in 1.2 million lights. Don't let anyone tell you there's no life in the Inland Empire.

Overrated, Overpriced, or Just Flat-Out Overdone

With the risk of being labeled knee-jerk, we are suspicious of any hotel anointed by the Type-A film industry and power-agent crowd—people so consumed by the need for power and recognition, they latch onto anything considered remotely "happening" without any regard to true excellence. Here are some examples.

› **Mondrian Hotel.** 8440 Sunset Blvd., 1 block east of La Cienega (Hollywood). ☎ 213/650-8999.

There's a lot to like about Ian Schrager's latest "face-lift boutique" hotel: a concerted lack of clutter, 360° views, Jean Baptiste Mondino's video of rolling ocean waves in every elevator, light installations by James Turrell, billiards. But the Royalton this is not. Rather, Mondrian is an L.A. version of the Paramount, with bright attentive wait staff, impeccably crisp and thoroughly conceived design elements, but lacking that certain something that once made other Schrager properties seem so in the now. Schrager—or, rather, his design lackey, Philippe Starck—seems to be replaying themes seen elsewhere: the long communal table (Morgan's Asia de Cuba restaurant), the beautiful white cloth draped everywhere (Royalton), the electronic gimmickry (Paramount), but gone is the ability to surprise. Oh, the scourges of branding.

› **Peninsula Beverly Hills.** 9882 Little Santa Monica Blvd., at Wilshire (Beverly Hills). ☎ 310/551-2888.

This hotel gets rave reviews from dubious sources, but we don't see how it is really all that different from other four-star chains like the Four Seasons. The decor, while handsome, is not innovative. Sure, there are bungalows in back, but they feel like Palm Springs condos.

Schragerland Observation

"Service is always the weak point at Schrager hotels. That's because the staff is not well trained. For example, the Mondrian used a casting agent when they were hiring for the hotel. That tells you something. They are hired for the 'look.' It's what Schrager has been doing all along. He can get away with it because the hotels are so well designed."

—Former Schrager Inc. muckety-muck, who will go discreetly unnamed

And, yes, there is a high degree of attentiveness, thanks to the iron-willed discipline of German-trained manager Ali Kasicki. But there's something horribly gauche about the clientele—drunk execs leering over fake-breasted hookers in the bar, CAA agents swarming the lunch room like it was a Condé Nast commissary, and beefy superstars flanked by squadrons of former cops. It all feels so nouveau Beverly Hills, so Atlantic City, so indiscriminately overpriced. Give it a miss.

RV Parks

› Dockweiler State Beach. 12001 Vista del Mar, at Imperial Hwy. (Playa del Rey). ☎ 310/322-4951.

There is one reason people stay at this RV Park: to be close to the city. While far superior in all ways, the Malibu Beach RV Park is just too far away, and, for many, too expensive. This 255-acre beach includes more than 3 miles of shoreline, with swimming and surfing areas, a playground, a picnic area, and a bicycle trail. A 118-site campground with laundry facilities, showers, and flush toilets is situated at the southern end of the beach (80 sites have RV hookups, with very reasonable rates). Residents who work at nearby LAX often stay full time. The children of these full-timers are the big lovers of Dockweiler—free to roam in the sands and the great out-doors. However, the adults look like they've been through the Invasion of Normandy. No small wonder—the giant, erotically apocalyptic Hyperion sewage treatment plant sits right behind the RV park, abutting a power plant, which abuts a refinery. And that is just the surface irony. Read the "RV Park from Hell!!!" essay

Michael Monk at Dockweiler State Beach

for the inside perspective on this quintessentially L.A. tableau of nature, oil, sewage, and NOISE.

Factoid: The waste from the toilets of Dockweiler Campground is pumped back to the Hyperion Sewage Plant to merge with the waste of all of L.A. (stars, agents, and Monks alike). The methane gas released from this waste is then sold to the next-door power plant, which powers huge areas of the city, including the Dockweiler campground, and the RVs and RV appliances plugged in there. When a Dockweiler camper flicks on his television, he is able to do so based on a visit to the loo he made earlier in the day. How's that for a media metaphor.

› **Malibu Beach RV Park.** 25801 Pacific Coast Hwy., at Corral Canyon Rd. (Malibu). ☎ **310/456-6052.**

We hate to give this gem away, but, Monksters, this is one of the best RV parks we've ever visited. Clean, well maintained, Gestapo security, resting on a bluff overlooking the beautiful blue Pacific, with the best fish shack in Southern California on one side and the fabulous Solstice Park on the other. It's the perfect place to park your American Legend Airstream, though not your funky monkey Monkmobile. We were kicked out because our graffiti-inspired exterior didn't mesh well with the Good Sam aesthetics of the guests.

World Class

A great hotel makes you want to be a great guest. All of these hotels operate on such high and exacting standards, it makes even the most punctilious and proper among us want to spruce up our act a bit. My mother always said you should surround yourself with people that challenge you to be your best. All of these hotels do just that.

› **Hotel Bel-Air.** 701 Stone Canyon Rd., at Hilgard (Bel-Air). ☎ **310/472-1211.**

Flowers, lots of flowers. Women, lots of gorgeous young women. Men, lots of fat rich men who like to see their young gorgeous women spending their money amidst all the beautiful flowers. Considered a romantic place for a tryst. Jackets required in the bar after 6. $350 a night for a king. $460 a night for twins. Bungalows start at $650. With 11 acres of gardens and discreet professional service, this is about as secluded as it gets.

› **Ritz-Carlton Huntington Hotel.** 1401 S. Oak Knoll Ave., at California (Pasadena). ☎ **626/568-3900.** www.ritzcarlton.com.

Built in 1906, this grand hotel is where "Subculture" star Carolyn Reese Crotty takes an occasional swim (occasionally accompanied by David St. James, star of Grant

In the course of our long nomadic history, the Monks have been to some pretty gnarly RV parks. T. O. Fuller State Park outside Memphis comes to mind (a white-trash haven for workers at the nearby Tennessee Valley Authority—the ferocious canines and the laundry hanging on the line did it for us), as does the legendary New Yorker Trailer City (alleged mercury beneath the soil and residents straight out of *Night of the Living Dead*). Yet, as uniquely horrible and perversely satisfying as those camping situations were, neither of them top the scenic, olfactory, and aural wonders of Dockweiler State Beach in Playa del Rey, California.

We got to this gem by taking 405 to the Imperial Highway exit. The Imperial was a treat in itself, especially driving it in the fog. Near the exit ramp were several yet-to-be-completed overpasses and absolutely no sign of intelligent human life. With the incoming mist, the lonely streetlights, and the cascade of cars, it was a riveting tableau—foggy Scotland meets *Blade Runner* meets Hitchcock. The drive down the Imperial took us past Los Angeles International Airport. Further down we passed a massive sewage treatment plant with smells far more intense than even those found in the Skunkmobile. And just beyond, at the end of the sacred highway, sat the Monk RV park of choice, Dockweiler State Beach. There was a busy runway to the right, a noisy thoroughfare running beside the park, that sewage treatment plant behind, and dozens of happy drunk campers lined up, compound-style, facing the blue Pacific. Campfires dotted the sand. We made the descent, passing shell-shocked state-park staff wearing ominously expressionless faces (this job clearly doesn't do much for one's mood).

We positioned ourselves somewhat away from the stream of jumbo jets careening overhead, but no matter where we parked, no matter how loud we played the relaxing sounds of Enya, no matter how tight we closed the windows, how deep we inserted the ear plugs, those planes were going to rock our world. And we mean ROCK!

VRRRRROOOOOOOOMMMMMMM! The DC-10 shook the Monkmobile to the core, literally moving it back and forth. We watched three motor homes in front shake from the assault.

Gottschall's *Howard Hughes in Hell*). The idyllic Japanese garden in back, the Jacuzzi hidden behind the trees, and its location near the Arroyo-Secco valley and the San Gabriel Mountains, far from the tumult of L.A., makes the Ritz-Carlton Huntington one of the most relaxing four-star options in the metropolis.

> **Ritz Carlton Marina del Rey.** 4375 Admiral T. Way, at Bali (Marina del Rey). ☎ 310/823-1700.

"It's okay!" Jim shouted confidently. "The park attendant said the planes wouldn't be coming that often at night." It was 10pm. Enya droned on sweetly with her harp and synth. We were getting into a groove. . . .

B O O O O O O O O O O O O O O O M M M M M M M M M M M M M - RRRRROOOOOAAAARRRRRBOOOOOOMMMMMMROOOOOOAR- RRRRRRVROOOOMMSHUSSSSHHHHHHHHROOOOOARRRRRRRRR!!!

The walls of the motor home were no barrier.

10:30: BOOOOOOMMMMMMMROOOOOOOOAAARRRBOOOOOM- SSHUUUSHHHHHHRRRRRROOOAAARRRR!!!!

"Meowwww!" Dolly screamed over the sounds of Enya. "Meowww, meowww!!!" It was clearly not getting any better.

10:45: BOOOOOOOOOMMMMMMMMMMROOOOOOOAR- RRRROOOOOAARRSHUSSHHHHHHHHHHHHHHHROAR- RRRRRRRRRRRRRRRRRRRRRRRRRRRRRR!!!!!

"You've got to be kidding!" Jim screamed to Mike in the back.

The sound of planes drowned out Mike's reply.

11:07: BOOOOOOOOOOOOOOOMMMMMMMMMMMMM- RRRRROOOOOAAAARRRBOOOOMMMMMMMROOOOOOAAR- RRRRRRBOOOOMSHUSSSSHHHHHHHHROOOOOARRRRRRRRR!!!

We were stunned that anyone could possibly sleep here, but even more stunned that the state of California would consider this a fine place for a *campground*.

ROOOOOOOOOOAAAAARRRRRRRR!!!!!

7am: Though we had just spent the most terrifying, shattering night of our lives, with planes flying over every 10 minutes, the next morning we woke to find the cheerful German and Mexican tourists frolicking in the sand, riding bikes, firing up the barbecue, as if nothing had happened at all. We were dumbfounded. Move over, T. O. Fuller, good-bye New Yorker Trailer Hell: You've definitely met your match.

As my dear mother writes, "You just can't go wrong with the Ritz Carltons." And how right Bev is. Fabulous views of the marina, excellent service, convenient. Plus full-tilt pool, two lighted tennis courts, workout room, and the kicker: a full length NBA-style basketball court. YES! While most guests come here to be near the overpriced shopping of Beverly Hills and Santa Monica, the Monk traveler comes to be near the far more compelling highlights of Dockweiler State Beach and the Museum of Jurassic Technology.

Addresses

Bacchanalia

› **Culver Hotel and Scarlet Restaurant.** 9400 Culver Blvd., at Washington (Culver City). ☎ **310/838-7963.**

A six-story flatiron classic, built in 1924, and just recently reopened. Famous because the actors who played the munchkins in *The Wizard of Oz* stayed here during filming, and their visit devolved into an extended bacchanal.

› **Playboy Mansion.** 10236 Charing Cross Rd., at Mapleton Dr. (Beverly Hills).

Hef parties on. His legendary Tudor mansion sits on a sprawling Bel Air estate, landscaped to the point that neighbors are completely obscured. It actually feels as if one is in the Alps, as all one sees are trees of green. The pool is a bouldered lagoon complete with waterfalls. Exotic birds walk proudly around the lawn. During our visit, the spider monkeys chattered away in their large cages, fed by scantily clad Bunnies coyly inviting you to do the same (Desmond Morris would have a field day with the implications). With 70 employees running the place, the Playboy Mansion is a carefully orchestrated celebration of the swingin' bachelor lifestyle, and one of the enduring icons of American popular culture. Tell someone you've been to a dinner at the White House, and you'd receive a nice, polite, "Oh, really?" Tell someone you've been to a party at "the Mansion," and they go into hysterics on the spot. Just ask Leonardo DiCaprio.

Celebrities' Residences or Residential Remains (Some Then, Some Now)

› **Houdini Mansion.** 2400 Laurel Canyon Blvd., at Laurel Pass Ave. (Hollywood).

Harry Houdini (nee Ehrich Weiss) lived here in the 1920s. The mansion was torn down in 1968, and the present owners of the property definitely do not want you poking around the ruins. Signs are posted everywhere demanding that you stay the hell away, but you can catch many of the mansion remains without trespassing. Then again, Mr. Houdini, the David Copperfield of his day, a man who hung straight-jacketed from skyscrapers and escaped from escape-proof prisons, would certainly have found a way to inspect the entire grounds without being caught. But most of us do not have such talent, so we advise that you keep your distance.

Sites of Death, Violence, or Other Mayhem

› **John Belushi.** Chateau Marmont, 8221 Sunset Blvd., Bungalow #2 or #3 (depending on your source), at Crescent Heights (Hollywood).

On March 5, 1982, actor/comedian John Belushi choked to death on his own vomit as he overdosed on a heroin/coke speedball.

› **Lenny Bruce.** 8825 Hollywood Blvd., at Laurel (Hollywood).

Where Lenny Bruce was discovered dead and naked in his bathroom, with morphine tracks on his arm. Drug abuse—so *romantic.*

› **Divine.** The Regency Suites, 7940 Hollywood Blvd., at Stanley (Hollywood).

Divine, a.k.a. Glen Milstead (transvestite star of many of John Waters's trash epics), was in L.A. to begin his first mainstream gig as a male actor when he died in his sleep. He weighed a mere 375 pounds.

› **Hugh Grant.** Corner of Sunset Blvd. and Courtney (Hollywood).

Where charming Brit thespian Hugh Grant (*Four Weddings and a Funeral*), was caught en flagrante with Ho-for-a-Day Stella Marie Thompson, a.k.a. Divine Brown.

› **John Holmes.** 8763 Wonderland Dr., at Green Valley Rd. (Beverly Hills).

Porn star John Holmes allegedly commandeered five coke-snortin' buddies to rip off wealthy club owner Adel Nasrallah, who, once he'd figured out who'd set him up, forced Holmes at gunpoint to the Wonderland house where, with backup, he clubbed the five sleeping thieves to death, allegedly forcing Holmes to watch.

› **Janis Joplin.** The Landmark, 7047 Franklin Ave., at La Brea (Hollywood).

Here, in October 1970, Janis Joplin overdosed on heroin, busting her skull when she hit the floor. Heroin addiction—so *CHIC!*

› **Rodney King, the Human Piñata.** Foothill and Osborne (Lake View Terrace).

Forever etched on George Halliday's videotape as the place where the LAPD bravely protected the citizens of L.A. from a huge, monstrous, superhuman, PCP-laced felon with a degree in martial arts and a penchant for early-morning fishing.

"I was just trying to stay alive, sir, trying to stay alive. They never gave me a chance to stay still."—Testimony of Rodney King in *U.S. v. Stacey Koon*

- Number of blows inflicted on Rodney King by the LAPD: 56.
- Number of lives lost in the Riots following the "Simi Valley verdict" in the first Rodney King trial: 52.
- Number of jobs lost because of the Riots: 11,000.
- According to former president George Bush, the breakup of the family was the number-one cause of the L.A. Riots.

> **L.A. Riot Flashpoint.** Florence and Normandie (South Central).

The southwest corner is still an empty lot. A former gas station, looted and in disrepair, still stands, as does a busted up bus bench, both of which are surrounded by a chain-link fence. Art's Famous Chili Dogs survives next door. Pep Boys is on the northwest corner, a new 76 Gas Station is on the southeast corner, and a liquor store on the northeast. Everything's in place for the next big eruption.

> **Leno and Rosemary LaBianca.** 3301 Waverly Dr., at Hyperion Ave. (Los Feliz).

One night after the Sharon Tate murders, and a few miles east of the Tate home, members of the Manson family cult tied up wealthy grocery-store owners Leno and Rosemary LaBianca with lamp cords and stabbed them to death in their home. "Death to Pigs" and the misspelled title of a Beatles' song, "Healter Skelter," were written in their blood on a wall and the refrigerator. A carving fork was protruding from Len's stomach, and the word "WAR" was cut in his flesh.

> **Diane Linkletter.** 8787 Shoreham Dr., at Cory (West Hollywood).

It was from a sixth floor window here, in 1969, that Diane Linkletter leapt to the ground, apparently distraught over a recent LSD trip in which she thought she was losing her mind. Kids do the strangest things.

> **José and Kitty Menendez.** 722 Elm Dr., at Elevado Ave. (Beverly Hills).

Where the loving, peaceful parents of Lyle and Erik met their maker.

> **Sal Mineo.** 8563 Holloway Dr., at La Cienega (West Hollywood).

Where actor Sal Mineo was knifed to death 2 days before Valentine's Day, 1976. He was getting out of his car when attacked by a couple of unidentified men. He died with the script of *P.S. Your Cat Is Dead* in his hands.

> **Marilyn Monroe's Suicide Pad.** 12305 5th Helena Dr., at Carmelina Ave. (Brentwood).

Bungalow where Norma Jean Mortensen allegedly put a stop to the whole big charade.

> **Marie Prevost.** 6320 Afton Place, at Vine (Hollywood).

Marie Prevost, a silent screen star out of a job when the talkies took over, basically drank herself to death. It was days before her body was discovered, and when the police broke in they found her half eaten by her dachshund.

> **Rebecca Schaeffer.** 120 N. Sweetzer, at Beverly (West Hollywood).

Actress Rebecca Schaeffer (*Radio Days, Down and Out in Beverly Hills*) received several fan letters from 19-year-old John Bardo, a mentally disturbed loner from Arizona. After she made the mistake of replying with a signed photo, ole John traveled to L.A., where on the morning of July 18, 1989, he rang the bell of Rebecca's building and shot her dead. In Tibetan Buddhism, "the bardo" is one of the realms where you can go after you die.

> **Bugsy Siegel.** 810 Linden Dr., at Lomitas (Beverly Hills).

Where Hollywood wanna-be and creator of Vegas was shot by disgruntled New York mobsters disappointed by the early returns from Siegel's desert casino, the Flamingo.

Studios

> **Demille and Lasky Barn.** 2100 N. Highland Ave., across from the Hollywood Bowl (Hollywood).

If the Hollywood Heritage preservationists hadn't gotten their hands on this landmark, it might have been flattened decades ago. As it is, a homeless arsonist nearly burnt the place down 2 years ago. Now, thanks to the fire, the former horse barn is up to code and ready for exhibits. Back in 1913 Cecil B. DeMille rented the Selma and Vine Street horse barn to make Hollywood's first full-length motion picture, *The Squaw Man.* The barn was later moved to Van Ness and Marathon Street, where it became Paramount Studios. After Hollywood Heritage took it over, the barn was moved again to where it now rests, across the street from the Hollywood Bowl. The Barn's exhibits are dedicated to the history of silent film. Its small theater shows features from that era.

> **Former Culver Studios.** 9336 Washington Blvd., near Culver (Culver City).

Now the home of Sony, this Culver City studio was once called "the Heart of Screenland." The Plantation House Greek Revival mansion now sits on the lot.

> **Triangle Pictures.** 10202 Washington Blvd., at Overland (Culver City).
☎ **310/244-4000.**

This studio was built in 1915 and later purchased by Goldywn. In 1924 it became MGM. Many of the original buildings and fixtures are still there, including the Yellow Brick Road that made its way to Oz and the rehearsal studio of Fred Astaire and Gene Kelly. In 1989, the studio was renamed Sony Pictures Entertainment.

Interesting for Reasons Other than the Above

> **Angelus Foursquare Temple.** 1100 Glendale Blvd., at Sunset Blvd. (Silver Lake).

The church of flamboyant evangelist Aimee Semple McPherson at the height of her fame and notoriety. Aimee was the first in a long line of eccentric Los Angeles spiritualists.

> **Batman Cave.** Bronson Park, end of Canyon Dr.; park in the parking lot, walk back down the road, and turn left onto the dirt road. Half a mile up the hill you'll come to the cave (Hollywood).

Where our heroes, Batman and Robin, lived, worked, and zoomed out of when they headed off to do battle with the Joker or Riddler. Independent of this pop-culture reference point, the cave, with its echoing walls and cool dark corners, is a captivating natural attraction in its own right.

> **Hawthorne High School.** 4859 W. El Segundo Blvd., at Inglewood (Hawthorne).

The Beach Boys' musical career began at Hawthorne High School in 1961, when Brian Wilson, his younger brothers Carl and Dennis, his high-school chum Al Jardine, and his cousin Mike Love (who attended nearby Dorsey High) decided to form a band. For almost 3 decades, the band generated a mystical vision of California coastal life through its unforgettable sun-drenched tunes. Brian Wilson reportedly was inspired to write the song "Fun, Fun, Fun" when he saw a girl driving by in her daddy's T-Bird as he stood at the Foster Freeze, 11969 Hawthorne Blvd. The Beach Boys' childhood home is at 3701 W. 119th St., in Hawthorne.

Trivia

Hawthorne High is also the alma mater of Greg Hetson of the Circle Jerks and Bad Religion.

> **Iglesia Universal.** 307 S. Broadway, at 3rd St. (Downtown). ☎ **213/588-9140.**

Home of frequent healing sessions—signs outside claim cures for anything from blindness to homosexuality—this former Million Dollar Theater was built in 1918 by Sid Grauman (of Chinese Theater fame).

> **Lookout Mountain Air Force Station.** Wonderland Ave., 5 min. off the Sunset Strip (Hollywood Hills).

Former home of a top-secret U.S. government film studio, which from 1947 to 1969 made propaganda films for the U.S. military, the Atomic Energy Commission, and other government and private weapons-related organizations. The American Film Institute recently honored the surviving "Atomic Cinematographers" of Lookout Mountain, which, in its heyday, employed over 250 people, working on about 2.5 acres.

> **Jayne Mansfield.** 10100 Carolwood Dr., at Sunset Blvd. (Beverly Hills).

Pink, very pink. Former home of Marilyn Monroe wanna-be, wife of Johnny Weismuller, and star of such hits as *Too Hot To Handle* and *The Girl Can't Help It,* Jayne Mansfield. The home was later owned by Ringo Star, Cass Elliot of the Mamas and the Papas, and then Englebert Humperdinck.

> **The Oak Tree.** 1100 Block, S. Hobart St. (South Central).

Cornelius Johnson, an African-American athlete who won four gold medals in the 1936 Olympics in Berlin, was snubbed after his wins by Adolf Hitler, who refused to shake hands with blacks. The U.S. Olympic Committee presented team members with 3-inch sapling oak trees. Today, Johnson's oak has grown to 40 feet and is visible from the street.

> **Ronald and Nancy Reagan.** 666 St. Cloud Rd., at Bel-Air Rd. (Bel-Air).

Though numerologically minded Nancy had the number on the house changed to 668, we will always think of it as 666 St. Cloud Rd. If Ronbo is "home" (which these days is a very tenuous notion, even if the former president is in actual residence), then you will see a cadre of secret service agents hovering outside. Nearby is the home of the Clampetts from the TV series "The Beverly Hillbillies".

> **Aaron Spelling.** 594 S. Mapleton Dr. (Holmby Hills).

The incredibly tasteful, cutting-edge, and brilliant producer of such mind-expanding TV fare as "Charlie's Angels," "Beverly Hills 90210," "The Love Boat," and "Melrose Place" built this monster shrine of unwitting high camp.

Animals

> **Bischoff's Taxidermy.** 54 E. Magnolia Blvd., adjacent to Interstate 5 overpass (Burbank). ☎ **818/843-7561.**

Though the heyday of the big-game hunter has long passed, their trophies have found a permanent home at Bischoff's. Opened in 1933, the place gained a reputation as one of the area's top taxidermy shops. While it's still possible to immortalize your Costa Rican jaguar under their able hands, the new owners have realized the lucrative potential of renting a full line of wildlife to photographers and film studios nationwide. The unimposing warehouse is not open to the public, but you can pass yourself off as a prop manager and gain easy entrance. As if in a disturbing "Twilight Zone" episode, you walk the floors surrounded by tigers, leopards, moose, wolves, boar, fox, kangaroo, elk, sheep, buffalo, and even a brood of chickens. Hundreds of species stand with open eyes, ready to pounce. Upstairs, a corner of discarded body parts, including a snout-torn coyote, seems eerily feral. Packs of wolves lunge near a banister. A clan of lions look dangerously alive, while a polar bear stands an impressive 12 feet tall with claws outstretched and jaws open wide. Jay Leno is propped monthly with wildlife from Bischoff's, as are pinups from *Playboy* and *Penthouse.* And what would you do if

. . . It's sort of a mix of *Bringing Up Baby* and that movie where they're dragging around the dead guy. We'll get Gwynneth to play the lead, and Steven Seagal to play the dead leopard . . .

even one of these beasts sprang to life? Take solace in the fact that at least the sharks are made of plastic and remain tethered to the wall.

Tip: For less bestial film props, try Burbank's **Tri-Ess Sciences,** 1020 W. Chestnut (☎ **818/848-7838**), home of snow machines, confetti cannons, and quarts of stage blood!!

> **Dog Parks.** See "Parks and Nature."

> **Hollywood Hounds on Sunset.** 8218 W. Sunset Blvd., at Havenhurst (West Hollywood). ☎ **323/650-5551.** www.HollywoodHounds.com.

This place may not seem like much on the outside, but oh-my-God, you won't believe what happens inside. As with their careers, their cosmetic profile, their cars, their villas (everything but their intellect), rich Angelenos are obsessive-compulsive about their pets. Like so many other businesses catering to the industry elite, Hollywood Hounds enables Angelenos in their absurdly indulgent behavior. Check this out: You can leave Muffy overnight when you go on a shoot, and Muffy can hang out with his Muffy pals watching Rin Tin Tin on TV. Muffy can also have a birthday party here, or even get married. Many lucky dogs have, often in the company of several of their canine pals. There's a wedding gazebo out back too, and a Rolls for the honeymoon. Julia Roberts is a regular. Hollywood Hounds on Sunset—just one more reason you gotta love L.A.

Art in Galleries or Museums

> **Bergamont Station Art Center.** 2525 Michigan Ave., near Cloverfield (Santa Monica). ☎ **310/829-5854.** Fax 310/453-1595.

We want to believe this collection of 21 galleries is the vortex of the L.A. art scene. And sometimes at gallery openings it definitely feels that way. But really it's simply the West Side's answer to the Brewery, with the same mercenary management, but without the living quarters.

> **The Getty.** 1200 Getty Center Dr., off 405 (Brentwood). ☎ **310/440-7300.**
Open Thurs–Fri till 9pm. Closed Mon. Free admission.

There's something off-putting about the Getty. It's not just its location on a hill. It's this sense that one has to make a reservation 6 months in advance to gain admittance.

That perception is actually inaccurate—you have to reserve *parking* that far in advance—but it's a perception that sticks because of the weird forbidding preciousness of the entire complex. The concept of the Getty is nothing short of miraculous: You are literally transported beyond your mundane concerns. The place requires a commitment, as great art should. Yet the overall feeling from being there is rather strange. Like a "Star Trek" episode. Like Biosphere meets the Cloisters. Like hanging out at some very rich person's version of a postmodern Acropolis. You should see it once, though like the L.A. Metro Rail, it's doubtful whether you will return again soon.

> **Municipal Art Gallery.** Barnsdall Art Park, 4800 Hollywood Blvd., at Edgemont St. (Los Feliz). ☎ **213/485-4581.**

In this largely flat metropolis, culture is often found on hilltops: witness the Getty Center, the Griffith Observatory, and the Municipal Art Gallery (a.k.a. "Muni"). Of all of these, Muni is the one cultural center known to locals but never visited by outsiders. Too bad. Housed in a Frank Lloyd Wright building atop "Mount Barnsdall," Muni is the one place in town firmly committed to developing local art talent. Be sure to catch the annual Open Call and Juried show, the highlight of the gallery's year.

Art in Public Places

We're big on public art. However, the whole business of getting one's art financed by the public is problematic. First, applying for a "grant" is inherently demeaning. The skills it takes to win a "grant" are often diametrically opposite of the skills it takes to produce world-class art. For me, great art has a "strangeness," to use Harold Bloom's excellent term, that renders it irreducible to the carefully delineated descriptions required of arts applications. The whole process kills the "art," not to mention the risk. Which is why we're always warmed by artists who defied what they proposed they were going to do, and actually put something out there that is original and challenging. Secondly, the nonprofit organizations and local, state, and county governments who pay for public art are conservative on the one hand (nothing that will encourage prurient sensibilities is allowed) and yet sickeningly politically correct on the other (murals celebrating the achievements of oppressed minorities often win approval). As a result, upbeat saccharine celebrations of "community" and "harmony" and "diversity" invariably get funded.

While this syndrome plays out all over America, it is particularly pernicious in Los Angeles, a growing arts capital, but one with a built-in bias towards feel-good projects. This view is no doubt engendered by the long-standing happy-ending mind-set of the sunny city's film and television industry, which has historically steered clear of challenging subject matter.

In such an unwittingly censorious environment, those artists who manage to create innovative public art should merit our attention. Here's some of L.A.'s best (and a few of the worst).

Graffiti

We are not about to send you all over L.A. to sample graffers' handiwork. Try the two centrally located examples below. If you find them intriguing, there's plenty more, including "L.A., Past, Present and Future" (4th and Spring, Downtown), the Palms Graffiti Wall (from the overpass on Motor, at National in Palms, climb up to the old railroad tracks) and the "Graffiti Pit" (Windward Avenue west of Speedway in Venice).

> **Graffiti Wall.** Northeast side of La Brea, at Melrose, next to Aaron Brothers and Yellowstone Clothing, and across the street from Pink's (Hollywood). Bombers: Saber and Tyke from AWR Crew, Phever from CBS Crew, et al.

Small science-fiction fantasy with the requisite buxom black babe. Not the best in town, but representative.

> **"Last to Stand."** Northeast corner of Pico and La Brea (Mid-Wilshire). Bombers: Spank from MBA, Mear, Phever, Siner and Retna from LTS.

East of Lucy's 24-hour Pastrami and Tacos and north of Canton Chef Express and Chief Auto Parts is an abandoned lot under development, with some graffiti walls that have not yet met the wrecking ball. The content of these walls is captivating—pyramids, man-birds, images of nature. The themes are ancient, futuristic, apocalyptic, though not thoroughly cohesive. But what do you expect—this is graffiti art, not Guernica. There seems to be a message to the whole scene, expressed by one graffer this way: "These styles must not be bitten. They must be understood. Reflect on this as yourself in a mirror. Then you will realize you are beneath the surface." Pretty damn Monk, if you ask us.

Murals

> **Farmer John's Mural.** 3049 E. Vernon Ave., at Soto (Los Angeles).
☎ 323/583-4621.

Entire wall mural of animals before they meet their packager. This is one of only a few remaining slaughterhouses near downtown L.A. They've been supplying

"Dodger Dogs" to the Dodger baseball fans since 1964. There is in fact no "Farmer John." The owners are named Clougherty and knew the public would never get their name correct. The murals are an attempt to sanitize what goes on inside this 10-acre factory of death.

> **Great Wall of Los Angeles.** Coldwater Canyon Blvd., between Burbank and Oxnard (Van Nuys).

Stretching for a half mile along the Tujunga Wash flood-control channel is the epic Great Wall of Los Angeles mural, depicting the history of people of color in California. One popular segment is Judith Baca's "Division of the Barrios and Chavez Ravine," chronicling the alleged forced eviction of "thousands" of poor Latino families in Chavez Ravine to make way for construction of Dodger Stadium. Little known to most Angelenos, this is a bit of an urban myth. As Robert Fiore made clear in a September 11, 1998, letter to *New Times Los Angeles:* "For all the good it will do, the truth is this: The land at Chavez Ravine was originally acquired by the city to build public housing. However, before the housing could actually be built, the political winds changed and rabid Red-baiters passed a referendum banning public housing from the site. All this happened long before L.A. was a gleam in Walter O'Malley's eye. By the time O'Malley came along, Chavez Ravine was something of a civic white elephant, and about 20 families were still living there, which could hardly amount to 'thousands.' From 1953 until 1958 when they were evicted, they were allowed to live in Chavez Ravine rent-free. Only one of those families, the Arechigas, had to be removed forcibly; later, it was revealed that far from being indigent, the family owned nine other houses in the city that they were renting out. . . . It should also be noted that as part of the deal the Dodgers developed 40 acres of recreational facilities in Elysian Park for free use by the public." Think about *that* the next time you feel the urge to trash Murdoch, er, Dodger, Blue.

> **Hollywood Stars.** Hollywood Blvd. and Wilcox, next to Playmates (Hollywood).

All the superstars of yesterday—Marilyn, James, Liz, et. al.—sitting in a movie theater looking down on the street. For some inexplicable reason, we just love this mural.

Sculpture

> **Ballerina Clown.** Northwest corner of Main St. and Rose (Venice).

Like it or not, this Jonathan Borofsky sculpture is one of the primary icons of Venice. And it deserves better treatment. If the city doesn't move to protect it, it could go the way of that other great pop icon of L.A., the fabled Chicken Boy.

. . . And in the big climactic scene, the two leads—we'll get Meg Ryan and Tom Hanks—meet at City on a Hill—you know, with that great view?—and . . .

› City on a Hill. Elysian Park, near Dodger Stadium; follow Stadium Way toward the stadium, turn left just before the parking lot, and climb up the hill (Downtown).

Commanding an impressive 360 degree vista, with downtown L.A., the Hollywood sign, and the ocean all within sight, this 30-foot-high Peter Shire sculpture was erected as a tribute to preservationists Grace Simon and Frank Glass. Towering concrete columns bare a colorful spinning appendage, while several cast-metal club chairs offer ringside seats to the panoramic views all around. Only a block away from the Police Academy and a favorite for late-night trysts, evidenced by the discarded condoms nearby.

› Triforium. Plaza of the Los Angeles Mall, Temple and Main (Downtown).

Really bad public art, with a vintage seventies feel. On occasion it plays music and flashes its disco-style lights. Essentially a $900,000 music box.

› The Welded Scary Monster. Martin Iron Design, 10726 Burbank Blvd., at Denny (North Hollywood). ☎ 818/760-3636.

Located in front of the Martin Iron Design shop, this looming Jurassic steel sculpture rises to monstrous heights,

Hollywood Trivia

Actress Peg Entwistle jumped from the letter H of the Hollywood sign in 1932.

threatening passing motorists. Welded by "Peter the Artist," the sculpture has changed hands several times over the years but now has taken up permanent residence on this busy thoroughfare. Its prominent, anatomically correct male member begs to be touched, though given the monster's broken tail and the fact that it's propped up by a two-by-four, one shouldn't yank too hard.

Water Art

> **Watercourt Fountain.** California Plaza, at the top of Angels Flight, between the Coopers and Lybrand Twin Towers (Downtown).

You've never seen a water fountain with a personality like this. It's a cross between a geyser and a goofy pipe organ, with a naughty circus clown thrown in. The thing will play songs and act depressed, ecstatic, and every other emotion in between. Perhaps the finest work of water art we have ever seen.

Yard Art

> **Garden of Oz.** 3106 N. Ledgewood Dr., at Rockcliff (Hollywood/Beachwood Canyon).

There is yard art and then there is YARD ART. Were you to landscape your backyard with representational metaphors from every daydream, fantasy, hallucination, and lucid dream you ever had, you might end up with a garden similar to the one found here. Painstakingly tiled halfway up a hill, the garden is glowing with rhinestones, vintage toys, ceramic figurines, and tchotchkes of every type. The owner gives Saturday tours of the Garden of Oz (by appointment—just leave a note), where you may view the Throne of Babe, the Wall of Toys, or the Bench of the Munchkin Luncheon. But if you can't wait, view the garden from the street. Just watch out for the speeding cars.

Bars

The idea that one can find compelling people at an L.A. bar seems to have died with the triumph of Dr. Bob and his 12 Steps of Alcoholics Anonymous. "The program" is riotously popular in a town of coke-snorting, speedballing, whiskey-downing Robert Downeys. As a result, the most original L.A. partyers, both in the industry and out, can be found in those bare-bones Christian "rooms," not at the local watering hole. Still, there are some great bars, if no longer consistently great bar clienteles.

> **Akbar.** 4356 Sunset Blvd., at Fountain (Silver Lake). ☎ **323/665-6810.**

Though the smirking, goateed hipster quotient can be overbearing at times, the Moorish decor of this Silver Lake watering hole offers surprising respite from the streets outside. Tall tables and stools crowd near the door, with more low-to-the-floor seating toward the back. The backlit bar delivers the requisite stiff martini with a fair share of cosmopolitans flying over the counter. The mix of artsy boho types, aspiring actors, and Los Feliz locals, both gay and straight, offer just the right edge without the pretensions of Hollywood watering holes like the Burgundy Room, Three of Clubs, Smalls, and the Good Luck Bar in Los Feliz.

> **Al's Bar.** 305 S. Hewitt, at 3rd St. (Downtown). ☎ **213/626-7213.**

See "Music Venues."

> **Argyle Patio Bar.** 8358 Sunset Blvd., at La Cienega Blvd. (West Hollywood). ☎ **213/654-7100.**

The art-deco history and decor, the patio, the metal palm trees are all nice, but the Sky Bar has a far better view, and does the elitist moneyed asshole thing far better. If only there were intelligent people worth talking to at these places.

> **Bar Marmont.** 8171 W. Sunset Blvd., at Crescent Heights (Hollywood). ☎ **213/650-0575.**

The same discreet celebrity quotient one finds in the hotel itself is palpably lacking here. Though we do like the feel—like a bar Burroughs might have stumbled into in Tangiers, with butterflies pinned to the ceiling, moody lighting, and big comfy chairs and sofas. It's no longer the secret hideaway it once was, swarmed now by valley types, and other people who are all dressed up with nothing to say.

> **Barbata's.** 20001 Ventura Blvd., at Winnetka (Woodland Hills). ☎ **818/340-5914.**

This is swing music so real, with old-time couples so bona fide, it scares away the wanna-bes in the burgeoning Swing Nation. Back in the days when Ventura Boulevard was called "Vegas of the Valley," this was the place. Their house band features Lawrence Welk's former accordionist, Kenny Kotswicz. The Christmas lights have been hanging since the seventies. An unforgettable treasure.

> **Bob Burns.** 202 Wilshire Blvd., at 2nd St. (Santa Monica). ☎ **310/393-6777.**

This boxy Republican fortress opened as a steak house in 1963. And while the cold war raged, the denizens of Santa Monica sipped on their gimlets within the dark windowless recesses of the Bob Burns. The impeccable upkeep affords one the opportunity to turn back the clock and sink into the black leatherette booths, stare

. . . The main thing is getting the right person to play Bob. Maybe Paul Sorvino . . .

at the wood-paneled walls, and imbibe. The bar's centerpiece is a grand piano where the blind Howlett "Smitty" Smith has been playing jazz and blues since before man landed on the moon. Unless you're really hankering for a piece of Des Moines, give the menu a miss and swap stories with the fur-wearing septuagenarians that frequently stumble in. Fortunately (or unfortunately, depending on your point of view), as the Bob Burns loyalists die out from old age, a recent influx of smart, smirking hipsters are picking up the tab.

> **Boardner's.** 1652 N. Cherokee Ave., at Hollywood Blvd. (Hollywood). ☎ 213/462-9621.

Original home of the down-and-out rocker. Grizzled local-music scenesters who look like they've been pouring themselves in and out of these same red-Naugahyde booths for the past 20 years, along with an assortment of kids looking for old glam-rock L.A. This is a shrine to faded dreams.

> **Dresden Room.** 1760 N. Vermont Ave., at Hollywood Blvd. (Los Feliz). ☎ 323/665-4294.

Favorite camp-lite watering hole for swinging straights in the know. Torch singing and the smoky air gives the place a strange 1940s ambiance. Which has fortunately not been diluted by the Dresden's starring role in recent Hollywood films.

> **H.M.S. Bounty.** 3357 Wilshire Blvd., at Alexandria (Koreatown). ☎ 213/385-7275.

Across the street from the illustrious Coconut Grove, and down from the old Brown Derby, this nautically themed restaurant and bar, with the great red burgundy booths, might have once been one of the classiest establishments in town. Given the jukebox is still loaded with Sinatra and Dorsey, and that the bartender and staff are low on attitude and high on genuine goodwill, this still might be counted upon as a dependable stopover. But its decor has seen better days—old maritime art, old carpet, old waitresses. And, unfortunately it's become a big drawing card for the über-ironic L.A. hipster brats, listening to big bands and smoking on cigarettes in the front room, in defiance of all smoking ordinances. Occasional club parties float through here, keeping the Bounty on the map. The residential Gaylord Hotel is just through a swinging door.

> **Lola's Martini Bar.** 945 N. Fairfax Ave., at Romaine (Hollywood). ☎ 213/736-5652.

Brit bloke about town Cash Peters writes: "a bit pricey, but boy! More varieties of weirdly flavored martinis than you've ever imagined (if you bother imagining martinis, that is)." Cash is right. French Kiss Martini. Three Strikes Martini. Mad Max Martini. Chollos Martini. Lemon Drop Martini. Rad Dad Martini. Lots of pretty martinis. But the crowd is so very Amateur Night.

> **Löwenbräu Keller.** 3211 Beverly Blvd., at Dillon (near Downtown). ☎ 213/382-5723.

The ultimate in German bar-and-restaurant camp—enough tacky, chintzy, schmaltzy kitsch to keep any ironic hipster in Smirk Heaven. I mean, this place reeks of it, from the fully armored knight at the head of the main table to the walls of mounted boar and deer to the giant cast-iron chandeliers. Go here to eat sausage. Go here to drink "bier." Go here because it is truly one of the great gaudy highlights of one of the most gaudy cities on earth.

> **Musso and Frank Grill.** 6667 Hollywood Blvd., at Cherokee (Hollywood). ☎ 213/467-5123.

Old Hollywood at its greatest, as long as you don't fall victim to the pricey menu. The low-lit rooms, aged wood paneling, red Naugahyde booths, and sweeping counter with stools scream Cocktail Nation. And, yes, in terms of martinis, this is the swinger's holy grail, even though Musso and Frank aspires towards the classic steak house. Offering a weighty choice between a $30 tenderloin and a $27 roast prime rib, they fall miserably short on delivery with whatever choice you make. Where they pick up the slack is in atmosphere and gin. Long before nineties hipsters began swigging Absolut, Musso was dousing the Hollywood elite with their perfectly chilled, double olive, gin and vermouth wonder. Upon delivery, the $6, thimble-sized conical glass seems a tad meager until they set a carafe at its side which holds the remainder. It's as ample and stout a martini as you'll ever need. Should you order another? Not if you have further business to conduct that day. The service is speedy, the ambiance is Mafioso perfect, the red-jacketed waiters just the right crusty; with the white tablecloths and deep seductive booths, if you don't hear Sinatra playing in your head by the second round then just try another and call a cab from the wooden phone booths near the back kitchen door.

> **Red Lion.** 2366 Glendale Blvd., at Silver Lake Blvd. (Silver Lake). ☎ **323/662-5337.**

Besides the brick and oak shuttered walls, the rafters lined with mugs, the upstairs beer hall, the huge stein near the bar, the cheesy karaoke, the clean and well-run Teutonic order to the place, the highlight of this ancient (by L.A. standards) German restaurant and bar is the beautiful fräuleins in sweet red dresses, happily here to serve you—that is, until the next singing or acting gig.

> **Re$iduals.** 11042 Ventura Blvd., at Vineland (Studio City). ☎ **818/761-8301.**

It has all the ambiance of a 1970s fern bar pickup joint, sans ferns and swinging singles. Though smoking, on the record, is forbidden in California, that doesn't keep half the clientele from lighting up and the staff from looking the other way. Sitting in the back of a strip mall, this is the unofficial after-work watering hole for low-ranking "industry" personnel. On any given night the bar is packed with gaffers, grips, production assistants, and rank-and-file writers who commiserate about their day with gin-and-tonic in hand. The walls are lined with the requisite framed, autographed star photos; the sound system blares golden oldies; and the intense insider gossip heard at every table is occasionally drowned out by a mediocre band.

> **Skybar and Grill.** In the Mondrian Hotel, 8440 Sunset Blvd., at La Cienega (West Hollywood). ☎ **213/650-8999.**

Much as we bemoan the egregious elitism of door policies, we always manage to make our way into these sort of places. Therefore, we can't tell you much about the door policy here. Hard to tell what sort of criteria they were using the night we visited anyway—lots of very tan Italian-American gentleman, a few Sean Penns, some crazy tall black character in a pigtail Afro, a few brokers, and lots of Valley women in cakes of makeup. Every woman seemed to be smoking (still allowed in California on outdoor patios), and many of the young men seemed to be posing for a slot as the next Steven Seagal, or maybe Luke Perry. We don't figure the irony quotient was quite high. Sample bathroom conversation: "I called her, but Jerry was doing the full court press on her. Something felt funny between Jerry and me, you know. So I laid off. I mean, Jerry's my friend, y'know. Jerry's my friend. So I quit calling her. But, I'll tell you what, of all the girls we've seen the last three days, she was the cutest."

"So, what's she doing with Jerry? The executive thing?"

"Nah, he's spending a lot of money on her. Got her into a Mariah Carey party."

"Mariah Carey's in town?"

"Yeah."

Breeders . . . where would we be without them?

There are a few saving graces at the Skybar and Grill: the surreal, extraordinarily large planters, whose flowers form an extraordinary archway over the dinner tables, and the large bedlike couches on the deck. Otherwise, like so much of L.A., with its emphasis on form over substance, wealth over warmth, it feels like high school all over again.

> **360 Penthouse.** 6290 Sunset Blvd., at Vine (Hollywood). ☎ **213/871-2995.**

There have been several stabs at turning this blight of a high-rise penthouse into a restaurant and bar, but each attempt seems doomed once the initial fanfare subsides. Whether 360 can pull it off remains to be seen, but the chief drawing card continues to be The View. The astonishing, unobstructed panorama gives the imbibers among us the perfect opportunity to get thoroughly sloshed while absorbing the aesthetic pleasures of another orange-brown L.A. sunset. The latest decor borrows heavily from the Philippe Starck school of "hanging white drapes," with walls that look like set flats that could come down in an easy 30 minutes. The blue seats and white linen table spreads continue the temporal, airy feel of the place. Chef Sean Studds promises to deliver a menu rich in "California-American" cuisine, though it bears a striking resemblance to hotel menus nationwide. Monk Lesson #23: No amount of polished aluminum or glossy floors can disguise an ugly building and unimaginative fare. But apparently the clientele hasn't noticed. As the hot spot du jour, the ubiquitous triumvirate of Madonna, DiCaprio, and Stipe has apparently given it a stamp of approval. Ordinarily that would be reason enough to stay away. But then again, there's The View.

> **Tiki Ti.** 4427 Sunset Blvd., at Virgil (Los Feliz). ☎ **213/669-9381.**

This pint-sized Polynesian bar has a devoted neighborhood following that possesses an overwhelming need to decorate. Tiki patrons have made a ritual of mailing in trinkets from around the world, creating a virtual rain forest of clutter hanging off the ceiling and lining the walls. Plastic skulls, shrunken heads, and blowfish are accented by an astonishing number of out-of-state license plates. A small, illuminated, water-filled grotto bubbles under the moderate tinkle of chimes hanging overhead. Polynesian masks line the wall, while the $7 boat drinks run the gamut from a classic Mai Tai to a fiery Electric Lemonade. The overworked bartenders can barely keep up with the thirsty, smoking crowd, so expect an easy 20-minute wait to get your clutches on a tropical drink before retreating to the center of the tiny room.

> **Ye Olde King's Head Pub and Restaurant.** 116 Santa Monica Blvd., at 2nd St. (Santa Monica). ☎ **310/451-1402.**

Occupying over six rooms and half a block, this re-created, gentrified English pub screams Universal City marketing concept. You might as well be downing a draft at Epcot Center. It sits right near the highly trafficked Third Street Promenade; just one more reason to steer clear on almost any given day—*except* Sunday, when Tom Sheehy crowds his oven with nearly two dozen legs of lamb for his weekly lamb special ($9.95). It's a tradition among the expats, and they pack the place with enough Brit wit to blush the queen. After a few beers and a slab of lamb you too might feel like you're back on the hills of Dover. Just ignore the sun.

On the Bus, Part 1:

Hand on the Wallet

It's been a long restless night at the Dunes Wilshire Motor Hotel, and afternoon has set in. The Monks jog down Wilshire and stop to catch a bus at the corner of Wilshire and Western. Under the towering hulk of the green, glowing Wiltern Building, in the glare of a smoggy, 90° day, Michael Monk determines that there's got to be a faster way to the beach than the car-stalled Interstate 10.

The green-tiled, chrome, postmodern architectural wonder of a subway stop sits adjacent. It's the last outpost of subway tunneling, so a hoard of passengers come out from its epic depths to catch the westbound buses that wait at the curb.

The long-awaited, highly coveted express bus to Santa Monica pulls up 40 minutes off schedule. The crowd crushes toward the door with the urgency of rats swimming to a raft. The driver is black. The boarding riders are Hispanic and carry the burden of Hancock Park on their shoulders, returning home from another slave-wage day of manicuring the lawns, cleaning the pools, washing the cars, and walking the dogs and children of their largely Caucasian employers. The debarking riders are Koreans who staff the seedy warehouse sweat shops east of downtown.

The door slams closed, and the bus pulls off with a smoke-belching lurch, forcing all standing passengers to fall half backward into the shoulders of whomever is nearby. In Mike's case it's a Korean lady carrying a backpack full of smelly fruit. Mike apologizes for bumping. She takes the unexpected interaction as a signal to ask for "dollar please, dollar please." When Mike doesn't respond with the requested "dollar please," she turns toward the remaining 50 Hispanic passengers and travels the length of the bus requesting "dollar please." At La Brea the driver tosses her off the bus for failing to pay the fare.

At La Cienega the Monks spot a girl wearing a pair of yellow jeans so tight the buttons promise to pop. The machismo Mexicans onboard, to a man, take notice of the fact that she is packing a mighty large rig in that bra. Her entrance is accompanied by the clicking of tongues as she ambles her way down the aisle. She wears the requisite Walkman, earphones dangling around her neck, with her hair parted so hard down the middle the scalp shines through. Her pant-popping, ass-shaking walk is further accentuated by two sizable chains that hang through the loops and cinch her waist even tighter than it already is. She carries an overnight bag and is sucking on a straw. Mike bets himself a fish taco that she's trade.

She doesn't stand for long as more than three crotch-grabbing boys near the back door of the bus offer her a seat in the midst of their hip-hop posse of pals. She takes the one closest to the door. The bus is now packed as tight as the girl's jeans. The boys crowd unbearably close around and are soon on the make, running through their lines. Though she doesn't accept, she doesn't decline. To each lewd comment she in turn responds with a lewdness so subtle it borders on the sublime.

She fingers a stack of CDs, removed from her bag with a touch so seductive it makes the skin tingle. The boys crowd nearer just to watch her ruby-red nails click one by one across the hard plastic edge.

One boy hangs against the pole, his eyes so dark they seem like half moon craters hanging under his brow. He begins making suggestive movements with his hip. Low guttural laughter peels off the back of his throat as he rubs his groin against the edge of her seat.

She coos. Coos like a pigeon on a building's ledge. There's a soft murmuring motion from the roundness of her lips that whispers deft cadence to the chugging bus. The boy proceeds with caution, making an apprehensive attempt to touch her on the head. She pulls back, her finger circling around and around a worn hole in her street-walking frayed yellow jeans.

"Puta," says the man next to Mike.

Puta thoughts are on the mind of every guy watching the slow-motion slip of her hand. She fumbles in her bag and pulls out a pack of gum, which she purposefully drops to the floor. It lands down behind the guy's feet. The posse of boys are chiding one another to pick it up. She pulls the bus stop cord while continuing to suck on the straw, puffing her cheeks until she looks like an inflatable doll. She shrugs as the gum sits there and, without words, pleads coquettishly with her eyes.

She's seriously messing with these guys. Just as the bus pulls over and a crowd gathers for the door, the dark-eyed boy turns quickly around, bending down to pick up the gum for her. Her fingers move quick. In a practiced move she's done hundreds of times before, she lunges forward out of her seat and, seen by only the most attentive eyes of a Monk, she makes for the boy's pocket. It's a move so smooth only the best in the trade could possibly have known. As the door flings open and a small crowd debarks, she swings away from the seat, takes her gum out of his hand, and in ass-waddling perfection, she's out the door.

Only two blocks later does the dark one with the increasingly large circles under his brow shout, "The bitch, she stole my wallet!"

And the posse of boys bound off the bus to chase a woman they'll never find.

Bookstores

> **Atlantis Books.** 144 S. San Fernando Blvd., at Olive (Burbank).
☎ **818/845-6467.**

The ultimate conspiracy book haven. Paul Hunt's dusty hole-in-the-wall has towering shelves stacked high, sectioned off by categories that include UFOs, Crime, and Conspiracy. Timely books on Clinton, Michael Jackson, and paramilitary organizations round out the eclectic selection.

> **Book City.** 6627 Hollywood Blvd., at Cherokee (Hollywood).
☎ **323/466-2525.**

Good art books and Hollywood biographies, but the service is abysmal (perhaps because they pay the help so poorly).

> **Book Soup.** 1818 W. Hollywood Blvd., at Larabee (West Hollywood).
☎ **310/659-3110.**

Though it is tiny and almost always packed, this might very well be the best bookstore in the city.

> **The California Map and Travel Center.** 3312 Pico Blvd., at 33rd St. (Santa Monica). ☎ **310/396-6277.** www.mapper.com.

An intrepid traveler's wet dream, with a healthy stock of maps from around the world. You can drop an easy hundred on a wall-size map of L.A., or, for the digitally minded, walk out with a Thomas Brothers' CD-ROM map to the Southland. Every major travel publisher is represented, with even obscure global destinations adequately stocked. The staff are well traveled and serve as virtual travel guides to the bewildering urban sprawl outside their door.

> **Koma (formerly Amok).** 1764 N. Vermont Ave., at Hollywood Blvd. (Los Feliz).
☎ **323/665-0956.**

B. Dalton's this is not. Koma carries everything PC culture says is not good for you, as well as plenty of titles the religious right would lose their lunch over. Selection runs the gamut—from conspiracy theories to effective homicide, riot control to suicide, scarification to very scary fiction. This is the vortex of literary high weirdness in L.A., though gradually falling apart since it changed ownership.

Midnight Special. 1318 Third St. Promenade, between Arizona and Santa Monica Blvds. (Santa Monica). ☎ **310/393-2923.** www.msbooks.com.

The traditional L.A. story seems to adhere to the following structure: Innocent comes to nasty cynical city, ends up selling soul, ends up accruing a flicker of fame and good fortune, has lots of sex, does lots of drugs, life starts to fall apart, still has lots of sex (but with the less powerful or beautiful), does more drugs, crashes, and, in recent treatments of the theme, is reborn through therapy, 12-steps, love, or leaving. A few of the following titles adhere to this overworked structure, often to entertaining effect, but, fortunately, several others skip the premise altogether. Here, in its loose totality, is the L.A. literary oeuvre.

FICTION

After Many a Summer Dies the Swan, Aldous Huxley

Anyplace but Here, Arna Bontemps

Ape and Essence, Aldous Huxley

Barfly, Charles "Hank" Bukowski

The Big Nowhere, James Ellroy

The Big Sleep, Raymond Chandler

The Black Dahlia, James Ellroy

Cadillac Desert, Mark Reisner

The Chinchilla Farm, Judith Freeman

The Day of the Locust, Nathaniel West

Death Claims, Joseph Hansen

Devil in a Blue Dress, Walter Mosley

Double Indemnity, James Cain

Eccentric People and Peculiar Notions, John Michell

Famous All Over Town, Danny Santiago

Farewell, My Lovely, Raymond Chandler

Get Shorty, Elmore Leonard

God Sends Sunday, Arna Bontemps

Helter Skelter, Vincent Bugliosi

The High Window, Raymond Chandler

Hollywood Days, Hollywood Nights, Ben Stein

How Town, Michael Nava

I'm Losing You, Bruce Wagner

Inhale: Gasoline & Gunsmoke, Donald Baker

Killing of the Saints, Alex Abella

L.A. Confidential, James Ellroy

The Last Tycoon, F. Scott Fitzgerald

Less Than Zero, Bret Easton Ellis

The Little Sister, Raymond Chandler

The Lonely Crusade, Chester Himes

Lonesome Traveler, Jack Kerouac

The Long Good-Bye, Raymond Chandler

The Loved One, Evelyn Waugh

Maiden, Cynthia Buchanan

Mother, Daughter, Carolyn See

The Moving Target, Ross MacDonald

The New Centurions, Joseph Wambaugh

The Nowhere City, Alison Lurie

Play It As It Lays, Joan Didion

Playing with Fire, Julia Taymor

Post Office, Charles Bukowski

The Postman Always Rings Twice, James Cain

A Single Man, Christopher Isherwood

Sleeping Beauty, Ross MacDonald

Soultown, Mercedes Lambert

Tortilla Curtain, T. Coraghessan Boyle

The Western Coast, Paula Fox

White Jazz, James Ellroy

NONFICTION

City of Quartz, Mike Davis

The City: Los Angeles and Urban Theory at the End of the Twentieth Century, Allen J. Scott and Edward W. Soja, editors

Crackpot, John Waters

Ecology of Fear, Mike Davis

An Empire of Their Own: How the Jews Invented Hollywood, Neil Gabler

Hello, He Lied, and Other Truths from the Hollywood Trenches, Lynda Obst

Hollywood Babylon, Kenneth Anger

Sex, Death, and God in L.A. (Stories and Essays), David Reid

Sex and the City, Candace Bushnell

Translating L.A.: A Tour of the Rainbow City, Peter Theroux

White Album, Joan Didion

The Los Angeles version of New York's St. Mark's Bookshop. Carrying on the Samo agitprop tradition, with Ginsberg, Burroughs, and anyone and everyone from the Marxist pantheon.

› **Skylight.** See description under "Los Feliz" in neighborhoods.

Buildings, Bridges,
and Other Visual Landmarks

L.A. architecture is a complete mess. It's like Seoul on a bad day. In fact, Seoul might have it more together. You'll find completely different architectural styles from one house, one building, one block to another, with no connection, no thread, no continuity between them. You can have a Hancock Park mansion and then two doors down a rickety wooden shack. You can have a Brady Bunch Moderne butting up to a Georgia O'Keeffe Southwest-style adobe. A four-star art-deco hotel adjacent to a nondescript tattoo parlor. It's a "do what you want to do, be want you want to be" kinda town. And the buildings reflect that. Moors, Egyptians, Spaniards, even Hansel and Gretel—all would find a home here. Those who enjoy the elegant harmony and consistency of cities like San Francisco and Santa Fe will find L.A. problematic. But, frankly, we've grown to love it. Here are our favorite buildings and structures in the most consistently shocking and innovative architectural city in America.

› **Bob's Big Boy.** 4201 Riverside Dr., at Alameda (Burbank). ☎ **818/843-9334.**
Oldest standing Bob's Big Boy in the country.

› **Bradbury Building.** 304 S. Broadway, at 3rd St. (Downtown).

A setting for the ultimate L.A. futurist film fantasy, *Blade Runner,* the Bradbury is the most remarkable work of indoor architecture in Los Angeles, a place so filled with surreal magic and mechanical surprise it left us gaping in awe. It features a beautiful sunlit interior court, glazed yellow brick walls, oak and mahogany paneling, ornate black wrought-iron railings and staircases, Mexican tile floors, the nation's first mail chute, and our favorite—open bird-cage hydraulic elevators leading up to the glorious atrium crowned by a skylit, peaked glass roof. Thank the pioneering wisdom of the architectural firm Levin & Associates, and developer Yellin & Associates, for the Bradbury's restoration—and the genius of architect/designer George Wyman, who

. . . We could do the chase scene in the Bradbury Building. Sort of an homage to *Blade Runner*. Yeah, an homage . . .

took the job in 1893 after getting a message from his dead brother through a Ouija board. On the ground floor, at Ross Cutlery, is where O.J. bought "the knife" (though show some consideration and don't ask the owner about it).

> **The Braille Institute Globe.** 741 N. Vermont Ave., at Melrose (Los Angeles). ☎ 213/663-1111.

Close your eyes and touch the large world globe in the lobby, and see if you can discover where America is. Tours of the institute begin every day in the lobby at 10am.

> **The Brewery.** Interstate 5 and Main St. Exit West (Downtown). ☎ 213/694-2911.

Not so much an artist colony as an impressive real-estate development populated by artists. The hard-edged, no-nonsense New York–born builder, Richard Carpenter, would probably switch over to some other concept if the artist colony shtick no longer paid off, but for now he's at full occupancy. A counter clerk at the on-site cafe confided that most of the art that comes out of here is mediocre at best, with the exception of a few stellar photographers and the occasional fine sculptor. We caught one of the sculptors at space number 688—great quasi-Godzilla metallic fantasies. A tour of the visually rich, and at times even artful, 287-space, 21-building complex is offered every spring. Call for info.

Picture this: The male lead—we could get Harrison—is working on a sculpture. The female lead enters. She's there to determine who gets funded. We could get Julia Roberts . . .

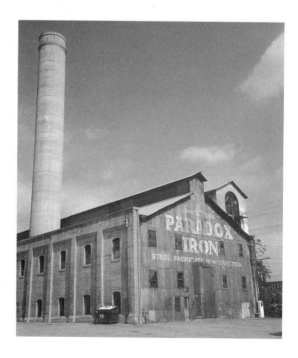

> **Bungalow Heaven.** N. Mentor Ave., around McDonald Park between Lake and Hill aves. north of Orange Grove Blvd. (Pasadena). Bungalow Heaven Neighborhood Association, ☎ 818/585-2172.

L.A. is big on bungalows, and these are are some of the best. The highlights are the airplane bungalow at 775 N. Mentor and another at 875 N. Michigan, which has an unusual entrance through a chimney.

> **Canyon Service and Detail.** 507 Entrade Dr., near the Pacific Coast Hwy. (PCH) (Santa Monica). ☎ 310/454-2619.

We adore this refreshingly old-fashioned service station, a cross between Edward Hopper and "Mayberry RFD."

> **Capitol Records Building.** 1750 Vine St., at Yucca (Hollywood).

Shaped like a stack of 45s with a stylus on top, and with a beacon that spells out "Hollywood" in Morse code, this is far and away the shining star of Hollywood, the ultimate example of L.A. vernacular architecture, and the big inviting landmark that greets all drivers as they enter Hollywood on the 101.

> **Central Library.** 5th and Hope (Downtown).

Dramatically renovated by Norman Pfeiffer in 1993 from the original Bertram B. Goodhue design (he of the Nebraska State Capitol in Lincoln). The highlights here are the elevators (the shaft and cars of which are papered with cards from the old card catalogue), and a glorious atrium inside the new Tom Bradley wing (grab a seat on the top floor that overlooks this vast yet colorful space). You would never know how huge this library is from the outside because the Tom Bradley addition descends four stories underground. The library is one of the clearest signs yet that downtown is definitely on the way up.

> **Chemosphere House.** 7776 Torreyson Dr., 1 mile past the intersection of Mulholland Dr. and Laurel Canyon (Hollywood Hills).

John Lautner's boldly futurist icon was immortalized in Brian De Palma's slasher send-up, *Body Double.* Built in 1960, it resembles a flying saucer caught in the trees. The drive to the house along beautiful Mulholland Drive is one of our favorites in the city.

> **Chiat Day Building.** 340 Main St., near Rose (Venice).

Outside, giant Oldenburg-style binoculars. Inside, the former home of renowned ad agency Chiat Day (the place is currently up for sale). Designed by Frank O. Gehry (Edgemar Shopping Mall, Wall Disney Concert Hall), the court architect of fin de siècle L.A.

› Chicken Boy. P.O. Box 292000, Los Angeles, CA 90029. ☎ **323/660-0620.**

Considered in all his wacky pop-art glory "the Statue of Liberty of L.A.," this humble roadside artifact has been brought to the attention of millions, thanks to the good karmic graces of Amy Inouye (of Future Studio fame). Originally resting atop a downtown eatery of the same name until said restaurant closed, CB's fate seemed sealed until Amy rescued and transported him to a place in Monterey Park. Here CB prayed for urban calm as he laid Buddha-like, caressing his sacramental bucket of fowl, his head John the Baptist–like between his legs, transmuting the negative energy put forth by a neighboring discarded school bus with the cryptic company trademark "Super White Power" emblazoned on its side. Though currently disembodied (his head is in Amy's studio, his torso in a friend's backyard), new plans call for our perma-glass hero to rise again, though only Amy knows when and where.

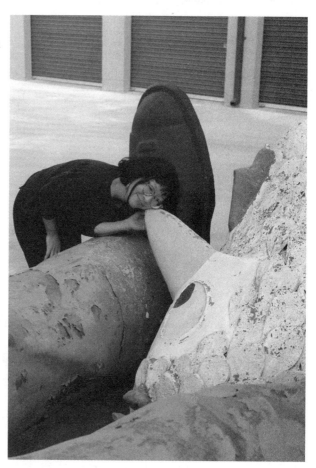

. . . It's a postmodern love story: Woman falls in love with a chicken statue. They'll love it in the cities . . .

. . . It's the world's first planned shopping mall, see, and the leads meet there—we'll get Leonardo and Cameron—and . . .

> **Coca Cola Company Bottling Plant.** 1334 S. Central Ave., at Pico (Downtown).

Streamlined Moderne Pop featuring two huge coke bottles at the corners of a massive ocean-liner exterior.

> **Crossroads of the World.** 6671 Sunset Blvd., near Highland (Hollywood).

A 1936 visual treasure patterned after a ship, it's the world's first planned outdoor shopping mall.

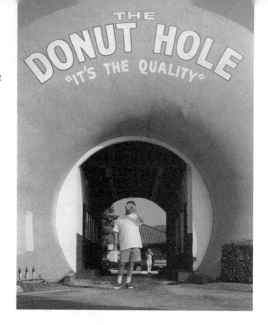

. . . It's a giant donut sculpture, see, and one of the leads is the sculptor—we'll get Leonardo—and he'll meet Cameron there while he's on his back on the scaffolding painting it, and . . .

> **The Donut Hole.** 15300 E. Amar, at Hacienda (La Puente).

The most delicious work of roadside art in L.A. Portly patrons make their way through the sacred donut center and purchase a variety of sugar-rich treats from a drive-up window.

> **Dunbar Hotel.** 4225 S. Central Ave., near Vernon

The structure ain't much, but the history around it is as important as any in L.A. This is where the great black jazz all-stars of the thirties and forties stayed, when Central Avenue was the scene and when downtown hotels were off-limits to blacks. The first hotel in the United States built exclusively for African-Americans, the Dunbar is being gradually turned into a symbol of community pride.

> **Forest Lawn Memorial Park Glendale.** 1712 S. Glendale Ave., near San Fernando Rd. (Glendale).

"A country club for the dead" featuring talking statuary and other kitschy funeral art. Celebrities buried here include Clark Gable, Sammy Davis Jr., Jean Harlow, Walt Disney, Humphrey Bogart, W. C. Fields, Gracie Allen, Errol Flynn, and Chico Marx, plus scores of other wackos and celebs, or wacko celebs, such as Aimee Semple McPherson, buried with a telephone (ostensibly to stay in touch with her faithful or with God, but more likely to stay in touch with her lawyer in case the cops finally decide to nail her for fraud). Of the three cemeteries in the Forest Lawn chain, this is by far the best. I mean, you gotta love a place whose internment options include "Vesperland" and "Lullabyeland."

> **4th Street Bridge.** 4th St., at Mission (Downtown).

Some writers consider this gnarly vestige of a beaux arts bridge "romantic." If your idea of romance is grungy industrial decay, then you bet, Betty. But with homeless feces in the alcoves, the pathetic denatured L.A. River rolling underneath, Hispanic graffiti all over the aqueduct's walls, and, below, nothing but railroad tracks and railroad yards, the word "romantic" might not be the first thing that comes to mind. But then you stand there awhile, and as the sun starts to set, as the Dragnet Building comes into view, as the trucks roar behind, as the ugly, foul, brackish, dark green L.A. River rolls steadily below, you say to yourself, "Hot damn, I love L.A."

> **Golf Man.** At Dominguez Golf Course, 19800 S. Main, at Del Amo; exit Main St. from northbound 405 (Carson). ☎ **310/719-1942.**

One of three giant triplets to grace the L.A. roadside. His brother, Lumberjack Man, can be found outside a hardware store on Long Beach Boulevard, and Gas Station Man is an attendant on 3rd Street in East L.A.

> **Historic Monument No. 624.** 3819–3827 Dunn Dr., near Washington Blvd. (Culver City).

A house, plus a couple of adjacent apartment blocks, that were designed and built between 1946 and 1970 by Lawrence Joseph in the so-called story-book style (the witch's house in Beverly Hills has the same idea).

Great L.A. Donut Structures

In addition to the Donut Hole (see review in this section), other great L.A. donut structures include **Randy's Donuts,** 805 W. Manchester Blvd., at La Cienega, in Inglewood (☎ **310/ 645-4707**), and **Kindle's Donuts,** 10003 S. Normandie Ave., near Century Boulevard, in South Central (☎ **323/ 756-8548**), both from the same 1954 design, though Randy's wins the coveted "Monk Award for Pride in One's Giant Rooftop Donut." They even sell Randy's Donuts T-shirts, though the sales help isn't nearly as pretty as at Kindle's.

. . . And we could do a sequel with a second donut sculpture, since the first one was destroyed by rebels at the climax of the first movie . . .

> **Madonna's House.** Best Viewed from Hollywood Reservoir—see "Parks" (Hollywood).

Though she has long since relocated to the more hospitable confines of Los Feliz, everyone still regards this mansion overlooking the Hollywood Reservoir as "Madonna's House." We've always liked her brother's paint job, which generated a fury of protest from neighbors. We snapped a photo of the Monkmobile in front of the pad—it seemed apropos to have the home of the Non-Material Boys shot before the former home of the Material Girl.

> **Santa Monica Pier.** Colorado St., at PCH (Santa Monica).

Vintage carousel, nostalgic penny arcade, great ocean view, and a towering Ferris wheel make this a favorite stop for all strata of Los Angeles. It's the location of the 1963 movie *Night Tide,* featuring Dennis Hopper as a sailor who falls in love with a mermaid.

> **Scientology Celebrity Centre.** Southwest corner of Franklin and Bronson aves. (Hollywood).

The Celebrity Centre is in one of the most beautiful buildings in all of Hollywood, with a nice view from the roof, but to call it a "Celebrity Centre" is such a hilarious stroke of simple-headedness, it makes us keel over with laughter. We love Scientology—it's the only "religion" that is perfectly in tune with the zeitgeist of Hollywood: unabashedly tacky, unashamedly overpriced, unquestionably low-brow. Message to Lisa Marie: *You get clear, girl.*

> **Self-Realization Fellowship Lake Shrine.** 17190 Sunset Blvd., near Palisades Dr. (Pacific Palisades).

Gorgeous meditative oasis, which safekeeps some of Ghandi's ashes. Founded by Indian guru Paramhansa Yogananda.

> **Shakespeare Bridge.** Franklin Ave. between Myra Ave. and St. George St. (Los Feliz).

A 1925 landmark (what is it with 1925 in this town?), with Gothic turrets and arches, the undeniably lovely and whimsical Shakespeare Bridge is probably the most beloved crossway in town.

> **Tower of Wooden Pallets.** 15357 Magnolia Blvd., near Sepulveda Blvd. (Sherman Oaks).

Built by Daniel Van Meter in his backyard from 2,000 platforms discarded by the Schlitz Brewery. Over 20 feet high, and visible from the street.

> **Union 76 Gas Station.** 427 N. Crescent Dr., near Santa Monica Blvd. (Beverly Hills).

With it's soaring roof, it looks like a more angular version of Le Corbusier's Notre-Dame-du-Haut or at least Noah's Ark. At night, it's lit by a gazillion lights and looks like blast-off is imminent. A classic in Atomic Age design.

. . . And we'll have the giant persecuted ape climb to the top of the Watts Towers, and have him attacked by LAPD helicopters. We'll get Brendan Fraser to play the ape . . .

› **Union Station.** 800 N. Alameda St., at Cesar E. Chavez Ave. (Downtown).

If you're looking to experience the feeling of L.A. during its 1940s prime, visit this extraordinarily clean, spacious, well-maintained (if underutilized) historical landmark. All train stations evoke a certain nostalgia, but Union Station more than most because it feels so California, so Old L.A. The Mission-meets-Mediterranean architecture has been ably preserved, including earth-toned walls, decorated beams, and courtyards of trumpet vines and fan palms. An anomaly in such a car-centric metropolis, Union Station serves the thousands of Angelenos who still commute by Metro-North. But just as importantly, it acts as the city's one true grand community space, where parties, weddings, and special events are regularly held. Go on any weekend, and you will find it buzzing on all cylinders.

› **Vedanta Temple.** 1946 Vedanta Place, near Vine (Hollywood). ☎ 213/465-7114. www.vedanta.com

We like this place. It's not the Taj Mahal. More like Taj Junior, or, as some say, "Little Taj." It features three onion domes with golden spires on top, and a sweetly contemplative ambiance inside. Developer William Mead deeded the property to the Vedanta Society of Southern California in 1929, and it has been used as a Ramakrishna temple ever since.

› **Watts Towers.** 1727 E. 107th St., at Willow Brook Ave. (South Central).

The Coral Castle of the West, Simon Rodia's dreamlike masterwork is an odd shrine in an even odder location. The cement-and-steel towers stand nearly 100 feet tall, and are imbedded with mosaics of seashells, bottles, and tiles. What is most strange is that no tagger has decided to leave his imprint—guess some surfaces are truly sacred. Take the Blue Line Light Rail to get there.

> **The Witch's House.** 516 Walden Dr., at Carmelita (Beverly Hills).

This place looks as if whoever lives there cooks questionable meals in a huge bubbling cauldron while chanting your name. Moved to this location because too many gawkers caused traffic problems at its previous spot.

Cafes and Coffeehouses

Merrill Shindler: "Where not very long ago (in geologic time), there were almost no coffeehouses in Los Angeles, it now seems as if there's one on every street corner. . . . I don't think a heck of a lot of many of them—hotbeds of lethargy in which people with rings through their noses serve poorly made espresso and desiccated carrot cake to other people with rings through their noses. Everybody smokes too much. I suspect a conspiracy between Maxwell House and Phillip Morris. . . ."

> **Cafe Interactive.** 215 Broadway, at 2nd St. (Santa Monica).
☎ **310/395-5009.**

When you're hard-pressed for cafe culture in L.A. and feel like you've just got to have that hit of bohemia, you might try elsewhere. But if downing a double tall in an interior so cool it intimidates, while sitting among the likes of Sean Penn and Al Pacino and surrounded by art so overpowering you feel like you're living inside someone's paradigm, then this is the place for you. Raw concrete floors, immensely tall ceilings, a wall of glass facing the street, and floral displays that reek of DESIGN are the only environmental hazards before you as you down your brew. The deli case has the tastiest display—sort of Mid-Eastern meets California nouveau—the juice bar has, well, really fresh juice, and the proverbial espresso bar delivers. If it weren't for that incessant need to see and be seen among the designer-shades crowd, these places wouldn't exist. But they do, and this might be the best. In case you bore of looking, there's a lone, unused, on-line computer in the back and a healthy display of magazines in nearly every language known to Monk.

> **Coffee Bean and Tea Leaf.** 135 N. Larchmont Blvd., at Beverly (Larchmont Village). ☎ **323/469-4984.**

Billed by locals as Main Street L.A., Larchmont Boulevard dares to act as if it's a quaint village tucked away in the big bad metropolis. The block-long commercial district between Beverly and First has lots of foot traffic and tree-lined sidewalks with plenty of stores and restaurants to pull you in, including this favorite latte bar. Order the Larchmont special—guaranteed to cure your hangover blues.

> **Electronic Cafe International.** 1649 18th St., at Olympic Blvd. (Santa Monica). ☎ **310/828-8732.**

Back in the early nineties, Sherrie Rabinowitz and Kit Galloway created this high-tech interactive playpen for the burgeoning number of cyberpunks in our midst, and outfitted it with on-line artworks, global info links, video phones, and a variety of other telecom toys. With a side of cheesecake and espresso to boot. Part of the 18th Street Arts Complex, which includes the legendary Highways Performance Space, ECI was (and still is) so far ahead of its time that most of us will take years to grasp its true significance.

> **Elixir Tonics and Teas.** 8612 Melrose Ave., at San Vicente (West Hollywood). ☎ **310/657-9300.**

The concept of Elixir Tonics and Teas is new and exciting: a beautifully designed and laid out Japanese-style teahouse in the heart of West Hollywood. It's ostensibly a quiet place to come and unwind from the cacophony of city life. But there's one problem: After experiencing this oasis, you might prefer life on the outside. Life inside Elixir is a form of hard-core spiritual hazing. Without the slightest solicitation on our part, the good-looking and friendly gentleman at the herbal bar never ceased explaining the various properties of each elixir, nor did he hesitate to offer quick on-the-spot diagnoses of what ails you (even though before you came in you didn't consider that anything really ailed you all that much).

I'm sure this is what he is trained to do by cofounder Jeffrey Stein, the elixir expert whom our herbal bartender kept hinting we should visit for more in-depth consultation. Stein appeared to be hovering in the background behind his arsenal of potions. Not very relaxing. More like an EST sales spiel. In fact, accompanied as I was by the beautiful Isabelle Bondi, I got the feeling one of the intentions of the brew masters at Elixir was to woo the unsuspecting with their warrior's knowledge of the Tao of the Gan Bei and other esoteric secrets. If you're looking to be caught up in this New Age babe lair, then by all means pay this place a visit. If you want a place to relax without being hounded like you just walked into a no-cover strip bar, then give this place a big miss.

> **G.A.L.A.X.Y.** Gallery and Chronic Cafe. 7224 Melrose Ave., at Alta Vista (Hollywood). ☎ **323/938-6500.**

The sheer outright cheekiness of this hemp emporium puts it on our list. There are no code words here. These folks sell BONGS. Big motherfuckin' water pipes, which everybody and their old lady know are used for one and only one viable purpose: *to bake like Betty Crocker.* What's neat about the Chronic is that it is so cleanly and meticulously run, with a bright, friendly, knowledgeable staff who are not completely baked themselves. This place is such a far cry from the head shops of yore it almost exists in a separate solar system. Besides selling every imaginable size, shape, color, and design of ganja paraphernalia, Chronic also carries other requisite hemp-related products, including hemp-seed treats and coffee, though any honest head will tell you straight up, brah, the goal of the Legalize Hemp movement is very simple: protecting one's right to smoke, eat, drink, or deeply inhale the kind green bud.

> **Lulu's Alibi.** 1640 Sawtelle Blvd., at Santa Monica Blvd. (West Los Angeles). ☎ **310/479-6007.**

So desperate is L.A. to latch onto the latte craze that this place has been way over-covered for what it really is—a decent and mildly trendy Brazilian coffeehouse next to the Nuart.

> **Namuhana.** 3377 Wilshire Blvd., at Alexandria (Koreatown). ☎ **213/480-1223.**

There is a distressing Balkanization in Koreatown, where the interaction between the Korean enclave and the rest of the city's populace is minimal at best. It is doubly distressing to find such isolationism among the area's teens. Undaunted, we regularly invade this hidden world. One great place to catch Korean youth in exile is this hip neon cafe and adjoining karaoke bar, located not just on top of but *in* the hat of the former Brown Derby. When we walked in, everyone turned and stared, as if we were a pair of black men walking into a KKK rally. We didn't linger long that night, but we will again. As Korean Zen Master Dae Seung Sunim might say, the only way to encourage integration is to "just do it."

> **Rose Cafe and Market.** 220 Rose Ave., at Main (Venice). ☎ **310/399-0711.**

On the surface one might say there is nothing all that special about the Rose Cafe—that is, until you realize that this place has been a major Venice gathering place since long before the cappuccino craze hit the country. And to this day it's a great place to spy on the range of yuppies and artists that still call Venice home. The desserts, from blueberry crumble pie to tarte tatin, are what keep the locals coming back.

> **Un-Urban Cafe.** 3301 Pico Blvd., at Urban (Santa Monica).
> ☎ **310/315-0056.**

Owner Pam Stollings and friends opened this brightly painted hole-in-the-wall oasis in 1994, taking the best of funky San Francisco attitude, the richness of a Dutch coffeehouse, and the remarkably good espresso of a Seattle cafe and combining it all on the outer fringes of Santa Monica to create a high-quality bohemian neighborhood gathering spot. Featuring acoustic music, comedy, and a considerably well attended evening of poetry and spoken word, their cafe is clearly a success. Local artists hang work on consignment while patrons donate most of the books and comfy furniture. It's a sweet, low-pressure vibe, where you might even curl up on a couch to read a book. How un-L.A.

Calendar

Unlike San Francisco, you wouldn't think Los Angeles would be the kind of town filled with groovy freaky annual events one must attend. But how wrong you would be.

> **Academy Awards.** Location varies from year to year. www.oscar.com/history/history_awards_ceremony.html. The actual ceremony is by invitation only.

You may malign it. You may find the whole film community shockingly shallow and self-obsessed. You may see right through the grossly inflated facade. But you have to go at least once, if only to stand outside in the bleachers as the parade of stars make their entrance. There is something immeasurably surreal about watching the larger-than-life likes of Claudia Schiffer, Richard Gere, Jane Fonda, Sharon Stone, Clint Eastwood, Gene Hackman, Sophia Loren, and more make their grand entrances, stepping from limousines into the hazing den of paparazzi and video crews from around the world. Save for the occasional political, business, or sports leader, these are the most famous faces on Earth. And gathered as they are at this one place on this one evening makes the Academy Awards the most pivotal event, anywhere, at any time during the calendar year. Inaugurals, World Cups, trials—none can compare for sheer star power. Don't miss it.

> **Doo-Dah Parade.** 11:30am Thanksgiving Day (Downtown Pasadena).
> ☎ **818/795-9311.**

A favorite Christmas tune was inspired by the 1946 Hollywood Christmas Parade. When Gene Autry rode his horse, Champion, down Hollywood Boulevard (or "Santa Claus Lane") and heard all the children yelling, "Here comes Santa Claus, here comes Santa Claus," he came up with the song he eventually co-wrote with Oakley Haldeman.

With hosts like Dr. Demento and participants that range from the Texas Chainsaw Orchestra to the briefcase drill team, this 23-year-old spoof of the Rose Parade has become an equally proud Pasadena happening. It's about as close as L.A. gets to the anarchic absurd spirit of San Francisco's Saint Stupid's Parade, though, in typical L.A. fashion, it's on a much larger scale, and includes elements that are not really so outrageous.

> The Hollywood Christmas Parade.
1st weekend in Dec (Hollywood).
☎ 213/467-1821.

We love this parade. It feels so hometown, so "civic," so wholesome, so darn Christian. And all the has-been stars, and B-list stars, make an appearance—including Loni Anderson, Debby Boone, Shirley Jones, Vicki Lawrence, Little Richard, Donny and Marie, Nancy Sinatra, and, of course, Dick Van Dyke. And controversial organizations find a way in under noms de guerre, such as Scientology's Concerned Businessmen's Association of America and its Happiness Club USA float (with its interesting claim that "over 12 million children across America have helped do projects based on the common sense moral values contained in *The Way to Happiness* booklet by L. Ron Hubbard"). Plus cheerleaders and marching bands from around the country. Remember: Christ was born in a region where it didn't snow a whole lot, so Christmas in Los Angeles isn't as absurd as it sounds.

For a complete history, photographs, memorabilia, go to **Hollywood Christmas Parade Archives,** Frances Goldwyn Hollywood Library, 1623 N. Ivar, Hollywood.

> Night of the Stars. Mid-July. Location varies (call for details). ☎ 818/348-9373.

Sponsored by the Free Speech Coalition, a loose organization of smut merchants committed to protecting the First Amendment, the Night of the Stars celebrates a variety of achievements in the year in porn, both on and off the screen. I have a feeling the awards ceremony in *Boogie Nights* was somehow modeled after this porn equivalent of the Oscars. Though the thrill of nuzzling up to provocative porn stars died for us about 12 years ago, for the right Monk, the evening probably offers its fair share of stimulating fun. As founder William Margold puts it, "No one's ever died from an overdose of pornography."

Celebrity Spotting

We consider stargazing about on the level of driving a Corvette—one of the tackiest, low-class things one can do. It's not so much that gazing at people worthy of respect is such a silly thing. If Ghandi, James Joyce, or the Buddha was strolling down the street, we might take a second glance. The problem with modern celebrity worship is that the subjects receiving such veneration are so unworthy of the attention. I mean, what do Demi Moore or Bruce Willis have to offer anyone? Ditto for Sly Stallone, Arnold, or Kathie Lee Gifford. These average talents are spectacles because their visage has been seen by millions. But they are neither brilliantly original nor really all that talented. They have contributed nothing of depth and substance to culture except their mugs.

Still, for the same reason that folks with Harvard PhD's still occasionally read *People* magazine, we offer the best—and *cheapest*—places in town to view Los Angeles's chief export to the world—the celeb. Maybe you'll get lucky and run into Michael Monk.

> Brentwood Community Market. 225 26th St., at San Vincente Blvd. (Santa Monica). ☎ **310/395-67154.**

Saturday mornings are a good time to catch the likes of Bob Redford and Michelle Pfeiffer.

> Cafe Luna. 7463 Melrose Ave., at Gardner (Los Angeles). ☎ **323/655-8647.**

A spot to spot stars from nearby Paramount Studios.

> Gelson's Market. 15424 Sunset Blvd., at Swarthmore (Pacific Palisades). ☎ **310/459-4483.**

As the local adage goes, "Celebrities have to eat too." Some actually shop for themselves. Sally Field and Billy Crystal are regulars.

Trivia

Lana Turner was discovered sipping a Coke in a malt shop on Sunset across from Hollywood High School.

"Anyone who's ever been around L.A. celebrities knows who Kato Kaelin is—he's the guy who gets the drugs. He's the guy who gets the girls, or the boys, whatever the case may be. All celebrities have someone like that around—there's not an unoccupied guest house in Hollywood."

—Fran Lebowitz, *Index*

> **Hughes Market.** 23765 W. Malibu Rd., at Pacific Coast Hwy. (Malibu).
> ☎ 310/456-2917.

Twenty-four-hour supermarket gets stars coming over from the Malibu Hills and the star-studded Malibu Colony—Martin Sheen and Carole King, for instance.

> **Hugo's.** 8401 Santa Monica Blvd., at King's Rd. (West Hollywood).
> ☎ 213/654-3993.

Great breakfasts, casual atmosphere, Hollywood players.

> **The Ivy.** 133 N. Robertson Blvd., at 3rd St. (West Hollywood).
> ☎ 310/274-8303.

Really nasty industry heavyweights in a country-inn atmosphere. Snobby and stiff door policies.

> **Mayfair Market.** Franklin Ave. and Bronson Ave. (Hollywood).

Hey, it's right across from the Scientology Celebrity Center (see "Buildings" above), so there are bound to be "celebrities" here, right? Well, for the most part, these are not super-well-known faces, but faces you know you've seen in some ad, on some show, but can't quite place. Hollywood is filled with these kinds of faces. They are the faces of bit-part actors, cameo superstars, soap-opera people. Folks who make a decent living as B- and C-level thespians, who might have had a big hit once upon a time and who made enough from that to buy a decent house in the nearby Hollywood Hills, but who aren't household names, and probably never will be. They are the bread and butter of the film and TV industry. And they shop at places like Mayfair Market.

> **Maurice's Snack 'N Chat.** 5549 W. Pico Blvd., at Fairfax (Los Angeles).
> ☎ 323/930-1795.

Funky soul food (brain 'n eggs and grits), and the occasional black actor or athlete.

> **Nate 'n Al's Delicatessen.** 414 N. Beverly Dr., near Santa Monica Blvd. (Beverly Hills). ☎ **310/274-0101.**

Homey Beverly Hills fixture, with motherly waitresses. The Naugahyde booths are where the celebs congregate.

> **Patrick's Roadhouse.** 106 Entrada Dr., at the PCH (Santa Monica). ☎ **310/459-4544.**

Billed as a place for "stargazing" (Arnold breakfasts there—even has his own seat), with opera on the jukebox. But the owner, a man who's actually called Bill, is "appallingly rude, a very abusive character," says one regular, though the stars love it. Makes sense.

The Lee Atwater Invitational Dead Pool

In a city that combines celebrity and death in such easy measure, and with such close proximity to Vegas, the Lee Atwater Invitational Dead Pool (http://stiff.com) seems like a dead winner. And that it is. Run by the brilliantly barbed twosome of Zachariah Love and his pal Grossman (no first name), the Lee Atwater was born of a simple bet between these two friends on which celebrities would drop dead in a given year. Atwater was the sole name both partners had in common, so the late Republican attack dog (and creator of the infamous Willie Horton ads) had the twisted Web site named in his honor. Since then, the site has grown considerably, offering many ways to play, with varying durations, sizable cash prizes, and more. The formula is simple: After laying down an entrance fee, each player makes a list of 10 celebs they consider likely to die within the time frame established by the contest (a list of who qualifies as a celebrity is found at http://stiffs.com/fame.html). Point values are attached to each pick, largely determined by the age of the celebrity (Liz Taylor obviously gets less points than Matt Damon), and celeb's health profile. Dead celebrities don't count even if you want them to die again (for a list of those who've already gone to the other shore, go to http://stiff.com/olderdeaths.html). Whoever predicts the most highly weighted celebrity deaths within the given period of time wins.

In *The Mad Monks' Guide to New York City,* we wrote that an obit in the *New York Times* is the final arbiter of whether one has lived a newsworthy life. We would now add to that a bicoastal caveat: being deemed a "celebrity" by the Lee Atwater Invitational Dead Pool.

Coda: We questioned Mr. Love on whether Iggy Pop, Annie Sprinkle, and Michael Monk would all qualify as celebrities. Sadly, Michael Monk did not make the cut.

> **Spago.** 176 N. Canon Dr., at Wilshire (Beverly Hills). ☎ **310/385-0880.**

The Hollywood Spago is reserved for tourists now. The BH location is where the real "playas" play.

> **UNOCAL Gas Station.** 9988 Wilshire Blvd., at Whittier (Beverly Hills).
☎ **310/276-3076.**

Watching celebrities get gas is a great Beverly Hills pastime. The proletarian quality of it is refreshing. Genuinely talented actors like Jack Lemmon and Cicely Tyson have been spotted here gassing up their autos.

Clubs

Comedy

> **The Ice House.** 24 N. Mentor Ave., at Colorado Blvd. (Pasadena).
☎ **626/577-1894.**

The party-line Monk point of view on comedy clubs is that they are low-brow strongholds filled with people with average jobs, average educations, and average cultural aspirations—the vast world of TV-land consumers; the kind of people who watched Comedy Central in its brick-wall early days. In other words, the perfect people for your average comic's naughty brilliance. But, on reexamination, we found strong salient reasons to visit a Comedy Club, namely, YOU ARE GUARANTEED TO LAUGH REAL HARD. And that, my friends, is therapeutic.

Which brings us to the Ice House. Now, we know a comic has to eat and a comedy club has to pay the bills, but let me tell you, you are going to pay handsomely here for those one-liners. Not only is there a sizable coverage charge, but a two-drink minimum (with drink prices that start around $6.50). So, if you decide to order food, you're looking at a $40 to $50 evening, minimum, and that's not cheap. Now, also keep in mind that the jokes the comics tell are pretty much centered around human sexuality, human excrement, female anatomy, male anatomy, and the occasional bestiality reference. The part of you that cries out for more sophisticated, intellectual, savvy fair will be raging inside. But, fortunately, the other side, which relishes sick jokes and crude bathroom humor, will be having a ball. You will howl. You will cry. You will keel over with laughter. And you will feel, in the end, you got all your money's worth. With a Hall of Fame that reads like a Who's Who of Standup—Billy Crystal, Robin Williams, Dana Carvey—the Ice House clearly has a formula that works.

Private

> **The Magic Castle ("A Museum of Old Houses").** 7001 Franklin Ave., near La Brea (Hollywood). ☎ **323/851-3313.**

This 1908 Victorian mansion was once the home of Rollin B. Lane, the original landowner of much of Hollywood. In 1963 the mansion was transformed by then owner Milt Larsen into a kind of Friar's club for magicians, their families and friends. Dinner and magic shows nightly, but you must be accompanied by a member and carry loads o' cash. *Tip:* While in the area, head up the hill behind the Castle to Yashamoro, a cheesy expensive Japanese restaurant, featuring blue drinks and a full-tilt view of the city.

Strip

More so than even Portland, Oregon, L.A. is the American capital of strip clubs. There are three reasons for this: (1) Quality of Life cleanup campaigns (à la Rudy Giuliani's New York) haven't struck the city; (2) there's an endless supply of failed starlets eager to strip for cash; and (3) this sun-drenched metropolis has sex on the brain.

> **Crazy Girls.** 1433 N. La Brea Ave., at Sunset (Hollywood). ☎ **213/969-0055.**

Crazy Girls has lots of good-looking swingers who make their way here, as well as the occasional Monk dork. There's a fair number of women with silicone implants, but a far larger number without. The place also has a pool table, a TV, and video games to ease the pressure somewhat. However, as door girl Carrie says, "It's still a high-pressure place."

> **Jumbo's Clown Room.** 5153 Hollywood Blvd., at Winona (Los Feliz). ☎ **323/666-1187.**

This small, low-rent, shockingly unsleazy strip club in the heart of Thai Town gained fame because Courtney "Where Is This Going?" Love danced here back in 1989. It's still the closest L.A. comes to the good-natured camaraderie of places like the Lusty Lady in Seattle. Most other strip clubs in town are run by a small cabal of owners who inflict a high-pressure drink policy that is hardly conducive to a relaxing good time. Not at Jumbo's, which doesn't charge a cover, has no pushy doormen, and has a decidedly low-key two-drink minimum. What's more, Jumbo's strives to create a feeling of community among the dancers and clientele that is quite refreshing.

Tip: After enjoying a sexy snack at Jumbo's, there's plenty of Thai food in neighboring Thai Town to fill you up in other ways. None of the places are particularly outstanding (and we've tried a few), but there's lots to choose from.

Film

There are moments one has in this town where you feel a flicker of hope that maybe the denizens of the film industry might know a thing or two about depth, quality, and character. Then something like the AFI 100 Best Films of All Time comes out, and you realize you are dealing with a town full of popular entertainers, not artists. Even if one makes a case that the AFI was only talking about English-speaking cinema, the inclusion of such mediocre efforts as *Dances with Wolves* and *E.T.* shows the myopia of this town's filmmaking community and the "entertain us at all costs" mind-set that shuts out less glamorous, less contrived, if far more authentic, efforts.

Having the film medium be centered in Los Angeles is like having the world literary mecca be centered in Tahiti—it's just a very bad match. In addition to its distance from Edison and his patent lawyers, the main reason the film industry moved to Los Angeles in the first place—the predictable, sunny, monochromatic weather—invariably produces a predictably sunny, monochromatic class of directors, writers, and actors.

Still, being Monks, we will make the most of a dire situation. So, here then, is our guide to the industry which defines this industry town.

Embarrassing Movie Mishaps

May 17, 1969. John Jordan, second unit director on *Catch-22,* plunged to his death during aerial photography when a gust of wind blew his plane off balance, sweeping him through an open door.

July 22, 1982. Actor Victor Morrow and child actors Renee Chen and Myca Dinh Le died during filming of *Twilight Zone: The Movie,* when a special-effects explosion caused a helicopter to crash into them.

Sometime in 1984. In a television mishap, actor Jon Erik Hexum of the CBS series *Cover-Up* died after accidentally shooting himself in the head with a "blank" pistol.

November 21, 1986. Stuntman Dar Allen Robinson was killed during a motorcycle chase scene in the Arizona desert for the movie *Million Dollar Mystery* after he plunged off a 40-foot embankment, hit a rock ledge, and was gored by a sagebrush limb.

May 30, 1987. Four Filipino soldiers were killed when a Philippine Air Force helicopter hired for the filming of a Chuck Norris movie, *Braddock: Missing in Action, Part III,* plunged into Manila Bay.

May 16, 1989. A helicopter carrying eight people filming another Norris action picture, *Delta Force 2,* crashed and exploded at the foot of a hill south of Manila, killing three American crew members and the Filipino pilot.

August, 1989. During filming of *Gone in 60 Seconds II,* director Toby Halicki died when a water tower fell on him.

June 25, 1990. Stuntwoman Heidi von Beltz was paralyzed from the waist down and lost the use of her hands during the filming of *Cannonball Run,* when a car that was supposed to narrowly avoid collision with five other vehicles crashed into a van.

September 24, 1990. Stuntman Jay Currin was killed during a 60-foot practice jump off a seaside cliff in Malibu during the filming of *Bikini Island* when he landed on the edge of an airbag and was thrown into the rocks along Point Dume State Beach.

November 10, 1990. Stuntman Jim Madieras was critically injured when he was thrown headfirst into a tree during filming of a scene for the Walt Disney movie *The Rocketeer.* Madieras and another stuntman were to simulate being propelled by an out-of-control rocket backpack and were supposed to land on a mattress.

March 31, 1993. A gun accident caused the death of Brandon Lee, son of martial arts film star Bruce Lee, during filming of *The Crow.* Lee's death was the sixth fatality in 11 years to occur on a television or film set.

Movies about L.A.

More than almost any other city, an understanding of L.A. requires an understanding of the movies made about it. In a city built on illusion, it is very important to understand the interpretations of that illusion. Here's a basic Monk primer.

American Gigolo (Paul Schrader, 1980)

American History X (Tony Kaye, 1998)

Annie Hall (Woody Allen, 1977)

Attack of the Killer Tomatoes (John De Bello, 1980)

Barfly (Barbet Schroeder, 1987)

Barton Fink (Joel Coen, 1991)

Beverly Hillbillies (Penelope Spheeris, 1993)

Beverly Hills Cop (Martin Brest, 1984)

Beyond the Valley of the Dolls (Russ Meyer, 1970)

The Big Lebowski (Joel Coen, 1998)

The Big Picture (Christopher Guest, 1989)

The Big Sleep (Howard Hawks, 1946)

Big Wednesday (John Milius, 1978)

Blade Runner (Ridley Scott, 1982)

Blue Thunder (John Badham, 1983)

Boogie Nights (Paul Thomas Anderson, 1997)

Born in East L.A. (Cheech Marin, 1987)

Boyz N The Hood (John Singleton, 1991)

Bulworth (Warren Beatty, 1998)

California Suite (Herbert Ross, 1978)

Chinatown (Roman Polanski, 1974)

City of Angels (Brad Silberling, 1998)

Clueless (Amy Heckerling, 1995)

Colors (Dennis Hopper, 1988)

Day of the Locust (John Schlessinger, 1975)

Dead Again (Kenneth Branagh, 1991)

Death Becomes Her (Robert Zemeckis, 1992)

The Decline of Western Civilization I (Penelope Spheeris, 1981)

The Decline of Western Civilization, Part II: The Metal Years (Penelope Spheeris, 1988)

The Decline of Western Civilization, Part III (Penelope Spheeris, 1998)

Devil in a Blue Dress (Carl Franklin, 1995)

Die Hard (John McTiernan, 1988)

The Doors (Oliver Stone, 1991)

Down and Out in Beverly Hills (Paul Mazursky, 1986)

Dragnet (Jack Webb, 1954)

Earth Girls Are Easy (Julien Temple, 1989)

Earthquake (Mark Robson, 1974)

Echo Park (Robert Dornhelm, 1986)

Encino Man (Les Mayfield, 1992)

Escape from L.A. (John Carpenter, 1996)

E.T. The Extra-Terrestrial (Steven Spielberg, 1982)

Falling Down (Joel Schumacher, 1993)

Fast Times at Ridgemont High (Amy Heckerling, 1982)

Forbidden Zone (Richard Elfman, 1980)

Forget Paris (Billy Crystal, 1995)

Get Shorty (Barry Sonnenfeld, 1995)

The Graduate (Mike Nichols, 1967)

Grand Canyon (Lawrence Kasdan, 1991)

The Grifters (Stephen Frears, 1990)

Head (Bob Rafelson, 1968)

Heathers (Michael Lehmann, 1989)

Higher Learning (John Singleton, 1995)

Hollywood Shuffle (Robert Townsend, 1987)

Jerry Maguire (Cameron Crowe, 1996)

L.A. Confidential (Curtis Hanson, 1997)

L.A. Story (Mick Jackson, 1991)

The Long Goodbye (Robert Altman, 1973)

Low Down Dirty Shame (Keenen Ivory Wayans, 1994)

Menace II Society (Albert Hughes, 1993)

Mildred Pierce (Michael Curtiz, 1945)

Miracle Mile (Steve DeJarnatt, 1989)

Mr. Wrong (Gaylene Preston, 1985)

Mulholland Falls (Lee Tamahori, 1996)

Nowhere (Gregg Araki, 1997)

People v. Larry Flynt (Milos Forman, 1996)

The Player (Robert Altman, 1992)

Poetic Justice (John Singleton, 1993)

Point Break (Kathryn Bigelow, 1991)

Postcards from the Edge (Mike Nichols, 1990)

Pretty Woman (Garry Marshall, 1990)

Pulp Fiction (Quentin Tarantino, 1994)

Rebel Without a Cause (Nicholas Ray, 1955)

Repo Man (Alex Cox, 1984)

Reservoir Dogs (Quentin Tarantino, 1992)

Safe (Todd Haynes, 1995)

Save the Tiger (John G. Avildsen, 1973)

Set It Off (F. Gary Gray, 1996)

Shampoo (Hal Ashby, 1975)

Short Cuts (Robert Altman, 1993)

Singin' in the Rain (Gene Kelly, Stanley Donen, 1952)

Slamdance (Wayne Wang, 1987)

Stand and Deliver (Ramon Menendez, 1987)

A Star is Born (George Cukor, 1954)

Star Maps (Miguel Arteta, 1997)

Sunset Boulevard (Billy Wilder, 1950)

Swimming with Sharks (George Huang, 1994)

Swingers (Doug Liman, 1996)

Ten (Blake Edwards, 1979)

Tequila Sunrise (Robert Towne, 1988)

The Terminator (James Cameron, 1984)

Terminator 2: Judgment Day (James Cameron, 1991)

That's Entertainment (Jack Haley, Jr., 1974)

Three Amigos (John Landis, 1986)

To Live and Die in L.A. (William Friedkin, 1985)

The Two Jakes (Jack Nicholson, 1990)

True Confessions (Ulu Grosbard, 1981)

Twilight (Robert Benton, 1998)

Valley Girl (Martha Coolidge, 1983)

Wag the Dog (Barry Levinson, 1997)

Welcome to L.A. (Alan Rudolph, 1977)

Who Framed Roger Rabbit? (Robert Zemeckis, 1988)

Zabriskie Point (Michelangelo Antonioni, 1970)

Coda: As a footnote to this list, one should add George Halliday's videotape of the beating of motorist Rodney King, probably the most socially significant film ever made about the city.

Support Services

› **Bischoff's Taxidermy.** See "Animals."

› **Ellis Props and Graphics.** N. La Brea Ave. at Beverly Blvd. (Los Angeles).
☎ 213/933-7334. E-mail: gotomikee@aol.com.

We'll tell you right from the start, like so many in the film industry, the folks who work this prop house do *not* mess around. They certainly can't be bothered with helping tourists. With that said, you should still check this place out, not just because you are a budding Alexander Payne, but to see Ellis's amazing collection of swords, guns, and police badges (all for rent with the proper studio I.D.). Lining the walls are posters of the films the place has outfitted, including the favorite of every shallow 30-something filmmaker, *Pulp Fiction*. Ellis also runs a side business in legal counterfeiting. Need a decent ransom note? Give them a call.

› **Tri-Ess Sciences.** 1020 W. Chestnut St., at N. Keystone St. (Burbank).
☎ 818/848-7838.

Science-fair kits, butterfly nets, everything you need to make smoke, fire, or fog. Confetti cannon, a snow machine, quarts of stage blood. You can rent or buy.

The Academy of Motion Picture Arts and Sciences

In all the hoopla regarding the Academy Awards, one can forget that motion pictures are not only an art form, they are also a science. As an art, they can be as intricate and subtle as a Nuryev ballet; as a science, they can be as technically complex as modern rocketry. We recommend a visit here only to put what you see at the metroplex in proper perspective, and to give a little more credence and weight to what passes as mere spectacle. It's located at 333 La Cienega, at Olympic Boulevard, Beverly Hills.

ACADEMY AWARDS TRIVIA
- The official trophy of the Academy Awards, known as Oscar, got its name from the Academy's First Librarian, Margaret Herrick, who commented on seeing it for the first time, "It looks like my Uncle Oscar."
- There have only been three circumstances that have interrupted the scheduled presentation of the Academy Awards: (1) 1938, when destructive floods all but washed out L.A.; (2) 1968, out of respect for Dr. Martin Luther King, Jr., who had been assassinated a few days before the awards presentation and whose funeral was held the day set for the Awards; (3) 1981, when the awards were postponed by 24 hours due to the assassination attempt on President Reagan.

. . . It's a Walter Mitty thing. We'll get Brad Pitt to play the tortured projectionist at the Cinerama, who imagines himself in all the movies. We'll get Brad to play those parts, too . . .

Theaters

› **Cinerama Dome Theatre.** 6360 Sunset Blvd., at Ivar (Hollywood).
☎ **323/466-3347.**

The largest non-IMAX movie theater in the country, this giant geodesic dome is also the focus of a recent landmark status hoo-ha. The owners, the Pacific Theatre chain, want to gut the current large flat screen to make it more appropriate for modern movie viewing, thereby killing the spirit of the theater (according to opponents). Also planned is a complex of stores and smaller film theaters, with the Cinerama Dome as the anchor. Mindful of what happened to several great L.A. landmarks, preservationists in town got a big head of steam going against the family that owns this theater, but the word at press time was that a compromise had been reached and construction will soon begin.

› **Fairfax Cinema.** 7907 Beverly Blvd., at Fairfax (West Hollywood).
☎ **213/653-3117.**

Before we were millionaire travel writers and world-famous celebrities (rent our video, *How Eating Brown Rice for Twenty Years Made Us RICH, RICH, RICH!!*), we saw all our movies here. Because of the bevy of *Chasing Amy* extras that seem to populate Fairfax Avenue? Because they show avant-garde cinema? No. It's mostly mainstream fair that either sucks or tanked at the box office. Why then? Because it's cheap! Only $2.50 a flick.

> **Mann's Chinese Theatre.** 6925 Hollywood Blvd., near La Brea Blvd. (Hollywood). ☎ **213/464-8111.**

Every tourist in the world knows about this place, but we recommend it because it truly is a thing of beauty. There's talk of bringing the Academy Awards back here. Wouldn't the greenhorns love that!

> **New Beverly Cinema.** 7165 Beverly Blvd., at La Brea (West Hollywood). ☎ **213/938-4038.**

New Beverly is the only reliable revival theater in L.A. Though art films make there way into the other venues such as LACMA, UCLA, Nuart, or the American Cinematheque, only New Beverly programs such a consistently eclectic mix every single night of the week.

> **The Old Town Music Hall.** 140 Richmond St., near El Segundo Blvd., just south of LAX (El Segundo). ☎ **310/322-2592.** www.nswwest.com (click on the Old Town icon).

A psychedelic 1925 Wurlitzer that's played before every show, no commercials, the occasional silent film, respectful filmgoers—yet another great reason to make the trek to fabulous El Segundo!!

> **The Tomkat Theater/Porno Walk of Fame (formerly the Pussycat).** 7734 Santa Monica Blvd., at Genesis (Hollywood). ☎ **213/650-9551.**

Compared to the Hollywood Walk of Fame, this walk of shame is decidedly half-baked and poorly executed. All that you have are hand and foot imprints (plus one penis imprint) in drab gray cement. By their signatures you shall know them.

And of all the porn-star notables memorialized here—John C. Holmes, Harry Reems, Marilyn Chambers, et. al—the sweet swirling penmanship of Linda Lovelace indicates she probably had the most fun. By the way, such mimicry of the Walk of Fame occurs all over Hollywood. For instance, check out the Community Area Police Station at 1358 N. Wilcox.

Food

Dining out in L.A. is a project. You have to drive everywhere that is even a wee bit interesting, and, after awhile, that becomes a drag. So, you tend to stock up at Ralph's and Trader Joe's, and cook a lot. Or at least we do. Nonetheless, there comes a time when even an abstemious Monk gets bored with miso soup, millet, and dandelion greens, and must venture outside his domain. To come to terms with not only dining out, but with almost any consumer decision in L.A., the Monk must do three things: (1) He must completely renounce everything he believes about restricting one's use of the automobile in the interest of environmental protection; (2) he must be comfortable with the fact that 5 miles here is the equivalent of 1 mile anywhere else; and (3) he must be willing to throw out culinary standards in the interest of expediency. Unless he remembers these three points, the Monk will become steadily frustrated at the 60 minutes he must travel to sample, say, that little take-out barbecue joint over in Leimert Park. The high incidence of road rage in this region derives precisely from such a simple but frustrating scenario. You can imagine then that the long distances one must travel gradually erodes the instinct to casually check things out in this town. Which is why this guide to L.A. food is so important. It will tell you in no uncertain terms whether the place is worth the inevitable hassle it will take to get there.

Note: See "Neighborhoods" section for additional restaurants not covered here.

> **ABC Seafood.** 708 New High St., at Ord (Downtown). ☎ 213/680-2887.

Cantonese seafood in bustling dining room. Not as humongous as NBC Seafood, but just as good. What could be more fun than dining in places named after dying television networks?

> **Andre's.** 6332 W. 3rd St., at La Brea (Hancock Park). ☎ 323/935-1246.

Ever get that hankering for loathsome cheap cafeteria food? Andre's is an Italian version of such a place. Hidden inside a hideous food court in the incredibly ugly Lucky/K-Mart strip mall across from the Farmer's Market, Andre's is a place you'd

There are some truly magnificent places to dine in Los Angeles. The assorted "Puckeries" (Spago, more Spago, still more Spago), the Puck Juniors (Patino, Pinot Bistro, and other assorted twists on Pinot and Patino), the Pucks in Training (Campanile, Abiquiu), and the über-Pucks (Valentino, Citrus, and Il Pastaio), but, we say, Puck Schmuck, Monk places are where you can get great food and original atmosphere, without spending a lot of bucks.

have to know about in order to find. And it seems lots of folks know about it. First off, let's make this clear: The place is cheap. Six bucks for a giant plate of spaghetti and marinara, with a nice-sized chicken leg, salad, and garlic bread. But it's a strictly fill-you-up affair because the quality is as low as a place can get before you have to call in the Health Department. Secondly, Andre's has a weirdly varied clientele. The night we were there our fellow diners included an assortment of poor Hispanics, dining businessmen, a hetero foursome all excited and dolled up for their big night on the town, two community organizers lost in some Sol Alinsky time warp, and some regular middle-aged mensches from nearby Park La Blah Blah. There was something so strangely Midwest, so gratifyingly populist, so industry-free about this assemblage, we actually found it heartwarming.

> **Alpine Village.** Harbor Fwy. (110) and Torrance Blvd. (Torrance). ☎ **310/327-4384.** www.alpinevillage.net

Proof positive you can find any ethnic cuisine in L.A. if you are willing to drive for it. Alpine Village is Kraut Kultur in all its faded glory. There's a lot going on at this mock Bavarian complex just off the Harbor Freeway in lovely Torrance. There's a beer hall-cum-restaurant with ugly old German women and Viagra-deprived German men doing a Demerol polka. There are loads of shops where you can buy all manner of German kitsch—beer steins, tacky Baroque paintings, and, in a politically incorrect twist, Nazi memorabilia. Yep, what those Krauts can't legally procure back in der Faderland, they can buy quite openly at the **Collector's Gallery** (☎ **310/532-2166**), which sells museum-quality daggers, swords, Nazi medallions, Nazi photographs, even Nazi tablecloths. No doubt you'll be hungry for some sauerkraut and head cheese after salivating over the wide selection of weird German foodstuffs at the Alpine Village Market. The place is well stocked, including rows of imported chocolate and candies, homemade sausages, and some German-speaking sales help. In addition to the sight of real live German-speaking Germans, the main highlight of Alpine Village is the wide selection of brown, black, and non-German white customers, who obviously thrill to the prospect of a dinner of knockwurst, bier, and brot, even though it won't be on a Nazi tablecloth.

> **Apple Pan.** 10801 W. Pico. Blvd., at Westwood (Westwood). ☎ **310/475-3585.**

Upon first inspection you may wonder, *What's the big deal?* In the shadow of the Westside Pavilion, this place threatens to be just another film prop with a contrived attitude. But that's far from the truth. This unpretentious burger joint is just that, a basic burger joint. In a diminutive, one-story cottage, 26 red stools wrap around a U-shaped counter with a big grill in the center (eerily reminiscent of the Peach Pit in "Beverly Hills 90210"). The waiters are soda-jerk perfect in their white shirts, white aprons, white paper hats, and big smiles. The stainless-steel and birch counter top serves as the communal table where your burger is slapped down on end, wrapped in paper sans plates. It's this minimalist delivery that lets the burger speak for itself. For this truly is the best burger in all of L.A. Reminiscent of open-grill burgers your granddad used to flip on the Fourth of July, these babies are juicy, succulent, and dripping with grease. The secret: They're not overcooked, the beef is choice, the onions tangy, and the buns fresh as can be. You can veer toward Southern Baked Ham, Egg Salad, and Tuna Salad sandwiches, but if you want the core of Apple Pan, get the $4.50 Steak Burger or Hickory Burger. And, as if that's not enough, the fresh-baked apple and pecan pies are waiting for you to take home.

Burger Trivia

Pasadena claims to have served the first cheeseburger back in the 1920s. Most of the major burger chains in the country—Burger King, In 'N Out, McDonald's, Carl's Jr.—opened their first outlet in L.A.

> **Astro Burger.** 5607 Melrose Ave., at Gower (Hollywood). ☎ **323/469-1924.**

Really really good garden burgers and fries. The guy who played Chachi in "Happy Days" asked for our autograph here.

> **Bahooka Ribs and Grog.** 4501 N. Rosemead Blvd., at Lower Azusa Ave. (Rosemead). ☎ **626/285-1241.**

Bad (really bad) Polynesian decor at this restaurant in the heart of Rosemead, featuring over 98 aquariums, including one with a fearsome carrot-munching barracuda. The paradoxical menu includes several items that didn't strike us as particularly Polynesian—onion rings, clam chowder, tuna melt, and New York steak to name a few. Oh, but they do wonderful things with pig and pineapple.

> **Barney's Beanery.** 8447 Santa Monica Blvd., at La Cienega (West Hollywood). ☎ 213/654-2287.

Hard to recommend a place that until 1985 had a bar sign and matchbooks that read "Fagots [sic] Stay Out." Then again, there is something so devilishly un-PC about that, we almost want them back. Barney's is remembered as the place where Janis Joplin hit Jim Morrison over the head with a bottle of Southern Comfort. Alcoholism—so *Bukowski!*

> **The Belvedere.** Peninsula Hotel, 9882 Little Santa Monica Blvd., at Wilshire Blvd. (Beverly Hills). ☎ **800/462-7899** or 310/551-2888.

This is the CAA canteen—home of the much discussed and highly overrated "power breakfast," with agents and talent in tow. Cursed with the singular disease of West L.A.: attitude over substance.

> **Canter's Deli.** 419 N. Fairfax Ave., at Rosewood (Los Angeles). ☎ 323/651-2030.

During the week, it's a large, charmingly ethnic place to kibitz with friends. Late on weekend nights, it's packed with young trendoids. At all hours, the prices are a little high (mediocre lox and bagel for 10 bucks—give us a break!). Clearly past its prime, Canters is beloved because it's the oldest deli in L.A., with the highest quotient of postmenopausal waitresses in the United States. However, Landers (7th and Alvarado, in Westlake) serves a far better pastrami, and the adjoining Kibitz Room is a far better bargain (nightly jams for free).

> **The Cooportunity.** 1525 Broadway Ave., at 16th St. (Santa Monica). ☎ 310/451-8902.

Given the disparity in price and quality among natural-foods stores in the greater L.A. area, this Santa Monica store comes as a refreshing surprise. After the deep-pocket shopping at Erewhon, Nowhere, and elsewhere, you don't even mind the cheesy New Age feel of the place. It's got a central deli case that rivals its competition at half the price. And the overwhelmingly organic nature of the produce and grains reminds us that natural foods are a movement as well as a way of eating. They've got the requisite masseuse off in the corner and the expected deluge of supplements and cruelty-free cosmetics, but the high ceilings, bright lights, and staff that actually speaks English and knows about the products make this second only to Whole Foods as the best natural-foods market in town.

. . . And we could get Billy Bob Thornton to play Dr. Hogly. Kind of a reprise of his *Primary Colors* character. There's the ribs connection . . .

> **Dr. Hogly Wogly's Tyler Texas B-B-Q.** 8136 Sepulveda Blvd., ½ block south of Roscoe (Van Nuys). ☎ **818/782-2480.**

God, we wanted this place to be good. All the way out in sketchy Van Nuys. And that name. Just gotta be authentic, right? I don't THINK so. First off, the place is packed. A good sign. But then, our waitress was menopausal. Blame it on the crowds, we reasoned. Besides, would you want to work at a BBQ joint in Van Nuys? The bottom line is the food. The ribs are allegedly hand-rubbed in spices, left to sit overnight, and then marinated all day. And they aren't baby backs either. These ribs are from full mature pigs, who've lounged around in the slop a bit. We ordered a bunch, plus some brisket and pork. How can we put this? The grub filled us up alright, it was pretty tasty, but it sure didn't match the promise of that name, or its sketchy locale.

Tip: Want authentic barbecue? Try **Maurice's Piggy Park and Pit Stop** in West Columbia, South Carolina, **Lucille's Bad to the Bone BBQ** in Boca Raton, Florida, or **Virgil's Real BBQ** in, of all places, Times Square, New York City.

> **Duke's Coffee Shop.** 8909 Sunset Blvd., at San Vicente (West Hollywood). ☎ **310/652-3100.**

In an area long on fakery and hype, Duke's is still the real deal, even if Ian Schrager likes it, and even if the prices have vaulted with the age of the scene. For scenes of rock-and-roll casualties, it's hard to beat.

> **Du Par's Coffee Shop.** 6333 W. 3rd St., at Fairfax (Fairfax area). ☎ **213/933-8446.**

Hard to believe, but right in the Farmer's Market, there is a real-deal coffee shop serving buttery pancakes the way Grandma Crotty used to make them. A very sweet place, with old-school waitresses who have zero interest, and zero hope, of landing work as models or actresses.

> **El Cholo.** 1121 S. Western Ave., between Pico and Olympic (Koreatown). ☎ **323/734-2773.**

Some Chicano food snobs may scoff at our inclusion of this old-time Mexican favorite, but we don't care. The place delivers awesome fajitas, in a festive and authentic setting. And, contrary to stereotype, the prices are quite reasonable for what you get. Besides, Dawn Moreno was once a hostess here. What more do you need?

> **El Coyote.** 7312 Beverly Blvd., near La Brea (Hollywood area). ☎ **323/939-2255.**

Without question the worst Mexican food we have ever eaten. Perversely popular because (1) the Margaritas are strong and cheap; and (2) it's where Sharon Tate and friends shared their last supper before meeting up with Charles & Company.

> **El Jalapeno.** Normandie and Beverly (Koreatown). No phone.

In all of this very Hispanic city, you would be hard-pressed to find a more ridiculous bargain than this funky taco stand on the northeast corner of Normandie and Beverly. The chef is a delightful, bright, happy Asian-Latino woman named Lee, who's very proud of her food, especially her pork tacos, and her hamburgers, which she forms by hand. "Unlike In-N-Out," she says warmly. That would be enough. But then Lee asked, "Where do you live?" I told her down the street. She then said, "I own the bar across the street." This came somewhat as a shock, since we'd noted, as we walked up, the run-down visage of this place called One for the Road, advertising out front "Girls, Girls, Girls" on one of those vinyl signs realtors use when they have lots for sale. We figured that on this decrepit stretch of Beverly a bar like One for the Road must see some pretty road-weary customers. Lee adds, "It's normally a $20 cover, but tell them Lee sent you and they will let you in for free." Well, there's a novelty: a taco stand owner who also runs a strip club. Unfortunately, however kind Lee is, we don't think we'd ever step in her One for the Road. That's because we think Lee's food sucked.

> **Encounter Restaurant.** LAX, 209 World Way (El Segundo). ☎ **310/215-5151.**

If the Jetsons, the B-52s, and the owners of Seattle's Gravity Bar ever got together to create their own special party space, Encounter Restaurant and Bar would be it. High above LAX, near the old Control Tower, the flying-saucer–shaped Encounter features an elegant yet retro groovy outer space decor, waiters in Star Trek uniforms, and groovy blue vodka drinks. Take a sip as you watch those daring young men and their flying machines.

> **Farmer's Market.** 3rd St. and Fairfax Ave., in the hub of CBS-land (Fairfax area). ☎ 213/933-9211.

Though some of the stands are a bit pricey compared to Grand Central, it still retains the original market charm—a rare achievement for a city built on novelty and illusion. Visit "Koffee Korner" and experience the legendary "Temple of June." Then grab yourself a paper at the Market's excellent newsstand, and get yourself a stool at the delightful Kokomo. The best Cajun breakfast feed in town.

> **Formosa.** 7156 Santa Monica Blvd., at La Brea (Hollywood). ☎ 213/765-8988.

Very old-school Hollywood hangout with requisite mediocre food. But no one goes here for the food; they go here for the history and the dark campy decor. Setting for the Lana Turner scene in *L.A. Confidential.*

> **Giovanni's Salerno Beach Restaurant.** 193 Culver Blvd., near Vista del Mar (Playa del Rey). ☎ 310/821-0018.

If you have an itch to drive through the foul wetlands of Playa del Rey out to Dockweiler State Beach to catch the thunderous roar of departing jets from LAX, then you must at least make a stop at Giovanni's. An otherwise unimposing, old-signage Italian food joint, upon entering it begs the question, *What sort of LSD-inspired nightmare were these people on?* It's the Christmas that never sleeps. For the height-challenged (in other words, if you're over 6 ft. tall) you'd better arrive and leave with your head hanging low, because from the ceiling and off the walls hang every conceivable variation on the Christmas theme. Layers of strung lights, thousands of tree ornaments, garland, pine cones, and such non-Xmas decor as jack-o-lanterns, flags, stuffed animals, and piñatas occupy every square inch of airspace. Almost as an afterthought—in case you forget you're in an Italian restaurant—there are bunches of plastic grapes, varnished bread loafs, and Chianti bottles by the hundreds hanging off the ceiling. It would be repulsive if it weren't so overdone. This is as close to eating in a thrift store as you can get.

The food? Well, it's most definitely an eat-at-your-own-risk kind of experience. Given that the maitre d' was reluctant to discuss the history of the place unless one sat down to order, we were treated to the Cliffs Notes version of how this place began only after downing what might possibly be the worst linguini with clams ever presented to us as food. But hey, the plate was overflowing. And with enough house wine in the system it really didn't matter.

As to the story behind the place: The namesake, one Giovanni, nearly 30 years ago got the urge to decorate the place for—yes, you guessed it—Christmas. Being too lazy to take it all down, the decorations stayed up. With each passing year the mess was expanded upon until it practically became a parody of itself.

Now there's no turning back.

> **Grand Central Public Market.** 317 S. Broadway, at 3rd St. (Downtown). ☎ **213/624-2378.**

This puts all other L.A. public markets to shame. Gorgeous neon, retro hip light fixtures, and not a tacky stall in the joint. And populated not by tourists, but by real ethnic Angelenos who use it as their primary place to shop. This 75-year-old food bazaar has been beautifully upgraded and restored by Ira Yellin of Bradbury fame, a rare developer who gives a good name to the sport. The place is a model of what can happen when people decide in earnest to rebuild L.A. And on the red line to boot.

Tip: Though Geraldine's, Flip Wilson's juice bar inside the market, has closed since Flip's death, other highlights remain, including China Grill, the cheapest Asian eatery in the city ($2.03 for pork chow mein, 50¢ coffee), and several meat vendors, which sell that Monk peasant delicacy, pig snout. Or as they say at the Grand Central Market, pig "snoot."

> **Hollywood Hills Coffee Shop.** 6145 Franklin Ave., between Argyle and Gower (tucked inside a Best Western Motel). ☎ **323/467-7678.**

We like this place. On the surface, you'd think we wouldn't. It is, after all, populated by pretty young actress moms, goateed and baggy-panted camera people, actors-in-training in designer shades. Hollywood Hills has the potential to turn into another version of New York City's model-friendly Coffee Shop, a vortex for nightclubbing industry brats, but due to the level-headed attitude of owner Susan Fine, it manages not to. Big Stars have eaten here—the walls are lined with a tasteful assortment of their signed mugs. Pitt, Bullock, Tarantino galore, plus framed posters of movie classics like *Reform School Girl.* Heck, Vince Vaughn wrote *Swingers* here. But the solid food—chili, turkey plate, meatball sandwich (they call it a "Luciano," and it was excellent)—the friendly, completely non-snotty attitude of the waiters, and, perhaps most importantly, its location inside a dowdy Best Western Motel, insures that the Hollywood Hills Cafe will remain a decent place to dine free of bogus Hollywood attitude. Now if the prices could come down a bit more, or if at least the portions could expand to match the current prices, it really would be a find.

> **Inaka.** 131 S. La Brea Ave., at 2nd St. (Hollywood). ☎ **213/936-9353.**

One of the last few authentic macrobiotic restaurants in California, if not America. Which means funky minimalist decor, and healthy if austere cuisine. Caveat: As

La Brea has gentrified over the last decade, the prices at Inaka have gone up stratospherically, though the sloppy funky decor remains. If you want far tastier gourmet macro cuisine at half the price, watch for the Monks restaurant chain coming to a city near you.

› **Joe's Restaurant.** 1023 Abbot Kinney Blvd., at Main St. (Venice). ☎ **310/399-5811.**

Name sounds more plebeian than the food. Fine cuisine in a clean, casually elegant space. Brunches are a favorite of Venetians in the know, though you can't beat dinner any night of week.

› **John O-Groats.** 10516 W. Pico Blvd., at Beverly Glen (West Los Angeles).
☎ **310/204-0692.**

The highlight (according to Michael anyway) of this pricey, extremely popular breakfast place was the superfriendly, supersexy Hispanic busboy, though for most people it's the grub. The pancakes are near perfection. Ditto for the eggs, sausage, and biscuits. Those Mexican Scots sure know how to cook. Unfortunately, the wait, especially on weekends, is atrociously long.

› **Kindle's Donuts.** 10003 S. Normandie Ave., near Century Blvd. (South Central).
☎ **323/756-8548.**

Nobody makes donuts like Cambodians. Then again, practically nobody but Cambodians owns California donut shops anymore. The Cambodian owners at Kindle's haven't done much to restore the monumental donut that is the symbol of donut eating everywhere, and don't really seem to get why that might be an important thing to do, but they've managed to sustain a quality product, with beautiful Cambodian women to serve you.

› **La Brea Bakery.** 624 S. La Brea, at Wilshire (next door to the highly touted Campanile Restaurant; Hancock Park). ☎ **323/939-6813.**

It would be the ultimate example of superficiality to dismiss the La Brea Bakery because they charge an exorbitant $5.95 for a pound of 9-grain cereal. Because, frankly, for a veritable canteen of gourmet stuff, in a tiny space, you cannot do better anywhere in L.A. Everything here is grand. Everything. Spicy country crackers, exotic olives, Scharffen Berger chocolate, gorgeous focaccia, candied ginger, hot pretzels to die for, raw Swiss Alpage cheese that you won't find in any other store in town, another cheese named in honor of David Amram, and, of course, the bread (soon to be sold at supermarkets around the city). Most importantly, the staff is downright fun and friendly. Shopping at this little oasis of excellence is an experience all visitors to the city must have.

> **La Hacienda Real.** 849 S. Broadway, at 8th St. (Downtown). ☎ **213/489-2399.**

This is it! The ultimate mecca for Mexican camp you've been dreaming of. The theme is red. And we mean red. Restaurant, bar, and club all in one, with a huge dance floor.

> **Malibu Seafood.** 25653 PCH, near Corral Canyon Rd. (Malibu). ☎ **310/456-3430.**

Basically a shack, with by far the best fast seafood in the city. The ahi-tuna burger is to die for. Ten percent discount on all items if you stay at Malibu Beach RV Park (see "Accommodations").

> **Mandarin Deli.** 727 N. Broadway, near College St. (Downtown). ☎ **213/623-6054.**

Both Kate Tews and Vaginal Creem Davis recommended. Cold cuke salad, stir-fried rice cakes, and scallion pancakes are the ticket. Friendly atmosphere and, most importantly, a bargain.

> **Maria's Ramada.** 1604 Kingsley Dr., at Santa Monica Blvd. (Hollywood).
☎ **323/669-9654.**

The way Maria's Ramada is situated, with its humbly lit nondescript entrance on Kingsley, it feels like a place you might discover in rural Mexico. Inside, it's the real José. A veritable carnival of delightful Mexican design: wooden benches, wooden trellises, and raw floors, with Maria herself, all timeworn and tired, sitting patiently in the corner. There are some slow nights here at Maria's, which doesn't ever seem to motivate the owners to advertise or maybe put a sign or entrance up on Santa Monica, so that the bulk of customers can see where they are. Maria's Ramada is humbly content with its station in life. After dinner we head over to Hollywood Star Lanes across the street (see "Sports and Recreation") to work off the lard. It's where the Brothers Coen filmed *The Big Lebowski,* dude.

> **May Restaurant.** 830 E. Valley Blvd., at San Gabriel Blvd. (San Gabriel).
☎ **626/288-5353.**

Whenever we are out in Asia Land, we stop in at this small, friendly, brightly lit oasis of excellent Taiwanese cuisine. The Taiwanese Slush variations are a mind meld in themselves. Choices include Grass Jelly, Tree Yam, and Love Jade. The best entrees are right there on the steaming trays, but for the adventurous there's also Chitterlings with Pig Blood Soup, Simmered Pig Feet, or Thousand-Year-Old Egg and Tofu.

> **Micelli's.** 1646 N. Las Palmas, at Hollywood Blvd. (Hollywood). ☎ **323/466-3438.**

A fixture in Hollywood since 1949, Micelli's serves midbrow Italian cuisine at decent midrange prices, with kindly paternal service to boot. But what makes it

Monk-worthy is the overwhelming sight of hundreds of wine bottles strung all over the railings and ceiling, and the overwhelming aroma of garlic emanating from the kitchen. We were here on an historic occasion: Jim Monk's 39th birthday, and the night the Bulls beat the Jazz in game six to win the 1998 NBA Title. Ice T sat nearby with his wife and kid. Thankfully, he let us eat in peace.

> **Oki Dog.** For the full grunge effect: 860 N. Fairfax Ave., near Santa Monica Blvd. (Fairfax area), ☎ **323/655-4166.** For a more congenial and cleaner ambiance: 5056 W. Pico Blvd., near La Brea Ave. (Mid-Wilshire), ☎ **213/938-4369.**

If you miss this pathetic raunchy dive, you've missed the very essence of L.A. The namesake Oki Dog, a goopy awful tortilla filled with chili, hot dogs, and pastrami, perfectly enwraps the three competing cultures of the city—Hispanic, Anglo, and Jewish. An absolutely essential rite of passage. But not for the faint of stomach.

... And we have a scene where the two characters—we could get Jackie Chan and Julia Roberts—stop at the Oki Dog for a snack . . .

> **Olson's Delicatessen and Gift Shop.** 5660 W. Pico Blvd., near Spaulding Ave. (Mid-Wilshire). ☎ **213/938-0742.**

It's distinctly possible this cute, clean, 42-year-old Scandie food and gift shop will be gone by the time you go looking for some limpa and Glogg. But, just in case Bertil and Helene Ohlsson are still around, come here to get your supply of caviar in a tube, Mills Ekte majones (mayonnaise), falukorv (German bologna), and ABBA-brand herring. The place is packed at Christmas.

> **The Original Pantry Cafe.** 877 S. Figueroa St., at 9th St. (Downtown). ☎ **213/972-9279.**

The best all-night option anywhere near downtown. But you have to come prepared. There's no menu. Everything's on the chalkboard. The selections are limited. The food is basic (meat loaf, T-bones, ribs, mac and cheese, ham and eggs). While the quality is mediocre at best, you get heaping portions of it, along with the complimentary radishes, celery sticks, and sourdough bread (be sure to have yours toasted). The place hasn't closed in 60 years, with great old L.A. ambiance. Owned by Mayor Riordan.

> **Original Tommy's.** 2575 W. Beverly Blvd., at Rampart (near Downtown). ☎ **213/389-9060.**

This original L.A. drive-in is famous for its extraordinarily good chili burgers and dogs, and 2am on a Saturday night features an eclectic mix of Hispanic and black gangbangers plus USC frat boys. Named after founder Tommy Koulax, it's the Nathan's of Los Angeles—or, better, the Original Ray's of Los Angeles, as there are copycats, like Tomy's and Fat Tomy's, all over town.

> **Pann's Restaurant.** 6710 La Tijera Blvd., at Centinela; 405 exit at La Tijera, make a right on La Tijera and you're there (Inglewood). ☎ **310/670-1441.**

A perfectly restored Googian landmark, it sends fifties conservationists salivating in vinyl and rock wall ecstasy. Pann's encapsulates all the elements of classic Coffee Shop Modern design in one locale. It's all here, from refrigerated overhead pie cases to Naugahyde cantilevered counter stools. If it's a slightly more gourmet breakfast you're after, in a groovy atmosphere filled with pretty young things from the industry, you may want to head to Susan Fine's Hollywood Hills Cafe (see above), but if you want that full-tilt supersonic ambiance, and real-people clientele, you gotta go with Pann's.

> **Papa Cristo's (a.k.a. C&K Importing).** 2771 W. Pico Blvd., at Normandie (Koreatown). ☎ **213/737-2970.**

This might be the best food bargain on the West Coast. The $5.95 lunch special gets you salad, excellent homemade pita, hummus, and THREE—COUNT 'EM—THREE LARGE JUICY LAMB CHOPS. The atmosphere is pure Greek—65-year-old Aristotle Onassis types in sandals, vericose veins, white shorts, and off-white hair with those big gold rings Roman emperors (or at least Telly Savalas) must have worn, with their big-hair young girlfriends wearing about 10 bracelets, shopping at the deli for olives, sweets, and other Greek delicacies. In addition, there's the requisite old women in black shawls, the Diamanda Galas lookalikes, and a scattering of non-Greeks who are on to the secret. The Greek sausage sandwich with tzatziki sauce also comes recommended, though anything at Papa Cristo's is bound to be great.

> **Philippe the Original.** 1001 N. Alameda St., at Ord St. (Downtown).
☎ **213/628-3781.**

A bit touristy now, but still retaining the look and feel of depression-era L.A. There are four gimmicks operating here: (1) Though Coles Buffet makes the same claim, ostensibly the French Dip sandwich was invented here in 1908 (get yours double-dipped); (2) the waitresses wear organza cupcake caps; (3) there's sawdust all over the floor; and (4) coffee's only a dime. Along with nearby Union Station, it's one of the true architectural highlights of downtown L.A. And the lamb sandwich is pretty decent too. For some odd, deeply nostalgic reason, we have frequent dreams about this place.

> **Pink's.** 709 N. La Brea, at Melrose (Los Angeles). ☎ **323/931-4223** or 323/931-7594.

We *loooove* this place. Mainly for its brightly lit exterior and retro ambiance. The dogs are very good, though not spectacular. You go to Pink's because you want a quick bite, because you want to schmooze around the open-air tables, because you want to experience a true cross-section of L.A.—from stars parked in limos to grip guys to gardeners to the inevitable struggling actor. Along with Canter's and the Farmer's Market, it is one of the long-standing culinary institutions in town. A veritable Nathan's of L.A., it's been in this location since 1939.

> **Rae's Diner.** 2901 Pico Blvd., near Cloverfield Blvd. (Santa Monica).
☎ **310/428-7937.**

This is a perfectly preserved classic L.A. diner. Unfortunately, the secret's out among the industry, as its interior has been used in a number of commercials and films. But the place has not lost its charm and remains virtually unchanged in look, character, and menu since its opening 40 years ago. From either booths or stools you can order the nightly $5.40 specials that deliver the tried and true liver and onions, pork chops, chicken fried steak, and veal. No one seems to leave unsatisfied, as the

Hispanic short-order cook has been practicing his craft here for nearly 20 years. And, unlike Phillipe's, there's no press on the walls.

> **Roscoe's Chicken and Waffles.** 1514 N. Gower, at Sunset Blvd. (Hollywood). Open weekdays till midnight, weekends till 4am. And almost always packed. ☎ **323/466-7453.**

Deep-fried chicken and other artery-clogging options, accompanied by waffles and cornbread, all of which are to be doused in artificial maple syrup—that's the formula at this funky, funky chicken place, the original of a citywide chain (other locations are 106 W. Manchester and 5006 W. Pico). The true "lizard king," herpetologist David Kizrizian, is a morning regular.

> **The Safety Zone.** 3630 Wilshire Blvd., at Harvard (Koreatown). ☎ **213/387-7595.**

Skip the cheesy restaurant in front (with tacky music and several TV's blaring) and head to the giant, clean "Barbecue Garden" out back, essentially a big tent with sides that roll down, filled with endless tables of Koreans drinking beer over tabletop gas grills. As atmospheric as Little Tokyo's Shabu Shabu, but with twice the crowd, the Safety Zone is the ultimate Korean 20-something hangout. As their takeout menu says: "Welcome to the Safety Zone. Have Good Time."

> **Superior Poultry.** 750 Broadway, at Alpine (Downtown). ☎ **213/628-7645.**

Vegetarians argue that if we knew how animals were butchered, we would turn vegan in a flash. Well, there were dozens of happy carnivores on our visit to Superior Poultry, all firmly aware they were buying recently butchered MEAT, and still, they walked happily away with their fresh kill. The brutal truth is that most humans are natural carnivores (I mean, what the hell did L. Ron Hubbard give us canines for—ripping into tofu?). And Superior Poultry slaps us in the face with the brute reality of this need. Walk in and you see cages of large and small critters—quail, Vietnamese chickens, checkoo, pigeons, guinea hens, ducks, regular ol' chickens, and silly wabbits—all waiting to be slaughtered (save for the cute white bunnies with the adorable pink ears, which are sold as pets—proving once again that it does all come down to beauty in L.A.). The prices are cheap ($2 per lb. of rabbit, $12 for an entire guinea hen), the floors surprisingly clean, the clientele Hispanic and Asian, the killing completely out of earshot. Got milk?

> **Tail O' The Pup.** 329 San Vicente Blvd., near Beverly Blvd. (West Hollywood). ☎ **310/652-4517.**

L.A. used to specialize in restaurants shaped like the food they serve. In this case it's a hot-dog stand shaped like a giant hot dog—well, actually it's a little more carnal than that, but we'll let it stand. One of the few functioning "vernacular" buildings

. . . Great idea: A love story that takes place at a poultry market. We could get Jennifer Lopez and Leonardo . . .

left in a town that used to have dozens. Get a shot of the manager answering on the doggie phone.

> **Thai Town.** Hollywood Blvd., between Wilton and Normandie (Hollywood).

It's hard to grasp how intelligent, generally tasteful friends can rave about Thai cuisine as if it was some paragon of culinary excellence. Like Vietnamese and Chinese food, Thai cuisine can be very tasty, but rarely is it world class. And the extremely funky places in which it is typically served usually tell you that from the start. If you happen to be cruising through East Hollywood late at night, that is the only time to dine in this area. The excruciatingly slow if 24-hour **Sanamluang** (5176 Hollywood Blvd.) and the nearby **Palms** (in the cheesy Thai Plaza, 5321 Hollywood Blvd., which features a Thai Elvis crooner) will both fill you up. Otherwise, despite the sweetness of the Thai people, despite the beauty of those tall, thin Thai waitresses, and the undeniable goodness of coconut Thai soup, you should give it a miss.

> **Versailles.** 10319 Venice Blvd., at Motor (Culver City). ☎ **310/558-3168.** Three other locations around the city.

I come in at 10:03pm. They'd closed at 10. "I am sorry, sir, we are closed." "But I drove all this way." "I am sorry, sir, we are closed." "But it's only 3 minutes after." "I am sorry, sir, we are closed." "Well, can I come in just to see what it looks like?" The waiter begrudgingly lets me in. Big mistake. Waiter number two appears. "I am sorry, sir, we are closed." "There's just me. I know what I want." "Okay, you can sit in the back." As I sit down, a third waiter appears. "I am sorry, sir, we are closed." "But that other waiter said I could sit down." "He thought you were going to visit friends." "But he said I could have something to eat." "I am sorry, sir, we are closed." "Oh, that's horrible." "Well, sir, maybe we can get you something to go." "That would be great." "I need to check with the kitchen." The kitchen is already breaking down for the night. The waiter returns. "I am sorry, sir, the kitchen is closed." "I'll just take your roast chicken with garlic sauce." He motions back to the kitchen. Within 2 minutes, a hefty bag appears. I pay $9, including tip, and walk away. "Thank you so much." "No problem, sir." I walk out to the mini-Monkmobile. I open up my Cuban treasure. Mounds of Cuban rice. The best damn plantains ever. And the chicken!! Practically an entire bird. And moist! With the most outrageously tangy sauce I've ever tasted. Along with Papa Cristo's, Versailles is the best ethnic dining deal in the city. I am sorry, sirs, but don't even bother arguing the point.

> **The Village Coffee Shop.** 2695 N. Beachwood, at Belden (Hollywood Hills). ☎ 323/467-5398.

This strangely homey, homespun, and hokey place is swarming with industry people, and the parking lot is full of their black Dodge Vipers. Cheesy American car, named in honor of a snake—can't get more Hollywood than that. Do they know? Probably not. Like, what are these people? Huddled together doing what? What are they discussing? What do they get paid to do? They are part of the mystery Hollywood workforce. Writers, actors, deal makers. Come and join them. They are looking for company.

> **Whole Foods.** 239 N. Crescent Dr., between Wilshire and Santa Monica (Beverly Hills). ☎ 310/274-3360.

There's no place in L.A. with the egalitarian good vibe, dirt-cheap prices, and enormous eclectic selection of natural foods found at San Francisco's Rainbow Grocery, the finest whole-foods market in North America. But this Austin-based chain, while clearly geared to a more mainstream upscale shopper (lots of sugar in those pastries), still has the best prices, selection, and quality in town. Nothing comes even close. And while your checkout girl is not likely to be a Rastafarian, you are likely to meet some groovy Angelenos, such as Mad TV's Terry Sweeney and the whiny if likable

Darby O'Brien of the late Ben Is Dead. Unfortunately, the large Whole Foods deli does not fill the need for a first-class gourmet whole-foods restaurant in town. Heck, we'd take the Source if it was brought back.

> **Zankou Chicken.** 5065 W. Sunset Blvd., at Normandie (Los Angeles). ☎ 213/665-7842.

The endless stream of customers from all demographics indicates this Armenian chicken place, in a funky small mall next to a Laundromat on Sunset, has a pretty good hype. The walls are plastered with the press they've received, indicating that food reviewers, in their desperate attempt to find something new to say, will invariably make a big deal out of nothing. Unfortunately, the delivery does not match the enormous hype. The chicken we had was dry and uneventful. The purple pickles were interesting but too strong. While the hummus was okay, the bulgur dish was so extra lemony it was almost impossible to eat. And the vaunted "garlic sauce," a scoop of seasoned lardlike substance that one was supposed to smear on one's chicken, was just weird. It wasn't a sauce, but a paste, and no matter how we tried to integrate it—in the pita, on the chicken, raw by itself, it still came out tasting like pure fat. The lovely Koo "Koo" Roo-sevelt raves about this joint, but maybe that's because her name is pronounced "coo." The old, resigned Armenian running the place adds a bit of poignant melancholy one rarely finds in the Sunshine City.

Note: For far better bird, though admittedly less atmosphere, we prefer the wood-fired variety at **Pollo Ala Brasa** (a rotisserie Peruvian chicken shack next to a car wash at 6th and Western; ☎ **213/382-4090**), and, yes, Koo Koo Roo (all over the city), hands down the finest fast-food chain in the country.

> **Zen Bakery.** 10988 Pico Blvd., at Veteran (West Los Angeles). ☎ 310/475-6727.

On the surface, this unassuming vegan bakery doesn't present much of a dazzling facade, but once you bite into one of those naturally sweetened muffins and tarts, you will swear by this place. Their philosophy is simple: "Use good stuff." How Monk can you get!

Language

Not everybody is writing a screenplay in L.A. Not everyone drives. And you haven't seen *every* stretch of this city on TV. Just the same, you won't hear every one of these words or expressions on a quick visit to Smog Angeles, but, if you stick around long enough, you're bound to encounter most.

Portions adapted from Jim Crotty's, *How to Talk American* (Houghton Mifflin, 1997) and the *USA Phrasebook* (Lonely Planet, 1995).

Amateur night: L.A.'s variant of New York's "bridge-and-tunnel people." "Looks like the show is sold out. Must be amateur night."

A.M.W.: Actress, Model, Whatever. A.k.a. "Wammie."

Angelyne: a surgically enhanced and guileless self-promoter who for nearly 18 years has used billboards and bus shelters to extol her availability. Not for sex or any other recognizable talent. But for being the fabulous glamorous "Angelyne." Used as in "Call Angelyne," or in reference to anyone determined to be famous in spite of their mediocrity. "She's so Angelyne."

The best-policed six square miles on earth: Beverly Hills.

Beverly Hills adjacent: Real-estate term for any rental unit remotely near Beverly Hills, even if it's a South Beverly Hills gang area. Also used tongue in cheek in reference to any other real-estate designation, whether coveted or not, as in "Hancock Park adjacent," "Burbank adjacent," "El Segundo adjacent."

The Big Orange: Los Angeles. A.k.a. "The Big Nipple." A.k.a. "La-La Land" (though no true Angeleno ever uses the latter).

The Blue Whale: The large, blue Pacific Design Center, in West Hollywood.

Boulevard boys: Male prostitutes on Santa Monica Boulevard. "Gas queens" are the gay men who procure their services.

Boys Town: The city of West Hollywood, the predominantly gay-male side of the metropolis. Gave birth to the Monk slogan: "He's not heavy, he's my differently sized lover." A.k.a. "WeHo."

Buk (pronounced "Booook"): The late Charles Bukowski, alcoholic demigod of 20-something poets and writers. Though he lived in Los Angeles for 50 years, the German-born Bukowski was most celebrated outside the United States, where his dogged pursuit of booze, whores, and the low life was romanticized as some sort of heroic gesture, rather than self-indulgent dysfunction.

But what I really want to do is direct: This is not only the ultimate big star cliché, it is also the preferred ironic expression in town right now. Used whenever one is discussing one's work or ambitions. "I am an assistant manager for Enterprise Rent-a-Car, but what I really want to do is direct." Alternately, one could substitute a variety of other menial occupations, but always with a smirk, as in "But what I really want to do is [wait tables, be a claims adjuster, work for Courtney Love]."

A California roll: Rolling through a stop sign without coming to a full stop.

Camp O.J.: The encampment of trailers and journalists behind the Criminal Courts Building in downtown L.A. during the 1995–96 "trial of the century" of O. J. Simpson for the murders of Nicole Brown Simpson and Ronald Goldman. The trial generated some other memorable O.J. vernacular, including "O.J. shoes" (Bruno Magli shoes allegedly worn by Simpson at the scene of the crime), and the "O.J. Projects" (on San Francisco's Potrero Hill, where Simpson ostensibly grew up).

Can't we all just get along?: The memorable line uttered by Rodney "the Human Piñata" King during the height of the L.A. riots. Now used tongue in cheek anytime there's a disagreement.

Carsonigen: Carson, a major oil refinery center. See "Harbor Freeway" under "Streets, Corners, and Highways."

Cattle call: A call for actors to audition. "I've never seen such a cattle call. I got there at 6:30 and it was packed. There were guys getting in fist fights for position."

Central casting: Fake. "Like a circus clown from central casting."

Closing the deal: Sexual intercourse. In a town of major "deals," it's an appropriate metaphor. A.k.a. "getting busy."

Coast 'n' toast: A drive-by shooting. The preferred way to settle scores in "Angel City."

Cocaine-contra: The alleged introduction of crack cocaine into the L.A. black community by CIA operatives trying to raise money for covert operations in Nicaragua.

Crips and Bloods: Two rival L.A. gangs who have maintained a truce since 1992. The Bloods wear red; the Crips, blue.

Cut to the chase: Get to the point. From the silent era in movies, when almost all dialogue was a pretext for an elaborate chase scene.

Devil winds: The Santa Ana winds—hot, dry, fast-moving gusts that allegedly wreak havoc with the psyche. A.k.a. "Santa Anas."

DGA: The Directors Guild of America.

Dialed in: In the loop, hip to what's going on. An appropriate metaphor for the City of Angels, given its residents' love affair with the telephone.

Fruit-and-nut run: What pilots call a flight to L.A.

Gated community: A real-estate term symbolizing L.A.'s paranoiac obsession with security.

A Gates man: A fascist cop. After the notorious former police chief Darryl Gates.

Get out of town!: You're kidding me. Used ironically as an expression of surprise or elation. Origin stems from a convergence of the classic New York expression, "Gedoutahea," and the standard 1930s Louis Mayer line, "You'll never work in this town again!"

Ghetto bird: A police helicopter. Ubiquitous in Angel Town.

Glassphalt: Bright speckles of stardust placed for the benefit of tourists on Hollywood Boulevard.

Going Richter: Blowing one's top, getting very angry. Refers to the Richter scale, which is used to measure the strength of earthquakes, of which there are plenty in Southern California.

Harsh a mellow: Mess up a calm or groovy mood. One is frequently called on it by earnest, irony-free Angelenos.

Heidi chicks: High-class call girls. After Heidi Fleiss, former madam to the stars.

The High Incident Bandits: Emil Matasareanu and Larry Phillips, who were documented live on television robbing the Bank of America in North Hollywood. Emil and Larry were also responsible for several other high-stakes robberies before dying in the Bank of America shoot-out.

Hispo-trash: Hispanics with mysterious sources of disposable income trying to emulate Eurotrash, of which there are thousands in L.A.

The Goal Is Not to Communicate

The M.O. of self-important people in this town is to avoid communication whenever possible. Since this is Los Angeles, such avoidance must be accomplished with the proper mix of sweetness, aplomb, and condescension. Here are some ways L.A. receptionists and assistants inform you that Mr. or Ms. Big Head is not interested in communicating.

- "He's in a meeting."
- "He's real busy right now."
- "Can she call you back?"
- "Can I take your number?"
- "I'll have her get right back to you."
- "He's on the other line."
- "Do you mind holding?"
- "Would you like to talk to his voice mail?"
- "He's out of town."
- "She just stepped out."
- "You just missed her. Can I take a message?"
- "He's got your message and will call you back later. Will you be in?"
- NO!!!

I'll let you go: *Please* let *me* get off the phone, already!

The industry: The film industry. As opposed to "the business" (i.e., television). If you are not somehow directly associated with "the industry," you are literally a nobody in this town. A.k.a. "Hollywood."

Juice: Power, influence, connections. If you got "juice," you "da man."

The Juice: The former football great and probable murderer O. J. Simpson.

Jurassic: Old-fashioned, no longer cool.

L.A. burn: A pain in the throat felt by new arrivals when they first encounter the intense L.A. smog.

The L.A. farewell: A smile followed by: (a) I'll call you ("get lost, you'll never hear from me again"); (b) Let's do lunch ("I like you, but you're a loser"); or (c) Let's do sushi (signifies the beginning of a serious commitment).

La-La Land: Another one of those taboo city nicknames. Its use is a dead giveaway you're some out-of-it dork from Poughkeepsie or San Francisco. Just don't use it.

Like: A word preceding every, like, well, almost, noun and verb. Sample sentence: "I was all like . . . and then he was all like . . . and then I was like . . ." This is the original Valley Girl expression—now spread across the country—where one is supposed to understand what the other is saying by the look or body expression they give you after "like." Resident scholars here at Monk interpret this peculiar phenomenon as the triumph of the media culture over imaginative speech, where popular images are so well understood, no one even has to make a comparison anymore. It is simply understood by the context of, like, "like."

Like, and, all, go: Popular L.A. transition words. "Like, I'm way into this new club, and she's all 'Yeah, but.' And I go, 'It's like way cool. Like, c'mon.' And she's like all into this regret trip. So I go, 'Babe, let's get in my ride and check out the sunset.' And she's all mopey. So I get all lovey. And she's 'okay,' and I'm all 'yowzer!'"

The Little One: The 1994 L.A. earthquake. For "the Big One," see San Francisco.

A Michael Jackson: A badly botched plastic surgery.

Miracle Mile: The continuous wall of tall buildings, and shopping emporiums, in the Wilshire District of West L.A.

Multiculti: Multicultural.

My boyfriend's in rehab: According to former smackhead Jerry Stahl (*Permanent Midnight*), the ultimate career-enhancing cachet for the upwardly mobile "d-girl."

My people/your people: A speedier version of the classic L.A. player line: "I'll have my people call your people." A.k.a. "my peeps/your peeps." Now used mostly tongue firmly in cheek. If not, it's a sure sign of a complete moron.

Normandie-adjacent: A real-estate term for young urban trendoids who really want that multiculti thing.

The Orange Crush: Where several major freeways (the 5, 22, and 57) intersect in Orange County. Heard on traffic reports.

Orange men: Street vendors, usually Hispanic, found at intersections all over L.A. selling bags of fruit and nuts.

Over the hill: The drive from the San Fernando Valley "over the hill" to Hollywood.

People: A celebrity actor's posse of publicists, agents, managers, handlers, and assorted sycophants. Major Hollywood actors are a cottage industry unto themselves. "You need to get in touch with his people to see if Tom can do the keynote."

The People's Republic of Santa Monica: The last holdout of 1960s L.A. consciousness, which has been almost thoroughly quashed by corporate development, real-estate speculation, and the Santa Monica Promenade. The only sixties remnants are the large number of homeless people scattered near the beach, pockets of rent control, and some juice bars.

Place: Mansion. "We've got a place in Malibu and another place in Palm Springs."

Power lunch (dinner, drinking, sweating, running, etc.): Nauseating L.A. yuppie term for doing anything with a high degree of intensity or dedication.

The Promenade: The Santa Monica Third Street Promenade. Has replaced Westwood Village and Beverly Center as the yuppie food, folks, fun, and annoying-street-performer destination of choice.

Ride: Your car. A.k.a. "wheels."

Rig: Fake breasts. "Man, check out the rig on that chick over there." A.k.a. "put on weight" (as in, "Looks like Cindy put on some weight recently"). L.A. is truly the "Silicone Valley."

Ro-day-oh: How to pronounce Rodeo Drive, the ridiculously overpriced shopping street that cuts right through "the Golden triangle," the wealthy Beverly Hills district defined by Santa Monica Boulevard on the northwest, Wilshire Boulevard on the south, and Canyon Drive on the northeast.

Sigalert: Traffic is completely stopped. Invented by a traffic reporter named Sigmund.

SUV: Sports utility vehicle. The monster truck of the industry set. As anyone who has ever been to Los Angeles knows, the hilly, snow-covered, rugged streets of this town require a vehicle of extraordinary size and strength. Of course, there are other reasons to own an SUV in L.A.: (1) it's a very effective ozone depleter; plus it shows you are not some limp-wristed Greenpeace vegan; (2) it's a status symbol; everyone immediately knows you are cool; (3) it's an incredible ego-booster—better than steroids!; (4) it makes a career girl feel more powerful; (5) it makes a weak man strong; (6) it obliterates other cars in accidents; (7) it's absolutely essential on those frequent off-terrain expeditions Los Angelenos take on the weekends. *NOT!*

Surfer U: Pepperdine University in Malibu.

The Swish Alps: Silver Lake, the second largest gay enclave in the city.

The 3 Bs: Brentwood, Bel Air, and Beverly Hills. Rich, white, star-studded enclaves.

"There it is. Take it": Immortal words spoken by Department of Water and Power (DWP) chief William Mulholland in 1913 upon completion of aqueduct bringing Owens Valley water to Los Angeles. This simple statement summed up the mind-set of that era: Screw everybody else.

Tradin' paint: A car accident.

TV parking: Finding a spot exactly where you want to be. A phenomenon that only happens on TV shows. A.k.a. "Kojak," as in "Nice Kojak!"

The Twin Towers: The gleaming new high-tech "correctional facility" downtown, immortalized on the cover of Mike Davis's *City of Quartz.*

University of California for Surfboarding: University of California at Santa Barbara. The school's beachfront location appears to attract students more interested in surfing than studying.

University of Spoiled Children: USC, the University of Southern California. Moniker derives from the fact that USC is an expensive private school with a reputation for fratheads and sorority babes with little creatively going on besides their rah-rah love of USC. Along with UCLA, it counts many film directors as former attendees. *Related note:* "Film director" is widely regarded as the profession of choice for spoiled rich kids.

The Valley: The San Fernando Valley. Home of, like, the stereotypical white middle-class Valley Girl, whose rad bitchin' mall lingo has spread around the, like, world.

>   **Valley Girl:** "Like, No Way!!"
>   **Monk:** "But it clearly has."
>   **Valley Girl:** "I'm so sure."
>   **Monk:** "No, really, I've heard Valspeak in Boise and Omaha."
>   **Valley Girl:** "Gag me with a silver spoon."
>   **Monk:** "But it's a sign of your cultural influence. Well, and surfers too."
>   **Valley Girl:** "I don't THINK so."
>   **Monk:** "You should be proud."
>   **Valley:** "Okay, fine."
>   **Monk:** "Really."
>   **Valley Girl:** "Whatever."

Weho: West Hollywood, L.A.'s answer to San Francisco's Castro. As Michelle Shocked sings, it's "Where the gay boys pose."

The Wizard of Westwood: The legendary UCLA Bruins basketball coach John Wooden, who won ten NCAA Division I championships—by far the most successful career of any college coach in history. His players included Lew Alcindor (a.k.a.

Kareem Abdul Jabbar), Jerry West, Bill Walton, and the all-time Crotty family sharpshooter of choice, Lynn Shackelford.

Yarmulke burn: The bald spot on the back of the head.

Libraries and Reading Clubs

People do read in this town. And not just scripts either. Here are a few of the more esoteric places to indulge one's literary leanings.

› Elysium Nudist and Naturist Archives. Topanga. ☎ 310/455-1000. Open by appointment only.

This library reflects the vision of the late Ed Lange, founder of the nonprofit Elysium Fields, L.A. County's only nudist colony. Lange left a collection of more than 10,000 still photos and hundreds of books and magazines that date to the 1920s.

› The Glendale Central Library Cat Collection. 222 E. Harvard St., at Louise, near the Glendale Galleria (Glendale). ☎ 818/548-2021. Officially open 1:30–5:30pm Sat only, though visitors can at any time request that Reference retrieve specific works from the collection.

Home to the world's largest collection of cat books and cat memorabilia. Over 20,000 items in total.

› The Marshall McLuhan–Finnegans Wake Reading Club. Mon nights at Abbot Kinney Branch Library. 501 S. Venice Blvd., at Abbot Kinney St. (Venice). ☎ 310/821-1769.

According to our inside source, Humphrey Chimpden Earwicker, the hand of Bob Dobbs is everywhere. Not the *real* Bob Dobbs, who isn't "real," but a creation of the genius warped mind of one Ivan Stang of Dallas, Texas. No, the manic, quite captivating Bob Dobbs of Toronto, Canada, a borderline nutcase (he once claimed his wife had discovered a "cure" for AIDS) who was funded for years in his mania by a Toronto trust-funder named Nelson Thull. Well, Dobbs has resurfaced in California, spreading his half-baked understanding of McLuhan and Joyce and melding a personality and communication style that appears to be a hybrid of the two. The result of his influence is this reading group, which, thanks to its founder, one Gerry Fialka, appears to be far more grounded than anything Dobbs could channel.

> **Paul Ziffren Sports Resource Center Library.** Amateur Athletic Foundation of Los Angeles. 2141 W. Adams Blvd., at Western Ave. (South Central). ☎ **213/730-9600.** www.aafla.org.

Ever wondered where that $200 million surplus from Peter Uberoth's wildly successful 1984 Olympic Games went? Ninety million of it went here. And it shows. This beautiful, meticulously maintained sports-history archive is one of the great undiscovered gems of the city, featuring large collections of sports videos, art, classic posters, autographs, and other sports memorabilia, plus an impressive selection of esoteric sports periodicals—everything from Blind Sports International (with articles on blind football, lacrosse, diving, and *fencing*) to Grit and Steel (devoted to the "sport" of cockfighting). With the bulk of the archives gathered from the late Helms Bakery Sports Collection, the library fields many research calls from the film and television industries, and its excellent staff of librarians will help you locate just about anything related to the history and culture of sports. Especially strong is their coverage of the Olympics. The relaxing, elegant grounds of the Amateur Athletic Foundation are in stark contrast to the testosterone-laden temples of sport like Nike World Headquarters and Nike Town. Open weekdays 10am to 5pm.

Museums

The typical Los Angeles tourist gravitates towards the Museum Mile, and the oft-covered (though still impressive) highlights of the George C. Page Museum of La Brea Discoveries, the Los Angeles County Museum of Art (LACMA), and, farther afield, the Museum of Tolerance in Century City and the Huntington Library, Art Collection and Botanical Gardens in Pasadena. The Monk traveler takes a different tack, as the selection below indicates.

> **Ackermansion.** 2495 Glendower Ave., near Cromwell, past entrance to Griffith Park (Hollywood). ☎ **213/MOON-FAN.** Open by appointment, and on Sat.

Forrest "Forry" Ackerman's extensive collection of sci-fi/horror props and memorabilia. (See Ackerman interview in this section.)

> **American Military Museum/Heritage Park.** 1918 N. Rosemead Blvd., south of Rush St. (South El Monte). ☎ **626/442-1776.** http://members.aol.com/tankland/musem.htm.

... And we could get Jim Crotty to play the disgruntled vet. You know, Jim Crotty? From the X video? ...

Put on a helmet, sit in the MASH tent, and let yourself drift back to the Land of Wars Past. All the menacing vehicles and launchers that make up the modern war machine are here to fill your memory, including dozens of tanks and other large weaponry, displayed in an orderly, if a bit crowded, fashion. For a more realistic setting—featuring tanks in their natural mucked up condition—visit the Patton Museum (see chapter 3). The Patton-like Don Michelson, who seems perpetually poised to share another war tale, and his son Craig, who's a little bit cowed by Dad, keep the place running, though the visitors seem to be few.

> **Banana Museum.** 2524 N. El Molino Ave., at Mariposa (Altadena).
☎ **626/798-2272.** www.banana-club.com. By appointment only.

A top-banana photographer named Ken Bananaster enthusiastically displays his banana-shaped treasures, ranging from banana pillows and banana liquors to the world's oldest petrified banana. (See Banana Man interview in this section.)

> **Center for Land Use Interpretation.** 9331 Venice Blvd., at Robertson (Culver City).
☎ **310/839-5722.** www.clui.org.

It's hard to know where to put CLUI—is it a museum by virtue of its ongoing exhibits, a library by virtue of its compelling books, a tour company by virtue of its one-of-a-kind sojourns to extraordinary ex-urban environments, or a massive

(continued on page 126)

Famous Monsters of Monkland:

The *Forrest Ackerman*

Interview

If the names Vampirella, Draculena, and Frankenstein send nostalgic shivers of adolescent adrenaline coursing through your veins, then Forrest Ackerman—and his house of many horrors—is your holy grail. Almost everyone who brought fantasy to print or screen has been handily influenced by him. As an agent to the literati of science fiction, an actor in such B classics as *Amazon Women on the Moon* or *Nudist Colony of the Dead,* and creator of the magazine *Famous Monsters of Filmland,* his faithful documentation of the rise of science fiction, in all its great and trashy forms, has kept an important genre from the dustbins of oblivion.

It's not everyone who can boast that robots from the films *Metropolis* and *Beverly Hills Cop* and the TV show *Battlestar Galactica* are part of their living room decor. Nor bookshelves that overflow with 250 editions of *Frankenstein,* including the original, signed *Frankenstein* by Mary Shelley, plus every book written on Atlantis, or volumes written in Esperanto, the global language that never was. Likewise, who has landscapes by Ray Bradbury, every horror magazine cover in print, an Abe Lincoln chair, and over 125,000 science-fiction photos just lying around? And who counts among his friends past Boris Karloff, Bela Lugosi, Peter Lorrie, Vincent Price, and Fritz Lang? We have just entered the remarkable home of Forrest Ackerman, a living legend, and the man who invented the term "sci-fi."

Monk: How did you make your living over the years?

Ackerman: The first job I ever had was with the government. I got a civil-service senior typist rating in the old days of the mechanical typewriter. Then at one point I went to work for the Academy of Motion Picture Arts and Sciences. In 1939 I was behind the scenes guarding the Oscars as they were being given out to *Gone With the Wind.*

After the war I had stories in print and virtually knew all the authors and editors. I thought maybe life had prepared me to be a literary agent specializing in science fiction. I edited and published Ray Bradbury's first story. He did let me resell overseas some of his work. And a young Isaac Asimov did the same. And A. E. Van Vogt did an extraordinary thing: He gave me some bottom of the barrel stuff. But I did so well for him—I had real enthusiasm for his work—for the next 40 years or so I was his agent. And I began to catch on. Before I knew it I had built up to 200 authors I was representing. I still do [represent them] as a matter of

fact, although about 99% of them are dead. Now I'm representing their sons and daughters, widows and estates.

I've also been in fifty-three films, just little fun cameos mainly, although I was president of the United States in *Amazon Women on the Moon.* Then in the next film I graduated from the president of the United States to president of the world. Then after two terms I was out of a job and all I could get was to be a judge in *Nudist Colony of the Dead.* Quite a come-down from president of the world.

In 1957 I went over to London to the world science-fiction convention and afterward I had a couple of spare weeks and went to Paris, among other places. And there on the newsstand I saw a magazine that ordinarily was about all sorts of movies, but this time it was on fantasy and horror. It had King Kong and Dracula, and The Man Who Could Work Miracles, and Frankenstein. So I just got a copy for my collection.

I got to New York and I met up with a chap named James Warren. He was publishing a poor man's *Playboy* called *After Hours.* He took one look at this French magazine. He was looking for a one-shot and wanted to rewrite it for an American audience. He took a chance and for 20 hours a day I was sitting at a smoking typewriter. It was smoking so bad I was afraid I was going to die of cancer before I completed the copy. And the publisher sat opposite me holding an imaginary sign in the air that said, "I am an $11\frac{1}{2}$-year-old. Forrest Ackerman, I am your reader. Make me laugh."

I had no intention of being funny with Frankenstein or Dracula, or anything, but that's what he wanted. And so the first issue of *Famous Monsters of Filmland* was born. Obviously it was a success and in the end I did 190 issues of it.

Barbarella was also very big at the time and I thought inevitably they're going to bring back Cinderella, and there will be a star girl named Esterella, and there'll be a triple-X film called *Beaverella,* and suddenly Vampirella jumped into my mind. And right next to her was her twin sister, Draculina. And I thought, "I wonder if there couldn't be a planet where instead of water there was blood." Not that it was coming from creatures or anything but that was just the chemical consistency of it. So I had a whole origin story in my mind of Vampirella. When I got back to New York we were off and running with Vampirella. Last year there was a Roger Corman Showtime movie of her on TV. They showed it three or four times.

So, what I've done to make a living has been agenting. I've had over fifty stories published. I just do everything and anything in life, what anybody wants of me that has anything to do with science fiction or films.

Monk: So tell us about your house here. How did this get started?

Ackerman: Well, believe it or not, in about 1930, if a little kid like me was to write off to a magazine and say, "Gee, I'd sure like that cover, you know," they'd say, "Oh, you want it, kid?" and they'd send it to you. Well, I never stopped collecting.

Since 1951, every weekend that I've had an open house, people drop in. By now approximately 40,000 people have visited me. One night I had 186 science-fiction people including Buzz Aldren and another astronaut here in my home. Basically, around forty times a year, as long as I'm here on a weekend, around twenty-five people show up. I would think everyone on earth has seen me three times by now, but they keep coming out of the woodwork.

Monk: Now certainly Spielberg has been here?

Ackerman: Yes, he was. Lucas never was, but Spielberg was.

> "An October 1926 Amazing Stories jumped off the newsstand and grabbed hold of me. In those days magazines spoke. And that one said, 'Take me home, little boy. You will love me.'"

Monk: You liked his movies?

Ackerman: I should say so. I had an epiphany when I saw *Close Encounters.* I'm an utterly irreligious individual but I felt full of spirit toward the end there when the beautiful little alien came out of the ship and man went off to the other world.

Monk: Do you believe that there's extraterrestrial life out there?

Ackerman: Utterly. There must be millions of them. So doggone far away I don't know if they'll ever get here. They'd have to come from a planet that had more or less the same gravity as we do and a breathable atmosphere. The chances seem too infinitesimal to me.

Monk: What do you consider the highlight, the prize piece of the Ackermansion?

Ackerman: Well, it isn't here at the moment, but it's the robot from my favorite film, *Metropolis.* It's a story 100 years in the future, which I have seen ninety times. So I have seen the robot in *Metropolis* destroyed ninety times at the end of the film. I commissioned a couple of fellows to spend a year and a half and 600 hours and they reconstructed her for me.

And also an October 1926 *Amazing Stories.* You'll see it downstairs. It jumped off the newsstand and grabbed hold of little 9-year-old me, and you're too young to know, but in those days magazines spoke. And that one said, "Take me home, little boy. You will love me."

And everything grew from that one magazine to 3,000 things that have consumed my life.

The Ackermansion *is located at 2495 Glendower, near Cromwell, in Hollywood. To arrange a tour, call ☎ 213/MOON-FAN. Also see listing under "Museums."*

>interview

pseudo-scientific prank? Like its neighbor, the incomparable Museum of Jurassic Technology, CLUI is all of these combined. Its books include *Hinterland* and *Route 58*. Its mission: to educate people about how the land is affected after folks abandon the structures they build (racetracks, factories, airplane scrap yards, nuclear test sites, hazardous waste dumps). Its Web site is a Monkish guidebook in its own right. Support these people.

› Frederick's Bra Museum / Frederick's of Hollywood. 6608 Hollywood Blvd., at Highland (Hollywood). ☎ 323/466-8506.

This place is more titillating when you first hear of it than when you actually visit it. Features the bras of such luminaries as Ethel Merman and Isabel Sanford.

› The Geffen Contemporary (a.k.a. "The Temporary Contemporary"). Museum of Contemporary Art. 152 N. Central Ave., at 1st St. (Downtown/Little Tokyo). ☎ 213/621-2766.

By most accounts, this downtown branch has more engaging exhibitions (not to mention better parking) than conservative main **Museum of Contemporary Art** at 250 S. Grand (☎ **213/621-2766**). Unfortunately, it closes for weeks at a time in between exhibitions, so call ahead.

› Jewish Sports Hall of Fame. West Side Jewish Community Center, 5870 West Olympic Blvd., near Fairfax (Fairfax area). ☎ 213/938-2531.

Historically, there's always been a stereotype that Jews don't become great athletes. Sandy Koufax, Mark Spitz, and Erwin Klein all repudiate that stereotype. Unfortunately, this exhibit is just a wall of names. There actually should be a full-tilt museum for Jewish sports heroes.

› The L. Ron Hubbard Life Exhibition. 6331 Hollywood Blvd., at Ivar (Hollywood). ☎ 213/960-3511. Open 10:30am–9:30pm daily.

God invented Scientology so EST graduates wouldn't seem so cheesy. L. Ron Hubbard, creator of the science of mind "religion" known as Scientology, is another American Spiritual Success Story, along the lines of EST founder Werner Erhard. Like Erhard, he borrowed extensively from the teachings of the world's religions, most notably the thinking of Theosophy and Buddhism, and crystallized his dharma into one book, *Dianetics.* There are 500 or so more books by the prolific writer, which our friendly perky tour guides never tire of mentioning, but it is *Dianetics* that first launched Hubbard to not only the top of the *New York Times* bestseller lists but also to world renown. The core of his teaching is palpably obvious to any beginning student of Zen: "All is made by mind alone"—or, in conventional lingo, "mind over matter"; or, in Hubbard's convoluted vernacular, "function monitors structure." From this premise, Scientologists are able to build cases against assorted enemies, including Prozac-prescribing psychiatrists. The great thing about this perversely entertaining exhibit, and about Scientology in general, is that despite the slavish deification of the engineer and science-fiction author from Tilden, Nebraska, they aren't pushy, at least not in the Mormon or Seventh Day Adventist sense, which the church and its followers somewhat resemble in style and aesthetics. You will undoubtedly walk away thinking the Ron-invented E-Meter, which measures thought forms and is one of the key therapeutic tools of the religion, is a piece of quackery akin to phrenology or Wilhelm Reich's orgonne box. And you will chuckle at the complete unoriginality of Hubbard's "20 Steps to Happiness" (which include such mind-blowers as "take care of yourself," "set a good example," and "do not steal"), not to mention the sliding wall of proclamations the Montana-raised eagle scout received. But, by exposing yourself to the core of the man's beliefs and his life's work, you will remove forever from your brain the belief that Scientology is primarily a litigious cult, bent on sussing out and destroying anyone who questions its methods or teaching. Now that's a religious thought.

> **Museum of Jurassic Technology.** 9341 Venice Blvd., near Robertson (Culver City). ☎ **310/836-6131.**

Either this is a brilliant practical joke, a pseudo-scientific spoof heralding nature's oddities and human superstitions as if they were subjects of compelling research, or it's totally sincere. Either way, the Museum of Jurassic Technology is unquestionably the finest, most disturbing museum-going experience in all of California. That it exists in Los Angeles is miracle enough. This collection of fascinating esoterica, a cross between the Mutter Museum, Barnum and Bailey, and the Smithsonian, should rightfully be positioned where large numbers of attendees are likely to appear, not on an ordinary street in Culver City, far from the tiny pocket of folks who actually do appreciate genius in this town. But the fact that it is situated precisely where it is, next door to the equally pioneering Center for Land Use Interpretation (see above), gives credence to the theory, expounded by Sirs Kassner and Munger of New York, that Los Angeles is the most culturally compelling city in America simply because so much of it remains unnamed and unclaimed. The Museum of Jurassic Technology is part of a tradition that goes back a hundred or more years—to early natural-history museums like Peale's in Philadelphia—when museums were collections of curiosities that wowed the spectator with the utter unfamiliarity of their exhibits. Go here immediately, before the Getty, before LACE, before anything. Take special note of the Monk-style exhibit on the history of motor homes (Galloping Bungalows), which looks at these vehicles as Edenic "land arks" originally built to withstand the coming Apocalypse, and Hagop Sandaldjian's world of microminiatures (seen only through the aid of a magnifying glass), which makes the Museum of Miniatures seem like clunky child's play.

> **The Museum of Miniatures.** 5900 Wilshire Blvd., near Fairfax (Fairfax area, Museum Row). ☎ **323-937-6464.** www.museumofminiatures.com. Open Tues–Sun 10am–5pm.

After the Museum of Jurassic Technology's exhibit on microminiatures, you might be a little nonplused by this far larger—yet far more quaint—look at the world of miniatures. But it bears viewing, especially as a history tour for young children, since the museum showcases a wide selection of miniature dolls in period costume. The highlights are a replica of the *Titanic* made from 75,000 toothpicks and 2 gallons of Elmer's glue, and a staggering reproduction of the 1982 Super Bowl between the 49ers and Bengals made out of chewing gum wrappers!! Carole Kaye started the museum a few years ago by building a dollhouse. But Carole's a perfectionist, you see, and her dollhouse turned out to be a mighty piece of real estate in its own right. After that, there was no stopping her. She came up with everything from the Palace of Versailles to the Vatican, all scale-models done in the most exquisite detail. Recently she gave the Museum of Jurassic Technology a run for their money with her own display of microminiatures, and now has several elaborately small miniatures as part of the permanent collection. The museum is definitely worth a visit, though it lacks the intellectual justification of the Jurassic or its bleeding edge sensibility.

> **Ralph W. Miller Golf Library and Museum.** 1 Industry Hills Pkwy., Sheraton Resort (City of Industry). ☎ **626/854-2354.** www.golftours.com/industryhills. Open Tues–Fri 9am–6pm, Sat–Sun noon–6pm. Free admission.

To hit a silly white ball around a golf course you have to be relaxed about life, with the money to indulge that state of relaxation. Golf is for people who deep down don't give a hoot about radically changing the world. The Ralph W. Miller Golf Library and Museum celebrates that status quo feeling. This handsome mahogany-paneled room inside the Industry Hills Sheraton Resort was built around the collection of the late Ralph Miller, a prominent L.A. attorney and renowned collector of golf books and memorabilia. The museum includes several small exhibits: photos of midget actor—and golf nut—Pat Bilon, who played E.T.; a shrine to the Harvard-educated Southern gent Bobby Jones, a lifelong scholar of Dryden, Swift, and Shakespeare (a far cry from Lee Trevino and Fuzzy Zoeller), who also won golfing's Grand Slam and is known for courageously living according to the golfing motto "play the ball where it lies"; a shrine to Mildren Ella "Babe" Didrikson Zacharias, who was nicknamed after Babe Ruth and who is known as the first woman golf pro, among other pioneering sporting feats; an exhibit on the evolution of the golf ball (the oldest ball dates from A.D. 1600 and is known as a "featherie"

(continued on page 133)

Mad Monks Meet Banana Man:
The *Ken Bananaster*

Up in the Altadena Hills, behind an unassuming storefront, the Banana Man, Ken Bananaster, throws open the door to his suburban landmark banana club. His polished smile, yellow-suited torso, and boyish charm are infectious. If you aren't smiling within one minute of entering the world's only known Banana Museum, you're hopeless.

From floor to ceiling hangs every artifact, kitschy replication, and piece of banana memorabilia known to mankind. The walls crawl with yellow plastic fruit. Display cases house the most thorough collection of banana products—everything from skin cream and soft candy to stationary, rubber toys, postcards, and wine. Primary yellow streaks through the room as the Banana Man drives home immediate food for thought: "Bananas are fun!"

Monk: How the hell did you become Ken Bananaster?

Banana Man: I was president of a manufacturing firm that manufactured photographic products and I started handing out banana stickers. People are too stressed out and people are going bananas in this world. We have to have a little more fun.

You hold this banana in the right position and you'll never leave the house without putting on your smile. First of all, you should eat a finger. That's one banana. I eat a hand a week, that's about ten. I eat about 250 pounds of bananas a year. Why? Because within the peel there is a meal. In this biodegradable bright-yellow curvaceous edible elongated herbaceous fruit we have the world's most perfect food. And that is not just Chiquita's slogan.

You've got no fat, no cholesterol. Vitamin A, B, B1, B2, B6, Vitamin C, a little iron, a little calcium, it helps things move through you with soluble fiber. And I'm telling you—are you ready for the big secrets about the banana?—you can treat your hair, treat your skin, relieve a headache, shine your shoes, and feed your bushes.

I am a young 59 years old. But you see, it's these bananas. If people got the word, if they really got the word . . . You don't need the Viagra, man. All you need to do is eat two bananas every day. There's so many things packed into these puppies. This is the answer.

Monk: So you think if the guys who are taking Viagra were eating the bananas they wouldn't need the Viagra?

Banana Man: You know, I'm not going to push it. If [someone] would get with it and sponsor the Banana Man I'd tell them all about the virtues of this fruit that they'd really like to hear. I've already done more as an individual than anybody else in the entire world to influence the perception of the bright yellow curvaceous edible elongated fruit. You don't have to spend a lot of money to stay in good health.

Monk: How many members are in your Banana Club?

Banana Man: There's 9,116 in this club from twenty-seven different countries. That's why you see all of these items in here, because people from all over sent one or two items.

Monk: Who's got the most Banana Merits in your club?

Banana Man: I can tell you who she is. On the wall over here you are seeing the world's only, hardest and oldest, petrified, hard-as-a-rock banana. It has been here in the Banana Museum for 24 years. It was found in a girl's closet. She told me about it and she said, "Ken, I've got a hard banana for you."

And I said, "You do?"

She said, "Yes, I found it in my closet."

I said, "Get it out of your closet, frame it, and send it to me!"

Monk: How many merits did she get for that?

Banana Man: One hundred BM's [banana merits]. And there was another guy who matched her. He lit himself on fire and got a hundred banana merits. I'll tell you, he didn't want to contribute anything, but he wanted that degree right away. He was a stunt man and he said, "Ken, if I come as a human banana flambé will you give me my masters degree?" And I said, "You got it." So he lit himself on fire, threw me a hot banana, and said, "Give me my BM."

Monk: This is the brightest place. It just makes you happy. Is this your full-time gig?

Banana Man: This is it. Nothing else. I'm working out of the house now and this is my office right here. Now a lot of people want to know how they can be part of this bunch, so we have a Web site, which is www.banana-club.com.

People come in here in groups. And yes, we have lots of visitors by appointment. This has been here since 1976. I've shown thousands of people.

Monk: Who are some of your famous members?

Banana Man: Well, now, President Reagan, he's part of the bunch. He's the P.B.: the President of Bananas. I asked President Reagan when I photographed him

"Another guy said, 'Ken, if I come as a human banana flambé will you give me my masters degree?' And I said, 'You got it.'

So he lit himself on fire. . . ."

with his friends, "President Reagan, do you remember me sending you your banana-club kit?" And he said, "Well, Banana Man, I don't remember!" But he's a member in good standing.

Oh, you know, guys like Steve Martin, comedians which I've sent the memberships to.

Monk: Let's talk more about the spiritual dimension of the banana.

Banana Man: Well, when you add the "S" on the end of the word itself, what does it mean to most people? It means out of control, crazy, straight out of their mind, or whatever. "He's gone bananas, they're going bananas." I think it's really got a bad rap. But you notice it hasn't suffered, because people keep eating more.

With no bones in these bananas—and they don't squirt, squeak, or leak—people have used bananas for so many different tasteful things. And we've covered most of them.

Monk: Well, it's obviously given meaning to your life.

Banana Man: I get a big charge out of seeing people smile and I think its important to stay happy, to be up, to be enthusiastic. So I've used this as a vehicle for myself to pass on to other people, so hopefully I have left people with a little better attitude.

Monk: Do you have banana dreams?

Banana Man: Yes I do, as a matter of fact. They're tasteful. I visualize myself in a big banana-building casino making appearances on a stage, getting everything started, getting everybody with a smile on their face and driving down the street in a banana car and everyone calling "Hey, Banana Man, Ken Bananaster, the Banana King."

Monk: We're in love with the banana.

Banana Man: I tell you, you're never going to forget this banana museum or me because every time you walk into a grocery store . . .

Monk: You're a deity now.

Banana Man: I like that.

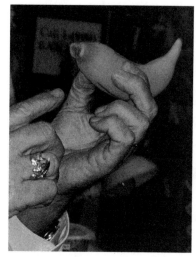

The Banana Museum is located 2524 N. El Molino Ave., at Mariposa, in Altadena. To arrange a visit, call ☎ 626/798-2272. Web site www.banana-club.com. Also see listing under "Museums."

>interview

because it was stuffed with feathers), plus a great poetic celebration of the game by a gentleman named Forgan. But the topper of this place is not the museum pieces, but the library: 5,000 books and periodicals and 20,000 photos in all, a total surpassed only by the USGA collection in Far Hills, New Jersey. A resource for golf scholars and sportswriters around the world, the library's highlights include the signed biography of Old Tom Morris, the native of Saint Andrews, Scotland, who was known as the "grand old man of golf"; Thomas Matthieson's *The Goff* (written in 1743, and now worth $40,000); and a 1597 Scottish Law Book, which documents laws proscribing golf dating back to 1457 (the game was outlawed because the government didn't want the citizen militia foregoing the practice of archery— see what I mean about golf being for people who don't want to change the world?). You will be assisted by two excellent and delightful women, library manager Marge Dewey (City of Industry's answer to Mrs. Krug of Omaha, Nebraska) and librarian Saundra Shefer, editor of Jeff Ellis's monumental golf tome *The Clubmaker's Art*. If you love *this* game, a visit to the Ralph Miller Library and Museum is as essential as, well, a relaxed view of life.

Music Venues

There's no longer a music scene in Los Angeles; there are simply music showcases. When the major labels are based right in your hometown, the whole notion of a scene gradually gets obliterated. Still, here are the best venues in Music Industry USA.

> **Al's Bar.** 305 S. Hewitt St., at 3rd St. (Downtown). ☎ **213/625-9703.**

This granddaddy of L.A. punk clubs has sponsored the likes of X, Social Distortion, Lydia Lunch, 7 Year Bitch, Beck, Tribe 8, Betty Blowtorch, and company. Three cavernous rooms, heavy on the graffiti, offer puked over, tore up, found-in-the-alley couches to sit on, and in the calm of late afternoon looks like the aftermath of an L.A. riot. If you could indeed open bars under bridges, this is what they'd look like. It's the sort of dungeonesque environment that college-town bars across America have unsuccessfully tried to copy. The sticky floor factor rivals the gnarliest bathhouse, the stage looks like it was dredged out of the L.A. River, and the bathrooms are at your own risk. But they keep packing them in for the best in unsigned talent, experimental theater, and ball-busting, hard-core rock and roll. Owner Marc Keisel bought the former truckers' bar in 1979 and provided a cultural vortex for the way-cool Outer Limits warehouse and industrial zone known as The Downtown Arts District. Though the downtown art scene has come and gone (and might come again), Al's Bar consistently soldiers on under the ironic glow of foxy bartender Stay-C.

> **El Floridita.** 1253 N. Vine St., at Fountain (Hollywood). ☎ **213/871-8612.**

Shall we dance . . . salsa? Ostensibly a Cuban/Puerto Rican musical form, this spicy elegant mix of Spanish classical form and African vavoom attracts devotees from across the demographic spectrum, including a few crazy Anglos. As one devotee eloquently put it, "Salsa is the most electric of musical forms. It is color-blind." If you want to dance salsa in L.A., you can do no better than El Floridita, a small Cuban restaurant nestled into a nondecrepit mini-mall. El Floridita, which took its name from a legendary Havana dance club patronized by and frequently mentioned in the writings of Hemingway, is run by the sharp, friendly, consummate young host Armando J. Castro, who took the restaurant/club over from his father 11 years ago. On Monday nights Armando's place becomes the hottest spot for Latin music in town. Spurred on by the spicy riddums of Johnny Polanco & Conjunto Amistad, regulars like Sandra Bullock, dancing madman Robert Duvall (if you saw what he pulled off in *The Apostle,* imagine what he could do on the dance floor), and Randa Haines (director of the Columbia-Tri-Star salsa flick *Dance With Me,* featuring Vanessa Williams) keep the tightly packed dance floor hoppin'. "Dancing is simply walking to the sound of the music," says one insider. After a few Mojistos (a smooth, tasty rum-and-whiskey combo, which is the signature cocktail of the house), you'll be hoppin' too. Though, if you are not a seasoned expert, you might feel a trifle intimidated. Especially when you spy the towering high-heeled Latin beauties, who flit about this place like nervous flies before hopping onto the floor with the next hot young stud. These girls can DANCE! Proper, proud, gorgeously coifed birds, they prance about the floor like tall flamingoes. If ever there was a reason to learn to salsa, the sexy senoritas of El Floridita are definitely it.

If you need to bring your mating dance up to snuff, contact **Albert Torres,** Johnny Polanco's promoter/manager, who offers salsa courses throughout the city (☎ **310/450-8770;** E-mail: Albert@salsaweb.com), including Salsa Sundays at the Boat House on Santa Monica Pier. El Floridita also has dancing Thursday, Saturday, and Sunday, though none of these nights compare to the intensity and sheer expertise of Monday. Make your reservation at least 2 weeks in advance.

> **5th Street Dick's.** 3335 W. 43rd Place, at Crenshaw (South Central). ☎ **213/296-3970.**

Owned and managed by tenor saxophonist Richard Fulton, this is a vibrant cafe in the heart of heavily African-American Leimert Park. From sweet-potato cobbler to tramp pot pies, the range of cafe grub is impressive, but the main dish here is jazz, 5 nights a week (plus poetry on Tues and Wed). Friday and Saturday the place is smokin'. After the house band closes at 1am, a steady stream of local legends hop upstairs for an impromptu jam session that lasts until 4:30 in the morning. The ambiance out front is like none other in L.A.—a bona fide sense of community, with men playing chess, young intellectuals debating the social importance of rap, and still others just enjoying an evening with friends. Very clean, no booze, and only the occasional whiff of ganja. As the locals will tell you, Dick's is the sort of small, packed, intimate place where jazz began. If you come to L.A. and don't visit, then you are missing the very soul of the city.

The Jazz Bakery. 3233 Helms Ave., at Venice Blvd. (Culver City). ☎ **310/271-9039.**

If you want an intimate yet raucous jazz ambiance, head to this smartly appointed *serious* jazz club in the old Helms Bakery complex. With renowned veteran performers like Clark Terry, Milt Jackson, Terence Blanchard, and Chuck Mangione, it's a place to come and *respectfully* listen. The managers don't even want you to whisper while the band is playing. For a looser, more barlike ambiance, try the **Catalina Bar and Grill,** 1640 N. Cahuenga Blvd., Hollywood (☎ **323/466-2210**).

> **McCabe's Guitar Shop.** 3101 Pico Blvd., at 31st St. (Santa Monica). ☎ **310/828-4497.**

Judging by the early lines around the block, Los Angelenos feel incredibly fortunate to have this low-attitude, low-volume, all-ages music venue to hear favorite acts. McCabe's has been around for over 4 decades, though owner Bob Riskin is quick to point out that it is first and foremost a guitar shop and music store. A 1969 concert with folk blues act Libba Cotton paved the way, and its reputation and following has been built since on the likes of Ritchie Havens, Elvis Costello, Joni Mitchell, and Tom Waits, to name a few. The modest 150-seat theater serves as a display room for guitars during the day, but at night, room is made for theater seats, folding chairs, and a place to sell coffee, tea and cookies. Given the size, it's understandable that most acts that pass through here might have a relatively small following, but McCabe's packs occasional surprises, including a 1994 appearance by rock legend Bruce Springsteen. In fact, McCabe's was doing the unplugged rocker thing long before MTV copied the idea. With no door policy, no bouncers, no smoking, and no alcohol, you couldn't ask for a more intimate setting for what continues to be the best folk club in L.A.

> **Spaceland.** At Dreams of L.A., 1717 Silver Lake Blvd., near Sunset (Silver Lake). ☎ **213/833-2843.**

Music Trivia

Beach Boy Brian Wilson failed a music class at Hawthorne High School when he submitted a song that would later become "Surfin' Safari."

If I was to put together a genuinely Monk Road Mix to the city, I'd toss aside most of the songs below and cut to the aural heart of this enjoyably crass, apocalyptic, deliriously monstrous, mad, and whacked metropolis. My Monk Mix would include commentary from radio monologuistic and playwright Joe Frank, helicopters hovering over 3rd and Western, the robotic monotonous beat of gangsta rap from a bass-heavy speaker inside a large black SUV heading west on Sunset. My mix would include conversations with employees who don't know the way to the restaurant they work at or the identity of Tom Bradley. My mix would contain a babble of actors on the make, pickup basketball players arguing over a call, Koreans, Thais, and agents (always arrogant, always moving far too fast). There would be the myriad of radio stations, all scrambling together, with bits of Spanish colliding with news reports, Oldies Rock, Christian jeremiads, KCRW fundraising spiels, and the latest Alanis hit. There would be barking dogs, juice blenders, cappuccino machines, buses, freeways, and those goofy honking horns that Hispanic street vendors use. It would be the true soundtrack of L.A. In lieu of that, I offer you the next best thang.

"Babylon Sisters," Steely Dan
"Blues on Central Avenue," Joe Turner
"Bob Says No," Pop Defect
"Born in East L.A.," Cheech & Chong
"Brutal Flower," Dirt Clod Fight
"Burn Hollywood Burn," Public Enemy and Ice T
"Butt Town," Iggy Pop
"California Blue," Roy Orbison
"Celluloid Heroes," The Kinks
"Chicken Boy Polka," Those Darn Accordions

"Church of Juniper," Anus the Menace
"Cop Killer," Ice T
"Court and Spark," Joni Mitchell
"Devil's Johnson," Ethyl Meatplow
"Do You Know the Way to San Jose?" Dionne Warwick
"Down In Hollywood," Ry Cooder
"525 UTSC," Sandy Duncan's Eye
"Fuck Compton," Tim Dog
"Glendale Train," New Riders of the Purple Sage

Adam of *Shithappy* doesn't like the owner, "the epitome of an asshole club owner. His dream of L.A. is pretty gross." Most alternative rock bands play here nonetheless. No cover on Monday.

> **Viper Room.** 8852 Sunset Blvd., at La Cienega (West Hollywood). ☎ **310/358-1880.** www.viperroom.com.

The sidewalk outside has the dubious distinction of marking the spot where River Phoenix OD'd on a heroin-coke speedball. Drug abuse—so *edgy*. Co-owned by Johnny Depp, the Viper Room features lots of celebs, lots of tourists, and a good sound system, all in a small intimate space. Plus a private little room where Johnny

"Go to Rhino Records," Larry "Wild Man" Fischer
"Heart Attack and Vine," Tom Waits
"I Hate the Rich," The Dils
"I Love L.A.," Randy Newman
"It Never Rains in Southern California," Albert Hammond
"Jane Says," Jane's Addiction
"Joe's Garage," Frank Zappa
"Join Me in L.A.," Warren Zevon
"L.A. Blues," The Stooges
"L.A. Freeway," Guy Clark
"L.A. Girl," The Adolescents
"L.A. is My Lady," Frank Sinatra
"L.A. Woman," The Doors
"L.A. Woman," Billy Idol
"Lexicon Devil," The Germs
"Linda Blair," Redd Kross
"Living in the City," Fear
"Lonesome Town," Ricky Nelson
"Los Angeles," X
"Los Angeles," Frank Black
"Los Angeles Blues," Lightnin' Hopkins
"MacArthur Park," Richard Harris
"MacArthur Park," Donna Summer
"Marriage," The Descendants
"Money I Owe," TV TV$
"Oki Dog," Youth Gone Mad
"Paradise City," Guns 'N Roses
"Peace in L.A.," Tom Petty
"The Promised Land," Chuck Berry

"The Promised Land," Elvis Presley
"The Promised Land," The Grateful Dead
"Redondo Beach," Patti Smith
"Rockabye," Shawn Mullins
"Rocking in the Kibbutz Room," Chuck E. Weiss
"Santa Monica Boulevard," Sheryl Crow
"Shaking Shaking Shakes," Los Lobos
"Show Biz Blues," JJ Cale
"Show Biz Kids," Steely Dan
"Sin City," Flying Burrito Brothers
"Steak Knife," The Angry Samoans
"Straight Outta Compton," N.W.A.
"Sunset Grill," Don Henley
"Take a Quaalude Now," The Eyes
"Trouble at the Cup," Black Randy
"Under," Babyland
"The Under Assistant West Coast Promotion Man," Rolling Stones
"Under the Bridge," Red Hot Chili Peppers
"Valley Girl," Frank Zappa
"Venice Beach," Jonathan Richmond
"Vine Street," Van Dyke Parks
"Walking in L.A.," Missing Persons
"We Never Close," The Paper Tulips
"We're Desperate," X
"Welcome to the Jungle," Guns 'N Roses
"West L.A. Fadeaway," Grateful Dead
"Whip It," Del Rubios
"You're So Square," L-7

and his partying pals can watch the action without being seen themselves. With all that said, the real hallmark of the Viper is that it is one of the few places in town where one can watch the likes of Johnny Cash, Tom Petty, and Iggy Pop up close and sweaty. Go Tuesday night at 9pm to catch drum-and-bass sensation DJ Carbo.

> **Wiltern.** 3790 Wilshire Blvd., at Western Ave. (Mid-Wilshire). ☎ **213/380-5005.**

An art-deco masterpiece with the mother of all ceilings, this ornate hall brings the most classic and classy acts to town, from touring ballet or opera to the likes of country folk legends k.d. lang and Nanci Griffith.

On the Bus, Part 2:

Our Lady of the
Transit Opera

The waves roll across Malibu beach, signaling it's time to head back into town. Jim dutifully gathers change. The bus takes *forever.* It's 30 minutes before the Monks finally realize that this isn't even a bus stop, but simply a place to sit and watch surf crash near the thunderous roar of the highway.

The real bus stop is a quarter mile down the road. The Monks sprint like a two-headed demon for the approaching 434.

"They should post signs. We thought that the bus stopped back there," Mike exclaims as he hops onboard.

An old man with bad hair whacks Mike good and hard with his gnarly green-and-white cane. "Shut up!" he snarls.

Inside it's immediately clear the Monks are the only gringos onboard. The regular passengers are Malibu's indentured servants—hailing from San Salvador and Mexico, earning their below-minimum unreported wage by picking the weeds and weaning the kids of the beautiful people. They all squeeze in tight. The bus is a marketplace of aromas, with hot chili breath breathing down backs.

At the next stop an aging prima donna sneaks through the back door. She's of that breed of flipped out, slightly self-absorbed women in their late sixties. She's wearing two unwashed wigs, which are totally askew and do not conceal the fact that her real hair is but a splotch of dirtier gray that hasn't seen the light of day—nor the head of a shower—since the fall of the Berlin Wall.

There is a fast exodus toward the front as ten Salvadorans give her plenty of room to sprawl in the back of the bus. She smells like last week's lasagna and wears yellow spandex tights with the seam pulled so severely up her crotch you can see the folds in her vagina, like two lips puckering for a kiss from the dirty bus floor.

"Oh, mama, cover it up," one black man pleads, and all silently agree.

Her skin is like beef jerky and you can just smell the salt under her arm. It's making Mike kind of hungry, but Jim's oblivious, absorbed in a newspaper, reading about the "Big Game." They grab a pair of vacated seats.

The woman is wearing a Walkman like half the boy whores in Hollywood, but she's listening to opera. Suddenly she starts singing at the top of her frail lungs, reaching for the highest note, following a tune which only she can hear.

"Visi D'arte! Visi D'amore!!"

Half the bus ignores her, but Mike is sort of touched by it all, until she really starts belting it out in the most ear-shattering, off-key, off-pitch operatic voice we've encountered since Chuck Yma Sumac.

"VISI D'ARTE! VISI D'AMORE!!!"

The ear drums are surfing the fringe, waiting to break, when it suddenly dawns on Mike that this woman who now sits up on her haunches on a small leather pack full of wigs and cassettes is experiencing some sort of musical satori, some sort of religious high. She's arched upwards in full passion, screaming every stanza from the depth of her soul, with no one able to carry on an even remotely sensible conversation.

"VISI D'ARTE! VISI D'AMORE!!!"

She's so out of tune and so into herself that the entire bus hangs between complete terror and total hilarity. The Hispanic women chatter at her painful lack of style, the Hispanic men chuckle over her disgusting crotch, and Mike secretly wishes he had the nerve to join in, off key and all.

Jim turns the crinkled page of the *Times,* happy from the previous night's scores. Mike wants a retake.

At Topanga Canyon Beach a nicely aged, sixty-something, still-a-stud beach hustler struts through the door. He's all muscles and forearms and owns a swagger that would send Tom Cruise scurrying for the ladies room. He heads for the back of the bus. He's got a few tow-behind junkies glued to him with long psychic cords. He's wearing urine-soaked Levi's and toting a knapsack reeking of brew. He parts a wave through the crowd with a fishy grin and makes for the only open seat, next to the lady of the transit opera.

She looks up, smiling. Her teeth aren't real.

He sits down thigh to thigh and puts a beefy arm across the back of the seat and settles in for the ride. As the bus lurches forward she resumes her operatic performance, broken by a belch, and begs a pardon from her lice-infested companion.

The bus gets quiet as he leans close.

"You're singing my favorite song," he advances.

"You're wearing my favorite cologne," she giggles, as her whole scraggly being opens up to a new dimension.

"I smell urine," Mike tells Jim. "That's urine, not cologne!"

Jim's oblivious.

She leans into him and starts singing in a softer falsetto.

"Caro mio ven, credimialmen, senza di te languisceil cor." Her fake teeth start clacking from a loose hinge.

"Get more glue honey, you're teeth are coming out," the hustler suggests.

She gets the drift and coyly shoves them back in and continues her song. He leans ever closer. The bus fills with new riders. She squirms in her seat, taking out a new tape at Sunset, adjusting her second wig even more off to the side. Feeling a bit faded before all the attention, she brings out the lipstick and slowly applies the lips. In a moment of brilliant inspiration she draws the tube of red across the corner of her mouth and up to her cheek, creating the effect of a clown on Quaaludes with a maniacal lip line.

He approves.

He begins to tap his wrinkled hand on her leg. By the third aria of the fourth act he begins to rub her thigh. She throws her head back, loosening the top wig. She chuckles at her faux pas and picks the wig up by the roots. In a moment of flamboyant reverence she kisses the stinking nylon hairpiece and gives it to her suitor like a gift of moss from a snout-rooting boar returned from the woods.

It's a contract for love.

She's dangerously near his lips, mouthing words of affection. The tear in his jeans is in just the wrong place. His growing bulge is making an embarrassing push for the waistband. If he holds her thighs any tighter, her knee caps might pop.

The bus rolls toward Santa Monica. She ups the volume of her tape and takes a comb to her tired old wigs, which are the only thing remaining between her and old age. She is smirking with her clown lips and slurping warm Coke from a can. Her legs are hot. She starts fanning herself and pulls a wad of gum from her mouth, pinning it to his forehead.

They kiss.

"Oh, se estan besando!" Two Salvadoran women gasp, crossing their legs.

A bus full of brown eyes turns to the back to watch. All eyes are hung between repulsion and attraction. And you can still hear her tape, squealing a high-pitched soprano from out of the earphones.

It's a big kiss, wet and dirty. Sand fleas are jumping out of her wig as his oily hands grope for her breasts. She pulls at the corner of his tangled beard. You can hear the buttons popping open from his trousers.

The flat landscape of the blue ocean passes at a dizzying speed as their pace accelerates. The seat is all theirs and the laws of nature move forward in synch with the blazing sun casting shadows across bus number 434.

The bus is in suspense. She dislodges herself from her corner and is now on his lap in full embrace. Her frail right hand pulls furiously at his ear while her left hand expertly changes the tape, opting for something softer. Her tights are stretching. The ladies in the bus have all but covered their eyes, though not a voyeur in the place has turned away.

"My god, I think they're like . . . doing it, Jim."

"With their clothes on?"

"Doesn't seem to stop them!"

She's old and she's hot and she's in love. And it shows.

Suddenly his buddies drag themselves down the aisle to warn that their stop is near.

"It's Broadway, man."

In a second he is disengaged and is holding her hand, kissing her flushed brow and pulling closed his torn jeans. They're locked at the forehead by a wad of gum as he gives his good-bye. She coyly demurs with her seductive eyes as her Don Juan exits the bus. The bus collectively sighs, relieved at the outcome.

She throws a kiss and pulls her wig back on, and the opera continues.

Neighborhoods

To speak of L.A. "neighborhoods" is to give the city too much credit. L.A. doesn't have neighborhoods. It has encampments. There is so little heart, so little pride in most of L.A.'s neighborhoods, it would be a disservice to the real neighborhoods of America to put the L.A. pretenders in such a class. On average, the only time a Los Angeleno even thinks of the word "neighborhood" is in association with "watch group." The average Angeleno is out to protect his own—Mike Davis is spot on in this regard. Still, people do live, play, and work in the following areas of the city. Some are quite compelling. Just don't go looking for a vibrant street culture, or anything that might resemble a "commonweal."

We've divided the metropolis up into four sections: West L.A. and the Baywatch Communities, the Real City (a.k.a. Old School L.A.), Behind the Orange Curtain (i.e., Orange County), and the Burbs and the Endless Sprawl (that is, the L.A. nightmare stereotype). Good luck!

(See also the "Streets, Corners, and Highways" section for an even more incremental L.A. breakdown.)

The West Side and the Baywatch Communities

The average tourist gravitates towards West L.A. The Monk tourist is far more skeptical. There are definitely attractions over there, but there are also loads of attitudinal, solipsistic white people, among the worst on the planet. To avoid contact with these soulless barbarians, we are very careful about when and where we venture west. We recommend the same for anyone who follows in our path. Just follow our motto: Don't Trust Anyone West of La Cienega, and you'll do all right.

› **Bel-Air.** North of Sunset Blvd., between Beverly Glen Blvd. and the 405.

Home of Ron and Nancy, industry Democrats, UCLA, and the Getty. But malign it all you want, it's still the only elegant refuge in the city. We'd live here if we had the bucks, and could stomach the money-grubbing neighbors hiding behind gated fences, brick walls, and innumerable face-lifts.

› **Beverly Hills.** From Sunset Blvd. to Olympic, west of La Cienega Blvd. to Whittier Dr.

Home of Monica, Courtney, and bratty UCLA coeds. A drive through here any night proves that well-to-do life is the same all over America: quiet streets, manicured lawns, cocktail parties, a social calendar, kids rushing around in their parents' expensive automobiles. It's like Bel Air without the Old School cache. Do you like slimy rich people in Bentley's, Jags, and Porches and their SUV-driving wanna-bes? Be our guest—live through *this*.

> **Brentwood.** Along Sunset Blvd. west of the 405.

Where O.J. got the girl. See "White People Only."

> **Culver City.** South of the 10, north of 90, east of the 405 to La Cienega Blvd.

Furniture, old movie studios, and Versailles, with a push for Third Street Promenade style redevelopment centered near the Helms Bakery. Other good reasons to visit are the renowned tamales at **Corn Maiden** (10301 Washington Blvd., 2 blocks east of Motor; ☎ **310/202-6180**), the astounding **Museum of Jurassic Technology** (see "Museums"), and the **Culver Hotel** (see "Addresses"), though the affordable rents are also making Culver City an okay place to live.

> **El Segundo.** South of the 105, west of the 405.

Where the Raiders trained before Art Davis broke faith and moved them back to Oakland, though its bigger claim to fame is that it's L.A.'s vortex of toxic tourism.

> **Hawthorne.** South of the 105, east of the 405.

Beach Boys and Mattel.

> **Holmby Hills.** Beverly Glen Blvd., south of Sunset Blvd., north of Santa Monica Blvd. (Beverly Hills).

Bel Air's evil twin. And the home of "Shrink to the Stars" (and Monica Lewinsky's own therapist) Irene Kassorla, author of the 1980s bestseller *Nice Girls Do*.

We wanted to leave this macabre, horrifically tragic episode completely out of this book, but we realize, for reasons of historical accuracy, such a major L.A. event could not be overlooked. We also know that most of you are decent enough to respect the privacy of others, as well as the memory of "Nicole and Ron." We'll tell you quite plainly: We believe O.J. Simpson deliberately committed these murders, and should have been punished accordingly.

1. **The Knife.** Ross Cutlery in the Bradbury Building, 3rd and Broadway (Downtown). Where O.J. bought "the knife."
2. **Sydney Simpson's dance recital.** Paul Revere School, 1450 Allenwood (Brentwood). Where Nicole snubbed O.J., forcing him to sit alone, away from the family. This made O.J. very angry.
3. **O. J. Simpson's House (and Kato Kaelin's crash pad).** 360 Rockingham Dr. at Ashford (Brentwood). Time how long it takes to get to Nicole's condo. Surprise, surprise—not much time at all!
4. **Nicole's Last Supper.** Mezzaluna (now closed), 11750 San Vicente Blvd. (Brentwood). According to an urban legend, before this restaurant closed one could order the "Nicole Special," i.e., rigatoni melanzane—what the victim ordered the night of her murder. One could also order some Häagen-Dazs, which Nicole only half ate. Ron Goldman was a waiter here. Not long after Nicole left that fateful evening, Ron brought to her condo the glasses Nicole had left behind at the restaurant.
5. **Nicole Brown Simpson's Condo.** 875 Bundy Dr., at Dorothy (Brentwood). On June 12, 1994 (just 2 days before Jim Monk's 35th birthday), Nicole Brown Simpson and her 25-year-old waiter friend Ronald Goldman were brutally murdered by a knife-wielding attacker, who to this day has not been formally identified.
6. **Nicole Brown Simpson's grave site.** Ascension Cemetery, 24754 Trabuco Rd. (Lake Forest). Nicole Brown Simpson was laid to rest here on June 16, 1994. Her grave is behind the cemetery office next to that of her grandfather, Josef Baur.

> **Long Beach.** Along the 405 west to the ocean, south of the 710.

Living in Long Beach is like living in Yonkers, New York. If you want to experience New York City, live in Manhattan. If you want to experience L.A., live in Los Angeles. That said, Long Beach does have a function: It's the farthest you can go from L.A. without falling behind the Orange Curtain.

> **Malibu.** Pacific Coast Hwy., 15 miles north of Santa Monica.

The town of Malibu is a big snore. But the surrounding beaches and mountains are not. Even with all its fame and celebrity cache, it's somewhat surprising that Malibu is not more overrun than it is. Go there to hike and swim. It offers the best of both in the L.A. area. It's also the best place in L.A. to watch rich people cry. Best times: during the winter-spring rainy season, when their multimillion dollar homes slide off the hills, or during the summer/fall fires, when the chaparral leads a blaze right through their living rooms.

Tip: Go to Point Dume above Malibu, the only place in L.A. where you can watch the sun rise *and* set over the water.

> **Pacific Palisades.** Pacific Coast Hwy. near Sunset Blvd.

Nice frontage. And with those high cliffs, nice place to commit suicide too.

> **San Pedro.** East of Rancho Palos Verdes at the end of the 110.

The first time we were through L.A., about 6 years ago, the city was too overwhelming to savor any of its parts. We kept hearing some good-natured, heartwarming voices from over there in San Pedro, but we were moving too fast to really pay attention. This time around we took the time to savor "Pedro." And we were not disappointed.

In a city overrun with speedy ersatz film types, it's gratifying to find a place that is so down to earth and real. "What Venice was like 10 to 20 years ago," San Pedro is home to an eclectic assortment of characters, including the late Charles "Hank" Bukowski, flutist James Newton, John Olguin (founder of the Cetacean Society), Mike Watt (leader of seminal L.A. bands The Minutemen and Firehose—check in on his life at www.hootpage.com/), and the indomitable Del Rubio Triplets, now "Doublets" since the death of one triplet (for a real treat, catch the girls shopping at the local Von's). A real sense of community still lives in this old fishing village. Check out **Sacred Grounds Coffeehouse,** 399 W. 6th St. (☎ 310/514-0800); the **Vincent Thomas Bridge,** a green version of the Golden Gate (from 110 take the bridge off-ramp, which crosses the L.A. channel); the **Maritime Museum,** at the foot of 6th St., Berth 84 (☎ 310/548-7618), one of the finest maritime museums in America; **Union War Surplus,** 355 W. 6th St., between Center and Mesa (☎ 310/833-2949); **Club Royale,** a true hole in the wall and the oldest hotel bar in San Pedro, which attracts a clientele of upper-crust boaters and deadbeats, and which no local wants us to list, so we won't; the wonderful **Korean Bell of Friendship,** South Gaffey Street at West 37th Street; the **Point Fermin Lighthouse,** South Gaffey Street, at Paseo del Mar; **Walkers Cafe,** 7000 West Paseo del Mar (☎ 310/833-3623), which was featured in the ultimate L.A. movie, *Chinatown;* and, at the end of Pacific

Avenue, the incredible **sunken city of San Pedro,** which was formerly Paseo del Mar Street until the Long Beach earthquake of 1933 sank that entire section of the street, destroying all buildings and leaving only the foundations). The folks at nearby Walkers Bar will tell you all about it. On top of all that, most of San Pedro has clean air, thanks to Hurricane Gulch, which blows all the gunk out to San Bernardino. People forget San Pedro is part of L.A., and that because it is, the city of L.A. can make the claim that it is a world seaport. Don't miss "Pedro," what *Random Lengths* editor called "the last un-yuppifed part of L.A." Go now before the peach and teal paint crews break in once and for all.

› Santa Monica

To butcher a bit of New Age vernacular, there has been a palpable vibrational shift in Santa Monica since the sixties era, when it was billed as "The People's Republic of Santa Monica." Though its representative in the state legislature is still Tom Hayden, and though the homeless and freaks still congregate near its beaches, Santa Monica has evolved into the entertainment hotbed of the west side. From the pricey groovy shops and restaurants along Montana, Main, and 26th, to America's most successful pedestrian thoroughfare, the Third Street Promenade, to the bevy of corporate entertainment conglomerates who now call this city home, Santa Monica has clearly been remade for the happy spendy bourgeoisie. Here you will find a lot of the same hetero male knuckleheads you'll find in San Francisco's Marina District and New York's Upper East Side, who've ventured in from places like Manhattan Beach, Brentwood, or Orange County because it now feels culturally safe to congregate here. The rise of Santa Monica breeders and nouveau riche is in direct proportion to the decline in Santa Monica freaks and funk. Fortunately, some great places still hang on, including **Vidiots, Bob Burns, Papa's Pizzeria,** the **Nu Art,** the **Un-Urban Cafe, Highways,** and neighboring **Electronic Cafe International,** but who knows for how long. Head east of 11th and south of Wilshire, where the old liberal Samo hangs on.

› Topanga/Topanga Canyon. From Pacific Coast Hwy., going north along Topanga Canyon Blvd.

We know Topanga from four people in four different periods of our career—from the highly dysfunctional Isis Goren pre-Monk era, from the Patricia Murray Macroneurotic days, from the hilarious Terry Sweeney Let's Go to L.A. and Get a TV Show "hyst-era," and from the just flat-out nutty Ed Lange and the Elysium Fields Nudist Colony daze. At every turn Topanga struck us as this little slice of Marin County. A wooded insulated retreat for people with an Aquarian consciousness and a bit of money to go and feel naturist and all Hot Tubby. You might say it's a poor man's Malibu. A middle-class Santa Barbara. But sweet. Very sweet.

And home to the romantic **Inn of the 7th Ray,** 28 Old Topanga Canyon Road
(☎ 310/455-131), the only place in California whose cuisine is influenced by the
teachings of Alice Bailey, and **Stoner's Grove,** an old artist colony hidden in a grove
of bamboo. So very Topanga.

› **Venice Beach Boardwalk.** Ocean Front Walk (Venice).

There's one word that sums up Venice Beach: testosterone. The testosterone of the
steroid-enhanced bodybuilders. The testosterone of the gangbanging b-ballers. The
testosterone of the hard-core surfers. Of the buzz-saw jugglers, of the tacky parade
of merchants, of the frenetic drum circle, of the intrepid bladers, of the paddle-
tennis regulars. Venice Beach is one of the last places in the L.A. metropolitan area
that, despite its obvious pitch to tourists, is still on the verge of dangerous explosion.
Everything ugly, tacky, unwieldy, grotesque, and sketchy in the city finds its way
here. Come here not to reject it for its palpable cheese but to celebrate its unique
and endearing populism.

Tip #1: Locals insist the best time to visit is during the week, when there are
fewer tourists. We prefer weekends because that's when the scene is completely over
the top. But don't get caught walking your dog to the beach. Due to recent fights
between the pit bulls of rival gangbangers, there are now serious animal restrictions.

Tip #2: There's an orthodox synagogue on the Venice boardwalk. For an "Only
in L.A." tableau, go at sunrise, when the homeless are waking up just as the Jewish
faithful are finishing up their morning prayers.

Tip #3: Don't confuse the Venice Beach boardwalk with the rest of Venice, which
is far more gentrified.

› **West Hollywood.** South of Sunset Blvd. to Beverly, east of Doheny Dr. to La
Brea Ave.

Boutiques, antiques, New Age books, and muscle-queen-clone homos that you wish
would just give it up and move to Palm Springs. Also known as WeHo. Also known
as Permit Parking Hell. Take away the large numbers of gay folk and this stretch of
L.A. is just a transition zone between Hollywood and Beverly Hills, whose demographic and aesthetic makeup contains a little of both. One day L.A. will have a
strong and popular mayor who will corral these renegade provinces into merging
with the city proper. WeHo, get back in the house.

› **Westwood.** Sunset Blvd. to Santa Monica Blvd., east of the 405.

Westwood is the home of UCLA. And for better or worse that is what completely
defines this very youthful, very collegiate slice of L.A. on the edge of Bel Air. Like college districts everywhere, Westwood is chock full o' chains, though it does contain

a few reasonably priced culinary surprises, including **Cowboy Sushi,** 911 Broxton (☎ **310/208-7781**), and a cheap Vietnamese take-out stand called **Saigon Street,** 978 Gayley Ave. (☎ **310/208-4038**). Tell Ken that Jim Monk sent you.

> **White People Only.** Along Sunset Blvd., west of the 405 (in other words, Pacific Palisades and Brentwood).

While certainly the greenest portions of the city, all that inviting nature is canceled out by the naked greed and rudeness of the inhabitants. As Adam Bregman of the excellent zine *Shithappy* writes, "This is the land of jerks in convertibles screaming into their cell phones and neighborhoods where if you're black or Latino and not a gardener or a maid, you're immediately a suspect of the neighborhood watch groups and private security firms."

> **Whitley Heights.** North of Franklin near Highland Ave.

This winding beautiful little hillside neighborhood was called the original Beverly Hills because of the old-school Hollywood royalty—Charlie Chaplin, Barbara Stanwyck, Valentino—who lived here in the 1920s. Now populated by B-list Hollywood wanna-bes in their requisite SUVs, Mercedes, and BMWs.

The Real City (a.k.a. Old-School L.A.)

Here is where anyone with memories of what a real city is like tends to congregate. It's hotter over here. It's multiethnic. It's economically diverse. It's very funky. There are minor street scenes. There's a large working class. There's Dodger Stadium. There's Griffith Park. And there are the remnants of old L.A.—**Union Station, the Bradbury Building,** the **Pantry,** funky old **Coles** at 118 E. 6th St. (☎ **213/ 622-4090**), and the grand old Victorians of Angeleno Heights. And, most importantly, the SUV-per-resident ratio is far less than on the West Side. If there's a future for L.A., and hope for a genuine urbane metropolis, it lies on the East Side.

> **Angeleno Heights.** Along Kensington Rd. and Carrol Ave.

One of the frequently heard L.A. clichés is that various L.A. neighborhoods look like film sets. Angeleno Heights is the one place where the cliché is true. This patch of turn-of-the-century Victorian homes is as delightful as it is surprising. It could be anywhere in America.

> **Broadway.** Downtown Los Angeles between 3rd and 9th sts. (Los Angeles).

L.A.'s version of New York's 14th Street, with discount Hispanic shopping, grand old movie palaces, and an eerie street scene of desperate crackheads. Go there now before Disney buys it up.

> **Chinatown.** North Broadway between Bernard and Sunset Blvd. (Los Angeles).

L.A.'s Chinatown doesn't hold a candle to its neighbor in San Francisco, but still, in terms of distinctive Chinese architecture, culture, and cuisine, it's worth a 2-minute tour.

> **Downtown.** Circled by the 110 to the west, the 10 to the south, and the 101 to the east and north (Los Angeles).

The home of grand ole L.A. and new financial L.A. interspersed with the wretched of the earth: women washing their hair in the street outside Grand Central Market, legless panhandlers in the Metro Rail station, crackies galore. L.A. has several artificial pedestrian zones like Santa Monica's Third Street Promenade, but the one true pedestrian zone might be downtown on Broadway, with its old movie palaces, landmark architecture, and streets crowded with third-world shoppers exploring the abundance of low-priced, low-quality merchandise.

East Side Angelenos want to like Downtown. They want a downtown, period. But L.A.'s downtown is still a long way from fulfilling its promise as a gathering place for the city, though the new **Disney Symphony Hall,** the **Staples Sports Arena,** and the redevelopment around the Biltmore and the library are bound to improve the area for the better.

> **Downtown Warehouse District.** East of Broadway toward the L.A. River (Los Angeles).

This area is the vortex of the Downtown art scene, though most say it's dead and gone. This warehouse district was converted into artist's studios decades ago and still remains the best place to live out a boho, Bukowskiesque fantasy if you don't mind the 10,000 homeless defecating in the streets below.

> **East Los Angeles.** Though generally refers to areas east of the L.A. River and downtown (such as Boyle Heights and Belvedere), East L.A. proper is near the 710.

This is basically La Raza in exile. Whittier Boulevard east of Indiana has traditionally been a popular cruise strip. Rule of thumb: East L.A. regularly comes over the bridges to L.A. proper, but West L.A. rarely, if ever, returns the favor.

> **Echo Park.** East of Glendale Blvd., south of Sunset Blvd. to the 101 (Los Angeles).

Nicknamed "Red Hill" during the 1950s because it was a haven for Communists trying to escape the McCarthy witch-hunts, today Echo Park is a lot like Silver Lake but without the cache. Check out the **kinetic bowling figure** at the Jensen's Recreation Center. The Echo Park Preservation Society got a 10-year grant from the city to keep it lit. Other Echo Park historic sites include Mack Sennett's **"Keystone Kops" studio** at 1712 Glendale Blvd. (in what was then known as Edendale), and **Walt Disney's first studio** at 4649 Kingswell (also in Echo Park). Also worth checking out is the reasonably priced French cuisine at **Taix**, 1911 W. Sunset Blvd. (☎ 213/484-1265), and the **Brite Spot Coffeeshop**, 1918 W. Sunset Blvd. (☎ 213/484-9800).

> **El Pueblo de Los Angeles Historic District.** Enter on Alameda Ave. south of Macy St. and across from Union Staton (Los Angeles).

Forget Hollywood, Beverly Hills, and Malibu; *this* is L.A. The historic 44-acre district is the site of L.A.'s original plaza, a Mexican zocalo. Includes the Plaza Church and the Avila Adobe. And, before we forget, there's the ultimate tourist trap: Olvera Street, lined with shops and restaurants that rival Tijuana any day.

> **Fairfax.** Fairfax Ave. between Melrose Ave. and 3rd St. (Los Angeles).

This long-standing old-world Jewish district has now become the hipster hangout du jour. And, actually, there are some pretty sound reasons for this. First, the fabulous **Kibitz Room**, 419 N. Fairfax Ave., at Rosewood (Fairfax area), a small, tight bar adjoining the famous and popular (if way overpriced) **Canter's Deli** (see "Food"). The Kibitz Room features rock and blues bands most nights of the week, jamming intensely and proudly, occasionally with audience accompaniment. And usually there's no cover. Secondly, the **Fairfax Cinema** (see "Film"), which shows mainstream Hollywood films a few months after they've had their run at the low cost of only $2.50 a show, in excellent theaters that are clean, clear, and well-maintained (quite a change from most low-budget movie theaters we've seen across the country). Third, the incomparable **Farmer's Market** (see "Food"), which still has fairly high authenticity value, even though the prices have gone up a tad. There are plenty of other Jewish bakeries, bookstores, and kosher restaurants and delis, too. Stroll around. You'll probably find your own little Yiddish treasure.

> **Fremont Place**

Tony gated neighborhood between Wilshire and Olympic near Hancock Park. Former residents include Muhammad Ali and Karen Black. Current residents include Dawn Moreno. For tours call The Homeowners Association at ☎ 323/935-8652.

> **Gower Gulch.** Area around Vine, Gower, Selma, and Sunset.

The history surrounding this stretch of Hollywood, original home to Adolph Zukor's Feature Play Company and the Nestor Film Company, has to be one of the coolest stories in Hollywood history. It seems that back in the early days of film (1891 to 1940), this street was where cowboy extras would hang out hoping to get work in one of the many westerns being shot in the area's studios. The "gulch" derives from the cowboy term "dry gulching," which means to shoot an enemy in the back.

> **Hancock Park.** East of Highland Ave. to Wilton, between Beverly Blvd. and Wilshire (Los Angeles).

Where the tasteful L.A. money class lives. Much older, restrained, and historic than West L.A.'s bastions of wealth, and surrounded by ethnic and economic diversity. Unfortunately, Hancock Park's main shopping thoroughfare, Larchmont, is slowly picking up the more egregious attributes of the West Side shopping corridors. There goes the neighborhood.

> **The Hasidic 'Hood.** Detroit Ave. from Beverly Blvd. to Third St. (Los Angeles).

You want Jews? We got Jews. Payes-wearing, long-bearded, kaftan and kippah Jews. Hasidic Jews. They live all around Detroit Avenue, off La Brea, between Beverly and Third. You see them at **Ralph's,** at the Jewish-owned (but Hispanic-run, of course) **Fish Grill** on Beverly, all over the 'hood on Saturdays. They are the only white people, outside of the homeless and hookers, who you regularly see walking the streets of L.A. They tend to stick to this neighborhood, though the businesses here are not as obviously Jewish as along Fairfax—but the *feeling* is actually more so. We love these people, though it is highly doubtful whether they love us. Or will love you, even if you are Jewish yourself. The Hasids are desperately trying to hang onto their centuries-old traditions, and look at contact with the non-Hasidic community as some form of contamination, a necessary evil best kept to a minimum. For this reason, the Hasids are more than a little insular, like the Amish and all other such traditionalists, but you gotta love the garb.

> **Hollywood.** North of Melrose to the 101 between Western Ave. and La Brea.

We absolutely love this perverse district of the city. Every loose-caboose nutcase chick who came to L.A. for stardom but ended up a tall thin homeless speed freak finds her way here. The place is a disheveled, raunchy, racy, and strangely inviting mess. All the excitement of the former Times Square but ten times safer because you can cruise it by car. It is often said that L.A. is a city where art imitates art, fiction eats fiction, where there's no "real life" to butt up against. Those who make this claim have not spent enough time in Hollywood, where reality is talking to itself right now, on six different channels.

> **Hollywood Hills.** West of Griffith Park, north of Franklin Blvd. (Los Angeles).

It's one of those elusive areas. Everyone knows it's there but aren't sure where. Case in point: We call the Chamber of Commerce, which is staffed by Hispanics who think it's somewhere north of L.A., but aren't certain and refer us to Parks and Recreation. Parks and Recreation think it's near Beverly Hills, but since it's out of their jurisdiction they refer us to the MTA. The MTA has no buses running there so they certainly don't know. We call a map company who strongly feel there *is* no Hollywood Hills and that it was created by realtors. We call Century 21 Realtors and are told by a British realtor it's near the L.A. River, somewhere. We call Yellow Cab and the dispatcher says it's near the Hollywood sign. Finally, someone making sense.

Though we could easily group parts of the Hollywood Hills area with those other West Side bastions of wealth, whiteness, and attitude, Hollywood Hills is in reality above where the Real People live. It's where old-school seventies and eighties industry people reside, as opposed to New School Los Feliz (that's "Loze—FEEE-liz") people. Its major redeeming values are its reservoir, its canyons, and some of its outrageous homes, but, rarely, its residents.

> **Koreatown.** South of Melrose Ave. to Pico Blvd. between Western Ave. and Vermont (Los Angeles).

Another self-contained L.A. ethnic enclave, in this case catering to the South Korean community in exile, with most stores containing Korean signage, and a little broken English as a nod to the resident Anglos, who are a clear and distinct minority. Notable features: really strange Korean food, really fun Korean golfing ranges, and very ambitious Koreans, with zero design sense. As opposed to the oh so nimble, oh so mindful Japanese, the Koreans took a look at the mantra "form follows function" and just left out "form" because it was too much of a bother. Besides, they were in a big hurry to get down to business. Which is probably why Tokyo has forward-thinking mass transit and Seoul prefers twenty-four–lane freeways. Funny how these old aesthetic battles get replayed in the New World.

As you might surmise, Koreatown is not very pleasing to the eye. In fact, the clash of unoriginal thrown-together signage can at times look downright appalling. Still, we lived here, for two years, in order to properly complete this book free of the far grosser excesses found on the West Side. Our conclusion? Koreatown is definitely an acquired taste.

If you're the average American culture snob, you may have little interest in learning about Korean culture, just as those self-satisfied Koreans show little interest in learning about ours. But a little effort can pay off in big ways here, for there are several salient reasons to dig Koreatown: the rents are cheap, the Koreans leave you completely alone, there's no bratty industry scene, it is centrally located, it's easy to navigate, and buried beneath the sea of tacky signage are some gems of old L.A., including **Taylor's Steak House,** 3361 W. 8th St. (☎ **213/382-8449**), **Beverly Hot Springs,** 308 North Oxford (☎ **323/734-7000**), and the old **Brown Derby** (well, actually the hat of the Brown Derby, which houses Namuhana, a Korean latte bar), 3377 Wilshire Blvd., at Alexandria. In addition, there's **Pollo ala Brasa,** the 24-hour Todd Nelson hangout **Pipers,** the **Wiltern Theatre,** and, the **Safety Zone,** the ultimate Korean 20-something gathering spot. Koreans are very open and friendly, once you break the ice. I know this from direct experience—both from the generous ladies who come Saturday nights to the Dharma Zen Center, and because of two Korean gentleman who lent me their AAA card when the Subaru broke down on Western. No wonder the Koreans are called "the Italians of Asia." Sit down for some Duk Manduguk and let 'em know you care.

> **Larchmont Village.** Larchmont Blvd. between 2nd St. and Beverly (Los Angeles).

We have a divided opinion—either it's a comforting slice of Main Street USA on the edge of Hancock Park, or it's just another yuppie pedestrian mall, with the requisite Jamba Juice, Starbucks, and pricey gourmet fare. If you can avert your gaze from the bevy of Paramount People and snotty chicks in their monster Range Rovers, then Larchmont is a tolerable place to shop, though take a second look for anything remotely alternative in outlook or appearance.

> **Leimert Park.** Southwest of Downtown, bounded by Crenshaw Blvd., Vernon Ave., Leimart Blvd., and 43rd Place (Los Angeles).

Now *this* is a neighborhood. With a congenial community vibe most African-American communities have lost in recent years. Forty-Third Street, which cuts right through the heart of the 'hood, is the Larchmont of black L.A.—minus the video stores, latte bars, and gourmet Italian eateries. Two small clubs, **5th Street Dick's,** 3347 W. 43rd Place (☎ **323/296-3970**), and **World Stage,** 4344 Degnan Blvd. (☎ **323/293-2451**), are the vortexes of the scene. Neither serves alcohol, but both offer exemplary jazz most nights. Near World Stage is the African cuisine at the **Elephant Walk restaurant,** 4336 Degnan Blvd. (☎ **323/299-1765**), home of Zimbabwe lamb chops and Tanzanian salmon fillet, and just around the corner is **Phillip's Bar-B-Que,** 4307 Leimert Blvd. (☎ **323/292-7613**), serving some of the finest ribs, chicken, and links in town. Also in the 'hood is the historic **Babe's and Ricky's Inn,** 4339 Leimert Blvd. (☎ **323/295-9112**), one of the original South Central blues bars, which moved to this vibrant community in August of 1997. Photos and posters from the old place line the walls, and 80-year-old proprietor Laura Mae Gross (a.k.a. "Mama"), who named the club after her nephew and son, still greets you as you enter. We told you this was a great neighborhood.

> **Little Tokyo.** At Central Ave. and 2nd St. (Downtown Los Angeles).

More than a century old, Little Tokyo maintains an aesthetic distance from the surrounding trash of the neighboring warehouse district east of Downtown. Its streets are clean, its store windows sparkle, and the pricey restaurants seem hell-bent on keeping the local homeless from ever entering their doors. Unexplored by most Angelenos, this little area is the largest Japanese-American community on the continent. However, times have been tough. This once thriving ethnic enclave was devastated by the World War II internments. After the war Japanese-Americans fled to the suburbs, far more committed to assimilation than other Asian groups. Little Tokyo became a place to occasionally eat Japanese cuisine and buy some Japanese-made products. Local boosters hope that pattern changes with the beautiful, newly expanded **Japanese American National Museum,** 369 1st St. (☎ **213/625-0414**), and the new **East West Players,** 244 S. San Pedro, between First and Temple (☎ **213/625-7000,** www.eastwestplayers.com).

Observations

"I was just over in Los Feliz. And I'm not going back. It's a hotbed of heterosexuality, connected to Silver Lake by the Shakespeare Bridge. People who were on Melrose ten years ago, with their hair dyed purple, now live here, with scary rugrats of their own."

—Mark Rosenthal, resident of West Hollywood, California

"I love Los Feliz, so don't write about it. I don't want anyone else moving here."

—Mark Kates, resident of Los Feliz

> **Los Feliz** (pronounced "Loze-FEE-liz"). Vermont Ave., north and south of Los Feliz Blvd. (Los Angeles).

It may have been discovered and promoted beyond recognition by the national media, but there is still something inimitably whacked about this neighborhood. It really comes down to the people manning the fabled establishments. Dan the Fidgety Neurotic, who, using money from an inheritance, took over fringe bookstore **Amok** (now Koma—see "Bookstores"), is completely gonzo, apologizing that he doesn't have enough money to buy new stock, no doubt alienating whatever customer base the store has left. The Reverend Robert Schaffner of **Mondo Video A-Go-Go,** 1720 N. Vermont Ave. (☎ **323/953-8896**), has been lifted from some strange Dobbesian universe. It's hard to believe business is actually transacted in the place, but it is. Mondo's selection of flat-out fringe videos is unparalleled (only

Vidiots in Santa Monica and Eddie Brandt's Saturday Matinee in North Holly-wood can possibly compare). Then there's the Japanese family that run the always popular, nondescript **Mako,** an unmarked restaurant at 1802 Vermont. They say they've been in the location for 13 years, but they barely mutter an intelligible word of English. And, of course, **Y-Que** (see "Stores/Shopping"), a small but tidy camp-lite emporium, and the far more ambitious **Soap Plant/Wacko/La Luz de Jesus Gallery** around the corner on Hollywood (which has the finest selection of counterculture/pop-culture books, cards, and artifacts in America and a fabulously bright and colorful staff, eager to serve your every demented need—see "Stores/Shopping"). **Skylight,** 1818 N. Vermont Ave. (☎ **323/660-1175**), is a warm, inviting independent bookstore that reminded us of Bailey-Coy on Seattle's Capitol Hill. It is an oasis in the city, as the nearest independent bookstore of any quality is Book Soup, almost 10 miles away. In short, the mainstreaming and prettifying of the funky fringe that has occurred in New York has yet to fully hit Los Feliz, or most of this city for that matter. Old L.A. is still a mess.

> **Silver Lake.** East and west of Silver Lake Blvd. going north of the 101 (Los Angeles).

Where old Hollywood lived, and middle-aged gays died. Now popular again with poor Hispanics and young hipsters. Ostensibly L.A.'s answer to New York's East Village, though that's a bit of a stretch. Buses don't really go here.

> **South Central L.A.** Crenshaw Blvd. east toward the 110 and south of the 10 (Los Angeles).

While it is undeniably true that at certain times of night everyone stays clear of certain L.A. neighborhoods (e.g., South Bureau—which averaged 429 murders, 502 rapes, and 12,914 aggravated assaults a year, before the decrease in crack use flattened crime rates nationwide), the overall stereotype of L.A.'s alleged "ghetto" is wrong. South Central is a polyglot in terms of language, race, and socioeconomic status. A mixed bag—hard to categorize. A smart and savvy Monk should be able to travel here at any time.

> **Thai Town.** Hollywood Blvd. between Western Ave. and Normandie (Los Angeles).

If decrepit filthy Thai Town was all you saw of L.A., you would definitely think this city is the pit-hole of the planet. Along a stretch of Hollywood Boulevard between Western and Normandie are a dozen or more Thai eateries. Most of them are tacky, filthy, and greasy. Some are compelling, like **Kanom Thai Ramsong,** 5185 Hollywood (☎ **213/667-2055**), with its exotic array of Thai desserts and vegetarian

- Estimates of hard-core gang membership in L.A. range from 10,000 to 100,000. The LAPD reports that 230 black and Latino gangs and 81 Asian gangs have been identified in the L.A. area.
- The first generation of black L.A. street gangs "emerged as a defensive response to white violence in the schools and streets during the late 1940's," according to Mike Davis, author of *City of Quartz* and *Ecology of Fear.*
- Names of early gangs in South Central L.A.: Businessmen, Slausons, Gladiators, Farmers, Parks, Outlaws, Watts, Boot Hill, Rebel Rousers, Roman Twenties.
- Unconfirmed theories for origins of the gang name "Crips": (1) "Crippled" style of walking affected by members of the 107 Hoovers, Crip predecessors; (2) acronym for Continuous Revolution in Progress.

food. Some, like **Palms,** 5273 Hollywood Blvd., at Hobart (☎ 323/462-5073), have talentless female singers, with cheesy eighties-style electronic backup. Some, like 24-hour **Sunanlang,** 5176 Hollywood Blvd. (☎ 323/660-8006), have a devoted following of alt.hipsters, whose taste we call into question. Almost all of them have gorgeous Thai waitresses, who are often supermodel thin with heartbreakingly pretty faces. A look around this 'hood and you get a snapshot of what Bangkok must be like. In fact, the area Harvard Motel advertises adult movies in the room. And it looks like you could order a lot more.

> **Westlake.** South of the 101 to the 10, east of Hoover St. to the 110 (Los Angeles).

Driving south down Alvarado, you get into the densely packed, very poor and desperate areas of Macarthur Park and Westlake, which has the highest homicide rate in L.A. The neon **Westlake Theater sign** is one of the last remaining icons from a time when this area had some class. Late at night there's a deliciously dark foreboding that pervades this area, but we wouldn't want to live here.

Behind the Orange Curtain

In Jim Crotty's slanguistic tome *How to Talk American,* Orange County is described as "Republican-land, with scads of white folk, a brand new airport named after John Wayne, traffic snarls for days, defense contractors, family values paranoia, and golf." While all of this is true, there is much more to see than first meets the superficial eye, including the perpetually snowcapped **Alpine Motel** (715 West Katella, in

Anaheim), the statue of **Harbie the Seal** (12262 Harbor Blvd., in Anaheim), the rock and rockabilly shows at **Linda's Doll Hut** (107 S. Adams St. in Anaheim), the oldest building still in active use in California, the 223-year-old **Mission San Juan Capistrano** (at Camino Capistrano and Ortega Highway in San Juan Capistrano), the humongous camera that is **Photo Express** (15336 Golden West St., in Westminster), the annual **U.S. Open of Surfing** held every August in Huntington Beach, **Nicole Brown Simpson's grave site** inside the Ascension Cemetery (24754 Trabuco Rd., Lake Forest), "the world's fastest can-can" at **Wild Bill's Wild West Dinner Extravaganza** (7600 Beach Blvd. in Buena Park), **King Neptune's Seafood Restaurant and Nautical Museum** (17115 Pacific Coast Hwy. in Sunset Beach), the **International Surfing Museum** (411 Olive Ave. in Huntington Beach), the **Richard Nixon Presidential Library and Birthplace** (18001 Yorba Linda Blvd. in Yorba Linda), the **Laguna Art Museum** (307 Cliff Dr. at Pacific Coast Highway in Laguna), cheese-phobic stewardess-harasser Robert "Do You Know Who I Am?" Schuller's **Crystal Cathedral** (a.k.a. Garden Grove Community Church, 12141 Lewis St., Garden Grove), the **Huntington Beach Zen Center** (5561 Tangiers Dr. in Huntington Beach), **Gustaf Anders,** the last great Scandinavian restaurant in the L.A. Basin (South Coast Plaza, near Sunflower Boulevard in Costa Mesa), and, of course, **Medieval Times** (7662 Beach Blvd., Buena Park), where knights joust while families eat lamb legs with their hands! (think Jim Carrey and Matt Broderick in *The Cable Guy*).

When and if (Attention publisher!) we do a guidebook devoted entirely to L.A., we will cover Orange County in depth. For now, you are free to move about the area. Huzzah!!

The Burbs and the Endless Sprawl

Not all these areas are suburbs per se, but they resemble as much, expressing standard suburban values one finds all over America, but with a peculiar L.A. twist.

> **Altadena.** North of the 210 above Washington Blvd.

Pasadena, but higher up.

> **Burbank.** North of the 134 between the 5 and the 210.

Theoretically part of the burbs, and definitely home of the Studios (but don't tell the tourists), "the Bank" has gotten to be so loved by locals it's been unofficially brought into the East Side family. Johnny Carson made a living mocking the place for years, but as Grand Royal Records poobah Mark Kates points out, "Burbank is still here, and where's Johnny?" Burbank has a little bit of everything—Media City Center, Ribs USA, Tri-Ess Sciences, the Sword and the Stone, Barrons Family Restaurant (home of the "best breakfast" in the United States, according to *Gourmet* magazine),

Crazy Jack's Tavern, Viva Fresh, and the groovy retro Burbank Airport. As Kates notes, contrary to stereotype, "Burbank is surprisingly versatile, plus it's freeway-adjacent."

> **Castaic.** East of the 5, 40 miles north of L.A.

When you hit Castaic, you know you're nearing the Grapevine, and are about to leave the gravitational pull of Los Angeles. For this reason, Castaic always has a kind of heart-warming and bucolic association for most Angelenos.

> **Chatsworth.** South of the 118 along Hwy. 27.

Headquarters of the American porn industry. Remember *Boogie Nights?* This is where it was set. And still is.

> **Glendale.** Between the 5 and the 2, north and south of the 134.

Main Street USA in the heart of L.A., with more Armenians than Fresno and more neo-Nazi's than Cour d'Alene. Check at the base of some of the old lampposts. Yes, those are swastikas. L.A.'s dirty little secret. As a sweet counterbalance, the **Glendale Central Library** (222 E. Harvard St.) is home to the world's largest collection of cat books and memorabilia (over 20,000 items in total). And the media noche at **La Cubana,** 720 E. Colorado St. (☎ **818/243-4398**), is outrageously good.

On a personal level, we remember Glendale from a cameo appearance we made in the 1993 X video "Country At War," directed by Spike Jonze of (the late) *Dirt* mag. The video features Michael Monk spilling groceries all over the Glendale pavement and Jim Monk in the very last frame, dressed in a scary black three-piece, tipping twenty bucks to Exene and the gang.

> **Hacienda Heights.** South of the 60, at Hacienda Blvd.

We've all been here, but we just didn't know it.

> **Lake Arrowhead.** From L.A., 10 east, 215 north, 30 east, 18 north, 189 east to the lake.

A semi-beautiful lake surrounded by semi-beautiful, semi-mid-American homes, filled with semi-Republican semi-retirees who live in this semi-natural locale because it reminds them of some semi-Idahoan pastoral ideal.

> **Lake View Terrace.** Off the 210, south of the 118.

Where Rodney "Why Can't Everyone Just Get Along?" King was used as a human piñata by the officers of the LAPD. Nearby Hansen Lake was probably where Rodney was heading.

> **Monterey Park.** East of 710, between the 10 and the 60.

Chinese and Vietnamese neighborhood known for Vegas-style, stadium-size seafood restaurants named after major television networks (see ABC Seafood under "Food").

> **Mount Baldy.** From L.A. 10 east to Claremont, exit Towne Ave. north, east on 66, north on Mills Ave., which turns into Baldy Rd. Follow to top.

Winter skiing, summer hiking, with killer views from 10,000 feet, and the renowned **Mount Baldy Zen Center** at 6500 feet (Leonard Cohen is known to "manifest" his "true nature" here on occasion).

> **North Hollywood.** Along the 170 north of the 134.

Over the hill and through the smog to New Jersey we go. Laurel Canyon is the equivalent of the George Washington Bridge. The 170 to the 101 south is L.A.'s answer to the Lincoln Tunnel. As with Joisey, there's some buried treasure: the **Atlas Sausage Kitchen,** 10626 Burbank Blvd. (☎ **818/763-2692**), the **California Institute of Abnormal Arts,** 11334 Burbank Blvd. (☎ **818/313-0479**), the incomparable **Eddie Brandt's Saturday Matinee,** 5006 Vineland Ave. (☎ **818/506-4242**), the **Hot House Cafe,** 12123 Riverside Dr., at Laurel Canyon (☎ **818/506-7058**), **Phil's Diner,** 11138 Chandler Blvd. (☎ **818/763-1080**), the **Steak Joynt,** 4354 Lankershim Blvd. (☎ **818/761-9899**), the **Wat Thai Temple,** 8225 Coldwater Canyon, and the **Welded Scary Monster,** 10726 Burbank Blvd.

We love Jersey. And we love North Hollywood.

> **Pasadena.** The north end of the 110, along the 210.

Pasadena is one of the few lovely, beautifully preserved sections of L.A. Maybe this has something to do with the fact that Pasadena is its own city, free to make its own rules. It's a strikingly genteel place, filled with large estates and stately mansions, but it appears neither suburban nor snobby. Sort of like Hancock Park, if Hancock Park had its own city—likable, though by no means racy or challenging. You live in Pasadena if you are a doctor, lawyer, mainstream journalist, or banker, not if you are serious about your entertainment career. It's where Angelenos looking for a semblance of Midwest normality go to breed. Highlights include the gorgeous **city hall** at Garfield and Walnut, the **Huntington Library and Botanical Gardens** (which is actually in San

Pollution Trivia

L.A. exceeds Federal Air Pollution Standards more than 100 days every year. The worst area for air pollution is Pasadena, which is also the wealthiest.

Marino), the annual **Doo Dah Parade, Cal Tech** (California and Hill), the **Suicide Bridge** (a.k.a. Arroyo Bridge, Colorado between Orange Grove and San Rafael), **Bungalow Heaven** (between Lake and Hill north of Orange Grove), breakfast at **Marston's,** 151 East Walnut (☎ **626/796-2459**), lunch at **Pie 'n Burger,** 913 East California (☎ **818/795-1123**), malts at the **Fair Oaks Pharmacy and Soda Fountain,** Mission at Fair Oaks Avenue (☎ **626/799-1414**), the lush curvy **Pasadena Freeway** (110), and the fact that Jim's sister Carolyn lives here. Downside: the predictably midbrow dining and shopping scene along Colorado Boulevard in "Old Pasadena," and possibly the worst smog in the city.

› **Playa Del Rey.** Culver Blvd. at Vista Del Mar, west of LAX.

Dreamworks and Dockweiler.

› **Rosemead.** East on the 10 to Rosemead Blvd./Hwy. 19.

Los Angeles County's equivalent of San Francisco's Richmond District, where large numbers of Asians live and play.

› **San Dimas.** East on the 210 to the 30.

Bill and Ted.

› **San Marino.** South of Pasadena in the vicinity of Atlantic Blvd. and Huntington Dr.

USC Republicans and the incomparable **Huntington Library and Botanical Gardens,** 1151 Oxford Rd. (☎ **818/405-2141**).

› **Sherman Oaks.** Along the 101 east of the 405.

As the strictly east of Western Avenue DJ Carbo explains, "If you've got Glendale and Pasadena, why do you need Sherman Oaks?" One bona fide attraction: **Reid Sherline's childhood home** (4477 Sherman Oaks Circle), right near the intersection of the 101 and 405 freeways.

› **South El Monte.** East on the 10 just west of the 19.

South, East, West, North—does anyone really care which El Monte we are discussing?

› **Studio City.** South of the 101 at Coldwater Canyon exit.

Where the studios used to be, and some still are. And, by some accounts, home to the best sushi place in L.A.: **Sushi Nozawa,** 11288 Ventura Blvd., 4 blocks from Vineland (☎ **818/508-7017**).

> **Van Nuys.** North of the 101 along the 405 to Sherman Way.

The Compton of the San Fernando Valley. High crime, high helicopter-to-resident ratio, and gnarly. Pronounced either "Van Noise" or "Van Eyes," according to some esoteric principle we've not yet fully grasped.

> **Woodland Hills.** Along the 101 at the 27.

Like Thousand Oaks, Sherman Oaks, and all those other Oaks and Hills: another innocuous Valley subdivision.

Parks and Nature

> **Bronson Park.** At the end of Bronson Ave. north of Franklin Ave. (Hollywood).

There is one salient reason to visit this Hollywood ravine that cuts up through the wilds of Griffith Park: It leads straight to the Hollywood sign. It's a long trek, mind you, likely to strain your knees and patience, but, once there, it's worth it. Along the way you will pass the cement walls of a former aqueduct, which are absolutely perfect for skateboarding, though no boarders were there when we visited. You will also pass plenty of our reptilian friends (and we don't mean CAA agents), so be careful where you step.

> **Castaic Lake.** 32132 Ridge Rte. Rd. near Lake Hughes Rd. (Castaic).
> ☎ 805/257-4050.

Set just far enough off Interstate 5 at the furthest outskirts of L.A. (and at about the point on the ascent where your car starts to overheat), this medium-size, man-made lake does a tolerable job of delivering a high desert oasis for the urban masses, with sizable swim areas, sandy beaches, boat launches, and parched desert mountain views to the north and east. Unfortunately, the masses swarm the area on weekends, and the water, already choking in parts with algae, takes on the extra burden of urinating kiddie swimmers and their hot-dog eating, Coca-Cola swilling, blubber-bloated parents wading on shore's edge.

> **Charmlee Park.** 2577 S. Encinal Canyon Rd., near Pacific Coast Hwy. (Malibu).
> ☎ 310/457-7247.

Big wide meadows, situated above Malibu, with an abundance of wildlife quite rare for L.A.

> **Elysium Fields.** 814 Robinson Rd., near Topanga Canyon Blvd. (Topanga Canyon). ☎ **310/455-1000.**

The only clothing-optional park in a metropolitan area anywhere in the United States. Dana Lange, the daughter of founder and nudist pioneer Ed Lange, oversees a motley crew of eccentric cohorts who effectively manage this rare and beautiful oasis in the heart and haze of Topanga Canyon. On weekends the religiously watered green lawn is covered with naked L.A. execs and professionals, who also partake in nude tennis, whirlpools, saunas, and, the riskiest of all naturist activities, cooking. But keep that tool under control—this is naturism, not a sex camp. See "Naked City Los Angeles" in the "Sex" section for that!

> **Griffith Park Observatory.** 1800 E. Observatory Rd. (Above Los Feliz). ☎ **323/664-1191** program information, 323/663-8171 sky information.

Site of the knife fight in *Rebel Without a Cause.* Plus, for only a buck you can get your very own space-shuttle souvenir using "the automatic miniature plastic factory." And 500 feet below the foot of the observatory is the fabled white layer of parfait. On a clear day you can see for miles and miles. As crowded as the place gets, it's still one of our favorite stops to get a big perspective on L.A. Nighttime is best.

> **The Hollywood Reservoir.** Southern entrance on Weidlake Dr. (Hollywood).

The story of L.A. is, in short, the search for water. No water, no L.A. There is not enough water here to support a civilization. It must be imported. Enter the Hollywood Reservoir, where a lot of that imported water is kept. The reservoir is like a European lake in the city. Like Lake Geneva. Like Lake Louise in Canada. A true blue oasis, surrounded by pine and sycamore. Those of us who come here regularly to make our 3.2-mile trek around the lake's perimeter are like a little eclectic community—all races, all sizes, all types. From moms and strollers to romantic couples to beleaguered execs to cross-trainers to screenwriting duos, actors, Monks, and more, all of whom know that the peaceful, clean, and beautiful environs of the Hollywood Reservoir are what make living in L.A. tolerable.

Best directions to the southern entrance: Take Cahuenga north 1 block past Franklin, right on Dix Street, left on Holly Drive, follow to the end, and follow switchback to right on Deep Dell Place, take first available left on Weidlake Drive, and follow to the top and park. Open 6am to 6pm.

> **Laurel Canyon Dog Park.** Mulholland and Laurel Canyon Blvd. (above West Hollywood).

Though the attention which Angelenos lavish on their pets borders on the compulsive, and though we've grown very tired of the annoying, cloying spectacle of

Women and Their Big Dogs, we have to admit this is the best place in the city to take your pampered mutt. Totally sweet and idyllic, with great views of the city. Other options: Silver Lake Dog Park, Runyon Canyon Park.

> **Pyramid Lake Recreation Area.** 53 miles north of L.A., off Interstate 5, in the Angeles National Forest. ☎ **805/295-1245.**

People come to this deep lake beneath mountains for boating, fishing, and swimming. Both day-use picnic and overnight campgrounds are available. Water comes from Plumas National Forest above Oroville Dam and is transported via the California Aqueduct. Not a great place to go unless you are into boating. Besides, Castaic Lake is closer to the city.

> **Robert H. Meyer Memorial Beach.** 12 miles north of the Malibu Colony on Pacific Coast Hwy. at Decker Canyon Rd.

Actually three beaches, El Matador, El Pescador, and La Piedra are collectively known as the Robert H. Meyer Memorial Beach. Film and video crews prefer the rugged, jutting rock formations at El Matador. Nudists prefer the less traveled, more secluded beaches at El Pescador and La Piedra.

> **Silverwood Lake.** Exit Hwy. 138 east off Interstate 15, 9 miles to lake (San Bernardino Mountains).

Such wonderful fishing opportunities, if your idea of a good catch is dead bass carcasses floating in a murky soup of chemicals and leeching metal from strange recovered contraptions that line the shore. This is the prototypical L.A. cyberpunk industrial nightmare. And the locals swear it's the cleanest it's ever been! If you want to see the differences between Oregon nature and L.A. nature, come here.

A Painfully Nasty Rash All Over Your Body

There are miles of magnificent beaches up and down the coast of greater Los Angeles. Unfortunately, some of the most popular are also some of the most polluted. Santa Monica, Cabrillo Beach, and Surfrider Beach in Malibu have all received "F" water quality ratings in recent years from Heal the Bay, a regional environmental group that monitors water quality in the area. The worst time to go in the water is during the winter rainy season, when contaminated storm drains flow into the ocean. As Abe Ingersoll, Monk.com Webmaster and recent star of MTV's *Road Rules,* attests, swimming in polluted ocean water can leave you with a painfully nasty rash all over your body.

> **Solstice State Park.** Pacific Coast Hwy., at Corral Canyon Rd. (Malibu).

Stunning views and clean rivers for swimming. A bit of a secret hideaway off PCH in Malibu.

> **Zuma Beach.** 9 miles north of Malibu on Pacific Coast Hwy. just before the town of Trancas.

If you've ventured as far as Malibu, you might as well go the extra dozen miles to one of the best beaches in all of L.A. Wide expanse of sands, radically good waves, and walking south you are beneath dramatic cliffs. A good place for watching surfers (and maybe a few dolphins). Drive back along Sunset Boulevard when returning to L.A. for a dramatically good cross-section of the city.

The Press

The most glaring defect in this city of earthquakes, fires, and riots is the general lack of wit. If your reply to a question is "Betty handles that," you will invariably be met with a blank stare. Oh, you have humorous people in L.A., but not necessarily well-read humorous people. L.A. goes for physical humor, sight gags, obvious buffoonery. It's funny that the British love it here, since so much of their rich rhetoric just goes right over the heads of most locals. That must get extremely disheartening after awhile. It certainly does for me. It's like dating a foreign woman who not only doesn't get your humor, but doesn't care to get it either. Jay Leno is based here. Letterman is based in New York. Say no more.

Now, I make this point about wit because I think the source of L.A.'s lameness in this regard is its lack of a genuine journalism culture. You have the venerable *L.A. Times,* which does an admirable job getting a handle on this unwieldy metropolis, and you have the predictably left-leaning and occasionally quite perceptive news weeklies, but you do not have richly entertaining publications like the *New Yorker, Esquire,* the *New York Observer,* the late *Spy* and its imitators, and a thriving, richly colorful alternative press, which all offer opportunities for smart, clever cultural commentary. Certainly, aware Angelenos strive to read compelling national magazines, but there is no respectable national magazine that grows out of this soil. You have the *Hollywood Reporter* and *Variety,* but they are trade rags that never stretch very far into bleeding-edge criticism. As a result, the agenda of discourse in this town, if there even is such a common agenda, is set by the *Times* and by local broadcast television, and to a lesser extent by radio. While we occasionally enjoy the provocative guests on Larry Mantle's "Air Talk" and Bill Maher's *Politically Incorrect,* along with the innovative blend of music and commentary on KCRW—and what Angeleno doesn't enjoy a good live helicopter chase scene on the local news?—the overall media mix does not provide a yeasty environment for sharp, droll, quick-witted educated observation. The most provocative journalism to come out of L.A. is from Matt Drudge, editor of the rather obvious *Drudge Report*. And you've heard enough about him.

The problem is, it's very unclear whether Los Angeles could handle, and even appreciate, its own version of *Spy* or the *New Yorker*. In addition, locals seem willing to convey star status only to actors, models, producers, and directors, not to editors, writers, and columnists. It's a good reason why journalism will continue to be the most poorly represented of the communication arts in this town, and why you shouldn't expect many locals to understand you when you say, "I was just trying to stay alive, sir. Just trying to stay alive."

Sex

> **HardArt Phallic Replicating Service. ☎ 323/667-1501.** By appointment only.

Owners Bill Hall and Jerry Lands make an exact, life-size replica of your erect penis. With over seventeen style options to choose from, including plaster or rubber, these guys make penis molding as easy as a trip to the barbershop. They've been casting male organs for over 7 years and have perfected a technique that seems to satisfy everyone from the senior citizen (looking for a more dependable way to satisfy his wife) to the novelty seekers (think incense burner on the mantel). These guys take the prize for their ability to normalize a rather touchy subject. Clients are invited to bring their wife, girlfriend, or significant other to encourage things along. With no pressure, the client takes his time until fully aroused. At that point, things get busy. Laying on a massage table face down (there's a hole in the center) the artists busily mix the molding agent and insert the organ into the mix, in what is described as a rather erotic experience. Three minutes in the mold and you're finished. The rest is up to them, and will take up to 6 weeks before they have immortalized your favorite member as a wall mount, a statuette, or your basic dildo. Prices range from $50 to $200, and, as they are quick to point out, "What you put into it IS what you get out of it." Bill and Jerry are professional, nonsexual (despite the circumstances), and possess a healthy sense of humor. For the erection shy they also have a home starter kit that you can do at your leisure. (See also "HardArt, Soft Lights" feature later in this section.)

> **The Hung Jury.** P.O. Box 1443, Studio City, CA 91614. No phone.

Founded in 1977 by Jim Boyd, this is basically a club for men with large members and their female admirers. Must measure a minimum of 8 inches when erect (underside of penis!). Holding at 2,000 members with 50% single men, 30% women, 20% couples.

If you are a remotely good-looking woman, you will have no problem finding a guy in this town—most likely a guy who drives a sports utility vehicle and has a fair amount of disposable payola. We can't guarantee spiritual depth, a profound sense of irony, or knowledge of Partch, Benjamin, and Duchamp, but we can guarantee a good tan and some nice clothes.

As for men, you have it much harder. In fact, L.A. has to be the very worst place for a straight guy on the planet. A good percent of the women who come here have one thing on their minds: stardom. As actresses, models, as anything that will put their name in lights. If you end up with one of these women, rest assured you are a mere stepping stone.

As a result of this simple, brutal Machiavellian reality of L.A. love, going to bars in this town is largely futile. Sure, there are pickup scenes, but they are filled with such overtanned Rolex-wearing knuckleheads you just don't want to bother. And the truly gorgeous women you are after rarely show up. And don't try picking up beautiful girls at the gym, at the reservoir, at Starbucks, or, worst of all, on the streets. Even more than in New York, A-list women in this town are perpetually on guard. They do the choosing. And they choose according to one very basic criteria: What can you do for me, baby.

With all that said, here are a few of the best places for the average Joe to catch that L.A.-10 dream goddess off guard before she has a chance to truly suss out your portfolio. You will lose in the end, but you can talk about the date for years to come.

1. **The Dog Park.** Primo pickup spot. Rule 1: Get a medium-size or small dog (with the exception of a few gangster rappers, only women are allowed to have extremely large dogs in L.A.). But don't get a nellie insect dog either. Rule 2: Be reasonably built up, but not so built up you're thought to be either gay or high on Andro. Remember: You're a rich L.A. asshole, out walking your dog. You just ambled out of the mansion, unshaven, in your ratty sneakers and

> **Naked City Los Angeles.** Box 2000, Homeland, CA 92548. ☎ **909/926-BANG.** www.ncla.com. In order to receive the password to get on their Web site, E-mail your credit card info to ncla@inland.net (the fee is $10).

From L.A., take 60 east, to 215 south. At Hemet take 74 east, 5 miles to Homeland. Turn left on Juniper Flats. Go 3 miles. Just before the road splits, make a left turn onto Juniper Flat again. Go 1 block till the dirt road on right, which is Quail Canyon. Go right on Quail Canyon for 3 blocks. You will come to a T. At the T go left for 1 block. After 1 block, make a right turn and head up "Mammary Mountain." When you're almost at the top of the mountain, there will be a fork in mismatched wardrobe. It doesn't matter what you look like, right? Good bet: Runyon Canyon Dog Park (Fuller and Franklin).

2. **Trader Joe's.** Unlike Ralph's, Von's, or Lucky, Trader Joe's is small, intimate, and clubby, and filled with well-heeled, gorgeous people who still have an eye for fancy food bargains. It's a latent democratic impulse, which is a big plus for guys with a lot of personality, tremendous spiritual depth, but not so much cash. Just stand around the produce looking totally helpless, and ask your gorgeous target, "Is this zucchini? Because it says squash." This will play into the latent mothering reflex in even the bitchiest L.A. babe. There is a segment of über-strong, über-fit, über-smashing L.A. women who will fall for your gambit. Women who long to nurture completely neurotic hetero doofus screenwriters. Even if you're not in any way tied into "the business," she will assume you are.

3. **Yoga Centers.** This is a longer seduction. Most Yoga classes are filled with women, so you will elicit more attention than you would at other classes. Unfortunately, you will probably elicit the attention of second-tier L.A. women, not the one you are after.

4. **12-Step Meetings.** Still the number-one place to pick up L.A. babes—assuming you want to date an L.A. babe with a serious, life-crippling addiction. The 12 Steps is very eighties in its healing modality, though it is very specific. There's AA (Alcoholics Anonymous), OA (Overeaters Anonymous), SMA (Self-Mutilators Anonymous), MA (Marijuana Anonymous), DA (Debtors Anonymous), CMA (Crystal Meth Anonymous), and, of course, CAA (Creative Artists Agency).

5. **Play the game.** Buy yourself a top-drawer suit. Get yourself a top-of-the-line makeover. Rent a ridiculously expensive automobile. And carry yourself with a palpable sense of superiority. Get invited to film openings and celebrity galas. And still lose.

the road. Stay left at the fork. There will be a sign saying NCLA. Keep heading all the way up the mountain. On top there will be another sign saying NCLA. Go past the sign. Down below to the left is a pool. Next to the pool is a diamond-shaped, mirror-covered building, where you check in.

Proprietor Dick Drost is a paraplegic, who owns this 22-acre adults-only nudist resort, featuring wide open sex of any variety you want, though mostly straight. If you've ever been to a nudist resort, with its peculiar no-sex-vibe morality, you can imagine this sort of freedom is positively revolutionary. As Dick's nubile young assistant, Barbie, explained, fees for a single guy are $30 per day on weekends, $20

(continued on page 171)

Hard Art, Soft Lights:

Michael Monk Visits the HardArt Phallic Replicating Service

The boner cloner answers the phone, lobbing clichés faster than spitballs, probing Michael Monk for details that no one but the devil should know. HardArt Phallic Replicating Service is doing brisk business, and while unanswered questions linger over call-waiting milliseconds, Mike resists the urge to slam dunk the phone before going too deep with these born-in-the-saddle "entrepornneurs."

Jerry Lands delivers the world's longest sound bite with subtextural self-promotion lingering under every breath. "We've got seventeen style options. You can choose basic plaster models, plain or with a bronze finish; fashioned into an incense burner; a wall plaque, though that's the deluxe; a jar with removable lid, which makes a great candy dish, condom holder, or whatever; and of course the rubber dildo, ethnically tinted by hand during the manufacturing process, if you like."

"Huh?" Michael is holding the phone at arm's length certain of only one thing: It'll be a cold day in hell before Jerry makes a copy of *his* most private member.

But Jerry Lands is a natural born salesman, and within 10 minutes what began as a curiosity call has culminated in the proverbial appointment at your local Penile Replicating Service.

"Simple as a trip to the barber," are Jerry's closing words.

>>>•<<<

That afternoon, Michael goes through the checklist. Trim the pubes or the plaster may stick, refrain from sexual activity, bring along some titillating porn, a girlfriend, or whatever, and don't forget to shave the balls if you want them included in the cast.

Don't think so, Michael thinks to himself on the ride over.

Walking up the stairs to the Silver Lake bungalow, a reality check stops him two inches from knocking on the door as the sudden prospect of disrobing before two total strangers settles in. *What in the hell was I thinking?*

Before he can change his mind the door has swung open and a barefoot, affable Bill is inviting the Monk in.

Expecting a more clinical setting, Mike surveys the infinitesimally small living room, cluttered with the urban consumerist chaos to be expected in the home of single men. One might assume that this surely must be the waiting room to a nice, clean, sterile casting studio out back.

Wrong.

Door closed, Bill makes no excuses for the clutter as he retreats to his computer to solve his latest HTML riddle on www.hardart-phallic.com. A bronzed mounted penis with wings hangs off the wall and throughout the room are assorted plaster erections. Jerry, the self-proclaimed bodybuilder, arrives straight from the gym and seems extraordinarily amped.

With tension already hanging in the air, Jerry's entrance pushes the stress meter another notch while he rages at Bill for not having the place set up. In between snide attacks on Bill's competence, he shoots Mike the occasional well-oiled marketing smile.

"You didn't bring a fluffer," he says.

"A what?"

"It's an expression in the porn industry. You know, someone to fluff you up!"

Performance anxiety sets in as Mike realizes that he really *didn't* think this through. No porn, no fluffer, and a decidedly unsexy atmosphere in this place.

As Bill the artist and Jerry the marketer busily set up, Mike stands awkwardly in a corner, waiting his cue, letting out a gasp when he sees the pint-size room convert itself into the pint-size penis replicating studio. A weight machine in the corner is replaced by a fold-out massage table with a conspicuous hole in the middle.

"Ready when you are," Jerry finally announces.

All eyes are on Mike. The silence doesn't help, so the suggestion is made for a bit of music to take the icy chill out of the air. Bill and Jerry engage in chitchat bordering on argument and it occurs to Michael that seven years must be a long time to be partners in a phallic replicating service.

"So, like, get naked?" Mike asks the obvious.

"Well, it's up to you. Leave on your shirt if you like, but we are going to need your fully aroused penis. As soon as you're ready we'll put you on the massage table face down and through the hole, and just try to keep it erect when we pull the mold on you."

"Okay," Michael answers, with little confidence left in his voice.

Somehow, with a stroke of luck, a minor conflict develops in the kitchen. While eyes are elsewhere the clothes come down and, throwing caution to the wind, Mike decides to get this show on the road before the fat lady comes stomping in and demands her money back.

"I'm think I'm ready!" says Mike, a few minutes later, wishing he could disappear through the woodwork.

"Are we raging!" shouts Jerry.

"Yep!"

The replicators come back in and suddenly the artistry of the moment surfaces. Jerry snaps on latex gloves while Bill busily fashions the mold, measuring and mixing the compound.

"So, are we doing the testicles today? Shaving's extra, you know!"

The comment seems strangely ordinary, but since the testicles haven't been shaven, and there is no desire to ever do so, the accommodating penis and testicle mold is discarded in favor of the simpler single-penis mold.

Mike hops up on the table, following the expert lead of Jerry's hands. In a snap, the two are busy underneath, filling the form with blue goop, the kind used in dental offices, and offering the friendly advice of "Don't let yourself go, 'cause this is going to feel really, really good."

No problem!

For the next three minutes, after the form snaps into place under the table and out of Mike's view, Jerry repeatedly says, "Think nasty thoughts." Whatever is going on down there is, well, hard to tell.

"Yeah, we get about 60% married men making it for their girlfriends to take home with them. And a lot of old guys, you know, they want it for their younger, sexually active wives. And for the shy, we have a home starter kit. But most people come on in."

The form is finally pulled off and the two are marveling at their work. "It's a perfect impression. Now if you want, we can enhance the replica a few inches, but that'll be extra. We need to know right away because that determines what happens next."

"Why, do I need it?"

"No, but, you know, some guys like to add a little for effect. I mean, you are immortalizing your penis, so you might want to compensate for any shortages."

Surveying the gargantuan plaster penes around the room, on the shelf, in the kitchen, mounted on the wall, it looks like most of the clientele opt for the $25 enhancement.

Michael dons his clothes, declining the option, declining their body-hair removal service, and declining to have anything more than the basic blue-light special, unaltered, untinted, white plaster replica with no wings, bronze, gold-leaf, or pedestal mounting. Plain and simple. Just what nature had in mind.

In the kitchen, Bill is cleaning dishes and Jerry is screening another client on the phone, and it suddenly becomes quite clear that for the HardArt Phallic Replicating Service it's just another day at the office.

"Don't forget, what you put into it *IS* what you get out of it," are Jerry's parting words.

during the week. For couples, $20 any day. $1 for a day pass for single women, who are obviously the prized commodity up here. If you merged Helendale's Exotic World with Elysium Fields you'd pretty much get the alternatingly cheesy and liberating essence of Naked City. Dick Drost is a nice guy, who, like many paraplegics we've met, has managed to create an imaginative way to get his sexual needs met. From Frank Moore to John Callahan to Larry Flynnt to John Hockenberry to Dick Drost, it now seems quite clear to us—chicks dig crips.

> **Pleasure Chest.** 7733 Santa Monica Blvd., near Fairfax (Los Angeles). ☎ **323/650-1022.**

San Francisco has its Good Vibrations, L.A. has the Pleasure Chest. All the leather and latex kink you could hope to find under one roof. Full walls of dildos, strap-ons, riding crops, whips, and yards of chain. Electric toys, butt plugs, condoms in all colors of the rainbow, and plenty of outfits to get you suited for your next kink-a-rama.

Strip Clubs. See "Clubs."

Spirituality

Every city has its patron saint. The saints of San Francisco, Saint Augustine, and Santa Cruz are obvious. The Hollywood patron saint is also obvious, though you won't find the answer in the name itself. The patron saint of Hollywood is L. Ron Hubbard, founder of Scientology. L. Ron *is* Hollywood. Ron's religion speaks to the needs of the city's primary occupational groups—actors, directors, and musicians. Like all patron saints, he stands above the city, proud of his great works. We pay homage to Ron throughout this guide, because, if we didn't we would be sued up the wazoo by his fanatical litigious minions. Praise Ron! Praise him from the mountaintops! Praise him in the valleys! Praise his good Texas name!

Here, by the way, is a list of the spiritual also-rans.

Observation

"Los Angeles is the only place in the world that you can find all forms of Buddhism. Not even Asian countries have all forms of Buddhism."

—J. Gordon Melton, director of the Institute for the Study of American Religion in Santa Barbara, CA

Buddhist

> **Dharma Zen Center.** 1025 S. Cloverdale Ave., at Olympic Blvd. (Mid-Wilshire). ☎ **323/934-0330.**

Only go straight, don't know, try try try for 10,000 years, save all beings from suffering, and then, only then, might you get your screenplay produced. Easygoing, friendly, Korean-style Zen.

Note: They also have a rural retreat center on 8400 Juniper Way in Tehachapi. Call ☎ **805/822-7776** for directions.

Rinzai-Ji Postcard of Wisdom

"We all want to be good people, but if one leaves out the devil, then one has just become a good fixated person. When we manifest a complete self then we have as our complete content both the plus and the minus, both the good and the evil. That's why they say when one manifests true wisdom consciousness, the complete doing that is knowing, then there is neither God nor the devil. . . . This experience of nothing to prefer, not needing to avoid or have anything particularly, is where one must start one's Zen practice."

—Zen Master Joshi Sasaki

> **Hsi Lai Temple.** 3456 Glenmark Dr., near Hacienda Blvd. (Hacienda Heights). ☎ **626/961-9697.**

The largest Buddhist temple outside of Asia was the site of a controversial 1995 fund-raiser attended by Vice President Al Gore. The veep's visit formed the basis of the Asian money scandal that briefly rocked the Clinton Administration. Connected with a large Buddhist organization out of Taiwan, Hsi Lai contains many buildings, many huge Buddhas, and an excellent museum of Buddhist sculptures and paintings. They also serve a vegetarian lunch every day in their dining room.

> **Rinzai-Ji Zen Center.** 2505 Cimarron St., at 25th St. (Los Angeles). ☎ **213/732-2263.** www.mbzc.org. To go to Mount Baldy Zen Center, home of the oldest Zen Master in America, call ☎ **909/985-6410** or E-mail office@mbzc.org.

In the folklore of Zen, Rinzai centers are considered harsh and militaristic—more samurai than gentle tea ceremony. This urban center of the more austere hardcore training facility on Mt. Baldy bucks

1. Show me your original face before the last chemical peel.

2. Three L.A. monks are standing outside the Beverly Hills Zendo, when the Zen Master comes up. One Monk says, "Master, you teach that all things have Buddha nature. Does that mean Scott Rudin has Buddha nature?" The Zen Master harangues the Monk for a good 20 minutes, crudely chastising him with every possible egregious insult known to humankind. The Monk attains enlightenment. What did the Monk attain?

3. A Zen Master asked an assembled multitude of pimps, prostitutes, and rap artists, "What is enlightenment?" The rapper Coolio immediately shouted, "chronic, Glocks, and Hummers!" The Zen Master replied, "You've attained the three treasures." What did Coolio attain?

4. After service one day a young student ran up to the Zen Master. "Sir, I have been practicing very, very hard, but I still cannot sell my screenplay. I've incorporated the best of *Armageddon, Deep Impact,* and *Something About Mary,* and, still, no results." The Zen Master replied, "Do you have a happy ending?" The student replied, "Of course!" The Zen Master said, "Then let's do lunch." The student immediately got enlightenment. What did the student attain?

5. A Valley Girl walks into the interview room to see the Zen Master. "Oh my God, like, you're supposed to be, like, enlightened!!"

   The Zen Master ponders her remark. "I am only a reflection."

   "No WAY!!"

   "Way," says the Master.

   "I'm so sure!!"

   "Fer sure."

   "Does that mean, like, you're not as grody as I thought?"

   "Totally."

   "Well, like you're a Zen Master, aren't you going to, like, make me answer some stupid koan?"

   "You already understand."

   "Whatever."

   "Exactamundo."

   And upon hearing that remark, the Valley Girl attained enlightenment. What did the Valley Girl attain?

The first Buddhist temple in the

nation opened in Los Angeles in 1904.

that stereotype. The place is positively good-hearted, though not at all officious. However, don't go looking for a feel-good bodhissavta cause to get behind. The teaching here emphasizes compassion as the fruit of a long life of practice. What is called "selfless compassion" as opposed to the more odious "selfish compassion" found littered throughout this Protestant land. No AIDS hospice here, bud. But do at least make it to the Sunday-morning lecture. As delivered by handsome head monk, Kido, or by the 92-year-old balls-to-the-wall Japanese Roshi, Joshi Sasaki, when he's in town, it's bound to shake up your dualistic world. Nightly meditation starts at 7pm. Morning meditation at 5am. And be sure to ask a monk to show you the hidden back staircase. It's where the original owner of the house used to come and go to see his mistress, who lived upstairs. And the baronial dharma hall was once used for large banquets. Also, be sure to get on their mailing list—their monthly postcards are concise gems of Buddha dharma.

› **Zen Center of L.A.** 923 S. Normandie Ave., near Olympic Blvd. (Koreatown). ☎ 213/387-2351.

Usually Zen centers are refuges from the samsaric storm. Not ZCLA, which invariably seems embroiled in one difficulty after another. Rocked a few years ago by revelations of the alcoholism of the late Zen master Maizumi Roshi (well documented by videographer Tiger Eye Hawthorne), it has managed to survive to endure a few more scandals, this time more sexual in nature. Now it's aligned with roly-poly Zen mensch Bernie Glassman and his precious PC dharma. Women's Studies majors and *Utne Reader* subscribers should feel right at home.

Christian

› **1st A.M.E. (African Methodist Episcopal).** 2270 S. Harvard Blvd., at 22nd St. (South Central). ☎ 323/730-9180.

Brought to town by the early settlers from the Midwest, who came here seeking not only a health cure but spiritual renewal, Christianity has a long, vibrant, often messianic history in L.A. But frankly, the excitement and creativity has not been the same since the city's most legendary Christian prophet, Aimee Semple McPherson, passed on. Today, you have your requisite ecumenical, Science of Mind, We Are the World, Glide Memorial clones over there on the West Side, and millions of traditional Christian believers in Koreatown, Pasadena, and all over Hispanic L.A., but nothing that excites us quite like tales of Aimee or the reality of Miss Velma (see

"Wacko-Fringe"). Still, once in awhile a Monk needs an old-fashioned hit of "love thy neighbor" without all that Nicene Creed dogma one gets in the Roman Catholic churches. This is when a Monk will seek out a traditional black Baptist congregation. And in Los Angeles, there's few better than AME, the social, political, and spiritual bedrock of South Central L.A., led by the charismatic Cecil Murray. Go to the rousing Sunday Healing Service (8am, 10am, or noon) and learn what it means to be saved. "Stand up!"

Jewish

Judaism is big in L.A. In fact, stars like Madonna, Sandra Bernhardt, and Courtney Love have made Kabala, the esoteric side of Judaism, seem almost hip. Judaism came out West with the early film pioneers. As documented by author Neil Gabler (*An Empire of Their Own: How the Jews Invented Hollywood*), men like Carl Laemmle (creator of Universal), Adolph Zukor (creator of Paramount), the Warner Brothers, Louis B. Mayer (founder of MGM), William Fox of 20th Century Fox, and Harry Cohn, head of Columbia, were all Jewish immigrants who helped transform a technological novelty—motion pictures—into the most powerful and influential mass medium of the 20th century.

These Jewish film moguls naturally brought with them their religion. Today, there are dozens upon dozens of synagogues in Los Angeles. Of all persuasions. We're particularly big on the Hasidic sect of Jewry (they have a few temples in the vicinity of Detroit and Third, near La Brea; plus a place out there in the Pacific Palisades). A lot of the power players head to Temple Israel, what a Jewish friend calls "the main joint" in town. Then there's Temple Beth Streisand, a temple on the Third Street Promenade, a Beverly Hills synagogue with an oil derrick covered in white-plaster housing, some sort of gay temple, and a little orthodox number right on the Venice boardwalk.

But even with all these excellent places to celebrate Shabbos, our favorite is still the **Beta Israel Temple Black Jewish Synagogue,** at 1101 Crenshaw (☎ **323/ 930-2027**). At this "synagogue," led by the 74-year-old Jamaican "Doctor" Ernesto A. Moshe Montgomery (a real traditional Jewish moniker there for ya), the emphasis is not so much on the Torah. No, no, at the Beta Israel Temple Black Jewish Synagogue, the emphasis is not on teachings of the past, but on predictions of the future. A graduate of the International Institute of Metaphysics, the good Doctor has a reputation for prophecy. Did you know that Doctor Montgomery was used by British intelligence during World War II to suss out the movements of German troops? Did you know that this man, now presiding RIGHT HERE in the Crenshaw District of L.A., was a major psychic player in the D-Day operation? How come that didn't end up in *Saving Private Ryan?* The things we're not told. Did you know that Dr. Montgomery predicted the acquittal of O. J. Simpson, the assassination of both Kennedys, and the death of Mother Theresa? What's more, the doctor predicts there will be a major earthquake in Los Angeles on October 17th, 2000. (Isn't that Diane "Baby" Raimondo's birthday?) Though you're not likely to get scholarly interpretations of the Talmud, or even Kabalistic interpretations of ultimate reality, Dr. Montgomery can read your aura, feel your vibration, and predict your future.

The Wacko Fringe

› **The Spiritual Rebel/Yesss Center.** 344 Indiana Ave., near 3rd Ave. (Venice). ☎ **310/ 399-0032.** www.westworld.com/~arhata/yes. E-mail: arhata@mail.westworld.com.

Run by the male-female twosome you will see any weekend on the Venice Boardwalk with placards of incendiary encyclicals on masturbation and orgasm, the Yesss Center is solid proof of how empty was the vessel created by the late Baghwan Shree Rajneesh. After his death, most Osho centers either died, fizzled out, or carried on with serious problems attached. The Yesss Center falls into the last category. In the words of the center's founder and leader, a long-haired, potbellied surferlike fellow named Arhata, "Most residents here don't come to the meditations. They only do the meditations right before they go to bed." Still, there are others who make the trek to the Thursday "Let Go L.A." blowouts, which essentially amount to a series of energy breath exercises followed by some guided meditation, interspersed with embarrassingly frank talk by Arhata and his latest bodhi chick on their extraordinary sex life. As cheesy as it all is, the meditations can only help.

› **Universal World Church.** 123 N. Lake, at Beverly Blvd. (Westlake).
☎ **213/413-3030.**

Don't be fooled: The drab exterior holds the doorway to another world. Inside, a deeply vaulted ceiling aims all eyes towards an altar overflowing with psychedelic Christian kitsch: It's one part medieval iconography and two parts down-market mall decoration. Queen of all she surveys, Miss Velma Jaggers sports an angelic silver coiffure and earnestly preaches arcane revelations to a diverse and slightly threadbare congregation. Holiday services are especially inspiring, studded with Vegas-quality performance breaks, and extra-shiny decorations.

From the L.A. Cacophony Society Web site (www.cacophony.org/la/): "Sunday, Dec. 20, 11 a.m.: Miss Velma is obviously not of this world. Seeing this woman ensconced in a confection of chiffon and crowned with gleaming white hair, you are barely surprised to hear her casually mention conversing with 12-inch angels seated on the foot of her bed."

(continued on page 183)

Galaxy Girl: A Cosmic Embrace from Astrophysicist of Love
Fiorella Terenzi

What do you get when you mix Cicciolina, Madonna, Stephen Hawking, and Angelyne? Answer: Dr. Fiorella Terenzi, the astrophysicist musician kung-fu master and author, whose carefully orchestrated style, sensuality, and beauty (Cicciolina) is matched only by her disciplined grasp of self-promotion (Madonna), enthusiastic appreciation of the cosmos (Hawking), and very L.A. determination to be a FABULOUS GLAMOROUS STAR!! (Angelyne).

Smiling. Always smiling. That is what this Monk came away feeling after a Venice, California, rendezvous with the delightful Fiorella Terenzi. The name itself conjures up images playful, light, and sexy—which, fittingly, is Dr. Terenzi's carefully controlled intention. The whole package, from the lovely but learned Italianate lilt to the winning graciousness and elegance, will draw even the staunchest cynic closer to the Fiorella Galaxy.

To her credit, Fiorella uses sex appeal to radically transform the image of scientists. Especially dear to her are young women, who might not pursue work in the field because of what she calls the male (or "Mars") dominated nature of current scientific inquiry. Her message to young scientists, eloquently delivered at every opportunity, is that you can do serious research, even fearlessly share the fruits of that research, and do it with flair, humor, and sensuality. As the testimonials of students and co-workers both here and abroad indicate, Dr. Terenzi has won many converts to her cause.

READY FOR HER CLOSE-UP

Like the late Carl Sagan (to whom she is often compared), Fiorella is a great popularizer, making an arcane and "technical" subject like astrophysics seem approachable and fun. It is this generosity of spirit that is at the heart of her much larger mission: sharing with the widest possible audience the magic and mystery of the cosmos and, through a variety of skillful means—including sound (*Music from the Galaxies,* Island), CD-ROMs (*Invisible Universe,* Voyager), the Web (Fiorella.com), and her recent book (*Heavenly Knowledge,* Avon, 1998)—motivating each of us to gaze up at the sky for beauty, love, and inspiration.

Fiorella: I came [to America as] a researcher at UCSD some years ago. And then I came back as a recording artist in 1991.

Monk: In that time period since 1991 you've continued to teach?

Fiorella: I resigned my position in Milano. . . . I was teaching full-time. Then I came back to America. I saw how things were, and I started to teach 2,000 people. So from a classroom of twenty-one I moved to a classroom of thousand. . . . Through the music, through the concert, through the lecture tour, through colleges, planetariums . . .

Monk: So you are a kind of full-time Fiorella industry now. . . .

Fiorella: Yes, I am.

Monk: And you see yourself as one of the stars in the galaxy. . . . Obviously you want to be a star yourself.

Fiorella: A galaxy. *[Laughs]*

Monk: You want to be a galaxy, not just a star *[she's still laughing]*. What are you, a Leo?

Fiorella: Veeer-go.

Monk: Virgo.

Fiorella: Yah!

Monk: So you're intellectual and grounded.

Fiorella: And Italian, which is everything in between.

Monk: So, if there's a galaxy out there that represents the qualities of Fiorella, what galaxy is that?

Fiorella: Well, it's my own galaxy. I try to do unique, original, innovative education, fun, entertaining, cool, hip, "glamorisch," sensual, feminine, elegant . . .

Monk: All of those things that you are.

Fiorella: Inspiration galaxy . . .

Monk: Is there a galaxy out there right now that corresponds to Fiorella?

Fiorella: No, because the best way that you can predict your future is to invent it. So, I am going to invent my own galaxy.

> *"The best way that you can predict your future is to invent it. So, I am going to invent my own galaxy."*

Monk: Literally speaking, we are going to find the Fiorella galaxy down the road?

Fiorella: Absolutely. But, actually, you know, it's still in big formation right now *[she smiles]*. It's starting to shine hopefully in its fullest form. I've been doing many things about that. . . .

Monk: You're using galaxy in the metaphorical or literal sense?

Fiorella: It can be both. Actually, it's a metaphor to say I would like to create my own galaxy. A galaxy is composed of many stars. I feel personally the need to be in more mediums. I feel very tied into the definition of being a scientist only. Likewise, I would not [want to] be a musician only. I cannot sing about "why did you leave me last night." I love to sing about stars. How stars fall in love. How stars attract each other. But I need to be grounded in astronomy. So it's perfect that I am an astrophysicist too. And vice versa. When I do science, I need the music. So it's perfect that I am a musician.

Monk: Madonna or Cicciolina. Who do you relate to more?

Fiorella: I love the popularity, the icon of Madonna. I wish I could have her crowd to be my crowd. But I would keep the femininity of Cicciolina. With the flower, and this loving things she has for men. Have you ever heard her talking to men? It's always in a warm and affective [way], it's never provocating. Cicciolina is always open, feminine.

ORBITAL PASTA

Monk: Do you do a specific spiritual practice to clear away the obstructions in your own perception?

Fiorella: I do the technique of the orbital mind.

Monk: The orbital mind! Trippy stuff. Go on, Fiorella, please.

Fiorella: *[laughs]* This is a space technique. Which means you have to close your eyes. You have to think about where we are, sitting at the coffee table, at the [Cyber] Java cafe. You have to close your eyes and visualize who is next to you. . . . Feel with your hand the table where you are sitting. Remember that you are with me.

Monk: Oh, I won't forget that.

Fiorella: Now, elevate yourself across the ceiling. Pass through the ceiling of this building. Go up and look down and see that you are sitting at a table with me. With a tape recorder in the middle.

Monk: So I'm on the ceiling right now looking down at you?

Fiorella: Go a little bit higher because I want you to see below you Venice, California. Go a little bit higher up, I want you to see Manhattan Beach. I want you to see Marina del Rey, Los Angeles, and a part of the Valley. And then I want you to go even higher up so you can see all California, all San Francisco, and a little bit of Seattle. Higher up, so you can see all United States of America, and higher up again so there it goes, planet Earth, spinning below down your feet. Stay there. Float there. Think about Monk. Think about everything with that vision. You are talking to the entire planet. You are one with the universe. That's the feeling of being the orbital mind. You are spinning around the planet, and the planet is spinning with you. And there are no frontiers, no barriers, no color, no accent, no problem, no anything. There is just the joy of breathing and being alive in the present time. Voilà! Come back!

Jim is still in a trance. She laughs.

Fiorella: That is the technique I do.

Monk: Do I have to come back, Fiorella? *[laughing]*

Fiorella: The other technique is you visualize water boiling. Hot temperature. Salt. Inside, boiling with the water *[she is starting to laugh]*.

Jim completely cracks up.

Fiorella: I don't understand. You said something. This is the technique. Remember the boiling water with the salt inside?

>interview

Monk: Got it.

Fiorella: Next we have to picture tomato with garlic and pepper, friends all around the house *[Fiorella and Jim are laughing again]*, put the pasta around the music, and this is the pasta meditation.

David, the bright, ever-present handler: *[laughing]* This is the orbital pasta.

Fiorella: *[Laughing, but determined to finish her explanation]* Some Italian music. Romance. Candle. Aromas.

Monk: You're beautiful, Fiorella.

Fiorella: A rubbing in the back while you are cooking pasta, and that's it.

Monk: What's in the back while I'm cooking pasta?

Fiorella: Rub. Massage . . .

Monk: I'm getting rubbed while I'm doing pasta. I'm into this. Can we do this one again?

Dave laughing.

Monk: Do you cook pasta at all, Fiorella?

Fiorella: Absolutely.

Monk: You're coming to our house. We're doing the orbital pasta for lots of people.

All laughing.

HUMANIZING THE COSMOS

Monk: But, seriously the skeptics out there might say, "Fiorella, you're so charming, you're as sweet as pie, I just love the way you make the cosmos come alive, but listen, hon, this is all anthropomorphic. You are applying human qualities to constellations. It's a beautiful thing, but it's just not reality."

Fiorella: The reality becomes reality once you attach a beautiful name to a celestial object. You attach a name that means something with you, and there it goes. You see, we cannot reduce the universe to be just a list of numbers—galaxies named only UGC-6697, UGC-3030. We should avoid that. You know the universe is not a catalog where you open, [see] model X Y Z, you know. The universe is a place with object that have their own communication, so I am proposing to rename celestial object with a name. Attach human property, and the object become real. So, if I think of Orion . . .

Monk: That's your lover. You're really hot on Orion.

Fiorella: I am. And I tell you why. I can do both. I can really chart Orion from my telescope and go and analyze all the chemical elements, distance, velocity. I can fly through the nebula. I can understand what's going on. Because I have an understanding, a fantasy attached to it. Orion is a mythological figure. Do not forget that mythology is a little bit at the base of everything in society, [and] therefore in reality. So I can fantasize about Orion, or write a song about Orion. I can do a music video. That is when the universe become real. But if you are going to name celestial object only with number, that is a universe that is unreal. That is a universe that doesn't have anything to say, is a universe that is a list of number that no one care about. That is the universe, that is the astronomy we have today. No one care about astronomy. No one care about science.

Jim: They care about astrology.

Fiorella: Absolutely! Because it personify. Because people need something they can use in their everyday life. I do, too. Otherwise, everything become too object-oriented. I think people want something they can approach. A scientist until today hasn't been approachable. A scientist is a scaring academic, nerd figure. I want to run away when I see my professor teaching me quantum physics. Was an extremely painful experience. And all the time you have pain you want to quit.

Monk: It's almost amazing that some people have even learned quantum physics. It's almost if they have to shut down their humanity to learn it.

Fiorella: That's right. Actually, I am proposing a vice versa. Bring out your humanity. Because through your humanity you can probably understand the universe. It is through your emotion. Everything I do is based on what I call emotional learning. When you learn via your emotion you learn forever. I am attaching a new image to a new scientist. I am attaching a new emotion to celestial object. I am attaching a sensuality, a femininity, to the universe that it didn't have before.

Monk: The devil's advocate will say, "That's beautiful, but . . ."

Fiorella: It's more than beautiful. It's more than wonderful. It's practical. It's key. It will open your mind.

>interview

"But then, nothing could surprise you after laying eyes on the sanctuary's glittering accumulations of altars and angels. In the program, you'll read that it's all gold leaf encrusted with precious stones, but in the glare of the spotlights, you'll also see gold paint and Mylar. It's like a cable-access version of heaven. Watch out for the giant angels with mechanized neon swords."

(For info on similar excursions with L.A. Cacophony, a satellite of the original San Francisco—surprise, surprise—Cacophony Society [though not as Monk-friendly], call ☎ 323/668-0080. Or E-mail to la@cacophony.org.)

Sports and Recreation

Pickup Basketball

> **Christine Emerson Reed Park.** 7th St. and California (Santa Monica).

For those tired of the waits and crowds at the Venice Beach courts, this little park, 7 blocks off Santa Monica Beach, is just the ticket. The talent isn't anything that'll wow a scout, but it does attract one Hollywood notable: Woody Harrelson. We're not big on Hollywood notables, but let's face it, you can't get a better example of art imitating life imitating art than the costar of *White Men Can't Jump* playing against trash-talking black players near where he had a pivotal scene with Rosie Perez. This, my friends, is the ultimate pickup-ball tableau. It's interesting to watch Harrelson in his trademark "Harvest Hemp Not Trees" T-shirt, scraggly beard and nonconfrontational demeanor. Off the court, he's a bit of a loner, quietly biding his time waiting for a chance to play. On the court, he plays aggressive, doesn't argue, and doesn't trash talk. Defenders play him hard, though not as hard as they might play a genuine talent like Jim Monk. When Harrelson's around, it's clear to all there's a major celebrity on the court, and no one wants to be responsible for ruining the cat's career. Weekends are best. And you can always get in a game, if you are willing to play on the second court.

> **Hollywood YMCA.** 1553 N. Schrader Blvd., at Sunset Blvd. (Hollywood).
> ☎ 323/467-4161.

Here you will find basketball games with the most talent, the most fun, and the largest number of struggling actors. In fact, at least one out of every two people you play with will have some connection to the business, which means the 9am and 2pm games (Mon, Wed, Fri, and weekends) will not only be packed, but will offer excellent opportunities to network. Saturday mornings occasionally bring out a posse of hip-hoppers, and occasionally little ole Mike Tyson (when he's not in jail).

› Sports Club/L.A. 1835 S. Sepulveda Blvd., near Santa Monica Blvd. (West Los Angeles). ☎ **310/473-1447.**

Fashioning itself as a day spa for L.A.'s entertainment elite, Sports Club/L.A.—part of a chain that also owns New York's Reebok Center—is a massive four-story complex that features everything from high-end massage, facials, a beauty salon, a dining room, and a snack bar to other things that actually have something to do with fitness, such as Pilates, transporters, spinning, wall climbing, every kind of workout machine imaginable, and, most importantly, basketball.

It was the basketball that drew me, mainly because I'd heard that members of the Lakers play here. The rumor, it turns out, is true (though, generously, Shaq only plays outside the key). Of course, the Lakers all have complimentary memberships (proof that the richer you get, the more free stuff you accrue). And they don't show up here all that often. The day I played, the games consisted mostly of loud, high-strung, endlessly bickering white guys; not what you'd call "sacred hoops." I actually felt somewhat at home, until I became the brunt of one Asian man's venom. But I was compassionate to his need to hector me for every minor mistake. The close-to-$200-a-month membership fee might make me a little venomous too. Of course, the big draw here is not basketball; as always at such palpably hetero clubs, it's "the scene." While everyone is admirably focused on chiseling the perfect frame, there's still plenty of that wandering eye. And with members like Sharon Stone and several Playboy bunnies, you can understand why.

› Venice Beach. Ocean Front Walk, near Venice Blvd. (Venice).

Just about any day of the week you can usually find a small group willing to play, with waits at a minimum. On weekends, though, fehgeddaboutit. One- to 2-hour waits to play a half-court game. Still, it's where all the tourists come to either play or watch. It's kind of nice having a young German couple watching your every move as you beat up on young Helmut, though the real draw is the full-court screamfests by the grandstand. Do not even think of playing on the full court unless you are good, you are strong, or you can really SCREAM. As always with Venice Beach in general, it's the testosterone, baby.

Other Courts

Other courts that come highly recommended by Monk advisors:

1. Carson Recreation Center (ask around)
2. Jim Gilliam Recreation Center, La Brea Avenue, South of Coliseum
3. Rogers Recreation Center, Eucalyptus and Hyde Park Boulevard (Inglewood)
4. Westwood Recreation Complex, 1350 Sepulveda Blvd., between Wilshire and Ohio (Tues to Thurs noon to 2pm, Fri nights 7:30 to 9:30pm)

Bowling

> **Hollywood Star Lanes.** 5227 Santa Monica Blvd., near Western Ave. (Hollywood).
☎ 213/665-4111.

Open 24 hours, with fifties sherbet neon and a seventies-style cocktail lounge, this is where *The Big Lebowski* was filmed, dude.

> **Montrose Bowl.** 2334 Honolulu Ave., at Ocean View (Montrose). ☎ 818/249-3895.

Tiny eight-lane bowling alley with over-the-lane ball return and snack bar. If business is slow, ask one of the German owners to bowl with you.

Firearms Training

> **L.A. Gun Club.** 1375 E. 6th St., near Alameda St. (Downtown). ☎ 213/612-0931.

While there are gun clubs in every major city in the country, when you consider L.A.'s paranoiac obsession with personal security, the L.A. Gun Club takes on added significance. Hunker down at the one place in town where rich Korean businessmen and inner-city gangbangers meet on neutral turf. Just after the riots their phone was busy for weeks. See "Monks with Guns" feature in this section.

Gyms/Spas/Massage

> **City Spa.** 5325 W. Pico Blvd., at Burnside (Los Angeles). ☎ 323/933-5954.

While a coterie of Angeleno friends recommend the plaitza and body scrubs at this very ethnic spa, where MTV's Pauly Shore is a regular, we found the place to be an obnoxiously chatty, loud, if humorous, throwback to New York's 10th Street Baths. That kind of aggravation we don't need! Unfortunately, the ubiquitous Asian places around town aren't much better.

> **East West Health Center.** 901 S. Western Ave., #105, at 9th St. (Koreatown).
☎ 213/737-6114.

IPO magician to the stars Michael Smith turned me on to this Korean Shiatsu massage, spa, and restaurant in the heart of Koreatown. Funky is the word—TVs blaring, slipshod food area, in serious need of upkeep—but the massage hit the jackpot. Talk about strong toes and feet: The no-nonsense women here work you deep and hard using an overhead wooden beam for support. However, the mercenary quality of these masseuses—they frown when you don't give a giant tip—sort of wrecked the relaxing spiritual afterglow.

A profound transformation happened at the L.A. Gun Club. I discovered I was a pacifist. It's one thing to see photos of gangsta rappers toting Glocks, or Mel Gibson brandishing one in a film, it's quite another to use one yourself. The L.A. Gun Club brought home to me the deadly violence of firearms. Since I do not trust myself to be balanced and socially appropriate at all times, I was very skittish about participating in this little game. Michael Monk, a Boy Scout from redneck rural Arkansas, had no such qualms. In Mike's childhood milieu, everyone used firearms. He grew up with them. Mike Monk may know how to dress in impeccable drag, sew a French seam, and design a bedroom, but, let me tell you, he can also pump a Walther automatic right into a target's forehead. Monk Lesson # 1: DO NOT, REPEAT, DO NOT EVER MESS WITH MICHAEL MONK. Like Atticus Finch, the lawyer in *To Kill a Mockingbird*, Mike may seem like a sweet and lanky guy, but he knows how to use a weapon if he has to. Naturally, Mike took to the firearms instruction at the L.A. Gun Club like a pig in a poke. I was raised a doctor's son in Omaha. Though my dear father was raised on a farm, he eschewed both hunting and fishing. My brothers didn't hunt. Nor did my friends. I never had much interest in gun culture, and looked down upon those who were part of it. The L.A. Gun Club changed all that.

I walked in completely scared of the place. The warnings on the wall were ominous. The display of guns—from 44 Magnums to little Saturday Night Specials—rankled me to the core. It took 30 minutes to calm down enough to grasp our friendly Korean guy's instructions. All kinds of frightening scenarios played out in my head—the gun recoiling so strongly I was bounced back, accidentally firing a round into my neighbor's stomach, the gun jamming my thumb, ripping out flesh, and then, my own double nature taking hold, and just for kicks, grabbing a gun and shooting the place up.

It's tough to rein in all these fears and demons. But I did. And with the help of my friendly assistant, Tack, I took my shots at the white target, putting bullets through the man's liver, heart, and arm, but missing the head. Sure-shot Michael Monk would never make that mistake. Which brings to mind Monk Lesson #2: Never underestimate the vengeance of Michael Monk. Woe unto those who have.

> **Gold's Gym.** 360 Hampton Dr., at Sunset Ave. (Venice). ☎ **310/392-6004.**

Some of the same Herculean freaks you catch on the Venice Boardwalk you can catch here, at the original king of bodybuilding emporiums. This is not the Original Gold's, which was at 1006 Pacific Avenue in Venice, but it is where the Arnold legacy is kept alive and pumpin', including plenty of connections for those behind-the-counter supplemental needs.

Running and Climbing

> **Griffith Park Run.** Take Vermont Ave. through main entrance, follow Vermont Canyon Rd. up to Griffith Observatory. Take dirt path on north end of parking lot. Above Los Feliz.

This is by far the most arduous uphill run in the city. As you jog up the dirt path, past others barely able to walk the steep slope, and gaze into the valley below, it feels almost mythic, like you're conquering Mount Olympus. As runners come and go, it feels you are all participating in the original Olympiad. Once at the top, there is a little patio and a wooden fence from which one can examine, Zeus-like, the kingdom down below. There is no satisfaction quite like making this climb without stopping.

> **Ultimate Stairway (a.k.a. The 4th Street Steps).** 4th St. and Adelaide Dr. (Santa Monica).

The Ultimate Stairmaster, to be more accurate. One hundred eighty-nine steps in all, with a gentle ocean breeze blowing through. Run up and down this thing about thirty times and you will reach some kind of satori. *Warning:* It can get crowded, and the serious runners get peeved if you wear perfume or jangling bracelets, or mess with their precious markers (branches, leaves, and rocks that demarcate how many "reps" they've done). But if you enjoy running in a beautifully green residential area, alongside some tight sweaty bodies, check this place out.

Volleyball

> **Manhattan Beach Volleyball.** Manhattan Beach Blvd., at Ocean Dr. Walk to beach. (Manhattan Beach).

Exercise Trivia

It has been estimated that jogging for 30 minutes in the heart of L.A. is the equivalent of smoking a pack of cigarettes.

We are not big on volleyball. We are not big on the sunburned Neanderthals you find playing volleyball at such locales. But if you want to experience the most thoroughly hetero beach scene L.A. has to offer—the San Francisco Marina meets New York's Upper West Side—then, by all means, get your breeder butt down here.

Water Flumes

> **Raging Waters.** 111 Raging Waters Dr.; take 10 west, 210 north, exit Bonita Ave.; follow signs (San Dimas). ☎ **909/592-6453.**

On the surface this might seem like a rather mainstream selection for such a refined and selective guidebook—and we'll admit that the place is crawling with folks who wouldn't know the Museum of Jurassic Technology from Jurassic Park—but there is something so mind-altering about a swift ride down a water flume, we feel compelled to include it. On the same day half of L.A.'s intelligent women were at Lillith Fair at the Rose Bowl, the Monks and three other male novitiates headed for some water bonding here. There were several highlights. For sheer mind expansion, try the Vortex—a dark tunnel ride, but not for the claustrophobic. For sheer terror, try the ten-story Drop Out. For pure, almost transcendental, relaxation, try the Amazon Adventure, one of the country's longest man-made rivers. Though our favorites were El Niño (absolutely no relation to the weather phenomenon) and Raging Rapids (five of you in a wild raft ride). High Extreme II, despite its towering height, is rather benign (the walk up is the scariest part). While you are waiting in line, there are plenty of barely legal bodies to scope out—though the lines are so long on weekends, even that gets old. We recommend a visit during the week.

Note: Raging Waters is not only the largest water theme park west of the Mississippi River, it is also the most pastoral, situated as it is inside the Frank G. Bonelli Regional Park.

Stores/Shopping

> **Busy Bee.** 1521 Santa Monica Blvd., at 15th St. (Santa Monica).
☎ **310/395-1158.**

We highly recommend the Busy Bee, the oldest hardware store in Santa Monica, where you'll meet owner, ah, we mean "steward," Don Kidson, a cosmic health nut who claims to be "The Juice Prophet." With his angular Viktor Kulvinskas–style

... It'll work right in with the retro thing. Think about it: A live-action Dudley Do-Right. We could get Harvey Keitel ...

frame and long gray mane, Don is a far cry from the standard image of hardware store owner we carry with us in popular mythology. Don claims to be 66. Now, whether he is telling the truth or simply saying that to beef up (or, rather, sprout up) the legendary power of juicing (not to mention the sales of Busy Bee's juicers), we do not know. Either way, he doesn't look a day over 59 or a pound over 120.

> **The Dudley Do-Right Emporium.** 8200 Sunset Blvd., near Fairfax Ave. (Hollywood). ☎ **323/656-6550.**

The life work of Jay Ward (creator of Dudley Do-Right, Bullwinkle, and Rocky), enshrined for all to purchase. His widow and daughter have run the playful spot for years, selling an assortment of lunch boxes, wristwatches, ties, production scripts, and more, all with Ward's imprint. But this is more than a memorabilia store. It's a cultural landmark. If you are in your late thirties or early forties you will realize how critical Mr. Ward's creations were to a creative happy childhood. Just imagine for a second if all you had to watch was Scooby Doo. No Rocky, no Bullwinkle, no Underdog, no Royal Mounties, no Boris or Natasha, no Nell! You'd be dumber than you think you are.

Factoid: What I didn't realize until recently was that Jay Ward helped create the characters behind my three favorite childhood cereals: Cap'n Crunch, Quisp, and Quake.

*Check out the **Los Angeles***

Department of Coroner Gift

Shop, *1104 Mission Rd.*

(Downtown; ☎ ***213/343-0760).***

> **L.A. Police Academy / L.A. Police Revolver and Athletic Club Cafe & Gift Shop.** 1880 N. Academy Rd., east of Stadium Way (Downtown). ☎ **213/221-3101** or 213/221-5222.

You have not fully understood L.A. until you visit this place. Dine with cops in the Academy Cafe, near the Jack Webb Memorial Showcase and the Academy brass-knuckle collection, then visit the gift shop and buy a bulletproof kevlar vest, a Hard Luck Cafe T-shirt, miniature LAPD police cars, LAPD banks, or some LAPD baby wear. Unfortunately, no more Riot Commemorative Mugs, stuffed piggies, or piggy banks. And definitely no George "Of The Jungle" Halladay videotapes. Complete your tour with the ultimate L.A. metaphor: a stroll through the peaceful Academy rock garden, appropriately adjoining a shooting range. Don't worry, there are headphones in the chapel to block out the sound of bullets.

> **Panoptikum.** 5050 Vineland Ave., near Camarillo St. (North Hollywood). ☎ **818/985-2837.**

Next time you feel like sleeping in a coffin, go see Patrick McGuire. Has he got a deal for you. Catering to the macabre, his store is a cornucopia of antique coffins, funeral-home furniture, and the stuff horror houses are full of. If wrought-iron fixtures, X-ray machines, or gothic swords are your idea of good taste, then you'll be a happy shopper. As with most collectors, he finally ran out of room and opened a store. His Chamber of Horrors features ongoing exhibits, a current one displaying mummy photos from Mexico by Simone Fox.

> **Soap Plant/Wacko/La Luz de Jesus Gallery.** 4633 Hollywood Blvd., at Vermont Ave. (Los Feliz). ☎ **213/663-0122.**

We absolutely love this place, which houses the finest collection of offbeat books and merchandise in L.A.: toys, cards, posters, folk art, religious items, you name it. The store moved to its present location when owner Billy Shire tired of the gentrification of Melrose.

> **Y-Que.** 1770 N. Vermont, at Melbourne Ave. (Los Feliz). ☎ **323/664-0021.**

Is Y-Que the Ruby Montana's of L.A. or vice versa? Not in the same class as the venerable Wacko, but a very clean, neat, and well-stocked camp-lite emporium. Trust Spencer—he wears Jim Monk's Buddy Holly frames.

Streets, Corners, and Highways

> **Franklin Avenue Strip.** Between Bronson Ave. and Tamarind (Hollywood).

Under the watchful eye of the Scientology Celebrity Center to the south and a Mayfair Market to the east, this couple-block stretch of Franklin offers one of the few cozy neighborhoods in the city from which to lounge on the sidewalk, sip your lattes, read your screenplay, and wait for the sun to set before heading home. Highlights include **Counterpoint Books and Records** (5911 Franklin Ave.; ☎ 213/957-7965), **Daily Planet Bookstore** (5931½ Franklin Ave.; ☎ 213/957-0061), **Hollywood Hills Coffeeshop** (6145 Franklin Ave.; ☎ 213/467-7678), **Tamarind Theatre** (5919 Franklin Ave.; ☎ 213/465-7980), and the happening restaurant **Birds** (5925 Franklin Ave.; ☎ 323/465-0175)—be sure to pick up one of their hilariously controversial postcards.

> **Fremont Place.** Between Wilshire Blvd. and Olympic Blvd. (Mid-Wilshire).

Tony gated neighborhood between Wilshire and Olympic near Hancock Park. Former residents include Muhammad Ali and Karen Black. For tours, call the Home-Owners Association at ☎ 213/ 935-8652.

> **Corner of Hollywood and Western** (Hollywood)

Crossroads for crazies. Charles Bukowski used to go down there and curse at the Bible belters. At the foot of a cavernous earthquake fault, which may explain the weird behavior found there.

> **Harbor Freeway (110)**

In a very close tie with the new 105 Freeway (which gives you an outrageous side view of LAX), the 110 offers an equally compelling vista, which will be of certain interest to the toxic tourist: On the 110 you get a complete panoramic view of the oil wells and refineries of Carson and Torrance (go at night when they glow like industrial casinos). Added bonus: The gangsta-rap proving grounds of Compton and Watts are not too far off the freeway, and at the end of the run is gloriously underrated San Pedro.

> **Lankershim Boulevard.** From Vineland Ave. to Victory Blvd. (North Hollywood).

Cultural vortex of the San Fernando Valley, if you can imagine such a thing. Some highlights: **Iliad bookstore**, 4820 Vineland Ave., at Lankershim (☎ 818/

509-2665); the **Blue Saloon,** 4657 Lankershim (☎ **818/766-4644**), **Circus Liquor,** 6417 Lankershim (☎ **818/985-0307**), and the **Eagles' Coffee Pub,** 5231 Lankershim, at Magnolia (☎ **818/760-4212**). Also in this area are many thrift and vintage-clothing stores along Vineland Avenue and fifties signage along Magnolia Ave.

> **L. Ron Hubbard Way.** At Sunset Blvd. 1 block west of Vermont Ave. (Los Feliz).

How could a leader of a half-baked religion get a street named after himself? Because the official religion of L.A. is Scientology—and because several prominent players in the entertainment industry are church members.

> **Mariachi Corner.** At 1st St. and Boyle (near Downtown).

Itinerant yet fully outfitted mariachi musicians hang out here waiting to get picked up and hired for gigs.

> **Mulholland Drive.** From Cahuenga Blvd. to the 405 (above Hollywood, West Hollywood, Beverly Hills).

The best views, the biggest stars, on the most pastoral roadway in L.A. The best stretch is the dirt-road portion in the Santa Monica Mountains, one of L.A.'s great natural treasures. This part of Mulholland feels the most detached from urban life, with roadside fruit vendors and huge chunks of land free of development. Take the drive with someone you love. Try Sunday morning.

> **Sunset Boulevard ("The Skank").** 7800–7200 blocks of Sunset Blvd., between Fairfax and La Brea (West Hollywood).

The place for prostitution. Despite the crackdown following the Hugh Grant bust, they've resurfaced. $40 for the full Monica.

> **Sunset Strip.** Sunset Blvd. between Doheny and La Cienega in West Hollywood.

Historically speaking, you will not find a more musically rich section of Los Angeles. It ALL went down here, and we mean ALL. Pick an era. The mid-sixties folk-rock explosion? Come to the Strip to check out the Turtles, The Byrds, and the Mamas and the Papas. Late sixties rock? Come to the Whisky-A-Go-Go to hear the Mothers of Invention, the Who, and Led Zeppelin. The seventies? Head over to the Roxy (9009 Sunset Blvd.) to hear Bowie, Springsteen, and Bob Marley and the Wailers. Or head down the way to Rodney Bingenheimer's English Disco (7561 Sunset

Now that we're mostly over our knee-jerk reaction against all things middle class, we can embrace the whole notion of "fun" and "entertainment" without running our Karl-Marx-meets-Herbert-Marcuse trip on everyone. These are L.A.'s top "fun" attractions par excellence. Lots of families and kids. Lots of European tourists. All of them enjoying themselves without a shred of irony. And now you too, like us, having stripped yourself of that late-eighties hyper-ironic stance only now filtering down to ads and TV programming, can, IN EARNEST, YES, EARNEST (remember that?), enjoy this stuff without guilt, without anger, without that smug little smirk you've been wearing most of your adult life. Have fun!!

- **Disneyland,** 1313 Harbor Blvd., at I-5 (Anaheim; ☎ **714/781-4565**). Fun!
- **Queen Mary,** Pier 1, at the end of I-710 (Long Beach; ☎ **562/435-3511**). Large!!
- **Universal City Walk,** Universal Center Dr., at 101 freeway (Universal City; ☎ **818/622-4455**). Commercial!!

Blvd.) to catch Queen, T. Rex, and, later, Blondie and the Ramones. The eighties? Try the glam-rock scene at Gazzarri's (9039 Sunset Blvd., West Hollywood). Just south of the Strip, the Troubadour (9081 Santa Monica Blvd., West Hollywood) was also a favorite sixties and seventies showcase for the likes of Peter, Paul, and Mary, Joni Mitchell, and Neil Young, and in the eighties for the likes of Guns 'N Roses. The eighties L.A. hard-core punk decreased the power of the Strip, as the indie music scene dispersed to venues like Club 88 (11784 Pico, West L.A.), Club Lingerie (6507 Sunset Blvd.), the Elks Lodge (now Park Plaza Hotel, 607 South Parkview), the Hong Kong Cafe (425 Gin Ling Way), Madame Wong's (949 Sun Mun Way), Al's Bar (305 S. Hewitt, at 3rd Street, Downtown), and the beloved Masque (Cherokee and Hollywood Blvd., Hollywood).

But the clubs in and around the Sunset Strip are like venerable Vegas casinos—they don't die, only the crowds and scenes keep changing. Or, according to some locals, *don't* keep changing. While in recent years the Strip has been stereotyped as a pricey haven for hard-rock fans from the Valley, it will, in time, find a reason to resuscitate and redefine itself all over again.

Caveat: While in the area be sure to check out the essential rocker hangouts, including Rocker Denny's, Rocker Ralph's, and the fabled Guitar Center.

Transportation;
or, Planes, Trains, and Auto Dependence

Yes, there are alternatives to the automobile in Los Angeles. Below are some favorites. Then again, until there's a major rethinking of alternative transport in this city, you're going to need a car. Naturally, we've pointed you to places where you can rent one.

Bikes

We're kidding, right? Riding a bike in L.A.? That's like driving a motor home around Manhattan. Precisely. We drove a motor home around Manhattan, and we've driven bikes around L.A. And we're here to tell you something you already know: IT'S NOT SAFE. At the same time, how else is L.A. going to become more humane, less aloof, less money-grubbing, unless courageous residents embrace a far more humble and ultimately more rewarding means of transportation? If you feel called to be among those at the front lines of change, contact **Critical Mass L.A.** at ☎ **213/953-9502.** They will plug you into their monthly rides, where bicyclists attempt to take back the streets from the auto-addicted hordes.

Buses

› MTA

If you insist on seeing greater L.A. by bus, you can contact the Los Angeles County Metropolitan Transit Authority at ☎ **800/COMMUTE** (which will suck you into voice-prompt hell), or simply go out on any major street, wait for a bus, and ask the driver for directions on where you need to go. The MTA bus lines have a reputation for bad service, though they offer an unparalleled snapshot of the sketchy underworld one doesn't get in standard glossy depictions of the city (see "On the Bus").

> **The Santa Monica Municipal Bus Lines (a.k.a. The Big Blue Bus).**
☎ **310/451-5444** (unlike the MTA, they answer your calls directly).
www.bigbluebus.com/bus.

If, however, you find yourself in Santa Monica, you should definitely hop aboard the Santa Monica Municipal Bus Lines. The Big Blue Bus is fast, clean, and reliable, and is often cited as a major reason why the entire West Side wants to secede from the city. Unfortunately, though the Big Blue Bus is calling us, it only has thirteen lines, mostly in Santa Monica and West L.A. It does have one express line to downtown Los Angeles, but it doesn't go to Hollywood, the heart of Beverly Hills, the San Fernando Valley, Universal City, Disneyland, or a whole mess of other destinations that the gargantuan MTA covers.

Incline Railways and Gondolas

> **Angels Flight.** Hill St., between 3rd and 4th sts. (Downtown).
☎ **213/977-1794.**

This might be one of the most charming attractions in all of L.A. A short little incline railway with old-fashioned wooden seats that, for a nominal fee of one

. . . And in the last scene the two leads—we could get Leonardo and Claire Danes—take Angels Flight, and it keeps going—like in *E.T.?*—and they fly away over the city. Fadeout. It's so L.A. . . .

quarter, takes passengers back and forth from the ethnic squalor of Downtown and Broadway to the shining citadels of commerce on Bunker Hill. Built in 1901 by Colonel J. W. Eddy, a lawyer and friend of Abraham Lincoln, Angels Flight is not only "the shortest railway in the world," but has carried more passengers per square mile than any other railroad on the planet.

› **Gondola Getaway.** 5437 E. Ocean Blvd., at 54th Place, Naples Island (Long Beach). ☎ 562/433-9595.

Authentic Venetian gondolas take passengers around the canals of Naples Island.

LAX

Los Angeles International Airport is often taken for granted by visitors to the city. Which is really too bad, since you will undoubtedly spend many days outside the airport searching out extraordinary attractions, when perhaps the most extraordinary attraction is right before you on your arrival and departure. The key to appreciating LAX is to arrive at least 2 hours early and to hang out for at least 2 hours more once you've arrived. Only when you take the time do you have the patience and stillness of mind to experience the walking, strutting L.A. clichés that pass through this complex. For starters, linger by the Platinum Gold top-dog ticket sections at one of the major airlines. You will undoubtedly catch a rising actress or model arriving at the last moment in her chauffeured town car. She will be GUARANTEED to be wearing sunglasses all the way from the car to the ticket line, where she will briefly take them off so that the First Class ticket line madame may indeed recognize her as the Big Star that she is and take appropriate ass-kiss maneuvers. Also rushing throughout the airport could be any number of transvestites, Marina del Rey moms with 5-inch white fingernails and on their fifth face-lift, their Santa Monica daughters in low-cut jeans and low self-esteem, innumerable Pamela Anderson clones, bona fide record-industry guys talking into their cell phones about how such and such "doesn't know anything about the business," *countless* prima donna big-star wanna-bes who are flying coach and taking it out on everybody, and the normal ragtag assortment of tourists from all over the world. It's a nightmare. It's colorful. It's positively insane. And that's just inside. The real thrills are outside—the groovy retro former control tower (now home to the neo-Jetson's Encounter Restaurant and Bar) and the long-term parking lots, where frighteningly loud jumbo jets fly extremely close to the ground (try Lot C). LAX may not be as architecturally astounding as Denver's International Airport or Chicago's O'Hare, or as refreshingly retro groovy as the Burbank Airport, but for a rare glimpse of thousands of Angelenos outside the protective wombs of their automobiles, it is the best scene in town.

Metro Rail

At this point it's more like a clean underused museum than a viable means of mass transit, but it's a big step in the right direction. Only two problems: (1) the trains keep running over people, and (2) the city is about to severely curtail Metro Rail funding. We understand the argument that money might be better spent on light rail and buses, but, if there's ever going to be an end-run around L.A.'s street-level transportation madness, certainly a subway system must play a role.

Rental-Car Agencies

You don't NEED a car in L.A. You can get by without one. In fact, you will unquestionably taste the true character of life in this town—its multiethnic funk, its surprising goodness, its desperation—if you forgo an automobile. Walking is by far the best option for tasting L.A. at ground zero. You won't believe the little finds you discover. You also won't get very far. If you eventually decide on public transit, you will need to keep in mind two undeniable facts: (1) for short distances of less than a mile, you're better off walking; and (2) for long distances, it'll take triple the time it would take by automobile.

Still, if you decide to take public transit, you should feel proud. In fact, you should feel a little self-righteous for confounding the prevailing car culture.

We think everyone who moves to L.A. should be required, by law, to walk and take public transit for the first month. We did. In fact, once every two years, Angelenos should voluntarily go on an automobile fast for a weekend. It would clue people in to just what automobiles and highways have done to destroy the subtle fabric of community here, and what little treasures await them if they just use their two feet.

For the visitor, we recommend the same experiment, even just for a day. Of course, after the experiment is over, you will want a car. And if you haven't brought one in yourself (hopefully not an SUV!!), you will want to rent. Compared to New York City and San Francisco, L.A. is a rental-car paradise. Here are our top recommendations.

> **Beverly Hills Rent-a-Car.** 9220 S. Sepulveda Blvd., at Lincoln, next to LAX (Los Angeles). ☎ 310/337-1400.

As one would expect, this rental-car agency is not geared towards the budget-minded Monk traveler. Rather, it's for the Monk traveler who has just signed a major movie contract to play a crack-addicted debate coach. Around $2,800 a day for the Bentley Azure. For a step down, $1,200 for the Ferrari 355 Spyder, and a mere $650 a day for a Porsche convertible.

The L.A. Problem

". . . lacking any sort of locus or geographic cohesion, our non-city forces its residents to suffer a freakish daily existence devoid of human contact."
—Brian Baltin, November 27–December 3, 1998 *LA Weekly*

As much as we like L.A. and believe strongly in its potential, we are also realistic about the sickness at its core. Because of our immediate awareness of this L.A. disease, we found ourselves holding back here, not wanting to drive the 30 minutes to see that funky bar on Hollywood or that friend over in Silver Lake, not to mention the 90-minute round trip to see that art exhibit all the way over in Long Beach. Like a hesitant lover, we just didn't want to give in to the L.A. M.O. Because if we did, then we would be "enabling" the city in its disease, and be guilty ourselves by association.

The L.A. problem is its love affair with the automobile. And whatever resistance we have to this city stems in no small part from our innocent belief that there is something wrong about a place where you literally have to drive *everywhere,* a place that's so spread out, a place that has so little street life, a place where folks are rarely forced to commingle with each other free of their automobile defenses, a place where the average actor, director, producer, gardener, clerk, agent, writer, chef, musician feels absolutely no pang of social conscience that there is something wrong with this picture. Where publications like *Los Angeles Magazine* are quite happy to go on at length about pricey Bentleys, Malibu mansions, and cocaine's renewed celebrity cache as if that validates L.A.'s historic role as home of the grotesquely decadent dilettante who has no conscience of the commonweal, and no need to worry about it.

The automobile assumption, which is at the root of the city's self-centered indifference and the lack of an active citywide debate on how to change it, is what troubles us about this town. The automobile assumption is the indirect cause of all the social evils here, from crime to alienation to pollution to congestion to the lack of a central core (of values, not just locale). One has to seriously question whether one wants to open up to a city that not only blithely feeds the automobile addiction, but attaches so much importance to the precise automobile one does drive. It seems like a very simple point. But the more one thinks about it, the more one realizes that L.A. can never become a Monk town, can never get close to the depth and aliveness of cities like New York, or even Portland, unless this issue is tackled in a very direct way. And, for that to happen, the city's journalists, style writers, and politicians need to quit tracking the inane clueless lives of the rich, famous, and lipo-sucked and get down to the far more serious task of revolutionizing the way Los Angelenos move about their city.

> **Budget Rent-a-Car of Beverly Hills.** 9815 Wilshire Blvd., at Santa Monica (Beverly Hills). ☎ 310/274-9173.

Contrary to what its name implies, this place rents out expensive automobiles in addition to the requisite Ford Escorts, Nissan Sentras, and Toyota Tercels. Tired of renting Chevy Cavaliers? Try Budget BH's Ferrari F-1 355 Spyder at a mere $1,400 bucks a day.

> **Cash Car Rent.** 1600 N. La Brea Ave., at Hawthorne (Hollywood). ☎ 323/464-4147.

In the wheeling dealing world of discount car rentals this is service with a smile. Cash deposits accepted, $150 for the week, and up to 1,500 miles. They pick you up, give you a back rub, whatever it takes to get you out the door in one of their run-of-the-mill Ford Escorts.

> **Enterprise Rent-A-Car.** 4550 Beverly Blvd., at Oxford (Koreatown). ☎ 323/962-5200.

Yes, there is one other reason to visit Koreatown and it's to grab a Cavalier from these folks and get the hell out of town. We list them only because they've bent a few rules to get us what we needed in a short amount of time. They pick you up, drop you off, and speak at least four different languages. $159 a week. Cash deposits accepted.

> **Quick Rent A Car.** 3900 Firestone Blvd., at San Juan St. (South Gate). ☎ 323/564-8650.

If you can get your butt all the way down past Anaheim then this is one of the best deals in L.A. Ford Aspires for $19.95 a day, cheap in and out. No frills. Cash deposits.

Trains

> **Union Station.** 800 N. Alameda, at Cesar Chavez Blvd. (Downtown). ☎ 800/872-7245 (Amtrak reservations).

This is possibly the most romantic, attractive, and lavishly furnished train depot in the entire West. The place simply exudes 1930s nostalgia. It'll cost you a lot more than road or plane transit to take the Sunset Limited from "N'awlins," the San Diegan to San Diego, or the Coast Starlight to Seattle, but it is worth it for the thrill of landing and leaving this pivotal L.A. landmark.

Views

> **The Bonnaventure Hotel Elevators.** 404 S. Figueroa St., at 4th St. (Downtown).

This is L.A.'s version of the Detroit Renaissance Center, but on a much smaller scale. The highlight is a series of cylindrical glass elevators that take one from ground-zero Bunker Hill through the roof and thirty-five floors up to the rotating Bona Vista lounge on top. The first-time rush is a major thrill, and the views on top are as good as any in town.

> **Bronson Park.** At the end of Bronson Ave. north of Franklin Ave. (Hollywood).

There is one salient reason to visit this Hollywood ravine that cuts up through the wilds of Griffith Park: It leads straight to the Hollywood sign, with tremendous views along the way (see also "Parks and Nature").

> **City on a Hill.** Elysian Park, near Dodger Stadium; follow Stadium Way toward the stadium, turn left just before the parking lot, and climb up the hill (Downtown).

Commanding an impressive 360° vista, with downtown L.A., the Hollywood sign, and the ocean all within sight (see also "Sculpture").

> **4th Street Bridge.** 4th St., at Mission (East Los Angeles).

The L.A. River rolls underneath, Hispanic graffiti is all over the aqueduct's walls, and, below, nothing but railroad tracks and railroad yards. The Dragnet Building comes into view along with a sweeping panorama of downtown L.A. (see also "Buildings, Bridges, and Other Visual Landmarks").

> **Griffith Park Observatory.** 1800 E. Observatory Rd. (above Los Feliz).

On a clear day you can see for miles and miles. As crowded as the place gets, it's still one of our favorite stops to get a big perspective on L.A. Nighttime is best, though you will have to elude necking Hispanic teens and busloads of tourists to gain any solitude (see also "Parks and Nature").

> **Highway 105 heading West of 110.** El Segundo.

The highlight of L.A.'s newest freeway is the side views of LAX as you approach the beach. Something about the angle gives you this incredible vantage point on the entire airport, with close-ups of the runway, jumbo jets, and the background mountains all in one panoramic sweep.

› Laurel Canyon Park. Mulholland and Laurel Canyon Blvd. (above West Hollywood).

Totally sweet and idyllic, with great views of the city (see also "Parks and Nature").

› Mulholland Drive. From Cahuenga Blvd. to the 405 (above Hollywood, West Hollywood, Beverly Hills).

Primo views on the most pastoral roadway in L.A. The best stretch is the dirt-road portion in the Santa Monica Mountains, one of L.A.'s great natural treasures (see also "Streets, Corners, and Highways").

› Santa Monica Pier. Colorado St., at PCH (Santa Monica).

Great ocean and sweeping city view, especially from on top of the Ferris wheel (see also "Buildings, Bridges, and Other Visual Landmarks").

› Skybar and Grill. In the Mondrian Hotel, 8440 Sunset Blvd., at La Cienega (West Hollywood). ☎ **213/650-8999.** (See Bars.)

› 360 Penthouse. 6290 Sunset Blvd., at Vine (Hollywood). ☎ **213/871-2995.**

The chief drawing card continues to be The View. The astonishing, unobstructed panorama gives you the perfect opportunity to get thoroughly sloshed while absorbing the aesthetic pleasures of another orange-brown L.A. sunset (see also "Bars").

Back on the Road

(with Jerry Maguire)

A tall woman sits on the pavement next to the on-ramp of Interstate 10. A haphazardly rolled sleeping bag, assorted luggage, a green nylon shoulder bag, a cage for two kittens, a litter box, and a couple of small boxes rest at her side. She is wearing tight blue jeans, a jean jacket, and a hat, which has an attached black veil that covers her face. She is also wearing dirty, scuffed, high-heeled granny shoes—not really vintage, just strangely out of style. She has ratty blonde hair which tumbles down her neck. Her fingers are long and bony, with manicured nails painted pink.

Inside the nearby gas station the Monk has just finished pumping gas and returns to his red Subaru. As he turns toward the on-ramp, waiting in traffic, he notices the woman sticking out a rather large thumb.

"This gal has way too many bags for hitchhiking! That's weird. Must be a wacko."

She had that wacko look. The veil over the face said it all.

The Monk slows to a stop.

"Where you going?"

"I need a ride to the Tuna Bowl. It's about 16 miles up the road," she says with a strange, somewhat Southern, little-girl voice. It is resigned, yet heartbreakingly sweet.

"I can take you downtown. That's as far as I'm going."

"Oh, no, I don't want to get off there," she says, followed by a soft disconnected smile.

The Monk is back on the freeway without her. He drives debating the wisdom of his move. Two sides are doing battle. *Why didn't you take her. What's 16 miles?* The battle rages on past each subsequent exit. *You could use a little diversion. You've gotten so predictable.* He gets off at Arlington, pauses, then turns around. He is going back to get her, all the while debating whether it's a good thing. *I can't believe I am doing this. I have to get back to work. I am not going to do this. I am getting off at the next exit.* He almost aborts several times. But something deep inside, a curiosity perhaps, a flirt with danger, keeps The Monk driving all the way back to Overland Street.

She won't be there. Some dude will have picked her up.

He drives across the overpass and can't see her. There is a sense of simultaneous relief and disappointment. Then, as the Subaru creeps further along, there she is.

Still sitting by the side of the road, her long legs positioned like a ranch hand, knees near the chest, spread eagle.

"I came back to pick you up. I didn't the first time because I thought it was strange for a woman to be hitchhiking. I thought you might kill me. And, frankly, this would be a very bad day for that. You're not carrying a gun, are you?"

"Oh, noooo." Her voice is sweet and coquettish. Not a modern L.A. gal's way of speaking at all.

"Here, let's put your bags in the trunk." The Monk picks up each bag, sussing out whether there is anything lethal inside. As he loads in the last of the luggage, a shoe box, she says it holds a pair of "Tom Cruise's slippers."

"Tom Cruise's slippers?"

"Yesss," she says with a smile.

In the car, she clutches her little white purse, about 10 years out of style. The Monk is wary of what might be inside the purse.

"You don't have a knife in there, do you?"

"Oh no . . ." she says softly.

Within minutes after hitting the freeway she is volunteering her life story. "My husband lives here. I'm going to see my boyfriend in North Carolina. My husband is okay."

"You mean you have a husband here and a boyfriend in North Carolina?"

"Yes, and he's running for president."

The Monk knows something is wrong here. She sits upright, one long leg crossed over the other. Her teeth are slightly bucked in that erotic way some women have. Her face is powdered white. She is bony, but beautiful. After a few minutes on the freeway she begins to rapidly free-associate. She is wired and can't slow down.

"I don't smoke pot because I don't like to be happy without a reason." The Monk, not one to partake himself, was relieved.

And then: "Are you Mr. Goodbar or Dr. Kildair?" The lovely spaced out Libran wanted to make sure she and her kitties were in safe hands.

The Monk can only catch fragments of other stories and conspiracy theories.

"I am Jerry Maguire," she blurts out.

Since she was clutching on a magazine article about Tom Cruise when picked up, this kind of made sense.

There is some other recurring rant about David Lee Roth, and a knife-wielding woman who wanted to kill her, and that she wants to head to Playgirls in Florida, and some other plan to be a stripper in Greensboro.

"Where are you from?"

"Texas."

The Monk drives down the freeway, heading east, debating inside what to do, still wary, still worrying that things might suddenly turn dangerous. Aware that with this woman, practically anything seems possible.

He decides to get off at Arlington, thinking, *I have to get this woman out of here.* As he makes a turn she says, "I'd like to kiss your butt."

"WHAT?"

"I'd like to kiss your butt."

He looks over as she unblinkingly stares through her veil.

"Are you sure?"

She nods.

The Monk takes a silent inventory and decides, *Hell, why not?* "Let's go somewhere a little more private."

"Oh, goodie. Where are we going?" She coos with girlish delight. "To jail?"

"No, we're going to go to a quiet, safe hotel."

"I like hotels."

The Monk takes her long and bony hand. She gives a slight squeeze to his fingers, but it isn't a firm, loving grasp. It is the thin grasp of someone completely tweaked inside. She stares straight ahead with a wide-eyed, slightly goofy look on her face, like a young girl's face when she's first fallen in love.

"I am a nun. We are the free holies. We will always love each other."

There's a pause, the Monk and Jerry Maguire holding hands. Minutes pass. Up near Wilshire, her smile now growing larger, Jerry Maguire suddenly blurts out invitingly, "Are you a passionate stranger?"

"Yes," says the Monk reluctantly, still torn between hesitation and his desire to jump into her game.

"We are passionate strangers, and we have always loved each other," she coos invitingly through lovable buck teeth.

"Who are you?"

"I am Jerry Maguire. And you are my beautiful lover," the smile still on her face. Moments pass, and then, "It's okay to seek pleasure. You need to learn self-gratification."

This was rather close to the bone. Where was she pulling this information from?

"I am a Monk."

"I am a nun. We are the free holies." She giggles. "We have a beautiful connection. It's so lovely and warm and beautiful. We will always love each other."

"How long have we known each other?" the Monk asks.

"We've known each other for many lifetimes, and we will know each other for many more. Always so beautiful and light and loving."

There is another pause, the Monk and Jerry Maguire just holding hands. Minutes pass. The red Subaru eventually pulls up a street and parks in the back of the hotel.

"I need my shampoo. And my kitties. I always go with my kitties."

Inside she intuitively heads straight to the bedroom, not even bothering to recognize the other Monk sitting there studying a map.

"She's crazy, but she's not dangerous. I'll tell you more later."

Back in the bedroom the Monk begins to nervously chat, asking more things about her life.

"Where are you going again?"

"To North Carolina to see my boyfriend. He's the president of the United States."

"I thought Bill Clinton was the president of the United States."

"No, that was staged. My boyfriend is the president of the United States. Can I kiss your butt now?"

She undresses quickly and crisply. She is a marvel. Leggy, clean, very pretty. With no foreplay, she goes right to work kissing that round Monk butt. There is no slow buildup in the Jerry Maguire universe. It is fast and mechanical.

"Here, let's slow down a bit."

"But I want to win the Best Butt Kisser Award," she girlishly replies.

She continues for another 10 minutes of what amounts to frenetic butt pecking, and then Jerry and the Monk turn face to face. She wants to let her kitties out of their cage.

"They like to watch," she says.

As she lets the kitties out, the Monk looks her over more carefully.

Her eyelids are painted green. Her cheeks are rosy. She's overdone her makeup.

Suddenly she's back to the job at hand. In between kissing she suddenly drifts into elaborate pontificating. At times, it is random. At other times, it is like she can read the Monk's mind.

"Every time I come back to Earth, my mind is up in the air."

"The mind forgets, but the body remembers."

"This is not a prostitute thing."

And then, "You are Logic. You must give me your number so that I can call up Logic and tell him I love him."

Logic wasn't about to give his number.

Suddenly she is up to take a long shower.

After she is dressed, she enters the bedroom and turns abruptly cold. She looks sad, like a dog whose owner had just died. The Monk talks to her, but she won't respond. She puts her face in a pillow and lays there motionless for 20 minutes.

The Monk decides it's time to leave.

>>>•<<<

The 16-mile drive to the Tuna Bowl, where Jerry Maguire is going to hitch a ride among the truckers, is just as eventful as all the moments before. Jerry Maguire cannot stop. They talk about her cats.

"I thought your cats' names were Black and Pinkerton," the Monk says in the car, as they head east on Interstate 10.

"They have lucky days. . . . Today is their lucky day so they are the Thompson Twins."

The Monk and Jerry finally arrive at the Tuna Bowl, a large Union 76 truck stop on the outskirts of Ontario. She is very alert and very adamant about what she wants to do. She can't be let off just anywhere. She might be spotted. She is let off in an open space between two trucks. She and her seven different pieces of small luggage are laid out neatly on the ground. After several good-byes she opines, "You pray for my safe journey; I'll pray for your salvation." It seems like the perfectly right thing to say.

As he drives away, the Monk realizes how deeply she has touched him. Jerry Maguire said some things that would always stay with him. She healed some wounds, transformed a few obsessions, and made a few worries disappear. The memory of her sweetness helped clean away the hurt of so many women who haven't been available, who refused to be "passionate strangers." He knows, too, he will never see her again. She will latch onto a trucker and make him feel like it's the very first time, like she loves no one but him, and that they have loved each other forever. Which will, of course, be true.

The Monk drives west on the freeway, remembering what Jerry Maguire said when they were first driving toward the hotel: "Did you like the beginning, middle, or end of the conversation?"

"Jerry," says the Monk aloud, "I loved it all!"

›san diego

When you first drive through San Diego, "America's 7th Most Kickass City," it appears to be the land of boring sun-bleached white people. Home of the sort of women one literally finds on old Beach Boys covers. And men who worship Junior Seau. A town completely apolitical, out of touch with social context and historical precedent. With millions in search of "the good life." In other words, another Orlando. Brewsky, please.

Compared to "Smog Angeles," the star-rich, riot-plagued megalopolis to the north, in whose shadow it will always remain, "S.D." feels safe, clean, Methodist. A city of endless suburbs. A city without edge, anger, or attitude (excluding Ryan Leaf, who fits San Diego about as well as Courtney Love fits Sisters of the Poor), without the urgency and unbridled careerism found elsewhere in the Bear Republic. Indeed, it seems to be as much a place for *relatives* of famous people (Philip Camberg, brother of Dame Muriel Spark, and Croce's Jazz Bar owner Ingrid Croce, widow of the late singer-songwriter Jim Croce and mom to rising music star A. J. Croce, come to mind). As *San Diego Union Tribune* reporter Jim Hebert explains, "Most people here have relinquished some part of their ambition and traded it in for quality of life. San Diego's the kind of place you can only make so much of an impact nationally. The town will never lend itself to launching major cultural movements. It reveals its charms slowly, but it's more interesting than given credit." In other words, let's drop the right-wing Republican rap, alright?

Over time you learn that San Diego's middle-of-the-road sensibility has a root, a context. The years of naval presence lent a square by-the-book conventionality to this sunny, mild-mannered metropolis. Case in point: native son and former California governor Pete Wilson. But underneath its Philistine facade, San Diego has always nurtured the weird and extreme, which bubble up continually in the form of cults, massacres, offbeat collections, outrageous personalities, and more.

For instance, the common stereotype is that L.A. and San Francisco are the home of wacko spiritual movements. But lifelong Californians know that San Diego has always been where fringe fanaticism flourishes. At the height of the New Age, believers here were always more fervent, and less given to irony and self-criticism. In addition, San Diego has provided fertile ground for ascension cults like Heaven's Gate and the Unarius Academy, wiggy channeling groups like Teachings of the Inner Christ, and more benign (though still colorful) communities like the Circle of Friends. It's also no surprise that Y2K survivalist groups and UFO societies flourish here as well.

And the city definitely has seen its share of individual characters, including lounge singer José Sinatra; Mojo Nixon (singer-songwriter of such classics as "Debbie Gibson is Pregnant with My Two-Headed Love Child"); the eccentric Loch David Crane of Ocean Beach, who's run for mayor several times, and is known for his Star Trike, a chopper-style motorcycle outfitted to look like the *Starship*

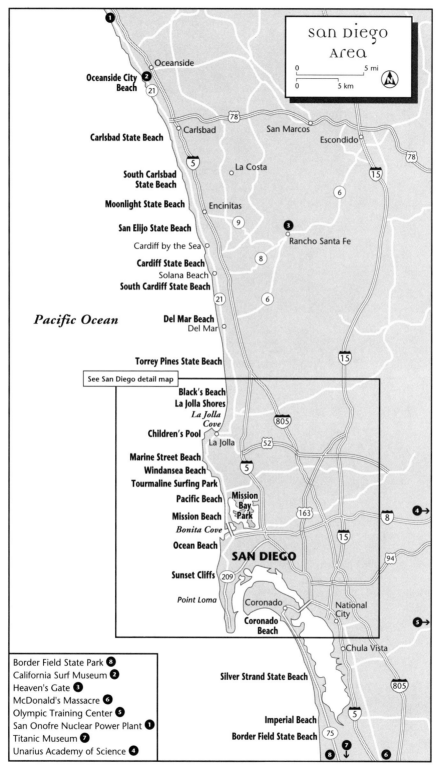

san Diego
Area

0   5 mi
0   5 km

1

Oceanside

**Oceanside City
Beach** 2

21

78

Carlsbad

San Marcos

Escondido

Carlsbad State Beach

5

La Costa

15

78

**South Carlsbad
State Beach**

6

Moonlight State Beach

Encinitas

San Elijo State Beach

9

3

Rancho Santa Fe

Cardiff by the Sea

Cardiff State Beach

8

Solana Beach

South Cardiff State Beach

21

6

Pacific Ocean

Del Mar Beach

Del Mar

15

Torrey Pines State Beach

See San Diego detail map

Black's Beach

La Jolla Shores

*La Jolla
Cove*

805

Children's Pool

La Jolla

52

Marine Street Beach

5

Windansea Beach

Tourmaline Surfing Park

Pacific Beach

**Mission
Bay
Park**

163

Mission Beach

Bonita Cove

Ocean Beach

SAN DIEGO

15

8

4

Sunset Cliffs

209

Point Loma

Coronado

National
City

94

**Coronado
Beach**

5

Chula Vista

Border Field State Park 8

California Surf Museum 2

Heaven's Gate 3

Silver Strand State Beach

805

McDonald's Massacre 6

Olympic Training Center 5

San Onofre Nuclear Power Plant 1

Imperial Beach

Titanic Museum 7

Border Field State Beach

75

Unarius Academy of Science 4

8

7

6

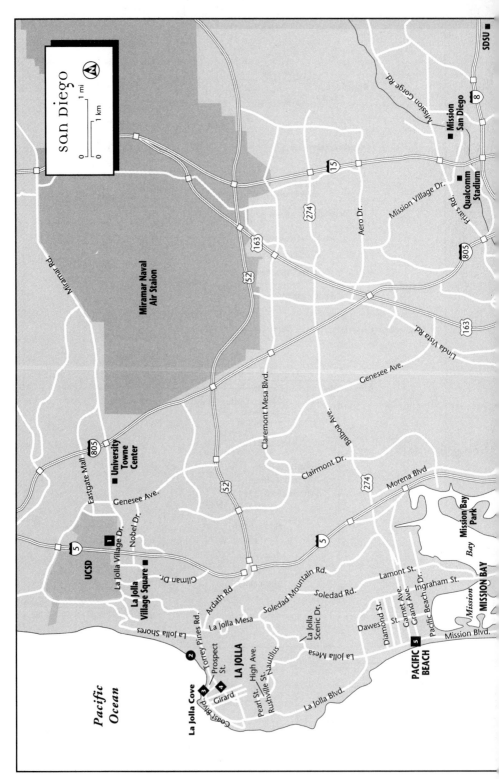

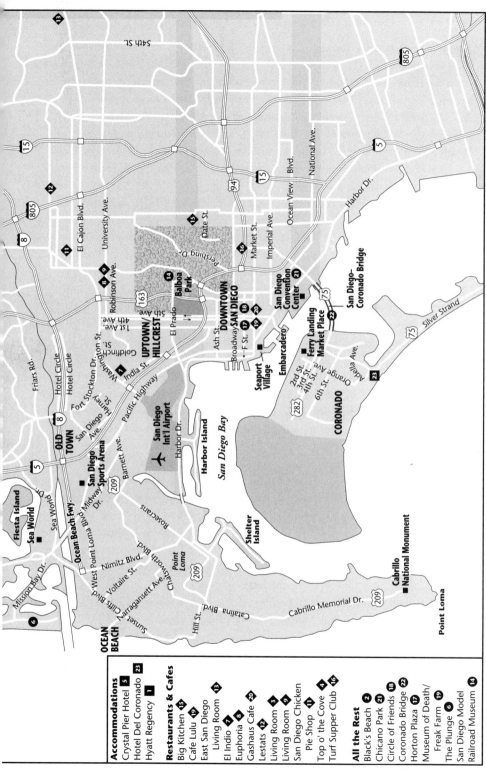

Accommodations
Crystal Pier Hotel **5**
Hotel Del Coronado **23**
Hyatt Regency **1**

Restaurants & Cafes
Big Kitchen **15**
Cafe Lulu **12**
East San Diego
  Living Room **13**
El Indio **7**
Euphoria **8**
Gashaus Cafe **20**
Lestats **12**
Living Room **3**
Living Room **9**
San Diego Chicken
  Pie Shop **11**
Top o' the Cove **4**
Turf Supper Club **16**

All the Rest
Black's Beach **2**
Chicano Park **21**
Circle of Friends **18**
Coronado Bridge **22**
Horton Plaza **17**
Museum of Death/
  Freak Farm **19**
The Plunge **6**
San Diego Model
  Railroad Museum **14**

San Diego   **211**

Enterprise; and Candye Kane, the bodacious and buxom porn star turned swing band sensation.

In the arena of collections, social-science teacher Jim Fletcher has the largest collection of presidential items west of the Mississippi, including a tremendous collection of Nixon memorabilia, at his **Museum of the American Presidency** (see by appointment by calling ☎ **619/270-0694**). J. D. Healy's outrageous **Museum of Death** is unlike anything else in the country. And the world-famous **San Diego Zoo** has some of the freakiest animals you'll see outside of San Diego's **Freak Farm**—how does an albino koala bear grab you?

In the 3COM tradition of sterile companies renaming beloved ballparks, San Diego high-tech firm Qualcomm Corporation, makers of the indispensable Eudora Pro E-mail software, paid millions to have San Diego's Jack Murphy Stadium— home of the Bolts and their inimitable mascot, "The Chicken," and the Pads and their inimitable announcer Jerry "I've Never Met a Malapropism I Didn't Like" Coleman—expanded and upgraded, with its name changed to Qualcomm Stadium, though San Diegans display their hidden contrarianism by continually renaming the stadium as they see fit. Qualcomm Stadium quickly evolved into "The Qualiseum," then into "The Q," and is currently known as "The Edifice Formerly Known as Jack Murphy Stadium" (a.k.a. "The Murph").

In terms of personalities, I'll bet you didn't know that Frank Zappa went to San Diego's Mission Bay High School, or that Denver Broncos running back Terrell Davis went to Lincoln High School, or that serial killer and Rancho Bernardo native Andrew Cunanan went to Bishop's High—though you probably do remember he spent significant time in Hillcrest, San Diego's tamer version of San Francisco's Castro. Then there's Brenda Spencer. In 1979, the 16-year-old San Diegan unwittingly launched a two-decade trend of school-yard shootings when she opened fire at the Cleveland Elementary School, killing Principal Burton Wragg and a janitor, both of whom were trying to shield the children from bullets. When asked why she did it, Brenda replied with the immortal line, "I don't like Mondays," which became the title of the Boomtown Rats' smash hit.

But the San Diego area isn't just home to murderers and freaks. After all, Dr. Seuss (a.k.a. Theodor Geisel) spent the latter part of his life in La Jolla (his wife Audrey still lives there). And inside trading pioneer Ivan "the Terrible" Boesky lived for many years on La Jolla's Mount Soledad (also rumored home of a midget colony). And Bob Crane, star of "Hogan's Heroes" and a predator in his own right, lived in La Jolla. Hogan's Beach, just north of Pacific Beach Point, might be named after him. And Sam Warren, head of the John Birch Society, hails from San Diego, as does Raquel Tejada (a.k.a. Raquel Welch), a one-time San Diego beauty queen, and Marion Ross, who played Mrs. Cunningham on "Happy Days," and Ly Le Hayslip, author of *When Heaven and Earth Changed Places: A Vietnamese Woman's*

Journey from War to Peace, which was made into the Oliver Stone film *Heaven and Earth*. And don't forget intellectual superstars like renowned cyber-sleuth Tsutomu Shimomura (of the UCSD Supercomputer Center), who achieved what no FBI agent could when he nailed rogue hacker Kevin Mitnick. Shimomura's book, *Takedown: The Pursuit and Capture of Kevin Mitnick, America's Most Wanted Computer Outlaw—By the Man Who Did It,* co-written with *New York Times* cyber-columnist John Markoff, describes it all in somewhat one-sided detail. And don't forget Bram Dijkstra, the wide-ranging Del Martian scholar, Georgia O'Keeffe expert, and author of several intriguing works, including *Evil Sisters: The Threat of Female Sexuality and the Cult of Manhood,* and Bram's wife Sandra Dijkstra, widely regarded as one of the most powerful literary agents on the West Coast. She represents Amy Tan and victim culture heroine Susan Faludi. And last, but certainly not least, Matt McMullen, of Abyss Creations in nearby San Marcos, creator of the $5,000 "Real Doll."

Finally, there's the San Diego music pantheon—bands like Drive like Jehu, indie scenester John Reese of the band Rocket from the Crypt, **Cargo Records** (for a real thrill, listen to the recorded voice prompts of their whacked male receptionist— ☎ **619/483-9292**), Mike Halloran, alt-folkie Cindy Lee Berryhill (catch her at Joseph Tabler Books in Hillcrest by day, performing around town by night), the encyclopedic Curtis Casella of **Taang! Records** on Mission Beach (706 Pismo Court, ☎ **619/488-5950**), and, naturally, coffeehouse queen Jewel.

So, you see, this sleepy naval town is not at all what it seems—just ask the residents of Rancho Santa Fe. Of course, with maturity and development has come a host of urban problems—smog, traffic congestion, sprawl—that has made sweet San Diego increasingly similar to its hard-core sister to the north. Still, San Diego remains a city of surprising excellence, history, and beauty. It is also more complex, more varied than its vaunted beach culture might lead one to believe.

Welcome to the Big Avocado, the home of the fish taco, the 1998 X Games, the first Spanish settlement in California, and the finest surfing on the coast.

DUUUUUUDE!

Accommodations

> **Crystal Pier Hotel.** 4500 Ocean Blvd., at Garnet Ave. (Pacific Beach). ☎ **619/483-6983.**

There is something eerily impressive about a hotel built upon a pier that has survived since the thirties exposed to 7 decades of corrosive salt air. Like, what if an earthquake, big wave, or misguided boat just happened to shake the pillars loose while you're in deep REM? And what about the mold? Apparently that question hasn't crossed the minds of those who've made the Crystal Pier Hotel their favorite lodging while visiting adjacent Mission Beach. Comprised of twenty old funky cottages and six newer models, this place has the style, look, and feel of those low-budget, white-trash motels you find lining man-made lakes throughout the South. But the novelty here is a chance to sleep above the pounding surf. And pound it does. It's your call whether the rhythmic crash of waves soothes you to sleep or locks you into an insomniac's nightmare. Over the years this place has run the gamut from sixties speed-freak haven to its current stab at respectability, featuring private decks and kitchenettes. Boogie boards, surfboards, and rental bikes are only a credit card away.

> **Hotel Del Coronado.** 1500 Orange Ave., at Dana Place (Coronado).
☎ **619/435-6611.**

The largest and oldest wooden structure in the United States, the "Del" is known primarily as the setting for the Billy Wilder film *Some Like It Hot,* starring Marilyn Monroe, Tony Curtis, and Jack Lemmon. Its most celebrated guest was King Edward VIII, who abdicated the English throne for the woman he loved, the twice-married Wallis Warfield Spencer—the very Wallis Spencer who was the Coronado-based wife of the commanding officer of the nearby North Island Naval Air Station when Edward made a pit stop at the Del in April 1920. It's a titillating celebrity factoid, one of many associated with this aging beauty.

In layout and decor, the Del is a cross between the ornate splendor of New York's Waldorf and the summer vacation ambiance of the Grand Hotel on Michigan's Upper Peninsula, though it is no longer considered the best hotel in San Diego. Years ago it gave up attracting a clientele worthy of its pedigree and settled for tacky tourists in shorts and perms and gold-chained Midwestern Chevrolet dealers in for a convention. A series of seven owners, a few of whom either stripped the Del of vital Victoriana or added inappropriate modern details, hasn't helped the old girl either. And yet, despite such architectural abuse, despite its obvious concession to the hoi polloi, the Del will wow you. The fantastic conical spires are said to have inspired author Frank Baum's vision of the Emerald City. The 33-foot wooden ceiling of the Crown Room, where many luminaries have dined, will leave you gasping in awe. And the white wood, red-roofed exterior of this gingerbread landmark reminds one of some of England's finest seaside resorts. In the right light it seems to come from a time of parasols, horses and buggies, and polo matches. We recommend a visit during Christmas, when the hotel is completely lit. But on any night you can still feel the magic. Just stroll along the long white Coronado beach, out of sight of parents and kids, and gaze back at one of those brightly lit spires, which are like lighthouses carrying the torch from when Coronado Island was a remote, pristine destination for would-be kings and queens.

> **The Hyatt Regency.** 3777 La Jolla Village Dr., just east of Interstate 5 (La Jolla). ☎ 619/552-1234.

Think of a giant mantle clock, with calming PoMo overtones, and you have University City's Hyatt. Though some think its expansive Romanesque lobby feels like a corporate mausoleum, for us this trademark Michael Graves design has a heart-thrilling grandiosity that lifts your head about 10 feet off the ground. The place is handsomely masculine, with a breezy entrance, sweeping halls, muted earthen tones, and—in keeping with the corporate neoclassical theme—a few headless statues. There are some cookie-cutter elements here, especially when you see your deep cherry, oak-wood furnished, vertical-striped room. But when it comes to cleanliness and crispness we'll take cookie cutter any day, especially when the cutter is so finely made. If you're feeling déjà vu while circling the hotel's perimeter, it's because you've seen a similar design by Graves at Disney World's Dolphin and Swan. But where Disney runs their hotels with a rote sugary smile, the demeanor at this slick Hyatt property is straight out of *Gattaca*. Though considered La Jolla (or, rather, Aventine), this freeway-exit neighborhood revolves around the flagship Scripps Hospital, with a dramatically surreal white Mormon Temple nearby and other mushrooming office parks—so if you're looking for local color, this isn't it. But if you're headed north from a three-day binge in Tijuana and just can't make another mile, this is your exit. With an Olympic-size swimming pool, state-of-the-art spa, and carefully articulated design, the Regency will make you feel like you've returned to civilization.

Addresses

> **Heaven's Gate.** Formerly 18241 Via Colina Norte, currently somewhere on Paseo Victoria, though it's best to look in an old *Thomas Guide* for the coordinates, since the street name has been changed several times (Rancho Santa Fe).

If it could happen here, it could happen anywhere. The community of Rancho Santa Fe is a sprawling, semirural urban refuge, several miles off the beach in north San Diego County. It's not a place one would customarily associate with cults. Yet, now, along with its assortment of boring millionaires, Rancho Santa Fe is known throughout the world as the place where 39 members of a group called Heaven's

Gate left their earthly vehicles and rode that Hale-Bopp comet to their spaceship in the sky.

The accoutrements associated with their bizarre departure are now part of San Diego folklore—the purple veils, the plastic bags, the Skyy Vodka, the Nike Air Ascenders, the Phenobarbital and apple sauce. The address of their last earthly abode keeps changing, due to attempts to keep the likes of us away. We acknowledged the neighbor's need for privacy and never actually paid a visit to the 13-room, $1.3 million mansion where Marshall "Bo" Applewhite (his partner Bonnie "Peep" Nettles died of cancer in 1985) and his fellow cyber phreaks committed ritual suicide, but we recognize that some of you will not be so guilt-ridden, so look in your *Thomas Guide* for 18241 Via Colina Norte. It will direct you to the right spot, even if the street's name is now changed.

Urban legend: A day after the Heaven's Gate tragedy, the *San Diego Union Tribune* quoted a Rancho Santa Fe local who said, "Well, I understand they were only renters."

Factoid: After the suicides, potential buyers had to pay a $250 viewing fee (proceeds were donated to charity). The eventual buyers recently hosted a "Heaven's Gate Halloween Party" for their 16-year-old child and Torrey Pines High School friends. The fee was $5 a head for the invited, $15 a head for the uninvited. Four hundred teenagers showed up, along with several sheriff's deputies, who broke up the festivities. Many parents were upset at the choice of party venue, though the party-givers did show a sliver of sensitivity: On the invitation, which featured a drawing of an alien figure, was this admonition: "Be respectful to the house, THOSE WEARING PURPLE CLOAKS WILL NOT BE ALLOWED INTO THE PARTY!"

> **McDonald's Massacre.** 522 W. San Ysidro Blvd., near Dairy Mart Rd. (San Ysidro).

James Oliver Huberty was having a very, very bad day when on July 18, 1984, at 4:30pm, the 41-year-old Ohio native randomly opened fire on dozens of Big Mac lovers. The first victims were two young boys running for their bikes. Minutes later, 21 people lay dead from Huberty's Uzi semiautomatic. The 22nd victim was Huberty himself, killed by a single police bullet. It was the worst single-day mass slaying in U.S. history. Not long after the slaying, the McDonald's was bulldozed and deeded to the city of San Diego with the stipulation that no other restaurant could ever be built there again.

Factoid: The McDonald's chain was founded by former San Diego Padres owner Ray Kroc.

Arts and Sciences

› Circle of Friends. 624 Broadway St., at 6th Ave. (San Diego). ☎ **619/233-3906.**

Who would suspect that a minor cultural explosion is underway in this unremarkable brick building on an unassuming corner at 6th and Broadway, near the Gaslamp Quarter? Known as "Nalanda" (or for the more literally minded, "the Loft") and under the caring hands and deep pockets of the nonprofit "Circle of Friends," this location has seen the transformation from bowling alley (Sunshine Lanes), to publishing house (*Hypno* and *Axcess* magazines), to a work station/art movement where the Circle of Friends, a chaotic, loose-knit digital commune, work out their vision of creating a meeting ground of spiritual consciousness and technology.

The Loft is but one of many projects under the Circle's protective wing. It is commandeered by a consortium of disparate voices, including Murshid, a self-styled yogi from Alabama. He and the Circle joined forces in the mid-1990s to create the space, offering technology to those who couldn't pay for it. With the financial backing of a mysterious Chicago affiliate, the building was bought for $925,000 and is now undergoing a slow transformation from funky art collective to funky art collective with freshly painted walls. As we learned on the impromptu tour given by an affable Sagitarian named Alia (who, like many members wandering the floors, had an intoxicating love vibe—a vibe canceled out by others who seemed like they were just 3 days sober), The Loft is open 24 hours a day to members, offering a maze of side offices, studios, large communal spaces, and more. On the second floor is a group of digital enterprises including the software company Digigami, which had an impressive array of high-end workstations. The third floor is more the loft of the building, hosting video and sound studios, a dance space, a makeshift yoga center and meditation space, a full-size weight room, art spaces, and personal cubicles for round-the-clock creativity or napping or both. Incense wafted through the third floor as Alia led us through an impromptu ten-minute guided meditation to clear our energy. The fourth floor looks like a thinly veiled party space, with a food bar under the watchful eyes of the spirited if slightly wiggy 82-year-old "mama" named Virginia, who happens to be Murshid's mother from Bama. We'll bet good karma this floor has been the site of ecstasy-fueled raves. Given that the Circle of Friends also owns a bookstore in north county Leucadia (Circle of Friends Bookstore, 704 N. Hwy. 101), and a 150-acre desert-retreat yoga center known as Liberty Advance (a combination of Arcosanti, Biosphere, and Rajneeshpuram in the making?) and money to back them up, they aren't as pie-in-the-sky as their laid-back demeanor, baggy pants, and flamboyant names might suggest. And at any rate, they give the greatest hugs.

In the 1960s, Hillcrest was the last of San Diego's neighborhoods to keep its beautiful neon sign up and functioning. Today, the rest of San Diego has caught on to the beauty and magic of such prominent visual landmarks. Now you will see gorgeous neon neighborhood signs all over town: Kensington (pink), the Boulevard (red), Normal Heights (blue). The large neon signs add a charm and class to San Diego that, in some ways, places the city a cut above its often cheesier neighbor to the north.

> **Ken Cinema.** 4061 Adams Ave. (Kensington). ☎ **619/283-5909.**

For well over two decades the *Rocky Horror Picture Show* played to a predictably raucous midnight crowd at this humble neighborhood theater in the heart of Kensington. With the closing of the Guild (formerly at 5th and Hillcrest), the Ken has become the last single-theater art house cinema in town. As a result, it's the likeliest place to view indie and foreign films, plus classic B films, from sci-fi to pure camp.

> **Self Realization Fellowship.** 215 K St. (Encinitas). ☎ **760/753-1811.**

This landmark meditation retreat center was once the home of the legendary Paramahansa Yogananda, author of *Autobiography of a Yogi*. Other than run-o'-the-mill out-of-body experiences, his greatest claim to fame was convincing thousands he was an enlightened guru—though just as important was his dedication to building beautiful relaxing meditative oases.

The Encinitas center (there are others in Los Angeles) sports an impressive golden lotus tower crowning a stunning arched white stucco temple. Like other SRF temples, it seems to have been heavily influenced by the aesthetics of a Hindu palace. The meticulously landscaped grounds sit right off the coast highway on a cliff overlooking the Pacific. And though there's a sincere attempt to create a serene atmosphere, the attitude of the staff and followers occasionally drips with self-righteousness. The maverick blue-hairs who run the place are curt to the point of rude, especially if you walk in wearing anything less than pants and a full length shirt. Fortunately, silence is the golden rule here, so at least you'll be spared any proselytizing as you wander the gardens amidst fellow seekers of solace. Yogananda, who "passed over" in 1952, was evidently a pretty cool cat, with his shoulder-length hair and penetrating brown eyes. He put out some decent books, and built some stunning temples. As with the Fellowship shrine on Sunset Boulevard in Los Angeles, this temple is definitely worth a visit, just steer clear of the devotees.

> **Unarius Academy of Science.** 145 South Magnolia, near Main St. (El Cajon). ☎ 619/444-7062.

Long before Lazarus and Shirley MacLaine were channeling ghosts from the past, Unarians were channeling Pleiadians from the stars. Long before. And in 1976 Michael Monk stumbled through their front door in the stranger-than-fiction Cajon Zone (a.k.a. El Cajon), initially drawn by the faux Roman columns, spinning globes, and purple drapes darkening this storefront "spiritual" center. Inside, the Unarians were actively involved in a costumed re-creation of a past-life melodrama in which one of its members had "channeled" that her boyfriend, also a member, had in a previous life been a Roman Centurion who sold her into slavery, where she lost her life in the arena. With numerous stand-ins assuming their parts, the unscripted session was carried out with such passion that Michael applauded at it's conclusion, much to his later chagrin. This was not theater. This was an earnest past life reenactment that formed the core of the Unarian teachings.

As if the reenactment itself weren't enough, a live Tesla coil was zapping sparks in the background, a miniaturized space city stood under a Plexiglas dome in the wings, and a regal, tiara-wearing Grande Dame—with velvet capes, white satin gloves, and a corseted maroon gown—strode through the door, seating herself on a gold-leafed throne. Michael, the newcomer, was summoned to "Archangel Uriel's" side to be introduced and blessed. With the clarity of a clairvoyant, the archangel proclaimed Michael a Pleiadian emissary whose presence was a sign from "The Moderator" that the Interplanetary Confederation was soon to land in a remote desert region near Alpine (just in time for the bicentennial) and that preparations for departure were drawing nigh. Excitement was in the air.

Welcome to the high-flying world of Unarius, a.k.a. Universal Articulate Interdimensional Understanding of Science. Michael later learned that before his arrival, Archangel Uriel (a.k.a. Ruth Norman, a.k.a. "the Space Lady") had been taking quite a few liberties with the writings and teachings of her deceased husband, Earnest Norman (a.k.a. Jesus, a.k.a. Archangel Raphael), a prolific writer who penned hastily scrawled tomes on reincarnation, interdimensional physics, and the like. And the flamboyant Uriel, a sort of Agnes Moorehead come to life, had responded to her husband's death by continuing his literary tradition. In fact, with a much younger member, Charles Spaegel, she collaboratively channeled a library's worth of otherworldly titles about the space brotherhood and past lives.

Now, husband Ernest may have been Jesus, but he seemed born of the same lunatic cloth as most apocalyptic televangelists. He certainly had a lot of gripes about who'd stolen his various ideas (one culprit: modern TV). And Uriel may have been an Archangel, but her penchant for outlandish costumes and a posse of men at her side definitely kept her in the running with the Queen of Sheba (who she also might have been).

Since Unarius has been around since the fifties, it has accrued its fair share of detractors. But the number-one reason why the faithful remain committed to this loony cult is the hope of being rescued from our God-forsaken planet by a fleet of Pleiadians in the year 2001. (Guess they couldn't find us in 1976.)

Michael's tenure as a space emissary didn't last long. He was summarily cast out when he challenged their beliefs. Spaegel received a transmission that Michael was an ambassador of Lucifer. As for Uriel: Rather than ascend or lift off in a space craft, Archangel Uriel just plain up and died in 1994. But the Unarians continue with their ever hopeful eyes toward the future when the true Conclave of Light will convene and they will be whisked away to join their distant kin. And you thought Heaven's Gate was weird.

Bars and Clubs

As in all matters, don't heed the recommendations of your average tourist guidebook: They will lead you clear away from the true highlights of the San Diego bar scene. Once you've exhausted our list, then you can go and have your fill at Croce's, Bahia, Topper's, and all the rest.

> **Alibi.** 1403 University Blvd. (Hillcrest). ☎ **619/295-0881.**

There are a few serious drunks who are permanent fixtures at this invitingly minimalist hole-in-the-wall. What connects the Alibi to the younger crowd is location. This stretch of University has become the hippest block in town. On any given night you'll find a dozen separate posses of 20-somethings dominating the pool room. The crowd is friendly, drinks are stiff, the tattoos ubiquitous, and by midnight the conversation decibel hits a peak that sustains itself until last call.

> **Arizona Cafe.** 1925 Bacon (Ocean Beach). ☎ **619/223-0847.**

Down the way from Pacific Shores is the next trendy dive bar in the making. Right now, it's the real deal, with portraits of legendary bartenders and customers from the forties and fifties lining the walls. Eighty-two-year-old "Tough Tony" Pandza still tends bar Tuesdays through Fridays from 6 to 9:30pm, and George Radovich, who opened the Arizona in 1943, still owns the joint. It's definitely a locals' place, with the trendoid quotient at a bare minimum. As the bartender told me one Friday morning, "If someone comes in here and orders a Mud Slide, they better go find themselves some mud." No microbrews? "No microbrews. Just standard stuff, the very best we can pour."

> **Casbah.** 2501 Kettner Blvd. (Downtown). ☎ **619/232-4355.**

When the San Diego music scene had its brief fifteen minutes of fame in the mid-nineties, the most likely place to fill your prescription of alternative rock was the Casbah. For that matter, it still is. Legends like Jonathan Richman, Dead Moon, Link Wray, Supersuckers, and Big Sandy and His Flyrite Boys make stops when they're in town. On the night of our visit the Loons served up the loudest rock and roll we'd heard since Blue Cheer. And that's no small feat considering you're under thundering earshot of commercial jets landing at the San Diego airport only a few blocks away. The long, outdoor patio entrance leads to a back-of-the-shack pool and game room. The meandering hallways, conversational cubby holes, and corner rooms offer up plenty of atmosphere. But the garage-size concert room offers little respite from the high-decibel assault of the evening's entertainment.

Hipsters, punks, and rockabilly scene-makers keep this place hopping every night of the week. For one of our favorite tableaus in all of San Diego, meander outside to the corner: If you wait long enough you'll catch a San Diego streetcar cruising along an elevated track, just as an airplane lands at nearby Lindberg Field. For a brief moment, San Diego feels oddly hip and cosmopolitan.

> **Live Wire.** 2103 El Cajon Blvd. (The Boulevard). ☎ **619/291-7450.**

Live Wire feels like a doublewide trailer in a weird sort of way. But a trailer park crowd this is not. Next to Casbah, Live Wire might be the likeliest place to suffer permanent hearing loss, as the low ceilings and narrow room really lock in the sound from the overly amped bands. A tight, friendly crowd bellies up to the bar. An Addams Family pinball machine greets you at the door. Ear plugs are provided by the bouncer.

> **Pacific Shores.** 5927 Newport Blvd. (Ocean Beach).

Ocean Beach is San Diego's nod to its sleazy sailor past. Unlike neighboring Mission Beach, Pacific Beach and La Jolla, things have never really taken off in O.B. And so, this five-block stretch of Newport Boulevard remains a wonderfully sad artifact of commercial decay. The Pacific Shores has somehow held on for over forty years as the most likely bar on the beach to hear fantastic war stories and tall tales. You can easily imagine the fights that used to break out on the streets when the marines, sailors, and surfing hippies would collide. Today, WWII vets have been replaced by both Vietnam and Desert Storm vets. Weekend hipsters have made a point of keeping the coffers full, partly for the camp factor from the prevailing nautical theme and partly for the stiff drinks and rocking juke box, which has the best selection of eighties New Wave in town.

> **Red Fox.** 2223 El Cajon Blvd. (The Boulevard). ☎ 619/297-1313.

Beverly has been folding cloth napkins at the same table for thirty years. This she does when business dies down. Her motivating factor behind folding napkins? "The boss told me to." What you have here are the remnants of what was once the city's premier steak house. The high-beamed ceiling, dark wood paneling, deep burgundy naugahyde booths, and chest-high fireplace reeks of romance, circa 1955. On the bar side you have a cozier atmosphere with Shirley at the piano. Shirley looks like she's been around, too. The clientele is old-school alcoholic with a younger Cocktail Nation crew soaking in the ambiance. Generally speaking, the food is at your own risk, though they definitely know what they're doing with a gin and tonic and choice cut sirloin.

Beaches and Parks

In popular folklore, Los Angeles is known for its beaches: Venice, Santa Monica, Malibu. But, in reality, the true blue beach culture is in San Diego. Ocean Beach (OB), Pacific Beach (PB), and Mission Beach—these are real beach communities, where surfers live year-round. More importantly, beach culture is so entwined with San Diego identity, locals even have names for the surfing breaks, such as the renowned Swami's in Encinitas, Pipes and George's in Cardiff by the Sea, Pillbox (a.k.a. Fletcher Cover) in Solana Beach, and Dolphin Tanks and Garbage near Point Loma and Sunset Cliffs. And if you tire of surfing, there's always cliff diving off "The Clam," a dangerous rocky promontory north of La Jolla Cove (but be ready for about a $300 fine if you get caught); body surfing at Boomer's, also near La Jolla Cove; or a visit to Border Field and Chicano parks.

> **Black's Beach.** Take North Torrey Pines Rd., park at the Glider Port, and walk from there (La Jolla).

Back when going nude was a sure sign of lunatic hippie fringe status, in the days before Frisbees, hang gliding off cliffs, triple-fin surfboards, and 36 SPF suntanning cream, there was a large faction of daredevils who'd risk hiking down the perilous cliffs of Torrey Pines to embrace the broad empty sands of Black's Beach in the buff. It was a community of sorts, where the risk of falling off the cliff (several did), being arrested by sly binocular-toting police for indecent exposure (many were), and getting righteously sunburned in all the wrong places was a clear and present danger. To the volleyballing, Frisbee-throwing, bare-ass multitudes that now run in the hundreds on any sunny summer day, the brazen efforts of those pot-smoking sixties pioneers seems like a trite footnote, given that nudity and Black's Beach now go so hand in hand. The phenomena of this beach, and the community of sun-worshippers it spawned, epitomizes everything the world loves and loathes about Southern California. They love the free spirit, the casual drift, the spread leg nakedness under an endless sun. Oh, to be nude and outdoors with hundreds like you!! By the same token, a phenomenon like Black's Beach is precisely what frightens the Puritan plurality right out of their shame-based minds.

Well, Black's makes it simple now. You park the car in the glider port parking lot, walk down a well-maintained path, stay within designated boundaries, unabashedly peel off your clothes, slather on the high-SPF lotion in all the right places, toss the Frisbee, chase the dog, splash in the rip-tide–prone surf, bury yourself in the sand with your nipples poking out, and wonder how there could have ever been a day when this was seen as anything other than good clean fun.

> **Border Field State Park.** Interstate 5, 15 miles south of San Diego. Exit Dairy Mart Rd., head south, turns into Monument Rd. going west. Follow signs (San Ysidro).

For decades, when it was considered the most notorious illegal crossing in California, this desperate, gray, and dangerous state park, straddling the Mexican border and within a stone's throw of the Tijuana Bull Ring, was an unfenced, under-patrolled hemorrhage, letting in thousands of illegal aliens a day. In fact, any deft enterprising Mexican or Central American could walk or hitch a ride into San Ysidro and all points north. Then, in 1994, after years of shootings, rapes, and robbery in this appropriately named "Borderlands" area, a steel fence went up covering the 5-mile no-man's land from the breakwater to Interstate 5. While not a deterrent (scores still jump the fence, or swim around the ocean bend), it has limited the flow to under sixty a day.

The park has a sweeping vista of the beach, the ocean, and San Diego to the north, and contains a flat estuary that acts as a wildlife refuge for endangered birds, and a modest parched grass area for picnicking and barbecuing. However, we love Border Field because of the rudimentary, toxic, forlorn ugliness of the place. The Tijuana River flows out of Mexico across a marshland so polluted that the surrounding beaches are considered hazardous for even the slightest human contact. (Imagine being an illegal and swimming this cesspool of filth and disease.) The combination of Tijuana's raw sewage overflow and its dumping of toxic refuse directly into the river on the Mexico side prompted the United States to build large pipelines and treatment plants in an attempt to limit the contamination before it flows out to sea. Other than the occasional picnickers, tentative tourists, and suspect

Though San Diego will never know the thrills and overkill of true cafe culture, we simply must rise to the occasion and defend what few legit latte joints exist—if only in response to *San Diego Magazine's* reader poll, which voted Starbucks the city's best cafe. Yikes! We're talking a handsome, if soulless, caffeine-dispensing joint at best and on other days a gentrified, culturally sterile corporate monster with a penchant for robbing neighborhoods of all redeemable character.

So San Diego, wake up and smell the beans!! If you're downtown, try **Cafe Lulu** (419 F St., at 4th), where in yet another raw concrete, high-concept, big flowers, and squiggly-lights-as-sculpture establishment you can slosh down a double and pretend you're a hip yuppie in Pasadena. The food's not bad and the LTC (laptop computer) ratio was a tolerable 1 in 12, which made for a passable scene.

If funk is your factor and you're still downtown, head over to **Gashaus Cafe** (640 F St., at 7th Ave.), and mingle with the nonchalant, baggy pant, slacker crowd. You'll feel right at home with the threadbare couches, ratty carpet, and multisaturated paint job adorning the funky rooms. It's got all the ambiance of a thrift store (same smell too), features three pool tables, and serves up the biggest bowl of cereal you've ever seen. That's right, Cheerios, Raisin Bran, Pebbles, Cap'n Crunch, Lucky Charms, swimming in milk. Oh yeah, and coffee too!

If you're gay (or even if you're not) and you haven't completely burnt out on Hillcrest, which is still coasting as a gay neighborhood after all these years (think the Castro but with low self esteem), then you should venture west on University, alternately jumping from **Euphoria** (1045 University at 10th Avenue), sampling their

gangbangers talking through the fence to their Mexican compatriots, the place is near deserted even on a nice, sunny weekend day. As you cross the dirt road watch out for snakes and beware of strangers asking for rides. Borderlands is San Diego's answer to Dockweiler, but even eerier. (See the interview with Border Patrol agent K. W. Thomas later in this section for more.)

> **Chicano Park.** Logan St., between Crosby and Evans (Downtown San Diego).

On the downtown side of the Coronado Bridge, painted on cement girders and highway overpasses, are some of the finest murals in Southern California. Immense, sprawling works of art that would make Diego Rivera proud. A small stage has played host to nearly three decades of neighborhood events, and despite the oppressive freeways, the place conveys a sense of cultural pride. Yet the whole point of this park has more to do with the historic resistance to the Coronado Bridge than anything else. An extension of the S.D. ghetto, Logan Heights once spilled its unseemly shadow espresso while kibitzing at the curbside tables, then on to the **Living Room** (1417 University at Richmond Street), where on certain nights you'll find yourself as close as San Diego can muster to a crowded cafe scene, with acoustical music, fresh pastries, and seriously good espresso. The Living Room has three locations, so you're in luck should your 2-hour parking meter expire. The East San Diego Living Room, 5900 El Cajon Blvd., near State College, has a wild and raucous study hall atmosphere from the nighttime student majority, while the Living Room in "the Village" of La Jolla, at 1010 Prospect, near Girard Ave., will put you in with the well heeled crowd, and give a view of the ocean to boot.

Though there are numerous places to top a double with foam along the beaches, most put food first, and have the uncanny feeling of soup kitchens, so we tend to avoid.

If a cozy, neighborhood cafe is your cup of Joe, then venture over to **Lestats** in Normal Heights (3343 Adams Ave. at Felton), where you can sink into the eclectic artiness of an offbeat coffee house featuring nightly entertainment (folk, sitar, spoken word) and hobnob in the garden patio where culturally literate types (thanks to nearby San Diego State) savor the bean with wacko psychics, Y2Kers, and yoga stretching housewives from the hood.

And then there's **Java Joe's** (4994 Newport Avenue, at Bacon) over in the sad-sack community of Ocean Beach. It's like a glorious Spanish mission inside, with a large space for acoustic and spoken-word performances.

And, hey, if all this trendy cafe culture is beginning to wear you thin, there's always Starbucks, "the city's best cafe!"

down Crosby Street to the bay. From the point of view of politicians looking for a place to plant the eastern approach to the Coronado Bridge, razing a downtrodden, crime-ridden neighborhood of Hispanics and blacks made total sense. But from the point of view of those facing eviction, a simple look on the map said there were a hell of a lot more shorter distances from which to connect the two sides.

"Chula Juana" native Michael Monk found himself wandering into a protest here in 1968 by sheer coincidence (these things routinely happen to "the Forrest Gump of the fringe"). As a member of the legendary Nitelites, a 10-piece nearly all-black soul band in which Michael played trombone, Sunday was the day to pick up the cash from the weekend gigs. The squirrely manager, Chuck, who was shacked up with lead singer cum soul-sister Sheila, lived in a ratty second-floor apartment on Crosby near the bay. After Michael retrieved his cash from Chuck, he ran head-on into a mob of local anarchists rallying the neighborhood to stop the bridge.

But bulldozers nearly always win. The bridge was built. While Chicano Park was a mere bone to appease the minority opponents of the bridge, the locals have made the best of it. Here, in this afterthought of a park, and thirty years after the neighborhood protests, you can picnic, walk your dog, swing your kid, stroll past the colorful murals crawling up the girders, drink your sloe gin, barbecue your meat, and dance beneath the murals as thunderous traffic rushes overhead.

> **Ocean Beach.** South of Pacific and Mission Beaches.

Ocean Beach is the drunk uncle of San Diego beach communities. This is where the sixties soared like an epic wave for one brief flicker, and it's been crashing ever since. The houses are dingier, the rents cheaper, the signage older, the businesses funkier than any other beach community in town. Those who never moved beyond their sixties drug-addled extremes are still wandering the streets like ghosts, as if in some unrelenting purgatory. For this reason we like Ocean Beach. It doesn't have the beer commercial ritualism of Pacific Beach or the gluttonous indifference of La Jolla. It's just a frumpy, dumpy, authentic beach community that never lies.

Bridges

> **Coronado Bridge.** I-5 south of downtown to the Coronado Bridge exit.

Before Coronado became just a ten-minute commute to downtown, you rode the ferry. Since the North Island Naval Air Station occupied the tip of the island, there were significant waits as thousand of sailors commuted from the end of Broadway to Coronado every day. There, in the overcast of the morning, you waited, watching the lumbering car ferries plow their way through the San Diego Bay. The initial idea of a bridge was met with mixed response. Opponents consisted of two strange bedfellows: on the one side of the proposed span were arch Coronado conservatives, admirals and their wives wanting to preserve their exclusive seaside village way of life; on the other side, across the bay, were the soon-to-be-displaced minorities at the base of Logan Heights, the city's most dicey ghetto. Both constituencies fought in vain— the conservatives with their behind-closed-doors power plays, the minorities with protests, rallies, and whistle blowing. Neither stood a chance since the opponent was "Progress," backed by the U.S. Navy. Case closed.

The bridge, as it now stands, is not exactly an architectural wonder. For example, it doesn't hold a candle (or a pillar or a beam) to the accessible splendor of Balboa Park's 1948 Cabrillo Bridge, which crosses the oldest freeway in the city (the 163). But the San Diego Coronado Bay Bridge, which opened August 3, 1969, is the most memorable bridge in town. This blue-sided metal-and-cement structure arches dramatically toward the sky like a roller coaster before landing on Coronado Island. What it lacks in ornamentation, it makes up for in astounding views. The smooth, near airborne ride offers a panoramic vista of the entire bay. And God is that a low railing on the side! To your north you see the waterfront downtown sweeping up into the hills, and to the south, through the labyrinth of docked Navy ships, the bay stretches to an indeterminable conclusion at the salt flats of Imperial Beach, with Mexico but a short ways away. Short of a steep landing at the downtown Lindbergh Field, this is the best ride in town. From this far up you'll momentarily agree that San Diego *is* paradise.

Note: You can still ride the **Coronado Ferry,** with none of the waits of yore. Head to 1040 N. Harbor Dr. (☎ **619/435-6029**). The ferry leaves San Diego on the hour and Coronado on the half hour. The cost is only $2 each way, and well worth it.

Food

> **Big Kitchen.** 3003 Grape St., at 30th St. (San Diego). ☎ **619/234-5789.**

Even though the Big Kitchen doesn't have a big kitchen, it does have a big heart, due to the matriarchal presence of owner Judy Forman. The legend of the place rests on former employee Whoopi Goldberg, who has since gone on to other things. But what keeps the neighborhood coming back decade after decade is the fact that you can't get a more tasty, straight-from-the-grill, home-cooked breakfast than this. (Or lunch: The place is open weekdays 7am to 2pm; weekends 7:30am to 3pm.) Situated on the back side of The Park (that's Balboa), east of the zoo, museums, and golf course but still under the ever-present thunder of approaching jets headed for Lindbergh Field, this oasis of folksy charm has been the consistent anchor in a neighborhood once considered a trifle rough around the edges, but now safe enough to stroll at night. The old counter and stools, the funky charm of the creaky door, the neighborhood recycling bin, and posters fluttering in the wind are all still there, but things have expanded to include a fair-sized dining room, a newly added trellised patio, and a menu that just gets better with age. Judy is what you call a beamer. She beams a feel-good, mile-wide smile, seems to never forget a face, and is positively adored by her patrons. On a Sunday morning you can guarantee a healthy 20-minute wait on the city-widened tree-lined sidewalk outside. Half of those who wait know each other, and for the other half, you'll soon be friends.

> **Blue Point.** 565 Fifth Ave., at Market (Downtown). ☎ **619/233-6623.**

Though by no means world class, the delivery at this street corner bistro is a noticeable cut above the otherwise mediocre strip of gentrified Fifth Avenue eateries. Two

Judy Forman of the Big Kitchen

years of trial and error have made Blue Point into one of the most dependable seafood restaurants in town. Though the decor is fairly contrived in its mid-nineties brass and mahogany elegance, the architectural brilliance of the building itself is guaranteed to impress your Chula Vista relatives. Be advised that thick wallets are required. Fortunately (or unfortunately) the bar will seat you for appetizers. As a result, you might catch a few loud, downscale sailor types in tees and shorts capping off a night of carousing with a shrimp cocktail. But you are in Diego, so get used to it. In the kitchen, eight line chefs, under the direction of Marshall Blair, get things right. You can watch the cooks across an open counter, where culinary activity rises to theatrical proportions. The mantra here is seafood. The oyster shooters are so fresh they're still squirming. The Seared Miso Marinated Bass comes with wild mushrooms in a lemongrass broth. The Griddled Mustard Catfish arrives with jicama slaw and jalapeño corn bread. Both were cooked to perfection. The Dean Martin–style double martinis (at ten bucks a pop) are strong enough to wrestle you to the ground. By your second round you might even take a liking to the soft jazz and big band tunes that persist from the muted speakers. And by the third, you might even take a liking to the obnoxious sailors being escorted to the door.

> **El Indio.** 3695 India St., near Washington St. (San Diego). ☎ **619/299-0333.**

In a town that has more tacquerias than most towns have cars, it's a tough call for what makes the cut above the rest. But when you start with the basics, take a look toward the bottom of the Mexican food chain, and evaluate the most overlooked yet essential part of a rockin' good Cal-Mex meal, it's the tortilla. And this is where they make them. Other than strolling the streets of Mexico, it's rare to get the full-headed aroma of hot tortillas churning off the press. Whether it's the big wheaty ones or the hot corn jobs, these babies just scream for melted butter and a dip in the salsa. Though in an ideal world they'd be like the hand-patted corn tortillas you find in sleepy Sonoran towns, these machine-made ones still do the trick. Factor in the cheesy quesadillas, crunchy tacos, and fair-size burritos smothered with avocado that come smoking out of the kitchen and you have some of the finest Mexican food in town. Judging by the long lines at both lunch and dinner, the secret's long been out. But they move you through at a rapid pace and before you're too bored you'll be face forward in a Styrofoam plate, shoveling down fistfuls of chips, salsa, beans smothered in sour cream, steaming rice, and those freshly built tortillas. The only thing to distract you from the feeding frenzy will be the sound of traffic on nearby Interstate 5 and another hot tortilla hitting the tray.

> **Mister A's.** 2550 Fifth Ave., top floor (Downtown). ☎ **619/239-1377.**

Everyone goes to Mister A's. You take your relatives there. You haul your prom date there. You take a business lunch there. And let me tell you, it ain't for the food. Nor the sassy waitresses in their push-up bras. It's *the view:* the ultimate 360-degree vista of the Big Avocado. Mister A's sits on the top floor of a Balboa Park office high-rise. It's a swank, old-world restaurant with all the opulent trimming that old-money San Diegans expect. Jackets required; jeans and t-shirts prohibited. The menu is pure steak house, and as can be expected from any "windows on the world" sort of place, it's overpriced. The drinks are weak and the stuffy attitude a bit out of sync. But have a seat on the outdoor veranda with views of the entire sparkling bay, adjacent Balboa Park, and neighboring downtown, and you'll be laughing with the seagulls in no time at all—especially when a jet heading to nearby Lindbergh Field passes so close it nearly skims the toupees.

> **San Diego Chicken Pie Shop.** 2633 El Cajon Blvd., near Texas St. (San Diego). ☎ **619/295-0156.**

We'll admit we're sending you here because it's something of a campy joke. Yet there is a practical side. When you can't bear to saddle up to one more taco stand, this is without a doubt the primo cheap dining experience in San Diego. Not so much for the decor—the room borders on a senior-center cafeteria with all the charm of a nursing home—but for the old-fashioned prices: $4.40 for a chicken pot pie, including bread, soup, whipped potatoes, vegetable, slaw, and dessert. Cheap, cheap, cheap. Coffee-shop food addicts will go ecstatic as the carts are rolled out with platter upon platter of nostalgia food: hot turkey sandwiches, chicken giblets, hot roast beef, and Jell-O for dessert. Such mediocrity doesn't prevent all manner of customers from waddling in from the boulevard. If it's not your basic street people loading up before a heavy night of panhandling, then it's your requisite slackers, senior citizens, and trailer-park families of eight. As for it's namesake, the Chicken Pie, what you see is pretty much what you get. Chicken, gravy, and crust. And for the side dishes, you can trust the vegetables are from the can, but who cares when you're eating out for less than a McDonald's Happy Meal.

› **Top o' the Cove.** 1216 Prospect St., at Torrey Pines Rd. (La Jolla). ☎ **619/454-7779.**

The singular caveat that sets this old-world, old-money, old-Republican holdout with a piano bar apart from the other old-world, old-money, classy joints lining this spectacular seaside village is that Michael Monk sipped his first glass of wine here, circa 1966. There were 10,000 bottles of wine in the cellar back then (still are), leaving the Monk plenty to choose from. Michael, having just turned a sweet 16, was being shown the town by the immeasurably neurotic mother of his high-school best friend. After doing the requisite overpriced gallery tour of La Jolla, Mike and his middle-aged companion settled into a late lunch at Top o' the Cove. The seductive charm of Mrs. Schramm had secured a choice bottle of chardonnay, despite the obvious presence of a raging hormonal teen at this table for two. The conversation centered around art, restaurants, and exotic tales from foreign lands, though it was obvious that Mrs. Robinson—er, Mrs. Schramm—had other things on her mind. By the time dessert was taken from the table and the last chardonnay consumed, her stocking feet were doing the tango with Michael's shoes.

Thirty years later Mike stopped by to see if the same magic was still there. He discovered that the attitude-rich wait staff take their job of serving wanna-be billionaires a little too seriously now. The sweet charm of the seaside cottage— shadowed by fig trees, warmed by fireplaces, and made just the right cozy for a candlelit dinner—just doesn't have the same luster it once did. But once you get away from the annoying glare of the wait staff, tucked into a corner with a view of the La Jolla Cove, and settle in for a promising (if expensive) meal of lamb or, God-forbid, veal, your second bottle of chardonnay just may turn back the clock to those days of playing footsies with the mother of your best friend.

› **Turf Supper Club.** 1116 25th St., at "C" St. (San Diego). ☎ **619/234-6363.**

Golden Hills is a neighborhood that was at one time considered the epitome of the good life, with grand homes overlooking the bay. In a later era it was the most likely place to score drugs and a gun up your ass. The slow revitalization of Golden

Hills to the point where it could support a retro, Cocktail Nation, hipster joint like the Turf Supper Club is nothing short of miraculous. Were this Cole Valley in San Francisco or Silverlake in L.A., a place like the Turf would fall between the ho and the hum. But we're talking San Diego, and few are the places that the post-ironic, pierced, tattooed, Betty-Boop-jet-black-hairdo crowd can sip martinis with a smirk and not feel threatened by the golden tan mob. In fact, judging by the general pallor of the clients, these people avoid the sun altogether, which isn't an easy trick under these perennially sunny skies.

However, we digress. The concept here is you cook your own meat. There is a selection of seasoned burgers, fish, chicken, steak, and token vegetarian kabobs. Choose one of these options and a beautiful waitress will bring out your respective skewer, plus some buttered garlic bread. You saddle up to the grill, daddy-o, and take care of the rest. At first the idea of cooking your own meat seems a bit labor-intensive, but, after a strong martini, you'll be way into it, and find that it is actually quite a hoot. As one regular put it, you never know who you're going to meet around the campfire. The original Turf Supper Club was started in 1950, and was relaunched in March of 1998 under new ownership. The horse-racing theme is beautifully articulated throughout, including on the menu, which is designed like a racing card. Turf Club co-owner Tim Mays is a famed local music impresario who launched the Casbah (the CBGB's of San Diego and "ground zero for local music") as well as the famed S.D. hangout the Pink Panther, now gone but not forgotten.

Museums

> **California Surf Museum.** 308 Pacific St., at 3rd St. (Oceanside). ☎ **760/721-6876.** www.surfmuseum.org. Free admission.

If you are decoy (nonsurfer), Benny (surfing novice), or Dido (surfing poser from inland, namely Escondido), and especially if you are a true-blue stylin' bare-backed free-ballin' surfing Beard (veteran surfer) and you're tired of riding the 25¢ tram out the 1,600-foot-long pier overlooking the nearby sparkle factor (the ocean), and don't feel like crossing eyes with one more furloughed Camp Pendleton Marine walking the hostile streets of Oceanside, then duck into this modest-sized tribute to wave culture. It's just for you, brah.

The primary visual marvels of this 14-year-old storefront museum (open 7 days a week, 10am to 4pm) are the tools of the surfing trade, namely the surfboard. There's a bodacious little history, too. Surfing was once a noble sport performed by Hawaiian kings, and in its humble origins was executed by strong seaworthy men on immensely long boards, who had a healthy respect for "the Big Mama" (the ocean) and for the consequences of a wipeout—namely, a quarter-mile swim to shore in order to retrieve the board. These mothers of all boards are displayed throughout the museum with their attendant lore, including an 1890 Hawaiian board, and possibly the oldest Californian board, dating back to 1917. You'll also get a roundabout education of just who brought this California pastime to its level of mass appeal, including the life of the ultimate boardhead, Tom Blake, who crafted the first hollow surfboard in 1932 and put the fin on in 1935.

Curator Rich Watkins is a most excellent wellspring of bounteous good vibes and a virtual encyclopedia of surfing, recalling the futile days of roping your leg to the board to keep it from flying to shore (it didn't work). It wasn't until 1970 that the leash was born, so have some respect for the long-boarders of old. You'll feel like a total quimby (loser) for ever tying a leash to your puny square tail twin-fin again. Yowza!

> **Museum of Death.** 548 5th Ave., just south of Market (San Diego). ☎ **619/338-8153.** $5 museum admission.

Now that St. Augustine's Tragedy in History Museum has bit the dust, this downtown museum might be the best place in the country to view death in all its naked, gruesome details. Housed in the basement of the first mortuary in San Diego (the esteemed Young and Young Furniture), owner J. D. Healy's long thin museum has immortalized the macabre in a series of rooms designed to SHOCK. Upon entering you'll pass Lady, an afghan sprawled on the floor in peaceful repose, except on closer examination you realize she's been sleeping for quite a long time (try ten years). The highlight is the starkly realistic photographs of Mel Kilpatrick, the late photographer for the Orange County Coroner's office, whose work shows the real face of fatality and the finer details of death none of us ever see even in the tabloids: gushing intestines, caved-in faces, gashes the size of ravines made by falling lawnmowers. This stuff is so extreme the teenagers viewing it could only deal by snickering, completely out of touch from the gross reality before them. The museum has several other highlights—a purple veil worn by a Heaven's Gater (the entire bedroom set, including Nike shoes, will soon be on display), memorabilia from the Manson murders with gory coroner's photos of all the victims (including a nude, bloody, and pregnant Sharon Tate), a casket room showing an eight-hour continuous loop video called "The Traces of Death" (watch a guy chained between two jeeps get his arm ripped away when the vehicles speed off in opposite directions), and the museum's prized possession, a Laotian Buddhist Funeral Float that was to be used for a high-ranking Laotian Monk. Because the city of San Diego wouldn't allow the burning of the entire pyre, a place had to be found for the funeral float. Why not the Museum of Death?

JD's museum is slowly becoming a repository for other items related to tragedy, including the notorious McDonald's Massacre in San Ysidro. With numerous photo essays and press clippings on the likes of Night Stalker Richard Ramirez, "Son of Sam" David Berkowitz (they even have David's letter, "13 Steps on How to Kill a Fat Lady," written DURING his trial for the murders he committed in New York), and Henry *Portrait of a Serial Killer* Lucas (recently moved off of Texas Death Row), you can spend hours scanning these walls.

JD himself comes across as an ordinary Gen-X Joe, kind of. With the requisite tattoos and piercings, and hard-core punk on the stereo, he sits at the counter, Monday to Thursday from noon to 10pm, Friday and Saturday from noon to midnight, cheerfully and speedily recounting horror death stories as if recalling last night's meal. For ten years he curated the Rita Dean Gallery in the same building, catering to extreme art and performance from the likes of Annie Sprinkle, Charles Gatewood, and Lydia Lunch. He rolled out the Museum of Death in 1995 when his death memorabilia began spilling out of the closets, and has been packing them in since. Now it's one of the primary draws of the Gaslamp quarter.

> **San Diego Model Railroad Museum.** 1649 El Prado, just west of Park Blvd., in the basement of Casa de Balboa Building (Balboa Park, San Diego). ☎ **619/696-0199.** www.globalinfo.com/noncomm/SDMRM/sdmrm.html. Adults $3, kids free.

If running your Lionel off the tracks at high speed was your idea of fun as a kid, then this railroad museum, the largest of its kind in North America, will send you into narrow-gauge ecstasy. It's enclosed in a 24,000-square-foot space on Balboa Park's overrated, indisputably Kodak-perfect El Prado Walk, and is open Tuesday through Friday from 11am to 4pm, Saturday and Sunday from 11am to 5pm. There are four permanent scale-model displays, each under the supervision of a local model-railroad club. Given the amount of volunteer time required to build and maintain these miniatures, it's safe to assume that the majority of workers are in their second childhood and way beyond the age of 60. When we were there, two 80-year-old pals were putting in an 8-hour shift and navigating from the center of the tracks, their shoulders hunched over, faces lit with glee and eyes following every turn.

Upon entry you are swiftly overwhelmed by the preponderance of detail in these elaborate miniature re-creations of Californian railroads. Desert landscapes complete with rock-strewn arroyos and multileafed scrub oaks, mountain vistas, bridge overpasses, and mile after miniaturized mile of telephone poles. But the crowning wonders are the trains themselves, modeled from the fifties after the transition from steam to diesel. These multicar re-creations capture in vivid detail the streamlined beauty of the Southern Pacific–Santa Fe, Arizona Eastern, and Cabrillo Southwestern lines, to name a few. Two of the more impressive sites of the museum are the huge scale model of Goat Canyon Trestle in Carriso Gorge, which is one of the largest wooden trestles in the world, and the old San Diego Depot, circa 1952, with it's Spanish-tile domes and terra-cotta roofs.

Most of the displays are so vast you lose sight of the train when it goes around the bend. And no matter how jaded you think you are, when you enter the Toy Train Gallery and see the hands-on throttles for a bona fide Lionel, our bet is you'll be choking the stick in no time as you strive to run her off the track—just for old times' sake.

> **Titanic Museum.** Coast Hwy., 2 miles south of town (Rosarita, Mexico). ☎ 011-52/661-40135.

In Halifax, Nova Scotia, one can visit the Maritime Museum of the Atlantic and relive the tragedy of the *Titanic* by viewing countless artifacts collected at the scene of the disaster, as well as tour the cemeteries where unclaimed bodies were laid to rest. In Rosarita, Mexico, one can visit the former site where *Titanic* the movie was filmed and view the warehouse were scant "artifacts" from partial sets were laid to rest. Guess which museum is more popular?

Judging by the reverential mood of those entering the former film set, you'd think this was an apparition of the Holy Virgin Mary. Slow lines of people somberly examine the mock coal furnaces, the mock drawing room, the mock table setting, and the mock statuary, and probe the guides with well-thought-out questions about the episodic scenes from this ridiculously over-heralded film. It's enough to make you scream.

After scouting locations around the world, Twentieth-Century Fox chose to film *Titanic* in Popotla, a small village just south of Rosarita, best known for a large arch off the road. The reason: freedom to hire cheap, nonunion help, and its proximity to Los Angeles. Hundreds of workers descended on the tiny village to construct what is possibly the largest open-air water tank in the world. The studio spent $5 million to construct a 770-foot, 80%-scale replica of the ship itself, another $8 million to dress her in period detail (from silverware to lifeboats), and even more for hotel rooms, meals, extras, lights, and electricity. The monumental boost to the local economy must have made Rosaritans very happy campers.

Given that these facilities now promise to keep almost all water-based movies out of the ocean and in the tank, Rosarita hasn't seen the last of this endeavor. And at $5 a pop to enter the museum they're going to continue squeezing every last buck off the *Titanic* bandwagon. So, even if there is a drought of water-based movies, they can at the very least maintain the extremely padded payroll of security guards—there were over a dozen working the time we entered.

What you get for your money is a short trailer of the making of the film, in a shed with folding chairs. Then you have access to a warehouse where the aforementioned "artifacts" are carefully laid out like priceless treasures from the sea.

Outdoors you see a scaled-down "hull" of the ship with TITANIC lettered on its side. And with some imagination you can picture where the eighteen-million-gallon water tank *might* be (it's off limits to the public), where the scale model *Titanic* *might* have sunk, and where the few thousand extras *might* have drowned at the bottom of a fictitious sea. At the very least it's good excuse to drive to Mexico.

Shopping

> **Horton Plaza.** 324 Horton Plaza—Broadway Circle between 2nd and 4th sts. (heart of downtown San Diego). ☎ **619/239-8180.**

Of all the malls we've seen across America—and believe us, we've seen our share—"Horton Hears a Customer" rates near the top. All the same chains are here—FAO Schwartz, Mrs. Fields Cookies, Gap, and Planet Hollywood—but they've been displayed and stationed in colorfully fun and inventive ways. The design is a sort of Postmodern Naif in that you find architectural motifs both ancient and new, brightly blended together with the childlike pastels one finds at the major hotels of Disney World. Though Isaac Asimov was allegedly involved in the design of the Plaza, it's really a place that would make Michael Venturi proud. Seen against the backdrop of the huge desert that surrounds this city, Horton Plaza is a strange and enticing mirage. A 6¹/2-block Middle Eastern Pop Art bazaar where folks from the Hinterland can come and feel the illusion of exuberant urbanity before heading back to their own cultural deserts. Horton succeeds where other malls fail—it is not only a brilliant original design, but you actually want to walk through it.

Sports

> **Olympic Training Center.** 2800 Olympic Park Way—drive south 805, exit east Telegraph Canyon Rd., go 8 miles and turn right on Wueste Road; 2 miles to the park. (Chula Vista). ☎ **619/656-1500.** www.olympic-usa.org.

Back in the day the only thing this far east of Otay (save Brown Field Municipal Airport) was wilderness. It was a time when the word "Otay" was synonymous with death. Because beyond the suburban navy homes of Chula Vista, among the sage brush, rattlers, and parched canyons, was a pig farm, or, more accurately, a slaughterhouse for pigs. On a good day, with a strong wind from the beach, you'd never know. But when the wind blew from the east, you could easily fall into a faint from the strong smell of porcine carnage. But thanks to the Olympic Training Center, opened in April 1995, Otay has been disconnected from its long association with butchery. Today, northeast of Otay's Brown Field is the astonishing 150-acre world-class training complex, the mother, father, and daughter of all sports centers. Fully equipped for field hockey, soccer, and track and field, it also boasts the nation's largest archery range. Every year, the center hosts a few thousand athletes and some plain old local school camps out for a spin on the world-class cycle course. It's an amazing transformation for this formerly parched killing field. In the distance you can stare mystically toward Mount Miquel, where, on adjacent Otay Mountain, Reba MacEntire's band lost their lives in a plane crash about ten years back. And as you watch the kayakers practice on Lower Otay reservoir you'll be among the select few that can state with a knowing smirk, "I know what this *used* to smell like."

> **The Plunge.** 3146 Mission Blvd., Belmont Park (Mission Beach).
> ☎ **619/488-3110.**

Back when swimming pools were the size of miniature lakes and the masses would come for water cures, saltwater spas like the Mission Beach Plunge were the social meeting ground for both rich and poor. Here, you could frolic in the seawater without those bothersome waves, float aimlessly on your back with no kelp beds in sight, and have faith that no sharks were closing in for the kill. Likewise, after the cure took hold you could throw out your spine on the neighboring Big Dipper wooden roller coaster overlooking the beach. The Plunge, and neighboring Big

Dipper, had a close call with the wrecking ball in the eighties, but preservationists fought hard (and successfully) to keep these two 1925 landmarks from giving way to condo mania. After laying dormant for a year (1987), the enormous splendor of the pool, its hand-laid tiles and its vaulted sky-high ceilings, have been fully restored, including new windows and a huge mural of orca whales at play by marine environmentalist/ painter Wyland (just Wyland). Gone, however, is the salt water, which made the Plunge "the largest indoor salt water pool in the world." Chlorinated city water has taken its place. Still, measuring over 175 by 60 feet, and at 84°, the Plunge remains a lap swimmer's dream. Be sure to catch one of their "Dive-In Movies," where you can float on your own raft as water-related flicks like *Jaws* are projected on the wall. Second-story mezzanines surround the pool, allowing one to view the swimmers, the movie, and the beauty of one of San Diego's finest architectural landmarks.

Like we said, once outside the Plunge, you'll be tempted to ride the Dipper. If you want to guarantee a place in the mental ward, or the Scripps Hospital Pain Center, then opt for the periodic Hurl and Whirl contest—the longest riding passenger takes home a prize of $50,000. The night we were there, twenty-four contestants had dropped to ten after a meager four days in the seat and 650 loops around the track. Those in line were opting for the privilege to sit next to one of the potentially hurling marathoners. Yellow windbreakers and barf bags were provided.

> **San Diego Surfing Academy.** P.O. Box 99938, San Diego, CA 92169-1938.
☎ **619/565-6892.** www.surfsdsa.com.

If you thought surfing was the exclusive domain of sun-bleached, bareback dudes doing raw aerials off a wedge, think again. In 1995 Pat and Lynne Weber had the foresight to open a surf academy in San Diego to make "shredding a pounder" accessible to the "smog monsters" of the world. And if Mabel Gudgel (age 81) or Molly Workman (age 12) can do it, then, well, by Kahanamoku, maybe you can too.

Catering to everyone from the extreme beginner to the near pro, this husband-wife team provide the wet suit, the board, the training, and, if you do the surf camp, some "grunts" as well. For starters, their day lessons are $45 for the first hour, $25 for the second hour, and $150 for the surf camp, a low-pressure two-day romp in the waves, with lodging, transportation, food, and photos to prove you did it. Both Pat and Lynne excel in putting even the heaviest land-lovers at ease. They start you with basic board handling, paddling, choosing the right wave, and riding the sucker until you fall off. They're near a zero in attitude quotient and big on surf etiquette and ocean and environmental awareness. Day lessons take you to San Elijo State Park Beach in Cardiff by the Sea. The camps get you to Baja. And, oh right, they're championship tandem surfers, Red Cross certified, and haven't lost a surfer to a shark . . . yet.

Over the Borderline: An Interview with Border Patrol Agent
K. W. Thomas,
Border Field State Park, San Ysidro, California

Spending your days parked beachside, listening to the roar of the waves with the sun on your back and wind at your neck, might seem like a dream job to some, but for the good men who stand watch at the Border Field State Park it's got more than it's share of hazards. A few years back, working the most treacherous crossover along the California border with Mexico, Border Field's fifteen understaffed agents couldn't come close to containing the weekly rush of thousands of illegal aliens who walked, ran, and crawled their way to freedom through this unfenced park to San Ysidro and all points north. The area of the State Park is eerily apocalyptic, with a desolate beach, low, sandy wetlands, and scrub brush and ravines crawling with snakes that feed off the barren rocky hills. Just a soccer-ball kick from the Tijuana Bull Ring, Border Field's monthly roundup of murders, muggings, and rape made it the most dangerous park in the state. And that was only half the trouble. Agents worked in one of the most environmentally hazardous areas of California, with toxicity levels in the Tijuana River so high it was declared unfit for human contact *of any kind,* and that includes the dust blowing in the wind.

The tide of public outrage finally made for sweeping change. Gone is the open border. In its place stands a towering steel fence that starts a few hundred feet out in the surf and marches 5 miles inland to the Port of Entry. With the addition of fifty more active agents per shift and a serious effort underway to contain and clean the Tijuana River, life at Border Field State Park has definitely improved. Even so, those troubled days are far from gone.

Surrounded by ocean to the west, vast desert to the north and east, and Mexico just to the south, San Diego truly is a border region between nature and foreign lands. As we learned from our interview with border agent K. W. Thomas, Borderlands State Park is where that San Diego/Tijuana border karma is most prominently played out.

Monk: This seems very bizarre. Anybody could swim around that. *[Pointing at the fence as it ends 200 feet into the surf.]*

Agent Thomas: They certainly do. They certainly try. They get in boats and go around it, swim around it.

Monk: You can't spot them if they're swimming, can you?

Thomas: Sure we can.

Monk: From the air?

> *"The fence is just a nondeterrent. You'd be amazed at how fast they can get over that fence."*

Thomas: We have various sites from where we can spot them.

Monk: You can do it electronically? You know if someone's swimming around that fence?

Thomas: We know if someone's out there 5 to 6 miles. And anything further out than that usually the Coast Guard picks up.

Monk: Do people still get through this park?

Thomas: Yeah. If you don't keep an eye on the people and count the number of cars, they'll try and pass kids through the fence and stuff like that.

>interview

Monk: It seems so flimsy. Why don't they make it an electric fence or something like that?

Thomas: Human rights violations.

Monk: The fence wasn't here years ago, was it?

Thomas: No, they put it up in '93.

Monk: Before that Mexicans could come to this park, right?

Thomas: Yep.

Monk: But was there another fence further down?

Thomas: No, just the river. And that's not much of a barrier at all. A couple of years ago this was a free-for-all out here. Border Patrol didn't even patrol this. From here to the Port of Entry back in '93 there were maybe fifteen agents on a shift. They had murders, robberies, all sorts of stuff out here all the time. People getting beat up. It was just insane. So the border's completely changed from what it was.

Monk: If I was trying to get into this country I'd just wait until there was a bullfight, with a big scene, a big commotion, then run over then.

Thomas: They haven't had bullfights there in a long time. But what they do is what we refer to as a Bonsai. They get like fifty or sixty and all jump at once. And we have two agents out [in this area of the park]. We usually can get backup in time to wrap them all up.

Monk: You can't shoot at them legally, right?

Thomas: Under certain circumstances we can. If they present a threat to either our lives or someone else's.

Monk: So it's still going on a lot, people trying to get over?

Thomas: Oh yeah. For the most part they wait until the sun goes down.

Monk: You mean, if I was here at around nine o'clock I would probably catch somebody? It would be that obvious?

Thomas: It depends. They're pretty good. They're pretty sneaky. They'll crawl right along the waterline at the surf. They'll go over the fence. Either that or dig a hole under it. Then they'll crawl right along the water line where the surf's hitting. They'll wear dark clothes so you can't see them.

Monk: Can't you pick up body heat?

Thomas: Yeah. But it depends where our cameras are set up.

Monk: Years ago couldn't you drive up here to the bullfight from this side?

Thomas: Yeah, you used to be able to do that. It used to be open. There used to be parties up here. The fence is just a nondeterrent. They can climb that fence.

You'd be amazed at how fast they can get over that fence. It's absolutely amazing. I'm amazed all the time at how quick they jump it.

Monk: Will most people coming in from Mexico come in from this area?

Thomas: No. This area is one of the tougher areas to cross now. Simply because we have more agents. Like I was saying, before '93 there used to be fifteen agents from here to the port of entry. Now we've got anywhere from fifty to sixty per shift. That makes a huge difference. We've basically pushed them out east. They're all going through El Centro. We used to apprehend anywhere from 1,500 to 2,000 aliens per night, just in this 5-mile stretch. And that was just who we caught. We had twice that many get away. You had fifteen agents out here working. It was a mob. Back then we had shootings all the time. There were people raped and stabbed. It was a mess down here. All of the houses up on Seacoast and all the way down were getting broken into, broken windows, it was a big problem.

Monk: Seems like now you could just bribe one of these houses on the Mexican side and build a tunnel underneath.

Thomas: They've done that. But they don't do it for people, they do it for drugs. That's where the big money is. If they're going to build a tunnel they're not going to mess with people. We have contact with the Mexican authorities and depending on how much merit you want to put in what they say we'll take some Intel reports from them [about suspected activity in border houses].

I'll tell you what they did a while ago. They had some strippers up in these brown houses right along here. They would open these windows and have the strippers up there at night. The border patrol agents would be driving by and they'd send some people up the beach [while the agents were watching the strippers].

Monk: That is so clever, you've got to hand it to them.

Thomas: Once in awhile, if you got some sprinters they make it to the river mouth before we can get them.

Monk: So the word has spread that this is just a bad area to cross?

Thomas: Well, if you cross here, if you make it, you've got 2 miles to run and you're in the city and once you get there it's over. We usually can't get them. If they go out east they've got mountains, they've got 20 to 30 miles, plus they've got to get a ride and pay more money. So they take their chances here. They know if they run up the beach and we catch them we're just going to drive them back to the port of entry and turn them back. If they spend 4 or 5 days walking across the desert in El Centro and pay all of this money out to smugglers and they get caught, they've got to start back at square one. They take their chances.

This area here is much better. Now we're catching fifty to sixty in a 24-hour period. We're not getting that many through now. But we do have getaways. We do have people get through. We've shored up the border quite a bit but people still get through. It's inevitable. You can't control everything all of the time. Out in El Centro they're catching a thousand a night and having that many get away. The smugglers have it down to a science out there. They cross the desert. They put a rock on the highway. The van stops. They load up and they're gone. Unless you're there to see them do it, it's almost impossible to catch them.

So now they're going to have to fortify out there, and it's just going to keep pushing it further and further east until one day, twenty years from now, the border will be sealed completely. Like I said, it's a lot of money to do this. It's expensive.

Monk: Are you still in favor of border control? After doing this so long do you sometimes feel like just opening the damn thing up?

Thomas: No. I think opening it up would be a big mistake. I know there are a lot of people for open borders and stuff. That'd be a huge mistake. The problems that we'd have here would be unbelievable. A lot of people look at the short term, "Oh, there'd be diversity, blah, blah, blah." Diversity is great to an extent. But overdiversity, especially with one population—I'm sure you've heard already, the Mexican population in the United States is almost not a minority anymore. In California it's not. It's becoming the number-one minority over blacks. It's just a matter of time. And you're already starting to see it in some areas where they're voting in their people, voting in their way of life. The whole thing about diversity is they're supposed to assimilate into the United States and the American way. But they're not doing that. They're bringing their culture over here and they're trying to implement their way of life, which is okay to a point, but if you're coming to the United States you need to be a United States citizen, speak the language, and be part of the United States. It's okay to keep some aspects of you're culture, but you're an American here.

You know what I will give to these people: They don't know the language. They'll jump these two fences. They'll hide in that river for hours, which during the winter is cold.

Monk: And probably polluted.

Thomas: Oh, don't even. I tell people don't even go in the ocean here. That water is really polluted.

Monk: They're dumping sewage in there?

Thomas: When that overflows it comes straight into the United States. Not only that, but they dump all of their toxic waste. We've set there on the levy and watched trucks just back up and dump green crap in the water. Who knows what it is. They've tested the water and it's got mercury, heavy metals, all kinds of stuff. It's bad news. The Border Patrol now has a lawsuit going with the government to get hazardous-duty pay because just working around in this area and breathing the dust from the riverbed when it's dried up is hazardous. It's a mess. But they're trying to clean all that up now. They've got a new sewage treatment plant and two more. They're trying to control all the water that comes across.

Monk: But you were about to say you hand it to the Mexicans.

Thomas: Oh yeah, because, they'll jump these fences, they'll hide in these bushes, they'll risk being bit by all kinds of snakes, rodents, and everything else, hide in that river, finally make it into the United States, get a job, and not bitch about it. Meanwhile you have people here in the United States that don't want to work for minimum wage. They're too good for that.

And generally, we give them every reason to come here. I tell a lot of them I catch, "Hey, I'm not blaming you. This is my job. If I was you with your kids, I'd be coming here, too." This is the land of plenty and our government surely hands it out. There's no reason for them not to come here. And generally speaking, they're great people. They're the nicest people. They're hard working. But their society obviously deals with things differently then we do. They're mostly based on bribes. But to have an open border in a short order of time would destroy the American way of life.

Monk: And we're not going to go that way, are we? There's no big push to—

Thomas: There are groups out there that can't stand the Border Patrol or INS and are for open borders. But I think the majority of people are against it. The problem you have is all of the border states are really up on what's going on with the border and immigration, but the states not on the border don't really see it as a problem because they're not affected immediately. Here in California, if we have a massive insurgence of people we see the effect immediately. The crime rate goes up, more cars are stolen, and all that kind of stuff. But other states don't see it. But they're starting to. My father-in-law is chief of police in Colorado and they did a road block and in one night, in Cortez, Colorado, they caught 136 illegal aliens. That's in one night in Colorado.

Monk: It's never the wealthy, highly educated people who try to cross anyway, is it? It's almost always poor people.

Thomas: Almost always. The wealthy, highly educated people can afford to pay the bribes to get their paperwork moved up and cross legally. They have border-crossing rights.

Monk: Do you have to do some military training to do this?

Thomas: No. Though a lot of guys that come in have prior military service but it's not a prerequisite. You have to learn Spanish. You have to go to five months of school to learn Spanish, learn immigration law, learn arrest techniques and stuff like that. Here it's not bad at all. But the border patrol seizes more drugs than all the other federal law enforcement agencies put together. On accident. We're not even looking for it when we find it.

Monk: They're called mules. Right? They just pack them in their stomachs, right?

Thomas: Not even that. Now they just do it in backpacks. Out in El Centro you'll see a train of twenty people all with these huge backpacks on. When we come up they drop the backpacks and run to Mexico. You just pick up bags of marijuana or cocaine.

Monk: But heroin, they don't mess with that, do they? It'd be too severe.

Thomas: They don't care. I mean, you've got an 18-year-old over there and you say "Here's $500, take this backpack over there." He doesn't care what's in it.

One of the most disgusting things was a drug lord who started stealing children, killing them, gutting them, and putting the drugs inside, carrying them across like they were asleep. They caught two guys doing it. I don't know how many more got across that weren't caught.

Monk: Wasn't there a major drug lord who built a mansion along the border and was taunting the border patrol?

Thomas: That wasn't here, that was out east. The same guy bought a warehouse on the Mexican side and the American side and dug a big tunnel. That was in Brownfield. That's just 15 miles east of here. It was like eight million dollars to build this tunnel. They had train tracks so they could push the stuff underneath. They had a real elaborate tunnel that came up in a room under a pool table. We have devices that we can run over the ground and check where there are anomalies in the ground, where there's no dirt or a big sinkhole. But they'd fill this thing with water. They had it where they could flood it and vacuum it out. So when it was not being used they'd flood it. If you ran something over, it would look like an underground stream or water source. And one time when they were transporting stuff we ran the device and found it. The tunnel was in operation for quite some time. If it cost them eight million to make, imagine how many drugs were going through every day. Hundreds of millions of dollars.

> *"I tell a lot of them I catch, 'Hey, I'm not blaming you. This is my job. If I was you with your kids, I'd be coming here, too.'"*

Monk: There's a guy surfing down there [pointing to a jet ski].

Thomas: Waverunner. They'll use those and come across here.

Monk: Now as soon as that guy crosses he's illegal, right?

Thomas: Well, he's made an illegal entry. But usually they do it at night. And then you have the people that come up from Guatemala and Honduras. And they know that we have repatriation where if they come all this way and for whatever reason they want to go back home all they have to do is jump the fence and give themselves up. We can't return them back to Mexico. We have to fly them all the way back to Honduras or Guatemala because Mexico won't take them.

Monk: What's the worst day of the year?

Thomas: Ah, New Year's we get really hit hard. During the day we don't get much because they're so hungover. But New Year's Eve the border is nuts. They're over there with rockets, guns, AK-47s. It will last for about four or five hours. I'm not kidding you. We just take cover. Everyone has guns and they're just shooting straight up in the air with no regard for what goes up must come down. As soon as it's midnight, fires, firecrackers, and lots of guns.

Toxic Tourism

> **San Onofre Nuclear Generating Station.** Interstate 5, San Onofre State Beach exit (San Clemente). ☎ **949/368-3000.**

If you're not driving an old rusty car or truck, chances are you'll cruise right through the immigration checkpoint on I-5 above Oceanside, since the so-called "coyotes" who smuggle illegal aliens across the border drive beaters for fear of losing newer and more expensive cars. But as you continue north toward San Clemente you might find yourself slowing to 40 as you gawk at the towering twin white globes of this controversial—though still awesome-looking—power plant. Though they resemble a pair of large silicone breasts catching the rays—which is something that actually does happen at a nude beach not far below—this troubled landmark is not the woman of your dreams. She's had her share of PR problems, not unlike a former neighbor, Richard Nixon, whose summer White House was nearby. In 1989, a study found that San Onofre's cooling system was killing off the massive offshore kelp beds and along with them millions of fish, eggs, and larvae. In 1991 the utility agreed to build an unprecedented 300-acre reef out of concrete slabs to protect the seaweed. But then there came the problem of those hundreds of sea lions and seals that got sucked into the cooling system intake pipe, arriving DOA inside the plant. Add to that the discovery of four radioactive atomic kittens born inside the plant—appropriately named Alpha, Beta, Gamma, and Neutron—who were found with alarmingly high levels of cesium and cobalt. As if that was not enough, there's the occasional degradation and corrosion of "generator water tubes," coupled with the earthquake potential of the region, and it's no wonder a few locals are a trifle skittish. Still, that doesn't seem to stop a thriving occupancy at neighboring San Onofre State Park and Campground (San Diego's answer to Dockweiler Beach in L.A.), not to mention the nearby nude beach, where sunbathers have to contend with a constant whirl of Marine helicopters strafing the area during fly-by practice runs. Then again, the sunsets are spectacular and the radioactive waves will ride you all the way to shore. Just look out for those intake pipes or you may be spending all eternity with four adorable atomic kittens and their glow-in-the-dark sea-lion friends.

The Big Sleazy: Tijuana, Mexico

For all of San Diego's attempts at morality, propriety, and by-the-book suburbanity, you have precisely the opposite just across the border. Tijuana is San Diego's shadow self. As Richard Brautigan put it, "a border town brings out the worst of both cities."

› Bambi's. Ave. Revolucion 910 (Tijuana).

If you've had the misfortune to accidentally wander into the Unicorn Strip Club, across the street where the skankiest girls in Tijuana work, then Bambi's will seem like a Miss America beauty pageant. But be forewarned: Bambi's is also the fastest hustle of any strip club in the known universe. When you enter from the street, disco pounds at your skull and before you can even adjust to the dark lights you're propositioned at least a dozen times with subtle, endearing lines like "Suckie-fuckie? Suckie-fuckie?" We were escorted by the top brass to a VIP booth overlooking the stage and promptly handed two ten-dollar beers. Before we could even get the bills out of our pockets there were no less than four wildly gyrating girls with enormous tits doing complete body slides up and down our torsos. Tijuana, in case you've been living in North Dakota all your life, places no restrictions on its strippers. Full-body contact and touching is, well, pretty much encouraged. We're not sure if the fingers down our pants were an attempt at arousal or a precursor to lifting a wallet, but praise Jesus only one of our posse was under the influence of Viagra. During the onslaught of sexual advances we had the wherewithal to secret our valuables away from curious fingers. If the girls weren't to our liking, then they were immediately replaced by another set. There seemed to be an unending supply of big-breasted Mexican beauties, though their personalities were noticeably lacking in the warm and fuzzy department. After eight ten-dollar beers (yes, each girl gets a beer) we were about to head off when our more adventurous pal Hank, throbbing from Viagra, decided to go for the two-for-one private booth special. He caught up with us half an hour later, claiming it was the freakiest sex he'd ever had.

› Cafe Especial. Ave. Revolucion 718, at the foot of the stairs below Hotel Lafayette (Tijuana). ☎ 011-526/685-6654.

Since July 17, 1952, Cafe Especial has been serving up original versions of basic Mexican fare, from their charcoal-broiled steaks to their famous steamed tacos. While still on Revolucion, this is one of the most overlooked of the Mexican food finds. You descend a long set of stairs to a classic alley of curio shops. Streams of sunlight fall three stories down through a canyon of colorful blankets, ponchos, hats, and leather goods. Inside the cafe you'll find atmosphere. *Lots* of atmosphere. Colorful tables and chairs. A deep dining room. Murals cover the walls. A crisp waitstaff dressed in white shirts, bow ties, and black vests are overly attentive and on their toes. Our food arrived within three minutes of ordering. To the average Jose this is a good thing. But it means, of course, that your meal was prepared hours in advance and is just scooped off the steamers. Margaritas are average, but across the alley you can get a pitcher full for a buck. And, yes, there's a mariachi band.

> **Grand Hotel Tijuana.** Blvd. Agua Caliente 4500 (Tijuana). ☎ **011-526/681-7000.** www.grandhoteltijuana.com.

To our shock and surprise, Tijuana has another face. A few miles beyond the ruins of disco-lined Revolucion and the unseemly barrios is a bona fide downtown. Here you'll pass American-style strip malls, banks, supermarkets, million-dollar mansions spreading up the hillside, and a surprising number of high-rises lining clean, well-paved streets. At the heart of this thriving commercial center is the Grand Hotel Tijuana, which, should you actually put some forethought into your debauchery, would be quite the self-esteem builder after an evening of crawling on all fours. This twenty-two floor glass tower faces a sprawling golf course, and each of its 422 rooms commands a panoramic view of the dusty metropolis below. There's a time-warp quality to the place, which comes dangerously close to the look and feel of a seventies Vegas hotel. Lots of mirrors. Cottage cheese wall paneling. Faux nouveau art. Aggressive attempts at coordinating drapes, carpet and bedspreads in similar (but not same) colors. For a hundred bucks it isn't a steal, but you'd be paying twice the price north of the border, and this way you don't have to face the commute when you hit the TJ fun curve.

> **La Villa de Zaragoza Hotel.** Ave. Madero 1120 (Tijuana). ☎ **011-526/685-1832.**

It's six in the morning and the first rays of light are hitting the neighboring Tijuana hills. You're in your car (if, at this point, you even have a car), hauling around a suitcase worth of leather goods, half-empty fifths of Tequila, and an armful of pharmaceuticals. Your friends, if there ever were any, have all disappeared. There is no relationship between your brain and most bodily functions. But you do know that if you don't fall into a bed soon you will ultimately lay your ass down next to the striped donkey under a pile of sombreros and pass out for good. That's where the Zaragoza comes in. Only a block away from the action, this is Tijuana's answer to a Motel 6: convenient, affordable, and it has clean sheets. With a basic room at $34.75 and a halfway decent attempt at Spanish Colonial architecture, this motel will definitely do the trick—especially when compared to places like Hotel Lorena on Revolucion, which rents rooms by the half hour. (Ten bucks an hour, in case you're interested. Girl not included.)

> **Medicine Store.** Ave. Revolucion 943 (Tijuana). ☎ **011-526/688-3535.**

Let's be honest. You're in Tijuana to break some rules. To aid in that quest there are more than a dozen pharmacies right on the main tourist drag. In the sixties this is where you bought your amphetamines, in the seventies your Valiums, and in the eighties your "happy pills." But at the turn of the century? It's Viagra, Bob. Almost every pharmacy advertises in bold signage this latest wonder drug. Naturally, we were doling out a few twenties for a half-dozen boxes of single 50mg doses. Before we'd even left the store, our pal Hank, along for the ride, had popped a few.

"What the hell did you do that for?"

"If I'm gonna do it anywhere, it might as well be Tijuana," he said.

Fifteen minutes later. "You feeling anything?"

"Nope."

Thirty minutes later. "How's it going?"

"Let's go visit a strip club."

A few tequillas and several kinky whores later, Hank had his fill.

Crossing the border was a cinch. We just stashed the Viagra in our camera and cruised on through.

›Road Trip:
The Desert

When the earliest battalions of God-loving pioneers crossed the barren stretches of California desert, they viewed every passing mile as the devil's curse. Even today, though the vistas inspire and the quietness restores, without four cylinders, bottled water, miles of tarmac, and frigid air-conditioning, this sparsely settled domain can easily lead to a brutal, tortuous demise.

Nonetheless, at a certain juncture in the aggressive conquest of the West, pilgrims began to eye the desertscape not with fear, but greed, seeing the barren terrain as treasure ripe for plundering. Since then, American Man has looked at the desert as a place to occupy and conquer, not a landscape worthy of protection on its own terms. From this viewpoint, the desert is merely a repository of resources, a place to be exploited, but otherwise avoided. A hostile enemy.

Until recently, the vast California desert made a mockery of such arrogant development. No more. Now, nearly two centuries after the very first pilgrims made their way across these lands, the great expanse of California desert has become an industrial windfall, envied by half the world. As a direct consequence of this consumerist view of nature, however, the California desert is slowly but surely becoming endangered, evidence of our historic disregard for the desert's sanctity and integrity. Even with measures like the 1994 Desert Protection Act, the situation is bound to worsen.

On the surface, as a playground, the area is still unrivaled. While the neighboring deserts of Arizona and New Mexico cover more miles, the California deserts are compact and manageable, with at least five distinct regions spreading across the southeast corner of the state. From the buggy rallies across the Imperial Dunes, to Anza-Borrego's parade of cacti and flowers, to Joshua Tree's Jumbo Rocks, to the Devil's Playground of Mojave, to the otherworldly low points of Death Valley National Park, each turn of the sun-buckled road gives way to an unparalleled panorama, energizing the most urban spirits.

Yet the sanctioned desert parks are merely the official facade for the thinly concealed pillage of all points underground. Beyond and even within the park system's borders sprawl enormous minefields where tectonic machinery hacks away at the earth. Whether it's the gold of Mesquite Mine, the borax of Boron, the gypsum of Plaster City, or the calcite near Anza-Borrego, countless commodities are violently extracted from the desert and by a convoluted path make their way into products worldwide. And because of this state's broad-minded quest for alternative energy, the California deserts are also home to the largest solar voltaic plants and windmill farms in America. Of course, not far from the windmills, parks, and goldfields, the U.S. military strafes huge areas of the desert in the largest war rehearsals on earth.

Whatever desert land the industrial-military complex hasn't claimed, the transplanted bourgeoisie have, building sprawling, unnaturally green golf courses, swimming pools, and air-conditioned shopping malls where desert hares used to run. As the textbook example, the sad, mindless opulence of Palms Springs crawls across the desert like a renegade virus, driven by the yearly increase in snowbirds escaping the cold. What desert is left after the resorts and the military have staked their claims is imperiled by increasing urban sprawl: Los Angeles will soon stretch to Victorville, San Diego to Julian.

Almost as an antidote come the low-tech cultists and survivalists seeking utopia in these valleys of rock and sand, seeking to preserve the salient virtues of the naked desert land—its solitude, space, beauty, and status as the ideal staging ground for cutting-edge art, performance, and community.

Indeed, for decades the California desert has been a magnet for the fringe. There is a Mad Max, desert-rat quality to the alternative types who brave the elements for a life in the dry heat. Spontaneous communities like Slab City, with winter populations numbering in the thousands, thrive on barren dirt, inhabiting camper shells, stalled cars, and aging RVs. Homegrown artists like Moby Dick and Leonard Knight (see interview later in this chapter) express their visionary hallucinations through the land itself. Felicity, the "Center of the World," proves that with enough money any nutball can start his own town. As corporate intrusions on this sacred land grow, so too will countercultural attempts to utilize the desert for artistic nonmonetary ends. Either way, the desert will increasingly cease to be desert, an area which by definition is sparsely occupied.

For better or worse, the California desert is already so far from empty space that to see it as such is to be blind. Every nook and cranny is teeming with creation, both natural and man-made. Follow our peculiar turns off the road and you'll discover that this is not only the ultimate California playground, but the ultimate California landscape, an astounding place to both nurture and amuse the soul. Just bring water!

East and South of L.A.

> **Anza-Borrego Desert.** Hwy. 78, west of the Salton Sea. Park Headquarters
☎ **760/767-5311;** Wildflower hot line ☎ 760/767-4684. www.anzaborrego.statepark.org.
For a tour of the park contact Desert Jeep Tours (☎ 888/BY-JEEPS).

This often overlooked desert should have been declared a national park ages ago but instead went the route of a state park. That's fine with us. As the mainstream German tourists flock to the more glamorous Death Valley, that leaves the Elephant Trees, Teddy Bear Chollas, and desert pupfish for Monks in the know.

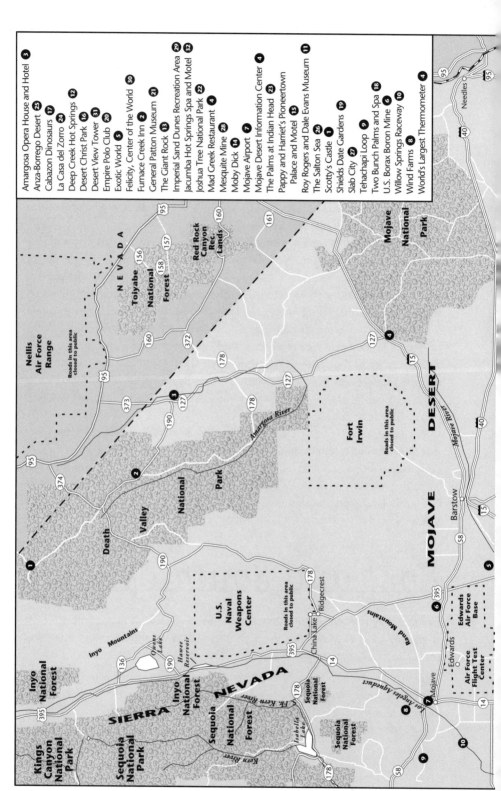

Amargosa Opera House and Hotel **3**
Anza-Borrego Desert **25**
Cabazon Dinosaurs **17**
La Casa del Zorro **24**
Deep Creek Hot Springs **12**
Desert Christ Park **16**
Desert View Tower **31**
Empire Polo Club **20**
Exotic World **5**
Felicity, Center of the World **30**
Furnace Creek Inn **2**
General Patton Museum **21**
The Giant Rock **13**
Imperial Sand Dunes Recreation Area **29**
Jacumba Hot Springs Spa and Motel **32**
Joshua Tree National Park **22**
Mad Greek Restaurant **4**
Mesquite Mine **28**
Moby Dick **14**
Mojave Airport **7**
Mojave Desert Information Center **4**
The Palms at Indian Head **23**
Pappy and Harriet's Pioneertown
    Palace and Motel **15**
Roy Rogers and Dale Evans Museum **11**
The Salton Sea **26**
Scotty's Castle **1**
Shields Date Gardens **19**
Slab City **27**
Tehachapi Loop **9**
Two Bunch Palms and Spa **18**
U.S. Borax Boron Mine **6**
Willow Springs Raceway **10**
Wind Farms **8**
World's Largest Thermometer **4**

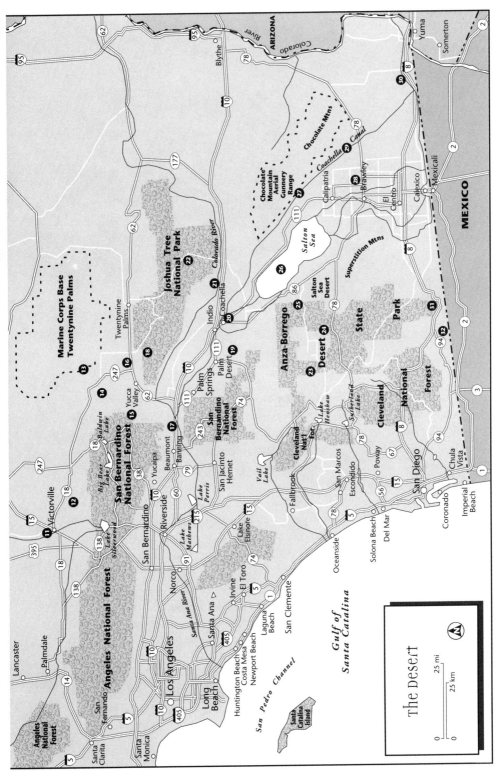

The Desert

25 mi

25 km

600,000 acres and hardly *any* German tourists

Anza-Borrego is a huge, 600,000-acre area that sprawls south of Palm Springs all the way to Mexico. It's bordered by several mountain ranges and the vast Salton Sea. If you think you're seeing Arizona in miniature, you are. The colors came from the inside of the Grand Canyon when millions of years ago it drained into this area. But forget the dirt—there's one spring event that draws people here: the desert flowers. They call it "In Season." That's when innkeepers charge double rates, few rooms are vacant, and bumper-to-bumper traffic is found up some roads. Still, March and April witness an astounding display of lavender, pink, orange, red, and yellow wild-flowers and blooming cacti, which totally carpet the desert floor.

The town of Borrego Springs is at the heart of the action. Adjacent to a state park, **The Palms at Indian Head,** 2220 Hoberg Rd. (☎ **760/767-7788**), is a holdover from the forties and fifties, when the resort was a secret hideaway for Hollywood stars (black-and-white photos scattered throughout the resort document the era). Thirty years ago, Borrego Springs was the ultimate biker-trash town and a great place to score speed. Now it's mostly upscale resorts and a shopping mall. What hot springs remained have now been sealed because locals "didn't like the element they attracted." When looking for a place to stay we were pointed to **La Casa del Zorro,** 3845 Yaqui Pass Rd. (from downtown Borrego Springs take Highway S3 4 miles, turn right Yaqui Pass Road; ☎ **760/767-5323**), as if it were the Holy Grail of resorts. The motif was Santa Fe–style. The clientele was fat Europeans. Relieved to be out of nauseating Palm Springs, we stayed. The food here is unquestionably the best in the area. Our Colorado lamb chops were succulent and tender. Ditto for the extraordinarily prepared halibut (a mighty trick, since properly cooking halibut can be a difficult feat). And the service—from our sweet and friendly Utah waiter, to the cordial and amenable front desk, to the manager himself—was top of the line. You will definitely be properly cared for at La Casa del Zorro. And, if you have any complaints, owner Helen Copley (of the Copley newspaper chain), lives just a few hundred yards away.

Though our rooms at La Casa del Zorro were very pleasant, after awhile we realized we were in the middle of this great desert landscape and we'd never know it from all the buildings, casitas, and tall tamarind trees. Our solution was to simply get out of the compound and hike. We discovered that there are so many trails, trenches, and deep ravines that you could get lost for months. But remember: Besides being an oasis of creosote, cactus, ironwood, and palm, Anza-Borrego is also an off-road-vehicle paradise, so watch out for those gas-guzzling SUVs (yes, for a small minority, they are more than status symbols).

At the entrance to the Anza-Borrego park coming up Road S22 sits an old guy next to his car with a sign that reads PEACE AND LOVE. He waves to all passing cars. Far out, man.

> **Cabazon Dinosaurs.** 50800 Seminole Dr., Main St. exit from Interstate 10 (Cabazon). ☎ **909/849-8309.** Gift shop open daily 9am–8pm.

The Cabazon dinosaurs are probably the most photographed and videotaped highway landmarks in the world, the ultimate example of roadside Americana. Built in the late 1960s by Knott's Berry Farm sculptor and sketch artist Claude Bell as a gimmick to get customers into the adjacent Wheel Inn Restaurant, these two life-sized concrete-and-steel reptiles loom over passing motorists, a hilariously huge and happy symbol informing all east-bound travelers that they're entering the desert and leaving the Herculean maw of L.A. behind. The Tyrannosaurus rex stands a menacing 55 feet high and bares a fair, though oversized, resemblance to his *Jurassic Park* cousins. "Dinney," the 150-foot-long, 40-foot-high apatosaurus, is slightly encumbered by the presence of a gift shop that resides in his belly. There's a high quotient of kids here along with packed tour buses of Germans and Japanese. Practice your T-rex roar and you'll scatter the crowd.

> **Desert Christ Park.** Mohawk Trail, at Sunny Slope Dr., next to Evangelical Free Church (Yucca Valley). From 29 Palms Hwy. go north on Mohawk Trail. Free admission.

One of Antone Martin's forty desert Jesuses

Antone Martin, a fanatical do-gooder with an obsessive Jesus fixation, spent his later years erecting an acre of ghostly snow-white concrete statues on this site overlooking the desert. You've got Jesus delivering his Sermon on the Mount, Jesus kneeling in the garden, Jesus talking to the children, Jesus hanging with the whores. Though the park is dedicated to Peace on Earth and the Brotherhood of Man, we're just a bit too cynical to look past the really bad handiwork and lofty ideals, without a mild snicker. Plus, the place has seen better days, due to the 1992 Landers earthquake that rolled a 7.6er through the valley and cracked off a few hands. The statues weigh in at up to 16 tons, with a few standing 12 feet tall. And let me tell you, these phantasmal characters are frightening. Under a full moon you'd swear they were creatures rising from the dead. But let's not be harsh. The setting does resemble old Palestine. And even if you aren't a true believer, you have to show Mr. Martin some props for the sheer monumental effort of erecting forty giant sculptures with his bare hands. The most notable piece is a 30-foot-long bas-relief wall where Martin carved the Last Supper. There is a cut-out window just above Jesus where you can peer over his shoulder and watch him bless bread. He's not only the rebel rabbi from Nazareth, he's a darn good photo-op!

But does the $700,000 include the dinosaur?

> **Desert View Tower.** Off Interstate 8 in Imperial County, 6 miles east of Jacumba on the In-ko-pah Park Rd. (Jacumba). Open daily 8:30am–5pm.

On a rugged hill on the edge of the Jacumba Mountains, looming thousands of feet above the Anza-Borrego Desert, stands a four-story tower made of rock and mortar, which houses a museum. From the looks of things a mop or broom hasn't been used around this "museum" in years. The level of spider webs and dust reaches spookhouse proportions. For a $1 entry fee you get to climb a spiraling stairwell, visiting several levels of Old West cowboy and Indian memorabilia in the form of badly framed lithographs and magazine cut-outs. But the view from up top is what you're paying for. From a vista that sweeps toward the far eastern horizon the entire desert floor is laid out before you. Gale-force winds rush through the mountain pass and whip fierce dust devils across the parched earth. Adjoining the tower are the "caves," where naturally eroded granite boulders were carved into skulls and animal forms by retired engineer W. T. Ratcliffe back in the 1930s. The "caves" have no particular relationship to the tower other than a possible marketing ploy to get more people stopping in. Of course, this is why we love this place: just another roadside attraction trying to make a buck. The tower itself was the work of a man named Burt Vaughn, who, impressively, built the whole thing with his own hands back in the 1920s. Ole Burt wanted to commemorate the pioneers who crossed the desert on their way to San Diego. Over the years it's seen many owners and at one point even hosted a restaurant but now limits its commerce to the gift shop and museum. Rumor has it the tower is up for sale. For a mere $700,000 it could be yours. Real-estate agent Ed Snively has the details.

> **Empire Polo Club.** 81800 Avenue 51, at Monroe (Indio). ☎ **760/342-2762.** empirepolo@aol.com.

Polo is a wonderfully elegant sport. It has majesty, grace, beauty. It is dignified. It seems proper to watch polo on a rain-swept field in England. In the desert, it's an obscenity.

The Empire Polo Club has 10 acres of emerald-green polo fields, with more sprinklers than you find on most golf courses. Across from the playing fields is an enormous oasis teeming with gorilla, elephant, giraffe, rhino, bear, lion, and a unicorn. Is it a zoo? Not exactly. The animal figures are made of bronze. They pose under the cover of tropical plants, palms, and flowers. Several arching bridges cross the oasis. Thatched-roof patios protect you from the blaring sun. In the middle of the lagoon is a sexy mermaid. For a brief moment, as you retreat under the shade from the 110° heat, you can almost suck water molecules right off the pond and through your pores. In the Southern California desert, all is fair.

> **Felicity, Center of the World.** Center of the World Rd. (Felicity). 10 miles west of Yuma, Ariz., Interstate 8. Exit on Sidewinder Rd.

When you arrive at the center of the world you know you're there because the sign says so. The town has its own post office, a cafeteria, several apartment complexes, a house, a 25-foot section of spiral staircase from the Eiffel Tower that travels into thin air, open-air desert bowling, and *no,* we repeat NO residents. At least not between the months of April and October, when the mayor and founder of The Center of the World, Jacques Andre Istel, moves back to France with his presumably beloved wife, Felicia. The town is either named after her or after a character in Istel's book, *Coe the Good Dragon.*

Other than his penchant for naming towns and defying the laws of science by declaring a surface center on a spherical planet, Monsieur Istel also has the distinction of being one of the fathers of recreational parachuting. At the center of "The

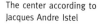
The center according to Jacques Andre Istel

In Felicity, The Center of the World

Center of the World" stands a pyramid that harbors a time capsule and a plaque indicating where you're standing, which, for those not paying attention, is the center of the world. (Actually, the *center* of the center of the world would be in the center of the pyramid, but we're dealing with the French here, so let's not get too anal, alright?)

Mr. Istel does have a passion for great art—a bronze Michelangelo's Hand of God points across a sundial toward the pyramid. He also offers all passing strangers the chance to immortalize their name on two parallel walls of granite, called The Wall for the Ages, which stretch a fair distance toward neighboring hills. Sir Jacques promises they'll be standing for a few thousand years, so cough up the dough and have your name engraved.

Established May 21, 1985, you'd think Felicity would have experienced the growth boom of similarly situated desert towns. Especially after the Imperial County Board of Supervisors agreed that "The Center of the World" was 114° longitude and 32° latitude and especially after the Institut Geographique National of France officially recognized Felicity as "The Center of the World" on September 14, 1989. Then again, maybe there is something to the Clintonesque distinction between "earth" and "world." Felicity is certainly not the center of the *earth*, which resides somewhere in the molten core. But is it the center of *the world*, which certainly must include the "billions and billions" of galaxies and infinite space Monsieur Sagan talked about? These Frenchmen are either pulling a giant Copernican joke or they know something we don't. Go make your own journey to "The Center of the World" and decide for yourself.

The California desert has historically been the home of spiritual visionaries. Among them, author Edwin Dingle and his Institute of Mentalphysics and its Sanctuary of Mystic Christianity and Caravansary of Joy; the former health resort of Zzyzx, built by evangelist Curtis Springer (no relation to Jerry); and, of course, Jacques Andre Istel's Felicity, "The Center of the World."

> General Patton Memorial Museum. #2 Chiriaco Rd. (Indio). 30 miles east on Hwy. 10, Chiriaco Summit Turnoff. ☎ **760/227-3483.** Open daily 9:30am–4:30pm.

From all known reports, General George Patton was a royal ass. But royal asses often make great generals. It's too bad this museum doesn't do this ass justice.

Back during World War II, before Patton took his troops to battle Rommel in North Africa, this was the headquarters of the Army's desert training center. The terrain is identical to North Africa, so it obviously gave Patton an edge over his Nazi counterpart. Over a million troops trained here, but all that's left is this small museum. (Hey, that sounds like a T-shirt. . . .) Outdoors are the tanks. Indoors are the uniforms, maps, a video that explains the African campaigns, and a small demonstrator tank, made to scale but never produced. The only personal item of Patton's is his fencing sword. The highlight of the place is the array of battered, used tanks just west of the museum parking lot. Now *these* are artifacts of war. Rusting, dented, forlorn, these remarkable examples of combat-tested machinery convey the feel of the desert campaign better than any museum ever could.

Outside at the
General Patton
Memorial Museum

The Giant Rock

> **Giant Rock.** Linn Rd. (Landers). From Hwy. 247, north of Landers, turn right on Linn Rd., which turns into a dirt road at the bottom of a hill. Take first dirt road to your left and follow out 3 miles. Veer right at major fork.

Finally, a place for those singularly obnoxious SUVs to kick into four-wheel drive and get off the friggin' road. Funny thing is, you only see vans and pickups out here on the sand (should tell you something about the overcompensating, undersized types who drive SUVs). Your mission, should you choose to accept it, is to drive off the highway into the middle of the desert, unaided by maps or markers, and, by sheer intuition, find a giant rock. Mind you, this isn't just any giant rock. Not only has this rock been the site of reported UFO activity, but it attracts thousands of ecstasy-fueled ravers on an occasional basis, though you don't have to be a drug user to appreciate the magic of this rock.

Though it got its start several million years ago, The Giant Rock's main claim to fame is that UFO abductee George Van Tassel moved his family under the towering geological formation in the late forties. There's a small cave that marks the spot. Apparently Mr. Van Tassel wasn't satisfied with his Integratron energy machine, which lies housed under a dome you'll pass on Linn Road. Out here, under the giant rock, he was able to talk directly with the stars.

Though the Van Tassels moved on, the less inspired (or gullible?) locals have kept coming for years, either to lose their virginity or to simply kick back and have "one for the road." Graffiti now covers a good deal of the lower portion of the rock's domed surface. One side has been severely blackened from the soot of one too many oversized camp fires. The discarded fridge, scattered car parts, and heaps of refuse lend a trailer trash aesthetic to the landscape.

Still, if you're lucky, and the ravers and locals are gone, maybe you too can make like Mr. Van Tassel and talk to the stars. Who knows, maybe you'll even get abducted.

> **Imperial Sand Dunes Recreation Area.** Hwy. 78 (Glamis).

A few miles west of Glamis you suddenly arrive at the California take on the Sahara Desert. Giant sand dunes drift in graceful ridges as far as you can see. The wind carves ripples across the crest as sand billows in the air. Just when you're capturing your Fuji Moment, suddenly, over the horizon charge two dozen dune buggies, flying over the peaks at top speed, spewing exhaust and sounding like a battalion of chain saws. It's frightening, horribly disturbing, but goddamn does it look like fun. You've just arrived at the nation's largest off-highway vehicle recreational area. On some weekends more than 30,000 motor enthusiasts show up, drink a lot of beer, and ride the dunes. When you're not getting sand flung in your face, you might also recognize the dunes from their role in *Star Wars*. Many of the desert scenes were filmed here.

> **Jacumba Hot Springs Spa and Motel.** 44500 Old Hwy. 80 (Jacumba).
☎ 619/766-4333.

If your vision of utopia is a limitless supply of healing waters, a funky cinder-block motel in the middle of the desert, and a bar that serves a mighty stiff drink, have we got a place for you. Just a quick sprint from the unpatrolled Mexican border, this motel dates back to the turn of the century, when there was a hotel-cum–health spa up the street that catered to the SoCal elite. But the hotel burned to the ground. Now, on the block-long street of Jacumba stands "The Spa." German-born Felix and Lisa Bachmier, along with Felix Jr., run this funky motel and smoky bar. Their rooms are cheap and clean. That's the best that can be said. Their restaurant is serviceable, leaning heavy on the prepackaged side of the food chain (unfortunately, this is the only place to eat in Jacumba). But the mineral pools more than compensate. A lap-size swimming pool is the centerpiece of the resort. The warm spring waters that feed the pool are both chlorine- and sulfur-free. You can easily get carried away with a long soak—floating on your back, staring blissfully at the dry blue sky. On the other side of the motel, near the entrance, is an indoor Jacuzzi, also fed from the springs. Here's where you make company with a steady stream of world travelers. Within an hour we'd met four Korean girls, a German family of three, two backpacking American students, a leather-skinned octogenarian with his bleached blond gin-guzzling wife, a high-testosterone trucker with more than soaking on his mind, and a healer named Thomas who gave the best impromptu shoulder rub

Felix Bachmier of Jacumba Hot Springs

we've had in years. On the trek between the pool and Jacuzzi you walk dripping wet in your skimpy bathing suit through the motel lobby and bar. The crusty men hunkered over their beer kind of stare you up and down. That gets a little weird, but hell, you're the only entertainment in town. There's a masseuse and tennis court on the premises, but who needs it. After a six pack and a 3-hour soak, you'll be so toasted Felix will be scraping you off the floor.

> Joshua Tree National Park. Cottonwood Entrance. Exit off Interstate 10, at Joshua Tree exit. ☎ 760/367-5500.

There's this tree, you see. Actually, it's not a tree per se, but a yucca, a proud member of the lily family. But it's usually called a tree, so we'll call it that too. It's a thorny, spiny, barrel-trunk tree with a lot of short stumpy limbs covered in pointy cactus leaves. It grows pretty tall. And when it stands against an azure sky near the end of the day, it makes for a great photo-op, with you standing in the foreground, of course. Because of the tree's bearded appearance and upraised limbs, Mormon travelers said it reminded them of the prophet Joshua, leading them on to the Promised Land.

Today the Joshua tree has its own park, though it's not the only plant around. There's lots of cacti. Lots of ironwood trees, smoke trees, creosote, desert willows, and small shrubs, too. The Joshua Tree itself only grows on the north end of the park. But that's OK, because most drivers enter the Park Loop Road from the north side at the town of Joshua Tree.

Now listen up: The recently canonized 800,000-acre Joshua Tree National Park is about the quietest place you're going to find in Southern California. Spread out over a mountainous terrain, it is absolutely wild in coyotes, mule deer, bighorn sheep, mountain lions, bobcat, badgers, gambil quail, roadrunners, and the majestic bald eagle. The roads through the park seem nearly desolate compared to those in its crowded neighbor, Death Valley. It's raw nature out here, without the frills. There are nine campgrounds. Self-guided trails take you to ghostly gold-mining camps. Frequent meteor showers take your breath away. Walk a few miles off the road to some quiet jagged vista and remember why you're alive.

› **Mesquite Mine.** Hwy. 78, 42 miles east of Brawley. ☎ **760/352-6541,** ext. 105.

A towering, heavy-gauge, barbed-wire fence slices through the desert landscape and is the first sign of man in this otherwise barren stretch of 78. Behind the miles of fencing is the largest gold mine in California, hence the Fort Knox level of security. Driving toward the entrance, you pass a mile-long, 200-foot plateau of waste rock. At the heavily guarded gate you are summarily scrutinized. If you've called in advance, you can take a hard-hat tour 350 feet down into the core of the mine to learn first-hand what the "heap leaching" process really is and how you too, with a little ingenuity and deep-pocket backers, could be pulling $100 million in gold annually out of these hills. The Mesquite Mine is owned by the second largest gold producer in the world, Newmont Gold of Canada. They attempt to counter the obvious damage they inflict on the landscape by proclaiming their land a protected zone for the endangered desert tortoise. Given the amount of cyanide solution used to leach the dirt, and the eroded hills that stretch toward the horizon, we don't entirely buy their environmental rhetoric.

Those refused entry can hike a trail ascending a hill overlooking the mine. From this vantage point you can see the vast outcropping of buildings, machines, pits, and storage pods, while contemplating the 87 tons of ore rock that must be moved to produce one ounce of gold. Something to ponder next time you put on a solid-gold necklace.

Joshua Tree artist Moby Dick

› **Moby Dick.** Hwy. 247 (Landers). 1 mile north of Landers on the left-hand side.

Old Moby Dick has been carving and painting the trunks of dead Joshua trees for well over forty years. From the looks of him it must have taken a fair amount of tequila to pull it off. Bordering the fence of his ramshackle roadside home, his comical tree trunks evoke hallucinatory images Walt Disney might have envied. Also scattered about are several outcroppings of junk that pass as sculpture, some made from discarded motorcycles. In his own intoxicated way, the man's brilliant. For a number of years he drove around in a truck with a huge sculpted whale mounted overhead, hence the name Moby Dick. Unfortunately, a drug deal gone bad (the facts were hard to follow) resulted in his prized possession meeting a fatal fire, burning it to the ground. His current plans involve a roadside tribute to Monica Lewinsky down on hands and knees. But first he's got a fire to light. Call it desert justice. He calls it revenge.

› **Pappy and Harriet's Pioneertown Palace and Motel.** Pioneertown Rd. (Pioneertown). From Yucca Valley, take Hwy. 62 west, turn north on Pioneertown Rd. ☎ 760/365-5956. www.pioneertown.com. Palace open Thurs–Sun, hotel open throughout the week.

When Harriet flips a steak on the grill she means business. She aims to please. The hundreds of regulars elbowing their way through this rustic restaurant/dance hall in the heart of the Mojave Desert are evidence that she has some mighty satisfied customers. But food isn't her only act. The big draw that pulls in folks from as far away as Reno is the music, liquor, and wild, raucous fun.

The setting of Pioneertown may look familiar to any film buff. It was established in 1946 as a movie set by Roy Rogers and Gene Autry and served as backdrop for the Gene Autry TV series, as well as the films *Cisco Kid* and *The Life and Times of Judge Roy Bean,* along with countless other cowboy flicks. A bowling alley, funky motel, and sprawling saloon served the card-playing, whiskey-drinking stars. Today Pioneertown operates under the slogan, "How the West Was." And damn, they come pretty close to getting it right, albeit end-o'-the-millennium–style. As you drive up the highway on a weekend night, you'll think you're completely lost among the yuccas when you suddenly come upon glowing neon beer signs, a mile of parked cars, a dirt parking lot full of campers, and an impromptu music circle. The Palace saloon is made of adobe and barn wood, with a tin roof. As you enter, you are greeted by a large wall-mounted moose. Weekends, the high-energy dance hall is bursting at the rivets, attracting an eclectic mix of local desert rats, bikers, businessmen, longhairs, and Marines on leave. If it weren't for the infectious goodwill of Harriet, things would get a bit rough, but they rarely do.

For several decades the Palace has been run with lots of love and folksy charm. After the decline of the town as a movie set, and after Harriet's mother Frances bought the place in the 1960s, the saloon became a notorious biker bar. Meanwhile, Harriet and her husband, Pappy, toured the country with their country blues band,

Harriet of Pappy and Harriet's Pioneertown Palace

Family Circle. In 1970, Harriet and Pappy took over the Palace. Pappy built onto the existing structure, attracting musicians to perform. They booked mostly country and rockabilly, though one night Donovan appeared. After extensive remodeling they invited country legend Lacy J. Dalton to play the house. In Harriet's words, "It was like she was opening a new day. When Lacy began to play, dust began to fall from the ceiling like a sign from above. She'd woke up the gods and the Palace was reborn!"

Though Pappy died in 1994, the legacy continues. Gene Autry came back to exchange hats, and film crews continue to shoot commercials. The adjacent motel is open throughout the week. If you're too drunk to drive back to Yucca Valley (which you will be), then one of these divelike motel rooms will have to do. Sunday nights local musicians jam to a house full of teens. Harriet dreams big and wants the saloon to outlive her and further the tradition for old musicians. "I'm the heart that rocks the Palace," Harriet says. "This isn't just a business, it's my heart, and when people come here they've come into my heart." If you meet Harriet, you'll believe her. Trust us, she's the real deal.

> **The Salton Sea.** Between Hwys. 86 and 111.

California is filled with strange bodies of water—Mono Lake with its trippy accumulations of tuff; the Owens Valley, completely sucked dry to supply the San Fernando Valley with chlorinated pool water; the completely mangled and denatured L.A. River; and, of course, the one-of-a-kind Salton Sea.

The Salton Sea is below sea level. It smells. There are trailer towns around the periphery. One such trailer town is North Shore, California. You do not want to live in North Shore. Unless you like the smell of rotting fish carcasses. Unless you like brown, smelly lakes.

People fish in this smelly soup. This sort of behavior is what makes me question the intelligence of fishermen. There are bait-and-tackle shops here, too. If someone opens up a Salton Seafood restaurant here some day, I'd advise you to stay away.

Why is the Salton Sea so foul and polluted? Because it's not a sea at all. It just looks like one. It's actually just a sandy depression in the desert, which got filled with water 83 feet deep and 45 miles long because of Colorado river overflow into the Imperial Valley back in 1905. The flood was stopped in 1907, leaving the present-day body of water, which has no outlets. The water is replenished by waters draining into the south end of the sea, and it stays constant, of course, by evaporation.

Why do we recommend a visit? Because the views at sunset are stunning. With the beautiful mountains behind, docks facing west, it's about as picturesque a tableau as one is likely to get in the Imperial Valley. But then, after your minute of sunset satori, you step back onto a decaying carp head and realize instantly why there's no rush to build condos on the Salton Sea.

The date-palm groves of

Coachella Valley produce 95% of

the world's date crop.

> **Shields Date Gardens.** 80225 Hwy. 111 (Indio). ☎ **760/347-0996.**

Date palms are one of the few sustainable crops grown in the dry land east of Palm Springs. There are thousands of acres of them. In fruit season, these noble palms droop heavily with clumps of succulent dates. Like the Monks, you'll pull off the road searching for a few dropped juicy dates only to find hard-as-rock rejects. That's where the cute, charming Shields comes in. They've been packaging and selling dates for seventy-five years and are hell-bent on educating the public about this luscious fruit. Walking into their center is an excursion into retro marketing, a campy dream come true. A darkened theater plays a short, grainy, continuously looped film entitled "The Romance and Sex Life of the Date." It elicits high smirk factor from everyone but the seniors who listen with rapt attention. The store carries every kind of date you can imagine: Super Jumbo Royal Medjool, Deglet Noor, Blonde and Brunette Dates. But you absolutely have not passed the date threshold until you've downed a large "World Famous" Date Shake for $2.95. Pure sugar. Sadly, outside of the Palm Springs Aerial Tramway (covered in every single guidebook to the area) and the above-mentioned Two Bunch Palms and Empire Polo Club, the Shields' campy Date Gardens is one of the few places we'd recommend visiting in the entire Palm Springs area.

> **Slab City.** Niland. From Hwy. 111, turn right at Gaston's restaurant. It's the only road in town. Follow to the end.

This is Rainbow Nation meets Mad Max meets a Good Sam Jamboree right in the middle of the Imperial Valley, not far from the Salton Sea, but not close either. It's desert out here. One thousand miles of government land. And it's free, baby. Which means every loser and loner with a vehicle and some spare cash can come out here and survive. Seasoned locals reckon two hundred dollars and some Milwaukee Best will get you by most months. A welfare or social security check, in other words. The name came from the fact that this former military training facility was decommissioned in 1946 and the wood and plumbing was sold off to local contractors. All that was left were the foundations. Thus, slab.

You want dysfunction? You got it. You want alcoholism? You got it. Still, residents prefer it to life in tract home suburbs or confining heavily regulated retirement homes. When entering, a small outpost welcomes you to Slab City with a crudely painted sign. Among the tumbleweeds and brush, the living quarters are fashioned out of cars, vans, trucks, and buses, some running, most not. Fire pits blaze away by

sunset as the dirty denizens huddle like post-apocalypse road warriors cooking their meals. Scrawny kids with ragged clothes and curious stares chase balls down deserted "streets." These full-timers have nothing but time on their hands and a defiant siege mentality, unwelcoming to strangers. However, winter months see the arrival of thousands of "snowbirds" in their fully outfitted RVs, Airstream pull-behinds, and over-the-hood camper vans. They soften the place up a bit. Somehow, this diverse transient community manages to get along. But when summer arrives, along with 100+ temperatures, only the hard-core remain. The desperate, gnarly edginess of these year-round Slab City citizens is worthy of a book, if not a poem.

> **Two Bunch Palms and Spa.** 67425 Two Bunch Palms Trail (Desert Hot Springs). ☎ 760/329-8791. *Note:* It takes studio (or at least divine) intervention to get through these gates if you're not a registered guest, so call in advance and plan a 2-day stay.

This renowned resort takes extra pains to point out the Al Capone bullet hole in the dressing mirror of the room in which he purportedly slept. And though they claim to keep their guest register secret, they relentlessly drop names in their promotional brochures. Yes, Jeff Bridges, Barbara Streisand, Mel Gibson, and Robin Williams stayed here. But any couple of yokels with a thousand to spend can retreat for the weekend. With its gauche, barely concealed elitism and enforced hushed tone ambiance, Two Bunch doesn't hold a candle to Tassajara or Harbin in authenticity or spirit. Still, Two Palms is the only Southern California hot-springs resort that comes even close to healing purity. And they are routinely voted one of the top ten hot-spring resorts in the world—if the *Condé Nast Traveler* definition of excellence means anything to you.

(continued on page 275)

God's Love in the Desert:
Leonard Knight
and Salvation Mountain

"I think the world needs a love story about little people just helping each other."

At the entrance to Slab City stands a "mountain." Actually it's a hill. From a distance it looks as if someone had draped a massive, multicolored canvas over the dirt and covered it with quotes from the Bible. Get closer, though, and the wash of colors become distinct patterns. To your astonishment, you realize the designs you see have been painted *on* the dirt.

For over thirteen years Leonard Knight has been painting religious icons and slogans on his three-story "mountain." GOD IS LOVE stands emblazoned at the top. LOVE is painted in pink. A tall cross stakes out the peak. You'd have to think the person behind this creation was a religious nutcase. Far from it. He's a lanky, soft-spoken lamb of a man with a delightful twinkle in his eye. Though he borrows heavily from scripture, his heart fairly bursts with goodwill and genuine compassion for all he meets. He is dedicated to this mountain. He works on it every day. And from a set of dirt steps painted in yellow, he explained to a passing Monk why Salvation Mountain is his life.

›interview

Monk: How did Salvation Mountain get its start?

LK: I came here in '84 and thought I'd just stay for a week. I had a hot-air balloon that had GOD IS LOVE on it, but it sort of rotted out and is back east. So I thought, *I'm going to have to put* GOD IS LOVE *on something else.* It just happened to be this mountain.

Monk: Was that the first thing you painted? GOD IS LOVE?

LK: No, I started with a big heart. Then I went up to love.

Monk: When you first moved here were you living in your truck?

LK: Yes, I had my '54 Chevy truck with my little house on the back and I was pulling my hot-air balloon around.

Monk: So what inspired you to come out here to Slab City?

LK: The weather. I was in Nebraska for four years from 1980 to 1984. I built that hot-air balloon in Nebraska. But it got so cold there in the winter. I said, "Boy. If I ever get this balloon built I'm going back to an island where it's a little bit warmer." So I think the weather had something to do with it.

Monk: So you had been here before.

LK: Yes. One year in '79.

Monk: And you were living in your truck then?

LK: Yes. But a different truck.

Monk: Have you always been an artist?

LK: No, never. I tried to paint cars for twenty years and could never paint a good one.

Monk: So the mountain was your first art project?

LK: Yes it was.

Monk: What was the inspiration behind it?

LK: In 1976, it was a Wednesday in the fall. One day I just said, "Jesus, I'm a sinner. Please come into my heart." I said that about fifteen times and tears started to come to my eyes. I really got to know Jesus real personal there by doing that and I wanted the whole world to know about it, but I wanted to be nice doing it. That's why "The Sinner's Prayer" is on the sides of my truck, it's on the mountain, it's on everything I do. *[Laughs]*

Monk: Are you part of a church?

LK: Not any religion whatsoever. I tell everybody, "If you love God, tell him so." And that's it. Nobody pushes anybody.

Monk: So it doesn't matter if they're Buddhist or Hindu. . . .

LK: Oh, it doesn't matter one bit. Let's just love one another and get along.

Monk: That's a good philosophy.

> *"I tell everybody, 'If you love God, tell him so.'*
> *And that's it. Nobody pushes anybody."*

LK: To my knowledge it cost about $17 to cover the mountain cause people gave me thousands of gallons of paint. So the whole thing don't cost hardly anything.

Monk: Do you carve these steps yourself?

LK: Yes. I shoveled the whole thing out to where I wanted it. I dig everything out or I build it up. When I wanted a flower I just take a big mucky bunch of adobe and just put my fist in it, make a flower, then paint it over.

Monk: How many coats of paint are on here now?

LK: Oh, I have no idea. I'd say twenty coats. Probably in some places forty.

Monk: Do you have people that help you?

LK: Not with the work, but they bring in the paint. It probably took three wheelbarrows full of adobe to make these letters. See how thick they are? *[Pointing to "God Is Love"]*

Monk: Well, what keeps you going? Why do you keep working at it?

LK: I just really wanted to put GOD IS LOVE to the world. God created the people and love and animals. If people talk about God's love or "let's just be nice," it thrills me a lot. I want to be a part of it.

interview

Salvation Mountain

Monk: So that's pretty much your message. That's what this mountain is about, to spread that message?

LK: Yes, that's right, to spread the message of love. And there are so many avenues of love.

Monk: Can you tell me some of them?

LK: Yes. There's a bus driver that we've been waving at with a great big smile for ten years. It's uplifting and I've never talked to the lady, hardly. She'll blow her horn at me and give me a big smile and I'll do the same. And it's beautiful. That's an avenue of love. I get excited talkin' about love because I think the world needs a love story about little people just helping each other. I've had many thousands of people come up here with 8 or 10 gallons of old paint and I'll say, "Well, I'll give you some gas money. I really like that paint." No, no. They don't want any money. They just want to help. I think the whole thing is just turning into a great big worldwide love story. And I'm excited about that.

Monk: Have you ever had anyone stay here with you?

LK: Years ago I did for a little while. But I seem to be a total loner on it. I have people come in, beautiful people. But they want me to do it their way. "No," I say, "just let me try to get in touch with love and do it my silly way." And I do it my way.

Monk: How do you survive here with all this heat?

LK: I do very little. In the morning for about two or three hours I can really move and then when it gets too hot I just take it easy. I feel the hard work is done so I can just relax. I don't push myself anymore. I never did push myself anywhere. I only worked when I wanted to.

Monk: Have you ever been married?

LK: Nope, not yet.

Monk: Not yet? Still looking for the right one?

LK: Yeah, but the older I get, the right one gets further away. *[Laughs]*

Monk: Now, you were one of the first residents of Slab City?

LK: No, they'd been coming in here ever since the '50s.

Monk: What sort of community is here? Would you say it's a peaceful group of people? People that get along?

LK: I definitely think so. I haven't locked anything for fourteen years. I can get on my bicycle at two in the morning and go and have coffee. I think it's a pioneer outfit. People leave you alone. You're free. If your neighbor has a loud dog you move half a mile so you can get along. Most all of the snowbirds are really friendly.

Monk: How is it that you survive here financially?

LK: The first eight years I really don't know how I did it. I've never had a penny come in. But the dump was open. You're free to scrounge around and pick up cans and I'd make enough for the day and just work on the mountain.

Monk: So you were recycling.

LK: Yeah, I recycle. But I never took all day to recycle. I just took two hours to get enough for coffee and right back to working on the mountain.

Monk: Do you have any future projects and visions you would like to work on?

LK: This is it. I just want to make it thicker and prettier and paint the whole thing four or five times with shiny paint so when the sun hits it every flower will reflect. I don't want it to get any bigger. I think it's big enough. If they leave me alone for one more year that paint's gonna shine! Now California's thinking this is a tourist attraction. Maybe I'm wrong here. It's just where I live. That's all it is.

Residing above the fray, overlooking the greater Palm Springs area, the former casino was named after two adjoining bunches of palms. A lookout tower, which no longer stands, was once used to spot approaching Feds. The grounds and buildings are deliberately rustic. The centerpiece is a turquoise grotto fed by 148° hot-spring waterfalls that cool down to a comfortable 100°. A small man-made lake is filled with ducks and koi. Running water meanders around the property into small pools and mini-waterfalls. You're far enough from town that you can see the stars at night and hear the wind blow through the tamarisk trees.

But the emphasis here is on the spa. Immortalized in the 1992 film *The Player,* in the scene where Greta Scacchi and Tim Robbins take a mud bath, the spa religiously delivers the best alternative therapies new money can buy. Besides the frequently requested Egyptian Clay Body treatment, they offer salt scrubs, aromatherapy, body wraps, deep tissue massage and Watsu, which got its start at Harbin Hot Springs and is an experience akin to returning to the womb (a hippy-dippy New Age Deadhead womb, but a womb nonetheless). But even with all the tender loving care, it seems the well-heeled *nouveau riche* and sunglassed celebrities still have a hard time achieving enlightenment, as evidenced by the heavy alcohol consumption in the Casino Dining Room. Should *you* begin to feel a little too blissed, don't worry, they've taken care of that too. It's called the bill!

East and North of L.A.

> **Amargosa Opera House and Hotel.** Hwy. 127, Death Valley Junction.
☎ **760/852-4441.** $10 for performance. Open Oct–May. Call for schedule.

In 1967, when Marta Becket got a flat tire outside Death Valley Junction, she fortuitously happened upon an abandoned run-down theater filled with dust, with an old calico curtain hanging on a stage. While most mortals would have curled their nose, changed their tire, and hit the road, Marta saw "magic." By 1968 she and her husband leased the place for $45 a month, renamed it the Amargosa Opera House, and began remodeling. Their first show drew only a dozen customers. Becket decided to paint an audience on the walls, as if by visualizing the crowds they would appear in the valley of death. In 1983 she joined forces with Tom Willett and now, from October through April, you have the best vaudeville in the desert—well, the only vaudeville in the desert, but still. The painting on the walls must have worked, as the audiences have definitely grown. Though she's in her early seventies, Marta's skits remain a blend of ballet and pantomime, with plenty of comedy thrown in. Broadway can take a hike. This is theater in the rough, miles from nowhere. The pure goodness and perseverance of Becket and Willett should definitely earn them a place in the American vaudeville hall of fame.

> **Deep Creek Hot Springs** (a.k.a. Bowen Hot Springs). San Bernardino National Forest (Victorville). From Interstate 15 take Bear Valley Rd. east. Far from town, turn right on Central Rd., left on Ocotillo Way (becomes dirt), and then right on Bowen Ranch Rd. Follow for 6 miles past other ranches. Last mile it narrows before ending at Bowen Ranch. *Note:* Be sure to leave a donation at the gate. (As one high desert local put it, "Greenbacks or green bud, makes no difference!!")

For most locals this is a secret that they'd just as soon keep to themselves because it's one of the most stunning hot springs in the country. But listen up! Take a flashlight and drinking water and be prepared to hike. Here's why: Once you pass through the Bowen Ranch gate—where owner Mike Castro collects 3 bucks a head to enter his property—you're going to park. And then you're going to hike a serious 3-mile descent into an incredibly steep ravine. On your way down you will be pinching yourself over the natural splendor the Monks have led you into. The dramatic back-side of the San Bernardino Mountains is a world removed from neighboring L.A. It's wild enough that mountain lions still roam. As you descend further, you'll begin to hear the midsize creek, which you'll ultimately have to ford.

The creek is frigid cold, but the half-dozen hot pools scattered along the cliffs on the other side are in some cases deep enough to soak standing up. There's also a ledge, where you can sit while a never-ending flow of shower-temperature water streams over your head and shoulders. It's pure nature with no frills, though there's evidence of a lot of care. The self-appointed local caretakers of the springs have spent years developing the pools, hauling sacks of concrete down to reinforce the sides and to build a few walls.

The majority of seasoned soakers are here in the buff. Conversations follow the gamut from industry types working on their latest "projects," to travelers making the hot-springs circuit, to local cowboy carpenters discharging from a hard day. But beware of two things. First, weekends bring an unruly crowd that includes a pre-ponderance of beer-swilling Visigothic jocks with their Valley Girl dates. Their clothes do *not* come off, they trash the grounds, and they're quick to condemn a portly torso. And second, there's the dark. By the time we left the sun had set. The pools were still crowded, so we didn't give it a thought. The strenuous trail up the ravine was easy enough to follow, as long as you didn't plunge a few hundred feet off the side. But once on top we took the foolhardy approach and headed up a nearby hill where we were certain the cars were parked. Wrong, wrong, wrong. Two hours later, after ascending many similar hills, we were hopelessly lost. We finally stumbled upon a drunk longhair on a country road who was, well, occupied with his date. We

The Ridgecrest Motel 6: They'll Leave the Trash Out for Ya

No question about it, it can get pretty "out there" in the desert. Those desert rats are often not the most hospitable people in the world. In fact, they're often downright ornery. Some hotel scenes can seem very similar to *Psycho*. Take the Motel 6 in Ridgecrest. My desk attendant was a fella named Chuck, who had lots of tattoos and a mild pompadour slowly losing the battle with baldness. Chuck looked like someone on the rebound. A guy who no doubt got into a whole mess of trouble once—maybe had a drinking problem, maybe even hurt somebody. A Jerry Springer candidate for sure. This Motel 6 gig was probably a plum job for Chuck—came with free room and board, decent though not spectacular paycheck, kept him out of trouble. I kind of admired Chuck, typing in my license number, phone number, and address, running me through the standard Motel 6 spiel—"Checkout is at noon, free coffee from 7 to 10am in the lobby, free local calls, dial 0 if you need the front office. Any questions?" He'd come a long way, and you almost felt that kind of satisfaction Christians must feel when they rescue a lost soul.

But then I turned the corner to head to the quiet nonsmoking first-floor room Chuck had secured for me. Along the way I passed Chuck's quarters. There was a serious party going on inside. Led Zeppelin was blaring. The wind was blowing. A ragged overweight chain-smoking half-man/half-woman was barking at her two dogs. Someone else was in the Motel 6 laundry room down the way, blasting discordant heavy metal radio. And here I was seeking the impossible—a quiet night in a godforsaken military town in the middle of the Mojave Desert. Robert Plant whined, "It really doesn't matter what time it isssss. . . ." Because Chuck and his posse were going to party all night, dammit, and Tom Bodett can just take a hike.

were miles off course and had to take a blind walk back down a gully. By sheer luck the car appeared. Like we said, flashlight, water, and be prepared to hike!

> **Exotic World.** 29053 Wild Rd. (Helendale). ☎ 760/243-5261. Open daily 10am–4pm. No admission charge, but at the end of the tour a donation would be appreciated. Directions: Take the Rte. 18 (Historic Route 66) exit from I-15 and go under the highway. Off Rte. 15 heading north, turn left at Helendale Market. At the 2 artificial waterfalls, turn right onto Helendale Rd.; after 1 mile turn right on Wild Rd. and look for #29053 and the large wrought iron gate with EXOTIC WORLD spelled out across the entrance.

Dixie Evans, "The Marilyn Monroe of Burlesque" in her day, is the caretaker of a most impressive collection of photos and paraphernalia about the fine art of

stripping. All the greats are depicted here—from Blaze Star to the Great Morgana, Gypsy Rose Lee to Exotic World founder Jennie Lee, Anne Marie to Buddy Hacket—Buddy Hacket?!, what's he doing here?! It seems, in true Hollywood style, proprietor Evans has thrown in several celebrity shots to add even greater sparkle to the lusty panorama on view.

But she's collected FAR more than photos, including Gypsy Rose Lee's trunk of costumes, Sheri Champagne's ashes, and Sally Rand's original fans, which "saved the 1933 Chicago World's Fair from financial ruin."

Every June, E-World hosts a hilariously wild and revealing strippers reunion and Miss Exotic Universe Contest (this year marks the 42nd anniversary). But be warned: The event is attended by loads of hard-drinking biker types who can be a trifle scary. Perhaps inspired by the nearby presence of the Leakey Early Man Site, the bikers feel compelled to act out prehistoric Neanderthal rituals. If you leave before it gets too dark, you'll be alright. If, however, you're really digging the aging stripper Neanderthal biker scene—and we can see how you might—then before you leave the area by all means stop in at the **Lost Hawg Saloon** (between Helendale and Oro Grande on National Trails Highway, a.k.a. Route 66)—the best biker-cum-stripper bar in the entire Mojave desert. Then again, it's probably the only biker-cum-stripper bar in the entire Mojave desert.

> **Furnace Creek Inn.** Hwy. 190 (Death Valley National Park). ☎ **760/786-2345.** www.furnacecreekresort.com.

This spectacular Mission Revival inn overlooking the heart of Death Valley has for over seven decades been a welcome retreat from the parched salt flats below. Furnace Creek boasts a stunning spring-fed pool, terraced gardens, deluxe hillside rooms, gorgeous stonemasonry, adobe walls, and the lowest-elevation eighteen-hole golf course on the planet. But, then, this is where we draw the line. We love this inn, we really do. But we were astounded by the flagrant waste of water spent on the golfing greens. Here you are in one of the world's most extreme, rugged, surreal landscapes, several hundred feet below sea level, surrounded by remarkable geological formations, and you have these morons sipping gin while brandishing the five iron?! Take a hike, you bourgeois yuppie jerks!! Death Valley is a pure raw spiritual experience. The Devil's Golf Course in the center of the national park, with its acres of severely eroded salt pinnacles, is where you ought to be swinging your club.

Yet, how could one even conceive of golf when Death Valley offers so many extraordinary other natural highlights? Down the road at Badwater you are 282 feet below sea level, the lowest point in North America. You will be standing in a veritable zone of silence. In addition, you can explore Artist's Drive, which borders a spectacular palette of desert colors. Or head to Dante's View, where you'll be 5,425 above the valley floor. You can spend days out in Death Valley, hiking the trails, mud hills, dramatic washes, and exotic rock formations. There's nowhere in the world like this, so it seems a little sacrilegious to never venture any further than the Furnace Creek pool, tennis courts, and fairways. But hey, it does get a bit toasty here in the summer when the place is swarming with those heat-seeking Germans. After *a good day's hike in the 120° sun,* not after a round of eighteen holes—*that's* when you've earned the world-class luxury of the Furnace Creek Inn.

> **Mojave Airport.** 1434 Flightline (Mojave). ☎ **805/824-2433.** From Hwy. 58, north on Airport Blvd. to airport.

There are many spectacular highlights in the California desert, but few compare to the sudden shock of seeing dozens of giant airplanes parked in the middle of

Mojave Airport, the world's largest airplane scrap yard

nowhere. As the Burning Man people well understand, the desert magnifies all that is placed on it. When first encountered, these planes seem monstrously huge and odd. Seen from a distance, they appear to be ancient aviation pyramids of totemic importance. In actuality, Mojave Airport is the world's largest airplane scrap yard, and what you see are decommissioned 747s, 720s, and old 707s, many of them used for parts (something to think about if you're flying Mexican and Spanish airlines, which are regular clients). In addition, many of the old bombers are wired to fly mechanically, then used for target practice.

With Edwards Air Force Base to the south and the China Lake Naval Air Station to the North, the Mojave Airport was once the epicenter of California aviation, and though this World War II Marine base is no longer used for commercial flights, space here is regularly leased out to store old commercial planes, to build faster planes, to test shuttle landing gear, and, naturally, to store decommissioned fighter craft.

The airport also has many firsts. The world sound barrier was broken here at the astounding speed of 4,200 miles per hour. This is where Dick Rutan designed the *Voyager* aircraft, which went around the world without stopping (he's currently at work in hangar no. 939). And currently under construction is a giant purple structure that will house a cutting-edge reusable rocket, which will fly into outer space and precisely return to Mojave Airport with one man aboard. For the aviation enthusiast, this is mecca, evidenced by a busload of British pilots who'd flown here on vacation just to see the airport.

However, though it is home to the Civilian Test Pilot School and a fascinating array of old fighter aircraft, including Phantoms, Drones, and Russian MIG-21s, the Mojave Airport is best known as a location for film and television shoots, and advertising shoots for the likes of Apple Computer and Kellog's Corn Flakes. The highlights of the $10 tour are the relics of those shoots, all contained in an area

Films Shot at the Mojave Airport		
Blue Thunder	*Hot Shots*	*The Stand*
Capricorn I	*The Long Kiss Goodnight*	*Tuskegee Airmen*
Diehard II	*Macarthur*	*Waterworld*
Dragnet II	*The Rookie*	*Yellow Rose*
Executive Decision	*Speed*	

known as "The Bone Yard." Kind, informative, born-again tour guide Javier Ruiz will gladly show you the rusted boat from *Waterworld,* the 707 blown to smithereens in the movie *Speed,* and an airplane from the movie *Executive Decision.* Inside the airport office is a gallery of historic shots featuring the airport, plus a scrapbook of clippings about the airport and its charismatic manager, Dan Sabovich. You'll learn that the tragically ill-fated Dorothy Stratten once appeared here in her glory days.

As you leave town, you'll feel the strong whistling winds that characterize this area. As you leave behind the chain stores and fast-food joints of Mojave, you find yourself in hard-core desert. In the distance you hear that most mystical of American sounds, the horn of a train. As the emptiness swallows you up, you think back on the staggering aircraft of the Mojave Airport, and marvel at the desert's strangeness.

› **Roy Rogers and Dale Evans Museum.** 15650 Seneca Rd. (Victorville). Exit Interstate 15 at Roy Rogers Dr., turn left on Civic Center Dr. ☎ **760/243-4547** or 760/243-4548. www.royrogers.com.

Put it this way: The trails weren't so happy for the hundreds of stuffed and mounted game. Elephant, lion, crocodile, rhino, water buffalo, hyena, African lizard, timber wolves, leopards—this guy liked to hunt. There are at least five rooms full of Safari trophies, but no sign of remorse for delivering the death blow to near extinct breeds. Though Roy and Dale also bit the dust, their legacy continues in this immense road-side edifice that exhaustively chronicles EVERY facet of their sugar-coated, gee-whiz, happy-trails lives. Shaped like a frontier fort, the squeaky clean, well-lit museum has kept the entire music-loving clan employed, with Roy Jr. currently at the helm.

Other museum features include an extensive gun display, saddles, old costumes, boots, Shriner fezzes, and the eerily preserved presence of their freestanding sidekick steeds Trigger, Trigger Junior, and Buttermilk, as well as Bullet the dog. Roy also parked his vintage cars here, including a 1963 white Bonneville convertible (driven only 23,000 miles); a silver-dollar Bonneville with large steer horns on the front grill, six-shooters on the door handles, and a saddle over the transmission hump; a

1964 Yellow Lincoln Continental convertible; and the 1923 Dodge truck that he drove with his family from Duck Run, Ohio, to California in 1930.

Every year the museum hosts the Cowboy Christmas, when you can hear Roy Rogers Jr. and the High Riders croon. For the converted, this is the Graceland of the Wild West. Ironic hipsters are going to have serious trouble swallowing the reverent attitude and folksy family values vibe, so you better shut your mouth and just hum along.

But it's worth a visit simply because it is so completely over the top. Just one big bodacious marketing ploy for the Roy Rogers Industry (i.e., his extended codependent kin).

> **Scotty's Castle.** Scotty's Castle Rd., Death Valley National Park. ☎ 760/786-2392.
First of all, it's not a castle. Secondly, Scotty didn't own it. Al Johnson did. But in terms of remote, original, and stunning vistas, this enormous Spanish Moorish hacienda gives San Simeon's Hearst Castle some fierce competition.

Half the fun is in getting there. A drive through Death Valley National Park is without doubt one of the ultimate American road trips. The park service road that leads to Scotty's is full of dips and turns as it travels through a geologically astonishing landscape. On our ascent to the castle we nearly plowed into a pack of wild coyotes and were given a 10-minute lecture by a park ranger for going 30 miles per hour in a 15-mile-per-hour zone.

The more official ranger lectures—er, tours—begin on the hour. Unfortunately, you have to listen to horrifically mundane trivia about the castle's furnishings, with an occasional bad joke told by a ranger in period costume. It takes an inquisitive Monk to elicit more compelling factoids. For example, Walter Scott (a.k.a. "Scotty") was a notorious swindler who in the early 1900s corralled wealthy Chicago insurance tycoon Albert Johnson and his wife Bessie into investing in his alleged Death Valley "gold mine." It took years before the truth emerged: There was no gold mine. By then, generous Al took a liking to Death Valley and decided to build a "castle." Being the forgiving type (or an incurable sap), Johnson remained good friends with Scotty, who, true to form, claimed the place as his own (thus the name "Scotty's Castle"). The Johnsons, being private types, went along with the charade. By 1925 the castle rose to include several buildings and an impressive turret, all constructed of concrete, redwood, and wrought iron. Steam power came from the nearby springs, and solar power was used to heat the water. It's assumed that only wackos move this far out into the desert, and dear Bessie certainly rose to the occasion. Her diminutive 4-foot, 9-inch frame was often clothed in flamboyant gowns with an ever-present tiara on her head. When she wasn't preaching from the balcony (she was a minister) she was busy playing the pipe organ, with its 1,100 pipes, in the mansion's "Music Hall." Still in operation, the pipe organ is loud enough to shatter an ear drum. As for Scotty, he never liked living here, though he had a permanent guest room. He became known for telling tall tales about the early desert mining days to gullible visitors.

The castle itself consists of two long buildings that surround a tiled courtyard with an overhead walkway. The walls are at least a foot thick. Given the lack of air-conditioning, you'd need to have been very committed to survive a summer up here. The Johnsons weren't full-timers, but when their fortunes in Chicago turned sour they rented out rooms and gave daily tours. The tours continued after their deaths, with most furnishings preserved exactly as they were. Outdoors, a massive pit marks the site for an incomplete pool, a rattlesnake trap if we ever saw one. The gift shop offers souvenirs to prove you survived the tour. But the highlight occurs only after you ditch the hokey tour, wander through the grounds, and breathe in the clean, mind-expanding desert air. Just watch for coyotes and the men with badges.

> **Tehachapi Loop.** Woodford-Tehachapi Rd. (Keene). From Hwy. 58, take the turnoff to Keene. Follow the Woodford-Tehachapi Rd. about 3 miles to the Loop Viewpoint, a monument located just above the loop at the siding known as Walong.

Serious rail fans worldwide speak of the Tehachapi Loop with the reverence generally reserved for classic steam engines and a shiny red caboose. Finished in 1876, this engineering marvel brought the Southern Pacific Railroad over a 4,000-foot summit of the Tehachapi Mountains by means of a rail loop. The tracks rise 77 feet as they cross over themselves at tunnel number nine. From the Loop Viewpoint you can stand all day watching mile-long trains and their engines work overtime as they make a full circle over themselves to gain altitude. An amazingly diverse crowd of people come and wait for the trains, including the heat-seeking Germans (who are always up for an engineering marvel), lots of British, and good ole boys from the South and Midwest out on a tour. Though plenty of wives were hanging out in the cars, we suspect it's the men in the bunch who persuade the ladies to come along. It's better than watching hubby playing with his Lionel back in Des Moines.

> **U.S. Borax Boron Mine.** 14486 Borax Rd. (Boron). Take Hwy. 58, exit onto Borax Rd. ☎ 760/762-7588. Open 8am–4pm daily in winter, 8am–6pm in summer (but call ahead).

Back when twenty-mule teams were pulling 4-ton wagons of "white gold" out of Death Valley, borax was primarily used for laundry detergent. You'll remember the commercials if you're over the age of 50. Since then, there's been a lot of digging, evidenced by this gaping, mile-long, 700-foot-deep pit. The mine was discovered in the twenties. You can go to the visitor center and look down through the observation window at the entire operation. It's the largest borate mine in the world, so things stay pretty busy. A million tons a year leave by boxcar. The mules are long gone.

Before borax made its way into soap, it was used by the ancient Egyptians to mummify their dead. The Chinese used it as a glaze in pottery. At the end of the millennium it's being used for everything you can imagine, including plastics, fiberglass, glassware, fertilizer, weed killer, bug killer, and nylon. In the center you can sample a chunk of borax—touch it, if you will, but don't stick it in your mouth. It's poisonous.

Once you've had your fill of watching fleets of trucks hauling the stuff away, you can drive downtown and visit the Boron Twenty-Mule Team Museum. Here you'll get a taste of the history of this desolate area and more propaganda on the almighty borax. If you're still itching for more of this mineral, drive Highway 178 toward the Panamint Valley through Trona, which is the second largest borate producer in the world. Trona is the meanest, ugliest, most desolate mining town in the entire West. The highway borders miles of borax flats. The industrial fumes from the smokestacks make Chernobyl seem like the Amazon Rain Forest. We didn't see a single living thing on our drive through town. Equally ominous is the valley terrain itself. This is Death Valley without hotels, souvenirs, and interpretive exhibits. Just raw, rugged, sunbaked desert. Full of borax.

> **Willow Springs Raceway.** 3500 75th St. West (Rosamond). Hwy. 14 north, exit west on Rosamond Blvd., right at entrance. ☎ **805/256-2471.** Open weekends only. Admission $10.

Willow Springs Raceway is the ultimate road-warrior proving ground, where the Winston-smoking, testosterone-driven carburetor crowd get their thrills on wheels, drink lots of Bud, and test their manhood on a 2.5-mile high-speed loop called "The Fastest Road in the West." Though we can't imagine anything more moronic than spending an afternoon watching grown men race their loud toys, the overall ambiance of the place is pure Wild West. Without the guns.

Situated in the greater Mojave Desert, just a scud shot from Edwards Air Force Base, the Willow Springs high-speed circuit throws nine sharp turns across the radical landscape. There's also a paved "Skid Pad," a three-eighths-mile dirt track, and an eleven-turn "Kart Track." In addition, on weekends the raceway hosts time trials, where competitors race their stock cars, motorcycles, modified production bikes, or just plain old karts. Anyone is welcome.

The spectators are a hardened, sunburned, Levi-and-sunglasses, tailgate-party crowd. Rows of RVs and SUVs are parked neck to neck, with lawn chairs staking claim to precious patches of dirt. Bored kids skateboard around the periphery while the hungry chow down at "The Fastest Food in the West." There's a certain gladiator mentality as drivers suit up in their racing leathers, boots, helmets, and sunglasses before mounting their vehicle. Half the crowd seems to be rooting for a spill. Given speeds of up to 120 miles per hour, they often get what they want.

Michael Monk at the Wind Farms

The heat can soar to 100+, making the tarmac soften underneath, so you'll want to bring lots of water. And remember to wear your hat, and for god's sake stay out of the forbidden Hot Pit Lane or you'll be roadkill. The spectators will probably love it, but we sure won't.

> **Wind Farms.** SeaWest Tehachapi, 7021 Oak Creek Rd. (Mojave). ☎ **805/824-4681.**
Throughout the desert passes you're going to repeatedly encounter majestic stands of wind turbines that gracefully spin in the strong desert breeze. Though Californians have grown used to them, to the first-time visitor these wind farms are so gratifyingly progressive it's hard to believe you're actually in the fossil-fuel-consuming capital of the planet. In the Tehachapi Pass area there are as many as 5,000 wind turbines, making this the second largest collection of wind generators in the world. Collectively known as the Kern Wind Energy Association, this stand of turbines is run by a consortium of private companies that collectively produce over 800 million kilowatt-hours of electricity a year. That's a lot of wind.

SeaWest Tehachapi Inc. is one of the Kern Wind–associated members and has close access near Mojave up a dirt road. When fully engaged, SeaWest's spinning propellers make a cacophony of sounds that travel the range from deep moans to

Factoid

California creates nearly 80% of the world's wind-generated electricity.

shrill high-pitched screams. They are almost extraterrestrial. And definitely worth a stop.

> **World's Largest Thermometer.** 72157 Baker Blvd. (Baker). *Note:* the Mojave Desert Information Center (☎ **760/733-4040**) is located under the thermometer. They will supply you with up-to-date weather information and a free topographical map.

There are two reasons to stop in this blink-of-an-eye town. One is to take a reading from the 134-foot digital thermometer, which registers up to the same number in degrees Fahrenheit. If you're German, you wait until the height of summer when the temperature hits the 120° mark. This silly amusement is an apparent rite of passage for Krauts—we're told it loosens them up, slightly. They flock through Baker, the "Gateway to Death Valley," when saner folks hit the Pacific surf. The thermometer is easily spotted from the Interstate and at night is illuminated in bright green neon. Next door is the 24-hour **Bun Boy Restaurant,** which makes for a fun chuckle but a really dull meal.

The second reason to stop in Baker is the "World Famous" **Mad Greek Restaurant**, on Baker Boulevard (☎ **760/733-4354**). For some inexplicable reason, those Mad Greeks decided to plant their Aegean cuisine in the middle of the Mojave Desert, so wayward travelers like ourselves could have a fairly decent alternative to roadside fast-food monotony. Passing into town, the Mad Greek's bright white and blue walls and Greek writing and signage immediately caught our attention. But we were prepared to carry on, until we saw the dozen semis parked at the curb. Now that was an endorsement. We pulled a U-turn faster than you can say "Nicomachean Ethics." Though the Mad Greek had a drive-through, we sauntered inside, sunk into the deep booths of the air-conditioned room, and ordered up the best babaganoush, lamb gyros, and baklava this side of Papa Cristos. In the neighboring booth sat a Native American Christian lady attempting to convert a trucker who was sucking down some dolmas. Those standoffish heat-seeking Germans were flocking in as well. We're not sure, but we think we saw one of them smile.

># road trip:
the central coast

It may be a cliché, but like many clichés, it has a strong ring of truth: The Central Coast of California is among the most beautiful coastlines on the planet. The girl is a bona fide supermodel. But, like many supermodels, the Central Coast is also schizophrenic. The closer you get to San Francisco the more progressive the thinking. The closer you get to Los Angeles the more bourgeoisie, rich, and cheesy. Smack in the middle is Hearst Castle. A drive straight down Highway 1 will clue you into the very heart of this extraordinary region. But be sure to take our detours, because that's where the good stuff lies.

North of L.A.

> **The Krotona Institute and School of Theosophy.** At Calif. 150 and Hermosa Rd. (Ojai). ☎ 805/646-2653.

For all you spiritual initiates, modern theosophy was the religious-philosophical combo platter of esoteric Eastern spirituality and Gnostic Christianity pioneered by the rotund Madame Blavatsky and pals back in the early part of this century. Some hallmarks of modern theosophical teaching include a belief in reincarnation and karma, "the presence of life and consciousness in all matter," the interconnectedness of all things, "the possibility of our conscious participation in evolution, the power of thought to affect one's self and surroundings, the reality of free will and

---

Krishnamurti and the Ojai Foundations

Krishnamurti, while an undeniably gorgeous mystic, was a bit of a self-centered stick in the mud, who wouldn't teach, or admit to knowing, anything in particular (guess he never heard of the bodhissatva vow). Not surprisingly, the foundation named in his honor is not open to the public, though the **Krishnamurti Foundation** can be contacted at www.kfa.org. Or by writing to Krishnamurti Foundation of America, P.O. Box 1560, Ojai, CA 93024-1560 (☎ **805/646-2726;** fax 805/646-667; E-mail: kfa@kfa.org).

For a far more open and happening spiritual center, try the **Ojai Foundation,** 9739 Ojai-Santa Paula Rd., Ojai, CA 93023 (☎ **805/646-8343;** fax 805/646-2456; E-mail: ojaifdn@fishnet.net). We visited here back in the early days of Monk, catching Robert Bly in his prime—getting shit-faced on Guinness before leading a homoerotic drumming circle for straight men. We also did a 1-day retreat with "Iron Joan" Halifax back in 1985, a headstrong dharma teacher with a nice smile. We like the place. It's similar to Taos's Lama Foundation, "a nondenominational land-based educational sanctuary" with equally astounding nature and views.

---

responsibility, and the ultimate perfection of human nature, society, and life." Though not a religion per se, theosophy performed a fairly important function in the development of late-20th-century American spirituality, paving the way for Krishnamurti, who set up shop in Ojai after studying at the Krotona Institute, and other Eastern teachers, including Suzuki Roshi, Chogyam Trungpa, and the many Eastern avatars who founded spiritual communities in the United States since the 1960s. While theosophy as a philosophical force has gone the way of other innovative-turned-dowdy international movements, such as the World Federalists and Rosicrucians, the grounds at the Institute are elegantly landscaped, offering a peaceful sanctuary for the earnest contemplative. There is also a bookstore containing many works from the theosophical canon should you want to explore the teachings of this often neglected force in the formation of modern American religious thought.

> **La Simpatia Cafe.** 827 Guadalupe St. (Guadalupe). ☎ **805/343-9284.**

In the heart of very Chicano, very sweet Guadalupe, California, is a little Mexican cafe. La Simpatia is its name. There are several elements that immediately draw you in—the comforting sign, the mariachi music, the yellow booths, chairs, and walls, the cleanliness! They even took our guacamole back because they decided it tasted too salty. This is a wonderful place, run by wonderfully sweet women, including owner Rosie Quiroga, niece of the late Frank and Maria Quiroga, who founded La Simpatia back in 1944.

> **Madonna Inn.** 100 Madonna Rd. (San Luis Obispo). ☎ **800/543-9666** or 805/543-3000.

God Bless Phyllis and Alex Madonna, the loving, generous couple who've brought us the campiest hotel in America. There is something indubitably Californian about their extravagant creation, which is why all travelers must see it. Fortunately, it's easy to visit, situated right off 101 near the town of San Luis Obispo, against the San Luis and Madonna mountains. What makes the Madonna Inn so worthy is Alex and Phyllis's unabashed, unapologetic love of color, chintz, and ornamentation. The

Madonna Inn Trivia

1. The Madonna Inn is the largest private employer in San Luis Obispo.

2. The first twelve rooms of the Madonna Inn were completed on December 24, 1958, and were given complimentary for that night's stay to a very surprised and grateful group of travelers.

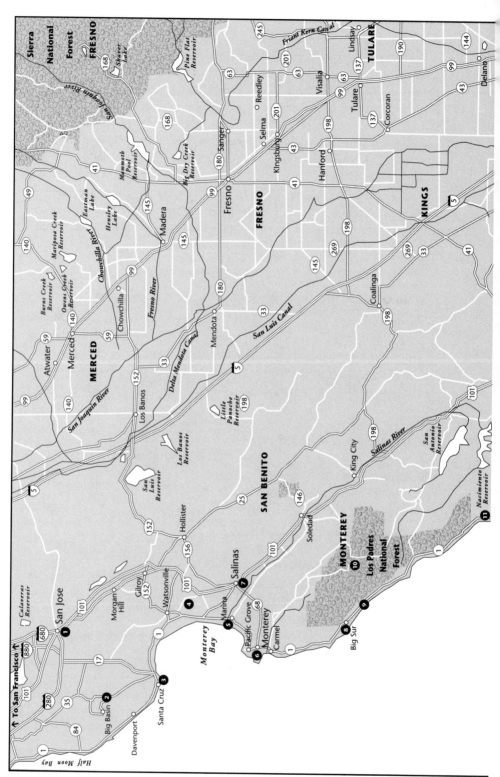

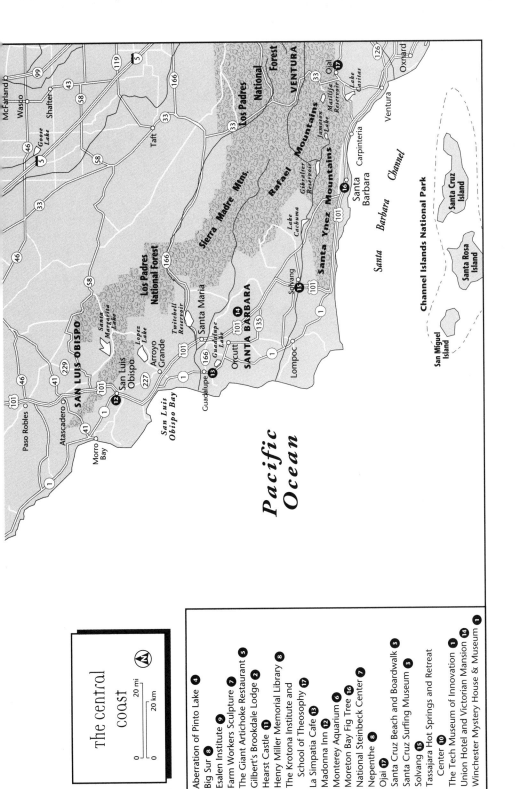

The central coast

N

0   20 mi
0   20 km

Aberration of Pinto Lake ④
Big Sur ⑧
Esalen Institute ⑨
Farm Workers Sculpture ⑦
The Giant Artichoke Restaurant ⑤
Gilbert's Brookdale Lodge ②
Hearst Castle ⑪
Henry Miller Memorial Library ⑧
The Krotona Institute and
    School of Theosophy ⑰
La Simpatia Cafe ⑬
Madonna Inn ⑫
Monterey Aquarium ⑥
Moreton Bay Fig Tree ⑯
National Steinbeck Center ⑦
Nepenthe ⑧
Ojai ⑰
Santa Cruz Beach and Boardwalk ③
Santa Cruz Surfing Museum ③
Solvang ⑮
Tassajara Hot Springs and Retreat
    Center ⑩
The Tech Museum of Innovation ①
Union Hotel and Victorian Mansion ⑭
Winchester Mystery House & Museum ①

The Madonna Inn

story goes that Alex Madonna, the locally raised, self-made cattle rancher, highway engineer, and bridge builder, created the architecture of the place, and simply let his wife go wild on the interior design. And did she go. Phyllis had no formal training. What she had was a unique and populist sense of beauty: from the year-round Christmas lights to the ultra-pink main dining room, which makes the Beverly Hills Hotel look like Motel 6.

Specifically, the dining room features large, pink, comfy, almost erotic Naugahyde booths, gold and pink red-flocked wallpaper, flying gold nymphs up above, a large fake tree in the middle that looks like a talking tree from the Wizard of Oz, and giant dolls swimming back and forth on electronic swings. Be sure to work your way to the downstairs men's room, which is set in a giant clam/geoduck shell motif, with a one-of-a-kind waterfall pissoir which makes the New York Royalton pissoir seem like a jailhouse stall. And be sure to visit the neighboring bakery and cafe. You have to love a place that lists "relish tray" as an item on the menu. Of course, the most famous part of the Madonna Inn is the 109 guest rooms. Each is designed according to a unique motif, starting with the legendary Caveman Room and culminating in such outrageously kitschy wonders as the Pick and Shovel suite.

The kindness and accessibility of Alex and Phyllis perfectly matches their extravagant and extraordinary friendly storybook interiors. The stained-glass windows near the front tell the history of Mr. Madonna's many achievements, though, like us,

Alex and Phyllis Madonna

you will come away loving the place because of the whimsy of Alex's understated wife, who in public takes a back seat to her commanding husband, but who added the childlike feminine excess that makes the Madonna Inn one of the ten Monk treasures of California.

Anecdote: Alex and Phyllis Madonna met at Elmers Cafe in Orchid, California. Phyllis was giving a friend a birthday cake. Alex said he'd like a piece of that cake. He didn't get the cake, but he got the girl. A sweet one at that.

› **Moreton Bay Fig Tree.** Chapala and Montecito (Santa Barbara).

One of the highlights of the Central Coast is a freak of nature. This giant expansive fig tree used to serve as a shelter for Santa Barbara's homeless, many of whom have etched their John Doe in the limbs and trunk. Today, it stands alone. No homeless in sight. A staggering natural wonder in a town filled with a fair share of artifice.

› **Ojai**

Ojai is a cross between Carmel and Sedona. With the wealth of the former and the chintz of the latter. It does feel like Shangri-La, or at least a beautiful Tibetan plateau, when you drive up to it on Highway 150 over the scenic Casitas Pass. But that idyllic fantasy is soon dispelled once you encounter the first Wendy's and the O-Hi Frostie. Sixty-three years ago, when Frank Capra filmed *Lost Horizon* here,

Creek Road. Starts at the south end of Ventura Street in Ojai and meets Highway 33 in Oak View. A picturesque country drive, which follows a stream shaded by giant oaks and sycamores.

Grand Avenue Loop. Go east on Ojai Avenue (Highway 150) to Boccali's Restaurant, turn left on Reeves Road and go 1 mile to McAndrew Road. Turn left (north) to Thacher School, then head back to Ojai on Thacher Road. The beautiful country roads take you through orange groves lined by stone walls built before the turn of the century by Chinese laborers.

Ojai Valley Trail. An ideal spot for walkers, joggers, bikers, and equestrians. The Ojai Valley Trail is a "rails-to-trails conversion of the 100-year-old railroad line" that moved trainloads of produce from local orchards to markets around the planet. It connects to Ventura's Foster Park 9 miles to the south.

Ojai truly must have been spectacular. Sadly, not so much today, with its various planned communities, soccer moms, and downtown tourist schlock. Still, the view atop the Dennis Grade can be heart-warming, especially during the frequent Ojai "pink moments" (for the best vista, follow Highway 150 east toward the Upper Ojai Valley, and drive to the back of the Dennison Campground up top). And there must be something in the air, as celebrated sculptor Beatrice Wood lived in Ojai until she was 106.

While nearby Wheeler Hot Springs is no longer in operation, Ojai does sport a few spas: **The Oaks at Ojai** (one of the top ten spas in the country, according to *Condé Nast Traveler,* for whatever that's worth) and the **Ojai Valley Inn and Spa.** There's also a few decent motels, such as the **Blue Iguana Inn** and **Los Padres Inn.** However, due to the "Carmel-ized" energy of the area, you don't need to spend a night here. If you arrive early enough, you can catch Ojai's major highlights: the **Krotona Institute and School of Theosophy** (see earlier in this chapter), the scenic drives, and **The Wheel** (16816 Maricopa Hwy., 6 miles north of town across from Wheeler Hot Springs; ☎ 805/646-4069), a legendary biker bar where Johnny Cash wrote "Ring of Fire" and Dudley Moore used to come play piano. Like so much of Ojai, those star-studded days are long gone.

› **Solvang.** Artificial Danish Village. Highway 246, 4 miles east of 101.

Can you say "awwwwww." You know, that long drawn out "awwwwww" we reserve for gazes at the little critter in the baby carriage. Scandinavian gingerbread architecture always brings out the "awwwwwws" in the Monk traveler. Of course, with tongue firmly in cheek. There is literally nothing to like about this completely disingenuous tourist trap, but there is tremendous guffaw potential in snickering at the gullible middle-class touristas and the clueless geriatric set who drive here to gnosh on sugary Danish pastries, day-old "fresh lemonade," and mediocre Danish fare. If you're a sucker for all things chintzy and precious, by Gawd, this place is Shangri-La. Or at least a reasonable facsimile of tourist Copenhagen.

> Union Hotel and Victorian Mansion. 362 Bell St. (Los Alamos). ☎ **800/230-2744** or 805/344-2744. Take U.S. 101, exit at Los Alamos, and head down the main street. You can't miss it. Rooms book up several months in advance.

We are not big on bed-and-breakfasts. Generally, they strike us as a little precious, far too contrived, and way too enamored with all that lacy, Stickley Victoriana. And though they claim historical authenticity, in most cases they are a far cry from it. Besides, do you really want an innkeeper overhearing your every word?

But there is something so ridiculously over the top about this B&B that it bears a visit, if not necessarily an overnight stay. Though there are plenty of handsome, if unspectacular, period rooms at the historic Union Hotel, the highlight here is the six original theme rooms in the adjoining Victorian Mansion, which are embellished in ways that only a lover of American kitsch would appreciate.

In the Fifties Drive-in Room, the bed is an authentic Cadillac convertible parked in front of a movie screen, showcasing *Rebel Without a Cause, American Graffiti,* and *Jailhouse Rock.* The Egyptian Room, accessed through a heavy stone sarcophagus, is designed as if for a harem, with a canopied bed, Oriental rugs, and a cavelike interior covered in hieroglyphics. The movie selections are *Lawrence of Arabia* and *Cleopatra.* In the Roman Room, marble steps lead up to a soaking tub, while Roman columns, busts, and murals of burning Rome surround the room. You sleep in a chariot. Your movie selections are *Ben Hur* and *Spartacus.* There's also a Pirate Room (your movie is Errol Flynn's *Buccaneer*), a French room (with views of a faux French countryside), and a Gypsy Room (your tub is a pool at the base of a rocky stream). In the morning, breakfast is delivered by dumbwaiter concealed behind yet another secret door. According to the owners, French tourists go wild for this place. And with the right attitude, so shall you.

South of San Francisco

> Aberration of Pinto Lake (a.k.a. Mother Mary Is Ready for Her Close-Up). Pinto Lake County Park, Green Valley Rd. (Watsonville). Enter the second park entrance on Pinto lake. Park in the large parking lot and walk through the soccer fields towards the path to the lake shore.

In terms of aberrations, this latest celestial visitation by the Holy Mother leaves A LOT to the imagination. On the peeling bark of a tree in a wooded area surrounding Pinto Lake is an unusual image of a ghostly face. If you happened to pass by the tree markings when no one was around, you wouldn't think anything of it. But, of course, the reality, or, rather, the aberration, is in the belief of the beholder (case in point: "The Face on Mars"). From a quick impression, it seems there's a lot who believe in this aberration. But before you go grab your rosaries and genuflect, genuflect, genuflect, remember that the largely Hispanic population of surrounding Watsonville has been praying their hearts out here for well over a year. So who knows if she's still listening.

The ride to the lake is half the fun. Driving around the suburban perimeters of Watsonville you won't meet with a single, disingenuous smirk as you ask for directions to the Mother Mary shrine. The locals reverently point you down Green Valley Road to the park entrance. Once inside the park, you might meet some confusion if you ask one of the Anglo soccer moms—"Oh yeah, I heard about that, it's around here somewhere. . . . Go Jimmy, go!!! . . . Sorry. . . ."—but ask any Spanish-speaking person within earshot and they'll fervently point the way. Once you arrive, you won't be alone. Dozens of aging Hispanic matrons, black lace veils draped over their heads, stand diligently at the base of the tree, chanting Hail Marys. Heaped around the base of the tree are candles by the hundreds, along with bouquets of flowers, crucifixes, and other Christian memorabilia Mother Mary might enjoy. There are even benches to sit on. The reverence is infectious, making it awfully hard for skeptical Monks to make a clear-headed call. After half an hour kneeling in the dirt at the base of the tree, with two dozen devout Catholics whispering "Santa Maria madre de dios" (i.e. "Hail Mary full of grace"), we think we saw the aberration crack a smile. Unfortunately, the Japanese-made camera showed nothing. But, heck, Christians throughout the ages have never bothered with issues like "proof." Who needs proof when you've got *belief.*

› Big Sur

Other guidebooks cover the 90-mile Big Sur region ad nauseam, so we won't here. You already know that this idyllic coastal area is home to Route 1, the finest scenic drive in America, and a positively mystical experience for the first-time traveler. You've also probably read that the village of Big Sur is gratifyingly free of banks, stop lights, shopping centers, and most other vestiges of tacky American commerce. For this reason, the town doesn't really appear to be "a town," and can be a bit disorienting to the often bewildered newcomer. For the true Monk, however, the village's vagueness is a welcome break from the chamber-of-commerce hard-sell one finds all over California.

There are many highlights in the Big Sur area. In addition to **Esalen,** the **Henry Miller Library,** and **Nepenthe** (all described elsewhere in this section), we recommend you check out two spectacular hits of nature: **Pfeiffer Beach** and **Julia Pfeiffer Burns State Park** (home of the 50-foot McWay Falls, California's only coastal waterfall). We also recommend you check out the amazing views, surroundings, and amenities at three accommodations: the **Post Ranch Inn** (☎ **800/ 527-2200**), **Ventana Big Sur Country Inn Resort** (☎ **800/628-6500**), and the more rustic **Deetjen's Big Sur Inn** (☎ **408/667-2377**). Giving directions here is futile. When you hit the "village" of Big Sur, just ask around.

Anecdote: In the late sixties Michael Monk made his first pilgrimage through Big Sur by thumb. Like many Haight Street refugees he was easily seduced by the intoxicating beauty of the coast, enough so that he constructed a 10-foot lean-to out of fallen brush, built a fire ring, and set up camp along with a few hundred other squatters who declared the Ventana Wilderness their rightful home. The hills were dotted with pitched camps, spent VW vans, and flimsy structures. The ocean was mesmerizing. The sky full of remarkable visions. The late-summer winds whispered mystical songs. Then the acid wore off.

Years later, Michael Monk coaxed a reluctant Jim to take a 10-mile hike up the trails of Pfeiffer–Big Sur State Park for that male-bonding-in-the-wilderness thing. He likewise convinced Jim that he should throw away his glasses and learn to *see* without them. That experiment lasted under a month. But the bonding thing lasts to this very day.

> **Esalen Institute.** Hwy. 1, 50 miles north of San Simeon, 11 miles south of Big Sur. ☎ **408/667-3000** or 408/667-3828.

Esalen is a cross between Harbin Hot Springs and Tassajara, with the funk of the former and the pedigree of the latter. We visited not long after El Niño destroyed Esalen's historic hot pools, which were situated down a 300-foot cliff overlooking the shoreline/breakers below. We soaked in the temporary pools, fed by a combination of springs and normal mountain water. Michael Monk, a regular Esalen visitor back in the day, said it wasn't the same.

Though Esalen has hosted such esteemed guests as Suzuki Roshi, Fritz Perls, Rollo May, and even Henry Miller over the years, the half-baked gathering of Terrence McKenna groupies while we were there suggests that Esalen has fallen a notch or two from its once hallowed status as the nexus of *intelligent* cutting-edge consciousness. Still, for the gorgeous grounds, the astounding views, and the highly rated vegetarian meals, it is definitely worth a visit, though remember: Esalen is primarily a group retreat and workshop center, not a spa, with only limited availability for regular overnight guests.

John Cerney's Farm Workers

> **Farm Workers Sculpture.** Hwy. 68 West, at Spreckles Blvd. (Salinas).

Situated by the side of the road, towering above fields of strawberries, these oversized sculptures loom over the toiling laborers nearby. The two-dimensional silhouetted plywood sculptures depict four migrant workers, stooped and religiously working over the crops. They are the work of local artist John Cerney, one of several artists commissioned by Chris Bunn, owner of the Crown Packing Company, to depict those who work for the company. You'll see Cerney's signature style on the side of various businesses throughout town, most with a similar nod toward agricultural themes, though a bit too happy for some tastes (picking produce is seriously hard work, and the physical and political struggles of migrant workers has never been a walk in the pasture). Nonetheless, the impact of this installation, and the shadow it casts over those in whose likeness it was created, gives an otherwise indistinguishable strawberry field new significance and meaning.

> **The Giant Artichoke Restaurant.** 11261 Merritt St., at Hwy. 156 (Castroville).
☎ **831/633-3204.**

Agriculture plays a big hand in the inland valleys south of Santa Cruz. As home of the Californian Artichoke, Castroville furthers the legacy of this edible thistle with a roadside diner shaped in its honor. Unlike the Olive Tree Inn and Restaurant in Lindsay (where olives are not utilized in either menu or decor), the giant green artichoke out front comprises only a small portion of the attraction. Inside, the artichoke theme is continued throughout the menu. You can get your fill of cream of artichoke soup, artichoke bread, artichoke quiche, an artichoke club sandwich, or the much heralded though slightly rancid (change that oil) french-fried artichokes. Next door, their vegetable stand sells—you guessed it—locally grown artichokes. Castroville's other claim to fame dates back a few decades to a young girl named Norma Jean who had a brief reign as Artichoke Queen. In fact, an Hispanic gay bar just a few blocks away is named in her honor. Nearby Gilroy hosts an annual Garlic Festival. And Watsonville plays host to the succulent strawberry, though neither of these towns have erected buildings shaped like their representative crops.

> **Gilbert's Brookdale Lodge.** 11570 Hwy. 9 (Brookdale). ☎ **408/338-6433.**

The 25-foot James Dean mural on the corner of this lodge is enough of a certifiable slice of Americana to justify pulling off the side of the road. But after you gaze, perplexed, at this ornate Hansel-and-Gretel-meets-French-Tudor-meets-Santa's-Village architectural wonder you reluctantly walk toward the lodge lobby thinking you're about to enter a David Lynch film come to life. The motel rooms and cabins are somewhat ordinary. But as you meander around the timber-stone lodge you'll stumble into the opulent Brook Room, which easily gives the Madonna Inn a run for the novelty. There, in the dining room, grow a few trees. The large stone walls, fussy table settings, and quirky antiques give it a Swiss Alps feel. All very quaint, kinda neat. But then you look further. And there, in the middle of the three-story room, complete with balconies and towering skylight, is an honest to God stream. We're not talking some meager, artificial trickle, recycled through water pumps. This baby comes roaring off the mountain and slices right through the ground floor, with cascading waterfalls to boot. In times past, dinner guests could, and would, fish for their meal. And though the fish do still swim through—imagine their surprise to be suddenly out of the wild and cast as momentary aquatic entertainment for the supper crowd—things are a little more civilized now.

The Brookdale Lodge dates back to the turn of the century when the San Francisco moneyed class came down for summer getaways among the towering redwoods. By the 1950s you had the entire NATO organization lodging here, as well as President Hoover and Shirley Temple. Fires and floods have caused the Lodge to be rebuilt several times. The most tragic was the fire of 1956, which destroyed most of the building. The Lodge's current incarnation dates back to that time, with all the grandeur and camp of old, including a glassed-in swimming pool where you can watch the swimmers from a below-level bar. The 1960s saw touring bands, such as Big Brother and the Holding Company, as well as luminaries like former Artichoke

Queen Marilyn Monroe. At one point a tunnel ran under the highway to cabins on the other side. According to local legend, the ghost of a young girl named Sara, who drowned in the creek in the fifties, still haunts the place. Given the caverns, crannies, and mazelike additions, it seems a likely hangout for ghosts, if you adhere to that paradigm. Unlike the Madonna Inn, there's really only one theme room. It's the Marilyn Monroe room, but, heck, since she actually stayed here, that should count for something. James Dean stayed here too, hence the large mural on the corner of the lodge.

> **Hearst Castle.** San Simeon, 42 miles north of San Luis Obispo, 94 miles south of Monterey. From San Francisco, take 101 to Paso Robles, then Calif. 46 west to Hwy. 1, north to the castle. From L.A., take 101 north to San Luis Obispo, then Hwy. 1 north.

It is tempting to treat the estate of William Randolph Hearst as another outrageous roadside attraction. As an architectural spectacle and nothing more. But even if one is cowed by the "Castle's" excess, one would be missing the overarching power and historical significance of its owner. What John D. Rockefeller was to oil, William Randolph Hearst was to mass media. He was big, ruthless, filled with blustery machismo. His ego matched his sprawling empire, which in its heyday included twenty dailies, nine national magazines, publishing houses, news agencies, and connections into radio, TV, and film. Though a Harvard dropout, he was a matchless propagandist, whose most famous and emblematic quip is forever etched in journalist lore: Upon hearing from a reporter in the Philippines that there was no war there, Hearst is alleged to have said, "You supply the pictures, I'll supply the war."

Hearst's brand of "yellow journalism" helped precipitate the Spanish-American War. He was a friend of politicians and Hollywood celebs, including his great love, "second-rate" Hollywood actress Marion Davies. He did not lightly suffer fools, or perceptive critics. Orson Welles, who directed, wrote, and starred in the profoundly scathing and thinly veiled portrait of Hearst, *Citizen Kane,* knew this all too well. Hearst mustered the weight of his vast media empire to almost completely blacklist Welles following the release of the film, even swaying the votes of members of the Academy of Motion Pictures, who selected *How Green Was My Valley* as Best Picture in 1941, rather than risk the enmity of the media magnate. *Citizen Kane's* later consecration as "the greatest movie ever made" did little to ameliorate the damage to Welles's career.

As Ned Beatty intoned to Howard Beale in the movie *Network,* "Mister Beale, you are messing with the forces of NATURE!" From the late 1890s through World War II, William Randolph Hearst was THE force of nature in American media. His ostentatious "castle" is a reflection of a time when such a pig-headed baron was allowed to run free in America. As you walk the grounds, past the pools, the banquet room, the artistic treasures of antiquity, remember that the days when such excessive opulence was uncritically tolerated are long gone. Even the wealthiest Americans of today—the Gateses, Buffetts, and Monks—wouldn't dare attempt what Hearst created at his castle, which in its mid-30s prime included a landing strip and a private zoo, containing giraffe, kangaroos, and herds of bison. Its grandeur was matched only by its beautifully lonely, and decidedly empty, isolation.

> **Henry Miller Memorial Library.** Hwy. 1 (Big Sur). ☎ **408/667-2574.** www.henrymiller.org. 1 mile south of the Big Sur Valley, 6 miles before the Julia Pfeiffer Burns State Park. Summer hours Mon–Sun 11am–5pm.

The Henry Miller Memorial Library is one of those places we must include because we'd be called to the mat and flogged if we excluded it. And we hate being flogged. We were reluctant to include it because it is hard to imagine a modern writer with greater hype than Miller. Akin to the humorless fans of the late Charles Bukowski, Miller's defenders border on maniacal. In both cases, the authors do not live up to the adulation. Still, Henry Miller lived in Big Sur, along with several other big-star authors over the years, including Jack Kerouac, Lawrence Ferlinghetti, and Robinson Jeffers. In fact, John Steinbeck's mother was a schoolteacher in Big Sur before she married. The Henry Miller Library, created by the late Emil White, a longtime friend of the author, is a focal point of various community events, including poetry readings, occasional afternoon concerts by the likes of Fred Frith, and annual arts and photography shows. Even if, like us, you find Miller overrated, you will find the library and its lush redwood-rimmed grounds to be a relaxing oasis. In the absence of a shrine to all of the Big Sur talents, this lovely house and meadow will have to do.

> **Monterey Aquarium.** 886 Cannery Row (Monterey). ☎ **831/648-4800.**

As far as aquariums go, this is the mother lode. In spite of the hordes of camera-clutching tourists, the effect of this huge marine sanctuary is positively transformative. "Touch pools" let you fondle purple sea urchin, decorator crabs, feather-boa kelp, and black abalone. An immense three-story kelp forest and adjacent simulated bay is teeming with jack mackerel, yellowtail, cabezon, dogfish, leopard shark, and wolf eel. A California sea otter swims laps in a two-story pool, while the million-gallon Outer Bay exhibit can be seen through the world's largest window.

With half an ocean dammed above your head, this is not a place to visit after an earthquake. Still, it makes a trek to beautiful though otherwise Disneyfied Monterey worth the visit.

Within this cavernous domain of concrete, glass, and sand, our favorite exhibit was, naturally, "Tiny Drifters." These delicate jellyfish come in all sizes and shapes, from the sea nettle doing their graceful slow-motion dance to the sea gooseberries that kind of clump in a pod. These creatures are in some cases so small and translucent they could easily pass for floating condoms. Clever backlighting gives some tanks an otherworldly feel, especially where the lobe comb jelly, egg-yolk jelly, and crystal jelly roam. With ambient music playing in the background, we sat transfixed for nearly an hour watching these pulsing ballerinas glide through the salt water. A total tour of the Monterey Aquarium could take as long as 3 hours, given space-outs like this. From the smallest (plankton) to the largest (seven-gill sharks), the Monterey aquarium gives you a good hard look at what's swimming underneath. Next time you hit the surf, you'll definitely think about it.

> **National Steinbeck Center.** 1 Main St. (Salinas). ☎ **831/796-3833.**

Shining like a beacon at night and the core of Salinas's redevelopment by day, this sprawling museum (opened June 27, 1998) honors the life of celebrated author and local contrarian John Steinbeck. The centerpiece of the 30,000-piece archive is Steinbeck's camper, "Rocinante," which he drove across America in 1961 in the company of his poodle, writing *Travels with Charley.* A vintage green GMC pickup, it hosts a custom-built camper that the author described as "A pick-up truck with a camper top, rather like the cabin of a small boat or the shell of a learned snail." One peek inside his galloping bungalow sums up the Steinbeck road legacy: a typewriter, a bed, a bottle of wine. What more could an alcoholic author want?

Wandering through the rest of the collection you'll listen to countless voice-overs reading from Steinbeck's early works. Several movie kiosks play loops of the films made from his books, including *The Grapes of Wrath* (with Henry Fonda), *Of Mice and Men, Winter of Our Discontent, Viva Zapata, The Red Pony, Tortilla Flat,* and *East of Eden* (with James Dean). Because so many of Steinbeck's short stories and books take place in agricultural settings derived from his early experiences in Salinas Valley, the museum gives you a palpable sense of the prewar desperation that ran throughout the valley when many itinerant workers drifted through looking for work. Nearby you can visit the **John Steinbeck Library** (350 Lincoln Ave.), where a 6-foot bronze statue of the author presides over the street. This is an irony, given that for the longest time Steinbeck had an ongoing feud with the town fathers and was not well liked. He wrote frankly about what he saw. And they burned his books. "His sympathies always go out to the oppressed, the misfits, the distressed. He likes to contrast the simple joy of life with the brutal and cynical craving for money," wrote the committee that awarded him a Nobel Prize for Literature in 1962. Now that he's dead and gone the town fathers seem quite content to cash in on his name.

> **Nepenthe.** Big Sur. ☎ **408/667-2345.** Hwy. 1, 30 miles south of Carmel, 5 miles south of River Inn.

You are definitely paying for the views here because the high-priced food definitely is not worth it. But what views! Over 800 feet above the gorgeous cliffs of Big Sur we sat, gazing out to sea, cogitating about our lives, about our direction, about the ordinary fish-shack tartar sauce that went with our average piece of salmon. Most of all, we cogitated about the two overtanned yuppie couples below us, sipping on wine, sipping on martinis, posing for pictures, with the men sniffing out the local dreadlocked teeny-boppers who happened by. There's not much to like about the many alcoholic citizens of Big Sur, nor the Bay Area bourgeoisie who make the trek down to overpriced places like Nepenthe, but the view, the goddamned view, is the best we've ever seen.

› Santa Cruz Beach and Boardwalk

We like to think of Santa Cruz as Eugene on the Beach, with the same progressive politics, long-hairs, hippie panhandlers, and drug use (and abuse) rationalized as "medicinal." A town of good vibes, good people, good bud, and great waves. There are two main highlights: First, the wonderfully atmospheric and surprisingly authentic Boardwalk, where the scene is Venice without the yuppies, Coney Island but not as decrepit, featuring the Giant Dipper, the only surviving wooden roller coaster on the West Coast, and the 88-year-old Charles Looff carousel, with its hand-carved wooden horses, 342-pipe German organ, and de rigueur brass rings; secondly, the beach, where the focus is surfing, brah.

Whether it's on Steamer Lane or Pleasure Point, Santa Cruz is widely recognized as one of the most classic, raging, off-the-Richter surfing destinations in the world. There's even a surfing program at the University of California at Santa Cruz. And if you ever tire of the Santa Cruz surf scene, just drive 3 miles north of Half Moon Bay to Maverick's, an offshore reef area with the "largest waves in the world": an average of 35 feet in winter.

Perchance to Surf

As I explain in my slanguistic tome, *How to Talk American* (Houghton Mifflin), surfing is the mother of all California-dude vernacular. What's more, to "surf" is not just a physical sport made popular in California, but a metaphor, born in the California Internet industry, for finding information fast (as in "surf the Web."). You want to see how pervasive the surfing metaphor is in California? Within a mere hour of each other you have the high-powered "surf engine," Yahoo of Santa Clara, and the legendary surf breaks of Santa Cruz. Killa Cali indeed.

> **Santa Cruz Surfing Museum.** Mark Abbott Lighthouse, West Cliff Dr. between Pelton and Columbia at Lighthouse Point (Santa Cruz). ☎ **408/429-3429.**

The setting is so California perfect that not even a rainy day could harsh your mellow. Perched on a hill overlooking Steamer Lane (one of California's primo surfing areas—named for the steamships that brought San Franciscans to the Santa Cruz wharf back in the day), this classic lighthouse is as peripatetic as the surfers outdoors. Built and relocated three times, the lighthouse's current mooring is the site of the city-operated Surfing Museum, allegedly the first of its kind in the world. The curators claim that surfing first started July 20, 1885, on *their* shores in Santa Cruz. They display crinkled photos and poorly made videos as supporting evidence. While other surfing museums up and down the coast may beg to differ, these folks just might be right. Trevor Cralle, author of *The Surfin'ary* (Ten Speed Press), argues that "the sport and art of surfing originated centuries ago (some claim A.D. 400) somewhere in the Pacific Islands, most likely Polynesia." But Trevor goes on to say that "Hawaiian Prince David Kawonanaokoa surfed Santa Cruz in 1885 and was probably the first person ever to surf in California." Cowabunga!

The lighthouse is dedicated to all young people who've perished through surfing misadventure. For instance, the museum has the ashes of surfer Mark Abbott, who ate a wave in 1965 at the tender age of 18. Also on display is a 4-foot, 6-inch belly board used by legendary 1930s boardhead Duke Kahanamoka. The highlight is a surfboard with a 17-inch shark bite that hangs in the center of the museum. When that shark bites with his teeth, dude . . .

> **Tassajara Hot Springs and Retreat Center.** 2 hr. southeast of Carmel Valley. From Carmel, take Carmel Valley Rd. till it becomes G16. Take G16 to Tassajara Rd., just past the 23.2-mile marker. Take Tassajara Rd. all the way to the Hot Springs. Call or write for more specific instructions. Reservation office: 300 Page St., San Francisco, CA 94102. ☎ **415/431-3771** for Tassajara overnight reservations; ☎ 415/863-3136 San Francisco Zen Center; ☎ 408/659-2229 or 415/431-3349 for day use only—line answered from 10am–noon and 1–4:30pm.

Opened in 1967 as the first Buddhist monastery outside Asia, the beautiful and remote Tassajara Hot Springs has taken on almost mythic status in the Bay Area. Located deep in the Los Padres National Forest near Monterey, it is the rural practice facility of the renowned San Francisco Zen Center, which means it is not recommended for the casual hot-springs habitué. However, for the true Monk traveler, it is an absolutely essential rite of passage. But before we get to the details of this meticulous place, let's cut to the logistics.

If you are interested in staying the night, you need to book months in advance, starting in early March (call ☎ **415/431-3771** for details). You will also need to make a reservation for day use (call ☎ **408/659-2229** to take care of that). This is the option we took. However, we recommend you get an early start because it's a 2½-hour drive from Carmel or Soledad, an hour of which is on a rocky dirt road filled with treacherous switchbacks. If you don't have a sturdy four-wheel drive, we recommend taking the Tassajara jitney. The folks in the office will give you times.

The drive to the Hot Springs is almost as inspiring as the springs themselves. You definitely feel you are delving deep into the heart of nature, far away from television, radio, and "civilization." Once at the Center, if you can get past, or at least learn to stomach, the occasional control-freak ball-busting Zenoid, and the less than conge-nial front-desk dude, you might very well enjoy your stay at this Zen Center–cum–summer hot springs "resort." Keep in mind that this is a serious Zen "practice" facility. And we mean serious. Therefore, the normal bum-kissing and hand-holding one would normally expect at a spa are missing. Yet you can tell zealous monks are running the place, because it is clean, organized, and artfully landscaped, with just-ly famous vegetarian cuisine. And the guest accommodations, including redwood cabins, Japanese-style tatami cabins, and elegant stone and pine rooms, are stun-ningly furnished and designed. They are lit only by kerosene lamps, and in some cases warmed by woodstoves.

But just because the environment is aesthetically serene, don't expect vapid ban-tering in the hot pools à la Harbin or Esalen. The air of meditative calm is main-tained in all sectors, except for the outdoor eating area, where things relax a bit and where you might have an opportunity to chat up one of the underpaid and over-worked young monks, who live here full-time without most of the samsaric distrac-tions of "home." They are wide-eyed and eager for deep and genuine contact. But don't get too relaxed, as the nearby stalking blue jays will steal whatever foodstuffs you brought in for the day.

Be sure to make the trek a few miles up the river to the pond, where the Zensters lounge and meditate in the buff (the river creates a flume à la Slide Rock in Sedona). And be sure to take in some zazen when you get back to the main area. Many great Zen teachers have done time at Tassajara, and the strength and elegance of their years of practice can be felt inside the zendo, if not out.

While Tassajara's overly precious reverence for all things Japanese borders on the ridiculous (even the cars in the parking lot are mostly Japanese), there's something to be said for Tassajara's stripped-down aesthetic of unadorned authenticity. It's refreshing to see so many middle-aged women deign not to dye their hair (and the way those middle aged Tassajara beauties tie their gray hair in buns is rather erotic). Unfortunately, if you are a straight guy, you're not likely to get much attention from the large band of power-tripping lesbians who seem to have found their way here. These anal contemplatives seize upon Tassajara's many rules—"shut the door," "shoes off," "quiet in the pools," "day-trippers can't eat with overnighters," etc.—as an opportunity to lecture and emasculate any free-spirited male who crosses their path. In the end, such arrogant disinterest in making the experience of guests comfortable, relaxing, and carefree partially nullifies the carefully maintained beauty of the place. If you want a real resort, try Two Bunch Palms in Desert Hot Springs. If you want real bodhisattva action, talk to Karimi, the Burmese attendant at the Millennium Shell, 1301 Broadway in King City. He's filled with the gusto, tolerance, and love of life that years of Zen practice can strip from many an unsuspecting practitioner.

San Jose

> **The Tech Museum of Innovation.** 201 S. Market St., at Park Ave. (San Jose). ☎ 408/795-6100. www.thetech.org. Closed Mon.

Until recently, a techie's tour of Silicon Valley might include a visit to the Hewlett-Packard garage (367 Addison Ave. in Palo Alto), the Yang and Filo trailer at Stanford (Yahoo resided on two computers named after Hawaiian sumo wrestlers Akebono and Konishiki), the Shockley Semiconductor building (391 San Antonio Rd. in Mountain View, "the Mother Road of Silicon Valley," according to writer David Plotnikoff), the Fairchild Semiconductor building (844 E. Charleston in Palo Alto, now a surplus office furniture store across from Sun Microsystems, "a shrine to the recyclability of Silicon Valley dreaming," says Plotnikoff), the ubiquitous Fry's Electronics (the full-tilt geek emporium, with wild architectural themes and notoriously lousy service), and occasionally the Jobs and Wozniak "garage" (actually, a bedroom in Jobs's parents' house at 2066—originally 11161—Crist Dr. in Los Altos, until the two wunderkinds moved out to the garage), concluding with a visit to the Apple store (Mariana and De Anza, in Cupertino) to buy some Apple paraphernalia and gaze at all those Macs you couldn't afford.

While diehards can still make that grassroots loop, tech-obsessed and culture-starved Silicon Valley now has something more to draw your interest than the eerily prophetic Winchester Mystery House, the loopy faux Egyptian grounds of the Rosicrucian Order (former Monk advertisers), the groovy retro decor of Joe's Restaurant, and the San Jose Historical Museum's half-scale replica of the 237-foot-high 1881 Electric Light Tower, which unsuccessfully attempted to illuminate most of downtown until it was blown over in a wind storm.

Opened in the fall of 1998, the 132,000-square-foot Tech Museum of Innovation is the buzz of Silicon Valley. At last, a museum worthy of our efforts!!

The subtext is: If you have a $96-million museum devoted to your trillion-dollar industry, it means you're legit, right? Well, sort of. We can say this much: Since computers are here to stay (despite what the Y2K paranoid schizophrenics have to preach) and most American guys, especially 12-year-old boys and their 12-year-old dads, love gadgets, this museum should be a guaranteed success.

First of all, Mexican architect Ricardo Legorretathe's stunning mango-colored building is a pomo cubist dream. Bold, blocky angles converge with palms and blue sky. Inside, past the crowds—and believe me, there are CROWDS—the high ceilings in this three-level museum are lit by overhead spots that wash the walls in pastel colors. A centerpiece art installation, called "Origin," employs a stunning mix of steel, gold leaf, terrazzo marble, silicon, and granite. A gold-leaf pillar rises toward a massive, domed, cobalt blue skylight. The utter simplicity and power of this piece is downright haunting. But we're not here for architectural excellence now, are we? It's the gadgets. And in this critical regard, "The Tech" goes far beyond the Intel Museum, the Computer Museum History Center, and other such attempts to provide a technological showcase in the Silicon Valley.

The upper level is extremely interactive, with the feel of a space-age casino. At the Inventors Workbench area you can build your own sensory-controlled device or experiment with CD technology. The Evolution Room steps you through the history of the microchip, an otherwise boring subject somehow made palatable, where you learn that the future of chip making will be human-free. In the Virtual Design Room you can make a 3-D portrait of yourself, scanning your head, altering the image, and taking a color printout home with you. The Tech Cyclone allows you to create and design your own cyber roller-coaster ride, after which you hop in a simulator and take off. The Transformation Booth takes your digital head shot and superimposes your head upon a sheep, a hippie, a hockey player (sounds like the chronological history of San Jose). Dumb tricks, but if you're a 12-year-old boy or dad, then you'll be yukking it up with the rest of them. The Life Tech area was my favorite display, where the fascinating world of DNA, gene splicing, and surgical advances are explained in ways that finally made some sense. Especially amusing is the Thermocamera that projects your transparent body up on a wall-mounted monitor where the unsuspecting suddenly appear colorfully nude. And in the basement you sample the outer limits in the Exploration gallery, with a simulated space walk (try the Jet Pack Chair), and underwater deep-sea robot diving. For all its technological brilliance and wizardry, its earthquake simulators and bunny suits, the artistry of the space itself is the key reason for coming to the Tech. Otherwise, you're likely to feel, as did I, that you've just eaten too much cotton candy at a high-tech carnival sideshow and have a really, really bad headache. Sort of like spending too much time on the computer.

> **Winchester Mystery House / Winchester Products Museum / Winchester Historic Firearms Museum.** 525 S. Winchester Blvd. (San Jose). ☎ 408/247-2101.

A forerunner of both the esoteric mystic Madame Blavatsky and the hyper-controlling hotel empress Leona Helmsley (only the little people finish houses), the capricious wiggy heiress to the Winchester gun fortune was ordered by the spirits of people killed by her late husband's repeaters to keep building and building this mansion to kill off the bad karma associated with hubby's namesake rifles. The spirits said that if she stopped building, she herself would die—a prophecy that did come true, of course. Sarah L. Winchester died friendless, though still not penniless, despite the ridiculous sums the nutty heiress spent doing and redoing her home. Years later it's clear there's no redeeming architectural merit in the unfinished 160-room structure, though there are plenty of goofball elements that belong in something like the mystery hole just south of here.

And yet, the spirit of Sarah L. Winchester haunts San Jose to this day. And not just because she was the first to blow millions without having a lot to show for it. Rather, Sarah's riotously out-of-control Victorian mansion (what the 1939 WPA Guide to California called "the externalization of a psychopathic mind") is the perfect metaphor for the unbridled growth of today's Silicon Valley. What's more, the various elements of the mansion itself find uncanny digital corollaries—Mrs. Winchester's paranoia led her to build little nooks where she could spy on her help (issues of on-line security anyone?), doors that open onto blank walls (fire walls?), and a staircase leading to nowhere (failed IPOs).

>san francisco

Hey, San Francisco, What Did You Do to Your Hair?

Twelve years on the road, traveling every two-lane highway across this country, we thought we'd never come back to what Chuck Yma Sumac called this "angel-food cake of a town."

There were many reasons we left San Francisco in 1986: the morbid gloom, the incessant crime, and Arctic summers to name a few. But more so, the frustrating reality of working twice as hard while paying for one of the highest cost-of-living indexes in the nation. That was enough to send us packing for good.

So why are we back?

We missed it. We wanted to see old friends. We felt long overdue in Monking *The City*. But also, and most importantly, because we needed a serious hit of that San Francisco edge. Not to be confused with the hard edges found in New York or L.A. But an edge that challenges one's relationship to time, space and, above all, reality.

It's an amorphous edge, not easily defined or understood. It promises ultimate freedom in expression, except you make all the rules. No road maps are given, no time limits set. Which is why anyone who is into transformation, radical expression, or just plain floating on fog will at one time or another do a stint by the Bay.

San Francisco is our nemesis. It seduces us with its pretty facade and its cosmic dance, then belts us from behind with its many lessons. And that is what brought us back. It was time for a reality check in ultimate reality.

The Cultural Petri Dish

There's something very appropriate in that it's named San Francisco. St. Francis, the most benevolent saint in the Christian hierarchy, was the archetypal caretaker of the wounded. His nurturing and tolerance allowed for healing and growth. Like its namesake, San Francisco opens its arms to all sentient beings. The emotionally and spiritually wounded, in particular, have always come here looking for freedom and change, for a place to grow and be themselves.

San Francisco is headquarters of the Rainbow Nation. Here you will find all races, orientations, and creeds coexisting far, and we mean FAR, more sanely than they do in any other American city. There isn't that nasty incessant battle for ethnic superiority one finds in the East. With the exception of the rather un–San Francisco neighborhoods of the Sunset and the Marina, people here don't even think in racial or ethnic terms. Other parts of the country, especially New York and Boston, seem weighed down by the legacy of their immigrant past. But San Francisco is the metropolis of possibilities. It is soft and misty. Like a dream. It seems beyond history.

San Francisco has always been and will always be the crucible where new thought is tested in America. If you come here to find a sense of solidity, continuity, and ancestry, you will be very disappointed. Like the tectonic plates beneath its soil, San Francisco is continually shifting in new and unexpected ways.

Time and again throughout its recent history San Francisco has completely remade itself. In fact, almost every major social transformation of the past five decades has had its roots in the Bay Area. This is because, unfettered by the rules and traditions of the East, San Francisco has been free to forge a new way.

In the 1950s, artists like Allen Ginsberg, Jack Kerouac, Lawrence Ferlinghetti, Kenneth Rexroth, and Gary Snyder gravitated to the city, where in North Beach bars and cafes the Beat movement found its defining voice.

In the early sixties, in nearby Berkeley, on the steps of Sproule Hall, the roots of the Free Speech and Antiwar movements were born. By the mid-sixties these political movements had merged with the acid dreams of the Flower Children and Hippies, creating on the corner of San Francisco's Haight and Ashbury the most influential "scene" this country has ever known: the Summer of Love.

By the late sixties, the roots of today's $14-billion natural-products industry were being planted by these same hippies who migrated north to the fertile growing regions of Sonoma County and beyond. While the original "crop" may have been cannabis, many of today's major natural-food companies—names like Fantastic Foods, Barbara's Bakery, and Traditional Medicinals—are still located in this region. In addition, for nearly three decades, Alice Waters has blended the organic wisdom of the natural-foods movement with her love of French cuisine at the world renowned Chez Panisse in neighboring Berkeley. From Alice and others' quest for fresh, locally grown organic food and medicine came a renewed commitment to stewardship of the land, air, and water, which quickly congealed into what we now call "The Environmental Movement," perhaps San Francisco's most enduring legacy.

By the early seventies the city had become the world mecca for gay liberation, then flourishing in the Castro and Polk Street neighborhoods. At the same time San Francisco was leading the way in the broader sexual revolution, crossing boundaries undreamed of only a decade before. Meanwhile, further south, Silicon Valley was spawning a revolution of a different sort with a small but mighty chip.

In the eighties, San Francisco led the way again in the fight against AIDS, as the back side of sexual liberation reared its ugly head. Long before President Reagan could even say the word "AIDS,"

Observation

"The Bay Area seems to give people permission to experiment, to go crazy, try something new. Then the ideas get packaged by the media in New York and are sent as myths to the rest of the country."

—Jerry Rubin

San Francisco's gay and lesbian community was heroically reaching out to those in need, creating hospices, meal programs, and persuasive pamphlets that quickly and effectively taught the hows and whys of safer sex. Those men and women were models of bodhisattva compassion, yet to this day they have not received their due in the nation's press, even though their pioneering work has saved thousands of lives, from all races and sexual orientations.

To its credit, the *San Francisco Chronicle* was the first paper in the country to have a regular AIDS beat, written by the late Randy Shilts, author of the seminal work on the AIDS epidemic, *And the Band Played On.* And say what you will about their overall journalistic quality, to this day the *Chronicle* and the *Examiner* have better coverage of gay issues than almost any paper in the country.

Also by the mid-eighties, San Francisco had leaped far ahead of the nation in the field of holistic health—while in many states it is still illegal to dispense herbs and practice acupuncture. San Francisco not only nurtured these powerful traditions at schools like the American College of Traditional Chinese Medicine, it spawned the first holistic medical clinic, the Quan Yin Acupuncture Center, to specifically assist people with AIDS. Meanwhile, San Francisco–based heart specialist Dr. Dean Ornish was courageously gaining mainstream scientific support for what was heretofore known as "alternative medicine."

In the 1990s and into the millennium, we have entered the exciting new world of interactive multimedia. And, once again, the San Francisco Bay Area leads the way. From the first large-scale digital be-ins, to Marin's Industrial Light and Magic, to the latest in Internet applications and content, Bay Area pioneers are reshaping how we look at ourselves and our world. Cutting-edge magazines like *Mondo 2000* (based at the legendary "Mondo House" in the Oakland Hills) and, more recently, *Wired,* based in the heart of SOMA's Multimedia Gulch, were covering and participating in the revolution long before most people knew what a modem was.

Interestingly, there has been a deep spiritual and psychological undercurrent running through most of these movements. On the spiritual level, the biggest influence has been Zen Buddhism, which came over with San Francisco's early Japanese settlers, but found its most noble expression in the work of Suzuki Roshi (*Zen Mind, Beginner's Mind*), who did more than any other teacher to bring ancient Buddhist teachings to the West.

From the beautiful and solid Zen Center at Page and Laguna, to the gourmet vegetarian cuisine found at the Zen Center–owned Greens restaurant at Fort Mason, to Issan-ji, the first gay Zen center/AIDS hospice, located on Hartford Street in the Castro, to even former governor and newly elected Oakland mayor Jerry "Moonbeam" Brown, Zen Buddhism has penetrated all aspects of the city, leading esteemed Zen Master Robert Aitken to remark that San Francisco is the "Buddhaville of America."

Remember EST, Esalen, and Primal Scream? In the 1970s, while the human sexual response was percolating on the streets of San Francisco, the spiritual traditions of the East were merging with the radical transpersonal psychology pioneered at such cutting-edge institutions as the California Institute of Integral Studies, the New College of California, and JFK University in nearby Orinda to form what was called "The Human Potential Movement" (later mistakenly grouped with New Age chicanery like crystals and channeling). It was out of this uniquely San Francisco home-brew of Zen-Taoist simplicity, high-tech innovation, and a can-do desire to creatively manifest one's innate potential that *Monk, The Mobile Magazine* was born.

In San Francisco, personal transformation has always been a political act, as Cal State Hayward Professor Theodore Roszak so ably explains in his books on American counterculture. San Francisco is a place where publicly sharing one's innermost thoughts has never been considered narcissistic or taboo.

Deeply affected by the San Francisco personalist tradition, autobiographical art has swept the nation in the eighties and nineties. From Annie Sprinkle to Karen Finley to Madonna Ciccone to the pioneers of the "perzine" (or personal zine), your humble narrators, the Monks, personal expression has moved far beyond baring

JUST DON'T CALL IT FRISCO: The Last Surviving Edict of Emperor Norton I

The first in San Francisco's long line of eccentrics was English-born Joshua Abraham Norton, who made a bundle in the gold-rush economy of 1849, and then lost it all trying to corner the rice market in 1852. After several years of reclusive penury, Norton emerged, unbalanced but unbowed, suddenly declaring himself "Emperor of the United States and Protector of Mexico," writing screeds against the republican form of government, even coining his own scrip, while parading about the city in an old uniform and military cap, a small sword dangling at his side, a stick or umbrella in one hand, trailed by two mongrel dogs, Lazarus and Bummer. Emperor Norton's most famous edict was against the use of the word "Frisco." He wrote: "Whoever after due and proper warning shall be heard to utter the abominable word 'Frisco,' which has no linguistic or other warrant, shall be deemed guilty of a High Misdemeanor, and shall pay into the Imperial Treasury as penalty the sum of $25."

Norton was accepted and even beloved by the local citizenry. He could eat and drink wherever he chose, free of charge. He could draw checks on local banks, using his own scrip!! And while possibly mad, he was also prescient. Norton was the first to call for a bridge across the San Francisco Bay.

Not surprisingly, thousands turned out for his funeral in 1880. He is buried in Colma Cemetery, his headstone affirming his rightful status as "Emperor of the United States and Protector of Mexico."

one's deepest feelings to literally baring one's most intimate parts. For better or worse, the intense focus on intimate personal expression we find everywhere from Jerry Springer to Oprah to the highly confessional string of films, books, and television about the drug and alcohol addicted, can almost all be traced back to the "let it all hang out" ethos of the San Francisco–based Human Potential Revolution.

But It *Is* Sort of Foggy Here

Now for the bad news. There's trouble in Paradise. Big trouble.

Start with "Da Mayor," Willie Brown.

The election of Mayor Brown perfectly illustrates everything that's fundamentally wrong with San Francisco. As much as we like the man personally, he lacks the courage to tackle the thorny issues of the city head on. Brown was elected in a landslide over former mayor Frank Jordan, an unimaginative, boring functionary with zilch for charisma. After four years of Jordan, San Franciscans longed for the colorful liberal mayors of the past, such as Feinstein, Agnos, and Moscone. They wanted a mayor with as much personality and charm as the city itself. And in Willie Brown they got it. A graduate of San Francisco State, Hastings Law School, and the Wilkes Bashford School of Snazzy Couture, Willie Brown is the ultimate San Franciscan. A man who, as the long-running speaker of the California House of Representatives, built a reputation as a short but mighty political insider, a debonair guy who always comes up looking stylish, vibrant, and concerned, all while doing the bidding of his large campaign benefactors.

Unfortunately, the deep-seated problems of San Francisco require more than stylish suits, entertaining rhetoric, and a dramatically refurbished City Hall (the costly "Taj Mah Willie"). What San Francisco needs is a hard-nosed crusader like New York's Rudy Giuliani. Unfortunately, San Francisco's historically anti-authoritarian populace would never tolerate a "Mayor Cop." So, the city is left with the less effective, though far more colorful, of the highly touted "New Wave Mayors."

The prognosis is not good. While Silicon Valley gazillionaires drive real-estate prices ever higher, the quality of life here continues to go downhill. The homeless situation in San Francisco is the worst in the country. You cannot walk more than one block in the Union Square, Civic Center, and Haight Street areas without being panhassled. You cannot safely park your car anywhere downtown without fear of being burglarized. New York's Giuliani put a firm stop to such intrusions on private space. Willie Brown doesn't have the guts. And though Brown is making modest improvements in Muni, the traffic situation in San Francisco is so increasingly intractable only a bold new transportation initiative is going to seriously improve it.

Then, there's the streets. Ten years ago we would have voted these streets the best-paved in the country. Now they look like a war zone. Potholes, ruts, incomplete repairs. That may be superficial, but it reflects a decay. A decay that's prevalent in all corners of town, right to the core of City Hall.

Dirty deals are abounding. The Presidio, a former military base and one of the most expensive pieces of real estate on the planet, is up for a land grab, and the rightful landowners, the public, are about to get screwed. As the *Bay Guardian* has diligently exposed, San Francisco can kiss good-bye any hope for sustainable development of the future "national park," thanks to the greedy machinations at City Hall. While the mayor's most outspoken critic, KGO talk-show host Bernie Ward, is naively one-sided in his vociferous attacks on Mr. Brown, Ward's allegations of Tammany-style corruption surrounding the new 49ers Stadium and Treasure Island redevelopment are worth exploring.

Furthermore, in a purely economic sense, the city is in increasing danger of destroying its fragile and enlightened diversity. For instance, San Francisco has become increasingly homogenized as most of its working-class base moves to Oakland or further afield. For those not following history, homogenization and the loss of a working class furthers the gulf between the rich and the poor.

Since the loss of its shipping trade and its once vital port, San Francisco has turned to the tourist dollar as its main means of support. While Mayor Brown touts sports complexes like PacBell Park and the new 49ers Stadium Shopping Complex as the saviors of China Basin, the Third Street Corridor, and Hunters Point, the city as a whole is in danger of

Observation

"San Franciscans tolerate high rents, bad traffic, and nonexistent parking because they believe that is the cost of living in a special, 'different' place. But the sad fact of the matter is that San Francisco is losing its unique character. The city that has always prided itself on being different is looking more and more like every other large city in America. Its residents are behaving more and more like people in every other large city in America.

And the myth of chain hatred is one of the reasons that fundamental shift in character has been able to occur with relatively little public debate. San Francisco has been 'chained,' almost sub rosa, at least in part because San Franciscans believe—quite falsely—that some law or regulation or bureaucrat or activist is out there preventing it from happening, or at least regulating its ultimate scope."

—Tara Shioya, *SF Weekly*, October 22–28, 1997

becoming a cliché of itself rather than a vibrant, economically diverse, forward-looking community.

It can be so nauseatingly provincial and detached here now you can grow moss between your knuckles chatting so amiably long about color schemes and IPOs. Visitors are still eager to buy the concept of the lush, green, beautiful cosmopolis—so fresh, so free, so sophisticated—but the real city is degrading behind the Victorian gingerbread facade.

In fact, at times it feels like this city is completely out of touch with reality. Sometimes you want to shake somebody and shout "Hey, wake up! The world's on fire!" You never have to do that in a city like Chicago or New York, where reality hits you in the face every second. It's almost as if San Francisco's beauty, balance, and tolerance is a curse. It can insulate you from what's really going on and what really needs to be done.

How to instill a sense of rawness and palpable realness to the city is a mystery. Outside of the occasional earthquake, the citizens are rarely forced to interact. This makes it transparently easy for gays and straights alike to come here, set up a nice bourgeois nest, and subtly distance themselves from anyone outside their own tribe.

For example, on playgrounds and in recreation centers throughout the city, generations of Asian-Americans stubbornly stick to themselves. There are adult gay men who haven't left the Castro in years. And where are the African-Americans? Conveniently tucked away in Hunters Point and Potrero Hill. If the L.A. Riots taught us anything, it's that separatism leads to despair and, ultimately, violence.

In the 1990s the once great city of Saint Francis smacks of a subtle insidious separatism that it pretends to ignore. And yet for the moment, everyone appears to get along. Are we dreaming? What is going on here?

Hope or Hype?

It is now quite clear that those neighborhoods that used to be the vanguard areas of the city have turned into cartoon caricatures of themselves. **The Castro** is a caricature of gay life. It has very little to do with how most gay people live their lives today. The restaurants on Castro haven't changed in two decades. Same old scene, same old clones, and that is depressing. It's lost in a time warp. The Castro wants you to believe that the seventies never died, that *Tales of the City* has just been written, and that disco, baby, is the latest rage.

The Haight is a spiffed-up caricature of the sixties. You have your head shops, your retro clothing, your groovy record stores—it's all so formulaic. The perfect trap for the young German tourists who flock there, guidebook in hand, thinking they're getting to see "hippies, *maaaan.*"

The only areas of the city that have any kind of realness are **the Mission** (quickly going the way of SOMA and the Castro) and the deliciously gnarly **China Basin** (whose raw edginess will soon be largely obliterated by the new PacBell Park). The

San Francisco Math Problems

1. Zelda and Jane were given a rottweiler at their commitment ceremony. If their dog needs to be walked 2 miles a day and they walk at a rate of three-quarter miles per hour, how much time will they spend discussing their relationship in public?

2. Sanjeev has seven piercings. If the likelihood of getting cellulitis on a given day is 10% per piercing, what is the likelihood Sanjeev will need to renew his erythromycin prescription during the next week?

3. Chad wants to take half a pound of pot to Orinda and sell it at a 20% profit. If it originally cost him $1,500, how much should Nicole write the check for?

4. The City and County of San Francisco decide to destroy fifty rats infesting downtown. If 9,800 animal rights activists hold a candlelight vigil, how many people did each dead rat empower?

5. A red sock, a yellow sock, a blue sock, and a white sock are tossed randomly in a drawer. What is the likelihood that the first two socks drawn will be socks of color?

6. George weighs 145 pounds and drinks two triple lattes every morning. If each shot of espresso contains 490 milligrams of caffeine, what is George's average caffeine density in mg/pound?

7. There are 4,500 homes in Mill Valley and all of them recycle plastic. If each household recycles ten soda bottles a day and buys one PolarFleece pullover per month, does Mill Valley have a monthly plastic surplus or deficit? Bonus question: Assuming all the plastic bottles are 1-liter size, how much Evian are they drinking?

8. If the average person can eat one pork pot sticker in 30 seconds, and the waitress brings a platter of twelve pot stickers, how long will it take five vegans to not eat them?

ADVANCED PLACEMENT STUDENTS ONLY

9. Katie, Trip, Ling, John-John, and Effie share a three-bedroom apartment on Guerrero for $2,400 a month. Effie and Trip can share one bedroom, but the other three need their own rooms with separate ISDN lines to run their Web servers. None of them wants to use the futon in the living room as a bed, and they each want to save $650 in 3 months to attend Burning Man. What is their best option?
   a. All five roommates accept a $12/hour job-share as handgun monitors at Mission High.
   b. Ask Miles, the bisexual auto mechanic, to share Effie and Trip's bedroom for $500/month.
   c. Petition the Board of Supervisors to advance Ling her annual digital-artists-of-color stipend.
   d. Rent strike.

Source: A bit of wisdom circulating on the Internet for months. No one knows the source.

rest of the city is either yuppified, guppified, or horribly Manhattanized. The quirky, funky little core of yore is disappearing fast.

We remember San Francisco as being a lot more flamboyant. With more of a picturesque street scene. And we never thought that the brilliantly creative gay community would become so predictable. Maybe that's what happens to all great movements. They settle down and settle in. That is certainly what has happened here. At times it seems like the only thing separating San Francisco from Middle America is that there's a chance the parents at a San Francisco PTA meeting might both be lesbian.

Perhaps S.F. has lost its fervor. Perhaps it's lost its direction. Or perhaps, just perhaps, it's simply conserving energy until it's time to birth the next revolution already germinating beneath the surface.

Perhaps, yet again, San Francisco can reclaim its status as the world's avant-garde breeding ground. This hope lies in the very nature of the digital revolution the city has helped create. For the values of this digital age are the same values the city has always held dear: democracy, freedom of expression, total access, empowerment of the average person, and decentralization of authority and control. It's what separates San Francisco from L.A.: inclusion versus exclusion. San Francisco is eternally looking for ways to empower everyday people. Los Angeles is not.

This appears to be to San Francisco's advantage, since the psychology (or, rather, pathology) of Los Angeles, which has been the cultural entertainment hotbed of the last twenty years, is out of step with the inclusive ethos of this new digital era. The entire Hollywood mind set, revolving as it does around a very small cluster of stars, directors, producers, agents, and other assorted players, is built on exclusivity. The whole mentality of what is called "the industry" and "the star system" is to exclude all but the chosen and well-connected few, who then parade their wealth and fame before the masses. L.A. is very eighties, a decade built upon the altar of self-aggrandizement. Like that decade, L.A. at its core does not have a very generous spirit.

By contrast, San Francisco has always been built upon a pillar of embracement, creating technology that everyone can use and creative space for everyone to play. Whether San Francisco remains the center of the present digital age depends largely on whether the digital age stays true to its egalitarian promise. On whether the values of San Francisco or L.A. prevail.

Then again, cyber space by its very nature needs no "center" or "scene." The digital frontier does not need this physical place called San Francisco. Though it very much needs the San Francisco state of mind.

Which is to say that maybe San Francisco will finally do what it's always threatened to do—lift off on a fog bank into a more expanded realm, where we will find it not in the flesh but in the realm of fantasy, a virtual city we can see and nostalgically be with in all its beautiful, tolerant, and noble perfection.

›Locked out
on the Road

After a final stop at Taco Bell, the Monks buckle up and hit the freeway on their way to San Francisco, bidding adios to Smog Angeles, steering through traffic, plowing through the Valley, passing cool-cat truckers at 80 miles per hour. With Magic Mountain in the dust, Mike cruises up the grade where boiling radiators spill drivers onto the sun-baked shoulder of Interstate 5.

Mike reaches down into his 99¢ Taco Bell cheese quesadilla, hungering for that first freeway bite. The music's blaring Morphine as his teeth chomp down into the soft white tortilla, anticipating the warm melt of bean and cheese . . . when a big green splat of liquid detergent squirts out of the folded tortilla and into his mouth.

"What the—?!"

There's an instant gag reflex as the lemon tang of dish-washing soap hastens down his throat and back up again. Mike leans sideways, tossing cookies out the window, splattering green and yellow across four lanes of traffic, as he struggles to pull over.

Close inspection of the offending quesadilla does indeed reveal a glob of green liquid ooze that has all the basic characteristics of liquid detergent meant for the sink, not as flavoring for California cheese.

Mike contemplates a lawsuit while continuing to wretch out the door. Ten minutes later the Monks are back on the road again, quesadilla saved for specimen possibilities should the need ever arise, though it is unlikely since neither Monk is litigious by nature.

Seven miles later, enjoying the end of smog and taking their first deep breaths of air in weeks, the Monks happen upon a narrow brush fire that burns dangerously close to traffic, rapidly climbing a hill. *Wonder why they're burning the brush,* ponders Mike, realizing seconds later that only an idiot would assume the fire was intentional.

The rear-view mirror reveals flames spreading out of control, with a few million acres of dry mountain in its path. Mike pulls off at the next exit to Pyramid Lake. Rushing the doors of the visitor center, he finds a taciturn clerk who's so completely absorbed in a romance novel that it takes a few repeated shouts to set off alarms in her sleepy head.

"Fire, Fire, Fire!!!"

She finally gets the hint and calls a ranger away from his lunch break. He walks outside to notice the darkening sky. He immediately radios in for local fire support, as Mike contemplates whether this act of bodhisattva compassion compensates for all those unpaid parking tickets hidden beneath the dash.

Nah.

Fifty miles later, north of Bakersfield, in the heart of the Sacramento Valley, another heavy smoke screen crosses the freeway. This time it's definitely an intentional burning of fields. The smoke cuts visibility, and traffic slows to 40 miles per hour.

Where's the air conditioner when you need it?

With windows up, vents closed, and an easy 100° heat outside, the Monks are sweating in the stale air. For the next 40 miles the smoke continues, leaving a nasty gray residue on the hoods of every car.

It's seven o'clock when the hyperventilating Monks finally pull across the cool Bay Bridge. Downtown San Francisco streetcars slice through the asphalt down the middle of the palm-lined streets. The heavy metal grind of the old green classic trains lends a thundering roar to the urban soundscape. The Monks drive up Market looking for an elusive parking space. Mike yearns to sit and get his bearings straight. At the intersection of Market and Tenth traffic comes to a sudden halt. Out of the four corners a plague of cyclists come bursting through like a pack of wild dogs. Motorists freeze nervously in place as a loud band of militant bike riders takes over the intersection. It's Critical Mass, San Francisco's monthly reminder that there are alternatives to four wheels and gas.

Helmeted, brandishing noisemakers, the eclectic group speeds by at a dizzying pace, shouting insults to the drivers who helplessly wait for the light to change. Ever the rebels, the Monks give a big thumbs-up to the parade on wheels, only to have a bearded eco-warrior acerbically shout, "Thanks for driving, asshole!"

"That wasn't very nice," says Mike, a veteran of every possible environmental protest in his four decades on Gaia.

It isn't until Church, a mile from downtown, that the Monks find a place to park in front of Cafe du Nord.

"The keys!" Mike screams after he absentmindedly closes the door. "Oh my God, I can't believe I did that."

There on the dashboard lay the keys. After a quick check of all the other doors, which naturally are locked, the Monks consider their options. After a few aborted tries using a borrowed coat hanger, Mike flips through a phone book and calls All City Locks. It's a busy night for the locksmiths as every member of the keys-locked-in-the-car crowd has apparently made a spontaneous convergence upon San Francisco. It could be a 2-hour wait at least.

"I'm hungry," says Jim.

The Monks walk over to Church and settle on Azteca. The place is packed. Wage earners are on downtime, with a weekend ahead. The Monks order and grab a table. Mike then heads to the men's room and pushes the door, but it only opens a crack. He tries again, and it springs open a foot. Someone's inside blocking the door. His arm can be seen lying on the floor.

While Mike contemplates calling 911, the door suddenly opens and out steps a stocky young guy, dressed in slacks, running shoes, button down shirt, and incongruent tie. His sleeves are rolled up and his face is quite red.

Inside, the toilet is full of paper towels. A full dispenser's worth fills it to the brim. A layer of paper towels covers the floor where the guy must have laid down. When Mike returns to the table the Paper Towel Man is sitting in the next chair. Without asking, he's taken a place and is bending slowly forward looking down at his hands, which are large and perspiring, the knuckles bright red.

"You okay?"

Paper Towel Man doesn't answer, but his tattoos do. From the wrist, traveling the length of his arm, he has a series of tattoos that go all the way up. Likewise, on his neck, above his collar, is the telling edge of another tattoo that spirals up from his back.

Mike busily eats his burrito. The uninvited guest sits slumped, unspeaking and perspiring heavily, dripping at the forehead. Suddenly he falls sidewise, his face on Mike's plate, crushing chips and burrito, splattering salsa, and drooling into the mess.

"Hey, hey . . ." Mike pokes at the guy, who has begun to shake. Suddenly the guy sits up straight, brushes chips off his face and mutters "Have a good day," as he bolts for the door.

"What was that all about?"

"Speedball," cracks a girl who is sitting close by. "He's in here all the time, shooting up."

"Oh right, speedball," says Mike, who suddenly has no appetite.

>>>•<<<

By the time the Monks return to their car, Steve O'Neil of All City Locks has double-parked his van, with a dog sitting shotgun.

"How much is this going to run me?" asks Michael Monk.

"Oh, it'll run you about the cost of a good meal."

"Cool," answers Mike, thinking thirty bucks sounds about right.

Eighty bucks later, Mike is opening the door.

"There goes our food money for the weekend," he says to O'Neil while he's packing his tools.

"Hey, next time keep a spare key in your wallet. In the meantime, there's always Taco Bell!"

The Top Ten Distractions in San Francisco

So, you got fogged in at SFO on a Sunday morning and have 12 hours to kill. S.F.'s a small town. You could practically walk it. But on the Monk trip you're gonna be cabbing because (a) there is no parking in San Francisco, (b) the buses are just too slow, and (c) walking sucks after two martinis. On our tour you'll be singing hallelujah; going to prison; paying your respects to dead people's ashes, a dead saint, and dead dogs; watching a flick; sitting Zen; dancing with transsexuals; looking cross-eyed at furniture hanging off walls; and, yes, drinking a really stiff martini. Sound like fun? Let's do it!

1. **St. John Will-I-Am Coltrane African Orthodox Church** (Western Addition). A small interracial congregation of believers in San Francisco's Western Addition consider jazz legend John Coltrane a saint. You get to experience the most unique liturgical celebration in the entire city (and that includes

Glide Memorial, Mrs. Bronstein-Stone). Love, Love Supreme, is the message of Saint John, and you can see it in the hearts and faces of almost everyone who attends. If there is one congregation that carries on the free-form spirit of sixties S.F. spirituality, this little church is it. All praise to God. (See "Spirituality.")

2. **Alcatraz Island.** If there is one tourist stop every sensible local will recommend, it is Alcatraz Island. We are not afraid to admit this is truly one of the most captivating highlights of the Golden State; proof positive that just because a place is recommended in every single guidebook to S.F. does not mean it isn't Monk-worthy.

The ferry ride over circles the former federal penitentiary, and if you go in a slight fog, as we did, the sight of thousands of seabirds circling the island as if it were a scene from Hitchcock's *The Birds* gives the place an unforgettably eerie and ancient melancholy. On the island itself, the buildings remain just as they were when "The Rock" was closed in 1963. The self-guided cell-house audio tour is impeccably realistic, featuring the commentary of inmates and guards who lived on this cold and windy fortress, reserved for the prison system's most dangerous and notorious. (See "Buildings, Bridges, and Other Visual Landmarks.")

3. **Columbarium** (Richmond Neighborhood). Urns line every wall of this four-tiered sanctuary. With stained-glass windows, a copper dome, and classical Muzak, it seems like an elegant wedding chapel. (See "Buildings, Bridges, and Other Visual Landmarks.")

4. **Holy Virgin Cathedral** (Richmond Neighborhood). Downstairs in this golden-domed Greek Orthodox Cathedral is the final resting place for the relics of Saint John, lying in state in the city's most ornate Gothic shrine. (See "Spirituality.")

5. **Presidio Pet Cemetery** (Presidio). Right under the S.F. side of the Golden Gate Bridge, near the thickly wooded aromatic heart of the Presidio, this sweet cemetery is where soldiers bury their fallen pets, such as Jason the Dancing Dog, Max Our Happy Puppy, and Baron ("He Lived to Love and Be Loved"). (See "Buildings, Bridges, and Other Visual Landmarks.")

6. **Castro Theater** (Castro). The ultimate movie-going experience in the city. A stunning 1930s movie palace, with Spanish Colonial architecture, a plaster ceiling that looks like a big tent, seating for 1,600, and organ music before major shows. (See "Theaters" in the "Film" section.)

7. **The San Francisco Zen Center** (Lower Haight). The guy with the pierced nose, ear, and tongue who cruised you at the S&M bar last night is likely to be sitting next to you calm as a cow. It's a place where Evan Dando 20-somethings who look like they shredded all last night commingle with itsy-bitsy Jewish

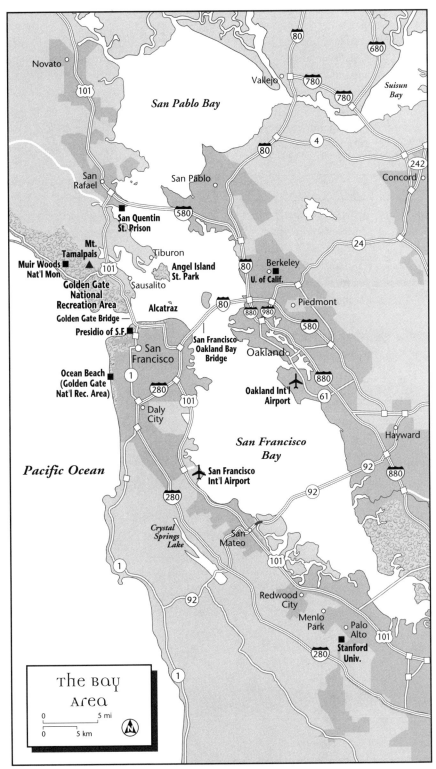

Novato

San Pablo Bay

Vallejo

Suisun
Bay

80

680

780

780

San
Rafael

San Pablo

101

242

Concord

580

80

4

San Quentin
St. Prison

Mt.
Tamalpais

24

Muir Woods
Nat'l Mon

Tiburon

Berkeley

80

U. of Calif.

Angel Island
St. Park

101

Golden Gate
National
Recreation Area

Sausalito

880 980

Piedmont

580

Alcatraz

Golden Gate Bridge —

Presidio of S.F.

San
Francisco

San Francisco
Oakland Bay
Bridge

Oakland

880

Ocean Beach
(Golden Gate
Nat'l Rec. Area)

1

280

101

Daly
City

Oakland Int'l
Airport

61

Hayward

San Francisco
Bay

92

880

San Francisco
Int'l Airport

92

280

1

Crystal
Springs
Lake

San
Mateo

101

Pacific Ocean

92

Redwood
City

Menlo
Park

Palo
Alto

101

1

280

Stanford
Univ.

The Bay
Area

0   5 mi

0   5 km

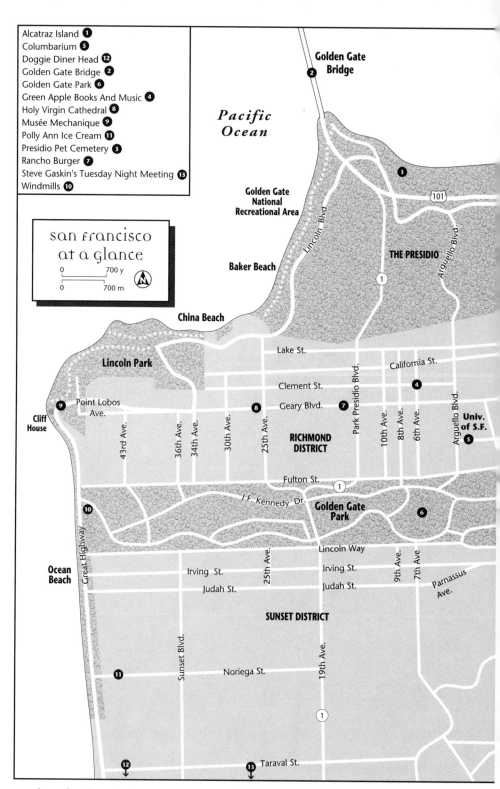

Alcatraz Island ❶
Columbarium ❺
Doggie Diner Head ❿
Golden Gate Bridge ❷
Golden Gate Park ❻
Green Apple Books And Music ❹
Holy Virgin Cathedral ❽
Musée Mechanique ❾
Polly Ann Ice Cream ⓫
Presidio Pet Cemetery ❸
Rancho Burger ❼
Steve Gaskin's Tuesday Night Meeting ⓭
Windmills ❿

san francisco
at a glance

0 ——— 700 y
0 ——— 700 m

Golden Gate Bridge ❷

Pacific Ocean

Golden Gate National Recreational Area

Baker Beach

THE PRESIDIO

❸

101

Lincoln Blvd.

Arguello Blvd.

1

China Beach

Lake St.

Lincoln Park

California St.

Clement St.

❹

Point Lobos Ave.

Geary Blvd. ❼

Cliff House

❾

❽

Park Presidio Blvd.

Arguello Blvd.

Univ. of S.F. ❺

43rd Ave.

36th Ave.

34th Ave.

30th Ave.

25th Ave.

10th Ave.

8th Ave.

6th Ave.

RICHMOND DISTRICT

Fulton St. ①

J.F. Kennedy Dr.

❿

Golden Gate Park

❻

Lincoln Way

Ocean Beach

Great Highway

Irving St.

Judah St.

25th Ave.

Irving St.

Judah St.

9th Ave.

7th Ave.

Parnassus Ave.

SUNSET DISTRICT

Sunset Blvd.

19th Ave.

⓫

Noriega St.

①

⓬ ↓

⓭ ↓ Taraval St.

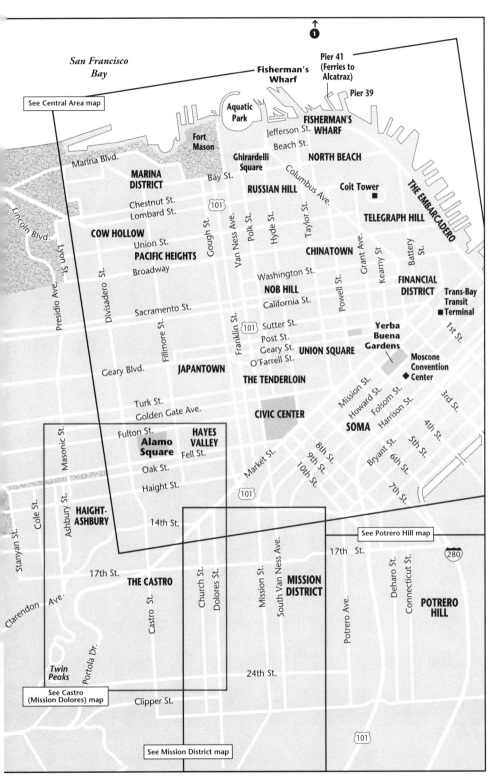

San Francisco
Bay

Fisherman's
Wharf

Pier 41
(Ferries to
Alcatraz)

Pier 39

See Central Area map

Aquatic
Park

Jefferson St.

FISHERMAN'S
WHARF

Fort
Mason

Beach St.

Marina Blvd.

Ghirardelli
Square

NORTH BEACH

MARINA
DISTRICT

Bay St.

RUSSIAN HILL

Columbus Ave.

Coit Tower

THE EMBARCADERO

Chestnut St.

Lombard St.

101

Polk St.

Hyde St.

Taylor St.

TELEGRAPH HILL

COW HOLLOW

Union St.

Gough St.

Van Ness Ave.

CHINATOWN

Grant Ave.

Kearny St.

Battery St.

PACIFIC HEIGHTS

Broadway

Divisadero St.

Washington St.

NOB HILL

California St.

Powell St.

FINANCIAL
DISTRICT

Trans-Bay
Transit
Terminal

Presidio Ave.

Sacramento St.

Fillmore St.

Franklin St.

101

Sutter St.

Post St.

Yerba
Buena
Gardens

1st St.

Geary Blvd.

JAPANTOWN

Geary St.

O'Farrell St.

UNION SQUARE

Moscone
Convention
Center

Lyon St.

Lincoln Blvd.

THE TENDERLOIN

Mission St.

Howard St.

Folsom St.

Harrison St.

3rd St.

Turk St.

Golden Gate Ave.

CIVIC CENTER

SOMA

4th St.

Masonic St.

Fulton St.

HAYES
VALLEY

Bryant St.

5th St.

6th St.

Alamo
Square

Fell St.

8th St.

Market St.

9th St.

7th St.

Ashbury St.

Oak St.

10th St.

Haight St.

101

See Potrero Hill map

Cole St.

HAIGHT-
ASHBURY

14th St.

17th St.

280

Stanyan St.

Church St.

Dolores St.

Mission St.

South Van Ness Ave.

Deharo St.

Connecticut St.

17th St.

THE CASTRO

MISSION
DISTRICT

POTRERO
HILL

Clarendon Ave.

Castro St.

Potrero Ave.

Twin
Peaks

Portola Dr.

24th St.

See Castro
(Mission Dolores) map

Clipper St.

See Mission District map

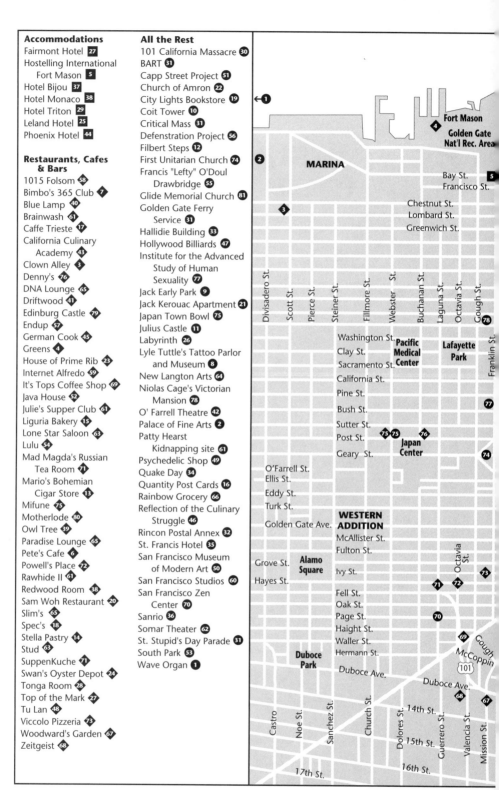

Accommodations

Fairmont Hotel **27**
Hostelling International
 Fort Mason **5**
Hotel Bijou **37**
Hotel Monaco **38**
Hotel Triton **29**
Leland Hotel **25**
Phoenix Hotel **44**

Restaurants, Cafes & Bars

1015 Folsom **58**
Bimbo's 365 Club **7**
Blue Lamp **40**
Brainwash **61**
Caffe Trieste **17**
California Culinary
 Academy **43**
Clown Alley **3**
Denny's **76**
DNA Lounge **65**
Driftwood **41**
Edinburg Castle **79**
Endup **57**
German Cook **45**
Greens **4**
House of Prime Rib **23**
Internet Alfredo **59**
It's Tops Coffee Shop **69**
Java House **52**
Julie's Supper Club **61**
Liguria Bakery **15**
Lone Star Saloon **63**
Lulu **54**
Mad Magda's Russian
 Tea Room **71**
Mario's Bohemian
 Cigar Store **13**
Mifune **75**
Motherlode **80**
Owl Tree **39**
Paradise Lounge **65**
Pete's Cafe **6**
Powell's Place **72**
Rawhide II **61**
Redwood Room **38**
Sam Woh Restaurant **20**
Slim's **65**
Spec's **18**
Stella Pastry **14**
Stud **63**
SuppenKuche **71**
Swan's Oyster Depot **24**
Tonga Room **28**
Top of the Mark **27**
Tu Lan **48**
Viccolo Pizzeria **73**
Woodward's Garden **67**
Zeitgeist **68**

All the Rest

101 California Massacre **30**
BART **31**
Capp Street Project **51**
Church of Amron **22**
City Lights Bookstore **19**
Coit Tower **10**
Critical Mass **31**
Defenstration Project **56**
Filbert Steps **12**
First Unitarian Church **74**
Francis "Lefty" O'Doul
 Drawbridge **55**
Glide Memorial Church **81**
Golden Gate Ferry
 Service **31**
Hallidie Building **33**
Hollywood Billiards **47**
Institute for the Advanced
 Study of Human
 Sexuality **77**
Jack Early Park **9**
Jack Kerouac Apartment **21**
Japan Town Bowl **75**
Julius Castle **11**
Labyrinth **26**
Lyle Tuttle's Tattoo Parlor
 and Museum **8**
New Langton Arts **64**
Niolas Cage's Victorian
 Mansion **78**
O' Farrell Theatre **42**
Palace of Fine Arts **2**
Patty Hearst
 Kidnapping site **61**
Psychedelic Shop **49**
Quake Day **34**
Quantity Post Cards **16**
Rainbow Grocery **66**
Reflection of the Culinary
 Struggle **46**
Rincon Postal Annex **32**
St. Francis Hotel **35**
San Francisco Museum
 of Modern Art **50**
San Francisco Studios **60**
San Francisco Zen
 Center **70**
Sanrio **36**
Somar Theater **62**
St. Stupid's Day Parade **31**
South Park **53**
Wave Organ **1**

Downtown San Francisco

0 .25 mi
0 .25 km

San Francisco Bay

Municipal Pier
Pier 45
Pier 43 1/2
Pier 43
Pier 41
Pier 39
Pier 35
Pier 33
Pier 31
Pier 27
Pier 23
Pier 19
Pier 17
Pier 15
Pier 9
Pier 7
Pier 5
Pier 3
Pier 1
Ferry Building
(World Trade Center)

Aquatic Park
Cable Car

Jefferson St.
Beach St.
North Point St.
Bay St.
Francisco St.
Chestnut St.
Lombard St.
Greenwich St.
Filbert St.
Union St.
Green St.
Vallejo St.
Broadway
Pacific Ave.
Jackson St.

Columbus Ave.
Embarcadero

NORTH BEACH
CHINATOWN
Tunnel

NOB HILL

Van Ness Ave.
Polk St.
Larkin St.
Hyde St.
Leavenworth St.
Jones St.
Taylor St.
Mason St.
Powell St.
Stockton St.
Grant Ave.
Kearny St.
Montgomery St.
Sansome St.
Battery St.
Front St.
Davis St.
Drumm St.

DOWNTOWN

San Francisco–Oakland Bay Bridge

Market St.

Stewart St.
Spear St.
Main St.
Beale St.
Fremont St.
1st St.
2nd St.

Geary St.
O'Farrell St.
Eddy St.
TENDERLOIN

Moscone Convention Center

Market St.
Mission St.
5th St.
3rd St.
4th St.

SOMA

Delancey St.

Howard St.
Folsom St.
Harrison St.
Bryant St.
Brannan St.
6th St.
7th St.
8th St.
9th St.
10th St.
11th St.
12th St.

Multimedia Gulch

Townsend St.
King St.
Berry St.
Channel St.
China Basin

S. Van Ness Ave.
Folsom
Harrison
Alabama
Potrero Ave.
Division St.
Alameda St.
15th St.

NEW MEDIA GULCH

4th St.
3rd St.
Illinois St.

6th St.
7th St.

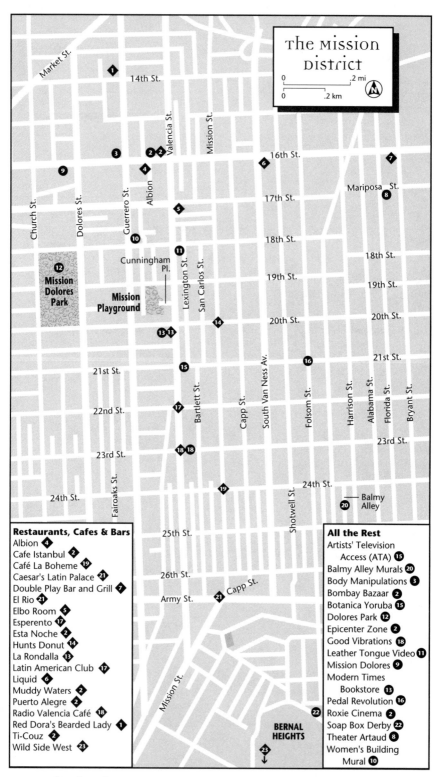

The Mission District

0   .2 mi
0   .2 km

Market St.
14th St.
Valencia St.
Mission St.
16th St.
Mariposa St.
17th St.
Church St.
Dolores St.
Guerrero St.
Albion
18th St.
18th St.
Cunningham Pl.
Lexington St.
San Carlos St.
19th St.
19th St.
Mission Dolores Park
Mission Playground
20th St.
20th St.
21st St.
21st St.
Bartlett St.
Capp St.
South Van Ness Av.
Folsom St.
Harrison St.
Alabama St.
Florida St.
Bryant St.
22nd St.
23rd St.
23rd St.
24th St.
Fairoaks St.
24th St.
Shotwell St.
Balmy Alley
25th St.
26th St.
Capp St.
Army St.
Mission St.
BERNAL HEIGHTS

Restaurants, Cafes & Bars
Albion 4
Cafe Istanbul 2
Café La Boheme 19
Caesar's Latin Palace 21
Double Play Bar and Grill 7
El Rio 21
Elbo Room 5
Esperento 17
Esta Noche 2
Hunts Donut 14
La Rondalla 13
Latin American Club 17
Liquid 6
Muddy Waters 2
Puerto Alegre 2
Radio Valencia Café 18
Red Dora's Bearded Lady 1
Ti-Couz 2
Wild Side West 23

All the Rest
Artists' Television
Access (ATA) 15
Balmy Alley Murals 20
Body Manipulations 3
Bombay Bazaar 2
Botanica Yoruba 15
Dolores Park 12
Epicenter Zone 2
Good Vibrations 18
Leather Tongue Video 11
Mission Dolores 9
Modern Times
Bookstore 13
Pedal Revolution 16
Roxie Cinema 2
Soap Box Derby 22
Theater Artaud 8
Women's Building
Mural 10

330   San Francisco

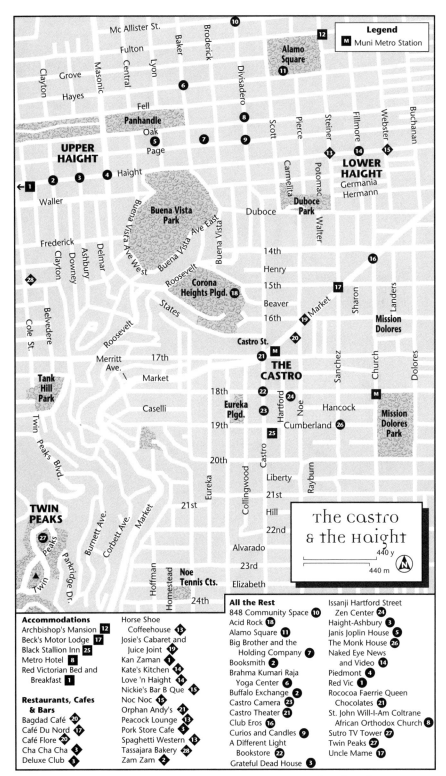

The Castro & the Haight

440 y
440 m

Accommodations
Archbishop's Mansion 12
Beck's Motor Lodge 17
Black Stallion Inn 25
Metro Hotel 8
Red Victorian Bed and Breakfast 1

Restaurants, Cafes & Bars
Bagdad Café 20
Café Du Nord 17
Café Flore 20
Cha Cha Cha 3
Deluxe Club 3
Horse Shoe Coffeehouse 13
Josie's Cabaret and Juice Joint 19
Kan Zaman 1
Kate's Kitchen 14
Love 'n Haight 14
Nickie's Bar B Que 15
Noc Noc 15
Orphan Andy's 21
Peacock Lounge 13
Pork Store Cafe 3
Spaghetti Western 13
Tassajara Bakery 28
Zam Zam 2

All the Rest
848 Community Space 10
Acid Rock 18
Alamo Square 11
Big Brother and the Holding Company 7
Booksmith 2
Brahma Kumari Raja Yoga Center 6
Buffalo Exchange 2
Castro Camera 23
Castro Theater 21
Club Eros 16
Curios and Candles 9
A Different Light Bookstore 22
Grateful Dead House 3
Issanji Hartford Street Zen Center 24
Haight-Ashbury 3
Janis Joplin House 5
The Monk House 26
Naked Eye News and Video 14
Piedmont 4
Red Vic 1
Rococoa Faerrie Queen Chocolates 21
St. John Will-I-Am Coltrane African Orthodox Church 8
Sutro TV Tower 27
Twin Peaks 27
Uncle Mame 17

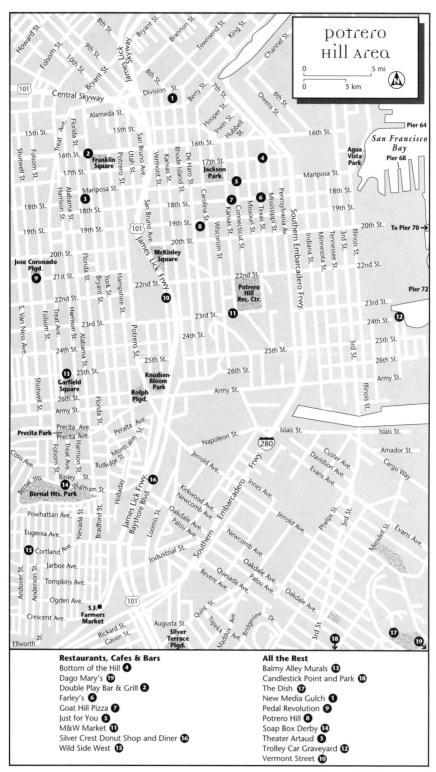

potrero
Hill Area

| 0 | | 5 mi |
| 0 | | 5 km |

Restaurants, Cafes & Bars

Bottom of the Hill **4**
Dago Mary's **19**
Double Play Bar & Grill **2**
Farley's **6**
Goat Hill Pizza **7**
Just for You **5**
M&W Market **11**
Silver Crest Donut Shop and Diner **16**
Wild Side West **15**

All the Rest

Balmy Alley Murals **13**
Candlestick Point and Park **18**
The Dish **17**
New Media Gulch **1**
Pedal Revolution **9**
Potrero Hill **8**
Soap Box Derby **14**
Theater Artaud **3**
Trolley Car Graveyard **12**
Vermont Street **10**

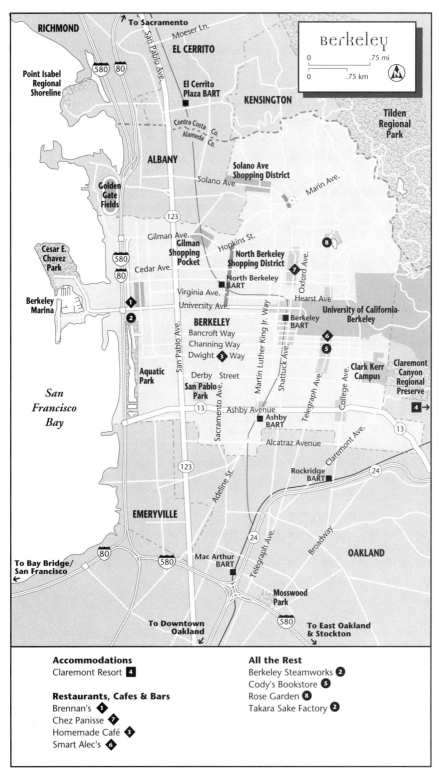

Berkeley

0   .75 mi
0   .75 km

RICHMOND

To Sacramento

Moeser Ln.

EL CERRITO

KENSINGTON

Point Isabel
Regional
Shoreline

El Cerrito
Plaza BART

Tilden
Regional
Park

Contra Costa Co.
Alameda Co.

ALBANY

Solano Ave.

Solano Ave
Shopping District

Marin Ave.

Golden
Gate
Fields

Gilman Ave.

Gilman
Shopping
Pocket

Hopkins St.

North Berkeley
Shopping District

North Berkeley
BART

Cesar E.
Chavez
Park

Cedar Ave.

Oxford Ave.

Hearst Ave.

Berkeley
Marina

Virginia Ave.

University Ave.

Berkeley
BART

University of California-
Berkeley

BERKELEY

Bancroft Way
Channing Way
Dwight ❸ Way

Martin Luther King Jr. Way

Shattuck Ave.

Aquatic
Park

Derby   Street

San Pablo
Park

Sacramento Ave.

Telegraph Ave.

College Ave.

Clark Kerr
Campus

Claremont
Canyon
Regional
Preserve

San
Francisco
Bay

Ashby Avenue

Ashby
BART

Alcatraz Avenue

Claremont Ave.

Rockridge
BART

Adeline St.

EMERYVILLE

To Bay Bridge/
San Francisco

Mac Arthur
BART

Telegraph Ave.

24

Broadway

OAKLAND

To Downtown
Oakland

Mosswood
Park

To East Oakland
& Stockton

Accommodations
Claremont Resort ❹

Restaurants, Cafes & Bars
Brennan's ❶
Chez Panisse ❼
Homemade Café ❸
Smart Alec's ❻

All the Rest
Berkeley Steamworks ❷
Cody's Bookstore ❺
Rose Garden ❽
Takara Sake Factory ❷

girls; a place where women who look like they are nuns straight out of the Sacred Heart and guys who look like reps for one of the Napa Valley vineyards meditate side by side with neurotic, eternally depressed victims of some sort of imagined childhood abuse. It's a true melting pot of Zen, and of San Francisco. (See "Spirituality.")

8. **Zam Zam** (Haight). Owner Bruno is the Soup Nazi of lounge-bar owners, and he's been behind the bar for forty-five years, and he doesn't take any shit. This place is almost too cool to describe. (See "Bars, Pubs, and Clubs.")

9. **Motherlode** (Tenderloin). This transsexual, drag-queen Tenderloin nightclub offers one of the wildest trips north of Tijuana. Just like TJ's seductively seedy strip bars, there is constant visual entertainment on the tiny corner stage, as well as tables full of working girls waiting for a young man to buy them a drink. Of course, all of these girls are trannies, but the dynamics of the deal are the same as they are on Revolucion Boulevard. (See "Bars, Pubs, and Clubs.")

10. **Defenestration Project** (SOMA). An installation that incorporates over thirty brightly colored household furnishings and appliances in gravity-defying positions on the walls and out the windows of this gutted, abandoned, six-story building. (See "Art in Public Places.")

Accommodations

Whether it's the lovely atrium and Rolls Royce chauffeur at the Pan Pacific, the understated class of the Mark Hopkins, or the Beat chic of the Hotel Boheme, everyone has their favorite San Francisco accommodation. Fortunately, we don't have to write for "everyone." Nor do we have to disguise our abhorrence for the shoddy service one routinely receives at San Francisco hotels. Whether it's because the city's hotels are routinely overrun by tourists or because of that perennial S.F. arrogance, service is generally not nearly as tight as in New York or Chicago hotels. Still, several accommodations manage to shine, and some actually care about each and every guest.

› **Archbishop's Mansion.** 1000 Fulton St., at Steiner (Western Addition).
☎ 415/563-7872. www.joiedevivre-sf.com.

Situated on the southeast corner of Alamo Square, near the string of overexposed Victorian gingerbreads known as the "Painted Ladies," sits the most dramatically over-the-top hotel in all of San Francisco. Not so much from the outside, which might go unnoticed in random passing, but from the Victorian inside, with its grand lobby and breakfast room, ornate wooden styling, 16-foot stained-glass dome, and playfully camp suites. We stayed in the Carmen suite (all of the rooms are named after operas), whose hallmark is an old-fashioned bathtub situated in the middle of one room (any spills lap up right onto the carpet—no mildew problems *yet,* we hear). The Gypsy Baron Suite has a double tub built into what was formerly the chapel of the house, where the Archbishop performed private mass. In addition to these eccentric touches, the highlight of the 95-year-old mansion, as with most, though not all, properties managed by savvy Joie de Vivre Hospitality (Hotel Bijou, Hotel Rex, Phoenix, et al.), is the service: helpful and professional, not officious and phony. Not a great place for the business traveler (this precious furniture isn't too suitable for desktop computers and the like), but otherwise highly recommended.

> **Beck's Motor Lodge.** 2222 Market St., at Sanchez (Castro). ☎ **415/621-8212.**

We really like the idea of a tacky, $72-and-up motel right in the Castro. We parked the Monkmobile in front of this place for a month; we were never told to leave and once even slipped into a recently vacated room to take a shower.

> **Black Stallion Inn.** 635 Castro, at 19th St. (Castro). ☎ **415/863-0131.**

A leather/Levi, clothing-optional bed-and-breakfast for gay men, this is the only Victorian we've seen that's painted black. If you're into wearing leather and all the customs that go with it, this is your spot. Otherwise, forget it.

> **The Claremont Resort.** 41 Tunnel Rd., at Claremont Ave. (Oakland). ☎ **510/843-3000.** www.claremontresort.com.

As with the Hotel Del Coronado, the Claremont has tremendous potential, but isn't fully exploiting it. Like an undervalued stock, its dramatic exterior, beautiful white facade, heart-stirring views, world-class spa, three-story tower suite, and prime location in the Oakland hills go largely wasted because of its illogical design mechanics and slipshod presentation. The new owners see it our way, as the hotel is now undergoing a top-down renovation to fully exploit its potential. Sarah Suggs, the hotel's charming marketing director, assures us that when the renovation is fully complete, the Claremont will return to its former glory as a resort destination for the truly elite. If only the Hotel Del would follow suit.

> **Fairmount Hotel.** 950 Mason, at California (Nob Hill). ☎ **415/772-5000.**

As with Alcatraz, the Palace of Fine Arts, and the Golden Gate Bridge, the Fairmount is one of those San Francisco landmarks that achieves canonical greatness despite its popularity with the tacky tourist set. It just has to be seen. The utter strangeness of its ornate, bright-red lobby is worth the visit alone. Throw in the

The Claremont Resort

delightfully gauche Tonga Room (where a band floats out on a barge into a South Pacific lagoon) and you have that rare aesthetic treat: audacious kitsch that's survived the test of time.

> **Hosteling International, Fort Mason.** Fort Mason, Building #240, enter gate at Bay and Franklin sts. (Marina). ☎ **415/771-7277.**

Bunk down with backpacking, goofy student types in gender-segregated, shared-bath, dormitory-style housing with killer bay views. Share a communal kitchen, do obligatory chores, and meet mostly foreign bunkmates. Great for lining up future crash pads when traveling Europe.

> **Hotel Bijou.** 111 Mason St., at Eddy. (Tenderloin). ☎ **415/771-1200.** www.joiedevivre-sf.com.

When I first learned about Chip Conley's boutique hotel built around the theme of San Francisco films, I was completely amped. Here were lodgings celebrating the spirit of a place in a very fun and direct way—how Monk! The lobby's movie palace design did not disappoint. Nor did the velvety off-lobby Le Petit Theatre Bijou, which plays two different San Francisco films a night (the only price one pays is regular interruptions by the staff grinding, pouring, or retrieving coffee—folks, move the coffee machine to another room!). But when I read that each of the guest rooms was "uniquely themed after a motion picture shot in San Francisco," I expected more than just archival photos of local movie palaces and a stock publicity photo from the film itself. While the 24-hour Film Hotline to current local filming locations and casting opportunities for "extras" was a nice touch, and the video library of sixty-five Bay Area films was impressive, the main highlight just might be the hotel's location next door to the ongoing nude performance art at the venerable Chez Paree.

> **Hotel Monaco.** 501 Geary St., at Taylor. (Tenderloin). ☎ 415/292-0100. www.hotelmonaco.com.

This colorful Moroccan-meets-art-nouveau hotel manages to be both cutting-edge and excellent, with the kind of friendly professional service Ian Schrager could only dream of. The executive suites, while not huge, are a vision of comfort, with exquisitely beautiful beds and couches, all mod cons, and a dash of delightful whimsy, which reminds you that you are spending the night in San Francisco after all, not Indianapolis. With such a strong design scheme, we wonder whether the Monaco will seem starkly anachronistic in a few years. For now, though, it is hands down the finest hotel in the city. And here's the kicker: not just a Gideons, but a copy of *The Teaching of Buddha* in every desk drawer. How San Francisco can you get!

> **Hotel Triton.** 342 Grant Ave., at Bush. (Downtown). ☎ 415/394-0500. www.hotel-tritonsf.com.

Triton is a more homey, more friendly, more tacky version of New York City's Paramount, with far less finesse and attention to detail. I doubt, for instance, that the Paramount would ever devote a suite to Jerry Garcia (adorned with eighteen originals of his surprisingly beautiful art—a step above tie-dye, for sure), or an entire floor that is ecologically correct (right down to the filtered shower water and recycled glass). The lobby has an architectural sitting area that looks like a tea party for the fashionably insane. Other rooms include a Joe Boxer–inspired tiger room. Where else can your underwear match the wall paper? While the Triton makes a nice attempt to attract indie stars and cold-hearted fashionistas, there simply is not enough Schrager-land fascism to completely pull it off.

> **Leland Hotel.** 1315 Polk St., at Bush (Polk). ☎ 415/441-5141.

Lots of male hustlers outside, which is like having a 24-hour security force. Clean rooms, shared bathrooms, and a European ambiance. And far enough up Polk Street to be out of the Tenderloin. Here you'll mingle with a hip clientele and occasional crazies.

> **Metro Hotel.** 319 Divisadero St., at Oak (Western Addition). ☎ 415/861-5364.

The best deal in town for a room with a private bath. Slightly trendy, on the border between the Haight and lower Haight, it has the feel of a hostel but the accommodations of a hotel. Ten years ago this was the hard-core ghetto and now it's tolerably hip.

> **Phoenix Hotel.** 601 Eddy St., at Larkin (Tenderloin). ☎ **415/776-1380.**

A former fifties motor lodge that's reincarnated as an ultra-hip, retro-Caribbean resort in the heart of the seedy Tenderloin, the Phoenix caters to the pop-rock crowd, including David Bowie, k. d. lang, R.E.M., and Billy Idol among others (or so says their propaganda—it's doubtful these stars are regulars). The Phoenix goes for the pseudo-tropical, "Gilligan's Island" effect with lots of bamboo, palms, and arty murals everywhere. Chow down on tasty world cuisine in Backflip or sip your martinis by the inner court lagoon. Meanwhile, the pimps and hustlers are only a holler away.

> **Red Victorian Bed and Breakfast.** 1665 Haight St., at Cole (Haight). ☎ **415/864-1978.** www.redvic.com.

Owner Sami Sunchild seemed like a borderline nutcase, and opined that Monk is aligned with "the dark forces," but still her bed-and-breakfast is worth the price even if just for the New Age schlock value. There are eighteen guest rooms with names that read like a flower child's kandy-kolored fantasies. Try the exotic Peacock Suite, the tie-dyed Summer of Love Room, or the Rainbow Room, replete with canopy and a bay view. Lot's of pillows, magic mirrors, redwood, feel-good colors, and a fish-tank toilet (shared, of course).

Addresses

The original home of the People's Temple may no longer be easy to find (the building was torn down), and who knows where Dan White bought those Twinkies, but the following are the addresses of the famous, infamous, and just flat out Monked of San Francisco.

> **Big Brother and the Holding Company.** 1090 Page St., near Stanyan (Haight).

Can there be a more underrated maven of the sixties S.F. music scene than Chet Helms? Predating the more hyped Bill Graham by two years, in late 1964 this transplanted Texan, living in a house on 1090 Page St., began to hold jam sessions in the house's basement ballroom. Big Brother and the Holding Company emerged from these jam sessions. One day, Chet introduced his pal from Austin, Janis Joplin, to the band. You know the rest of that story. Helms went on to host concerts at large halls like the Fillmore (before Graham took it over) and the Avalon Ballroom (1268 Sutter), and organized the first Be-In in Golden Gate Park on January 14, 1967. Interestingly, Austin, Texas, continues to play a pivotal role in American popular music to this very day.

> **Castro Camera** (now occupied by the Skin Zone—plaque out front let's you know this is the spot). 575 Castro St., between 18th and 19th (Castro). ☎ 415/626-7933.

"My name is Harvey Milk and I'm here to recruit you."

—Standard stump speech opener of Harvey Milk, first openly gay person elected to the San Francisco Board of Supervisors

This is the camera shop of the theatrical, charismatic pioneer of the gay rights movement, Harvey Milk (nee Glimpy Milch). It was from this location that the colorful Milk launched his political career, helping gay and nongay constituents alike get what they needed from the city bureaucracy. After several unsuccessful attempts at winning elective office, Milk was finally elected to the San Francisco Board of Supervisors. Only eleven months into his term, on November 27, 1978, Milk and then mayor George Moscone were assassinated by conservative antigay supervisor, Dan White, who had crawled through the basement window of the City Hall soil-testing lab on McAllister (at Van Ness) to avoid metal detectors. White had resigned his seat on the board following the enactment of a gay civil rights bill he had opposed, and was angered that Milk and Moscone would not let him have his seat back after he had changed his mind. In May 1979, the jury found Dan White guilty of voluntary manslaughter, buying the defense's argument, in what became known as "the Twinkie defense," that the junk food White consumed that day made him do it. White was sentenced to 7 years and 8 months for the double murder. Enraged by the light sentence, on May 21, 1979 (the eve of Harvey Milk's forty-ninth birthday), thousands marched on City Hall. The demonstrations quickly erupted into riots and a concomitant police counterattack on the gay community, including the near complete destruction of the Elephant Castle Bar (now Harvey's on Castro). The evening became known as "White Night," and to this day is remembered as one of the key turning points in the city's political history.

Just nine days before his assassination, Milk had tape recorded his political will, which he labeled, "To be read in the event of my assassination." On the tape he said, "If a bullet should enter my brain, let that bullet destroy every closet door."

Though it took his death to do it, San Francisco is today the most "out" and gay-tolerant city in America.

> **Condor Club.** 300 Columbus Ave., at Broadway (North Beach).

Every plastic surgeon knows the name "Carol Doda." The San Francisco cocktail waitress and actress was the first well-known woman to sport silicon-enhanced breasts. On June 19, 1964, Carol ushered in the California "Topless Era" when she exposed her artificial "mams" at the former Condor Club in North Beach.

> **Grateful Dead House.** 710 Ashbury St. near Haight St. (Haight).

Victorian house where the Grateful Dead (originally the Warlocks) lived during the sixties, the era that defined them, and stereotyped them, for eternity.

> **Haight-Ashbury.** Corner of Haight St. and Ashbury (Haight).

Media-created cultural vortex of the sixties. Certainly the most recognizable symbol of that era, if not the actual vortex (which was everywhere and nowhere), and now the location of Ben and Jerry's ice cream.

Note: If you want to see the spot where diehard San Franciscans believe the sixties *really* began, head to **Longshoreman's Hall,** 400 North Point at Mason. Between January 21 and 23, 1966, celebrated author Ken Kesey and his band of Merry Pranksters served up some LSD-laced punch. The long-guitar-solo movement was born.

> **The House.** 3929 19th St., at Sanchez (Castro).

A three-story "Swiss Family Tree House" perched above the street with over ninety steps to climb, where in 1985 the Monks and their cats, Nurse and Nurse's Aide, slept, baked, and entertained before making that fateful decision to sell everything they owned and hit the road. A.k.a. "The Monastery."

> **Invention of Television.** 202 Green St., at Sansome (North Beach).

We told you San Francisco is where big ideas germinate. Not only was the foundation for motion-picture technology laid here by photographer Eadweard Muybridge's animal locomotion studies, but television was launched here too. At this address, on September 7, 1927, Philo T. Farnsworth transmitted images using the first cathode-ray tube.

> **Jack Kerouac Apartment.** 29 Russell St., at Eastman St. (Russian Hill).

Where the Beat author lived, drank, and drugged while writing *On The Road.*

> **Janis Joplin House.** 112 Lyon St., near Panhandle of Golden Gate Park (Haight).

Where the late rock singer Janis Joplin and Country Joe McDonald once lived. Would NOT have wanted to experience this pad. Bring a bottle of Southern Comfort and imagine the dysfunction.

> **Mission Fire Hydrant.** 20th St. and Church St. (Mission).

This gold-painted fire hydrant is the only hydrant that kept pumping after the great earthquake of 1906, saving the surrounding Mission from ruin.

> **Nicolas Cage's Victorian Mansion.** 1945 Franklin St., near Washington St. (Pacific Heights).

Not that he doesn't have other cities to live in (he has five homes at last count). It's very unlikely you'll find him sipping latte out on the curb.

> **101 California Massacre.** 101 California St., at Front (Financial District).

On July 1, 1993, gunman Gian Luigi Ferri was having an incredibly bad day. He sprayed fourteen people with his semiautomatic TEC-CD9 in the high-rise law office of Pettit and Martin. Eight people bled to death before police knocked off Ferri.

> **Patty Hearst Kidnapping Site.** Above Julie's Supper Club, 1123 Folsom St., at 7th St. (South of Market).

Above this trendy yuppie bar and restaurant is the closet where a blindfolded Patty "Tania" Hearst was held hostage by the Symbionese Liberation Army. *Note:* One of the capitalist targets hit by Tania and her SLA comrades was the Hibernia Bank at 1450 Noriega and 22nd Avenue. Since then, the bank has gone through an interesting transformation, first to a Bank of America and now to a Blockbuster Video, where you can rent Paul Schrader's film about the gun-toting debutante, *Patty Hearst.*

> **Steven Gaskin's Tuesday Night Meeting.** San Francisco State Student Union, 1600 Holloway Ave. (Sunset). ☎ 415/338-1111.

Steven who? This is the ultimate litmus test of whether any of those pseudo-hippie dinosaurs who say they were "there" (the Haight/Summer of Love) were actually there. It's like this. Steven Gaskin was a prof at S.F. State, who looked like Jesus, rapped an incredible, transcendental rap, and over the course of 1967 grew his audience from a meager classroom to an auditorium full of thousands of devotees chanting in unison and hanging on his every word. Believe me, this was in many ways the true beginnings of sixties consciousness, because out on the street, where the drugs flowed freely, it wasn't always a pretty sight. Gaskin focused all of that wild, psychedelic energy into something tangible you could build a vision upon. He taught us to be responsible to each other, the environment, and to ourselves. He broke down barriers and initiated a hell of a lot of kids into the bigger picture of planetary consciousness. In fact, he might have been the first to speak of "planetary consciousness." Aum circles began here. So did open, multipartner marriages. And so did structured anarchy with an emphasis on love. One day, a thousand or so Gaskinites hopped on some buses and headed through Boulder toward Tennessee, where the largest American intentional community, the Farm, continues to this day.

The People's Temple

1859 Geary Blvd. between Steiner and Fillmore. Though the temple building has been torn down, you can go to this site and envision the scene.

Along with the Donner Party cannibals and the Manson Family murderers, the People's Temple faithful are the crucial third piece of the California Triptych of the Macabre. The rise of James Warren Jones from humble Indianapolis preacher to San Francisco Housing Authority appointee to violent leader of a Guyana Kool-Aid klatch is one of the most twisted stories from a most twisted era. As weird as California gets, it doesn't get much weirder than this. Jones (known as "Dad" to his followers) first brought his congregation of 900 to Ukiah, California, after an investigation into his Indianapolis mission for the sick and homeless discovered that Jones was promulgating bogus cures for arthritis, cancer, and heart disease. As with many doomsday cults of the sixties and seventies, Jim Jones preached that the end of the world was nigh, and eventually moved his Mission from Ukiah to San Francisco, where he found plenty of confirmation for his beliefs and plenty of need for his outreach work. Jones was quite popular in S.F., until an exposé on abuses within the Temple by *New West Magazine* prompted the charismatic leader to move his congregation to Guyana, where the town of Jonestown was created in his honor. Jones developed a belief called Translation, wherein he argued that he and his followers would all die together and move to another planet and live a peaceful loving life there. In one of his more mind-blowing acts, Jones had his Guyana posse routinely practice mass suicide. These trial runs involved followers pretending to drink poison, then falling to the ground dead. Gradually, news of Jones and his Guyana shenanigans spread to Congress. In November 1978, Representative Leo Ryan went to investigate reports of human rights abuses on the compound. Ryan was shot to death as he and four former cult members waited at the airstrip. Fearing the inevitable crackdown on his jungle fiefdom, on November 18, 1978, Jones persuaded 910 members of the People's Temple to drink some grape-flavored Kool-Aid laced with potassium cyanide, liquid Valium, and other pharmaceuticals. This time it was for real. And they all knew it. All 638 of his adult followers and 276 children died, some by suicide, others by gunfire. A few fled into the jungle and lived to tell this harrowing tale.

Note: One of the more startling facts that came out of survivor reports was the sight of followers waiting in line for their poison long after others had died.

Art in Public Places

The biggest problem with San Francisco art, and why the city will never be taken seriously as a world art center, is because of the blinding political correctness of the city's major arts organizations, benefactors, and media. It seems San Francisco arts professionals are so deathly afraid of offending any self-designated group of victims, outcasts, or ethnic minority, the city ends up mounting exhibits and supporting programs of monumental mediocrity purely out of fear. If your particular art form is Queer Jewish comedy, aboriginal dance, Ceremonial arts of the Amazon, a documentary about a homeless man who ran for Santa Monica City Council—if you wear your particular ethnic or victim identity on your artistic sleeve, you are more likely to get funding in this town, and publicity too. Some of this art is pretty good, but a little goes a long way. Fortunately, there are a few examples of San Francisco public art that cannot be claimed by any one ethnic and/or oppressed minority, though, as the following list indicates, these are few and far between.

› **Balmy Alley Murals.** Balmy Alley, between 24th and 25th sts. (Mission).

This block-long alley features the volunteered works of celebrated Hispanic muralists. Funky, folksy, and political. The Day of the Dead parade ends here every November 1.

› **Candlestick Point Park.** Gilman St., opposite 3Com Stadium (Candlestick Park, Hunters Point).

The highlight is the Orchestra for the Natives of the Future, a sound sculpture of metal drums installed near the center of the park on the bay. After you get all your percussive ya-ya's out, watch police cars speed around obstacle courses in the stadium parking lot across the street or spy on couples fornicating in cars to the south.

› **Capp Street Project.** See "Museums."

› **Defenestration Project.** 214 6th St., at Howard (SOMA). ☎ **415/626-7549.** gog@sirius.com.

Brian Goggin and a group of fellow artists created quite the stir in 1997 when they erected this sensational installation that incorporates over thirty brightly colored household furnishings and appliances, such as couches, chairs, tables, and refrigerators in gravity-defying positions, bolted, welded, and rigged on the walls and out the windows of this gutted, abandoned, six-story building. At first glance it appears as if an earthquake has shaken the building's contents out the windows and toward the

(continued on page 350)

Jerry Brown,

Mayor of Oakland

Underneath the gruff attack dog veneer, Jerry Brown is completely, delightfully mad. Such a man of the people, he positions folks in the most unlikely of places. When you walk in the door of his office-cum-campaign-headquarters-cum-communal-living-quarters in the heart of Jack London Square, you are greeted by a short black woman. She is sweet. Bright. Eager to help. Capable. She is also near totally blind. I am sure this woman, were she able to smile at herself, would have to acknowledge that only Jerry Brown would hire a blind person to be a receptionist for a major mayoral headquarters. It is positively revolutionary. An act of enormous breadth and compassion. It also might be regarded, in any other political campaign in America, as very, very stupid. But that's conventional politics for you.

Jerry Brown is not about conventional politics. He is not a member of either political party. He is independent—fiercely independent. It is his independence that allowed him to triumphantly win the 1998 Oakland mayoral election with a majority of the vote, obviating the need for the customary run-off in November. We spoke with Jerry Brown six months before he took office. He used that time to drum up support for a ballot initiative that would grant greater power to the mayor's office. At the time, the Oakland mayor was a figurehead, just another member of the city council, with no veto power. Jerry wanted to change all that. One of many great ideas of the consummate idea man, but an idea that had to be implemented if Brown could hope to achieve any of his dreams for Oakland.

Monk: I want to start with some focus on the place of Oakland. How would you describe the spirit of Oakland?

JB: Oakland is working class. It was the shipping-factory center for the east side of the Bay Area. In fact, the planes stopped here. You went by ferry boats to San Francisco. It was a rail head and it's more in the spirit of production, like other cities, with high concentrations of poor people and minorities. But unlike Baltimore, it didn't lose hundreds of thousands of people. Not like Detroit. It's more real. Integrated. Highly diverse and yet it really expresses what America is all about.

Monk: So in ways it's more like the old industrial strongholds than other California cities.

JB: Yeah. But it's near San Francisco. It's in the Bay Area. It has lakes, which give a Marin County feel to it.

Monk: One of the bigger challenges you face then is trying to bring it back economically?

JB: And be a safe place.

Monk: So, the main thing concerning people is crime?

JB: Yes.

Monk: New York is considered one of the safest cities in the world per capita. Except some people say that [Giuliani's] strong-arm tactics are a violation of freedom. How do you preserve freedom and diversity while attaining quality of life?

›interview

JB: By emphasizing community policing. By recruiting locally. By building bridges between the community and the police. And linking them together as a self-governing community. Freedom is destroyed when people are afraid to leave their house at night. Freedom is destroyed when you can't open a store without hiring a guard. So, it's a two-way street. And concern about overbearing government is a legitimate one, abuse of power. But, the principal abuse today in Oakland is the violation of individuals' rights by criminals. Not by the police.

Monk: How would your approach be different than Giuliani's?

JB: Well, I don't know all his approaches. But we're certainly going to encourage the police to focus on those areas of the highest crime and make sure that presence of both the police and the organization of the community is such that crime is not tolerated, [as well as] this sad reality of drug houses operating flagrantly with drug dealers on the streets protected by their intricate system of runners and lookouts. I want that to change.

Monk: By community policing alone?

JB: No. By whatever has to be done. Oakland has to be cleaned up. Oakland is losing hundreds of millions, maybe billions of dollars. Its citizens are losing their freedom. They have lost their freedom. I've talked to people who are afraid to go anywhere at night. Now that isn't everybody, but there are people who live in the hills who say we can't come down to Lake Merrit. It's not safe. Well, some of that is exaggerated fear and some of that is real. So we've got to create the reality of a wonderful safe place called Oakland.

Monk: Now Giuliani has instituted this plan to fine and arrest people for minor quality of life violations on the theory that if you dampen this environment of crime, if I stopped you from blaring your boom box, or if I stop you from smoking a joint, or if I stop you from jumping a turnstile on the subway, if I fine and arrest you for these so-called petty crimes I might find you've got a long and serious criminal record. Is that a tactic you would employ?

JB: Well, I'm certainly going to look at that. The main thing people are afraid of is violence. They are disgusted by people trashing parks or streets. I envision citizenship as not just a bundle of rights, but a set of duties. And we have to make that work voluntarily.

Monk: Now the police are very demoralized. I've read quotes in the paper that say they don't want to live in the city. What are you going to do to improve the morale of the Oakland police?

JB: Meet with them. Support their legitimate work and understand that from their point of view people's rights *are* protected.

Monk: Now, if you were to talk about Oakland, historically speaking, if you had to put a pantheon of Oakland figures together, who would that be?

JB: Richard Stein. Jack London. Earl Warren. Maxine Kingston. Ishmail Reed.

Monk: Looking back, who are the people that you are influenced by?

JB: Since I consider the political system broken, I'm not able to find among politicians anyone to point the way. I am looking very carefully at the founding concepts of America. And the federalists who say that if people group into factions, this has to be controlled by various mechanisms. Checks and balances. There is something missing in an aspect of the American political idea, and in our idea of virtue or friendship or the good. From the founding, the influence of Locke and Hume remains a great atomizing influence. Very hyper-individualistic. The possessive individual facing the world. Hobbes said that life is short, nasty, and brutish. So you have that world of atomization. Now after a few hundred years, we're looking at other societies and other more collaborative kinds of community in society. That's an idea that doesn't show up that often.

Monk: Right.

JB: Abraham Lincoln had a vision. He didn't look to the Constitution, which was this mechanism to control the vices of greedy individuals. He looked to the Declaration of Independence, the Revolution. He took the ideal of equality. Lincoln in his Gettysburg Address reformulated the original understanding. So you have the Declaration and then you have the Constitution, which was a very different kind of document. And then you had Lincoln saying, wait a minute, we have to look to the Declaration of Independence, which puts equality as our goal. And in another place Lincoln said, the great test is whether we can prove that popular government is not an absurdity. That's the continuing anxiety. Can the popular government work? And so, I'm looking at people who have something to say about this. Gandhi is a political figure. Martin Luther King. We have to reformulate the basics of political society. And right now we're at the end game. With little focus on the heart of the American cities, with many places [which are] crime-ridden. Depressed. With a lack of a connect to the environmental constraints. Every city from New York to Chicago to Oakland, if it isn't emptying, if it isn't diminishing, it's still spreading out. So the metropolitan footprint is bigger than ever. People need more and more space. They need more cars. More pavement. More air-conditioning. More water wasted and all the rest. So, the possessive individual is the accumulator of a wagon with stuff to put in his or her house, imported from wherever. That's the [basis] of the American idea. And that idea is inadequate. Because it's not an idea that everyone can plainly copy. If everybody copied America, with 200,000,000 cars for 265,000,000 people, then we would need four more planets. So we have a nonreplicable idea and [yet], by principal, you should be able to universalize what it is you're doing. And if you can't, it lacks moral authority. Moral validity. We cannot universalize the American experience. So we have to [change] if we're going to be a good society among other societies in the world. So that's what I see. Look back to this great discussion of the federalist period where they were all discussing what is the nature of government: What should be the role between the central state and the community state? We need that kind of discussion [today].

Monk: So maybe your administration is an incubator of ideas and an attempt to create a prototype that could be replicated on a bigger scale?

JB: Well, that sounds more grandiose than we can deliver, but that is the direction. That's a direction we want to be pointed in.

Monk: Your life, the way you try to live here for example, is kind of communal?

JB: Convivial!

Monk: A convivial atmosphere that you would like to see in society.

JB: More friendliness. And certainly more friendliness in Oakland. More accessibility. More efficiency. Not just efficiency as a bureaucratic term. Not wasting.

Monk: You talk about an ecopolis, right?

JB: It was really an idea to take into account the ecological aspects of Oakland. To make it more sustainable. And to involve the citizen in thinking about it. Because its a great place to be. The weather is great. We're closer to San Francisco than San Francisco is to itself. Many parts of San Francisco are further from its downtown than we are. So we are strategically placed. The rent's cheaper. The weather is better. And you are more accessible to the whole Bay Area.

Monk: You have an initiative on the ballot.

JB: Yes.

> "The great test is whether we can prove that popular government is not an absurdity. That's the continuing anxiety. Can the popular government work?"

Monk: What will this initiative do, how will it change government in Oakland?

JB: It will, for the first time, create a separation of powers between the executive and the legislature. Today the City Council hires the city manager, who is a chief executive. That has created confusion and a lack of a mandate. [The executive is] accountable to the legislative body and the legislative body is a poor executive. So that's what my initiative does—takes the mayor off the council and designates him as the chief, as the person responsible for the executive branch as an independent elected official. It makes the mayor accountable.

Monk: And he is then the chief executive in fact, not just in theory.

JB: He's not in theory now. He merely presides at the city council. That's his only function.

Monk: So he's just one vote among many.

JB: That's all he is. It's an honorific title.

Monk: Before we quit, can we play a little game here. It's called the name game. I'll name a person and you give me a little one sentence description.

Monk: Willie Brown. Mayor Brown.

JB: Elegant energy in motion.

Monk: Bill Gates.

JB: Reaching.

Monk: Ken Starr.

JB: Ill-fitting suits.

Monk: Hillary Clinton.

JB: Focused.

Monk: Exactly. You know I got really perturbed about what a columnist wrote about you the other day and pulled out the old stereotypes saying Jerry Brown is a little different because he eats brown rice for breakfast. And I just thought, *Well, what's so weird about that?*

JB: Right. I don't know that I've had brown rice for breakfast. Although I more often have it for dinner. Along with vegetables.

street below. But they hang in calm repose, perhaps waiting for the wrecking ball before they decide to complete the leap to the ground. What is Defenestration? According to Mr. Goggin, "It is the act of throwing something or someone out of a window." Only in San Francisco.

Note: If you are interested in buying the Defenestration Building, the price is only $2.5 million. Fax the I. M. Patel family at 415/621-8436 if interested.

> **The Labyrinth.** Grace Cathedral, 1100 California St. (Nob Hill). ☎ **415/749-6310.**

At the east entrance of Grace Cathedral is a meditation maze of geometric swirling patterns. This "labyrinth" is a replica of the one at Chartres Cathedral, which was laid in stone in 1200. Those who wish to walk it are required to remove their shoes. The neo-Gothic cathedral itself is an imitation of Notre Dame and took 53 years to complete.

> **Reflection of Culinary Struggle.** Corner of Leavenworth and Golden Gate sts. (Tenderloin).

Finally, a mural for the oppressed San Francisco minority of busboys, waitresses, and short-order cooks. In the heart of the Tenderloin.

> **Wave Organ.** Marina Blvd. and Baker. Walk out the jetty at the tip of the marina, right on the water (Marina).

The Wave Organ

East of the Golden Gate Yacht Club on "the point" is a truly "organ-ic" work of public art. Go during high tide, sit down in the lovely alcove, or put your ear to one end of the pipes, which submerge into the bay, and listen to the deep bellowing organ-like sounds of the water. The stone used in the construction is from a cemetery in Laurel Heights.

> **Women's Building Mural.** 3543 18th St., near Guerrero (Mission).
☎ **415/431-1180.**

One of the most PC murals on one of the most PC buildings in one of the most PC cities on the planet. And yet, despite what we said at the beginning of this section, it's definitely worth seeing. Mainly because it colorfully demarcates a key landmark in San Francisco history: the first community center in the United States to be completely owned and operated by women. Managed since 1979 by the San Francisco Women's Center, the Women's Building has spawned similar centers all over America, and is the one guaranteed place in town where a Hispanic woman could refer to herself as a "lesbian feminist of color" without a shred of irony.

Bars, Pubs, and Clubs

> **Albion Club.** 3139 16th St., at Albion (Mission). ☎ **415/552-8558.**

The anchor of the 16th Street I'm-trying-hard-not-to-look-clean scene that includes a handful of hip hangouts on the block between Valencia and Guerrero. Albion sports three pool tables in back and a women's room that deserves a quick peek by the dudes.

> **Bottom of the Hill.** 1233 17th St., at Texas St. (SOMA). ☎ **415/626-4455.**

We won't have to do this again. The potato salad was tasty—had that sweet conventional mayo quality one should always expect from potato salad. The curried noodles were a little weird. The bean dip was way funky and overly sour, like it had been sitting around since last week's all-you-can-eat $5 Sunday buffet. The barbecued chicken was good, and the bangers too. The guy on stage was playing a long somber dirge. In the back room late 20-somethings, some with goatees, others clean-shaven and in Levi's, one with mutton chops and short-cropped hair, another short and squat, were all clustered around playing pool. A few token gals shot, too, one a red-head with curls, in black, with granny boots. Another more Marina, smiling, like she worked in the art world somehow. The boyfriend was solid, well built. He wore nice glasses. They all drank hearty brown beer out of big glasses. Some smoked cigarettes. Camels it looked like. If the scene was an ad campaign, it would be Lucky Strike meets Zima meets Airware. Something pitiful and rote about it all—folks clustering around to talk about what? Day jobs as couriers, Copymat clerks, law students, financial planners? We just love the "Friends" generation.

> **Cafe Du Nord.** 2170 Market St., at Sanchez (Upper Market). ☎ 415/861-5016.

Cindy Johnson opened this downstairs restaurant and bar eight years ago, and has made it into the classiest music venue on upper Market. Dark wood paneling and a long, dark bar set the tone for this underground, yet unpretentious scene. Du Nord scores heavily with its diversity of entertainment, from Tuesday Salsa night to Sunday swing. But their notoriety may still lie in the drag presence on Mondays. From the inimitable Elvis Herselvis, the Andrew Sisters, and the unforgettable Patsy Cline, you're likely to see pop hits of yesterday's swooners with a nineties gender twist thrown in.

> **Caesar's Latin Palace.** 3140 Mission, at Army St. (Mission). ☎ 415/648-6611.

If you want to shake your maracas, there's nothing like this. Get there early on Fridays for free salsa dancing lessons.

> **Double Play Bar and Grill.** 2401 16th St., at Bryant (Mission). ☎ 415/621-9859.

Want a slice of the San Francisco Old Goys Network? Come here. That's one-eyed Warren Hinkle at the bar, nursing a cocktail, with a stack of papers nearby—impressive cosmopolitan choices like the *New York Observer* amidst the *Chron* and *Times*. And who's showing off those pictures? Some developer, no doubt. Looks like that Aliotto babe coming in. And there's some big Christmas party in the banquet room. Of course, the appeal of the Double Play goes far beyond back-room muscle and fitness. This bar has been around since 1909, and is lined with mementos from that golden era, including an overhead black-and-white shot of Seals Stadium (inspiration for the bar's name), plus a shot of Marilyn Monroe and Joe Dimaggio (a former Seals slugger), other celebrity photos, an actual Seals uniform above the bar, and the highlight: loads of leather gloves lining the upper parts of the walls. Oh, and there's a framed Hinkle campaign poster, when the former Ramparts editor ran for mayor. This is San Francisco's version of Chicago's famed Billy Goat Tavern, but cleaner, better preserved, and strangely beautiful. An absolute must visit.

> **Driftwood.** 701 Geary Blvd., at Leavenworth (Tenderloin). No phone.

"You wanna date?" is a frequent query at this murky oasis deep in the Tenderloin, where hookers and pimps hang for a drink while on duty. Barren and dark, it gets our vote for the city's most dead-end bar. The only thing to do here is quietly observe, kick for a bit, then split quick.

> **Edinburgh Castle.** 950 Geary Blvd., at Larkin (Tenderloin). ☎ **415/885-4074.**

Even the bartender has a Scottish accent in this Saxon-style drinking hall. The two levels afford enough space for large groups of merry toasters in what is still somewhat of a locals' secret, though the hipsters have definitely caught on.

> **El Rio.** 3158 Mission St., at Army (Mission). ☎ **415/282-3325.**

Girls' nights, boys' nights, or both anytime, with a World Beat soundtrack. Just a narrow bar area, but there's a great urban courtyard out back for the Sunday salsa parties.

> **Endup.** 401 6th St., at Harrison (SOMA). ☎ **415/357-0827.**

Overall mixed crowd. The Endup has hosted some of the most wild parties in recent years. Not only was it the site for the annual Ms. Uranus (the most vile drag competition on earth, bar none!) but also the long-lived Girl Spot. The parties are continually changing, though. Two bars, a sunken room with fireplace, and outdoor deck with a waterfall where you can watch the action on the small dance floor. Lives up to its name on Sunday mornings.

> **Esta Noche.** 3079 16th St., at Valencia (Mission). ☎ **415/861-5757.**

Ain't nothin' like a little Latino drag bar to confuse your impression of the macho Mission. Tuesday nights and weekends fill this small bar with greeters, gawkers, and pretty men with tiny mustaches.

> **Latin American Club.** 3286 22nd St., at Valencia (Mission). ☎ **415/647-2732.**

Small, crowded, and yet still comfortably slack. Cool neighborhood bar with enough funky touches, such as the flashing red SIN sign, to make it interesting. The cramped placement of the pool table ensures that you will meet people if you play. Unofficially endorsed by the late Red Man, a middle-aged hunk who walked around painted red.

> **Liquid.** 1925 16th St., at South Van Ness (Mission). ☎ **415/431-8889.**

It doesn't require much to create a bar du jour. Just take a long, cavernous, concrete

Question

"Why does everyone keep asking me why I'm red?"

—The Red Man

hole in the wall, throw a pool table in front, a long brushed-aluminum bar and long shelf of backlit spirits down one wall, a row of Naugahyde diner seats against the other, a pint-size dance floor, a raised platform, a blacklit DJ, and a lax smoking policy. The surly bouncers ID everyone, even aging hipsters, and a constant stream of squad cars patrol this notoriously seedy crack corner. The place has just what the breeders love: high energy, impending danger, and the chance to drop fistfuls of twenties for high-priced drinks while slumming in the Mission. Liquid has been pouring to a steady crowd for over a year and despite its trendy trappings, they get decent crowds on weeknights. Outside the door it's the real deal: The ten-dollar blow jobs, the crack vials in the curb, and the human excrement in the alley prove that the appearance of a South of Market bar in this 'hood hasn't changed a thing.

› **Lone Star Saloon.** 1353 Harrison St., at 9th (SOMA). ☎ **415/863-9999.**

The South of Market lair of really big, hairy gay bears with lots of tattoos, gnarly beards, and biker vibes. But they're all pussycats just waiting to be stroked. The urinal hides behind a leather curtain and the decor screams "Danger! High Voltage."

› **Motherlode.** 1081 Post St., at Polk (Tenderloin). ☎ **415/928-6006.**

This transsexual, drag-queen Tenderloin nightclub offers one of the wildest trips north of Tijuana. Just like TJ's seductively seedy strip bars, there is constant visual entertainment on the tiny corner stage, as well as tables full of working girls waiting for a young man to buy them a drink. Of course, all of these girls are trannies, but the dynamics of the deal are the same as they are on Revolucion Boulevard.

› **Nickie's Bar B Que.** 460 Haight, at Webster (Lower Haight). ☎ **415/621-6508.**

Lower Haight hole-in-the-wall that serves strong sounds without the attitude of the big dance clubs. Their long-standing Monday Grateful Dead Night brings out the tie-dye. Wide range of parties, including funk, soul, hip-hop, and reggae.

› **Noc Noc.** 557 Haight, at Webster (Lower Haight). ☎ **415/861-5811.**

A postmodern cave that is on the edge of being trendy but still retains a lot of the appeal from the time when there were no identifying markers outside the club. Fake rock walls, dashes of stainless steel, and young lower Haight denizens that sit on the pillows and drink in the nooks.

› **The Owl Tree.** 601 Post St., at Taylor (Tenderloin). ☎ **415/776-9344.**

Total knickknack explosion. Owl everything. Clocks, prints, stuffed feathered corpses. The decor resembles what your grandmother's living room would look like if her collectable hobby turned into a freakish fetish. James, the weekend bartender, entertains in this tight Tenderloin spot while a thousand owl eyes watch.

> Rawhide II. 280 7th St., at Folsom (SOMA). ☎ **415/621-1197.**

The ultimate country/western gay dance bar for the boot-and-Stetson set. On weekends there's a sea of happy dancers two-stepping it across the floor. Five-dollar dance lessons on Wednesday nights. Almost as much fun as a hayride.

> Redwood Room. Clift Hotel, 495 Geary Blvd., at Taylor (Downtown). ☎ **415/775-4700.**

An art-deco cocktail lounge that is the benchmark of old-school sophistication. Customers in high-backed chairs drink from snifters and smoke cigars as elegantly as a cigar can be smoked. The space is movie-set melodramatic, with deep redwood walls, a long mahogany bar, tall fluted columns, gorgeous Gustav Klimt reproductions, and a tower-high power ceiling. Black-tie table service completes the image to Cary Grant–like perfection.

> Spec's. 12 Alder St., at Columbus (North Beach). ☎ **415/421-4112.**

Tucked in a half alley off Columbus in North Beach, the walls at Spec's serve as a museum of San Francisco and maritime memorabilia. A mixed crowd packs the place at night; entertainment comes from your ability to eavesdrop. The captain of this rickety craft is a big-bearded guy named Frank, hailed by many as one of the best bartenders in town. If you're lucky, and still able to write, you can have your handwriting analyzed by a wonderful crazy lady.

> The Stud. 399 9th St., at Harrison (SOMA). ☎ **415/863-6623.**

Once almost exclusively the realm of gay boys, the Stud is reinventing itself for the decade to come through the efforts of owners Michael McElhaney and Ben Guibord. Killer parties are once again attracting the severe queer and pierced set. The long-standing Wednesday-night oldies party still packs them in. The tunes are varied throughout the week, though there seems to be a design to revive the garage house party on Saturdays. Heklina's ongoing Tuesday-night Trannie Shack is the best party in town with midnight performance by the cream of drag queens, including occasional drop-ins by the visiting Lady Bunny (of Wigstock fame). Co-owner Michael also fronts a male belly-dancing troop called Ultra Gypsy, who occasionally perform at the Stud!

> 1015 Folsom. 1015 Folsom St., at 6th (SOMA). ☎ **415/431-0700.**

Always in a state of flux, you just need to get the word from the street to find out what's going down here. Rave babies, multisexual scenesters, and up-till-lunch energy make this upstairs/downstairs party lounge happen.

› **Tonga Room.** Fairmont Hotel, 950 Mason St., at California (Nob Hill).
☎ **415/772-5278.**

The 1940s landmark Tonga Room is the mother of all tiki lounges, and the standard by which all others—from Trader Vic's to Bahooka—are judged. The tropical decor and excellent cocktails are only the first level of greatness. Throw in tropical rainstorms, thunder and lightning, and a band that floats out into a lagoon on a raft, and you have the ultimate Polynesian bar experience. Go for happy hour when the drinks are cheaper. Band starts at 8pm.

› **Top of the Mark.** Mark Hopkins, 999 California St., at Mason (Nob Hill).
☎ **415/616-6916.**

You will hear folks who say they prefer the Mark to the eye-popping excesses of the Fairmont. But that's like preferring Carson City to Vegas. Blandness has its advantages, but if you've gotten as far up as Nob Hill, the highest point in arguably the finest city in North America, why settle for the sort of handsome restraint one can find in Kansas City. Which is not to detract from the one salient advantage of Top of the Mark: the extraordinary panoramic view of the city.

› **Wild Side West.** 424 Cortland Ave., at Andover (Bernal Heights).
☎ **415/647-3099.**

The old wood floors and red walls instantly bolster the western feel when you walk in and around the peach-colored pool table. It's just like being in *Bad Girls,* except in this version, Drew and the girls are dykes. Two pinball machines line the wall, conversations flow from one corner to the other, and when the bartender steps outside for a smoke she tells you to pull your own draft as she watches from the door. Excellent Bernal Heights bar that caters to any orientation, but saves its best for the women.

› **Zam Zam.** 1635 Haight St., at Clayton (Haight). No phone, dammit!

Owner Bruno is the Soup Nazi of lounge-bar owners. These are Bruno's rules, and if you don't follow them, he will throw you out: (1) Do not sit at the few tables, sit only at the semicircle bar, so Bruno does not have to walk too far; (2) order a martini, preferably gin—anything else and Bruno would have to crack open one of the dusty bottles; (3) Bruno has been behind that bar for forty-five years, and he doesn't take any shit. This place is almost too cool to describe. Art-deco decor, Lynch-like lighting, and the smoothest jukebox in the City (Fats Waller, Benny Goodman, Xavier Cugat). If you don't believe the rules, just try breaking them.

> **Zeitgeist.** 199 Valencia, at Duboce (Mission). ☎ **415/255-7505.**

A great, tough drinking spot. One long bar, one pool table, a patio out back, and a crowd that digs on being too far down Valencia for the 16th Streeters. Winner of the coolest Mission jukebox competition. Motorcycle not required but appreciated.

Bookstores

> **Booksmith.** 1644 Haight, at Clayton (Haight). ☎ **415/863-8688.**

Though Booksmith opened its doors a good decade after the Summer of Love, the spirit lives on in this Haight Street landmark. Their visiting authors read like a Who's Who of the sixties including the late Allen Ginsberg, the late Timothy Leary, Grace Slick, Robert Anton Wilson, Maryanne Faithful, and those debunkers of at least part of the flame, yours truly, The Monks. Hunter S. Thompson had them wrapped around the block. "No injuries were reported, but apparently it came pretty close," says owner Gary Frank. Packed into 3,300 square feet, with over 40,000 books, they appeal to a lot of ex-hippies, multimedia types, and a healthy PC contingent. Their magazine section carries over a thousand titles. And their Altered States section contains every drug-related book one would ever care to read. But then again, if you're on drugs, will you be reading? Be sure to collect their author trading cards—the Monk card is quite rare.

> **City Lights.** 261 Columbus Ave., at Broadway (North Beach). ☎ **415/362-8193.**

Along with nearby Vesuvio Cafe, this is one of the last remaining icons of the Beat era, and they show no sign of slowing down. Owned by the occasionally irascible Lawrence Ferlinghetti, the store opened in 1953 when Ferlinghetti was an active supporter of the Beat movement and a poet in his own right ("An Elegy to Dispel Gloom," written in November 1978 after the assassinations of Mayor George Moscone and Supervisor Harvey Milk, is one of the more touching poems about the city). The chance to see both Ferlinghetti and the store has become a rite of passage for many visiting bibliophiles. City Lights stocks a healthy collection of poetry, art, and political commentary. The fabled poetry readings continue to this day. And Jack Kerouac Street (more of an alley) is right out the door.

> **Cody's Bookstore.** 2454 Telegraph Ave., at Haste ☎ **510/845-7852.** New store at 1730 4th St. at Delaware (Berkeley). ☎ **510/559-9500.**

Cody's is the grande dame of countercultural bookstores and has the battle scars to prove it. Established in 1956 by Fred and Pat Cody as an academic bookstore servicing nearby UC Berkeley, over the years, and especially under the current ownership of Andy Ross, they've become more general interest, with a decidedly alternative bent. Cody's will always be dear to our hearts because back in September 1986 they were the first store ON THE PLANET to carry the first installment of *The Monthly Monk*. They are also the largest independent bookstore in town. Situated right on Telegraph Avenue, they've definitely seen their fair share of the action—from the political upheaval of the 1960s, when tear gas exploded in the store as antiwar protesters sought refuge from the club-wielding "Pigs," to the bombing of the store in 1989 when an Islamic fundamentalist reacted to the presence of Rushdie's' *Satanic Verses* on their shelves. Through it all, Cody's has remained a front-runner in the fight for free speech. Mr. Rushdie himself paid a very emotional visit in 1997 to personally thank Cody's for enduring a bomb on his behalf. Their visiting authors have included every major writer of the late 20th century, including Mailer and Ginsberg, as well as minor lights like the Monks. On our 1993 tour for *Mad Monks on the Road* we were greeted at the door by the Naked People, a collective of free-thinking Bezerkley-ites (and Frank Moore acolytes), who in the grand Telegraph Avenue tradition were fighting a local ordinance against public nudity. Though today there are less naked people, there are certainly more books—150,000 titles at this writing— and a righteous determination to not let the big chains win the numbers game. Long live Cody's!!!

> **A Different Light.** 489 Castro St., at 18th St. (Castro). ☎ **415/431-0891.**

If you just *happen* to be a member of the Gay-Lesbian-Bi-Transgendered community, this is *your* local bookstore. Not that you won't find healthy coverage of this lifestyle in every other bookstore in town, but, as their 14,000-plus titles attest, A Different Light is exclusively focused on authors from the gay community or subjects of interest to the community. They also have over 400 gay periodicals, many from around the world (*J & L* from Taiwan, *Out* from New Zealand, *Outright* from South Africa), as well as an admirable assortment of gay-friendly zines such as *Gerbil, Teen Fag,* the *Daily Plague,* and *Driver Side Airbag.* The S.F. store has remained one of the premier gay bookstores in the nation since it opened its doors in 1987 (the flagship store opened in L.A. in 1979) and to this day is regarded as one of the hottest places in town to cruise the same sex without appearing completely obscene or out of place. Downside: The staff can sometimes be outright bitchy, and rarely will bend over backwards to help a customer in need (well, figuratively speaking).

Great Books and Poems of the San Francisco Bay Area

The Abortion, Richard Brautigan

And the Band Played On, Randy Shilts

The Annals of San Francisco, Frank Soule, John Nesbit, and John H. Gihon

Big Sur, Jack Kerouac

The Dain Curse, Dashiell Hammett

Desolation Angels, Jack Kerouac

Dharma Bums, Jack Kerouac

El Dorado, or Adventures in the Path of Empire, Bayard Taylor

"An Elegy to Dispel Gloom," Lawrence Ferlinghetti

Final City/Tap City, Lew Welch

From Satori to Silicon Valley, Theodore Roszak

Japanese by Spring, Ishmael Reed

The Joy Luck Club, Amy Tan

La Mollie and the King of Tears, Arturo Islas

The Making of a Counterculture, Theodore Roszak

The Maltese Falcon, Dashiell Hammett

The Mayor of Castro Street, Randy Shilts

McTeague, Frank Norris

Microserfs, Douglas Coupland

More Tales of the City, Armistead Maupin

Old Tales of San Francisco, Arthur Chandler

"A Strange New Cottage in Berkeley," Allen Ginsberg

Tales of the City, Armistead Maupin

Tripmaster Monkey, Maxine Hong Kingston

The Whole Earth Catalog, Stewart Brand

> **Green Apple Books and Music.** 506 Clement St., at 6th Ave. (Richmond). ☎ 415/387-2272.

Every starving artist intimately knows this bookstore as a primary source of supplemental income. They have a generous buy-back policy for used books and CDs. On any given day you'll find long lines of sheepish-looking locals with their grocery sacks, boxes, or day packs full of used books, which the Green Apple will pay for in cold hard cash. As a result of their reputation for saving so many people from bouncing yet another rent check, you'll actually find some amazing deals. They're exceptionally strong on the arts as well as floor-to-ceiling stacks of best-sellers and trashy novels. So before you toss out this Mad Monks' guide, keep in mind "The Apple," where you can get 15¢ on the dollar. Not a total loss. And it beats panhandling.

> **Modern Times.** 888 Valencia St., at 20th St. (Mission). ☎ 415/282-9246.

Far from a clean, well-lighted place, this funky, dusty, ramshackle store has remained the epicenter of left-wing political correctness, carrying a healthy inventory of the PC Canon—women's studies, African-American, countercultural, labor, world lit, progressive Hispanics, Marxist dialectics, they have it all. In addition to radical politics, their focus since opening the door in 1971 has been on small-press books. One of their top best-sellers was *Girls Guide to Taking Over the World: The Zine Revolution*. Their 28,000 other titles along a similar anarchistic vein might not fare too well in Tulsa or South Dakota, but Modern Times has never lacked for a constituency in this politically charged neighborhood. Long before the chic restaurants and club crawlers hit Valencia Street, Modern Times was the de facto community center for this post-hippie/Hispanic block, complete with bulletin boards, literary events, and plenty of intellectual justification for those who believe the revolution isn't so much over, it's just been postponed.

Buildings, Bridges,
and Other Visual Landmarks

› **Alcatraz Island.** Take the Blue and Gold line from Pier 41, Fisherman's Wharf. Ferries leave daily at 9:30am, 10:15am, and every 30 min. thereafter to 4:15pm. The more comprehensive evening tours leave at 6:15 and 7pm Thurs–Sun. Expect to spend about 2 hr. on the island. Call ☎ **415/773-1188** for ferry prices and updated schedules. www.nps.gov/alcatraz.

If there is one tourist stop every sensible local will recommend, it is Alcatraz Island. This is truly one of the most captivating highlights of the Golden State. The ferry ride circles the former federal penitentiary, and if you go in a slight fog, as we did, the sight of thousands of seabirds circling the island as if it were a scene from Hitchcock's *The Birds* gives the place an unforgettably eerie and ancient melancholy. On the island itself, the buildings remain just as they were when "The Rock" was closed in 1963. The self-guided cell-house audio tour is impeccably realistic, featuring the commentary of inmates and guards who lived on this cold and windy fortress, reserved for the prison system's most dangerous and notorious. Men like Machine-Gun Kelly and Al Capone spent time here, as well as the irascible, though brilliant, ornithologist Robert Stroud, loose subject of the film *The Bird Man of Alcatraz*. The most staggering fact is that out of hundreds of attempts, only three escapees went uncaptured. It is believed they either drowned in the cold swift currents of the bay or were eaten by sharks (though some believe the escapees might be alive today, reasoning that if Jack LaLanne could swim the distance *hand-cuffed*, certainly a highly motivated convict could too). Alcatraz was closed in 1963 when then attorney general Robert Kennedy discovered it cost the same to keep a prisoner at Alcatraz as it would to put him up as a guest at the Waldorf Astoria. Native Americans occupied the island in 1969 for eighteen months, and still believe it belongs to them, so every attempt is made to present a PC facade. Run with reverence and intelligence by the National Parks Service, the park's only weakness is its inability to laugh at itself (we were banned from doing a cover shoot on the island after one park ranger realized we would be posing with surfboards).

> **Bay Bridge.** See "Views."

> **C & H Sugar Factory and Carquinez Strait.** 830 Loring Ave., at Rolf (Crocket). ☎ 510/787-2121.

Almost every visitor who comes to the Bay Area finds a reason to drive north on Highway 80 across the Carquinez Bridge towards Reno, Tahoe, or the Sacramento Valley. And most comment on the imposing, strangely un–San Francisco sight of the C & H Sugar Factory that lies perched on the southern side of the Carquinez Strait right below the Carquinez Bridge. What these travelers don't realize is that here is a stop that is as intriguing as any place they are heading. The Carquinez Strait is where the Sacramento River floods into the San Francisco Bay. It was the eroding force of this river, roaring almost 2.5 million years ago between the peaks of the Coastal Range, that formed today's bay and golden gateway. The Carquinez has seen lots of traffic since its creation. To this day, you can view giant ships heading through the passage from atop the hills of the captivating town of Crocket, or down at the **Nantucket Seafood Restaurant (☎ 510/787-2233)** at the foot of Port Street on the Crocket Marina.

> **Chinatown Side Streets.** Chinatown.

While the magical essence of Chinatown has been destroyed by unchecked tourism, the subtle mystery of the Old World can still be felt once you get off the main drags. Try **Ross Alley** (a.k.a. "Gau Leuie Sung Hong"), home of the infamous Chinatown opium dens, gambling rooms, and brothels back in the 1870s, and **Waverly Place** (between Grant and Stockton), the yin to Ross Alley's yang, filled as it is with many Chinese temples.

> **Columbarium.** 1 Loraine Ct., at Anza (Richmond). ☎ 415/752-7892.

The ultimate place to stash your ash. A treasure trove of urns line every wall of this four-tiered sanctuary, which, oddly, served as a polling place during the last presidential election. With stained-glass windows, a copper dome, and classical

Dead Stars

"Yeah, I've got maps to all the dead stars' homes. It's called 'The Map of the Dead Stars' Homes.' But some aren't dead yet."

—Stannous Flouride

The Columbarium

Muzak, it seems like an elegant wedding chapel, and is the only place you are literally going to find Prince Albert in a can. The head caretaker, Emmitt Watson, leads a fabulous impromptu tour. On it you will see some of the more famous urns in the Columbarium, including those of the Shattuck Family, the Eddy Family, and, yes, the Folger Family. Open 9am to 5pm Monday to Friday, 10am to 2pm on weekends, this is one of the true gems of San Francisco.

› **Doggie Diner Head.** 2750 Sloat St., at 46th Ave. (Sunset). ☎ **415/564-6052.**

This doggie-head-on-a-pole diner once dominated the cityscape, serving up wieners at various locations. Thanks to gentrification, only one Doggie head remains, across from the zoo atop the Carousel Restaurant. It needs a serious face-lift, but in a victory for preservation it's been declared a historic landmark and cannot be removed.

› **Francis "Lefty" O'Doul Drawbridge.** 3rd and Berry sts. (SOMA).

This is one of two remaining drawbridges in San Francisco (there's another one on 4th Street) and the only one that's still in regular operation. O'Doul was a New York Yankee who became manager of the San Francisco Seals, where Joe DiMaggio started back in the 1940s. The sight of this black iron structure against the setting

The last of the Doggie Diner heads

sun of the bay is one of our favorite S.F. tableaus. Near PacBell Park, the new Giants stadium currently under construction, and the late San Francisco RV Park, where the Monks used to park the fabled Monkmobile.

> Francis Scott Key Monument. Music Concourse, Golden Gate Park.

Erected in 1888, this is the first monument in the United States dedicated to the composer of our unsingable national anthem.

> Golden Gate Bridge. See "Views."

> Hallidie Building. 130 Sutter St., at Kearny (Downtown).

It's the world's first glass-wall building, constructed in 1917, and represents the birth of modern architecture. The glass facade is adorned with decorative railings, balconies, and stairs.

> Julius' Castle. 1541 Montgomery St., near Union (Telegraph Hill). ☎ **415/392-2222.**

Just because it's tacky doesn't mean it's affordable. This eccentric pink palace on Telegraph Hill houses a totally overpriced restaurant with a killer view. The architecture alone is worth the visit. It's the sort of place you bring a date on prom night or your grandmother on Easter.

> **Mission Dolores.** 3321 16th St., at Dolores (Mission). ☎ **415/621-8203.**

Over 5,000 Costanoan Indians are buried in the cemetery, victims of early displacement through disease and cultural genocide. The actual church was completed in 1791. It's the oldest building in San Francisco, with 4-foot-thick adobe walls and redwood-log support beams.

> **Palace of Fine Arts.** 3601 Lyon St., between Bay and Jefferson (Marina).

A neoclassical Roman rotunda with two curved colonnades overlooking a small park and lake replete with fountains and swans, the Palace of Fine Arts is the most breathtakingly beautiful structure in all of San Francisco, and the ideal place to take a prospective lover or just a leisurely stroll. Built by Bernard Maybeck as a temporary structure for the 1915 Panama-Pacific International Exhibition, it was the last remnant of the dream city built on the present-day marina for the World's Fair. In the 1960s financier Walter Johnson put up the $2.5 million to restore it. Today the Palace seems like the ideal set for a coronation, but houses the Exploratorium (an interactive science museum) instead. Just what are those women looking at anyhow?

> **Presidio Pet Cemetery.** Crissy Field Ave., near McDowell (Presidio).

Humbly located on a small plot of land right under the S.F. side of the Golden Gate Bridge near the thickly wooded aromatic heart of the Presidio, this sweet cemetery is where military personnel bury their deceased animal friends. Enter through a

Presidio Pet Cemetery

white picket fence to an ominous warning: "Caution: Hazardous Waste Area." Inside you'll find a touching array of pet shrines, some with more trinkets than a queen on parade. Our favorites are those dedicated to Tyson "T-Bone" Brooks, Jason the Dancing Dog, Max Our Happy Puppy, Miss Dusty, Radar, Fifi, Jet, Birdie our Parakeet, and Baron ("He Lived to Love and Be Loved"). From a glance at the remarks on the sweet white crosses, it seems the "owners" loved their pets as much as, if not more than, their spouses and family.

> **Rincon Annex Post Office.** Spear St., at Mission (Downtown).

Built by the WPA in 1940, this phenomenal masterpiece houses historic murals with possible Communist sympathies. The lobby holds an 85-foot-high skylighted atrium. Adjoining shops and restaurants aim for the corporate set, but the eight-story-high waterfall is as refreshing as a walk through a rain forest.

> **St. Francis Hotel Glass Elevator.** 335 Powell, at Geary (Downtown).
> ☎ 415/397-7000.

The city's best ride to the stars, it's an E-ticket ride. Walk straight through the lobby toward the elevators. Ride up at 1,000 feet per minute. If this leaves you begging for more, ride the elevator in the Fairmont.

> **San Francisco Museum of Modern Art (a.k.a. "SF MOMA").** 151 3rd St., between Mission and Howard (SOMA). ☎ 415/357-4000. Open 11am–6pm Fri–Tues, Thurs 11am–9pm. $8 adults. Half-price on Thurs 6–9pm and free the first Tues of every month. Museum is closed on Wed.

Mario Botta's giant air-vent ashtray design makes this the most stunning new work of architecture in this city since the TransAmerica Pyramid. We just love it. Whimsical, humane, bold, humorous, minimalist yet richly rewarding, it's simply amazing how this delightful structure conveys the many attributes of not only the city but of modern art in general. An absolute must visit, even though the prices are a little steep.

> **San Francisco Studios.** 375 7th St., between Harrison and Folsom (SOMA).

What do Phyllis Diller, Whoopi Goldberg, and Cliff Robertson have in common? They and a dozen others put their foot and palm prints in concrete to launch the ill-fated star walk in front of this short-lived attempt at Hollywood North.

> **Sutro Bath Ruins.** Northeast of the Cliff House on the Great Hwy. (Richmond).

In 1863, Adolf Sutro, a wealthy ex-mayor and the first in a long line of S.F. reformers, so loved the people of this city that he built a grand oceanfront bathhouse where they could come and frolic in the therapeutic salt waters of the Pacific. The staggeringly large Sutro Baths consisted of seven 500-foot-long swimming pools, 500 changing rooms, and space for 24,000 visitors. For grand gestures, it doesn't get grander than that. Though the baths burned down in 1966, visitors still come to explore the ruins. And damn fine ruins they are too.

> **Sutro TV Tower.** Top of Mount Sutro (Twin Peaks).

If you think about it, this TV antenna dominates the entire city by virtue of its elevation. Its tripod form and size looks like a giant insect surveying the bay. Why hasn't someone made a sci-fi classic using this as an alien space invader?

> **Trolley Car Graveyard.** Warm Water Cove Park, east end of 24th St. (China Basin).

The final resting place for dead trolley cars, all spray-painted and forlorn. Under the shadow of a PGE power station, the abandoned trains date back to the fifties.

> **Vermont Street.** Potrero Hill.

The crookedest street in the city is Vermont, not Lombard. Go south over the hill, which overlooks I-5 and S.F. General Hospital, and watch out for skateboarders. Perfect for cars with no brakes. We couldn't make the switchback turns in the Monkmobile.

Cafes and Coffeehouses

> **Brainwash.** 1122 Folsom St., at 7th St. (SOMA). ☎ **415/861-3663.**

There's now the equivalent of a Brainwash in almost every major city in the country— a place that combines cafe and entertainment with a Laundromat. In some cases, the mix is video store/Laundromat or art gallery/Laundromat, but the common denominator is always cleaning. Of all of these hybrids, Brainwash remains the most fully executed and aesthetically compelling. The aim of this place is to give patrons something to do besides read newspapers while soaping their skivvies. It's a perceptive concept, given that the American Laundromat might be one of the last remaining gathering places where people actually hang and wait without much pomp, circumstance, or distraction. Of course, there's a mercenary aspect to such community-building. Like a full-service supermarket, Brainwash doesn't want its groovy customers spending their money elsewhere while waiting for their ripped jeans to dry. So thorough is their approach, they've even adorned the bathrooms with original quotations, so one never has to feel bored or uninspired. Like us, you still may end up preferring the bare-bones blah of a conventional Laundromat sans entertainment, which helps clear the head while cleaning the clothes, but if you are less Monkish, then this arty, punk, industrial design cafe/Laundromat with loud rock 'n' roll, high-priced treats, and South of Market attitude is the very best in its class.

> **Cafe Flore.** 2298 Market St., at Noe (Castro). ☎ **415/621-8579.**

Cafe Hairdo, Cafe Dish, call it what you like, it's really just a small-town beauty parlor with a zillion scrutinizing eyes monitoring your every move. Complete with dizzy gossip, diverted glances, and an oversupply of really bad eighties hairdos.

> **Cafe La Boheme.** 3318 24th St., at Mission. ☎ **415/643-0481.**

The historical meeting place of the Monks, where at midnight, April 1, 1985, following the weekly Barefoot Boogie, Mike and Jim sat discussing dysfunctional families, life, and food. Anarchy hasn't worn well for the funky, worn interior of this neighborhood cafe, though it's still an excellent testament to its countercultural roots, with flyers for every imaginable cause adorning the walls. With ringside seats to the downtrodden, drug-dealing circus outdoors, this may be the last bastion of true Mission—Hispanic, hippy, punk—as its patrons stall for time, clutching a copy of the *Realist* and a double tall espresso.

> **Caffe Trieste.** 601 Vallejo St., at Grant (North Beach). ☎ **415/550-1107.**

Full of aging wanna-be writers with hairy ears who sit all day cruising chicks while contemplating their next paragraph as they absorb the cultural significance of being in this historical cafe where truly great writers once met.

> **Farley's.** 1315 18th St., at Texas St. (Potrero Hill). ☎ **415/648-1545.**

It's a clean, well-lighted place to read a book and act adult. On top of ultra-hip Potrero Hill, there's a certain neighborly charm that makes it feel small-town. Lots of the people know each other by name, books with important-sounding authors abound, and you almost feel like taking off your shoes and lighting a pipe.

> **Horse Shoe Coffeehouse.** 566 Haight, at Steiner (Lower Haight). ☎ **415/626-8852.**

If ever there was a place you could spit on the floor and no one would notice, this would be it. Actually, you could *puke* on the floor and few would notice.

Observation

"San Francisco is a mad city—inhabited for the most part by perfectly insane people whose women are of remarkable beauty."

—Rudyard Kipling, 1889

It's funky, smoky, and a total freak fest day and night, a place that pulls all the despairing elements of the lower Haight together in one big room. Out on the sidewalk, junkies slump near the entrance.

> **Internet Alfredo.** 790 Brannan St., at 7th St. (SOMA). ☎ 415/437-3140.

There are Internet cafes with only a token computer, poor connections, and no techno geeks behind the bar, and then there are INTERNET CAFES whose primary focus is the Net and all points in-between. This is one of the latter. Upstairs from a photo studio and only a block away from the courthouse, the T-1 connections, the highly informed computer wizards, and the K-mart prices make this the most reliable connection for all of your net needs. Full design stations with scanners are available, as are live video-cam feeds. The amicable kingpin (a.k.a. Big Daddy, a.k.a. Alfredo) is the primary driving force behind this venture and he and his cohort Jessica make a point of making everyone feel quite at home.

> **Josie's Cabaret and Juice Joint.** 3583 16th St., at Market (Castro). ☎ 415/861-7933.

It's our favorite alternative to Cafe Hairdo across the street and also has the best cabaret in town. But during the day, before the performances start, it's a great place to hang with a friend and talk—the food's great and you don't feel like everyone is watching you.

> **Mad Magda's Russian Tea Room.** 579 Hayes St., at Laguna (Hayes Valley). ☎ 415/864-7654.

The owner, David, works the counter. We like that. He's an opera singer, slightly flamboyant, and has giant hats coming out of the wall. It's cozy and serves great Russian pastries made by ladies from the Richmond. The fortunetellers out front are really, really good at predicting the future.

> **Mario's Bohemian Cigar Store.** 566 Columbus Ave., at Union (North Beach). ☎ 415/362-0536.

It's not pretentious. Just a plain Italian coffeehouse with a few tables and serious espresso. They also make their own campari. Italian is spoken here because the old men hunkered around the tables like it that way. So do we.

> **Muddy Waters.** 521 Valencia St., at 16th St. (Mission). ☎ 415/863-8006.

This is by far the most down-home cafe in the Mission, especially now that a statewide indoor smoking ban has cleared the air. Great for taking a half-hour snooze while sitting propped up like you're reading a book. Don't forget to order something.

> **Pete's Cafe.** San Francisco Art Institute Cafe, 800 Chestnut St., at Leavenworth (North Beach). ☎ **415/771-7020.**

Plop the interior of this rooftop cafe down on any street in town and it wouldn't warrant a mention. But it makes our highly selective list because of a very simple truism: location. Of the many cafes in town, Pete's has indisputably the best view of the city and bay. What's more, you get to hang with groovy academic artistes, which can be *soooo* heady. You're also inside, or, rather, atop, the oldest cultural conservatory in the West, the San Francisco Art Institute, which mounts consistently high-quality events and gallery shows. And then there's that Diego Rivera mural. The downside: They're only open when school is in session.

> **Radio Valencia Cafe.** 1199 Valencia St., at 23rd (Mission). ☎ **415/826-1199.**

This ultra-cool–sounding weekend jazz place is always packed and has that sort of radical chic that hints of the East Coast.

> **Red Dora's Bearded Lady.** 485 14th St., at Guerrero (Mission). ☎ **415/626-2805.**

When Harriet, Lori, and Lynn opened this place they probably didn't know they were going to have the hippest and hottest girl place in town. Sure, boys can come here too (it's a gender-free zone) but the feel is dyke, and the scruffy, pierced, tattooed crowd is even friendly. Great shows on weekends.

Calendar/Events

> **Anon Salon.** Events every 6 weeks (SOMA). No phone. www.anonsalon.com. E-mail anon@sirius.com.

Every 6 weeks it's a really big theme bash where the digital-world geeks party down for a night. Rich, costumed "bohemians" come to get drunk and mill about as if an orgy might happen, but it never does. It's in a big ten-room flat that Marcia Crosby and Joe Bullack repaint for each party to match their mood. Sometimes it's scary, sometimes cosmic, though it always struck us as a bit contrived, trying a little too hard to be "avant-garde."

> **Critical Mass.** Foot of Market St. (Downtown). Last working Fri of the month.

It's a spontaneous gathering of hundreds of cyclists on the last working Friday of every month. They meet at the end of Market for a massive show of spokes, then everyone cycles west, shutting down traffic and demonstrating the beauty of alternative transportation. Every decade since the sixties in America seems to have had

(continued on page 378)

Interview: San Francisco Mayor
Willie Brown

If one were to look at fashion sense alone, Willie Brown would be considered the perfect San Francisco mayor (well, the perfect mayor working with a 1970s design palate). Factor in open-mindedness, a willingness to buck a few canons of social convention, and a refreshing candor, and you're talking the ultimate San Francisco mayor. But underneath the glossy, ring on the pinkie, Top O' the Mark veneer, what many locals wonder is whether this most San Franciscan of mayors is just another smooth dealer oiling the gears of the corporate money machine, or whether Mr. Brown has the pluck and temerity to tackle the knotty quandaries of this complex metropolis, even if it makes this most image-conscious of politicians look a little, shall we say, unfashionable. The Monks, never afraid to ask the tough questions, went straight to "Da Mayor" for the answers.

The moment he enters the room you sense two things: (1) the public face; (2) the private self-assurance. Though he might not be as revolutionary as the other Mayor Brown across the bay, Mayor Willie Brown of San Francisco never leaves even a shred of doubt that he is, indeed, "Da Mayor." While traces of insecurity and hesitation occasionally leak out, it's reassuring to find someone who feels entitled to this pivotal civic station. Even if you don't totally agree with him, you *want* to believe him, mainly because he so firmly believes in himself. And in today's political world, that's half the battle.

Monk: What is the spirit of San Francisco, according to Mayor Willie Brown?

WB: Well, it's very difficult to define exactly what the spirit of San Francisco really is because San Francisco is so eclectic. There's some of everything and everybody here. And there's a level of mutual respect. Mutual appreciation and sensitivity. I would tell you probably in one word, absolute and complete freedom.

Monk: So, freedom being the kind of ruling principal of the city, you also have some very difficult problems, possibly as a result of that freedom. Homelessness. Crime. Now, other mayors—say, Giuliani in New York—have curtailed freedom a bit in the interest of improving quality of life. Do you see those two, freedom and quality of life, always having to be in opposition to one another?

WB: Not at all. We don't really restrict and curtail anybody's freedom. It's just the opposite of what the personality of this city really is. But we also do not tolerate

people adversely impacting upon [others]. So when someone wishes to sleep on the streets, they can't do that. The streets are to be used by all of us. So there is no tolerance of one occupying the streets or the public parks exclusively. I took a little bit of heat for removing the encampments in Golden Gate Park. The park is for everybody. The park cannot be sectioned off for just folks who happen to be poor. We don't tolerate that. So, you do strike a balance, but that balance must always have a relationship to freedom.

Monk: Let's get to the specifics of that. Having lived in both cities, here and New York, we wanted to look at the two different styles. In New York, the mayor would actually arrest people for minor quality-of-life violations. And, in so doing, the police uncovered people who had long criminal records. They'd bust people for these little things and catch bigger fish. As a result, crime is down. Now we walk around San Francisco and there's still panhandling on Haight Street, in the Mission, in the Tenderloin, and we have this feeling that if you were to take the kind of steps that Giuliani has taken to really reduce the crime level here, you would alienate San Franciscans.

WB: Well, first of all, I don't think that anybody should be arrested for offenses for which you can cite people. Give people tickets. The cost of processing someone who's been arrested is astronomical. Doing the citation is just as effective. If there are multiple citations then there may be a point at which you become a public nuisance and you use the public-nuisance process to remove [them]. You can't just go out and arrest folks for real insignificant acts where there are no victims.

Monk: So you would not go out and stop people from panhandling?

WB: Our merchants [are] of great assistance. In the Castro the merchants are telling the people [not to] give money to the folks. Give them these coupons that entitle them to food. And, invariably, that has dramatically reduced the number of people who are panhandling. In addition, we have an elaborate set of nonprofit organizations who render services for folks. They are all in walking distance and they all have fabulous menus and as a result of that, we have outreach workers that constantly go out and say to panhandlers, don't do it. So you've got to be very careful on how you strike that balance. You are never, however, going to remove everybody.

Monk: This issue is very interesting to us—freedom versus quality of life. We travel to every city and this seems to be the dichotomy going on. How do you preserve both? For instance, in other cities they are trying to eliminate the sex districts, sex shops. Times Square in New York is a classic example of that. Will you ever go that far in terms of restrictions on the freedom to sell merchandise?

WB: No. I don't think we will ever get to the point where we would try to impose, for the lack of a better word, religious values on what may be entertainment for others. We certainly would want to be sure that it is not offensive to others who don't go that route. But, at the same time, we would want to make sure that people who do go that route can do so in a safe, healthy environment.

Monk: Let's talk a little bit about diversity. Because when it comes to freedom, that's a big quality we have here in San Francisco. Now some people argue that Mayor Brown, in his attempt to bring business to the city—the two stadiums, encouraging bigger developers to come into Union Square, mall developers, et cetera—that, in effect, what you're doing is the same thing that's happened in New York, which is a mallification of the city, trampling on some of the quirky stores that always made San Francisco so unique. How would you answer that criticism?

WB: I'd answer that criticism very directly by saying take a look at our neighborhoods. That's where the uniqueness of our neighborhoods [reflects our] diversity. Chinatown hasn't changed one iota. And it will not change one iota. Westport, which is the western part of the city, that hasn't changed. The only thing that's happened is many Asians have moved in and there are now Asian signs and Asian businesses and Asian restaurants. The same goes for the back part of Geary Street. So those neighborhoods have not altered themselves at all. The fact that Bloomingdales wishes to put a store in downtown San Francisco has absolutely no effect on these neighborhood stores. On the other hand, the struggle still goes on to try to make sure that the chain stores don't happen in San Francisco.

Monk: And how do you prevent them from coming in?

WB: Well, your planning laws and your zoning laws are literally designed to keep the neighborhood's character as it is.

Monk: The rest of the country looks at San Francisco as this unruly stepchild of high weirdness. Now you have from Washington attempts to curtail some of the strides you've made to be tolerant in public policy; for example, the recent House of Representatives resolution, which is somehow going to stop protection of gay rights in the workplace. And also legislation trying to stop the cannabis clubs of this city. Let's start with the gay rights measure. How can you do an end run around that?

WB: We're not going to do an end run around it. We're going to face it head on. We believe local autonomy has been the cornerstone of Republican politics in this nation for years. And to suddenly decide that one city in the whole universe of cities and states should be blacklisted and denied assistance, we will answer that question and I think we will defeat that effort. Congress has enough trouble being the city council of Washington D.C., let alone [governing] the municipalities that exist throughout this nation.

Monk: What is your feeling on medical marijuana? Do you think it was a good idea?

WB: Absolutely. I supported the proposition which was on the ballot. I supported the efforts in the halls of the legislature on more than one occasion. The authorization and availability of that substance as a medical ingredient. And I still have that opinion. The voter's will [has now been overturned] by the federal authorities. The state of California can't go its own way and chart its own course on this issue, in that there may be criminal violations and criminal penalties associated with [the cannabis clubs]. I don't intend to have myself or any person connected with the government of San Francisco indicted for any criminal activity. And so we are trying to work with the federal government to find a way around that. Because there is clearly a medical need for marijuana.

Monk: Do you ride a bike ever? Because today is Critical Mass.

WB: Yes it is. But don't encourage them. It's a nightmare. Traffic is tied up in the city. Traffic is difficult already. I've instituted all kinds of rules and regulations in this city. I'm so gung ho on trying to keep the traffic flowing and when these bicyclists come along and take over the streets, when they run stop signs and what have you then public safety becomes threatened and, in that regard, you cannot tolerate it.

Monk: So you're trying to find a balance here between cars and bikes.

> *"If you live here, you can't help but enjoy. [It's] a place where every day of your life you're happy to get up."*

WB: We are. We may not be doing it as quickly as they wish it would be done. Their requests, according to the commission's evaluation, were a bit unreasonable. So there are some tests that are being run. This business of bike lanes in San Francisco has to track with level streets. Bicyclists can't handle the hills. Regular bicyclists. So we carefully have to do a network of streets for bicyclists to follow. And we've got the proper signage and we're doing all those kinds of things. We are encouraging people to use bicycles. We put a considerable number of our policemen on bicycles now. We patrol the Tenderloin on bikes. We patrol the Mission on bikes. We patrol the Haight on bikes. We are patrolling all the parks on bicycles. So our bicycle police force has grown considerably. And it's kind of a dramatic thing for them because tonight they too will be out in force for Critical Mass.

Monk: Do you have a religious belief?

WB: Oh, absolutely. I'm a Protestant. I go as regularly as I can to my own church, which is United Methodist over on Fillmore. But as an elected official I make sure that I visit many other churches.

Monk: Okay. Good. Hallelujah. Now, is there a philosopher or a spiritual thinker in your development? Any great books? Any great authors?

WB: I'm more of, you might say, an entertainment reader. I am really into escapism. So for me, whatever Grisham does, being a lawyer, that's great escapism. I can imagine myself being in Susan Sarandon's shoes in *The Client*. I can imagine all that scene. I also [read] almost anybody's biography or autobiography. And then, finally, I'm a student of Winston Churchill.

Monk: Are you looking back to people like Churchill?

WB: My reference to Churchill only has to do with his intellectual capacity. And his incredible command of words and the symbols that go with those words. And the master of the put-down. I am a great student of the prime minister's speeches. I absolutely love the give-and-take of that combat. As far as a deliverer of pure speech you could not beat Martin Luther King. So there are some people in history, and events, that you have to reference in order to get where you're going. But I've got to tell you, I don't know anybody, frankly, that practices that as carefully and cleverly as Bill Clinton.

Monk: What does he do that others don't do?

WB: Well, he has a full set of brains. He has a core of beliefs—he doesn't always follow [them], but he has a core of beliefs and an understanding. He can [consume] a vast amount of information and understands every ounce of it. He is a great reader of people. He has an ability to focus on an issue, and he has superior listening skills.

Monk: Well that's funny you should mention him because we play this little thing called the name game. We'll name a person and you give us your little aphorism or little quick answer of what you think. Eddie DeBartolo.

WB: He is the prototype of a pro franchise owner. A wheeler-dealer merchant in the world who has a yearning to win.

Monk: Ken Starr.

WB: Maniac.

Monk: Elvis Grbac.

WB: Oh, I got in real trouble. *[Laughter]*

Monk: We know about that. The tour de faux pas.

WB: Elvis has the potential to be a great quarterback. And that's the best I can say.

Monk: Bernie Ward.

WB: Confused.

Monk: Can you elaborate a little bit more on his confusion?

WB: He knows not what he is. He knows what he would like to be. But he does not know how to get there. Therefore he is constantly in turmoil about his own identity, his own beliefs.

Monk: How about a word of advice for Bernie Ward on how to get to where he should be.

interview

WB: Get out of the journalism business.

Monk: Now let's talk about a couple of things that are uniquely San Francisco. If you had to name your three really quintessential San Franciscan places, things that you'd love to see preserved over time, what would they be?

WB: Well, almost any piece of this city is worthy of a protection effort. What do I enjoy? Well, being the mayor, you've got to, literally, sample every restaurant. There are restaurants I eat in more often than others. I eat at the Black Cat. I go late night to Top of the Marriott because of some singers there. I go to the Mark at 8:00 because there is a great piano player there. I go to Compass Rose at the St. Francis Hotel because Abe Battat has been playing there forever. He's a buddy. So there are places that I move around in with some regularity, but I would not want to preempt those places as the only places. Every Sunday I eat lunch at areas in Union Street and I've been doing that since about 1968. I also eat at a soul-food restaurant called Powells. And, believe me, every Friday at 1, I'm in a bistro on Bush Street called Le Central. And I've been doing that with my friends and it has become part of the lure of the city. They actually now have tour buses that come by looking because they know that's where we are going to be. From 1 to 3 every Friday. And we've been doing that forever. If I'm really going uptown for dinner and what have you, I'll go to the Fleur de Lys. I'll go to Stars, or Hawthorne Lane. There are just so many. If I want a burger I'll go to Moose's. Or I'll go to the Balboa Cafe. And if on a Sunday, I'll go to Pier 23 and listen to some music and sit outside on the dock and feed my face with squid. And if I'm really into fish, I'll end up at Aliottos on the waterfront. Or Eighth Street Grill. Particularly, if I'm hanging out with some journalists, they seem to just love the Eighth Street Grill. And then if I'm going to the opera I'll eat at Jardinieres, which is right around the corner here with great Creole 7 nights a week. Guys in the tuxedos. A room that holds only maybe forty, forty-five people. Very intimate with a great wine list. And it's walking distance to the opera. Walking distance to the symphony. Walking distance to the ballet. So, it's the favorite place for that kind of activity. So when you say where do I go, what do I do, I do it all.

Monk: What San Franciscans—besides yourself, of course—represent the spirit of the city?

WB: Oh, well, Harry Denton.

Monk: Why Harry Denton?

WB: Because Harry was first a bartender. Then a piano player in a bar. Then a bar owner. Then, of course, he fell from grace briefly because of some tax problems and what have you. He's come rolling back. He's partnered up with a guy who runs all the boutique hotels and they put major restaurants in these boutique hotels and Harry has gained 700 pounds and lost 1,500 pounds. And Harry is into being the poster boy for Viagra and being interviewed. He is a symbol of this city.

Monk: Any woman in that list?

WB: Oh, yeah. The woman that runs Tosca, Jeanette Estridgen, who is a walking encyclopedia of every movie that's ever been done. And on any given night, you will see Nicolas Cage and Francis Ford Coppola and Phil Kaufman and Robin Williams.

Monk: Sharon Stone?

WB: Sharon Stone's husband more than Sharon Stone. You'll see Kevin Spacey in there. And you'll see Sean Penn bartending in there. Jeanette runs it with an iron hand. I don't think the walls have been touched in seventy years. Because I can still see the lines in there. And there's never any light in the place. They do not light the place. They line the coffee drinks up, and this was a speakeasy joint in prohibition. And it was the only joint in the city where you could get booze. Because they disguised it in this drink and everybody in San Francisco would go there to drink. We still serve that drink there. With the disguised booze. So, that's part of what this crazy city is all about and Jeanette represents just that.

Monk: What I get from talking to you is that I've barely seen a better match between the spirit of a city and the spirit of a man. I really think you enjoy the richness of this city in a way that few predecessors have.

WB: But if you live here, you can't help but enjoy. [It's] a place where every day of your life you're happy to get up. Because you know there is something exciting that's going to happen. Politically. Socially. Financially. Something unusual is going to occur in this city. This city is like a news capital. Every day of your life.

Mayor Willie Brown can be reached at DaMayor@ci.sf.ca.us.

>interview

"Bike messengers run red lights because they're so stoned on marijuana that they're color blind."

—Meter maid, when asked why cyclists run red lights

its vanguard political movement. What the highly creative ACT-UP was to eighties radical protest, Critical Mass is to the nineties. Only problem is that Critical Mass lacks the cohesive strategy and singular focus of ACT-UP or even Queer Nation, and thus events like those on July 26, 1998, when Critical Mass cyclists defied the planned route and created city-wide chaos, are bound to mar the movement's effectiveness. Anarchism is a wonderful catharsis, terrible for reaching one's goals. Some locals have gone so far as to label Critical Mass "Critical Mess," since the loose-knit organization has succeeded in pissing off their wider constituency of people—who use cars for absolute necessity but desperately want to find a better way. In fact, if the self-righteous barbs directed by some bicyclists at car drivers continues, a few former supporters have half-jokingly threatened to create a counter-movement called Critical Gas. Still, for the most vibrant ongoing act of agit-prop, Critical Mass is the main event in the city right now.

> **Quake Day.** Lotta's Fountain, intersection of Market, Kearny, and Post (Downtown). Apr 18.

Each year on April 18, 5:12am, the remaining survivors of the 1906 quake gather at Lotta's Fountain at the intersection of Market, Kearny, and Post to commiserate. At this point any survivors are well into their nineties and it's the closest thing we get to the shamanistic tradition of cataclysmic storytelling.

> **San Francisco Cacophony Society.** ☎ 415/665-0351. www.zpub.com/caco/index.html.

Carrying on the free-spirited Bay Area tradition laid forth by the Merry Pranksters, the San Francisco Mime Troupe, the Suicide Club, and, of course, the First Church of the Last Laugh and its annual Saint Stupid's Day Parade, and acting as a pivotal force in the shaping of Burning Man as we know it today, Michael Michael's San Francisco Cacophony Society is for grown-up funsters who rightly presume that the whole city is a playground and life is an acid test. Members get their thrills from absurdist field trips like the underground sewer walk (formal wear only), dinner parties on the Golden Gate Bridge, Santa rampages, and over-the-edge excursions into the underbelly of urban dada madness. Very refreshing when it first appeared on the radar in 1986/87, Cacophony, while inspiring chapters from Portland to Brooklyn to L.A., has ironically accrued a kind of knee-jerk prankster predictability of its own. Definitely join the party if you're bored with life and seeing monotone, though don't expect a whole lot of sincere deep dialogue.

> **San Francisco Lesbian-Gay-Bisexual-Transgender (but, God, forbid, No NAMBLA) Pride Parade (a.k.a. SFLGBTP).** 1390 Market St., #1225, San Francisco, CA 94102. ☎ 415/864-FREE.

While the NYC Pride Parade is more enjoyable (there's nothing like driving down Fifth Avenue to the roar of thousands), the S.F. Parade carries more personal significance, since it was our first Pride Parade (1985), and because San Francisco, like it or not, is still regarded as the spiritual home of the gay rights movement. In the 1994 S.F. Pride Parade, our Bounder, the Monkmobile, won "Best Wheels." However, we haven't been back, since the S.F. Gay Rights parade, much like the Castro's formerly eccentric Halloween, has turned into a midbrow gawk fest for the entire liberal family. The edge, the flamboyance are gone, leaving in their wake a set of predictable rituals that might grab newcomers to the movement, but no longer interest old fogies like the Monks.

> **St. Stupid's Day Parade.** Begins at the base of Market, at Embarcadero (Downtown). Apr 1.

In the grand tradition of S.F. merry pranksterism, hundreds of really, really creative and smart people "stupidly" celebrate their patron saint by swarming the Financial District on April 1 and following the sacred rituals of their "stupid" predecessors. Begins at the base of Market (at Embarcadero) around noon, and includes the sock exchange at the Stock Exchange and a penny toss at the Bank of America. Loud, jubilant, poignantly satirical, and the site of Mike and Jim's first day together over fourteen years ago.

At the St. Stupid's Day Parade

Prince with Leather Gloves

at the Dore Alley Street Fair

He rolls into Kaffe Kreuzberg on the corner of 9th and Folsom in a silver-plated wheelchair, front wheels spinning in the air. Black leather driving gloves grip the rims as he moves toward the table where Michael Monk sits, two sex workers by his side.

Outside, the block is closed down, barricaded from end to end and with a posse of police watching the street. It's the Dore Alley Street Fair, a South of Market leather fest where San Francisco unfurls its signature style. Two blocks of raunch sweats under the scorching sun. Leather daddies walk the perimeter with their slaves, bound at the wrists, strapped in harnesses, necks collared in chains.

Inside, the man, who calls himself Prince, rolls toward the table, interrupting a conversation that isn't his.

"Excuse me, I'm sorry to butt in like this, but I need some help."

All eyes turn to the big black man in his big wheelchair. He leans forward, a crucifix dangling from his neck. As he talks, his porcelain white teeth, capped in gold, flash through his pleading smile.

"Yeah, whatcha want," says Liz, one of the whores, who's sucking iced coffee through a two-barreled straw.

"You all from around here?" He's apologetic from the start, with a face twisted up in knots, puzzled forehead, glancing side to side.

Michael Monk gets the feeling he's about to ask for spare change except that his well-groomed battle-gray jumpsuit seems a bit too nicely pressed.

"I live in Richmond and, you know, I'm married."

"So . . ." says Liz.

"Yeah, yeah, but, like, I haven't had sex in over ten years. You know, on account of this"—he points to his lifeless legs—"and I'm getting tired of it. So I thought I'd come over here and see if I could get something going. What's this all about?" he points outside.

He leans over in a low hush. "How do I get somebody to have sex with me? What's it I'm suppose' to say?" His near whisper carries to the other tables and a few snickers are heard around the room.

"How much you want to pay?" says Liz. "I'm not that cheap!"

"I don't want to have to pay. I just want to have some sex. I mean, what d'you got to say to get one of those girls out there? You just go up to them or what?"

All eyes turn toward the window, observing the street. It's a hard-core leather scene, primarily men, and what few women roam are either staunch dykes or joined by chain to their masturbating men. It's the biggest raunch fest, period, a capacity crowd of self-proclaimed refugees from the Folsom Street Fair who intend to reclaim the sleaze.

"Listen, you want some sex, I'll do you. But nothing's free."

"I'm not paying! They don't have to pay," he motions out the door. "Why should I? Why don't we just go in the room there, you know. I'm not all that bad, am I?" Prince sits there unbuttoning his shirt down to his belly button. A ripple of scars outline his gut below the waist line.

"Look, if you want something, you just ask for it. That's all there is to it. They're either gonna say yes, or they gonna say no," answers Liz.

"Then what about you?"

"Well, I'm saying no. Cause I'm a work-for-hire kind of slut. That's just how I am."

Liz and friend get up and drag their attitudes out the door.

Prince rolls close behind, wheeling through the maze of people. On the street, heavy-bass techno thumps out of sky-tall speakers at the end of the block. A mass of leather clad, shaven-head masters with harnessed slaves parade around. Serious tribal tattoos convert the pink-white flesh of leather hipsters into a mosaic of Escher patterns off their well-muscled limbs.

Michael Monk follows at a safe distance, drawn like a voyeur into the wake of Prince, who sets out on his solo mission.

"Just ask for what you want," he seems to be muttering.

Michael Monk plods carefully across the sticky asphalt, which smells like a petri dish of spent bodily fluid, baking in the tarmac like a primordial street stew. The brick walls up Dore Alley are braced by a bevy of leathermen in thigh-high black boots, muscles cinched by metal-ribbed leather armbands, throats tight from the pull of chokers, wheezing for breath in the stifling noonday blaze.

A crowd gathers around a telephone pole, its height obscuring what exotic action lurks beneath. A ring of corseted babes, their waists cinched small by rows of stainless-steel eyelets, surrounds the pole. A crowd seems to thicken, pulling tighter to the center as moaning rises from below.

Michael narrowly squeezes through, stepping on steel-booted toes, parting through the sea of leather, as he catches a quick glimpse of a leather boy slave, bleach blond, shackled and collared, who's got his tongue stuck seriously deep up the rear of a total stranger.

Further up the alley a long-haired gent is raising some serious hell on the bare back of his blond cohort, who barely conceals the pain. He whacks her hard with a riding crop, slapping her ruby-red thigh, welts rising like craters across her tortured flesh. She comes up for air and begs for a nipple, *doesn't matter—right or left*. He submits his left to the edge of her teeth and she slowly consumes it, barely coming up for air.

Down the street, a crazy chick chants at the top of her lungs, wearing a bow tie of nipple rings, cock rings, and lacerated handkerchiefs. She presides near the whipping booth, where in a low-back chair recipients hunker down awaiting the lick from a 4-foot cat o' nine tails that comes cracking down, raining blood-curdling pain upon the willing backs of fellow masochists.

Through the cracks, Michael hears a familiar voice.

He turns to see Prince still making the rounds. Singling out the hot babes, he rolls forward, braking within arm's reach of an unsuspecting arm. Prince motions the person toward him, drawing an ear to his mouth, where he whispers his improbable invitation, only to be summarily declined.

On and on he goes, down the street, curb to curb. He chases his fantasy, rolling after those slow enough to catch, repeating his well-rehearsed plea only to be met by a broad shake of the head and a polite brush-off.

"Having any luck?" Michael finally asks when he comes face to face with Prince.

He produces a handful of phone numbers, some on business cards.

"Oh my God, you've got to be kidding me. That many?" Michael stands back surprised.

"They all want money," says Prince with a sigh.

> **Soap Box Derby.** Bernal Heights Speedway, Bernal Heights Blvd., at Folsom (Bernal Heights). No phone. 1pm, 3rd Sun of every month.

From Memorial Day to Halloween on the third Sunday of every month, motorless race cars take to the hills in the fastest derby in the world. Sponsored by the San Francisco Illegal Soapbox Society, all you need to do to enter is build a car and show up. Just follow Folsom Street past Army and all the way up. Bring Band-Aids.

Film

Movies

After the Thin Man (W. S. Van Dyke II, 1936)

American Graffiti (George Lucas, 1973)

The Barbary Coast (Howard Hawks, 1935)

Basic Instinct (Paul Verhoeven, 1992)

Being Human (Bill Forsyth, 1994)

Birdman of Alcatraz (John Frankenheimer, 1962)

The Birds (Alfred Hitchcock, 1963)

The Black Bird (David Giler, 1975)

Bullitt (Peter Yates, 1968)

The Competition (Joel Oliansky, 1980)

The Conversation (Francis Ford Coppola, 1974)

Copy Cat (Dave Fleischer, 1941)

Crazy Quilt (John Corty, 1966)

Cujo (Lewis Teague, 1983)

Dark Passage (Delmer Daves, 1947)

Days of Wine and Roses (Blake Edwards, 1962)

Dim Sum (Wayne Wang, 1984)

Dirty Harry (Don Siegel, 1971)

The Doors (Oliver Stone, 1991)

Escape from Alcatraz (Don Siegel, 1979)

The Fan (Tony Scott, 1996)

Fearless (Peter Weir, 1993)

Final Analysis (Phil Joanou, 1992)

Fog Over Frisco (William Dieterle, 1934)

48 Hours (Walter Hill, 1982)

Foul Play (Colin Higgins, 1978)

Freebie and the Bean (Richard Rush, 1974)

The Game (David Fincher, 1997)

Gattaca (Andrew Niccol, 1997)

The Graduate (Mike Nichols, 1967)

Greed (Erich von Stroheim, 1928)

Guess Who's Coming to Dinner (Stanley Kramer, 1967)

Harold and Maude (Hal Ashby, 1972)

Heart and Souls (Ron Underwood, 1993)

The House on Telegraph Hill (Robert Wise, 1951)

Hustler White (Bruce LaBruce, 1996)

Innerspace (Joe Dante, 1987)

Interview with the Vampire (Neil Jordan, 1994)

Invasion of the Body Snatchers (Philip Kaufman, 1978)

The Jagged Edge (Richard Marquand, 1985)

The Jazz Singer (Richard Fleischer, 1980)

The Joy Luck Club (Wayne Wang, 1993)

Junior (Ivan Reitman, 1994)

Lady from Shanghai (Orson Welles, 1948)

Lenny (Bob Fosse, 1974)

Magnum Force (Ted Post, 1973)

The Maltese Falcon (John Huston, 1941)

Maxie (Paul Aaron, 1985)

Mrs. Doubtfire (Chris Columbus, 1993)

The Net (Irwin Winkler, 1995)

9 to 5 (Colin Higgins, 1980)

Nine Months (Chris Columbus, 1995)

Pacific Heights (John Schlesinger, 1990)

Petulia (Richard Lester, 1968)

Play It Again, Sam (Herbert Ross, 1972)

The Presidio (Peter Hyams, 1988)

Psych-Out (Richard Rush, 1968)

The Right Stuff (Philip Kaufman, 1983)

The Rock (Michael Bay, 1996)

San Francisco (W. S. Van Dyke II, 1936)

Sister Act (Emile Ardolino, 1992)

Sneakers (Phil Alden Robinson, 1992)

Star Trek IV: The Voyage Home (Leonard Nimoy, 1986)

Take the Money and Run (Woody Allen, 1969)

THX-1138 (George Lucas, 1971)

Trenchcoat (Michael Tuchner, 1983)

Vertigo (Alfred Hitchcock, 1958)

A View to a Kill (John Glen, 1985)

What's Up, Doc? (Peter Bogdanovich, 1972)

When a Man Loves a Woman (Luis Mandoki, 1994)

Theaters

> **Artists' Television Access (ATA).** 992 Valencia St., at 21st (Mission). ☎ **415/824-3890.** http://www.atasite.org.

There are a few vortexes in town where the various S.F. subcultures intersect: Rainbow Grocery, Burning Man, and Artists' Television Access. Open Monday through Saturday (10am to 10pm), ATA is a media-arts center with a large viewing room for experimental videos and film. You can also use their editing machines really cheap and find out what the other twisted minds in town are producing. The only problem with ATA is its weakness for work by the self-anointed "oppressed" (women in search of "empowerment," Asian-Americans, Mexican-Americans, and all sorts of other hyphenated Americans).

> **Castro Theater.** 429 Castro St., at Market (Castro). ☎ **415/621-6120.**

A stunning 1930s movie palace, with Spanish Colonial architecture, a plaster ceiling that looks like a big tent, seating for 1,600, and organ music before major shows, this majestic landmark offers the ultimate movie-going experience in the city. For once, a theater to take a same-sex date and not receive attitude for holding hands, though just as many hetero couples make the scene as well.

> **The Red Vic.** 1727 Haight St., at Cole (Haight). ☎ **415/668-3994.**

It lacks the charm it had when it was down the street in the Red Victorian Bed and Breakfast, but it's still a great film house with those cozy couches toward the front and the best in brainy films (*Manufacturing Consent* is always a big draw).

> **Roxie Cinema.** 3117 16th St., at Valencia (Mission). ☎ **415/863-1087.**

A totally casual, arty film house in the heart of the Mission, showing standard classics, foreign flicks, and the best bad movies in town. We viewed *Four Flys on Green Velvet,* possibly the worst horror/murder flick ever made, and never laughed so hard.

Food

> **Bagdad Café.** 2295 Market St., at Noe (Castro). ☎ **415/621-4434.**

It's like eating in a fish bowl while you cruise the natives. A full glass-plated corner cafe serving deluxe meals at deluxe prices. A decent veggie meal can be had here if you're in the mood. They're open 24 hours.

> **Brennan's.** 4th St., at University (Berkeley). ☎ **510/841-0960.**

For drunk Micks with a remnant of class, Brennan's is the E-ticket ride. Historically, it's been a huge working-class bar with a working-class cafeteria serving working-class Hofbrau-style grub (ham, corned beef, frankfurters, turkey sandwich, turkey neck, even turkey carcass to take home), but a mid-nineties makeover—including a freshly painted kelly-green ceiling, 1950s light fixtures, and recessed fluorescents shining on a rust-colored background—now make this an attractive stop for folks from any income group. Across the street from Spenger's (the popular fish restaurant) and trendy 4th Street, where you can breakfast at **Bette's Ocean View Diner** (1807 4th St.; ☎ **510/644-3230**).

Trivia

The fortune cookie was invented by Makota Hagiwara at the Japanese Tea Garden in Golden Gate Park in 1909. He didn't patent it and the idea was quickly adopted by the Chinese restaurants in town.

> **Cafe Istanbul.** 525 Valencia St., at 16th (Mission). ☎ **415/863-8854.**

Big Middle Eastern plates and really thick Turkish coffee. Plop down on the pillows near the windows or sit at the brass tables along the wall. Exotic aromas and sounds so genuine you'd swear you can smell the camels. Go see the Fat Chance belly dancers at their sister restaurant, Amira, across the street.

> **California Culinary Academy.** 625 Polk St., at Turk (Tenderloin). ☎ **415/771-3536.**

Monday through Friday, from 6 to 9pm, go downstairs to the Academy Grill for the most decadent all-you-can-eat dessert buffet of your life. Or, if you're really hungry, have the full dinner buffet, which includes dessert (but don't forget these are students cooking). Sort of embarrassing to be caught here pigging out in such a formal setting, but it's a great way to try all the saucy dishes you can't otherwise afford in the better eating establishments around town.

> **Cha Cha Cha.** 1801 Haight St., at Schrader (Haight). ☎ 415/386-5758.

What's with all the altars on the walls? This is a very trendy tapas joint where you have to spend $8 per person (says so on the menu), but we like it. The crowds are lively and they definitely deliver great tapas. Spanish atmosphere and tiny plates with big food.

> **Chez Panisse.** 1517 Shattuck Ave., at Cedar (Berkeley). ☎ 510/548-5525.

At Chez Panisse, in the heart of Berkeley's former "gourmet ghetto," the message is clear: (1) fresh, organic, locally grown food is good for you and good for the planet; (2) growing, preparing, and eating fine food together is a ritual that deepens community; (3) eating out shouldn't be a comfortable experience (for these prices, one should get better than hard austere benches, however beautiful); and (4) great food, lovingly prepared, is expensive. The chefs here were very friendly. Some were even drop-dead gorgeous. And Alice Waters, the Goddess of the gourmet Zen approach to cooking (a.k.a. "California cuisine") is a decent spry woman, with her heart and head in the right place. But girl, lose the personal assistant. Talk about arrogant. This woman acted like they were doing *us* a favor, and we were the ones paying for the damn meal! Never have we seen such impudence, petulance, and snottiness in a person whose function is to create a positive impression for a business. And we aren't the only ones who carry this impression. (Madam, there was a rather influential handicapped lady you snubbed—she hasn't forgotten either.) The short, brusque, and outright snide way in which we were treated by this one person caused us to reevaluate our entire Chez Panisse experience—for all the hype, for all the precious rhetoric about the magic of organic purple tuti fruit peppers, sandpiper raspberries, and earthbound fava beans, maybe the Chez Panisse era has passed. Maybe the restaurant is riding on its laurels. Maybe Hawthorne Lane, Post Rio, and a slew of other San Francisco eateries are better after all. Maybe Alice Waters needs to reexamine whether her message of love and community is trickling down to the subordinates. Still, STILL, and this is a very exceptional "still," we won't let such gross effrontery stand in the way of telling you that the food here is quite special, particularly the salads, fruits, and soups. However, while relying on the stand-alone flavor of organic fruits and vegetables is fine, doing the same with meat and fish might be a mistake. In other words, the flesh could have used a bit more—dare we say?—seasoning. Nonetheless, the professionalism, precision, and enthusiastic good cheer of the chefs—who are, after all, the stars of this show—overcomes all deficiencies, even though the funky casual attire of your average Berkeley dinner guest might leave a more refined visitor a little unnerved. Monday nights in the downstairs restaurant offers a reduced prix-fixe menu. Closed Sunday.

> **Clown Alley.** 2499 Lombard St., at Scott (Marina).

Down-home goodness with a hip diner environment. This mom-and-pop place offers the least expensive late-night dining around (its famous twin on Columbus closes early). The back of each menu offers a horoscope to pass the time while-u-wait.

> **Dago Mary's.** Hunter's Point Naval Shipyard, at the end of Evans St., right after the gate to the Naval Shipyard (Hunters Point). ☎ 415/822-2633. Only open for lunch and special banquets.

A stone's throw from where Burning Man enthusiasts toil away at Headless Horse Point Warehouse sits a classic restaurant named after an Italian woman, Mary Chiorzio, San Francisco's version of "Diamond Lil," who ran a whorehouse and then a restaurant out of this joint back in the 1930s. We like it for two reasons: (1) its obscure location at the entrance to the Naval Shipyards in sketchy Hunters Point; and (2) its Victorian decor—red velvet drapes, gold-flocked wallpaper, chandeliers—which hits you like a typhoon when you enter the door. The bay views aren't bad either, though the real drawing card is the clientele. Chef Rick Bruno, who used to cook at Bohemian Grove on the Russian River, says regulars include members of several fraternal organizations, including Godfathers and the Sons of Sicily. It ain't called Dago Mary's for nuthin'.

> **Denny's.** 1700 Post St., at Buchanan (Japantown). ☎ 415/563-1400.

This isn't your regular Denny's. It may look and feel like a Denny's, but, located in the heart of Japantown, they offer Japanese and Hawaiian breakfast specials such as Hawaiian Portuguese sausage, Oriental noodles with ham and fish cakes, and the topper: Spam on rice!

> **Esperpento.** 3295 22nd St., at Valencia (Mission). ☎ 415/282-8867.

On the subject of tapas, try this place. It's a bit cheaper than Cha Cha Cha's and they definitely deliver a sparse but extremely yummy meal in a trendy setting.

> **German Cook.** 612 O'Farrell, at Leavenworth (Tenderloin). ☎ 415/776-9022.

A touch of Germany in the heart of the Tenderloin. All the sauerkraut, knockwurst, and hot potato salad you've ever wished for. Go in on an empty stomach and come out with a lead belly.

> **Goat Hill Pizza.** 300 Connecticut St, at 18th (Potrero Hill). ☎ 415/641-1440.

As far as pizza joints go, they're one of the best in town, though we also have a fondness for Vicolo, behind the Hayes Grill. Order you're own gourmet pizza from a long list of extras, and they will build it for ya.

> **Greens.** Building A, Fort Mason. From Marina and Buchanan sts., enter parking lot (Marina). ☎ 415/771-6222.

Open since 1979, they are the granddaddy of S.F. vegetarian restaurants. Though no longer completely run by the San Francisco Zen Center, they are still run with Zen Buddhist grace and efficiency. Don't expect a pig fest because the small servings are pricey (and they don't serve pig), but the taste treat goes the extra mile and you'll be oinking approval in their stunning bathrooms.

> **Homemade Cafe.** 2454 Sacramento St., at Dwight Way (Berkeley). ☎ 510/845-1940.

Tom Dalzell, self-taught lawyer and slanguist of the oppressed, told us about this breakfast joint, and we're glad he did. As Tommy D put it, "It has a great mix of working people from the flats, lesbians, and aging hippies." Our target market. The French toast is truly the best we've ever had—buttery, somewhat soggy, *sweeeeeeet.* The eggie weggies and apple sausage were also satisfying. Most importantly, our waitress was warm yet efficient. Don't miss it.

> **House of Prime Rib.** 1906 Van Ness Ave., at Washington (Polk). ☎ 415/885-4605.

Prime rib paradise for bottom feeders. Feels like Omaha with big booths, soft lights, and cart-loads of meat. Select a cut of beef, nurture your cocktail, and swoon to the elevator music in this classic dinosaur of a steak joint.

> **Hunts Donut.** 2400 Mission St., at 20th (Mission).

Open 25 hours. Drug deals are going down all night long, so watch your back. Great cinnamon rolls.

> **It's Tops Coffee Shop.** 1801 Market St., at Octavia (Upper Market). ☎ 415/431-6395.

Since 1952, this family-run, knotty-pine hole-in-the-wall goes for the country kitchen cabin feel. About the size of a boxcar, you get the best trailer-trash meals on Market here. Working the grill since 1947, they've got the requisite jukebox, a counter with stools, and homemade pies accompanied by the biggest scoops of ice cream in the city.

> **Java House.** Pier 40, off Embarcadero, near the end of Townsend (Downtown). ☎ 415/495-7260.

This dive sits right on the water overlooking a yacht harbor and offers a good, basic, cheap but skimpy bay-side breakfast, and flavorful characters in the early hours. Also, don't miss **Red's Java House** (on Embarcadero, at Brannan Street), a rickety old dive for dockworkers on a break. Most of the regulars order burgers and Budweiser for breakfast.

> **Julie's Supper Club.** 1123 Folsom St., at 7th St. (SOMA). ☎ 415/861-0707.

Despite the fact that it turns into a total yuppie fest on weekends, it's got a funky, fifties, retro character and serves up an interesting menu. Plus, upstairs is where Patty Hearst was held hostage in the early weeks of her infamous kidnapping. Who could ask for more?

> **Just for You.** 1453 18th St., at Connecticut (Potrero Hill). ☎ 415/647-3033.

This long, narrow slice of real-estate delivers one of the best breakfasts in the city if you don't mind the wait. With only two tables plus ten stools at a polished wood counter, the 10-by-20-foot cafe can only seat sixteen. The raw floor and high ceiling with skylight lend a light, airy feel as you watch the rock-and-roll hipsters working at the classic grill. Owner Arienne Landry hails from Louisiana and imports such culinary riches as Creole crab cake, flavorful grits, fresh corn bread, and Longanisa (Filipino sausage). The menu has a warm, Southern feel too it, the seasoned home fries, scramble tofu, and fresh baked scones are beyond standard fare, and the Italian Omelet is worth a repeat visit anytime. The regulars, all known by name, are diehard fans and would just as soon keep this little kitchen all to themselves, but sorry, word is out.

> **Kan Zaman.** 1793 Haight St., at Schrader (Haight). ☎ 415/751-9656.

A nice attempt at opium-den dining, with floor seating under a pseudo tent complete with pillows, carpets, burnished copper, and terra-cotta walls. It's supposed to conjure up images of a 14th century Moorish palace. Sorry, nice try. Best feature, though, is the hookah with your choice of apricot or honey apple tobacco. The grub is down-home Middle Eastern fare. If you can sit in the window, it's great.

> **Kate's Kitchen.** 471 Haight St., at Fillmore (Lower Haight). ☎ 415/626-3984.

Push through the druggies, sign your name at the door, and by the time you get inside you'll be ready for the best breakfast in town. Good country cookin', including delicious cornmeal pancakes and sausage, right in the middle of the lower Haight. A Christine Clausen standby.

> **La Rondalla.** 901 Valencia St., at 20th (Mission). ☎ 415/647-7474.

Year-round Christmas lights and mariachi bands make this the most festive Mexican eatery in the Mission. Not just your standard enchilada joint, they get into wild variations, including goat meat. They have late night hours, and the margaritas soar.

> **Liguria Bakery.** 1700 Stockton St., at Filbert (North Beach). ☎ 415/421-3786.

Stand in line for focaccia, the potato chip of North Beach. This small place bakes and sells *only* focaccia, in three simple varieties, without all that yuppie inventiveness found elsewhere, and it is *sooooo* cheap. The aromas will knock you over with Italian wholesomeness. For an additional treat, head across Washington Square (where there's a time capsule buried under a statue of Ben Franklin) to **Mario's Bohemian Cigar Store Cafe,** which uses Liguria's focaccia in making its incredibly savory sandwiches.

> **Love 'N Haight.** 553 Haight St., at Fillmore (Lower Haight). ☎ 415/252-8190.

A hole-in-the-wall take-out joint serving basic but very tasty Middle Eastern fare. They serve a total meal and they don't skimp on the hummus. Everything's made from scratch, the dolmas is moist, and they sell fresh juice. When Jim lived in the lower Haight, he ate here at least twice a week.

> **Lulu.** 816 Folsom, 4th St. (SOMA). ☎ 415/495-5775.

There are many fine gourmet yuppie eateries in S.F., serving all sorts of dishes with femmy French names. Of all of these, Lulu is the best, not only because it goes easy on the femmy Frenchness, but because the food is terrif. I had a quick lunch during the *How to Talk American* tour with John Alderman, late of *Wired News,* and though we had to zorch through our soup and entree while discussing the size and breadth of the American mono-culture, we both left feeling like we had sampled some of the most exquisitely flavorful and most beautifully presented food in the city. If you are in a quandary over whether to dine at Post Rio, Stars, or Lulu for your big night on the town, choose Lulu.

> **M & W Market.** 23rd and Arkansas sts. (Potrero Hill). ☎ 415/550-0603.

A bright white light illuminates the pavement on 23rd street outside this nondescript corner market in the interzone between the "O.J. Projects" to the east and south and the sea of middle- to upper-class yuppie apartment dwellers all over Potrero Hill. Looking down from the park, which adjoins the Potrero Rec Center above, one can watch the endless stream of black customers who frequent this outpost on the edge of the hood. Inside are fairly normal neighborhood market goods—soap, snack food, soft drinks, and a whole variety of alcoholic beverages. So many options that the Middle Eastern store owners have stocked even more beverage selections inside the deli case. These customers clearly are not coming for the babaghanoush.

› **Mifune.** 1737 Post St., at Webster (Restaurant Mall, Japantown).
☎ **415/922-0337.**

We're not prone to the obvious, but if you want your basic Japanese fast food, they serve almost every type of noodle dish you've ever dreamed of.

› **Orphan Andy's.** 3993 17th, St., at Castro (Castro). ☎ **415/864-9795.**

A tiny little 24-hour place in the heart of the Castro with a friendly menu for the blurry-eyed. If you're looking for interesting times, just listen to Virginia the waitress, who says, "When you come in here, you take your life in your own hands." Words of wisdom from a woman who knows.

› **Polly Ann Ice Cream.** 3142 Noriega St., at 38th Ave. (Sunset). ☎ **415/664-2472.**

Here in the outer Sunset, you'll find the weirdest ice-cream parlor ever, where they serve a flavor called "Durian" that smells like gasoline. And that's just the start. They've got a wall of unheard-of flavors and a spinning roulette to help you decide.

› **Pork Store Cafe.** 1451 Haight St., at Ashbury (Haight). ☎ **415/864-6981.**

Former butcher shop turned trendy breakfast joint. You can smell the bacon a block away from this neighborhood pig trough. It's not the cheapest, but it's got everything pork you might want.

› **Powell's Place.** 511 Hayes St., at Octovia (Hayes Valley). ☎ **415/863-1404.**

Owner Reverend Powell has been serving a mix of chicken and gospel music for decades. This neighborhood kitchen has resisted the urge to upscale like everyone else on the street. With funky Southern charm they serve up banana cream pie, corn bread, and choose-your-own chicken parts to order. Has a bit of a rehab feel with the employees, but otherwise you get a good level of grease and gospel, which you just can't get enough of sometimes.

› **Puerto Alegre.** 546 Valencia St., at 16th St. (Mission). ☎ **415/255-8201.**

There's at least 300 tacquerias in S.F. and they almost all serve the infamous, oversize San Francisco burrito. Using price, atmosphere, and sauce as our guide, we found over twenty in the Mission that do the trick, all along Valencia and Mission or down 24th. This one is family-run, with grandma's picture on the wall. They'll do anything to order, have great green sauces, a counter, and upholstered seats. Very funky and very south-of-the-border.

> **Rainbow Grocery.** 1745 Folsom St., at Division (Mission). ☎ **415/863-0621.**

This is the most progressive people's food store in the country; a daily celebration of natural foods, and the community that goes with it. After eight years on the road sampling mediocre pill shops, co-ops, and natural-foods chains from coast to coast, we wept when we walked back into this treasure. True, the style is a little dated, but the spirit of the people that work here is purely tribal. There's an immense eclectic range of products (some of the most esoteric health food in the world), all with an eye on the earth. May they prosper and proliferate like wildflowers across our barren land.

> **Rancho Burger.** 5121 Geary Blvd., at 16th Ave. (Richmond).

A wooden plaquefest adorns the walls with talking hot dogs and pies. It's a visual treat with not-too-horrible, bare-bones, fast-food fare. They've kept the cool jukebox and booths, and are managed by a sweet Asian family.

> **Rococoa Faerrie Queen Chocolates.** 415 Castro St., at Market (Castro). ☎ **415/252-5814.**

If a meal could be made of chocolate, then this is your cocoa-bean smorgasbord. It's like the Fairy Godmother on mushrooms. Watch out for the jalepeño fudge.

> **Sam Woh Restaurant.** 813 Washington St., at Grant (Chinatown). ☎ **415/982-0596.**

An infamous Chinese dive up from Grant, open till 3am. Walk through the hot kitchen and up the narrow stairs to the dining rooms. There you're greeted by old Chinese waiters with white-trash attitude and dumbwaiter service. If this doesn't do your Chinatown jones, try **Tong Kee** at 870 Washington, which has less attitude and better food, or the always popular **House of Nanking,** on Kearny near Columbus.

> **Silver Crest Donut Shop and Diner.** 340 Bayshore, south of Army (Bayshore). ☎ **415/826-0753.**

An around-the-clock diner on the more industrial side of town. It's your basic burger, donut, and meat-loaf sort of place, but with really old booths and jukeboxes.

George, the short-order cook who also happens to own the joint, serves up grub from behind his horseshoe counter. Step to the rear to an adjoining bar where George the bartender (same guy) offers the traditional shot of ouzo to first-time offenders.

> **Smart Alec's.** 2355 Telegraph Ave., at Durant (Berkeley). ☎ 510/704-4000.

We don't think much of Telegraph Avenue, and, generally speaking, the sight of wiggy stoners and gutter punks causes us to lose our appetite. But this vegan fast-food joint ain't half bad. In the tradition of McDharma's, Smart Alec's offers vegetarian versions of standard American cuisine—veggie burgers, air-baked french fries, and, instead of a Coke, a fruit smoothie.

> **Spaghetti Western.** 576 Haight St., at Steiner (Lower Haight). ☎ 415/864-8461.

Lower Haight's take on the Old West. People tend to start piling in there pretty early, probably because they haven't gone to sleep yet. The two-egg omelets sometimes come with three eggs. Don't even bother coming on a busy Sunday morning.

> **Stella Pastry.** 446 Columbus, at Green (North Beach). ☎ 415/986-2914.

Sometimes a good hit of sugar will do the trick. This is the Graceland of Italian pastry joints in North Beach—everything's done in excess. Since the forties they've been perfecting sacrapantinas to an orgy of sweetness.

> **SuppenKuche.** 601 Hayes St., at Laguna (Hayes Valley). ☎ 415/252-9289.

We tried on several occasions to eat at this Hayes Valley German restaurant, but always ended up arriving a minute too late. Germans are punctilious about time, even though there are very few Germans who work in this place. When we finally did dine here we discovered that the cooking was not done by Germans, but by Mexicans. Take nothing away from Mexicans, who do most of the cooking at most big city restaurants in the country today, but the food here is not as scrumptious as one would hope from a glance at the meticulously realized German decor. They do have a fine range of German dishes, and the bread is good and hearty, but after you're done, feeling as stuffed as Helmut Kohl, you'll realize why the Germans are not known for world-class cuisine. As with many Hayes Valley restaurants, come here for the look and feel—clean and strong wooden benches and tables, Mittel Europa design touches like the big crucifixes in the corners, and tall steins of bier.

> **Swans Oyster Depot.** 1517 Polk, at California (Polk). ☎ 415/673-2757.

They've been around since the thirties and as far as we're concerned you can skip the frills at the other oyster palaces and just dig in for some fresh fish at this place. And they serve steam beer.

Tip

For Vietnamese in the East Bay, try Le Cheval on 10th and Clay, in Oakland.

> **Tasajara Bakery.** 1000 Cole St., at Parnassus (Cole Valley).
> ☎ 415/664-8947.

The freshest, best bread in the city. There's almost always a line but it's totally worth it for this super-healthy Cole Valley treat.

> **Ti-Couz.** 3108 16th St., at Valencia (Mission). ☎ 415/252-7373.

Still in the Mission, it's a regional French restaurant serving two kinds of crepes: savory or sweet. Totally wig out on building your own crepe from a long list of ingredients. Michael went for a white-chocolate, cheese, mushroom, and orange-sauce crepe with extra fresh cream. If you're lucky, maybe you'll see a puppet show.

> **Tu Lan.** 8 6th St., at Market (Mission). ☎ 415/626-0927.

A sleazy, fluorescent-lit, Vietnamese diner just down from Market Street that is so killer even Julia Child dines here. The open kitchen with counter seating is a grease fest, with flaming pans, crackling sesame oil, and tall stacks of bird-nest noodles. Chow down on portions so huge they're embarrassing. But watch out for the homeless camped in the doorway.

> **Vicolo Pizzeria.** 221 Ivy St., at Franklin (Civic Center). ☎ 415/863-2382.

It's California pizza at it's best. But you pay for it. They've got these great cornmeal crusts with exotic toppings in a very eighties metal-and-glass setting. Something about the bright lighting, the incredibly high quality, and its dreamy location in an alley near the Opera makes us return to Vicolo over and over again.

> **Woodward's Garden.** 1700 Mission St., at Duboce (Mission). ☎ 415/621-7122.

Disciples of Chez Panisse pioneer Alice Waters run this small corner restaurant, strategically if irritatingly located right beneath the 101 freeway and adjacent to busy Division Street. If the noise doesn't get you, the pollution will. The restaurant drowns out the sounds of autos by playing jazz and classical at relatively high volumes, and the food, always fresh and often organic, will more than compensate for whatever damage you are doing to your lungs dining "al fender."

Language

Here is the language of "the good life." Here is the vernacular of "the most beautiful place on earth." Here is the slang of my beloved spiritual home. Portions adapted from Jim Crotty's *How to Talk American* (Houghton Mifflin, 1997).

The Barbary Coast: Legendary name for the Marina and Embarcadero areas of turn-of-the-century San Francisco, when it really was raunchy and bawdy.

Berserkeley: Berkeley, home of the University of California at Berkeley. Because of its legendary history of radical student protest, crazed hippies, and even weirder shenanigans since the sixties, the decade that made it famous.

The Big Four: Collis P. Huntington, Mark Hopkins, Charles Crocker, and Leland Stanford—four robber barons who made their fortune building the Central Pacific Railroad in the late 1800s and whose names live on in major city landmarks (the Huntington Hotel, the Mark Hopkins Hotel, the former Crocker Bank, and Stanford University in Palo Alto).

The Big Game: Annually, Stanford versus Cal in college football. Held the Saturday before Thanksgiving.

The Big One: The inevitable earthquake that will one day level the city and kill us all.

The Bonnie Baker: The Bay to Breakers. San Francisco's "Aren't we wacky? Aren't we zany? Aren't we multi-culti?" road race held every May.

Breeders: Heterosexuals. In general, this city's are the best behaved in North America, owing to the mistaken notion that they are in a distinct minority (even though they represent 75% of the population). The gay ethos is so pervasive here that some straight men unconsciously strive to look and act gay just to fit in. Then again, there are those breeder males who seem intent on being as boorishly obnoxious as possible in order to signal to breeder females that they are not, in fact, "fags." Like all such ploys throughout history, this really turns the "ladies" on.

"Buds, doses": How to greet someone on Haight Street. Alternatively, "bugs and roses."

Buyers club: The Marijuana Buyers Club, where a terminally ill person in this pot-crazed town can buy weed "for medicinal purposes only." A state initiative now makes this practice legal. But, as Jay Leno observes, "If marijuana was truly medicinal, Jerry Garcia would still be alive today."

Café Hairdo: Café Fleurs. Owing to a late-eighties article shot at Fleurs called "Hairdos of Castro Street."

Cal: The University of California at Berkeley. For the rest of the UC system, the town in which the branch is located is cited (e.g., UC Santa Cruz), but not here.

The Cardinal: Nickname for Stanford University's sports teams. Once called the Indians, before political correctness changed all that. Ironically, the Native American who served as the mascot was very disappointed to lose his job because he performed real Indian war dances during games. One of the new names suggested by the student body was the Robber Barons (recalling founder Leland Stanford). It was, of course, rejected by the administration.

Castro clones: Gay look-alikes in denim jeans, work boots, and flannel shirts who prowl the Castro Street bars.

Chinatown express: Muni's no. 38 Geary bus, which heads from Chinatown to "the new Chinatown," the Richmond District. So named because of the large infusion of Asian residents into the Richmond in the early 1980s.

The City: San Francisco—the cyber-gay-hippie-yuppie mecca that is dead set on looking fabulous at all costs. Well, you are, dahling, YOU ARE! However, its image as a tolerant haven for good-natured creative genius is being seriously challenged by the growing ranks of outright mean and abrupt real-estate jerks capitalizing on the tightest rental market in the world. A.k.a. "San Fran." Never ever ever "Frisco."

Coitus Tower: Coit Tower. Shaped like a fire-hose nozzle. Financed by a woman with a big-time fireman fetish. Or so the story goes.

The Comical: The *San Francisco Chronicle,* the biggest joke in town. And, ironically, the one paper everyone reads cover to cover. A.k.a. "The Moronical."

Di-Fi: Dianne Feinstein, the former mayor and current senator, known for shepherding through the ban on automatic assault weapons.

The Emperor: His sartorial Highness, Mayor Willie Brown. A.k.a. "Da Mayor."

Fascist: Anyone to the right of the *San Francisco Bay Guardian.*

Five & Tens: East Bay residents (area code 510).

The 49ers: (1) the early settlers of San Francisco, who came west in 1849 in search of gold in the nearby Sierra Nevada foothills; (2) the local pro-football franchise.

The Freakway: Brad Wiener's term for the Safeway at Church and Market, the most eclectic and culturally diverse supermarket in America. If you want a snapshot of what San Francisco is really all about, linger at the checkout stand here at any hour.

Glamour slammer: The spanking-new jail adjoining 850 Bryant.

The Glass Coffin: Twin Peaks, an over-fifty gay bar on Castro near Market, surrounded by windows.

Goatee Gulch: Columnist Jack Boulware's nickname for South Park, where the young, beat, and invariably goateed assistants to the assistant Web masters hang out and utter profundities such as "We tweaked this and we tweaked that and then whoaaaaaaa!" Also generally applied to the faux Beat thing sweeping the city. A.k.a. "Info Gulch."

Gourmet Gulch: That part of Berkeley's Shattuck Avenue that includes among its pricey shops and restaurants Peet's Coffee and Tea, the Cheese Board Collective, and the restaurant that revolutionized California cuisine, Alice Waters's world-renowned Chez Panisse. A.k.a. "gourmet ghetto."

Haightball: A particularly intense brand of pickup basketball found in the Panhandle near Haight Street.

Harbin: Harbin Hot Springs, the quintessential hippie hot springs up in Middleton, where the Bay Area counterculture goes to chill out amid beautiful mountains, excellent trails, and flabby New Age couples floating each other in the hot pool. A.k.a. "Watsu World," home of the "Watsu People."

Hella: Very, really, excellent, extreme. "I got hella food, you hungry?" "I went hella fast to get here." The signature East Bay term.

Hella sketchy: Really weird or scary.

Herb: The late San Francisco Comical columnist Herb Caen, whose bad puns and provincial observations entertained locals for decades.

The Herpes Triangle: The Golden Gate Grill, the Balboa Café, and the Baja Cantina—three "breeder" pickup bars in Cow Hollow. The only places in town where it's acceptable to order a Coors Light.

The hills and the flats: Two distinct socioeconomic and geographical areas of the East Bay.

Jerry: The late Jerry Garcia, lead singer and guitarist for the signature San Francisco hippie band the Grateful Dead. Not to be confused with "Jerry" Brown, mayor of Oakland.

Joe: Joe Montana, former quarterback for the 49ers. Still deified in these parts as well as in the town of Joe, Montana.

The Jukebox: The Marriott on Mission. A.k.a. "the Wurlitzer."

KGB: Killer Green Bud. A San Francisco, by way of Humboldt County, word for "pot."

The King of Torts: The legendary San Francisco pugilist Melvin Belli, whose main claim to fame (besides his many wives) was defending Jack Ruby, the killer of Lee Harvey Oswald.

L.U.G.: Lesbian Until Graduation. Very East Bay.

The Lexus Freeway: Highway 280 on the Peninsula, a scenic cruise strip for the super-rich of Silicon Valley. A.k.a. "the Mensa Freeway."

Manie (pronounced *mane*-eee): Very crazy. For example, a friend goes to a Sausalito boat party and gets so drunk he's unable to drive home. He asks his friend, who's high on acid, to do the driving instead. Both gentlemen might describe that car ride as rather "manie." Popular in Marin and parts of San Francisco.

The Mayor of Castro Street: Harvey Milk, San Francisco's first openly gay supervisor and charismatic pioneer for gay rights. Along with Mayor George Moscone, he was felled by assassin Dan White.

Mount Tam: The revered Mount Tamalpais, just across the Golden Gate Bridge in Marin County. The Bay Area's answer to Mount Shasta.

Multimedia Gulch: The South Park area south of Market, thought to contain the best and brightest in the burgeoning field of multimedia. See "Goatee Gulch."

Muni: The San Francisco Municipal Railway. Where "service" is a dirty seven-letter word. A.k.a. "Muniserable Railway," because of the nasty, almost sadistic, tone of some of its drivers.

No doubt: A way of agreeing without really listening. It beats "uh-huh."

Nowhere Valley: The Noe Valley neighborhood. "Leave It to Beaver" meets the Isle of Lesbos. So named from its moms-and-strollers Presbyterian provinciality.

The O.J. Projects: What white residents of Potrero Hill call the neighboring projects, where O.J. made his start into a life of violence, deception, and crime.

Pacific Graft and Extortion: PG&E, the local power company. A.k.a. "Pigs, Ghosts, and Elephants."

The Painted Ladies: The row of pastel Victorian homes that line the east side of Alamo Square on Hayes Street Hill. The ultimate San Francisco "photo op," experienced by busloads of European visitors daily.

Polk: A gay hustler sleazoid mecca. Where the married queers from the Castro go to cheat on their husbands.

Practice random kindness and senseless acts of beauty: Like so many cultural innovations of the last four decades, this movement started in the Bay Area— Sausalito, in fact. Anne Herbert wrote these words on a restaurant place mat. They have since become a mantra for do-gooders around the country and the cornerstone of a growing movement known as "guerrilla goodness."

The Pyramid: The TransAmerica Building. The most striking downtown visual landmark.

Rainbow: Rainbow Grocery, one of the last great natural-food cooperatives in America now that corporations dominate the natural-foods industry. Along with Zen Center and "the Freakway," one of the vortexes of city life.

Right on: You know what it means, and it's back in style in the city, but with a distinctly understated slacker pronunciation and delivery.

Sacto: Sacramento, the comparatively conservative and low-key state capital to the north.

St. Maytag: St. Mary's Church, on Geary and Gough. Resembles a washing-machine agitator (a.k.a. "Our Lady of the Spin Cycle").

Sandalistas: An East Bay term for activists in search of a righteous cause. Named after southern Mexico's Zapatista National Liberation Army, whose insurgence reinvigorated an international network of human rights activists who'd been shopping for a cause since the civil wars ended in Nicaragua and El Salvador.

SOMA: South of Market Street. Also known as "south of the Slot," for the cable-car track that used to divide Market Street.

Specific Whites: Pacific Heights, the upscale yuppie part of town.

The Stick: Candlestick Park, a windy, cold, yet beautiful stadium where the 49ers and Giants play. Now called 3Com Park at Candlestick Point after Silicon Valley's 3Com Corporation, part and parcel of the trend away from ballpark names that actually have some emotional resonance with the public.

The Swish Alps: A predominantly gay neighborhood in the hills above the Castro.

Tour de faux pas: Willie Brown's fabled yet ill-fated trip to Paris in November 1996, during which da mayor signed a sister city act with Paris, expanded trade and tourist opportunities, convinced leading AIDS researcher Luc Montagnier to locate a new AIDS research and treatment center in San Francisco, and called 49ers quarterback Elvis Grbek "an embarrassment to humankind" after the team's loss to Dallas (unbeknownst to Brown, Grbek's baby had undergone surgery for spina bifida the day before the game).

The Twelve Tombs: A sixties nickname for the Berkeley dorms.

The Twinkie Defense: The macroneurotic defense plea ("the harmful additives in my junk-food diet made me do it") first used by supervisor and policeman Dan White, the assassin of Mayor George Moscone and gay supervisor Harvey Milk. It worked. Pleading "diminished capacity," White was sentenced to only 7 years and 8 months, the maximum allowable for manslaughter, spawning "the White Night Riot," the largest gay uprising in San Francisco history. Upon his release from prison after five years, Dan White committed suicide, inspiring decades of seriously dysfunctional behavior under the pretext of bad food choices.

The Twins: Vivian and Marian Brown, San Francisco's delightfully campy identical twosome who've come to represent the spirit of carefree consumerism that has now become this city's hallmark.

Wiggin': Stressing or freaking out. Heard mostly in the Haight.

William Hurts: Men who try to get laid by being pitiful, sympathy-inducing wrecks.

The Wine and Cheese Heads: The San Francisco 49ers. As opposed to the Cheeseheads, the Green Bay Packers.

The Wine Country: Mission Street between 5th and 8th, a prominent hangout for winos. A play off the real Wine Country, populated by gourmands and wine connoisseurs, in the Napa Valley.

The Zam: The *San Francisco Examiner,* an afternoon and Sunday paper. Tends to have more hard news than "the Comical" but is less beloved. Published by husband of Sharon Stone, beefy Phil Bronstein.

Museums

> **Barbie Hall of Fame.** 433 Waverly St., at University Ave. (Palo Alto).
☎ **650/326-5841.** Open Tues–Fri 1:30–4:30pm, Sat 10am–noon and 1:30–4:30pm.

Mrs. Evelyn Burkhalter's massive collection of the perky anatomically correct blond doll, with her clothes, accessories, and, like, everything! The museum has it all, from the first Barbie to the present-day physically challenged Barbie (in a wheelchair, no less). This is the largest Barbie collection in the world that dares to open its doors to the public.

> **Capp Street Project.** 525 2nd St., at Federal (SOMA). ☎ **415/256-2900.**

This gallery hosts the most provocative installations in the city, often bringing in a resident artist to completely reformulate the Capp Street space. We especially loved the Glen Seator installation, "Approach," which perfectly duplicated the Capp Street Project facade, including the sidewalk and curb outside, complete with graffiti, potholes, and telephone pole. It caused us to reexamine "the original" with beginner's eyes, and to reevaluate what is meant by private and public space. An amazing work of art in an amazing gallery.

> **Lyle Tuttle's Tattoo Parlor and Museum.** 841 Columbus Ave., at Lombard (North Beach). ☎ **415/775-4991.** Mon–Thurs noon–9pm, Fri–Sat noon–10pm, Sun noon–8pm.

The now retired Lyle displays an interesting collection of early tattoo equipment and designs in this active parlor. Tuttle's decades of inking have seen everyone from Janis Joplin to Cher.

> **Musée Mechanique.** 1090 Point Lobos, behind the Cliff House (Richmond).
☎ **415/386-1170.** Mon–Sun 10am–8pm.

Dozens of antique, mechanical, coin-operated amusement machines. Our favorite is the Unbelievable Mechanical Farm complete with suckling pigs. Around the corner is the Camera Obscura (one of only two left in the United States) and nearby are the eerie old ruins of the Sutro Baths. If it's a full moon, visit the Statue of Dianna in adjacent Sutro Heights Park and witness impromptu pagan rituals.

> **New Langton Arts.** 1246 Folsom St., at 9th (SOMA). ☎ **415/626-5416.** Wed–Sat noon–5pm.

An all-in-one space featuring exhibits, spoken word, theater, film, and performance art. To date they've had their share of controversy, the least of which was *Amnesia,* a show that dealt with in-your-face sexuality. A definite "brains on toast" sort of place.

> **Burlingame Museum of Pez Memorabilia.** 214 California Dr., at Broadway (Burlingame). ☎ **650/347-2301.** www.spectrumnet.com/pez. Tues–Sat 10am–6pm.

A whole museum devoted to Pez dispensers. There's over 280 in all.

> **Takara Sake Factory.** 708 Addison St., at 4th (Berkeley). ☎ **510/540-8250.** Mon–Sun noon–6pm.

We're not big on sake. Sure, it's the perfect warm accompaniment to the cool freshness of sushi, but it doesn't approach the subtle complexity of wine or even beer as a stand-alone drink. Still, the folks at Takara Sake take their rice and plum wines seriously, and offer free tastings from noon to 6pm every day of the week. And it's worth it. For the clean spotless quality of the tasting room. For the one-of-a-kind small museum, which showcases the fascinating wooden tools used in turn-of-the-century sake production. And, yes, for the endless supply of sake, "the happiness you can pour." Try the Ginjo, a premium smooth import, which runs $160 a bottle.

Music Venues

> **Bimbo's 365 Club.** 1025 Columbus, at Chestnut (North Beach). ☎ **415/474-0365.**

Huge, ornate old hall, set up with tables for dinner shows or cleared out for bigger acts. The lobby and bar are from an era of gangsters, not grunge, but varied bookings claim everyone.

Trivia

Both the Beatles and the Sex Pistols gave their last concerts in San Francisco.

> **The Blue Lamp.** 561 Geary, at Jones (Tenderloin). ☎ **415/885-1464.**

One of the few blues bars in The City. Tight, smoky, comfortable lounge.

> **Bottom of the Hill.** 1233 17th St., at Texas (Potrero Hill). ☎ **415/626-4455.** See "Bars, Pubs, and Clubs."

When you tire of the likes of Dracula Milktoast, the Brian Jonestown Massacre, Minnie Pearl Necklace, Full Metal Chicken, The Screaming Bloody Marys, Ovarian Trolley, JFKFC, Fag Bash, Manson-Nixon Line, Heavy Into Jeff, and other recent bands from the S.F. indie music scene, listen to this ultimate cross-generational list of songs about the "city by the Bay."

"Boogie at Russian Hill," John Lee Hooker

"Brother Esau," Grateful Dead

"California Über Alles," Dead Kennedys

"Common Market Madrigal," Jefferson Airplane

"Dock of the Bay," Otis Redding

"Embryonic Journey," Jefferson Airplane

"Fogtown," Michelle Shocked

"Frisco Blues," John Lee Hooker

"Golden Loom," Bob Dylan

"Golden Road to Unlimited Devotion," Grateful Dead

"Grace Cathedral Park," Red House Painters

"Hello San Francisco," Buddy Guy

"I Left My Heart in San Francisco," Tony Bennett

"I Left My Heart in San Francisco," The Residents

"I Think He's Gay," Pussy Tourette

"Jump For Joy," Kingfish

"Kid Charlemagne," Steely Dan

"Luv & Haight," Sly and the Family Stone

"Mean Ole Frisco," Eric Clapton

"Mean Ole Frisco," Arthur Crudup

"Mission in the Rain," Jerry Garcia

"Picasso Moon," Grateful Dead

"Ride Captain Ride," Blues Image

"Russian Hill," Jellyfish

"St. Dominic's Preview," Van Morrison

"San Anselmo," Van Morrison

"San Francisco Bay Blues," Jesse Fuller

"San Francisco Days," Chris Isaak

"San Francisco Nights," Eric Burdon

"San Francisco," Judy Garland

"San Francisco (Be Sure to Wear Some Flowers in Your Hair)," Scott Mackenzie

"San Francisco Fan," Cab Calloway

"San Francisco Mabel Joy," Joan Baez

"She's Your Lover Now," Bob Dylan

"Standing on the Moon," The Grateful Dead

"Tiny Montgomery," Bob Dylan

"Warm San Francisco Nights," Eric Burden

"We Built This City," Starship

"When the Lights Go Down in the City," Journey

> **Deluxe Club.** 1509 Haight, at Ashbury (Haight). ☎ 415/552-6949.

A unique, forties-style swing pad. The bartenders and acts seem like extras from a Russ Meyer flick, and the young crowd plays along. Pervasive is the sexy smell of slicked hair, and the retro attention to detail even extends to suspenders, handbags, and cocktail dresses. Check out St. Vitus Dance, the "Sex Pistols of Swing," when they play.

> **DNA Lounge.** 375 11th St., at Folsom (SOMA). ☎ 415/626-1409.

Great, grungy place to see bands. The large main floor is surrounded by a balcony level that affords a perfect vantage for those who want to watch, play pool, and avoid the pit.

> **Elbo Room.** 647 Valencia St., at 17th St. (Mission). ☎ **415/552-7788.**

Too often crowded, but its popularity is deserved. The tiny area upstairs from the main bar promotes local bands, including top-floor jazz.

> **Paradise Lounge.** 1501 11th St., at Folsom (SOMA). ☎ **415/861-5121.**

Three stages make this the hub of the SOMA club scene. If you find the first floor too cramped by the power crowd, go upstairs to mellow out in the funky upper bar/pool zone.

> **Peacock Lounge.** 552 Haight, at Steiner (Lower Haight). ☎ **415/621-9850.**

By day a club for old lower-Haight blues dudes, this spot turns into a garage-rock pit on weekend nights. The closest thing to seeing a band play at a living-room party.

> **Slim's.** 333 11th St., at Folsom (SOMA). ☎ **415/255-0333.**

One of the top venues for bigger acts. The sound is supreme, and the long hall affords good "checkin' the band" spots. The crowd can vary greatly depending on the act, although the SOMA flair is always there.

Neighborhoods

The San Francisco Bay Area is not only the most beautiful city in America, but also the true home of Hollywood's creatively intelligent elite (Robin Williams, Francis Ford Coppola, Barry Levinson, Sharon Stone, Whoopi Goldberg, Philip Kaufman; Tom Hanks was born in nearby Oakland), as well as literary lights like Evan S. Connell (*Mrs. Bridge*), Barry Gifford (*Wild at Heart,* which was made into the David Lynch film), and Nobel laureate Czeslaw Milosz (*Facing the River: New Poems*). It is often billed as "the city of neighborhoods." Unfortunately, more and more, those neighborhoods are ruled by money, not by community, as the young loft contingent are pricing out whatever vibrant reasonably priced neighborhoods remain. See for yourself.

> **The Avenues (Sunset and Richmond).** Two districts bordering Golden Gate Park from Stanyan Blvd. to the Great Highway. Richmond to the north. Sunset to the south.

San Francisco produces the most original creatives in the West, but it also produces the most normal "Normals," as these two districts attest. You move to **the Sunset** when you want to die on the vine. Culturally, it's the suburbs with a weird, arctic-zone beach life deprived of any sort of sun. People who would rather be in the Midwest but could never get back because they've done too many drugs move here. You can tell a native because they have that dour blank look of the light-deprived. More self-help books sell in the Sunset than anywhere. The pluses: Golden Gate Park and the cold beaches. Minuses: Frank Jordan territory (former S.F. mayor who drew a lot of support from here) and a very low irony quotient (in a city dangerously low as it is).

The Richmond is an old Russian enclave almost completely colonized by Asians. More like a suburb than any part of the city, which is why families dig it.

> **Bernal Heights.** Percita Ave. to Cortland Ave., south of Mission St.

A liberal hillside sanctuary for upper-middle-class whites who don't get nervous being in close proximity to the Mission's Hispanic multitudes. The San Francisco dream without the pedigree and costliness of "Snob Hill."

> **The Castro.** Market St. between Diamond and Church up to 22nd St.

Home of the plug and play "gay demographic." After years of AIDS, and a wide panoply of gay lifestyles and points of view, the Castro still settles for the

Observations

"This place is so small you can't toss a bottle over your head without it hitting someone your ex-boyfriend just slept with."

—Don Baird

"People say they're moving to San Francisco to come out of the closet. Well I'm sorry, they've got it all wrong. San Francisco is the closet! A really big gay closet. If you want to come out of the closet, you'll have to leave San Francisco."

—Cornelius

"I'm straight, I'm married, and the most erotic thing I've ever done is run around the house naked with my wedding ring on!"

—Anonymous straight man living in the Castro

stereotypical mind set of "let's par-teee, girlfriend!!" Even though the real party's moved on, the neighborhood can't get over itself or its self-importance. It remains a Madame Tussaud's of 1970s gay life, with the tired old clichés still actively in place: clones, leather, disco balls, and rainbow flags (in fact, there's a giant rainbow flag waving from a flagpole at Castro and Market—YUK!!). Okay, we get it, the gay/lesbian/bisexual/transgendered movement will forever be indebted to this street. And we'll never forget our first collective moment when we, the denizens of the hinterlands, took our first walk through a totally gay neighborhood. But the best three things about the Castro are Cliff's Variety Store (with a store full of queers who know all about electrical wiring and plumbing), the Castro Theatre, and the 24-hour Walgreens. Otherwise, take your Hot 'N Hunky self and head somewhere real.

> **China Basin.** South of King St. to Army St., west of 280 freeway.

This is one of the last vestiges of unmanicured, ungentrified real estate in town. No Victorians. No parks. Just industrial ruins, open fields, and an old drawbridge that reminds one of Pittsburgh, not San Francisco. From the PacBell Ball Park to 3rd Street redevelopment, China Basin is about to undergo a complete and total makeover, effectively eliminating one of the last funky aspects of the city. Hunters Point, here we come.

> **Chinatown.** Bush St. to Broadway, Stockton St. to Kearny St.

You're angry. You're Chinese. You're a member of the most discriminated-against group in California history. There's no way you're going to blend with those white Anglo-Saxons, who kept your great-grandparents from crossing Market, who treated them as slaves, called them "coolies," and imposed miners' taxes and other indignities. As a result of your aversion, you're permanently stuck in this tourist trap excuse for a community, making a modest income serving chop suey and chow mein to silly rubberneckers. The best you can hope for is that your children's children will learn English and bust out of the Chinatown-Richmond ghetto for good.

> **Civic Center.** McAllister St. to Hayes, east of Gough to Market.

While the standard tourist knows Civic Center as the home of impressive San Francisco cultural landmarks like the **War Memorial Opera House,** 301 Van Ness Ave. (☎ 415/864-3330), the **Veteran's Building,** 401 Van Ness (☎ 415/392-4400)—which houses not only the Herbst Theatre but is where the United Nations charter was signed—the **Louise M. Davies Symphony Hall,** Grove and Van Ness (☎ 415/864-6000), the fabulous new (if low on shelf space) **Public Library,** Larkin and Grove (☎ 415/557-4400), and the "Taj Mah Willie," the expensively revamped **City Hall,** 400 Van Ness Ave. (☎ 415/554-4000), those who live here realize that the character of Civic Center is shaped primarily by the countless street freaks who call this area "home." It's often enjoyable to sit on the desecrated green grass and watch the frenetic tweakers rush off in response to one imagined crisis or another. Unfortunately, it's a pathetic commentary on the lack of courage in City Hall that nothing is ever done to fully resolve a glaring problem that sits right on its doorstep.

> **Downtown Financial District.** Market St. east of Powell St.

You're boring. You're white. You work in something vague like "financial services." You go to "singles bars." You used to live in the Marina District. You now live here.

> **Fisherman's Wharf.** On the bay, at the foot of Embarcadero.

If you are a typical San Francisco tourist, you will head here. And you will enjoy it—for the views, for the fish mongers, and, if you are a little savvy, for the Medieval Dungeon (107 Jefferson St., at Mason), a rather graphic re-creation of 140 torture devices. Locals find more than a little irony in the placement of the Dungeon at the Wharf, a place they rarely, if ever, visit. What is never made clear to tourists is that Fisherman's Wharf is not really an active wharf, nor is it used very much by fisherman. It is, however, a great place to have fun with the tourists. After disembarking from our eventful tour of Alcatraz, dressed, naturally, in full prison drag, we were propositioned by several happy tourists, eager to give us tens and twenties if we would pose for a photograph. There's something heartwarming about these people—so easy to please, so hungry for any sign of San Francisco eccentricity, without a clue on where to really find it. As a public service, if you stumble upon a sweet happy-go-lucky tourist, do the bodhisattva thing and steer them to this guidebook.

> **The Haight.** Upper Haight: Haight St. and adjacent area west of Buena Vista Park. Lower Haight: Haight St. and adjacent area east of Divisadero to Webster.

The Summer of Love street that will never ever be able to get another life. Why? Because three decades later its commercial success stems from reinventing the sixties over and over and OVER again. As the birthplace of Flower Power and the Dead, it's evolved into a big nauseating pig trough, including burnouts, skinheads, and loads of shoppers, who are confronted with the same ethical quandary on almost every block: Do I enable this burnout loser in his obvious addiction or do I tell him to get a freakin' life?! There are two Haights. The lower is where you get gritty, shoot dope, and hang. The upper is where you spend cash, cruise by car or foot, and panhandle for the cash you will need to shoot dope and hang on lower Haight.

Coda: For a more historical view of the neighborhood, we recommend **The Haight-Ashbury Flower Power Walking Tour,** Tuesdays and Saturdays and by appointment (call ☎ **415/863-1621**).

> **Hunters Point.** East of 3rd St., south of Evans Ave.

You're black. You're depressed. Your granddad used to work in the Naval

Observation

"Buds, doses."

—Every fifth person on Haight

Shipyards during World War II. Life here has sucked ever since. Jobs are few. Half your neighbors are on welfare. Gangs control the streets. Your son, if he's lucky, has a concession gig at 3Com. You elected Willie Brown because he promised jobs, a new ballpark, and a train line. You're cautiously hopeful, though you're bound to get screwed again.

> **Manillatown.** Kearny between Columbus and Market.

Only diehard long-term San Franciscan activists remember that the stretch of Kearny between Columbus and Market comprised the largest Filipino enclave in the city, centered primarily around the International Hotel at Jackson and Kearny. Soon there will be a Filipino-American museum on the spot of the old hotel, plus a new hotel, hopefully to house some of the residents evicted when the last hotel was demolished back in 1978.

> **The Marina (a.k.a. "Breederville").** North of Lombard St., west of Van Ness Ave.

Come here when you're ready to come down from your hip and refined San Francisco high and confront the folks who increasingly make up the dominant constituency of this town. If you drop your judgments, there's lots to experience here. There's the nightly breeder pickup scene in Cow Hollow. There's breeder-ball (a.k.a. volleyball) on Crissy Field or further down near the yacht club. There's breeder men's basketball at Moscone Park—lots of Bruce Willises in training there. And breeder bonding at the nearby Safeway. If you miss them here, you are now likely to find plenty of their ilk all over town, including North Beach, the Financial District, SOMA, and, yes, even the Castro (well, just on Halloween). Chug, chug, chug, chug!!!!!

> **The Mission District.** Mission St. and adjacent area going south of Duboce Ave. and 101 Skyway.

South of the border but north of L.A., it's the ultimate Hispo-hipster melting pot. "The Mission" was an Irish Catholic neighborhood with a distinctive New York accent until Mexican Catholics moved in and converted Mission Street into a kinder, gentler Tijuana, with the cheapest lamps, sofa beds, and rents in town. Original Mission District highlights abound, including Red Dora's Bearded Lady, Muddy Waters, the Roxie Theatre, Bombay Bazaar, the Elbo Room, and Esta Noche (the hard-core Latino transvestite bar). However, the main commercial buzz these days is on Valencia, which in a short seven years has become the trendiest strip of cafes, bars, restaurants, and clubs in town. It's comical to see yuppie diners slumming it on Valencia while fresh vomit stains the sidewalks from the indigenous derelicts.

> **Multimedia Gulch.** Townsend St. to Folsom St. between 2nd and 4th sts.

Media term originally applied to the digital start-ups in early-nineties South Park—essentially Townsend to Folsom and 2nd to 4th. Now, due to the expansion of the S.F. Internet industry, the term is applied to the entire SOMA area, which includes such successful Internet companies as Macromedia (makers of Shockwave and other leading Internet tools). See "South Park," and "New Media Gulch."

> **New Media Gulch.** Between the 101 and the 280, south of Townsend St. to 17th St.

A more hip, though less expensive, locale for digital start-ups, in the south Mission, between SOMA and Potrero Hill. A similar South Park–like cafe and restaurant scene is springing up. Popular hangouts include the **Atlas Cafe,** 20th and Alabama (☎ **415/648-1047**), **Blowfish Sushi To Die For,** 2170 Bryant St. (☎ **415/285-3848**), and the much more reasonable **Hung Yen,** 3100 18th St,, between Harrison and Folsom (☎ **415/621-8531**), an authentic Vietnamese restaurant.

> **Nob Hill.** Leavenworth St. to Stockton St., Jackson to Bush.

You either own a ridiculously high-priced condo across from the cathedral or live in a modestly priced building a few blocks down the street. Such is the schizophrenic character of "Snob Hill," home of several notable San Francisco landmarks: Grace Cathedral, the Fairmont Hotel, the Mark Hopkins, and, of course, those cable cars.

> **Noe Valley.** Noe St. and adjacent area from Douglas to Dolores St.

Known as designer baby buggy–ville, with more baby buggies per capita than any other neighborhood in town, it's the best area for spotting post-sixties middle-aged professionals who finally decided to do that family thing. Either that or Mission burnouts who finally got their life together and moved up the hill. If the omnipresence of political correctness doesn't make you puke on the pavement then you might actually enjoy a stroll down 24th.

> **North Beach.** Columbus Ave. and adjacent area going toward the bay.

Welcome to the Italian Disneyland and home of City Lights bookstore. Little Italy, as it's affectionately called by tour guides, has got the charm of really fancy toilet paper in a run-down boarding house. If you need your Italian pastry, Italian coffee, and Italian gelato, you live here. Even the streetlights have Italian stripes on them. Sure, there are lots of Italian restaurants, but the residents are mostly Chinese. The old Italians are either dead or alcoholics who never come out of their rooms.

> **Pacific Heights.** Broadway and adjacent sts. west of Van Ness Ave. to Presidio Park.

A matching linen, crystal, and china sort of neighborhood. It takes a trust fund, really deep pockets, or a corporate expense account to live in this postcard-perfect village on a hill up from the Marina. It's so clean you'll want to take off your shoes lest you track in dirt from the Tenderloin. The most deranged, bloodthirsty panhandlers can be found at Pacific Heights's teller machines. Even so, the streets are relatively safe, as evidenced by the many late-night single women walking their dogs.

> **Potrero Hill.** South of 17th St. between 101 and 280 freeways.

The neighborhood of choice for radical chic liberals who are racist at heart. If you don't believe us, just watch the smiles disappear when a few homies walk the street. An elite hillside island, it has astounding views, and is filled with transplanted bohemians and increasing numbers of Marina scum who don't realize there's a gun in their back. That's because on the south side of the hill, just out of sight, is the city's biggest project, where Orenthal James Simpson got his start. The white residents of Potrero Hill live a comfy existence dining on gourmet pizza and Napa Merlot. Meanwhile, the poverty time bomb ticks.

> **Russian Hill.** From Pacific to Bay and Polk to Mason.

Nob Hill's quieter sister, without the razzle-dazzle hotel scene, but with more extravagant gardens and stylish high-rise apartments. Plus, the much-heralded Lombard Street, the *second* most crooked street in the city (Vermont on Potrero Hill is number one). There's still lots of old white money up here, but Chinatown has taken over the east flank and is moving in for the kill.

> **SOMA.** South of Market from 1st to 12th sts.

You want to be in New York but you're not, so that's why SOMA is for you. Hell, it even sounds sorta like SoHo. Oddly enough, there's nothing even remotely New York about the area, other than the clubs, loft theaters, and wide, flat streets near old piers. Once cheap, it's now overpriced but still an acceptable address for artists who don't want to deal with the Mission, or, more likely, for Silicon Valley gazillionaires who don't want to acknowledge they work in San Jose.

Originally a swamp, then a slum, then a hotbed of multimedia, SOMA is quickly emerging as one of the cultural vortexes of the city, as the Yerba Buena Complex (1993), SFMOMA (1995), Sony Entertainment Center, Mexican Museum, and Jewish Museum all attest.

> **South Park.** South Park Ave. bet. 2nd and 3rd. sts.

Rarefied, full-of-itself neighborhood, in the transition zone between SOMA and downtown, where many Internet players allegedly reside. The most famous is, of course, *Wired* and its offspring (*Hot Wired, Wired News,* Suck.com, et. arrogant alia), but there's also Ziff-Davis, NetNoir, and allegedly a host of others we don't care much about. Frankly, we've never quite bought into the hype around this tiny 'hood, and beyond the *Wired* brats, are often hard-pressed to name a culturally compelling company that has come out of it.

Still, if you're looking for the S.F. equivalent of the industry bar and restaurant scenes of L.A., come to that sweet oval green space known as South Park. **Ristorante Ecco,** 101 S. Park St., between Bryant and Brannan and 2nd and 3rd (☎ **415/ 495-3291**) and the **South Park Cafe,** 108 S. Park St., between Bryant and Brannan (☎ **415/495-7275**), both cater to the goateed digeratti set.

› Telegraph Avenue. Berkeley.

Everything that was annoying, disgusting, and just flat-out lame about the sixties lingers and loafs along this thoroughfare south of the Berkeley campus, which is the source of this street's perverse appeal. Interspersed among newer, cleaner, more homogenized eateries and cafes and the perennial grunge are some of the old stand-bys—**Le Mediterraneum,** where a fat, whacked Wiccan woman wears a button that says "weird and proud" and sells her mediocre poetry books at a card table at the front; **Moe's,** the old literary hangout featured in *The Graduate,* now sucked of all its character by a recent renovation; **Cody's,** still a decent bookstore (one of the first in the country to carry *Monk*), which, in answer to the Modern Library's list of the 100 Best Books of the Century, has a sheet asking patrons to list their own picks—naturally, prominent members of the oppressed womyn of colour pantheon, Alice Walker and Toni Morrison, have books near the top, along with lesbo leading-light Gertrude Stein; the **Annapuna** head shop, around since 1969 and looking it; two excellent music stores, **Amoeba** and **Rasputin; Blondie's Pizza,** near where Jim had an acid meltdown in 1984 (the workers wear tie-dye tees); and an assortment of fried Ken Kesey and Wavy Gravy clones and other messed up casualties of over three decades of anarchy, giving the street the feel of a Dead concert gone awry.

› The Tenderloin. East of Van Ness Ave., south of Geary Blvd. to Market St.

West of downtown, it's just what it sounds like: a tender loin. Taking its name either from a prewar practice of bribing cops with tenderloins of beef to overlook the rampant sex and gambling scene, or because cops who worked this dangerous beat were paid higher salaries (and thus could afford choice cuts of beef), it's S.F.'s contribution to high-density urban blight. You'll get everything you want and more in this 'hood, including drive-by shootings, $25 blow jobs, abundant crack, and really cheap restaurants. Outside of Bangkok, the best transvestites in the world work the streets of the Tenderloin. And only a scant few blocks from the tourist scene around Union Square.

> **Western Addiction (er, Addition).** East of Divisadero St. to Buchanan, south of Geary Blvd. to Hayes St.

You're either an old black family on your way out, a hipster just passing through, or a middle-class yuppie looking for a bargain on real estate. Your neighborhood runs the gamut from the pristine San Francisco Zen Center to the smackheads outside the Horseshoe Cafe to the Panhandle of Golden Gate Park. Nagging at your soul is the realization that you live in a real-estate designation, not a community.

Parks and Nature

> **Dolores Park.** 18th St. to 20th St. bet. Dolores and Church (Mission).

This is one of those parks with an ongoing identity crisis. Sloping up towards 20th Street with one of the most sweeping views of downtown and the Bay Bridge, it has an odd mix of neighbors. On its western edge is the Castro. On any given warm sunny day the gay boys are out in full force improving upon their tanning-booth tans. Meanwhile, the Yuppies to the south haul their dogs off of Noe Hill to poop and scoop. From the east come the Mission hipster contingent with their multiple piercings and freak-show tattoos; for God's sake let these folks through cause you know they need some sun. And then you have the Mission Hispanic moms and a zillion kids deconstructing the kiddies playground, plus a mixture of blacks and whites going at it on the basketball court, with maybe a Mormon tandem watching on the sidelines waiting for a slip in someone's self-esteem. One big San Francisco melting pot. Only thing missing are the Chinese.

But before you start thinking utopia, here come the homeboys to ruin everyone's party. Long before all the respectable citizenry took to the park, this was a sure place to get mugged or gang-banged, or to score a bag. The gangs still hang, especially after Mission High, on the north side of the park, lets out. There's heavy police patrol around the perimeter, a strong indication you still want to think twice about strolling through the park late at night. Back in the mid-eighties it was one of the most likely places to find a dead body, as Michael Monk did one early morning on his jog around Dolores Park. Dead as in overdose from the readily available heroin down on 16th Street and Valencia. The body count has gone down but the needles are still to be found.

> **Golden Gate Park.** West of Stanyan between Fulton St. and Lincoln Way (Sunset/Richmond).

Yeah, so, it's the most beautiful city park in the country. Landscaped up the kazoo with millions of tax dollars spent keeping its green hills from returning to their original state, which was sand dunes. Everyone loves this park. The Richmond Jews love the park, the Asians love the park, the Russians love the park, the UCSF med students love the park, the blue-haired flower sniffers love this park. But no matter how often you've traipsed through the rose garden, toured the Conservatory of Flowers, gone artistic in the De Young Museum, rowed a boat on Stow Lake, or thrown rocks at the Buffalo past Spreckels Lake, you cannot really know Golden Gate Park until you've harvested some 'shrooms. Psylocybin, that is. Altered states. Hippie chicks. Groovy, man. 'Shrooms grow wild throughout "the Park" (thanks to a little help from some friends), which is the main reason Golden Gate Park will forever be immortalized in Michael Monk's mind as the place where his Summer of Love really did begin. Back in the day, on any given day, this is where you'd find several thousand freaks completely stoned on multiple doses of acid, peyote, or the aforementioned 'shrooms, literally frying their sockets seeing God, angels, and the park's hallucinogenic plant life that makes funny sounds in the wind. You had love-ins, you had drum circles, you had people in tents, people in turbans, naked people in long big daisy chain snake lines with knots of flowers bunched in their lice-infested hair dancing madly across the park making love to the big pimp god and his holy rollers up on high. You had the park carousel spinning like a wild mythological nightmare, it's ponies taking on Goliath proportions, with longhairs scaring off the little kids. The butchered amputee limbs of the coral trees took on threatening postures summoning up visions of deformed gladiators from some foreign world. Every tree, shrub, and blade of grass took on a personality during those trips. Countless barefoot wanderings toward the beach became epic journeys of the soul from which you'd later proclaim "I made the beach!" Having survived a solid summer of tripping through Golden Gate Park, Michael Monk will never, ever be able to walk through those grounds again with a straight face. Neither should you. Bag some 'shrooms.

> **Jack Early Park.** On Grant, Between Chestnut and Francisco sts. (Telegraph Hill).

On the east side of Grant, climb the stairs to this thin tiny park with a sweeping view of both bridges. Peek down into neighboring windows and watch rich people pick their noses.

> **Presidio.** East entrance at Lombard and Lyon (Marina District).

There's so much current debate about what to do with the Presidio, but really the solution is quite simple: Bring it back to the roots of the settlement but with a postmodern PC twist, featuring an upscale gourmet restaurant called Acorns, serving Acorn Soup from acorns hand-cracked and blended by the descendants of the original Ohlone Indians. A brew pub called Padres, in honor of the 21 missions scattered up and down the El Camino Real, featuring beers of Spain and Mexico, brewed by descendants of the original settlers and first converted Christians, the

Ohlone Indians. A gambling hall featuring all manner of games of chance, including the Native American game of sticks, run by the descendants of the original settlers of San Francisco, the aforementioned Ohlone Indians.

> **Rose Garden.** On Euclid, between Eunice and Rose (Berkeley).

Though nothing compared to Portland's impeccably well maintained Rose Test Gardens, this smaller, looser, less vibrant, amphitheater-shaped Berkeley rose garden still is a welcome retreat for many, including Julia "Rose" Dalzell, who used to play Pooh Sticks by Strawberry Creek at the bottom of the garden. A tunnel under Euclid goes to Codornices Park—full of nannies with their charges on weekdays, third world on the weekends. Adjoining the rose garden is the Gertrude Jekll tennis court. There might be a "there" there, but we keep changing our minds.

Sex

With a sexual diversity unmatched by any other Western city outside Amsterdam, San Francisco carries the legendary sexual proclivities of the Barbary Coast, Beats, hippies, and gays into the 21st century without a trace of shame. For many outsiders, a trip to "The City" is synonymous with debauchery. Given the preponderance of North Beach strip clubs, Polk Street and SOMA video book stores, city-wide gay sex clubs, dildo shops, porn theaters, and the nation's only sex institute (where you can get a degree in Sexology), San Francisco definitely lives up to its name as "Sin City," though it's still a lot easier to get unpaid action as a gay man or woman than as a hetero guy.

> **Berkeley Steamworks.** 2107 4th St., at Addison St. (Berkeley).
☎ 510/845-8992.

Established in 1976, this is the only full-service gay bathhouse in the Bay Area that survived the AIDS-era shutdowns. Tucked away in an industrial neighborhood, this sprawling complex is a no-holds-barred, down and dirty sex emporium with nearly a hundred private rooms, sauna, Jacuzzi, steam room, and a huge maze called the Outback where all sorts of group groping goes on in the dimly lit halls. As a sensible concession to the ongoing AIDS crisis, there are ample safe-sex resources, condoms, and workshops to educate the promiscuous male.

> **Club Eros.** 2051 Market St., at Church (Upper Market). ☎ 415/864-3767.

This is the cleanest, best-lit sex club in the city for gay and bisexual men, with the occasional lesbo girl party thrown into the mix. While most sex clubs in San

I can say with confidence: San Francisco still leads the way in sexual perversity. Upon my arrival here, I was given a site-specific sleaze tour of where to go to have sex. Within 24 hours I'd been invited to three orgies, saw two performance artists take off their clothes, bare their souls, and share some bodily fluids, and then met the queen of erotica herself, Susie Bright. As far as I can tell, *sex* is the main selling point of this town. Not computers. Not tourism. It's almost pathetic to watch these denizens of the Midwest, Asia, and Germany flock here and settle for the Wharf, the Bridge, and Chinatown when they could be *balling their brains out*. Go figure! If they'd only peer into history they'd learn about the Barbary Coast origins of the town. There was a time, during the gold rush, when San Francisco was the biggest fuck-fest since Rome. More than a century later, it still is.

It's easier to get laid here than in any town in the United States, especially if you're gay, or at least open to it. And for all the residents who may disagree, go check out all points east of here and you'll see what I mean. My first honorary dinner party included an extravagant Saturnalia for dessert. The classic San Francisco handshake involves shaking below the belt. Here, sexual identity moves far beyond the convenient labels. The paradox of gender is thrown out the window. Whether you arrive gay, straight, bi, or transsexual, San Francisco sets the stage for a total redefinition of your sexual being. And it lends an air of support and acceptance to whatever bold experiment you want to try. For example, there are more surgically made penises in this town than anywhere in America. There are more silicone implants on boys than girls. And there are more sex clubs, sex shops, open-house orgies, and sex in alleys here than in all of North America. AIDS has transformed the experiment, but not halted it. Safe sex has become an art form. Like water making its way down hill, the residents of San Francisco are committed to finding their way to orgasm, no matter what course they have to take.

I like that. It makes for compelling eye contact and creates that slippery edge. That's why we call it the Amsterdam of the West. You can get anything you want, if you only take a look.

—Michael Monk

Francisco depend on raunch and anonymity to attract their patrons, the glass-plated doors of Eros open right onto busy Market Street across from the Freakway (i.e., the legendary Safeway). The congenial, communal atmosphere inside feels more like an upbeat health club than a den of iniquity. There is a European steam room, a sauna, and showers, as well as the requisite maze and playrooms. Towels are provided, as the clothes *must* go off. Nonsexual massage therapists are always on call and special events are held throughout the week. Wednesday nights are for the hirsute crowd when the "Bears" turn out in force.

> **Good Vibrations.** 1210 Valencia St., at 23rd St. (Mission). ☎ **415/974-8980.**

This is the most sex-positive, progressive dildo shop in the land. Why? Because it's owned and run by chix. From vibrators to butt plugs, thigh harnesses to nipple clamps, Good Vibes always has "the right tool for the job." The staff can be extremely helpful, providing lots of explicit sex education without a trace of shame. Staffer Nao had us down on all fours in doggie collars. Their motto: "If you want something done right, do it yourself." Be sure to check out their vibrator museum.

> **The Institute for the Advanced Study of Human Sexuality.** 1523 Franklin St., at Bush (Pacific Heights). ☎ **415/928-1133.** www.iashs.edu.

Opened in 1976, the institute is one of the world's only accredited schools of sexology, with extensive libraries and academic training for budding sexologists. They have the largest collection of sexual artifacts in the world and have archived an immense storehouse of contemporary sexological materials, including books, porn magazines, porn videos, and films. They gained notoriety by offering cutting-edge classes such as the "fuck-o-rama," which projected hundreds of explicit and erotic images at the same time across sixteen screens in an attempt to challenge one's biases. Open to the public.

> **O'Farrell Theatre.** 895 O'Farrell St., at Polk St. (Tenderloin). ☎ **415/776-6686.**

Opened since 1969, this is the Carnegie Hall of public sex in America. Riding the sixties "free love" wave that crashed over the city, The Mitchell Brothers launched this wildly successful theater as a movie palace to showcase their adult films, including the sensational Marilyn Chambers in *Behind the Green Door* (1971). In 1976 they launched a totally nude revue to the consternation of city fathers (who ordered the dancers to put on panties at least). Also in the 1970s, Hunter Thompson was their night manager.

The Mitchell Brothers were to strip clubs what Larry Flynt is to publishing—unrelenting advocates of smut. As a result, they often found themselves in court. The last court date was the 1991 trial of Jim Mitchell for the murder of his younger, drug-addled brother, Artie. It seems Jim was found walking a few blocks away from the home of a very dead Artie. Jim had a rifle in one pant leg and a pistol strapped beneath his jacket. Jim Mitchell was found guilty of manslaughter, but is now a free man.

These days the O'Farrell showcases their exotic strippers on a set of stages called the Kopahagen, Ultra Room, Green Door Room, and New York Live. Though their

(continued on page 422)

Interview:

Carol Queen,

Doctor of Sexology

From her small-town roots in Glide, Oregon, to her newly acquired doctorate in Sexology, Carol Queen, the saucy, seductive San Franciscan educator, has strived for two decades to make a sex-positive mark in a sex-negative world. In the last decade Carol has been writing, speaking, lecturing, and teaching in various contexts about sexual-diversity issues. She's known within the sex-worker community, has done peep shows, S&M, prostitution, and explicit posing. She's authored or edited several books, including *Exhibitionism for the Shy, Switch-hitters, Real Live Nude Girls,* and *Pomosexual.* Her most recent work, *Bend Over Boyfriend: An Adventurous Couples' Guide to Male Anal Pleasure,* is intended to teach women how to penetrate their men with strap-ons. "Let me show you with my body as well as my brain," she is apt to say.

As the Director of Continuing Education at Good Vibrations, on the board of advisors of San Francisco's Sex Information hot line, and as one of San Francisco's wittiest sex researchers, Dr. Queen (yes, it's her birth name) certainly deserves a pedestal in the Aphrodite Hall of Fame. Given the context of her refreshing liberality, it comes as no surprise that her path to sexual enlightenment traversed a road rich in experience and personal insight.

Carol: How I got here was by growing up in a very small town. Knowing for sure that I was from Mars. I mean, actually, I think that's a pretty good upbringing for an adventurous and unusual child. Because you get to learn early on that you're going to be a little different from the people around you and you might as well run with that. I came out as bisexual when I was 15. As a lesbian when I was 17. Mainly because there was no support of bisexual community that I had access to at that point. And if I wanted to follow my fascinations for girls, I had to be a dyke to do it. And so I was for ten years. And I was politically active in that community (Eugene, Oregon), and pretty much landed with both feet on the ground. Which really helped me politicize sexual issues. It also introduced me to a notion of identity politics. And its limitations. Which is some of what I've done in the nineties. Sort of both explore and honor our sexual identities and also help to raise consciousness about the fact that just knowing what someone's sexual identity is isn't necessarily going to be enough in terms of forming coalitions. In the eighties, in addition to getting my degree in sociology, which also gave me a social-cultural vantage point to look at these issues, I also started to do AIDS work. And it was through AIDS work that I realized that this business of saying I was a lesbian was all well and good, but I loved and cherished many men, many of whom I was on the verge of potentially losing. And that sort of brought me back up to the notion of bisexuality and that I wasn't really honoring my full sexuality by just calling myself a dyke. And that brought me back to San Francisco. I've lived in the Bay Area now for about thirteen years. So, I can't quite imagine living anywhere else.

Monk: How would you define the current sexual climate of San Francisco?

Carol: Well, I definitely see that San Francisco, in the last five years or so, has undergone a pretty striking change. Not just the art and sexuality communities. It's really been influenced by Silicon Valley money. South of Market, which used to be a playground of the sexual underground and then a hip artist space, is now condo-izing about as fast as anybody can manage to throw up buildings. The expense of the city is really difficult for people who live on the margins economically, as well as culturally and sexually. The fact that at one time you could live fairly cheaply in San Francisco and also do your art and your work and affiliate

>interview

with a lot of other people who were somewhat like you or, at least, somewhat interesting to connect with, I really would say that those days are compromised. And the sex community to me feels in some way as though it's dispersing. Partly because those organizations and clubs that had leather gatherings or sex parties or what have you, they are having a harder and harder time finding places that they can rent and occupy. There is still a lively sort of polymorphism community centered around the San Francisco sex scene. So we are in some sense increasingly serving the mainstream more than we have in the past. I think people come expecting a particular kind of San Francisco sexual culture and are surprised to see how many mainstream people there are. But San Francisco, nevertheless, is still a place in the country where, for example, a task force on prostitution could sit for two years, be taken fairly seriously by the media and the citizens of the city, and come out saying that it recommended decriminalization of prostitution. I don't know that there are very many cities in the United States now where that would, in fact, happen. And so the sex-worker community is still politically engaged. So that does still make San Francisco a form of mecca for others. And what I would hope is that San Francisco now is exporting its politicized and artistic sexual culture to cheaper cities. The different sorts of sexual minority organizing that happened in the sixties and seventies in San Francisco happened in the seventies and the eighties everywhere else. So I don't see that it's going to lose its strength in that respect.

Monk: More than most cities, San Francisco can be distinctly defined by the decades. The Beats came out of North Beach in the fifties. The hippies out of the Haight in the sixties. In the seventies the Castro spawned the gay movement. The eighties San Francisco Bay Area certainly cultivated the digital revolution. Now, with the whole emphasis on Internet and community, is the overall hallmark of nineties San Francisco more of a culmination of all previous decades?

Carol: I think that each community and movement was informed and inspired by the movement that proceeded it in many, many respects. I think the alternative sexual culture that we think of as epitomized by the hippies still had an awful lot of Beat involvement. And, of course, we can think of somebody like Allen Ginsberg, who was an avatar of all of those movements in many ways, especially the first three. And so there were always people who had roots in the social movement or community preceding the one that's most active in any given time period. And I know that one of the things that's been most extraordinary for me moving to San Francisco is that I've gotten to meet a lot of those people. Talk to them about what it was like in the decade that they're best known for. And find out what they think of the changes that occurred. And so I also think it's sort of a pre-millennial coming together of tribes. In a lot of ways the Beat, the hippie or free love, the gay freedom, and the digital and artistic freedom movements have all attacked what Bob Dylan called the gray-flannel dwarf. The person in the center who lives life in a certain mainstream way in order to have certain privileges and one of those privileges is sort of the freedom of not being noticed. And, of course, one of the things that I know from the kind of work I do is that the gray-flannel dwarfs go for the Misters and the Ms. Because the women have joined the gray-flannel–dwarf class thanks to the work that feminism has done. Maybe not what it had in mind to begin with, but that's been one of the effects. Those people also are sort of struggling with their own sexual issues and their own sense of limitation and fear and fright about going too far. I think that's always been true and it's now possible for the extreme sexual players to sort of turn back and give a little bit of education and support. Sort of a hand up to the people initially we thought of as our polar opposites. Those people don't do any of these things in their bedrooms. They're frightened and they want to be middle class. I think that's beginning to break down to some degree.

"Anything that can make a person go from one orgasm to eight, I think deserves respect."

Monk: If there was a defining moment in your life in San Francisco, what would it have been?

Carol: Well, my trimester at the institute, three things happened in pretty rapid succession. So if I can condense those into one moment. Because they were all very interrelated and worked in separate, interconnected ways on my psyche to sort of shoot me in a different direction than I had been going before. I entered the institute still lesbian-identified. Although I was a lesbian-identified bisexual, or however we were terming it there in the late eighties, I had become sexual with men again but not very much, and I didn't know exactly where to be with all of that. And in rapid succession at the institute three things happened. I heard the term "sex positive" for the first time. And many people now have heard the term sex positive and maybe aren't even thinking very hard about what it means. To me the term sex positive automatically makes me think of the term sex negative. From that I've had to struggle to get more okay about sexuality. To fight with the people around me who aren't okay with my kind of sexuality. To look at the ways that the laws and mores of this country reinforce sex negativity in many, many respects. And so it automatically for me opens up a deep suitcase of the tangled spaghetti sex culture that we all live within, none of us being able to completely separate ourselves away from the straighten-up-and-fly-right culture that wants to mold us into those gray-flannel dwarfs. And so that really got me going. Just the term. And it's one reason that I included the term in the subtitle of *Real Live Nude Girls.* I want to let it be known that there's an alternate way of thinking of sexuality that isn't contextualized only in the gay movement or only among swingers or whatever, that there's some overarching. A really philosophical way of thinking about sex that has a lot of implications if we delve into it.

Two, I sat through the fuck-o-rama. The fuck-o-rama is sixteen or more separate screens, video and 16-millimeter projection and slides going on all at the same time. It's an educational tool at the institute. The fuck-o-rama shows so many images, so many diverse explicit and erotic images at the same time, that the brain can't process and recognize all of them at once consciously, but you get it all, nevertheless. And it's sort of a booster rocket for a person to recognize what their biases and freak-outs are. And we rarely get that. You know, it's part of the legacy of identity politics to separate people out into subcommunities. To try to convince us that we don't have as much in common with the people over there in that subgroup as in our own subgroup. And the fuck-o-rama just blasts through all that. And the images are changing all the time. The slides click on, click off. The 8-millimeter loop runs out and they start a new one of something else. It's a good half hour. And with music playing in the background. And in the fuck-o-rama, I saw pictures of dicks on the wall. Pretty big. Moving. Doing things. And I realized that I had never kept my eyes open and looked at a penis for any length of time in my entire life. I had sex with plenty of men in high school and college. Never kept my eyes open. Now, why not? I thought of myself as a relatively sexually adventurous woman when I was 16 years old. Why didn't I keep my eyes open? That sort of played into the whole notion of what I was thinking about sex positively, and let me understand, in this really supportive and educational environment, that I was carrying around my own freak-outs. Fears. Assumptions. Biases. And if I started to unpack those, I would be better off.

Third, I went to the first ever Jack- and Jill-Off party, where I got to see sexual diversity on the hoof, not just on the wall. What I remember about that Jack- and Jill-Off was, one, that in sitting on a sofa, playing with myself, having people all around me playing with parts of me that didn't usually get played with while I was playing with myself alone, watching a semicircle of guys jacking off, say 6 feet away from me, I became multiply orgasmic for the first time in my life and it was clearly about exhibitionism, voyeurism. More stimulation than usual. All the things that people go to a sex party to experience. And I had no idea that all those things were deeply implicated in my own eroticism because I hadn't had a chance to explore them before. But now I knew. And anything that can make a person go from one orgasm to eight, I think deserves respect. And further exploration. So that led me into the work and play that I have done in group-sex environments and group-safe-sex environments because not only was it an orgy, it was an orgy with great purpose. And I've continued to do some of that work with Robert, my partner. And it let me know how important exhibitionism was to me. Which led me directly to school.

So all of those things taken together happened within probably a span of two weeks. Close enough to a moment historically. It really let me see a vision of sexual possibility that had to do with not drawing lines, but erasing them. Respecting difference, but letting it be all around one to give yourself more options. To inform what you choose to do even with the things that you don't choose to do. All of those things it seems to me can be looked at on the one hand as significant multicultural influences on us. Positive influences. Or they can be looked at, as I think much of the country does, as threatening, disgusting, different, misunderstood, that you have to keep at arms length. So, the degree to which I had actually done the "I don't want to look at that," even thinking of myself as sort of a sexually liberated and hip person, came home to me and what could be possible from switching over to a positive viewpoint was illustrated to me in a completely embodied way. So that's the moment. That's what sort of turned me and let me go in a different direction than I had been going before. That's been the importance of San Francisco. So my mission is not to have that sex negativity be such a profound influence on all our lives.

shows are now no different than the industry stock and trade, this is still the grand-daddy of San Francisco strip clubs and worth a visit as long as your wife or girlfriend doesn't mind.

> **Windmills.** Golden Gate Park, West End, near Pacific Coast Hwy. (Sunset).

Also known as Queen Wilhelmina's Tulip Path, these are the cruisiest windmills in the country. Follow the path that runs the width of the park from windmill to windmill. Plenty of sex in the bushes, trees, and open spaces. Also plenty of unsuspecting tourists, which makes for humorous afternoon drama.

Spirituality

> **Brahma Kumari Raja Yoga Center.** 401 Baker, at Hayes (Western Addition).
☎ 415/563-4459.

Do yoga and sit straight.

> **Church of Amron.** 2254 Van Ness Ave., at Vallejo (Pacific Heights). ☎ 415/775-0227.
Get metaphysical.

> **First Unitarian Church.** 1187 Franklin St., at Geary (Cathedral Hill).
☎ 415/776-4580.

Emperor Norton went here.

> **Glide Memorial Church.** 333 Ellis St., at Taylor (Western Addition).
☎ 415/771-6300.

Cecil Williams brings you home to Jesus.

> **Holy Virgin Cathedral.** 6210 Geary Blvd., at 26th Ave. (Richmond).
☎ 415/221-3255.

Downstairs in this golden-domed Greek Orthodox cathedral is the final resting place for the relics of Saint John, lying in state in the city's most ornate Gothic shrine.

> **Issanji Hartford Street Zen Center.** 57 Hartford St., at 18th St. (Castro).
☎ 415/863-2507.

A queer zendo and former hospice, founded by the late Issan Dorsey—the charismatic author of *Street Zen*. Beat poet Phillip Whalen is Roshi in residence.

The San Francisco Zen Center

I *love* Zen Center because the guy with the pierced nose, ear, and tongue who cruised you at the S&M bar last night is likely to be sitting next to you calm as a cow. It's a place where Evan Dando 20-nothings who look like they shredded all last night commingle with itsy-bitsy Jewish girls; a place where women who look like they are nuns straight out of the Sacred Heart and guys who look like reps for one of the Napa Valley vineyards meditate side by side with neurotic, eternally depressed victims of some sort of imagined childhood abuse. It's a true melting pot of Zen, and of San Francisco.

I *like* Zen Center because they keep everything running smoothly without resorting to Gestapo tactics. Because they leave you to your own experience, but gently introduce you to the dharma through lectures and courses you want to drink. I like Zen Center because they recognize the importance of beauty, even though this very neat, well-maintained and elegantly precise center is at times a bit too precious and anal about ceremony and aesthetics. I like Zen Center because the quality of people who attend are a cut above in intelligence, character, and depth.

I *dislike* Zen Center because it has devolved into the most militantly PC Zen Center in continental America (Aitken Roshi's social activist bunch in Honolulu might still take top honors). Telltale signs: Betty Shabazz's name was placed on the altar after her death; the latest writer in residence was a woman who wrote a book about "Buddhism after patriarchy"; and, to top it all, if you examine the bulletin board outside the zendo you will find a little posting that reads, "Multicultural Collection Available in Zen Center Library. Take affirmative action into your own hands, head and heart. Appreciate other cultures as well as your inherited and acquired ones. Learn how to challenge unearned privilege and injustice." Help!!

Many of my beliefs might be considered extremely liberal, but I don't sit Zen to deepen an ideological agenda. I hope that my Zen practice takes me beyond the often false dichotomies of public policy debates. Not to take anything away from Zen Center's "outreach work" on behalf of the homeless, people with AIDS, and prisoners. It is all very beautiful, if you tow their cliché liberal line. Unfortunately, it's murder if you try to buck the arrogant matriarchy.

The San Francisco Zen Center is located at 300 Page, at Laguna. ☎ **415/ 863-3136.** www.zendo.com/~sfzc.

> **St. John Will-I-Am Coltrane African Orthodox Church.** 351 Divisadero St., at Oak (Western Addition). ☎ **415/621-4054.** www.saintjohncoltrane.org. Divine liturgy at 11:45am.

When one reflects upon the fact that Yahweh was a literary figure largely invented by a prominent woman in King Solomon's Court, and that Jesus, while a living, breathing man at one time, is largely known today because of the extraordinary myths built up around him by a series of highly imaginative poets and writers, it should come as no surprise that a small interracial congregation of believers in San Francisco's Western Addition should consider jazz legend John Coltrane not only a saint but an embodiment of spiritual values equal to those literary figures mentioned above. When one attends service at this small vibrant storefront church, one is experiencing the very same grassroots passion that led to the deification of that rebel rabbi from Nazareth. What is more, you get to experience the most unique liturgical celebration in the entire city (and that includes Glide Memorial, Mrs. Bronstein-Stone). The standard musical expectations one carries from years of Christian liturgy are inverted here—where one anticipates a resolution, there comes another variation; and where one expects variation, there comes a sudden resolution. Love, Love Supreme, is the message of Saint John, and you can see it in the hearts and faces of almost everyone who attends. If there is one congregation that carries on the free-form spirit of 1960s S.F. spirituality, this little church is it. All praise to God.

Sports and Recreation

> **Candlestick Point.** Gilman St., opposite 3Com Stadium/Candlestick Park. (Hunters Point).

The mother of sailboarding locales. Intense howling winds shoot through the gap of the adjacent San Bruno Mountains producing board speeds up to 45 miles per hour. The incredibly rough water makes it near impossible for anyone not sufficiently advanced.

> **The Dish.** Hilltop Park, off 3rd Street and LaSalle (Hunter's Point).

This hilltop cement bowl in a sketchy part of Hunter's Point is the only place in the city specifically designed for skateboarders. Great views. And, on the bright, sunny weekend we were there, not a soul in sight. We were ultimately stopped by a carload of churchgoers wanting to know if we were from City Hall. When we think back on why we could never live in San Francisco again, it's because we remember the depressing insularity at the root of those churchgoers' question, which spoke volumes about the forlorn emptiness at the heart of this seeming paradise.

> **Filbert Street Steps.** East side of Telegraph Hill, Filbert St. (Telegraph Hill).

Hoof your way down from phallic Coit Tower. The terrain is so steep that the street becomes steps. We counted 455 steps the first time, 438 steps the next time, and

397 steps the final try. So go count them yourself. Also, it's a veritable urban jungle, where a flock of thirty-eight parrots live amidst overwhelming greenery and stunning views.

> **Hollywood Billiards.** 61 Golden Gate Ave., at Jones (Tenderloin).
☎ **415/252-9643.**

Burgers and snooker. It's a large place that sneaks up on you once you get through the door and up the stairs. There's an enormous bar, a solid menu, dozens of tables, and not a warped cue in sight.

> **Japan Town Bowl.** 1790 Post, at Webster (Japantown). ☎ **415/921-6200.**

No matter how many times you do it, bowling is still weird. Here they have forty lanes and hundreds of young Asians yukkin' it up. Japanese is definitely spoken. Crash the pins for 24 hours on weekends. For glow-in-the-dark bowling, try Tuesday, Saturday, and Sunday nights when they turn off all lights, turn on lasers and fog machines, hand out glow-in-the-dark balls, and turn the alley into a bowler's laserium. Kind of trippy.

> **Mission Bay Golf Center.** 1200 6th St., at Channel (China Basin). ☎ **415/703-6184.**

Surrounded by major freeway overpasses, industrial warehouses, and transient squalor, this prefab driving range maintains a country-club attitude despite its neighbors. Next door visit the Mission Creek houseboats and feed the barnyard pet ducks.

Stores/Shopping

> **Body Manipulations.** 3234 16th St., at Guerrero (Mission). ☎ **415/621-0408.**

If piercing your clitoris isn't enough, this small shop will go the extra mile and brand you with a geometric tribal motif. With two studios, owner Vaughn continues to offer complete scarification services as well as a remarkable line of earplugs.

> **Bombay Bazar.** 548 Valencia St., at 16th St. (Mission). ☎ **415/621-1717.**

Long before the hipsters were driving the real estate up on this block, even before the crack vials had hit the curb and you could still find parking on Valencia, there was the Bombay Bazar. Open for more than twenty-three years, it's the ultimate Indian supermarket, with a massive selection of chutneys, curries, tandoori paste, pickled limes, pickled chilies, bulk cardamom, pure mustard oil, masala, jasmine tea, and gallon jars of ghee. With pop singer Lata Kishor wailing over the sound system you can browse an entire aisle of Krishna postcards, another aisle of Indian movies, another aisle of incense, and when you're finished, sample their cardamom, fig, or mango ice cream in the adjacent cafe. Servicing over 15,000 Indians who work in the hotel business and who primarily live in the Tenderloin, the greatest irony is that the tremendous mural on the wall of Indian motifs was rendered by a Mexican artist.

> **Botanica Yoruba.** 998 Valencia, at 21st St. (Mission). ☎ **415/826-4967.**

Our all-time favorite Santeria shop, with a crucifix for every occasion.

> **Buffalo Exchange.** 1555 Haight St., at Clayton (Haight). ☎ **415/431-7733.**

Buffalo is the best and cheapest of the used-clothing emporiums. They buy your used clothes, or take them in trade.

> **Curios and Candles.** 289 Divisidero, at Page (Western Addition). ☎ **415/863-5669.**

Magic made commercial, with a complete supply of love potions, money incense, and everything for your bewitching needs.

> **Epicenter Zone.** 475 Valencia St., at 16th St. (Mission). ☎ **415/431-2725.**

A totally cool drop-in center for the baggy-pants crowd. Includes a very funky library to sit and read, a bunch of bins from which to buy really obscure music, and plenty of space for radical events. They also have an on-again, off-again community switchboard. Serious fun.

> **Leather Tongue Video.** 714 Valencia St., at 18th St. (Mission). ☎ **415/552-3131.**

Some of their videos are so hard-core even we didn't have the guts to view them all. Decent zine collection too, including *Zapruder HeadSnap,* but, overall, it doesn't compare to the selection and atmosphere at Naked Eye.

> **Naked Eye News and Video.** 533 Haight St., at Fillmore (Mission). ☎ **415/864-2985.**

Besides running one of the best alternative news racks in the city, including zines even *we've* never heard of, owner Steve Chack and his cohorts have also cornered the market on obscure films for your video pleasure. Most importantly, you can be guaranteed to find a copy of *Monk* in stock.

> **Pedal Revolution.** 3085 21st St., at Folsom (Mission). ☎ **415/641-1264.**

This Mission bike-repair shop trains homeless in bike repair and is the shop of choice for local bike messengers.

> **Piedmont.** 1452 Haight, at Masonic (Haight). ☎ **415/864-8075.**

At first glance you might think that this is just a glitzy showgirl shop—which, in fact, it is. But many of the girls who shop here happen to be guys. For twenty-two years they've been dressing strippers and drag queens. And they've got a great catalog called the *Drag Rag.*

> **Psychedelic Shop.** 1098 Market St., at 7th St. (Tenderloin). ☎ **415/621-0357.**

The reincarnation of the original Haight store is a mecca for rock posters, Grateful Dead memorabilia, and obscure recordings, buttons, tie-dye T-shirts, Hackey Sacks, pipes, papers, and psychedelia.

> **Quantity Postcards.** 1441 Grant Ave., at Green (North Beach).
☎ **415/986-8866.**

One of the finest postcard shops in the country. From the classic fifties cards to tacky Americana to today's string of satirical zingers, Quantity has them all. They also have an earthquake simulator that can give a rise.

> **Sanrio.** 39 Stockton St,, at Market (Downtown). ☎ **415/981-5568.**

Hello Kitty. The cult of cuteness starts here. A product proliferation of cheap things to send to friends when you want to smother them with saccharine.

> **Uncle Mame.** 2241 Market St., at Sanchez (Castro). ☎ **415/626-1953.**
www.unclemame.com.

Clearly the hands-down emporium for useless kitsch that has somehow worked its way into every hipster pad across America. Pulling heavily on nostalgia, you find sock monkeys, Wondergirl lunch boxes, Tweety Bird, Kermit the Frog, Donny and Marie Osmond dolls, Elvis bubble gum, rubber peanuts, wax lips, candy cigarettes, Fizzies, and more. Uncle Mame (a.k.a. David Sinkler) runs the place like he's master of ceremonies at a three-ring circus, and given the primary-color scheme and the visual cacophony throughout the store, the elephants might be just outside the door. There are vintage televisions playing videos of such classics as Eleanor Roosevelt's margarine commercial and good ole Lucy. Likewise, Mame has one of the largest collections of Pez dispensers, over 400 Lucite snow domes, a black-and-white–photo booth, and holy-water bottles. It's a riotous trip down memory lane, though some of those memories might best be left behind.

Abie in the Abbey,
Monks in the Mission

It's a late-night crawl through the dark zone of the Mission, where the true deals are made. Girls work the streets, popping blow jobs for a dime. Their shadow-faced pimps hang in the doorways of a row of dive bars. The Monks park at the intersection of South Van Ness and 16th near the flashing lights of a police car that casts blue-red grids across the oil-stained streets, its siren on low squeal.

The cops have a junkie up on the hood who only moments before was holding patrons of Liquid, the latest bar du jour, at knife point as he gathered a wallet or two. The slightly rattled curbside crowd is very Nordstrom, out slumming in Crack Central for a Saturday-night buzz. Inside, Liquid has the requisite props (concrete floor, brushed aluminum bar, pool table, postage-stamp dance floor, squiggly sculptured lights) . . . enough to send the Monks screaming for the pierced tat-tooed crowd.

Outside, the junkie is in the back seat of the squad car, headed downtown for the night. As the cops hunch over their radio, calling in the report, right beneath their nose major deals are being made.

The Monks cross Mission toward Valencia Street, passing seventy or more loiter-ers who are doing a brisk trade. Chiva, speed balls, and crack are stuffed in bal-loons and held inside the mouths of hyper-alert dealers, who suspiciously eye every new face that walks down the street.

The Monks cross Valencia and are hustled, spare-changed, offered crack, offered smoke, offered tar. They kick past needles and vials thrown to the curb. Wild-eyed crackies on a five-day binge troll the streets, scooping up dropped quarters, looking for cars that beg for a break-in. Tin-foil mamas stand in the shadow of stoops, renting their makeshift crack pipes for a buck to the brain-blown frat boys taking a walk on the wild side. There's a black cat calling, "what'cha want, what'cha want, what'cha want." Girls with bruised skin cruise the alley, chattering through speed-riddled teeth, so tweaked they'd take a punch in the gut for a rock. "Get me high, daddy," they continually say. "Get me high, daddy."

The Monks walk across the filmy sidewalks into Gen-X Valencia domain. Hipsters out for the night prowl with a gin-and-tonic buzz, their bottle-dyed hairdos, thrift-store clothes, and Little-Lulu-lunch-pail fantasies deliciously in check. The chicks scuff the sidewalks in their patent-leather baby-doll shoes wearing ripped nylons and flowery print smocks, Courtney Love–style, now seven years out of date. Their disingenuous love-patch boyfriends posture alongside, emulating pop, trash, thrash, punk; in their pockets, Gitanes. With the predictable buzz cut or slick back 'do, their skinny pipe-leg pants confine cocks shriveled up from too much meth.

Down the streets they go, jangling stainless steel from their pierced scrotums, nipples, and bellies, asymmetrical hardware running out of their nose. They're branded in the armpit, holes carved in their souls, cruising for smack, crack, or a dungeon whack. They sport bisexual, trisexual, three-day-bearded, peanut butter crusted, cum-stained, attitude-rich smirks that at times translate into smiles.

Their lives are fucked, and they know it.

Jim slows the pace, picks out a pair of shoes being sold on the street — shiny shoes, military shoes, J.C. Penny-go-to-Sunday-Baptist-Church, singing-in-the-choir, spit-shined, daddy-o pimping shoes.

Jim hustles the guy down a buck from the five dollar deal and off he walks, stolen shoes in hand. Turning Guerrero, the slack-jawed Gen-X slummers thin out, as do the hustlers, crack addicts, junkies, porch mamas, et al. Guerrero's a tad suburban, if you want to look at it that way. Victorian buildings bulge their bay windows out over the street. Cars scramble round and round for the thrill of just parking. Commercial space thins out to but a few corner markets, a tattoo parlor and a store selling zines.

A church slices the sky with its steeple, its doors flung open on the corner of Camp Alley, bluish light streaking on the sidewalk illuminating globs of tar, blood, dog shit, spittle, and a crushed vial or two. Inside, a clean man, a man with tall broad teeth and frizzy black hair, smiles benevolently from underneath the garb of a priest. Is it real or just a costume?

A line of people wrap around the corner. It's a casual, clean-cut, Old Navy, cotton-pleated sort of crowd. Could be a bible thumper going on inside. But on a Saturday night? The priest is named Abie. He's a low-key huckster with an amiable grin, swaying the undecided to plunk down a fiver and come sit for a spell.

"Nine by Nine Industrial" read the posters at the door. It's a community of sorts, authors of books, authors of poems, authors of fantastical journeys through the mind. Simpler put, it's your basic poetry read.

Inside, the old, unused church reeks of mahogany, its brown wooden fixtures gracefully aged. A conglomerate of geeks converge upstairs in the high-ceilinged auditorium full of odd-angled pews. At the back, wine is being sold. Imbibers grab their seats amid the indeterminable buzz, where here, safe from the streets, thrives another urban scene. The hip quotient is refreshingly missing, faces a little too scrubbed. Glaringly absent are buzz-cut girls and goateed gents with their condescending 'tudes.

The listeners sit down for a spell and the show begins with a thud, as an addled shy guy reads from his notes with a horribly shaken voice, lamenting all the love lost upon his hopelessly bland life. The pace is slow but the crowd is polite as what few hecklers there are excuse themselves downstairs. Suffering four more poets, the Monks are on the verge of dismissing the whole inconsequential scene when a second-act poet, a vein-popping, swaggering, stubble-faced man, a man from Russia no less, with the intoxicating name of Eugene Ostashevsky, storms the stage and grabs the mike, growling, snarling, forcing air through the lungs in dramatic intake as he begins to recite a long string of lines, delivered unbearably distinct, punctuating the air in a moaning, junky drone, lobbing the eardrums with plaintive outcries.

I want to be an American marching for
various Campbell's cans!
The country I was born to makes me nauseous!
It's full of Igors and strung-up Natashas.
I was in a guilty house of love
amongst see-through walls I would live.

The Monks sit up and the crowd bends forward as this mad Russian poet sucks the mike through his throat and out his pores, melding thought with word, anxiety with sound, sleepless nights with manic days. His whines emanate from the root of all suffering. His smoky voice mines the depths of his subtextual thought factory as he tells us all in so many words to go screw ourselves for being so predictable and uncool.

I turned this house into Fort Apache.
In my head, I heard melodies.
I went blind. Misguided souls.
I have no native language!
I can't judge. I suspect I'm like garbage.
Learning in a dialogue where they hear dead
    men talk.
But their thrashing in their words made me cry
    out toilless.

The Russian has the crowd wrapped around his little finger, howling, chanting, anxiously wrestling with the ghost of Ginsberg. His rant consumes the remainder of the show, as the audience laps up his verbal pigsty, staggered by the onslaught. And when it's over, its over. The Marina-like crowd pours down the stairs into the church, out onto the streets—streets swept clean, foggy clean, like a million other nights. The blue haze of late night creeps through the alleys. Domestic-violence calls go out like fireflies over 911. Squad cars race the lights to put an end to murderous intent in the neighboring projects.

And the Monks cruise down Mission with a new pair of black shoes.

>on the road

Theater and Performance

> **848 Community Space.** 848 Divisadero, at McAllister (Western Addition).
☎ **415/922-2385.**

A cool living-space-turned-theater, co-owned by performance fixture Keith Hennessy. Now in their seventh year, they have fostered the irrepressible careers of countless performers, actors, and risk takers who, in predictable S.F. fashion, continually push the envelope toward the rougher edge of art.

> **Josie's Cabaret and Juice Joint.** 3583 16th St., at Market (Castro).
☎ **415/861-7933.**

One of the hottest stages in town, with the best of gay/lesbian comics, performing artists, and touring cabaret. Current home of Joan Jett Black's evening talk show. (Also see listing under "Cafes and Coffeehouses.")

> **Somar Theater.** 934 Brannan St., at 9th St. (SOMA). ☎ **415/863-1414.**

This giant warehouse of a space South of Market has been host to some of the more bodacious and LARGE performances in the Bay Area of late, including the occasional Burning Man/Cacophony extravaloonza.

> **Theater Artaud.** 450 Florida St., at Mariposa (Mission). ☎ **415/621-7797.**

Founded in 1972 by a group of artists as the performance center of Project Artaud (one of the largest artist live/work spaces in the country) and incorporated in 1984 as an independent theater, it was named after French visionary Antonin Artaud, and influenced by his philosophy of breaking down cultural barriers in traditional theater. Their mission has from the beginning been to support the vision and development of contemporary performing artists. Now approaching three decades of productions, they have definitely met that goal. The theater is housed in the old American Can Company factory, and sports three-story ceilings and nearly 11,000 square feet of space.

Transportation

San Francisco is not a car town. Despite that warning, almost everyone who lives here drives a car. Otherwise you're very dependent on a crowded, fickle, and notoriously obstreperous public transportation system.

But it's a no-win compromise. Sure, Boston and New York are parking nightmares, but San Francisco has *the hills!* What's more, because most San Franciscans adamantly oppose a crosstown freeway, or sensible expansion of the current Central Freeway, it literally takes longer to go from the Golden Gate Bridge to China Basin than it does to go the far longer distance from downtown Los Angeles to LAX. In addition, those S.F. meter-maids are overweight terrors on electric wheels. And the parking police in San Francisco are the toughest, tow-happy bureaucrats in the country. The Monks have been towed no less than SIX TIMES in the past few visits to the city. To top it all off, Mayor Willie Brown's live and let live approach to law enforcement means that, despite the radical decrease in crime nationwide, San Francisco remains the one major city where you are very likely to have your car busted into. We have been broken into three separate times recently. And just forget about finding easy quick parking in the Haight, the Castro, or Union Square. It just ain't gonna happen.

Which is why we politely recommend some of the following alternatives to getting around town.

BART Tour

> **Bay Area Rapid Transit.** Go underground at Market St. at the Embarcadero.

This silver-bullet underground subway rises above ground in the East Bay for an excellent, and cheap, 4-hour tour of the entire area. Buy a dollar ticket at the Embarcadero station on Market, board westbound to Daly City, return eastbound to Concord. Return toward the city, changing at MacArthur. Go north/south to Richmond and Fremont. Then again, change at MacArthur back to the city. Disembark at Montgomery (one stop from Embarcadero). In the works is an extension to the airport. BART is the best mass transportation option west of Chicago.

Cable Cars and Streetcars

> **California Line.** Market St. at Embarcedero, California St. at Van Ness Ave. **Powell-Hyde Line.** Powell St. at Market St., Northpoint St. at Hyde St. **Powell-Mason Line.** Powell St. at Market St., Bay St. at Taylor St.

Despite your carefully inculcated Monkish aversion to standard tourist traps, if you're a first-time visitor to San Francisco, you'll want to ride a cable car. The locals have a love-hate relationship with the contraptions, but, secretly, everyone admits San Francisco would not be the same without them. Along with the Golden Gate Bridge, they are the definitive icons of the city. The ride up California Street on a

(continued on page 444)

Larry Harvey:

The Last Burning Man Interview You Will Ever Need to Read

(This Year)

WHAT IS BURNING MAN?

Pyrotechnic, neo-pagan, dadalike, surreal. Absurdist, anarchistic, celebratory, real. Dreamlike, ritualistic, archetypal, ephemeral. It's Mad Max meets Zabriskie Point. Tribalism meets technology. Apollo meets Bacchus meets Thor. However we define it, Burning Man remains defiantly indefinable, a doorway to don't-know mind. Still, we continue to try.

Burning Man might be described as a celebration/performance piece/"God for Satin" mind meld held near Bruno's one-blink-and-it's-gone town of Gerlach in the middle of northern Nevada's Black Rock mesa, where nothing lives, not even insects, and where S.F. phreaks and their L.A.-to-New York followers come together every Labor Day Weekend to build temporary community around the simultaneous satire and celebration of community, each year doubling in size and notoriety, drawing in journalists from around the globe who attempt to see in it some trend or theme, which isn't there intrinsically yet is there through the bug-eyed vision of the beholder, those who toss off their clothes and wallow ecstatically in the dust, those who have made the event into a self-regulating nomadic village with a large word of mouth following, with a meaning as wide as the playa itself—from a pyromaniac's wet dream to a goddess's worst nightmare—with enough explosives to power a medium range rocket back to Reno, and enough inspiration to keep all sectors of your brain buzzing 24 hours a day, including existential boxing, a drive-by shooting range (Barney was one of the targets), art cars, pirate radio stations, a mock German beer garden, drag races in drag, eccentric sunbathers, rampaging postal workers, billboard liberationists, fire-breathing dancers, loose-wired pranksters, exploding chimneys, cacophonous clowns, an All-Star tag team wrestling match between the forces of Light and Darkness in which Joan of Arc foils Tricky Dick with the display of a missing eighteen minutes of tape, a battle in which Albert Camus is rudely sacked, to the Church of the Camera Obscura, The Cargo Cult, The Little Chapel of the Playa, the Deconstruction Bicycle Camp, the Temporal Time Ice Sculpture (a 10-foot high ball of ice with clocks and time pieces frozen inside), a 14-foot rocking horse, a Nebulous Entity, to a long procession of kerosene poles leading to the sacramental and sacrificial figure upon which we place our collective

›interview

aspirations, good, bad and ugly, the figure which acts as a Christ-like container of all life, as well as a symbol of birth and decay, to the pièce de la no-resistance, the ceremonial burning of this four-story 40-foot wood-and-neon effigy of a man (think Wicker), originally constructed on much smaller scale by Larry Harvey on San Francisco's Baker Beach back in 1986 as a way of exorcising the demons of a failed relationship (though the party line is that it had something to do with the solstice), doubling in size and complexity each year, with the help of Michael Michael (a.k.a. Danger Ranger) of the San Francisco Cacophony Society, the insanely brilliant Kimric Smythe (the fabled "Exploding Man") of Survival Research Laboratories, and technician craftsman Dan Miller (the "Man's Man"), to become the most original and free-form festival of its kind in America, touching long-buried synapses in the global art psyche, conjuring up the neglected spirits of Ernst and Marinetti and Ubu and Duchamp and, of course, Dali, and sending out an olive branch to all those struggling within the prison of the prevailing mono-culture and the suffocating sameness of the so-called "alternative" culture, running circles around any remotely similar celebration, whether it be Woodstock or Loserpalooza or the treasured Drainbow Gathering ("I Love You Drainbow Brother!"), because at its core it is so fundamentally inclusive (like its city of origin), and, more importantly, not full of itself, showcasing at its best a rare combination of heart and absurd humor, and at its worst noisy and unorganized silliness, lacking in focus and soul, what John Bogard, that old desert curmudgeon of nearby Planet X might call "druid puke," what the earnest disaffected Siteworks bunch might admonish as a great concept gone awry, what serious ritual freaks might dismiss as child's play, with lots of snafus thrown in too (firecrackers that don't go off, satellite phones that don't arrive, a man that burns too soon, the occasional mindless Neanderthal here for the "party," not the community), yet somehow always pulling people back because of its visionary promise, because of the transformative power of the desert locale—a totally "flat 400-square-mile hardpan alkali expanse" where 40-mile-per-hour dust storms and sudden torrential rainfall can kick the shit out of your site and your psyche, a place where water is nonexistent, where everyone and everything diminishes in scale and yet magnifies in epic beauty—and also because of its powerful edict of "no spectators," challenging us to make it great and of the highest quality without any intermediaries to filter the experience, challenging us not to rip on the dopeheads and the mud people and the cult-like ravers and the pistol-pack'n gun freaks and the cerebral gearheads and the passive consumers, and embrace everyone as equal without all that New Age gobbledygook and sappy psychobabble, in the process birthing a new kind of co-existence, built on the high altar of creativity and the bedrock truth of impermanence, for, in the end, the party does stop, and the radio towers do come down, and the art cars drive away, and the man does burn, and every last bit of his ashes, and every last piece of debris, every last piece, is carted completely off the playa, not with a lot of environmentalist rhetoric or mother-earth mysticism but with a level-headed respect for the land, the people, and the event, which happens but once a year, with a beginning, a middle, and a glorious end.

We are sitting in Larry Harvey's darkly lit, completely trashed Alamo Square apartment. There's a pile of uncleaned dishes in the sink, masks and artwork aplenty, and enough papers, clothes, and assorted refuse thrown around to make Horse Badorties feel right at home.

But Larry Harvey, the titular head of the Burning Man nation, is not a slob. Well, by his own reckoning he is, but it's not what one first sees. Instead, what one sees is Harvey himself, a tan, big-eyed impresario of the weird, with big circles under those big eyes, smoking cigarette after cigarette as if it's his duty to keep world nicotine consumption up.

Everyone knows Harvey as the guy with the Stetson. He's not wearing his Stetson now. As a result, we can see for the first time the full handsomeness of the man's face, head, and hair. We're catching Harvey the day after an extraordinary event— the overflow reception of "The Art of Burning Man: An Incendiary Exhibition at the San Francisco Art Commission Gallery," and the ensuing procession, led by sixteen monk-like figures bearing a flaming brazier, to Lech Walesa Alley, where the Burning Man has been erected in an empty lot.

Harvey is proud of this milestone in the twelve-year history of "the man." It's the first time the event, the movement, has received official sanction from the city (Mayor Willie Brown was there to launch the exhibit) and the first time the Burning Man contingent has managed to take over a major city park or plaza. It's the ultimate tribute to Harvey, whose solid demeanor and clear-headed Oregon core has allowed him to move between two very disparate worlds—the artsy boho pyromaniacal geniuses of the S.F. counterculture to the more brass-tacks establishment of sheriffs, BLM (Bureau of Land Management) bureaucrats, mayors, and city councils he has to petition to gain permission to stage his yearly festival in the desert, and the now almost weekly series of benefits, performances, and extravaganzas that have grown up around it.

Larry Harvey sits at the kitchen table, answering questions in between the frequent telephone calls. There's a gathering this afternoon in Hunters Point, where a band of Burning Man artists, including a few Silicon Valley boys Larry is proud to have onboard, are constructing Harvey's latest madcap design, the Nebulous Entity.

Twelve years into this world party, which has drawn press and followers from around the planet, and which has spawned dozens of Burning Man chapters in cities all over the continent, the pipeline still runs through a portable phone to a smoking man in a ramshackle San Francisco apartment.

As we watch him light each new cigarette, we see that each match is a small fire lighting Harvey, the literal burning man. Every few minutes Harvey lights up, and every few minutes another soul is lit with the fire of his creation. In observing the power of this simple mind-to-mind transmission, we start to realize we are possibly dealing with a demigod here, though Harvey has done everything he can to eschew such an old-world archetype.

We decide to take his photograph. Larry Harvey does not want to be photographed without his Stetson, which sits but a foot away on the table. He reaches for the hat, but we talk him out of it. We did the standard Burning Man story several years ago. We have the pictures of Harvey in his Stetson, playing patriarch to the masses. We're older now, and hopefully wiser. We want Harvey the man, not

the public icon. We want to really know, long before the now canonized dates in the Harvey legacy, how all of this, how all of him, actually came to be.

Monk: So yesterday was a historic event in San Francisco, wasn't it? Burning Man came to the streets in a big way. Was that the first time?

LH: No, we did a thing a couple of years ago. The significance of this was that we virtually engulfed the Civic Center. And with the blessings of the Art Commission and the mayor. That was what was historic about it.

Monk: So let's describe it. Let's start with a basic question. In 1986 you decided on a simple gesture. You decided to burn an effigy of a man on a beach?

LH: Typical San Francisco shit. Just a gesture.

Monk: And all of this came out of the subconscious of Larry Harvey! Twelve years later, this little gesture, this little thing that came out of this little act, just blossomed into something huge. What is it now?

LH: It's turning into a populous social movement. It's certainly an arts festival out there. But it's more than that. It's certainly a party out there. But it's far more than that. It has turned into a community now that's beginning to extend across the nation. Primarily through the medium of the Internet. And very potently through word of mouth. It's now reaching a point in the exponential curve where it's going to be perceived to be taking off at this extraordinary rate.

Monk: So, it's this movement. Does it have a name anymore? Is it still called Burning Man?

LH: It's always been called Burning Man.

Monk: But the Black Rock Desert Festival?

LH: My point is it exceeds the boundaries of the event. That's the next big story that's going to be told. We came out of the mulching bed of San Francisco bohemian culture. The same city that produced the beatniks and the hippies. This couldn't have happened anywhere but San Francisco. If you went to any other city—if you went to New York or if you went to L.A., you'd find everyone on a career track. And everybody would be whimpering in their little trench and their horizon would be limited by their career designs. They'd be scrambling up the ladder for success and competing with one another and stomping on each others' fingers as they clambered up the rungs. San Francisco isn't like that. People come to San Francisco to find themselves and go broke. I don't think the mayor would put it that way, but it's what creative people do. They come here because they think, *I can't do what I want to do. I can't express what I am in some unique way where I am. But I bet I could in San Francisco.* So they end up here. And you've got a lot of creative types who are self-directed. New York would gobble up all the excess energy in a minute. Bang! And all the talent. The performers would be in Broadway shows or trying to get into an off-Broadway show.

L.A., the metabolism down there would all be the entertainment industry. Only in San Francisco. I mean, where else could I get all these people to work for nothing? They'd all want their professional rate. And, secondly, it's been a classically bohemian scene. And bohemians are strange creatures. During the eighties, as America was becoming increasingly commodified, in which every social relationship was being gobbled up by market values, the bohemians were operating in their own funny little economy, which is essentially a gift economy. Very different from a commodity marketplace. When people get poor enough they have to share or pool resources. And if they're acting to a creative end, self-directed, it turns out that ideals are very infectious. People are putting themselves aside for the passion they invest in their work. Then it makes all kinds of cooperation possible. The boho economy is based on sharing scarce resources. Recycling resources. That is, finding, using society's cast-offs that nobody ever found any value in. And transfiguring them into useful items.

Monk: Give us an example.

LH: Well, look at what Mark Pauline (Survival Research Laboratories) did for years. They just go out there and find what people have thrown away or no one is using.

And they would then appropriate that to a greater and higher good. We've incorporated that in the Burning Man. Essentially, you do each other favors all the time. In a market economy the whole point of any transaction is that you don't have any connection with the other person. Which is good. It frees you to go about your business. You don't want a relationship with the guy selling gum at a subway. You want to get your gum and get on the train. Gift economy is different. Gift economy implies connection. When somebody gives, you are [obliged]. That's why you refuse gifts sometimes. Because you don't want to be obliged to somebody. This means your inner community is primarily organized and funds itself through an exchange of gifts. You know that if you give a gift, you'll get a gift. It's not barter. It's beyond barter. It will just come back to you somehow or other. And what that does, it forges a really intense sense of community among people. So, all through the eighties, living at the bottom of the economic pile, the artists were basically operating completely outside the normal monetary system. In large part we came out of that. We never had a grant. We never had any funding. For years I was living way beneath the poverty level. And I funded it somehow. And as we got bigger, more people would contribute gifts. And, in contributing a gift, they would become a member of the community. What we have done out there is we've created this huge city that's based entirely on gift giving. People drive in there with semitrucks full of a whole world they assemble on-site. And they never asked us for anything. People ask me, "Are you going to sell out to Disney?" How could they buy us? You can't buy stuff if it's for free. We couldn't sell out to them. We couldn't sell that process to them. There isn't any way they could run it. There's no point in making the offer. We couldn't deliver. Even if we wanted to. Which, of course, we wouldn't.

So then you have this city that's based, primarily, on the exchange of gifts. And in all these ways, people give out tokens. People create theme camps. We fund a little of the art that has a really public aspect. Some landmarks [that] dress the civic landscape. And then only we tend to give people about half the money they need. And then they have to go out and raise more. But when they go out and raise more they do a benefit. When they do a benefit, then suddenly they are connected to all these people who are giving them gifts. The community grows. So we kind of said to people, this is your chance to go out and live like an artist. And that turns out to be for the sake of self-expression and at the very edge of survival. Because that's how the artists have always lived. And that's the romance of the bohemians. This is a chance for everybody to experience that. We're the world showcase for outsider art. It's stuff that doesn't turn up in New York [galleries]. A significant amount of stuff that's actually pretty good has been produced by people that had no notion that they could do anything. And they produce things that they could begin, if they wanted to, an art career on. Then it gets down again to the economic question. They say, well, you're not paying the artists. And what do they get out of it? How do you live in an economy like that if you're not willing to live underground for the rest of your life? Which is not a particularly attractive prospect. I think it comes in just finding a balance between the two.

Monk: I think the secret why Burning Man has become so huge and people are willing to contribute to it is that you just always kept it wide open. It was never about you personally, Larry Harvey.

LH: That's the classic mistake that hipsters in the scene make. They self-fabulize and tell themselves stories about how great they are. And you're great because you're unknown. Just wait for one hipster to get known and all the rest of them will turn on them. We always kept the damn thing open. We said anybody can do this. Anybody at all. There was some dissension in the ranks a couple of years ago. There was debate that went on whether we wanted uncool people. And, frankly, I don't know who uncool people are. I mean anybody's cool who is authentically expressing something. And, as a result, our demographics are out of this world. First there was us and then there came a younger crowd. And then there came sort of a middle-aged crowd. Then the RVs showed up. And then people's parents started showing up. And then the children started showing up. And now it's everybody.

Monk: Do you build the Burning Man every year?

LH: It's my design primarily. They still operate off of my original drawing, but every year, the builders add little love touches. And innovations. And I just let go of it after a while and they come, and ask, is this okay? And we talk about it, but they've got the lead. In a normal art situation everybody would be jealous about their entitlement. Their authorship. Their credit.

Monk: Their intellectual rights.

LH: Yes. Because they are operating in an economy of scarcity. Everybody is competing with one another. It's hard to collaborate in a situation like that. With this, it's an economy of creative abundance. They're egomaniacs, but for the most part artists are on the erotic side of the spectrum. And they tend to merge and collaborate really easily. If you just give them half a chance. So I design the Man and yet other people—I just wait for them to make little suggestions and they love it. It's theirs. So let them have it.

Monk: So the secret is, you've studied, to some extent, past social movements.

LH: The last few years I have.

Monk: You suddenly found yourself in the middle of a social movement. And what you've seen, your recipe for success, is to constantly stop the judgments. Stop the tendency to become exclusive.

LH: Yeah. Because we preach community, but one thing communities will do is they will close their ranks and they won't let anybody else in at a certain point. They're always doing that. And that's the downside of community. And that's the thing that we've labored to eliminate. We've [created] a very intensive community experience, but we tried to eliminate that provincial aspect of it. And we've largely succeeded by keeping very porous. I think there is a countercultural agenda that's yet to be realized. What helps in our case is that the people who are leading it are in their forties and fifties. Depending on youth to lead the way was perhaps a mistake in the past. I got a 16-year-old kid. I can tell you it would be a mistake. And I mean most of [the Burning Man leaders] were pretty wild in their youth. They are still pretty wild by most standards. But the difference is that we've had experience in the real world. The beatniks were actually led by a somewhat older group. It was the hippies that, though they actually had a lot of wonderful ideals and there was a lot of beautiful energy that went into it, succeeded in giving the counterculture a bad name for thirty years.

This is not a love-in. We are still trying to overcome that. And I think that the time is ripe for it. If you suddenly give people an idea they can passionately rally around that has all of these things that the system so conspicuously lacks, then great changes are quite possible. I mean, it's kind of funny. Burning Man doesn't have any competition. It's just wide open. It's really strange. And pretty soon there's going to be more and more people imitating us. It's going to grow like bacteria in a virgin culture.

For information call the Burning Man Hotline at ☎ **415/561-9377** or go to www.burningman.com. Luddites write to P.O. Box 420572, San Francisco, CA 94142-0572.

sunny day is the ultimate Rice-a-Roni treat with simply incomparable views. The ride at sun-up or sundown borders on sublime. The downside of the cable cars is they are a veritable circus, which is why most San Franciscans rarely hop onboard. There are long lines of tourists. The conductors have a well-honed shtick, which borders on obnoxious. And you'll be asked at least a dozen times, "Will you take our picture please?" But putting all this aside, it's still one of the best rides in town. Catch it at California Street and Van Ness Avenue for the shortest wait in line.

> **The China Express (a.k.a. 30 Stockton, Muni).** Chinatown.

If you want the experience of suffocating from the crush of flesh while enduring an exceedingly strong odor of ginger, ride the 30 Stockton bus from 3rd and Townsend streets all the way into Chinatown. You'll be amazed at the sheer number of Asian immigrants that squeeze in, elbows pointed and arms loaded with bags. Just when you think not another soul can possibly board, in steps another twenty ladies fresh from the sweat shops of SOMA and China Basin. They love to talk. They love to push. And they love that ginger.

> **F-Market Line.** Muni (Downtown).

These little darlings of Market Street are perfectly restored 1930s streetcars that run from the Embarcadero to the Castro. They are not to be confused with the Metro Streetcars that labor above and below ground shuttling San Franciscan's proletariat from the Financial District to outlying neighborhoods. These historical landmarks on wheels are practical, especially for making a quick trip up or down Market Street without descending into Muni subway hell. Unlike the cable cars, they do not have long lines. They hold sentimental value for Michael Monk because in his hippie teens, when the green-and-cream–colored cars were on their last derelict legs before being retired to pasture, he used to jump the bumper of the N Judah near the Haight and ride at considerable speed through the Duboce Tunnel hanging on for dear life on his way to the Fillmore West to catch the likes of Janis, Jimi, and (Mike's favorite) Blue Cheer.

Bikes and Blades

> **Critical Mass.** Foot of Market St. (Downtown). Last working Fri of the month.

It's a spontaneous gathering of hundreds of cyclists on the last working Friday of every month. They meet at the end of Market for a massive show of spokes, then everyone cycles west, shutting down traffic and demonstrating the beauty (and ecological necessity) of alternative transport. (See "Calendar/Events.") But beyond the strident political ambitions of Critical Mass, biking is a thoroughly viable way to see the city. Plus you will get a complete workout navigating the hills. (See "Calendar/Events").

Note: If you prefer a more regular celebration of alternative transport, check out the **Midnight Rollers,** a group of roller bladers who take to the streets every Friday night in groups ranging from 5 to 100.

Ferries

› **Golden Gate Ferry Service.** Foot of Market St. San Francisco Ferry Building (Downtown). ☎ 415/923-2000.

You are surrounded by water. One of the most beautiful bays in the entire world is at your feet. And if you have slim chances of hitching a ride on one of the thousands of sailboats and yachts docked at the many marinas around town, then this is your ride across the bay. On a par with New York's Staten Island Ferry, San Francisco's Golden Gate Ferry gets you a spectacular 30-minute ride from downtown San Francisco to Sausalito. On the way you get a close glimpse of Alcatraz, see the Golden Gate Bridge in all its glory, and catch a stunning view of the downtown waterfront.

Cars, Sort Of

› **Soap Box Derby.** Bernal Heights Speedway, Bernal Heights Blvd. at Folsom (Bernal Heights). 1pm, 3rd Sun of every month, Memorial Day to Halloween.

The fastest derby in the world. (See "Calendar/Events.")

Views

In a city built on hills, the coveted apartment with a view is the end goal for most urban dwellers on the fast track to material success. But in San Francisco views come in all kinds and shapes. You can have a city view, bay view, bridge view, ocean view, Civic Center view, park view, skyline view, cathedral view, cable-car view. In other words, if the Realtors can coin a view and raise the price, they will. We're very egalitarian about views. We think they should be available to everyone. So put on your Docs, get out your binoculars, and take a look around.

> **Acid Rock.** Museum Way, Roosevelt Way, Corona Heights Park (Buena Vista).

The best alternative view of downtown when you don't want to schlep up Twin Peaks. Michael Monk took LSD here in 1967: hence its name. Just climb the red rocks and soar.

> **Alamo Square.** Hayes St., at Steiner (Western Addition).

This park, across from the overly heralded "Painted Ladies" (a row of colorful Victorian houses), has seen a remarkable transformation in the past twenty years from ghetto to yuppie haven. Ever since the neighboring projects came down, Alamo Square has become one of the most sought-after neighborhoods in town, especially with its solid Downtown and Civic Center views. Busloads of shutter-happy tourists add to its friendly good-natured allure.

> **Claremont Resort.** See "Accommodations."

> **Coit Tower.** From Lombard St., at Grant St.; follow signs east on Lombard to top of hill (Telegraph Hill).

Despite the heavy circling of tour buses and cars, the parking area below the tower is still one of our favorite views of charming Russian Hill, the bay, Downtown, and the Marina and bridges. Spectacular at sunset.

> **Golden Gate Bridge.** 101 North to bridge (Presidio).

One need not wonder why a foot crossing of *the bridge* is a rite of passage for any newcomer to the city. The blend of earth, air, sky, and water against the shimmering white backdrop of buildings of the distant San Francisco hills is soul-reviving, if not soul-shaking. Just resist the urge to jump.

> **Golden Gate Ferry Service.** Foot of Market St. (Downtown).

To understand San Francisco and where it really got its start, better take to the water. Before airlines and interstate highways, most travelers arrived at this busy port by ship. From the vantage point of the ferry you'll have a stoic view of the hills and sky-line from water's edge. Best seen near dusk when the lights start to twinkle.

> **Interstate 280.** Going north into S.F., take 6th St. exit (South of Market).

Sweeping, panoramic view of downtown, the bay, and Twin Peaks as you take a frighteningly high exit ramp.

> **Pete's Cafe.** See "Cafes and Coffeehouses."

> **Potrero Hill.** Top of 20th St. (Potrero Hill).

Just follow any of the state streets (Vermont, Kansas, Rhode Island) to 20th and you'll have a lovely, beautifully comforting view of the massive downtown skyline and Bay Bridge.

> **St. Francis Hotel.** 335 Powell St., between Post and Geary (Union Square).

In terms of standard tourist vistas, the view from the outdoor glass elevators of the esteemed St. Francis Hotel is de rigueur. However, there are more macabre reasons to note the Saint Francis. On October 23, 1950, Al Jolson died of a coronary occlusion while playing rummy in his suite. And on September 22, 1975, Sara Jane Moore fired a shot at President Gerald Ford. The second bullet was deflected at the last second by an ex-Marine.

> **San Francisco–Oakland Bay Bridge.** Driving west on the bridge, entering San Francisco (Downtown).

What an entrance! As soon as you pop out of the Yerba Buena Island Tunnel the city springs into perspective with a stunning view of the Downtown skyline, the bay, and the not-so-far-away Alcatraz Island. Nothing quite stirs the heart like this spectacular arrival into the magical metropolis.

> **Top of the Mark.** See "Bars, Pubs, and Clubs."

> **Twin Peaks.** Top of Twin Peaks Blvd. (Twin Peaks).

There's a reason why every tour bus in the city makes a pit stop here: The Twin Peaks are the highest elevation in the city, and a veritable Mount Olympus, from where you can view the entire city and bay. Buried in these hills are two copies of the very first issue of *Monk: The Mobile Magazine.* The power of that original vision resonates from this sacred spot to this very day. But beware of fog.

Monks on the Road,
Hot Chick on the Roof

Five circles around the block, and the Monks are still jockeying for a coveted parking space on the streets of San Francisco on a late afternoon.

"Quick, grab it," shouts Mike when he eyes a car pulling out in his rear-view mirror.

Jim sprints out the door to the abandoned parking space, standing guard as Mike races around four blocks of one-way streets to finally return to an impatient Jim.

Outside, the sun creeps behind layers of fog, robbing the day of its remaining light. A mob of costumed celebrants pack tightly toward the center of a drumming circle in front of the stately War Memorial Building on Van Ness. Two stories above, Mayor Willie Brown presides. But here on the street, an assembling parade is squeezing the creative nerve of the city. Today is a reception for Burning Man, a historic event. After twelve years of thriving underground and out in the Nevada desert, the Man is erected 40 feet tall in its city of origin, as if reclaiming its rightful domain. This is the beginning of a monthlong festival celebrating the Burning Man art movement that has spread like mutant fungus across the nation. And the apocalyptic hipsters have taken to the streets.

Mike and Jim elbow their way through the mob to get a closer look. The crowd throbs with excitement at the visceral convergence of artists, jitterati, and modern primitives, commencing their orgiastic tribal procession down Van Ness to Lech Walesa Alley.

Most of the onlookers are a converted crowd. But in their midst is a family of four, tourists to the core, Gap-outfitted, clutching city maps, camera, camcorder, and a day's worth of shopping bags from Union Square. Dad clutches Mom by the upper arm, his Midwestern eyes bulging at the exotic sight of male belly dancers and a red-turbaned diva who stands licking her coal-darkened lips, an 8-foot boa curled around her neck. Their tourist son, a shade before puberty, looks slightly bored, like he'd rather be playing video games at the corner store. But their hormonal teenage daughter, dressed in high-buttoned blouse, perky breasts on high beam, crimson lips chomping on a wad of gum, looks like a mare at the starting gate, ready to pounce on the first bare-chested male.

The parade penetrates the crowd, led by sixteen black-robed monks hauling an impressive cauldron of fire. The cloaked men march to a silent cadence, followed by ashen-faced women, scantily dressed in ribbon-torn black gowns, their exposed nipples bandaged with electrical tape, bundles of incense held in their palms, shrieking before the flames. Tourist Dad is turning the eyes of young Tourist Son away from the naked breasts, but Tourist Girl is already losing herself to the rhythm, tapping her pearly nails on the edge of her Macy's bag, her top button undone.

The night air is filled with drumming. Percussionists bang on every conceivable surface, sending thunderous rat-ta-tats into the canyons of the Civic Center. As the parade crosses Van Ness, the crowd follows, drawn by a primordial urge, drawn by the moving cauldron of fire, drawn by the towering glow of the Burning Man.

Across the street he stands tall in a vacant pit, between two buildings opposite the towering dome of City Hall. Here artists have turned an otherwise unsightly hole of urban refuse, a dumping grounds for homeless waste, into a den of artful hedonism.

The Monks are in the heat of the parade. Behind them comes Tourist Girl, eyes wide as a tiger, hair slightly tossed, and another button undone. She tows her reluctant clan, who are dragging their feet.

"Honey, we'd better go; we have ten o'clock tickets for the Plush Room," says chirpy Tourist Dad. Tourist Mom is cupping her ears and Tourist Son's bored grimace is beginning to crack as the spectacle before him looms larger than his small suburban mind.

The procession files into the pit, spiraling around the base of the Burning Man. He appears omnipotent, comically wise, as if constructing a plan for a leap across the street and a sprint to the beach. He's lit in neon, his skeleton pulsing ruby red and lavender streaks of light. At his feet throngs of dancers writhe in ecstasy, pounding the dirt, heaving their bodies forward in a staged, paganistic ritual that white hipsters imitate so very well. Spider men appended by ropes from a neighboring building crawl down the walls in slow twisted movements, their bullhorns sending cryptic messages toward the crowd.

Hundreds of onlookers press against a fence, looking down into the pit. The Monks are sandwiched between an unsavory group of gutter punks and the tourist family, who are huddled together in a protective clutch.

"People of earth, people of earth, the end is near!" shout the spider men.

"Kewl" says Tourist Girl, who has spit out her gum and is now dancing around, yet another button undone.

"Honey, mom's getting sick, so we have to go," says the stressed Tourist Dad.

Not on your life, she says with her eyes.

The Monks wander around the block to the alley where the carnival begins. Strolling through the mob, they cross fortunetellers, belly dancers, cyber freaks, and a mad margarita maker who's plugged a mixer into a six-cylinder, flaming manifold that shoots columns of fire 3 feet high into the misty night air. For each new drink he fires up the engine, blender rattling, flames shooting, and near-naked girls dancing to the sound of crushing ice.

The Monks descend into the pit. The dust is kicked up high as a cloud, pearls of sweat making mud beads on the earthen dance floor. The black-robed men with their cauldron of fire are throwing ashes to the wind. Conga lines, dozens deep, trance dance in circles to the deafening roar of the primal beat. It feels like Egypt, maybe ancient Cairo, on a Saturday night, long long ago.

Walking out of the pit, the Monks cross the tourist family, only they're missing the girl. Anxiety is written on Tourist Dad's brow. Tourist Mom has stuffed tissue in her ear and Tourist Son stands mesmerized by the fire-spewing Blender Man.

Mike peruses the alley following the gaze of the bewildered dad. Cyberbus sits parked on the curb, its rooftop crowded with flamboyant dancers rocking the chassis. Gypsy-skirted chicks twirl barefooted across a muralized hood. Tourist Dad bends forward in a squint, peering at the faces climbing onto the bus.

Suddenly, there she is. Tourist Girl. She's up on the bus, untethered from her folks, dancing ecstatically with a bare-chested man. As Tourist Dad lurches forward, pulling family behind, he begins yelling at the top of his lungs.

"Get down from there! Cindy, get down . . ."

But his voice is drowned out by the cacophony of sound. And with a pop of the wrist her blouse is finally undone.

›Road Trip:
The North Coast

The north coast of California contains a surprisingly eclectic mix of highlights. Not only mystical coastal scenery, but outrageous Buddhist shrines, groovy hot springs, goofy drive-through trees, colossal lumber mills, and serious environmental activism. It's rainy and cool here a lot of the time, adding a poignant realness and melancholy to a state that often strikes visitors as endlessly sunny and bright. To get into the vibe of the North Coast, you need to sink into the mist, give in to the wet, and take a deep breath of incredibly fresh sequoia air.

North of San Francisco
(Marin, Sonoma, Napa, and the Rest)

West Marin

If you do nothing else in the surrounding Bay Area, visit West Marin—staggering in its natural beauty and unique in its commitment to the land, where the local Wendell Berries know a thing or two about culture, as well as how to make world-class cheese.

The long-term residents here like the organic life. They like to raise dairy and beef cattle, and sheep. They like to grow organic produce, maintain vineyards, even run an oyster farm. The residents of West Marin know they have the most unique living situation in the Bay Area. They are an hour's drive from one of the most beautiful and cosmopolitan cities on the planet, yet they are also right near extraordinary parkland, the ocean, beaches, whale watching, mountains, intelligent neighbors, the Green Gulch Zen Center, incredible restaurants, Scott Egide, and farmland too.

However, the residents of West Marin live in the Bay Area, where land prices are skyrocketing faster than blue-chip Internet stocks. Actually, the digital gold rush down in Silicon Valley has a thing or two to do with area land values. Because Marin's land prices are astronomical, there is an increasing disincentive for folks to stay in the ag business. It's far more lucrative to sell that property to a development company that's all ready to transform those gorgeous fertile fields into low-density luxury spreads for the rich and famous, who have essentially taken over the town of Ross and are building "trophy homes" in neighboring communities. Rural low-density development has been the loophole by which high-end developers have circumvented Marin County's strong laws against urban sprawl. When "A-60 zoning" was passed in 1972 (A for agriculture, 60 for 60 acres—only one house would be allowed on each 60 acres of land), it seemed like a solid protection for local agriculture. No one at that time envisioned a day when that large a parcel wouldn't be an

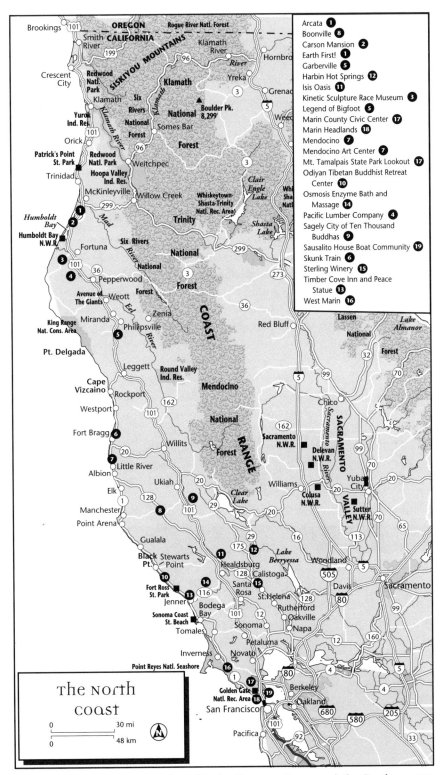

Arcata ❶
Boonville ❽
Carson Mansion ❷
Earth First! ❶
Garberville ❺
Harbin Hot Springs ⑫
Isis Oasis ⑪
Kinetic Sculpture Race Museum ❸
Legend of Bigfoot ❺
Marin County Civic Center ⑰
Marin Headlands ⑱
Mendocino ❼
Mendocino Art Center ❼
Mt. Tamalpais State Park Lookout ⑰
Odiyan Tibetan Buddhist Retreat Center ⑩
Osmosis Enzyme Bath and Massage ⑭
Pacific Lumber Company ❹
Sagely City of Ten Thousand Buddhas ❾
Sausalito House Boat Community ⑲
Skunk Train ❻
Sterling Winery ⑮
Timber Cove Inn and Peace Statue ⑬
West Marin ⑯

The North Coast

0 ————— 30 mi
0 ————— 48 km

obstacle to non-ag buyers. Today developers are engaged in a tense, competitive game, engendered by the extraordinary sums of money to be made in Bay Area real estate.

What's gratifying is that locals in towns like Point Reyes Station, Olema, Bolinas, and Inverness have not taken this situation sitting down. They teamed together in 1980 to create the Marin Agricultural Land Trust (MALT), a coalition of ranchers and environmentalists that works to preserve Marin County farmlands for agricultural use. MALT purchases conservation easements in voluntary transactions with landowners, preserving the land for posterity as a place for agriculture.

There are many educated, wise, and talented back-to-landers all over California, but nowhere is there such a clear reality check as in West Marin. If that land isn't used to grow food, it will certainly be used for development. And if growers are not given a sizable incentive to keep that land in production, even the most selfless may be tempted to go for the big-time development bucks. The results are everywhere in the county. According to Elisabeth Ptak, MALT's communications director, "Most of Post-Coast Miwok Indian Marin was farmland. Anywhere you look on the developed east side of Marin was once dairies or ranches. A few remain along Highway 101 between San Rafael and Petaluma, but their days are probably numbered. The former Freitas Dairy is now home to the Northgate Mall."

Fortunately, there are leaders like Star Route Farms, Straus Family Dairy and Creamery, the Corda Winery, and McEvoy Ranch, all organic farmers vigilantly working to preserve West Marin's endangered way of life. In addition, many other ranchers and farmers are the fourth or fifth generation of their families to carry on Marin's 150-year-old tradition of family farming.

But the fight is not just about agriculture, it's about aesthetics, and, just as importantly, a mindful and spiritually rewarding lifestyle. It's funny: While many

The Marin Problem

While we advocate West Marin in a big way, Marin County has a problem. A nasty glaring problem, which will hit you not long after you cross the Golden Gate Bridge: TRAFFIC. It's *baaaaad* over here. Interstate 580, Shoreline Highway, East Blithedale Avenue, Sir Francis Drake Boulevard, and especially 101 are slow-and-go good chunks of the time. And if you have to commute from the North Bay, say up around Petaluma or Novato, to San Francisco, you're looking at the worst traffic jam in the country. No kidding. Something to consider if you plan to do some sightseeing in this area.

Hey, Marin: Mass transit is admirable, but Californians love their cars. They aren't going to give them up. EVER. Widen the damn roads.

At the Pine Cone Cafe

concerned West Marin residents are not well-to-do by any stretch, some West Marin residents come from serious wealth. They know about that life, and don't want it here. And they certainly don't want to end up like so many towns up and down the California coast—Carmel, Mendocino—which have sold their souls to the highest bidder in order to become rural playpens for America's corporate and entertainment elite. A situation where the locals end up in the role of indentured servants—running saccharine bed-and-breakfasts and cheesy chintz and T-shirt shops, or waiting tables at the local four-star eatery.

West Marin is a great place to visit mainly because it is *not* a tourist trap. Fortunately, the tourist accommodations that currently exist are a cut above the rest. **Manka's Inverness Lodge,** while not possessed of the cordial interested service found at the nearby **Blackthorn,** is clearly one of the top little hotels in the state. The rustic arts-and-crafts design brings one back to the feel of *A River Runs Through It* or the roar of the hunting camp. The **Pine Cone Cafe** in Point Reyes Station not only serves excellent food, but one of the waitresses has a habit of following the Monks across the country. She served us macaroni and cheese at the original Bistro Montage in Portland and lemonade and salad here. Across the way, Sean Penn and

After their sports utility vehicle was hijacked in L.A., Robin vowed to not raise her kids in the City of Sports Utility Vehicles. They decided to move up to Marin to live like "regular people" (muffled laughter, please). Always a fantasy of Hollywood "big stars," and almost always impossible. Still, the passionate twosome and their offspring are making a go of it, much to the chagrin of Marin residents who would prefer that area land values not soar through the roof. Penn and Wright will definitely have more privacy than in L.A. because (1) San Franciscans, as a rule, don't give a rat's ass about celebrities; and (2) Few Bay Area photographers have the moxie to mess with Sean Penn.

Robin Wright seem to enjoy **Tomales Bay Foods** and the **Bovine Bakery** (though don't get all affable with any Zen Center employees—they get buggy when you try to be overtly friendly; it's one of the unfortunate side effects of following your breath). In keeping with Point Reyes's commitment to the agricultural life, the **town clock** (at Main and 2nd) "moos" the hour at noon and 6pm.

West Marin: the epicenter of not only the San Andreas Fault, but the struggle over sustainable development in California.

Highlights of West Marin

1. **The Epicenter of the Great San Francisco Earthquake.** Go to the Bear Valley Visitors Center west of Olema. Follow the Earthquake Trail past the displaced fence.

2. **Bolinas.** Off Highway 1, 5 miles north of Stinson Beach. Home to alcoholic aging hippies and their dysfunctional offspring. Richard Brautigan (*Trout Fishing in America*) committed suicide here in 1985. Nice beach too.

3. **Green Gulch Farm.** Never mind the uptight samurai babes you often encounter in places run by the S.F. Zen Center; a drive to Green Gulch makes for the ideal Sunday outing. You do a little sit, hear a little talk, and chow down outside. As always, the food, overseen by the learned hand of author Ed Brown (*The Tassajara Bread Book*), is exquisitely flavorful, no doubt due to the Green Gulch organic farm, which supplies the produce to Greens restaurant in "the city."

4. **Industrial Light & Magic and Lucas Film.** ILM is the special-effects capital of the world film industry (*Titanic, Forrest Gump, Star Wars, Terminator 2, Schindler's List, Saving Private Ryan, E.T.,* et al.). Lucas Film has produced

five of the top twenty highest grossing films of all time. Both are situated on the gorgeous Skywalker Ranch.

5. **Ross Post Office.** No one can have mail delivered to their homes in Ross, so even gazillionaires and big stars have to retrieve their *Monk* subscriptions from their local P.O. box. Hang around, you never know who you might run in to.

All the Rest (Marin, Sonoma, Napa, et al.)

> **Harbin Hot Springs.** 18424 Harbin Springs Rd. (Middletown). ☎ **707/987-2477.** Go north on Hwy. 29 to Middletown. Once in town turn left on Hwy. 175. Go 3 short blocks and turn right on Barnes Rd. Follow for 1.5 miles up an incline. At the Y in road take the left option. You are now on Harbin Springs Rd. Another mile and a half will bring you to the Harbin gate.

Say what you will about Harbin's New Age, paganistic, rainbow-nation vibe, this is the most well run, big-hearted, egalitarian hot springs resort you may ever find, bar none. For over three decades Harbin has served as the alternative healing vortex for San Francisco freaks in the know. While neighboring Calistoga offers the packaged tours, mud baths, and water cures, Harbin takes the more organic approach, with less glitz, no neon, and a clothing-optional policy.

There's something refreshing about human nakedness in all its vulgarity. Flabby, skinny, old, young—everyone blends. Watching Harbin mature over the past thirty years from its barely concealed pothead beginnings to its current level of folksy elegance has been like watching a wayward child become an astute and caring friend. We love Harbin. It's a state of mind. The waters are smooth as silk and the five pools range from hellishly hot to icy cold, which is great for the hot-to-cold ritualistic crowd who spends hours sampling the extremes.

Now for the bad news: the Couples. There's just one too many freaky lovebirds doing the gushy stuff in the damn pools. On any given weekend evening you're going to find some serious coupling action to the point of embarrassment and floating sperm. Yeah, it's discouraged, but you just can't stop libido. And Harbin can't exactly afford to go Gestapo on these people either. While daylight brings more of a rainbow family feel, with groovy octogenarians, Berkeley scholars, Haight Street gutter punks, computer geeks, goddess types, gays, lesbians, zendoids, and kids, as soon as the sun sets, those cheesy pickup lines start darting across the pool. By evening's end the pools are so full of clichés ("What's your sign?") that barely a genuine word can be heard. Help!

But then, just when you're close to swearing off Harbin and its pothead woo-woo crowd, vowing never to return again, something remarkable happens that changes your mind. You take a hike through 1,200 acres of private land and have a personal epiphany. You meet your soul mate over casual dinner in the Stonefront Restaurant and, despite your cynicism, are soon "coupling" with the best of them. Or you've just had one of the most amazing water-immersion massages—called Watsu—and feel completely restored, despite how unbelievably tacky that whole Watsu thing looks. Chances are when you leave Harbin, whether you've camped overnight or stayed a week in their high-end luxury suites, you'll feel a good deal better than when you first entered the gate.

> **Isis Oasis.** 20889 Geyserville Ave. (Geyserville). ☎ **707/857-3524.**

Welcome to the Temple of Isis. Within earshot of the roaring freeway, this 10-acre estate is the epitome of New Age in all its tacky, cheesy glory. At the entrance a purple obelisk pulls you off the road into the compound where you'll find a pyramid, giant yurt, teepee, dome, and an Egyptian temple dedicated to Isis. A lodge and several cottages accommodate overnight retreaters, as does the wine barrel room. The centerpiece of the property seems to be a 500-year-old Douglas fir where many candlelit ceremonies transpire. A heavy-set woman with intense eyeliner—also, coincidentally, named Isis—owns and runs the place. Since the late seventies her "church" has been ordaining priests and priestesses, who are heavily indoctrinated into Goddess worship, rituals, and mythology. The grounds also serve as a retreat center where in a misguided moment Michael Monk once took a 3-day workshop in the early eighties with transpersonal psychologist Lynn Lombard to explore the "inner child" thing. As movements come and go, the Isis Oasis holds down the fort for all those myth-making, overweight, sex-deprived, middle-aged Goddesses who want a break from their mundane world of chocolate and Häagen-Dazs. It's easily the campiest retreat center in California.

> **Marin County Civic Center.** 3501 Civic Center Dr. (San Rafael). ☎ **415/473-3500.** Exit Hwy. 101 at San Pedro Rd. Take San Pedro Rd. to Civic Center Dr.

Beautiful, sunny, marvelous San Rafael has one reason, and one reason only, to pull off the road, and that's this Frank Lloyd Wright masterpiece. Wright's motto was "a good building is not one that hurts the landscape, but is one that makes the landscape more beautiful than it was before the building was built." He certainly hit the mark with the Marin Civic Center. This long horizontal building links three separate hills, utilizing colored composition tile, walkways, and stairs of terrazzo marble, and a barrel-arched roof of precast blue concrete that blends with the sky above. Though the building is more impressive from a distance, you should feel honored to walk the halls. Frank Lloyd Wright never did so himself. He died at the age of 92 and never saw the completion of the Civic Center.

> **Marin Headlands.** Near Golden Gate Bridge. ☎ 415/331-1540. North of bridge, exit Alexander Ave. Go left under highway and head west to Golden Gate National Recreation Area Marine Headlands.

The waves crash, birds squawk, and people walk barefoot in the grainy sand. It's all so predictable (Rod McKuen poetry please). Don't you just wish sometimes that an oil spill would come along to muck things up? At least it would be a change from the same ole sandy-beach-and-wave scene. Bunch of dead birds floating in oil. Smelly waves with gray foam. People in rubber shoes gingerly walking through the mess looking for birds to resuscitate back to a pointless seagull life. Why are we all here? Is there really any purpose to flying? What about those feathers? Something to ponder for the brain-dead hand-holding day-trippers from the city who occasionally get a stick up their butt to go see the world outside, but rarely get further than the parking lot of the Marin Headlands, in the back of their muscle car, porking Maria Sanchez, the neighborhood slut.

The headlands, fortunately, has never had a spill, but 2 pints of Jack should go down easy as you enjoy this perfect Californian scene. It really is amazing to have such a gorgeous stretch of green so close to a major city. Know any fish jokes?

> **Mount Tamalpais State Park Lookout.** Mill Valley. North on Hwy. 101, take Stinson Beach/Hwy. 1 exit. Follow shoreline about 2.5 miles and turn left onto Panoramic Hwy. After 5.5 miles turn right onto Pantoll Rd. and continue a mile to Ridgecrest Blvd. Follow to parking lot.

As any San Franciscan can attest, for well over three decades Mount Tamalpais has been a sacred place for countless hippies, New Agers, and pagans. Which means Mount Tam has undoubtedly sustained more hallucinogenic trips per capita than any other state park in the nation. I know at least 40 of my 309 trips were from the Lookout, including the one where I saw rocks turn into vaginas, and snakey appendages that looked vaguely like trees chant incomprehensible passages from the Koran toward the sky above. Such frequent trips are possibly one reason for my predilection for run-on sentences and odd grammatical choices (which my editor sometimes fixes and sometimes not). But I'm not the only one. On any given weekend in the sixties you could find clusters of dosers absorbed *with* the view; in the eighties you could find clusters of ecstasy-fueled visionaries absorbed *by* the view; and in the nineties you can find clusters of Y2Kers absorbed *in themselves*. Mount Tam is the place where mountain biking got its start, though if the militant Mount Tam hikers had their way, mountain bikers could just go to hell and stay there. This is a hiker's paradise. People take their hiking serious here. You gain perspective on Mount Tam (in fact, one of the early Monk projects, The Cookie—a precursor to the Clif Bar [see *Mad Monks On the Road*]—was conceived up here). And on clear days, of which there are many, you can see literally see forever.

> **Odiyan Tibetan Buddhist Retreat Center.** 33755 Tin Barn Rd. (Cazadero).
☎ **510/548-5407** (Dharma Press in Berkeley). From Stewart Point, go 4 miles up Stewart Point Springs Rd., turn right on Tin Barn Rd. and go approximately 4 miles to gate.

The drive through the redwoods takes you past an odd trailer-trash encampment on the side of the road, but by the time you arrive at the Odiyan gates you've hit nirvana. You've arrived at the renowned 1,500-acre monastery of the Nyingma School of Tibetan Buddhism, whose headquarters are in Berkeley. Though the monastery is rarely open to the public, the breathtaking roadside view of its astounding yellow-gold domed temple and fluttering yellow prayer flags is definitely worth the stop. Opened in 1975, the temple is an ongoing construction in progress, whose main purpose is the preservation of original Tibetan art, scrolls, and architecture. There is a small Buddhist community of monks and nuns who live inside the gate, some of whom are engaged in solemn three-year retreats. When not doing their prostrations and mantras, they are actively involved in the painstaking restoration of ancient art as well as the transcribing of text from scrolls. Just as the Celtic monk scribes were the hinges of Judeo-Christian history, it seems Tibetan monks have become the hinges of Buddhist history.

There are occasional public events and shorter 7-day retreats open to the public, but you have to join their mailing list to be informed. From outside the towering, barbed-wire fence you are invited to ring a bell for thirty seconds to let them know you're there. Rarely is there a response other than the bark of gnarly guard dogs who parole the perimeter. This thwarted our plan to squeeze between a gap in the gate. For those occasional times they do open the gate to visitors you'll be treated to one of the most amazing monastic digs in the nation.

> **Osmosis Enzyme Bath and Massage.** 209 Bohemian Hwy., near Bodega Hwy. (Freestone). ☎ **707/823-8231.**

Leave it to Northern California to reinvent the spa. Sure, you've had your mud baths, salt rubs, aromatherapy, and eucalyptus scrubs, but bet you haven't had an enzyme bath, now have you? This unimposing roadside retreat is a day-only spa with the requisite soft lights, music, and friendly atmosphere. Inside you'll find a squeaky-clean reception area with all the personality of a doctor's office. The fun begins out in the Japanese tea garden, where they serve you a cup of hot brew before getting you to completely disrobe and hop into the cedar troughs. Lying down, you'll be completely covered in steaming hot cedar and Douglas-fir chips, rice bran, and more than 600 enzymes derived from plants and vegetables. The point of all this is to completely detox your system, aid digestion and circulation, and provoke deep relaxation. After twenty minutes under the chips, with the metamusic sounds of the Monroe Institute (designed to further balance the hemispheres of your brain) you are Jell-O. From there you'll get wrapped mummy style in a private room to completely chill out before a pair of healing hands rub your last worries away. Is this heaven? No. It's Osmosis.

> **Sausalito House Boat Community.** Bridgeway and Gate 5 Rd. in Sausalito.

While the rest of Sausalito has sold out to the highest bidder, the original spirit of the place hangs on at this funky houseboat community. The legend of these boats goes back to Kerouac and the Beats, who spent lots of time here. Many of the squatters from that era still live here in outrageously outfitted "arks." Our friend Annie Sprinkle recently lived here, near one of the larger houseboats, the *Vallejo,* which was owned by sculptor Joseph Varda, who threw many outrageous parties in the fifties and sixties, and had many illustrious guests living there over the years, including Alan Ginsberg, Anaïs Nin, and Alan Watts. A little ways down the beautiful bike path that runs along the bay is where the Grateful Dead used to record. And a little further on down is where Otis Redding wrote "Sittin' on the Dock of the Bay."

While the beautiful Sausalito Bay is tranquil most of the time, things do get out of hand here on occasion. In December 1998, it seems Ms. Cathomas Starbird, a member of the Sausalito School Board, pleaded guilty to punching, jumping on, and biting another woman in an April 1998 altercation precipitated by the victim's refusal to perform oral sodomy on Ms. Starbird's husband. All three had just returned from a dinner celebrating the husband's birthday.

> **Sterling Winery.** 1111 Dunaweal Lane off of Hwy. 29 (Calistoga).
> ☎ 707/942-3300.

There are at least a hundred reasons to completely avoid Napa Valley's celebrated wine district. At the top of the list is the in-your-face marketing shtick that assaults you at every turn in the road. The same crowds that stay in bed-and-breakfasts, float hot-air balloons, and get married in gazebos flock to this valley, which is why we generally avoid it. Besides, if you were a connoisseur of fine wines and worthy of sampling some of the world's finest vino, there are dozens of better boutique wineries than the crass, sterile, mediocre wines put out by Sterling. So why do we give this the coveted, highly selective Monk seal of approval, for which wineries, restaurants, and tourist authorities routinely bribe us with food, lodging, and women? The view. Not a free view either. You earn this view after shelling out six bucks and hopping on an aerial tram that carts you 300 feet above the valley floor, where you disembark, walk around the picture-postcard-perfect Mediterranean-style winery, and take in the panoramic scene below. Grapes. As far as the eye can see. Obviously you won't be alone up here, and, in fact, if herd instinct grabs you like it did the Monks, you'll soon be hoofing through the self-guided tour, which delivers a surprisingly comprehensive survey of how wine is made, start to finish. But don't you dare walk away with one of their expensive wines. They've already got you down for six bucks. Instead, belly-up to the tasting room and get your money's worth.

> **Timber Cove Inn and Peace Statue.** 21780 N. Coast Hwy. 1 (Jenner).
☎ **707/847-3231.**

This eye-catching 72-foot-tall obelisk is as good a reason as any to get out of your car to stretch and gawk, after miles of switchback turns. It stands above the rocks behind Timber Cove Inn and was erected by the now-deceased Beniamino Bufano back in 1969. It's got the Madonna, some children, and an ominous hand painted on its side and is dedicated to world peace and the United Nations. Quaintly universalistic in its way. The artist sounds like he was a real lunatic, though, as most guys named Beniamino who build giant obelisks to world peace usually are. It took him seven years to erect the thing. He lived a monastic life and had an aversion to handling money; that is, if you're to believe the bar napkin with the full story, which a bartender thrust in our face when we inquired inside. Now that brings us to the other reason for stopping. Timber Cove Inn looks like a throwback to some obscure Reaganesque ocean lodge with "fine" art, "fine" food, and gallons of "finely made" vino. The redwood inn has that sort of tacky decorum that men in golf pants and their permed-hair wives seem to enjoy. Big cars were parked out front. The cocktail crowd inside, all in their upper seventies, seemed a bit sloshed for the middle of the day. The tall, redwood-beamed cathedral ceilings, floor-to-ceiling stone fireplace, and walls of glass suggest a cliff-hanging spaciousness. Of the fifty-one rooms, also maxed out in redwood, you have nifty balconies, big windows, and stunning views of the rocky coastline below. If ever there was a place to hole up during a storm, get plastered, and screw your brains out, this is the place. Cozy? Yep. Fireplaces? Yep. Jacuzzis in every room? Pretty much. Some of the rooms are built around rock formations, with lofts, skylights, and sauna. Downstairs things feel a tad pretentious in that gold-chain-and-Cadillac sort of way. They've got some resident raccoons that hang around begging for food. Entertaining! Also a grand piano. If you can't bear dropping a couple of big bills for a night's sleep, then take the tour of the obelisk, make a toast to peace, and be on your merry way.

Middle North

Mendocino

There is absolutely no denying the staggering natural beauty of the drive up Highway 1 from Point Arena to Mendocino. The scraggly, windswept quality of the oceanfront conjures images of *Wuthering Heights* and the crags and moors of Cornwall, England. When the fog rolls in, as it often does, it feels like ole Ireland too, perhaps one reason a lot of Irish settled in nearby Boonville and surrounding regions. Today, however, despite the mystical melancholy of the surrounding trees, sand, and water, the area is of questionable interest, overrun as it is by the quaintness bug that has infected every small town on the California coast. Blame it on the midbrow tourists (our favorite target) who come in search of this contrived sugarcoated Victoriana, and the folks around here who seem intent on establishing one coast-long branch of Bed, Breakfast 'N' Things—the more lace, the more cozy comforting quaintness, the better.

The town of **Mendocino** itself can make you sick with its precious tourist schlock, much like an overdose of saltwater taffy. Amidst the middle-aged couples in their J Crew attire, you will find the highly praised **Cafe Beaujolais** (emphasis on the "booozh"), 961 Ukiah St. (☎ **707/937-5614**). While the decor is syrupy—everything has to be flowery and Frenchy and femmy in these parts—the food is not. The corn and chili chowder was solid—thick, creamy, and incredibly tasty, with homemade corn chips to sprinkle on top. Ditto for the seared tuna with mango-chutney and Chinese noodles in peanut sauce. I had several world cuisines fighting it out in my stomach, and, at the end, there was peace throughout the kingdom. Don't expect much entertainment value from the clientele—ordinary Americans one and all, taking an ordinary vacation from their ordinary jobs, ordinary children, and ordinary lives.

If you're the sort of person that can savor "wine and cheese" without irony, get all gushy over twee Victoriana, shop without embarrassment for predictable paintings of orca whales, and sincerely like staying in neat-as-a-pin bed-and-breakfasts, then Mendocino is your burgh, baby.

Three—Count 'Em, Three—Places to Visit in and Near Mendocino

> **The Corners of the Mouth.** 45015 Ukiah St. ☎ **707/937-5345.**

It's a health-food store in a former Baptist Church that was built by a lumber baron for his daughter's wedding. The baptismal is full of beans.

> **Mendocino Art Center.** 45200 Little Lake St. (Mendocino). ☎ **707/937-5818.**

Just when we were on the verge of giving the town of Mendocino a big thumbs-down for selling out as a nauseatingly predictable bed-and-breakfast tourist trap (which, by the way, it is), we stumbled into the Art Center, and the town was redeemed. First of all, Tony Moretti, a transplanted New Yorker, was hitching down the highway with the fiercest smile we've ever seen, and we stopped to pick him up. As an artist in residence, he insisted we come take a quick tour of his current home, which we did. What we found was a seriously profound art collective with ten studios and eight resident artists who are well on their way to becoming world-class successes.

Back in 1959, Bill Zacha bought the existing property for next to nothing and opened up the center, where he both painted and taught. With his wife Jennie and fellow artists, he single-handedly developed this town as an art colony, pulling Mendocino out of its loser sea-village persona. Sounds like the Zachas were having a hell of a good time back before the tourists descended. Despite the ridiculous commercialization of their town and the local galleries loaded with mediocre "coastal art," the center has remained a steadfastly innovative force in the world of art. There's a strong community spirit among the artists. And the sculptors, including Mr. Moretti, are exquisite craftsmen. It's definitely worth a peek, as is the neighboring Mendocino Headlands loop road, where you go to watch whales and sunsets.

> **Skunk Train.** Foot of Laurel St. (Fort Bragg). ☎ **707/961-4414.**

Train-buff alert. Train buffs arrive like lemmings during summer months to ride these vintage motorcars, some of which are the only remaining trains of their kind (a 1925 MS-100, for example). Trains are cool. Unfortunately, people that ride trains are sometimes not. In other words, expect to contend with a buttload of bed-and-breakfast types. What grabbed us about the Skunk Train was, number one, the name. Seems that back in 1885, when they were used for hauling massive redwood logs to sawmills, the common remark about the gas engines was, "You can smell 'em before you can see 'em." Hence skunk. OK. Kind of funny. Kind of lame. But should you feel the itch to ride the rails and don't mind parting with $35, the Skunk Train takes you on a truly amazing 40-mile loop, around 381 curves, through two deep mountain tunnels, and across thirty bridges and trestles on its way to Willits and back. Along the way you chug through the heart of redwood country, get to ride in both open-air or closed cars, and get to breathe deep forest air without the hassle of hiking through the messy woods. The Skunk line has hauled loggers, freight, passengers, and stupid tourists along the same route for over 100 years. Nicolas Cage and Sean Penn took a turn while filming *Racing with the Moon*. Most folks favor Steam Engine no. 45, painted a splashy red with gold trim. But we liked the "Super-Skunk," a high-polluting diesel-powered locomotive that really lives up to its name.

Sagely City of Ten Thousand Buddhas

We've visited just about every type of Buddhist center you can possibly imagine, but nothing comes even remotely close to the interior of the temple at the Sagely City of Ten Thousands Buddhas, 2001 Talmage Rd., in Talmage, near Ukiah (☎ 707/462-0939; fax 707/462-0949; E-mail: paramita@dnai.com).

Leave it to the Chinese to build the most outrageous meditation hall in all of California. Ten Thousand—you can count 'em—*10,000 freakin' Buddha statues* are enclosed in Plexiglas along the walls, the ceilings, and behind the altar. In this tall space over 100 Buddhist monks and nuns (mostly Chinese, though there are other nationalities), and a smaller number of lay practitioners chant, bow, sit, then chant, bow, and sit some more. The whole experience is positively trippy, even if you've sat meditation for years. What's more, this truly is a little city. In fact, it's part of a growing American trend towards multimillion-dollar Buddhist complexes. Like the $30-million Hsi Lai Temple near Los Angeles (site of the Al Gore fundraising scandal), and the 125-acre Chuang Yen Monastery in New York, the 488-acre Sagely City has its own Buddhist University, Buddhist research-and-translation institute, international Buddhist convention center, stores, living quarters, and, most importantly, a growing number of well-trained and highly disciplined monks and nuns (especially nuns). There's also an excellent, clean, and exceptionally friendly vegetarian restaurant on the property, which is popular with local Ukiahans. As you walk amidst the beautiful hills, seventy buildings, and wandering peacocks, you will concur: There is no better evidence of the mounting strength of traditional Buddhism in America than the epic Sagely City.

Boonville and the *Anderson Valley Advertiser*

The drive to "Boont," as the old-timers who speak the native dialect of Boontlin call it, is more scenic then the town itself, which is your run-o-the mill tourist schlock-o'-rama. Rather than the original Scots-Irish Boontlin speakers who first made this town famous, Boonville is now known more for the rantings of the *Anderson Valley Advertiser*, which operates quite literally according to the Joseph Pulitzer motto: "A newspaper has no friends." It seems some locals don't find editor Bruce Anderson too amusing—or fair or accurate, for that matter. However, such criticism may be due to Anderson's clearly left-wing, pro-union political stands, which, to his credit, he doesn't require the other writers on his staff to ascribe to (for instance, Arthur Winfield Knight's movie reviews could not be considered politically correct). What's more, the *Anderson Valley Advertiser* is just that—an advertiser. And the highlight of the paper is the diverse range of local ads—everything from backhoe services, portable saw mills, and septic cleaning to lawyers "specializing in Marijuana Defense" to the United Farm Workers to the Boonville Church of Christ. It's a cranky, colorful (though black and white) and thoroughly entertaining weekly locals' paper (like Huntsville Arkansas's *Madison County Record,* but with attitude), where a diverse range of readers—some quite profound, some bordering on brain damaged—get actively involved. The paper ably keeps alive Boonville's reputation as a vortex of ornery and creative expression. (Subscriptions: $38/year to **Anderson Valley Advertiser,** 12451 Anderson Valley Way, Boonville, CA 95415; ☎ **707/ 895-3016;** E-mail: ava@pacific.net.)

The Far North

Humboldt: Land of Disenchantment

Humboldt County, like much of rural Northern California, is filled with aging boomers who rebelled against the system in a big way (read: grew pot) only to realize that the system won. Today they are reluctant members of the workaday world. And finding themselves amidst the rat race, with mortgages, child support, car payments, and health-care bills, they are very bitter the revolution failed. And they are very bitter they are perennially broke. And they are very VERY bitter that the Feds just busted one of the local hydroponics farms. That Humboldt hippie angst leaks out everywhere you go in these parts. Folks aren't nice and cuddly up here. At times

they're downright paranoid and suspicious. The dream is over, and a few locals are taking it out on everyone. Be warned.

Rules for engaging Southern Humboldt County: Watch for the poison oak, don't feed the bears, go to all the stupid big-tree tourist stops, and don't ask anyone how they really make their money.

Arcata

Good ole Arcata, a Mother Jones wet dream come to life. You want politically correct? They live it right down to the campgrounds for deadbeats (or in Arcata-babble, "urban travelers"). Voted the best place to live in the United States by the knee-jerk folks at *Utne Reader,* Arcata is an eco-warrior's dreamopolis—a Green Party mayor, the renowned Humboldt State Environmental Studies department, a major co-op, a weekly newspaper in which almost every article has some ecological connection, dreadlocked Deadheads, hippie chicks with names like Feather and Flower, the chaotic if well-intentioned Earth First! prominently working the local fair, hemp everything (clothing, food, and, of course, da kine green bud), and truly fantastic nature from here all the way to scenic Trinidad.

Of course, "best place" endorsement or no, radical chic Eric Utne would never live in a place with so many gutter punks, the bastard offspring of tolerant liberalism. These scummy potheads don't believe in work, freely scrounge from the bulk bins at the co-op, beg for the scraps left over at the local fair, and defecate wherever they please. They are disgusting, and, what's far worse, extremely self-righteous. Every attempt to rein them in is seen as an oppressive crackdown by the hegemonic capitalistic superstructure. There's nothing worse than someone doing the George Orwell "Down and Out" number who's misread some Gramsci.

Then again, if you like Berkeley's Telegraph Avenue, you'll dig Arcata. Like Telegraph, and the Haight, Arcata seems as if it is locked in some sixties time warp. It doesn't feel progressive, but, rather, regressive, as if the town had missed out on most of the major cultural revolutions of the past thirty years. Punk, rave, rap, ACT-UP, digital culture, all have made their minor mark here, but your average Canyon, River, and Sunshine still harkens back to the ethos of the alive and well Rainbow Nation. As one Humboldt State coed adroitly put it, "The Arcata definition of hip is to wear nothing that's leather and be a bisexual vegan."

Alas, Arcata does have one advantage over most other college towns in California: better nature, and more of it. For example, **Redwood Park** (at the east end of 11th and 14th streets) is breathtakingly beautiful. Ditto for the adjoining 600,000-acre **Community Forest,** and the lovely **Arcata Marsh and Wildlife Sanctuary** at the foot of I Street on Humboldt Bay. Arcata citizens are deeply invested in their natural environment, halting the creation of a Wal-Mart in nearby Eureka, blocking off-road vehicle access on neighboring beaches, and pioneering a wastewater treatment system that allows citizens to "flush with pride." If the city was populated by folks with a little more belief in hard-nosed law enforcement and a little less faith in libertarian socialism, it just might become one of the best towns in America.

Places and Things to Check Out in and Near Arcata

What other town of 15,000 do you know of that can support two huge natural-foods stores? In Arcata's case, there's the **Arcata Co-op** at 8th and I and its brighter, cleaner competitor, **Wildberries,** 747 13th St. (☎ **707/822-0095**), whose founder, Phil Ricord, in a bit of Arcata irony, created his own upscale natural-foods store because he "wanted a nice car and to eat sugar without guilt." Other area culinary vortexes include the **Cafe Mokka Coffeehouse** (5th and J), the friendly **Los Bagels** (1061 I), the vegetarian **Wildflower Cafe and Bakery** (1604 G at 16th Street). Despite the raves of locals, though, none of them are anything special in either food or decor. The real action, the real scene, the real sense of Arcata, is back at the Arcata Co-Op, where the homeless gutter punks are always out front ready to recycle your trash.

› Arcata to Ferndale Cross-Country Kinetic Sculpture Race. Arcata to Ferndale. Memorial Day weekend. www.roadtripamerica.com/places/ferndale.htm.

Every Memorial Day weekend the towns of Arcata, Eureka, and Ferndale host the Arcata to Ferndale Cross-Country Kinetic Sculpture Race, a colorful three-day

---

Arcata, I Think We Have a Transient Problem

Excerpt from the September 6 Arcata Police Report, reprinted from the September 17, 1998, *Humboldt Beacon:*

SUNDAY, SEPTEMBER 6

12:13am: A transient woman well known to Arcata's finest was cuffed for her drunken state and the puddle she left in public.

8:00am: Three transients camping in Redwood Park left at an officer's request.

8:21am: A Santa Rosa woman left her campsite in the 1200 block of F Street at an officer's request.

12:33pm: Three transients harassing customers at the Fourth Street Market were told to cut it out.

12:40pm: Another transient was told not to take items from the trash at the same market.

12:45pm: A Eureka woman reported that a transient's dog bit her daughter the previous day at the Co-Op.

---

costume ball/race that requires kinky bicycle/tank/boats to navigate varied terrain, including solid ground, sandy beach, and water. It's a cross between the Doo-Dah Parade and Bay to Breakers, and next to the requisite arrival of aging folk artists like Joan Baez at nearby Humboldt State, one of the highlights of the calendar year.

> **Carson Mansion.** 2nd St. and M (Eureka).

This is one of our favorite mansions in all of California. It was built in 1884/85 (it took 100 men two full years) as the home of lumber magnate William Carson, who had it boldly stationed right next to his lumber yards. Strikingly ornamented in a range of styles—Italianate, Stick, Eastlake, and Queen Anne—it is now a private club, so, naturally, most visitors meekly stand outside the gate taking photographs. Not the Monks. We don't bother with conventional protocol. We just walked right into the Carson Mansion, as if we belonged. We walked upstairs to the private parlors, through the dining room, and back out again. Nice mansion. Real nice mansion.

> **Earth First!** Corner of K and 8th St., in the Croatan Gallery (Arcata).
☎ 626/825-6598.

Does a storefront full of flea-ridden secondhand furniture, backpacks spilling across a floor, dozens of banners, flyers, stacks of boxes, unshaven unshowered scruffy guys, and hairy-armed chicks eating brownies sound like the headquarters of an organization capable of bringing the North Coast's most powerful industry to a halt? Not exactly. But then Gandhi was kind of a slouch too when you think of it. Though Earth First! has no official center, or leader for that matter, this thrown-together office near downtown Arcata is a major vortex for the in-your-face anarchists that populate this region. Visitors are welcomed and then put to work stapling, labeling, or filing. Anarchy moves at it's own imperceptible pace, so even when it seemed like absolutely nothing was happening during our visit, the flyers on the walls announcing countless actions belied the judgment. Ever since David Chain, a.k.a. Gypsy, was killed by a falling tree in the autumn of 1998, things have gotten extremely intense around Earth First! headquarters. Their poster child, Julia Butterfly, the longest-running tree-sitter in the world, recently passed the one-year mark, achieving cult status among the eco-warriors. Because of the tremendous publicity given to Julia's sit, the numbers of tree-sitters continues to grow, especially at their current camp in the woods, near Carlotta, deep in Grizzly Creek Redwoods State Park, where the tree-sitters train. Also thanks to Julia, the main focus of their efforts in this region—saving the last remaining stands of old-growth redwoods—is starting to gain major international recognition. Heretofore written off as the tree-spiking fanatical fringe of the environmental movement, Earth First! is, dare we say, getting respectable. So before you write this motley crew off as a bunch of pot-smoking, vegan, unshaven Deadheads (which many of them are), remember that many Earth Firsters are also educated, extremely articulate, and dedicated to one hell of a noble cause: KEEPING JULIA UP IN THAT TREE!!

> **Kinetic Sculpture Race Museum.** 580 Main St., at Shaw St. (Ferndale). ☎ 707/725-3851.

Ferndale may have its quaint Victorian houses, but the reason for this town's place on our map is the annual Memorial Day Ferndale, Eureka, Arcata Kinetic Sculpture Race. If this doesn't prove the effects of too much pot on one's brain, then nothing will. For three days across a 38-mile course, hundreds of mobile sculptures hit the streets in what many consider the most outlandish road race in the world. The rules are as follows: the sculptures must be human-powered, capable of traversing roads, sand, mud, and water, but cannot pose a danger to society. This leaves a pretty wide playing field. What you get are monster machines like the 3-ton Quagmire Queen that takes up to twenty-eight people to power. The brain behind this madness is Ferndale artist Hobart Brown who in 1969 spent a weekend deconstructing his son's tricycle, transforming the three-wheeler into a five-wheeled bright red creation that he took to riding down Main Street. Apparently this started a trend and soon the mad artists of Ferndale were attempting to outdo one another with their mobile sculptures on wheels. Now the race attracts an international following with entries such as the Pencilhead Express, Nightmare of the Iguana, and the Leprechaun Limo. A downtown storefront hosts a yearlong exhibition of previous contenders that includes the Highway Patrol Car, the Top Banana and the remarkable People-Powered Bus. They say every vehicle floats, but we'd suggest returning on Memorial Day to see for yourself.

Note: Once you tire of the Victorian utopia of Ferndale, make sure you take a drive out Highway 211 to Cape Mendocino's refreshingly isolated "Lost Coast," one of the last undeveloped shorelines on the West Coast.

> **The Pacific Lumber Company.** 125 Main St. (Scotia). ☎ 707/764-2222.

Perched along the banks of the Eel River at the northern end of the Avenue of the Giants is the mill where those behemoth coastal redwoods meet their maker. This is hands down the biggest, meanest, loudest lumber mill in the world, and Scotia is the last remaining company town in California. Pacific Lumber built it all and owns it all, from the blocks of white houses, schools, and church to the shopping mall and marketplace. The mill employs a good portion of the 1,000 souls who live here, and they are pretty up front about their operation. You can take a firsthand look at how those mega tree trunks are converted into lumber, paneling, and chips. You might want to get yourself in the mood by popping on a tape of Throbbing Gristle,

Pacific Lumber Company

drinking a quart of Jack, and donning a full-cover flight suit with helmet, because a trip through this mill is the equivalent of standing on the exhaust end of a 747 just before takeoff. To start the tour, get your pass at the museum located in the middle of town at 124 Main St., then follow the signs to the visitor's entrance. You begin your self-guided tour at the bucolic Anadromous Fish Learning Center and from there yellow lines lead up the stairs of Mill B. From an overlook you watch the first phase of redwood deconstruction as mammoth tree trunks roll across the debarker—huge rotating gears with Godzilla-sized teeth—and are sprayed down by a hydraulic hose at 1,600 pounds per square inch, sending bark flying across the yard. At that point the barkless trees are forced into a head-rig where serious 60-foot band saws begin slicing away at the once noble trees, sending boat-sized planks down convey-or belts for further cuts and sizing. Not a shred of timber is wasted in this mill—every particle of tree becomes product in one form or another. As you follow the yel-low line across a catwalk and in through the mill you have a bird's-eye view of the hundreds of workers, grim faced, haggard, and worked to the bone. They toil below, sorting, marking, stacking, and operating the controls of machines. The sound of saws ripping through redwood brings to mind prehistoric hornets on a death binge. Loud thumping, incessant clacking, nauseating pounding and screeching of machines. We loved it. Finally something bigger than us that overpowered all mind chatter. Our jaws slacked, our eyes bulged wide, and our knuckles turned white. It's as good as a slaughterhouse, if you like that sort of thing. By the time we got to the other end we felt like we'd just had five multiple orgasms or took a hit in the head from a 3-foot sledgehammer. Oh, um, maybe we should have donned the earplugs they provide at the beginning of the tour.

The spirit of Julia Butterfly hangs over the North Coast like an apparition of the Mother Mary. Having lived in an endangered California redwood since 1997, without even *once* touching the ground, she's become the patron saint and martyr of tree-huggers everywhere (there's even a Web site in her honor—www.lunatree.org). Julia has a cell phone, allowing her to do periodic interviews with the press, and she has a fantastic support team of Earth Firsters. She is committed to her cause, though some argue that maybe she should just be committed. What brought Ms. Butterfly to this juncture?

Allegedly, she was in a terrible car accident, which not only wounded her but shook loose her reason to live. When she encountered the giant redwoods, her spirit was revitalized.

When we first learned of Julia Butterfly we were charmed. What a sweet, innocent soul, staying in a tree she loved in order to protest the logging of ancient forests. We also thought she might be a little nuts. There were reports that her car accident had, in fact, rendered her a little deficient in some areas, but, still, what innocent moxie, what sweet courage. The tree-spiking anarchist in us rooted for her success.

As always with such pure souls, there is a whole industry set up around them, at first to protect them, but over time to gain maximum ideological mileage out of their heroism. This is clearly the case with Julia, who is first and foremost an Earth Firster, at least judging by the group that's her biggest defender.

Not surprisingly, her tree-sit has drawn unprecedented attention to the pivotal struggle in Northern California—the interests of big lumber versus the values of environmentalists seeking to preserve the last and largest remaining unprotected grove of ancient redwoods on earth. It is a "versus" situation, unfortunately, due to unyielding positions taken by both sides. So, as a counterbalance to the steadfast position taken by our wizened logger friend Mr. Zimmerman (see interview in chapter 7, "Road Trip: The Mountains"), we were naturally curious about the young and determined Madam Butterfly.

She was born Julia Hill, and her father was an evangelistic preacher, which might explain some of her zeal. It was in August, 1996, while a bartender in Fayetteville, Arkansas, that Julia had a near-fatal accident, which ultimately resulted in her pilgrimage to California the following summer to reassess her life. It was here, in Arcata, that she first ran into activists from Earth First!, the controversial environmental group that has used almost every tactic in the *Anarchist's Cookbook* to save old-growth forests. Julia, who adopted the name "Butterfly," was soon volunteering to climb a tree, despite her aversion to heights.

On December 10th, 1997, when Julia was only 24, she climbed 180 feet up an ancient redwood and began what has become the longest recorded tree-sit in history—or at least North American history, given that the Siddhas of India have been known to hang in, around, or off of trees for decades at a time until their legs shrivel into match sticks. In the grand American tradi-

tion of civil disobedience by "lady conservationists," she soldiers on, month after month, 15 stories up the 200-foot, 1,000-year-old giant redwood she calls "Luna."

From her lofty view, on an 8'×8' platform, she overlooks snowcapped mountains, the Pacific, and a massive mud slide, caused by the Pacific Lumber Company's clear-cutting, that destroyed nearly ten homes in nearby Stafford. Pacific Lumber, which is owned by Houston-based Charles Hurwitz, has used every tactic imaginable to dislodge her, including round-the-clock floodlights, air horns, guards to cut off her supplies, chain saws felling trees around her, and a helicopter, caught on video, which buzzed so low it was stirring nearby branches as a man shouted from below, "Get ready for a bad hair day!"

When she's not clinging on for dear life (40-m.p.h. winds once nearly blew her off the tree), she's busy writing poetry, climbing barefoot through the branches for exercise, or cooking stew over her one-burner stove. Julia hauls up supplies from her doting ground crew by a long rope and swabs herself down for the occasional bath. Occasionally Luna talks to her in a calming, powerful voice. It's a girl tree, 'natch.

At Pacific Lumber headquarters they are a bit skeptical that the tree's had much to say and are just patiently waiting for the day when Ms. Butterfly will fly away and they can convert Luna into $600,000 worth of board feet for home paneling, outdoor decks, and a few more redwood hot tubs.

And what does Madam Butterfly say to that?

"I gave my word to this tree, the forest, and to all the people that my feet would not touch the ground until I had done everything in my power to make the world aware of this problem and to stop the destruction."

She's not coming down.

Garberville

A former logging town now a tourist stopover point, Garberville feels redneck hippie. In other words, it's live and let live up here in the redwoods, where it gets real hard telling the rednecks from the aging freaks, since there's a little of each in most of the residents. For instance, that nice portly 55-year-old fellow making your sandwich at the Subway carries a gun. Maybe that's why he's so easygoing; he has sure-fire backup.

True cutting-edge culture is hard to come by in these parts. You're far enough north to be above any high-brow urban influence. Like other isolated parts of the country, folks up here feel free to be their tacky wacky American selves. Burl, baby, burl.

Garberville is America's equivalent of Medellin, Columbia. More than a few of the businesses are fronts. The main gig is *weeeeeeed*. The local papers carry a "bust barometer." There's a hemp shop, rather odd for a town of only 1,400, a **Hemp Festival** in November, plus a sinsemilla-friendly **Reggae on the River** fest at nearby French's Camp every August. The hardware store sells grow lights and hydroponics equipment (don't ask why). Oh, and that 55-year-old guy again? The one making you a sandwich at Subway? He drives a brand new $55,000 truck. Betcha didn't know you could make that kind of money slapping provolone and bologna onto whole-wheat buns.

> **Legend of Bigfoot.** 2500 U.S. 101 (Garberville). ☎ 707/247-3332.

Yet another roadside schlock shop, this time with a Bigfoot theme. Read the wall clippings and brace yourself for a close encounter with the legendary Bigfoot, the part man/part ape who's allegedly been terrorizing the locals for the past five decades. Other than some questionable photos of the naked big-footed fellow, the highlight of the store is the life-size replica of Bigfoot that stands front and center. You'll also find immeasurable chuckle factor in the tacky redwood lawn ornaments, redwood planters, redwood birdhouses, and carved redwood deer.

›road trip:
the mountains

Beaches, deserts, the tallest trees on Earth—you'd think the Gods would have stopped there. But they went one notch higher: "The Mountain Region" of California.

While many consider the Colorado Rockies to be the cream of continental highlands, the California mountain ranges hold their own. For instance, along the 400-mile eastern corridor of the state, you will regularly encounter the Sierra Nevadas—the steepest mountain range in the Lower 48, reaching their pinnacle at the 14,494-foot Mount Whitney, the highest point in the continental United States. In addition, the mountain region's volcanic Cascades—Mounts Lassen and Shasta, and Medicine Lake Highlands—are filled with thousands of amazing lava tubes, cinder cones, ice caves, natural bridges, craters, obsidian flows, and faults. What's more, the rock 'n' roll tectonic plates that forced the Sierras to their remarkable heights created North America's third deepest lake, Lake Tahoe. The views from the valley floor of Yosemite inspire millions of visitors every year. And the little known Lava Beds National Monument above Shasta offers one of the most surreal landscapes in the world. Need we say more?

In fact, we do. Because prior to the four-lane highways that now cross these mountain passes, the California mountain ranges were a major obstacle to early settlers doing that "go West young man" thing. In point of fact, for the first half of the 19th century California mountain areas were generally passed over in favor of the low-lying Californian delta and coast. But by the time the Donner Party finished smacking their lips from a hard-earned meal, all that changed. Gold was discovered at Sutter's Mill, and the news spread like wildfire through every town in America, and many around the globe.

Not since the Crusades had so many wild-eyed souls relocated in such a short period of time. The rugged mountains soon sported booming mining towns, but by 1855 most of the surface gold had been panned, causing disheartened prospectors to kill themselves off at the rate of 1,000 per year. When the big mining companies came in for the final rape, pillage, and settlement, the Californian mountains were a done deal. Good-bye pristine unpopulated wilderness. Hello op-por-tun-ity!

The Sierra Nevada and the Mount Shasta / Mount Lassen Cascades arguably made the single most important contribution to putting California on the world map. Without "the gold in them thar hills," San Francisco would have been nothing but a smelly little port with lots of randy sailors, and L.A. just a mediocre version of San Francisco, but drier. Gold turned San Francisco into the darling city of the West and the snow-fed rivers turned Los Angeles into the borrowed-water urban-sprawl mecca that it is today.

With gold, lumber, minerals, and water, it didn't take long before the mountains became prime commercial real estate. Fortunately, a few visionaries had the foresight to set aside most of the natural splendor. From the sheer rock walls of Yosemite, to the alpine scenery of Kings Canyon and Sequoia, as well as Mount Shasta (14,162 ft.), Lassen (10,457 ft.), and Whitney (14,495 ft.), most of this area's richest natural treasures are relatively unspoiled and accessible to all.

Highway 395

You'll be using this highway a lot in this region, but before you take it for "granite," remember it is a highlight in its own right. The 395 takes you along the eastern side of the Sierra Nevadas, past a series of compelling attractions, all prominently demarcated by highway signs. From the eerie emasculated Owens Lake (see below), to the Still Life Cafe (see below), to the Alabama Hills in Long Pine (where many a Hollywood epic has been filmed, including *Gunga Din,* and where the Long Pine Film Festival is held every year) to the giant tuffs of Mono Lake (we challenge you to find a more bizarrely beautiful lake in all of America), to Bodie (the finest ghost town in the West—go east of 395 along 270) to a Japanese internment camp far up near the Nevada border, 395 has it all. Because of its diversity of climates and terrain, amazing scenery, and compelling roadside distractions, 395 rates as our favorite highway in the entire state.

As we traveled thousands of miles, winding in, out, and around these mountains, it became clear that without these impressive ranges California would be nothing more than a long dry desert with some bodacious beaches. Our road trip through this region covers both the outstanding nature and quintessential road stops to prove that even at higher altitudes, California quirkiness is alive and well.

The Northern Mountains

The northern portion of our Mountains chapter focuses on the Crown Jewels of California—Lassen and Shasta. Unlike Yosemite, Napa Valley, and most other natural gems of the state, these two mountains are largely undisturbed by tourists and development, and remain about as pure and untrammeled as you're going to find in this state, revered by spiritual seekers and nature lovers around the world.

› **Lake Siskiyou.** Mt. Shasta City. ☎ **530/926-2618.** Exit I-5 at Central Mt. Shasta exit. Go west to stop sign then turn left on Old Stage Rd. Follow road to Y, veer right and continue to park entrance. You will be at the Lake Siskiyou Campground. Signs will point you to the lake.

The confident grandeur of Mount Shasta seems to inspire wiggy spiritual quests. For instance, over the years Shasta has attracted countless New Agers searching for those elusive Lemurians supposedly hiding out inside the mountain. In 1986 the Harmonic Convergence brought thousands of seekers to the mountain's base, all hoping to catch a glimpse of the mother ship. In earlier times the mountain attracted loggers and miners. But for the nature lovers among us who aren't inclined to dig for minerals or sit Zen at the Shasta Abbey (next to a roaring freeway), you will get a hit of satori by simply pulling off the road and heading straight for Lake Siskiyou. We all have our favorite pristine mountain lakes. For the Monks, Lake Siskiyou has been our preferred road stop for every northbound trip through California for the last thirteen years. Under the towering shadow of Mount Shasta, this lake has water that looks so pure you want to drink it, but really shouldn't because boats, people, birds, and babies populate the beaches on warm days and could introduce unwelcome intestinal critters. Get yourself an inner tube and float out to the middle of the lake, gaze up at the magnificent peaks, and know deep inside that you don't need space visitors to whisk you away to a better life. Paradise is right here.

› **Lava Beds National Monument / Captain Jack's Stronghold.** Hill Rd., east of Dorris. ☎ **916/667-2284.** Go east on Hwy. 161 for 20 miles. Turn right on Hill Rd. and follow signs to Lava Beds National Monument Headquarters for specific directions to the site of Captain Jack's Stronghold.

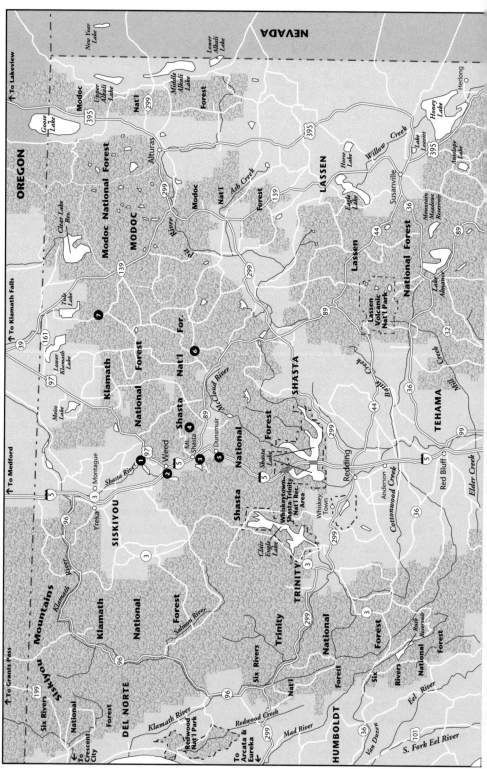

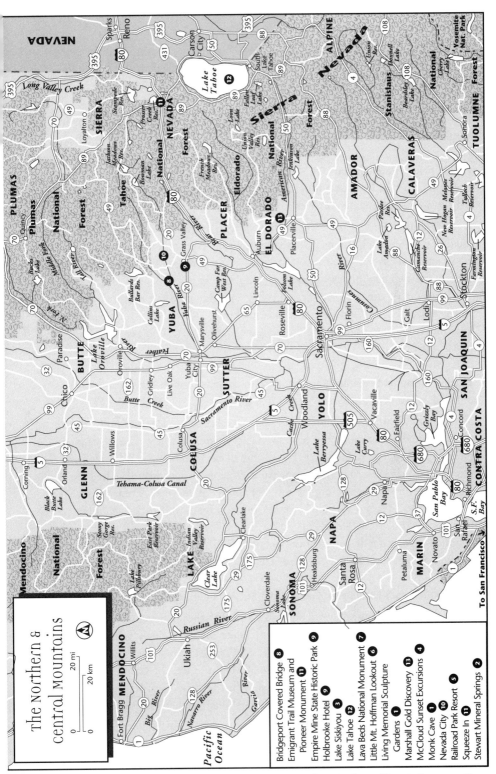

The Northern & Central Mountains

Bridgeport Covered Bridge **8**
Emigrant Trail Museum and Pioneer Monument **11**
Empire Mine State Historic Park **9**
Holbrooke Hotel **9**
Lake Siskiyou **3**
Lake Tahoe **12**
Lava Beds National Monument **7**
Little Mt. Hoffman Lookout **6**
Living Memorial Sculpture Gardens **1**
Marshall Gold Discovery **13**
McCloud Sunset Excursions **4**
Monk Cave **1**
Nevada City **10**
Railroad Park Resort **5**
Squeeze In **11**
Stewart Mineral Springs **2**

The bleak landscape, surrounded by cone-shaped mountains, should alert you to the fact that you're in prime real estate for dormant volcanoes. Though the last active eruptions were 100,000 years ago, the after-effects have made for one nifty national monument, with over 70 square miles of underground caves. There are literally over 300 lava caves, lava tubes, and ice caves in this vicinity, and the rangers will even loan out flashlights for unlimited miles of exploring. Don't miss the petroglyph rock drawings.

> **Little Mount Hoffman Lookout.** Medicine Lake, north of Bartel. ☎ 916/964-2184. From Hwy. 89 take Rd. 15 north and then right on the Medicine Lake Rd. Follow the signs for approximately 4 miles.

Under ordinary circumstances you might balk at paying $35 to sleep in a cabin that requires you to bring bedding, garbage bags, cooking utensils, and your own matches. But the inconvenience you suffer affords you a 360° view of Mounts Shasta, Lassen, and McLoughlin, as well as of the neighboring volcanic landscape. Situated 7,309 feet up, this historic 1920s cabin comes equipped with a woodstove, two cots, an ax, shovel, bucket, and fire extinguisher. There is no water (you must bring in your own). There is an outhouse. If you want that Kerouac *Dharma Bums* feeling, this is your spot.

> **Living Memorial Sculpture Gardens.** Hwy. 97 (1 mile north of Hwy. A-12), north of Weed. ☎ 916/938-2218.

With Mount Shasta and miles of open range as a backdrop, Dennis Smith created the ultimate outdoor gallery for his astounding sculptures. These towering masterpieces constitute one man's vision of war and all the suffering it brings. However, this is not some cheesy, patriotic theme park. These exceptionally well crafted pieces represent a truly authentic display of compassion. At the park entrance you are greeted by the "Peaceful Warrior." From there you drive down a rock-lined dirt-road loop to view the "Flute Player," "The Why Group," the "Nurses," and others. Each sculpture is packed with provocative symbolism. Mike Monk's favorite was the fornicating couple, appropriately entitled "Coming Home."

> **McCloud Sunset Excursions.** End of Main St. (McCloud). ☎ 530/964-2142.

We love train rides, but, unfortunately, so do all the other schmucks who wax nostalgic at the sight of a steam locomotive. While most old-timey train rides are nothing more than a ride around the block, McCloud takes you on a jaw-dropping 3-hour, 40-mile excursion around the base of Mount Shasta. McCloud was once a company town, and the train, originally called the McCloud River Railroad, follows tracks that were laid for logging the area forests. They still operate minimal freight trains along with their weekend dinner loads. We suggest giving the $70 gourmet

At the Living Memorial Sculpture Gardens

dinner a skip and opt for the $9 open-air excursion train, where the views beat out the indoor dining car anyhow. Beware of tourists who show up wearing turn-of-the-century clothing for that added nostalgic edge.

> **Monk Cave.** Rte. A-12, north of Weed. From the intersection of Hwy. 97 and A-12, go approximately 1.7 miles north on A-12. Look for dirt road on right. Follow about one-tenth of a mile and stop at rock outcropping surrounding small pit in ground.

O.K., so it's really named Sand Cave and is part of the Shastina Lava Caves, but in 1986 a vital piece of Monk history occurred at the mouth of this 991-foot-deep cave. Camped in our trusty Ford Econoline van, the Monks made this spot one of our early overnight camps. While cats Nurse and Nurse's Aide staked out territorial domain by spraying every rock in sight, we performed our first ritualistic shaving of the heads to achieve that authentic Monk look. After the shave we noticed the outcropping of rocks, and the pit. Sans flashlights we entered the pit, discovered the cave entrance and spent the next few hours stumbling blindly in the dark down this remarkable hole. Being that hot lava once carved out thousands of these portals to the underworld, it's not that unique for the region. In fact, the local Weed Tourism Department will direct you to the Pluto Caves, which are much bigger. But hey, it's our cave, and you can take a hike into subterranean Monk history if you dare.

Interview:

Elmer Zimmerman,

Retired Lumberman and Curator of the Lumber Town Museum

We're standing in the former courthouse, now turned Lumber Town Museum, in downtown Weed. Elmer Zimmerman, dressed in lumberjack plaid, seems pretty chipper for his 88 years. He's waiting for us at the door, and has turned on the stove to take the chill off.

Elmer gives a quick tour of the museum, taking his time explaining the old tools of the trade. He finds exceptional amusement in showing an old ax that was sunk so deep in a tree that the logger couldn't get it out. The tree ultimately grew over the ax, and now that section of the tree is in the museum. He came to town in his twenties, while the Great Depression was in full swing. For the next several years he clung to his job, despite lack of pay, just so he'd have a roof over his head and food in his belly. It was a company town and he, like thousands of others, were unwittingly made into indentured servants. The company owned the stores, the forest, and essentially the men. But the forest treated him well, and he stuck it out for the next fifty years, as manual lumbering was ultimately replaced by the big machines. It's been a long haul, and it shows. But Elmer's only complaint about his life in the trees is just one: Those damn environmentalists.

Monk: What got you out to Weed?

EZ: Oh, I was just moseying around the country during the Great Depression. I'd heard the company here was hiring and logging seemed like steady work. It was the Longbow Lumber Company. They were nationwide. In fact, they were worldwide. They had lots of Ponderosa Pine here, and this town was nothing but a logging town owned by that company. Everything north of Division Street for the next hundred miles was company.

Monk: So when you got here you were immediately hired?

EZ: Yes. I started with minor jobs out in the woods. There was an awful lot of hand labor including laying tracks. But mostly the Mexicans laid tracks. They had hundreds of men in the woods. In the woods it was all hand labor. The log rolling [the movement of logs], however, was by railroad.

Monk: So they built rails all through the woods?

EZ: Right. They'd haul the men out to the woods and then at night they'd haul 'em back in again. In much later years they bought gasoline-powered railroad cars to haul the men out. Once they got you out there in the woods, you were cutting down trees by saw and ax. It wasn't until 1941 before they bought any power chain saws, and the first ones in those days were not good at all. Finally, during the war they fixed us up with 10-horsepower electric saws. The motor was only about 8 inches in diameter and about 15 inches long but it had a real high torque. But we had to mount big generators on the side of a tractor to run the saws. Those generators were pretty heavy.

Monk: How many men would be involved in the falling of a tree?

EZ: The men work in pairs. You must understand that they've got to be compatible to work together. They usually work year-round falling trees. The foreman laid out 300-foot-wide strips away from the train track. He'd make miles of strips [i.e., areas], marking the trees. The men would each have their own strip and fall all the trees. That strip might take them a week or maybe two weeks to cut up, depending on the timber stand.

Monk: What sort of tools would they be using back then?

EZ: A saw, a sledgehammer, and wedges. You have to use wedges, so if the tree is leaning a little bit they drive wedges in there so it would fall in a certain direction. The main thing is to not cross trees. You never cross trees when you fall them down because you'll break 'em all to hell.

Monk: Was there a lot of competition between the teams? Would there be rivalry?

EZ: Oh, yes. That always goes on to see who could cut more than the other one to brag about it. They got paid so much for every tree they put down. A set of fallers fall a tree, up till noon. In the afternoon one of those two men starts to do the limbing. He'd chop all the branches off of the trees. And the other one would do the bucking. He'd measure and cut the tree in 32-foot log lengths. That is the toughest job in the woods, falling the timbers and getting it worked up. It's hard to even understand how hard it is. They also had to carry a hammer, wedges, and saw oil. It's nothing more than diesel oil that they used to sprinkle on the saw when they run into tree pitch to keep it lubricated.

Monk: What was your job back then?

EZ: I worked skidding and loading. They had just discontinued the horses when I came here and started using winches on these big machines. When I got here they built a camp 42 miles from Weed. It wasn't a camp, it was a regular town named Tennant. They furnished everything. They put in a real big steam-powered plant that served the whole town, all the shops and everything. They built 100 family houses all alike. Two-bedroom houses. And they had a big cookhouse to serve 200 men.

Monk: What was it like to live in a company town?

EZ: It was very interesting. The depression was at the worst, and the market for Douglas fir up north just went flat. The pine market was bad, but the fir market was just dead. We kept operating here. We went down to three days a week, but it was enough to keep bread on the table. The manager we had, Mr. White, they gave him orders to shut this down, but he said, "We've got to keep the people alive." So he kept it going three days a week for several years. It was tough. Our wages went down to nothing. We basically worked for food and shelter. If you weren't married, you lived in sort of a bunk house. They built a hundred-bed rooming house.

Monk: When things went from manual labor to machinery, how did this affect the men?

EZ: There was a crew of maybe three men and a foreman for skidding and loading. Those fellas, when they started to swing over to tractors, didn't like that. They weren't mechanically inclined anyway so there were a lot of problems. They just didn't know what to do with the tractors. They couldn't see how the tractor was the right way to go even though they were a lot more productive with a lot less injuries.

Monk: How would injuries happen?

EZ: The skidders would run a line out 2,000 feet to the trees. The guy out there, he don't see anything because he's so far away. When these logs moved, they have tremendous power, and you'd better watch out. There'd be fatalities and they'd brag about it. They'd just leave him there in the forest till the shift was done.

> *"When these logs moved, you'd better watch out. There'd be fatalities and they'd brag about it. They'd just leave him there in the forest till the shift was done."*

Monk: You're kidding! Somebody drops dead and you just leave them there?

EZ: Till the end of the day.

Monk: Wow. Till the end of the day! So back in those days did they have reforesting programs such as they do now?

EZ: Longbow Lumber Company was the first company that I knew of up here on the West Coast that started that. They built their own seed orchard out at Tennant, raised their own seedlings, and started planting them. I'll admit that it was a failure because they didn't know what they were doing. You've got some terrible winters and you've got some awful dry summers. They sent those foresters up there to do this job and they just couldn't get going.

Monk: So they weren't very successful.

EZ: Where they cut the most, that part usually took care of itself. They left seed trees to put out the seed. They got plenty of new stuff coming in that way but it was where they had big fires that they had problems. Fire was the number-one enemy of forestry.

Monk: How long did you work in Tennant?

EZ: Tennant was our headquarters. Then we got too far out of there to transport the men back and forth every day. So we put up a stag camp. They moved the men out 50 miles away and kept the women in town. Whether it was five days a week or six, they stayed there all week and the company would haul them back to headquarters on Saturday night, take 'em back out to stag camp Sunday afternoon. The married men were home for just one night. So you can understand why they called those trains names. The one that brought the men in, that was the Stiff Pecker Special. And Sunday afternoon, the Limber Prick brought them back out to the camp again. We operated out of Tennant up until 1957. Then we had some stands of timber left, but it didn't justify keeping the railroad, so they shut Tennant down completely and moved all the men into Weed. That was one year after International Paper bought everything. They bought the whole company. Everything up and down the West Coast and all the timber lands.

Monk: At what point did the environmental movement begin affecting your industry?

EZ: It didn't do much here until recent years. When the state passed a law that said you couldn't cut a tree that was under 18 inches in diameter, that's when problems started. But we had good people at the head of our company. You have to be careful on your skidding not to do damage to the reproduction that's there.

Monk: You said you started having trouble more recently with environmentalists?

EZ: It's just a terrible thing. They stopped us from cutting old growth and they cannot get it in their head that a tree does not live forever. It's just so stupid. These trees get old, die, and stand there for a few years, and finally they get rotten on the stump and fall over on the ground. You can't even go in there and take that dead tree out of there. It has to lay there and rot. It's so ridiculous. We're the most wasteful country in the world with wood and it's terrible. It's ridiculous the way they're doing it.

Monk: So you think a lot of these laws are just too extreme?

EZ: Yep. And when it falls down it's sometimes a wind blowing them over. You could still salvage something out of it but nope—you can't touch it. They say it provides feed for the other trees. Well, you've already got 6 inches of crap on the ground there. You've got so many needles off these trees and little limbs that the seed don't get down to the ground.

Monk: What's your view of Earth First! and environmentalists in general?

EZ: They're just too ignorant. They think they're doing a good job and they mean well but they just don't know a damn thing about forests. They don't understand that the forest doesn't need these old trees to rot and decay on the forest floor. People been working the forests for longer than any of them been around. Those damn environmentalists should just leave us alone because we know what we're doing. They don't understand the forest. But we do!

The **Lumber Town Museum** is located at 303 Gilman St. in Weed (☎ **530/938-2352**).

The Caboose Motel

> **Railroad Park Resort.** 100 Railroad Park Rd. (Dunsmuir). ☎ **916/235-4440.**

We call it the Caboose Motel because what you get in this novelty act masquerading as a resort is a parking lot full of cabooses circling a swimming pool. The individual cars sit like forlorn monuments, oddly detached from their choo-choos. Each car is restored beyond perfection and has brass beds, color TVs, full baths, and nifty little overhead sitting areas where the brakeman used to smoke his pipe. Beyond the motel lies the stunning **Castle Crag State Park** and the source of the Sacramento River.

> **Stewart Mineral Springs.** 4617 Stewart Springs Rd. (Weed). ☎ **916/938-2222.** North of Weed on I 5, Edgewood exit. Go under freeway and turn right on Edgewood. 1 mile turn left on Stewart Mineral Springs Road. Follow to end.

The teepees are a dead giveaway that this place marches to a different drummer. Especially when the purification sweats led by a Karuk Medicine Man commence. This 100-plus-year-old spa was healing the afflicted long before the hippies, New Agers, and hot-springs connoisseurs made it their stomping grounds—its healing mineral waters were legendary among Native Americans. When Henry Stewart arrived in 1875 and was miraculously restored to health, he showed his appreciation by taking possession of the springs. There are now over eighteen buildings that include cabins, dormitories, an **A** frame house, and the aforementioned teepees. Park Creek flows through the middle of the property. But if you're dreaming of a soak under the stars you'll have to settle for old-fashioned bathtubs inside a bath-house. Stewart Springs is rustic and looks every bit the age they claim it to be. If you don't mind a little rust, rot, and the occasional naked sunbather, the pristine mountain setting and nearby Mount Shasta gives this hot springs that extra healing edge.

Lake Tahoe and Surrounds

With an average depth of 934 feet and water so pure you can spot a red condom floating 20 feet below, Lake Tahoe is the perfect remedy to the nearby casino debauchery. A 72-mile loop will give you a full-day workout at the wheel. A few hundred miles of hiking trails will take you through bubonic-plague rat-infested forests. The nightlife in Stateline will have you cheek to cheek with gold-chain ski trash from Sacramento and points west. But the water! Sparkling emerald green and lit like diamonds by the radiant sun. For those not inclined to dive in, there's the *Tahoe Queen,* at Ski Run Marina, Stateline (☎ **530/541-3364**), a stern-wheeler with large indoor viewing decks, room for 500 passengers, and a glass bottom for gazing into the watery depths. There's also the *Tahoe Gal,* a full-scale paddle wheeler that leaves from the Lighthouse Marina in Tahoe City (☎ **800/218-2464**), with cocktails served onboard. But for the radical Monk, there's only one option: put on a wet suit, stuff some cash inside a waterproof pouch, dog-paddle across the eighth deepest lake in the world, take a hike through pristine forests, then cross into Nevada to dump your money down a slot machine. The casinos won't care that you're all wet and look like Sasquatch. They just want what's in that water-proof pouch. Give it to them.

> **Bridgeport Covered Bridge.** 17760 Pleasant Valley Rd. (Bridgeport). Hwy. 49 north out of Nevada City, then left on Pleasant Valley Rd.; go 8 miles.

We like covered bridges. We really do. But let's face it, they're just a little too precious. And as far as covered bridges go, New England has the corner on the market. Still, California hosts the longest single-span covered bridge in the United States. The Golden State may not always do it better, but invariably it does it bigger.

If you don't drive off the mountain on your way down the treacherous switch-back road, you'll arrive at this perfect Kodak moment, awestruck by the bucolic setting. Fresh mountain air, roaring river, chirping birds. Ah, wilderness! Measuring in at 251 feet, Bridgeport is one of only nine covered bridges in the state, and at first glance it seems rather dowdy. But what matters here is *size,* and the Bridgeport definitely lives up to its rep. It rests on massive granite blocks crossing the swift South Yuba River. It has a "Warren truss with an auxiliary Burr arch and is covered in Sugar Pine shake roofing," whatever the hell that means. Closed to vehicular traffic, its open walkway takes you across the river. Inside, you realize what an enormous project this was back in 1862, especially hauling all of the lumber from neighboring forests. You can peer down at the rapids from open portals and watch bass and trout leaping upstream. If you're feeling lucky, you can pan for gold.

> **Emigrant Trail Museum and Pioneer Monument.** 12593 Donner Pass Rd. (Truckee). ☎ 530/582-7894.

They came, they camped, they ate. Each other. It was 1846, and George Donner was having a really bad winter. The Paiute Indians were being mean. The snow was 22 feet high. The route through the Sierras was impassable. And fellow traveler Lewis Keseberg ate Donner's wife. Not that Lewis Keseberg was that bad of a guy, it's just that the menu on Truckee Lake that winter was very limited. It included oxen, oxen bones, rawhide, snow, shoestrings, and, for the main course, human flesh.

This legendary and macabre tale of California cannibalism makes the Emigrant Trail Museum worthy of a stop. For the uninitiated, the full story goes like this. Inspired by Lansford Hasting's *Emigrants' Guide to California,* the Donner Party took off from Springfield, Illinois, in the spring of 1846 and, after a few ill-fated detours, dug in at Alder Creek during an early November freeze, 6 miles from Truckee Lake in the high Sierras. By December their hastily erected cabins were buried in snow, and the food had run out. Several attempts were made to traverse the pass, most ending in death and cannibalism. Rescuers who set out to find survivors often met with their own deaths and subsequent cannibalism.

The museum houses recovered artifacts that include shovels, rifles, books, flasks, powder horns, a fully loaded wagon, and knives that could have been used to fillet human flesh. Outside is a huge sculpture of a pioneer family. Of the ninety-one members of the Donner party, forty-nine survived. The other forty-two died of starvation and, when hunger overcame grief, were then served for dinner. The leader, George Donner, died of an infection from a cut on his hand and got a lake, a mountain pass, and a road named after him. Lewis Keseberg never lived down rumors that he killed and ate George Donner's wife, Tasmen.

The Donner Party saga is without question the most remembered episode in all of California history, what author Wallace Stegner called "one of the nightmares of the American dream." While not honest, detailed, or forthright enough for our tastes, the Emigrant Trail Museum and Pioneer Monument is the only opportunity we have to examine the remains of this pivotal California tragedy. And for that reason alone, it is an essential stop.

Trivia: Lansford Hasting was never called to the mat on his faulty travel information. One of the original California eccentrics, in 1847 he tried to establish a Confederate Republic in Brazil, and in 1870 died while leading a revolt by ex-Confederates back in the United States.

> **Empire Mine State Historic Park.** 10791 E. Empire St. (Grass Valley).
☎ 530/273-8522.

If you are smitten by gold fever and don't have the patience to go panning on the river, then visit the site of the oldest, richest hard-rock gold mine in California. From 1850 to 1956, over 5,800,000 ounces of gold were extracted from the 367 miles of underground passages of the Empire Mine. The success of this and other California hard-rock mines is largely attributed to the immigration of miners from Cornwall, England, where similar hard-rock mining for tin and copper had gone on for over a thousand years. At Empire Mine you'll watch a cheesy twenty-minute video about the history of gold mining, then wander above ground on a self-guided tour past the cyanide plant (cyanide was used to break down the rock), the refinery room, and the head frame (the structure over a mine opening), and then peer down a 2-mile vertical shaft that once delivered miners to this subterranean world. An electric train will soon take visitors down a few hundred feet.

Nearby **Malakoff Diggins State Historic Park,** 23579 N. Bloomfield Rd., Nevada City (☎ **530/265-2740**), allows a view of the largest hydraulic mining pit in California, where you can see the damage done in the name of gold, as well as the remains of a mining town.

The **Sixteen to One Mine,** 356 Main St., in Alleghany (☎ **530/287-3330**), takes the mining experience a step further. For a fee ranging from $95 to $500—depending on the tour—you can don a hard hat, boots, and gloves and descend through the main portal, ride the man-skip into the depths of the mining operation, walk the tunnels, witness active mining, and tour the Underground Gold Miners Museum. With a little luck you'll be the first to view virgin gold ore as it's pulled from the earth. Plus, you'll be given the opportunity to purchase gold specimens for a whopping 5% discount!

> **Holbrooke Hotel.** 212 W. Main St. (Grass Valley). ☎ **916/273-1353.**

Grass Valley boasts an affluent past. From 1850 to 1940, an annual average of eight million dollars in gold was extracted from its neighboring mines. Now that the mines have closed, Grass Valley serves as the business center for the Gold Country. In the historic downtown stands the Holbrooke, one of the aging relics of the gold-rush days. Built in 1862, this fully restored hotel has entertained such guests as presidents Grant, Harrison, Garfield, and Cleveland, as well as Mark Twain. In its heyday the hotel was a notable stopover for lucky miners who crossed the street after cashing in their findings at the Gold Exchange. Like most structures of its time, the hotel was fortified against fire damage with iron doors and a foot-deep layer of dirt on the roof. The saloon features a stunning redwood bar back. The cage elevators take you one floor up to twenty-seven guest rooms, including the Mark Twain Room. It was here that the cantankerous author of *The Roar of the Mining Camp* spent many nights penning words, smoking cigars, and vigorously dreaming under the canopy bed. Legend has it several ghosts roam the building and have been sighted in the restaurant at table fifteen. The lingering smell of cigars has also been reported by countless guests. Apparently Mr. Twain's ghost can't read the NO-SMOKING sign now posted on his door.

> **Marshall Gold Discovery.** 310 Back St. (Coloma). ☎ 530/622-3470.

This is where the California gold rush literally began in 1848. Near the site of Sutter's Sawmill, James Marshall, an employee of Sutter, found gold in the South Fork American River. Marshall made the mistake of bragging about his discovery in town. Word got out, and the largest gold rush in history ensued. Soon after, the surrounding valley filled with greedy miners staking out claims, often killing each other in the process, making California the number-one destination for the get-rich-quick crowd (it hasn't changed since). The mill site is now nothing but a monument. Flood waters ripped the original mill off its foundation in 1924. Several yards away a small marker points toward a side wash in the river where Mr. Marshall panned his first gold. The river's a stunning sight, but you have to use your imagination to get the historical significance of where you're standing. For $5 you can cross the bridge, get down on hands and knees, and try your luck at panning (no picks or shovels allowed). A replica of the sawmill was constructed near the Sutter's Mill marker and is an accurate copy of the original. Across the highway stands the **Gold Discovery Museum,** which offers a compelling history of the gold rush. And up on the hill is the towering bronze-coated James Marshall Monument erected over the discoverer's grave in 1889. Mr. Marshall, the father of the gold rush, died a pauper.

> **Nevada City.** From Interstate 80, exit at Hwy. 49 north for 30 miles.

Tales of corruption, greed, prostitution, and political graft abound in this cozy mountain village full of aging hippies, yuppie transplants, and rustic mountain men. Founded in 1849 during the heyday of hard-rock mining, Nevada City was known for its network of tunnels that worked their way under city streets, where gold, girls, and booze were transported between hotels and brothels. As a town of 10,000, it was initially called Deer Creek Dry Diggins and hosted the busiest red-light district in the

West. Today the entire Nevada City downtown is a designated National Historic Landmark, presenting a squeaky clean, perfectly restored, Disneyfied Victorian image to the throngs of tourists that crowd its streets. Not a trace of the whores or gold can be found. However, the **Stonehouse Brewery,** 107 Sacramento St. (☎ **530/ 265-3960;** www.stonehousebrewery.com), is a reminder of the town's boozing past, when at least a half-dozen breweries fermented beer. Founded in 1882, the Stonehouse's towering stone walls give a monastic feel to the pub, while the mahogany bar, pine floors, and open beam ceiling add an Old West flare. Upstairs is a less impressive restaurant that misses on the food front, with basic bar food dressed and priced to appear gourmet. In the back of the brewery is a cave burrowing into the hillside and a series of passageways that go under the street. While the Stonehouse is the perfect setting for downing a few pints of organic beer, the **National Hotel,** 211 Broad St. (☎ **530/265-4551**), has a saloon that kicks ass in the hard-liquor department. The National is the oldest continuously operated hotel west of the Rocky Mountains, with a line of horse and buggies out front to cart you around town and an old-as-God hotel night clerk who possibly dates to the gold-rush era. Up the street is the **Nevada Theater,** 401 Broad St. (☎ **530/265-6161**), which is the oldest continuously operated theater in the nation. And as for the vaunted Nevada City tunnels? They've been boarded up ever since those drug-crazed hippies moved to town.

> **Squeeze In.** Commercial Row (Truckee). ☎ **530/587-9814.**

While contemplating cannibalism at nearby Donner Lake you're likely to work up a healthy appetite. Should eggs come to mind, then you've struck pay dirt at the Squeeze In. Peanut-butter omelet? They've got it. Chicken-livers-and-cream-cheese omelet? That too! Established in 1974, the Squeeze In's been cracking eggs for throngs of ski bums who pack old-town Truckee on weekends. Fifty-seven omelets with names like Trippy Thomas, Princess Pammy, Racy Tracy, Screamin' Beaman, and Dirty Dick leap from the menu. An old bicycle hangs from the ceiling, and Art Linkletter signed the wall. But so did 2,000 other wanna-be taggers, whose names are scrawled on the cluttered wallboard.

Yosemite on Down

And on the 27th day Jesus said, "Let's do it right." And so Jesus created Yosemite, the perfect natural attraction, filled with birds, bears, mountain lions, lakes, trees, steep mountain climbs, awe-inspiring beauty, and visitors from near and far. And Jesus was happy. Very happy. You see, no matter what you've heard about the

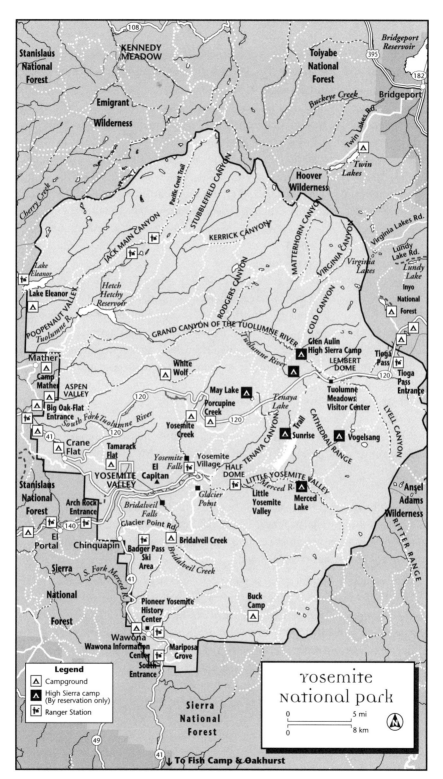

traffic, the pollution, the noise, the endless busloads of tacky tourists, you MUST visit Yosemite, one of America's great natural treasures (and this is a country whose main highlight IS natural treasures). From almost any vantage point in the park, one can catch the major natural attractions—Half Dome, Mirror Lake, and El Capitan (the largest piece of exposed granite on Earth). And oftentimes you can witness several others, including Royal Arches, Yosemite Falls, and even Bridal Veil Falls. If you rent the right room, as we did at the reasonable though not spectacular **Yosemite Lodge,** Yosemite Lodge Drive, at North Side Drive (☎ **209/372-1274**), you will have a comforting scene of trees and grasses right out front your balcony. Though there are neighbors right next door, it feels about as pastoral as a hotel can get, unless one stays at the far more expensive (though worth every penny) **Ahwahnee Hotel,** 1 Ahwahnee Dr. (☎ **209/372-1407**), whose massive wood-beamed dining room exudes gusto, pride, and fortitude.

There are many excellent guidebooks and park-service literature that elucidate all the trails one can hike, rocks one can boulder, and sheer rock faces one can reconnoiter in Yosemite, but our recommendation is rather simple: Get a simple map of the area and just start exploring. Nothing wrecks a trip into nature like too much information. Above all, don't tote any books (including this one) around with you. Yosemite offers that rare opportunity to drop your mental agenda and just soak in the staggering brilliance of nature at her finest. *One final note:* It is best to visit Yosemite during the late spring or early fall before the peak tourist season. We also insist that you take a dive into one of the park's many rivers. Yes, it's cold, very cold, but nothing puts you more quickly in touch with nature then sampling the water. Like Yosemite pioneer and Sierra Club founder John Muir, Monk travelers are no wussies.

> **Ancient Bristlecone Pine Forest.** From 395, take Hwy. 168 West, then White Mountain Rd. to Schulman Grove. Ostensibly closed from Halloween to Memorial Day due to weather and road conditions (though we went at the beginning of Jan). Motor homes not recommended.

There's something biblical about the long drive up into the Ancient Bristlecone Pine Forest. You're winding up a steep incline to pay homage to a species of tree known as *Pinus Longaeva*—or, in lay-Monk's terms, the bristlecone pine. Many of the *Pinus Longaeva* found at this 11,000-foot elevation are more than forty centuries old, outdistancing those old sages, the Giant Sequoia, by at least 1,500 years. And, let me tell you, these trees look their age: brittle, stark, weathered gray bushlike formations that have defied the odds and hung on out of spite. The bristlecone is the hook, but what will really rotate your world is the panoramic view.

> **Erick Schat's Bakkery.** 763 N. Main St. (Bishop). ☎ **619/873-7156.** Another location in Mammoth Lakes.

When you first walk into Schat's Bakkery (yes, two "k's"—they're of Dutch descent), you think it's just another cheesy sugar factory, and while they do have their share of dainty little treats, their homemade energy bars are simply out of this world. Completely natural and completely addictive. You have never tasted anything like these babies. On a par with the crunchy chewy sourdough raisin bread Jean Ponce once made over in Chico. Before you head off to hike, load up on energy food here.

> **Mammoth Mountain Ski Area.** From Hwy. 395 take Hwy. 203 east 5 miles.

In our pantheon of cultural Neanderthals we put a certain strata of ski-resort people pretty dern near the top. Up there with frat boys, certain ad culture people, and people who drive obnoxiously large sports utility vehicles. In the case of Mammoth Lakes, all three sectors come together in one neat dislikable persona.

The Mammoth area is beautiful, especially the underappreciated lakes, but the people are not. The area attracts the requisite drunk-ass party-hearty ski-resort folks, with pedestrian intellectual aspirations and no spiritual consciousness. It's a real shocker coming from the beautiful Bristlecone Forest and nearby Deep Springs, with all the high-minded talk of Harold Bloom and Henry David Thoreau, to then encounter the boorish attitudes here. We're just not sure this is what John Muir et al. had in mind when they lobbied for protection of these noble mountain ranges.

> **Owens Lake.** On Hwy. 395 between Highways 136 and 190.

The delightfully barren, eerie, emasculated Owens Lake was drained during the first part of this century to feed San Fernando Valley lawns. One's innocent appreciation of the lake's surreal beauty is modified by an awareness of its sad history. Fortunately, it is slowly coming back due to environmental protests from Owens Valley farmers displaced by Mulholland's fabled aqueduct. To this day, the people here suffer a disproportionately high number of lung ailments from the dust bowls in the Owens Valley region. To get a clear sense of who and what had to die in order for L.A. to live, it is imperative that you visit this area.

> **Owens River Walk.** In Bishop, go east of 395 to Line St. (one of many gateways to the area). For information on fishing and other outdoor recreation in the area, call the Bishop Chamber of Commerce at ☎ **760/873-8405.**

We can do without the family-values vibe of Bishop, but the Owens River Walk is one of our favorite walks in the state. On a clear winter day, with the towering Sierra

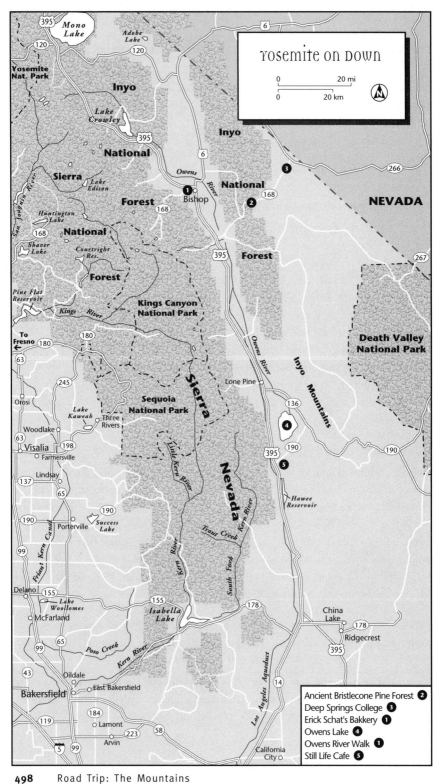

Yosemite on Down

0	20 mi
0	20 km

Mono Lake

395

120

Adobe Lake

120

6

Yosemite Nat. Park

Inyo

Lake Crowley

395

Inyo

6

266

National

Owens River

National

168

NEVADA

Sierra

Lake Edison

Forest

Bishop ❶

168

❸

❷

Huntington Lake

168

National

395

Forest

267

Shaver Lake

Courtright Res.

San Joaquin River

Forest

Pine Flat Reservoir

Kings River

Kings Canyon National Park

Owens River

Death Valley National Park

To Fresno

180

180

63

245

Sierra

Lone Pine

Inyo Mountains

Orosi

Lake Kaweah

Three Rivers

Sequoia National Park

136

Woodlake

63

❹

Visalia

198

Farmersville

Little Kern River

395

190

190

Lindsay

137

65

Nevada

❺

190

190

Success Lake

Porterville

Kern River

Trout Creek

South Fork

Kern River

Hawee Reservoir

99

Friant Kern Canal

Delano

155

Lake Woollomes

McFarland

155

Isabella Lake

178

China Lake

178

65

99

Poso Creek

Kern River

Ridgecrest

395

43

Oildale

East Bakersfield

Bakersfield

Los Angeles Aqueduct

14

119

184

Lamont

223

58

Arvin

California City

5

99

Ancient Bristlecone Pine Forest	❷
Deep Springs College	❸
Erick Schat's Bakkery	❶
Owens Lake	❹
Owens River Walk	❶
Still Life Cafe	❺

as a backdrop, it uncannily resembles one of those impossibly beautiful backdrops for a mainstream beer commercial. Plus, it's easily accessible, free, and OVER 80 MILES LONG, with 22 miles of the river open for year-round fishing. How pristine can you get!

> **Still Life Cafe.** Hwy. 395 and State (Olancha). ☎ 760/764-2044.

Just south of the junction of 395 and Highway 190 to Death Valley sits a small inviting French cafe with a decidedly crunchy granola moniker. Inside it's all French: French owners, French diners from the nearby Crystal Geyser plant, and even a little French attitude. You never know where French attitude is coming from. Is it that we had the gall to interrupt their French lunch with some questions? Is the mere sight of an American an affront to their sensibilities? Are they afraid we might note their hygienic habits, recently reported to be about what we'd always assumed? Or is it that they don't understand English? In such a situation, it's customary to smile. The French don't see the need for this—they'd rather have you squirm. In fact, as I left the Still Life Cafe, the pairs of French eyes that wouldn't look at me as I was standing in the middle of the restaurant now followed me to my car, watching me drive away. They were like the eyes of one of those nasty rural folk in *Straw Dogs,* exhibiting barely concealed anger. Why do I say all this? Because the presence of such authentic French attitude in the middle of the rugged Old West is what makes the Still Life worth a stop. It represents one of those incongruous California tableaus we so dearly enjoy. And, what's more, owners Malika and Michel Patron serve the finest gourmet food within a hundred miles.

Go Deep, Young Man

Jim Monk at Deep Springs College

Deep Springs College is in the middle of a stunning 50-square-mile valley in the high desert of eastern California, an hour's drive from the nearest town. Founded in 1917 with an initial endowment of $1 million by industrialist L. L. Nunn, the 2-year liberal arts program has an average of 24 students and six faculty members, its program structured around thirteen terms. It would be like any small alternative liberal arts college in America except the students at Deep Springs work twenty hours a week on the college's 30,000-acre cattle ranch, all student and campus conduct is left up to the student body (including censure, expulsion, and the selection of all faculty, students, *and* visiting Monks), and (get this!) it's totally free.

But, before all you pot-smoking hackey-sacking vegan Rainbow slackers get excited, let us inform you that Deep Springs is among the most discriminating colleges in the nation, with an admissions process that requires a series of interviews, seven essays, and extremely high SAT scores (1,500 is the standard). Plus, you're competing against a few hundred other applicants for only two dozen slots. Deep Springs is for that rare young man of 18 or 19 looking for a college experience that actually educates his whole being, not just the parts above his neck and below his navel.

I was drawn to this oasis after reading that Deep Springs had the highest-rated campus food in America. That was an interesting endorsement. What kind of school goes out of its way to serve great food to the student body? I decided to explore. What I found is the kind of school a Monk like me would have applied to had I known about it twenty years ago.

I visited with the Deep Springs students on the last day of class. The guys were understandably tired of the grind. It's a lot of responsibility being a student here, including milking the cows, feeding the horses, growing the alfalfa, and maintaining the buildings, all while simultaneously taking a demanding academic load, not to mention being present for regular meetings that can last upwards of six or seven hours. And though the students speak as one mind about what they are getting out of the experience, one can only surmise it's a little trying just the same.

After the formal interview, I participated directly in Deep Springs life. Skeptics will shake their heads, but I found earnestness here, and, what Zen masters call "try mind." I set gopher traps with Dmitri from New York City by way of Moscow, who in a year would be on his way to study social science at Harvard. I visited Graham, who lives in what students call "the Harold Bloom suite." A letter Graham wrote to Mr. Bloom and Mr. Bloom's clever reply appear on the door. It was so gratifying to see deification of *academic* superstars for a change. And I talked after lunch with Mark and Conner, two students who told it like it is.

Mark: Other colleges—Harvard, Yale, Princeton—were sending me all these books and catalogues and I got the feeling it was the exact same thing from college to college, except with different pictures. Of course, all the students were happy. It was always autumn. It was always a perfectly blue sky and the students were always very multiethnic and diverse.

Monk: [Laughs]

>interview

Mark: I just got the feeling they were trying to put one over on me. I kind of thought that Deep Springs really had an idea behind it besides *Let's make some money.*

Monk: How did you hear about it?

Mark: When my parents were researching colleges for my older brother they found out about it and they really liked it. My brother had gone to an all-male high school and he was like, "Yeah, right."

Monk: Yeah, I went to an all-male high school too.

Mark: So that was not an option for him [for college]. But then when I was being recalcitrant about getting applications and not wanting to go visit colleges, they mentioned it and I called and got the application. It was great because one of the things that really made it attractive and distinctive for me was that I went on this spree one morning calling colleges and asking for brochures and applications. It was always some young, female voice answering the phone, "Hello. This is Princeton." Blah blah blah blah blah. I called Deep Springs. The phone rings about five times and some guy answers the phone, "Uh, hello. Yeah, uh, Deep Springs."

Monk: *[Laughs]*

Mark: There was talking in the background and he said, "Can you hold on a second? Hey guys! Would you shut up?" And then a week later the brochure comes with my name scrawled in crayon. Obviously it was the only thing he could find [to write with]. To this day I haven't found out who it was. It came with my name and address in crayon. I just thought that was so cool.

Monk: I see.

Mark: I think just the fact that it was distinctive and that there was really an ideal behind [the school].

Monk: How do you define that ideal?

Mark: It's a fairly nebulous concept: The ideal of service to humanity. We're theoretically here to learn and to serve. It's a weird sort of dichotomy.

Monk: So you're somebody who could have gone to an Ivy League school.

Mark: I only applied to three other schools. Harvard, Princeton, University of Rochester.

Monk: Rochester. Why there?

Mark: They have a fantastic music program. And they also offered me a lot of money.

Monk: And so you got accepted to all those and chose Deep Springs. You realize that's quite an endorsement for Deep Springs.

Mark: Yeah. I'm certainly not the only one. But, see, I like it [here] because you can get the best of both worlds. I can come here for two years [and then go to a regular college]. You can stay here longer than two years; you just need to ask permission of the student body and you usually have to have a fairly specific compelling reason to stay.

Monk: So you chose to come here as opposed to going to an Ivy League school, and you liked its informality, and the interesting combination of working in nature and academics. You guys are cattle ranchers I understand?

Mark: Of Alpine cattle.

Monk: That's certainly atypical. That's certainly not something that happens at other schools. So it's kind of a better balance of mind and body than you find at most places.

Mark: Yeah. We have what people call the three pillars, which are academics, labor, and self-government. Theoretically they are all equal. We give them equal attention.

Monk: Some people might say this is Evergreen-in-the-desert or Bennington West. Very liberal, self-governed . . .

Mark: I don't know if they'd call us very liberal.

Monk: Are you pretty diverse in your political views here?

Mark: Well, I don't know. I'm kind of leaning toward conservative-moderate. There are some pretty radical leftists out here. It's kind of a weird mix.

Monk: That's great to see because usually when you have self-government and it's tied in with environmental studies you get a stereotypical kind of student. I've been to Evergreen. I've been to Reed in Portland. Most of the students would probably describe themselves as left-wing. Not here then.

Mark: We certainly have our share. There's no doubt about that. But there are also staunch, staunch defenders of all things capitalist. The environmental classes are always fairly self-selected. I mean, the people who are in that are in that because they're pretty green. But there are also people in [those classes] who definitely would not agree with a lot of the things that seem to be consensus there.

Monk: Is there anybody here who would support impeachment of the president? [The interview was conducted during 1998, The Year of Monica.]

Mark: Absolutely. Especially when you take into account staff and faculty.

Jim turns to speak to another student.

Monk: What's your name?

Conner: Conner.

Monk: Jim Crotty. Nice to meet you. Okay. I'll ask you the big question. Chicks. No chicks?

Conner: No chicks.

Monk: Is that cool? I mean, how do you guys deal with that? Do you go get some prostitutes over in Nevada and bring them in?

Conner: Actually I don't know of any Deep Springs students going there, but if you take the bus in from Vegas the place you have to get off is called Lida Junction. All Lida Junction consists of is the Cottontail Ranch.

Monk: But at 19 and 20, my hormones were raging.

Conner: I think people come out here looking for an intense experience. You throw that in with no alcohol, no drugs, [the intensity] never stops. The Deep Springs experience is 24-7. I think there's a realization that you probably won't get an experience like this ever again and we're very lucky to be out here in the first place.

Monk: Amen brother, I'll tell you from personal experience.

Conner: For me anyway, just the idea of that sacrifice was really attractive to me, because, first of all, that right there means that everyone who's even applying, and, second of all, who actually end up coming out here is really fucking serious about being out here. It sucks sometimes.

Monk: But you have to deal with that. You can't always get what you want, right?

Conner: Yeah, and it's [just] two years.

Monk: Do they teach you skills like meditation? Is there a spiritual quality to this?

Conner: Not in any formal sense. Whatever keeps you sane.

Monk: Do they teach you skills to keep you sane?

Conner: Lots of people find it by wandering off into the mountains. A lot of people find tranquillity working really, really hard. You find your own ways and I think it's not something that can be taught.

Monk: You search and you'll find it. To me, one of the great things about going out to the desert, one of the reasons I like going out there, when you get there it's like washing your brain out of all the crap and all the stimulation of the city and you can get very clear about your life. I once did a 90-day silent Zen retreat—it was nothing like what you guys do out here, two years in nature—but it was pretty revolutionary for me. When I went back into the city it was like this alien world. Tell me what happens when you guys go into the city. What's the experience you have of it?

Conner: I don't know yet because [going to] Bishop doesn't really count. I haven't been home since I came here in June. So when I fly home in two days that will be the first time I've been out of the valley for any substantial amount of time. We went through Vegas when we went on our field trip to Hoover Dam. In fact, many of us go to Vegas to catch flights home. Springers usually wander around the street all night waiting for their flights to leave, sleeping in movie theaters. You don't want to spend your money on anything so you sleep in the casinos.

Monk: You said there are policies against drug and alcohol use, but obviously it has to go on, right?

Conner: No.

Monk: Zero pot?

Conner: Zero.

Monk: That's got to be the only college in America.

Conner: See, the reason it works is because it's self-enforced. The faculty and staff doesn't have any say in it. It's all within the SB [student body]. Technically, I guess we only have one administrator who works within the college. We have Iris who works in the office.

Monk: No kidding. That's pretty wild.

Conner: All student conduct is left, almost exclusively, up to the student body. Censure and expulsion are pretty much within the realm of the student body.

Monk: But somebody has to . . . has it happened that you've seen somebody censured for smoking pot?

Conner: In the past it certainly has. It [the drug and marijuana ban] is relaxed on breaks. We don't enforce it on breaks.

Monk: You're excited about this?

Conner: It's been awhile.

Monk: *[Laughs]*

Conner: But during the term people take it very seriously and no one dicks around with it.

Monk: In an all-male environment, how do you deal with gay issues? How does that come up and how is it dealt with? Is it open?

Conner: Yeah. There's an openly gay student on campus. He's just gay.

Monk: But he's the only one.

Conner: People have all kinds of theories about repressed homoerotic desires at Deep Springs, but I wouldn't say it's ever been dealt with in any way. It's what it is.

Monk: Did you apply to Ivy League schools?

Conner: Yes.

Monk: Is that pretty typical?

Conner: It's pretty typical, but there isn't a real stereotypical Deep Springs student. We're pretty diverse. We're mostly white, middle-class kids [smiles].

>interview

Monk: Is there an attempt to bring in black kids or Hispanic kids? You don't have an affirmative-action policy?

Conner: No, we don't have affirmative action mostly because the application process is so personal and based pretty much solely on—I think the committee ignored SAT scores this year.

Monk: Ignored them?

Conner: Yeah, and pretty much ignored grades. Applicants come out here for four days. There are seven application essays that are read by every member of the application committee. It's a pretty intensely personal thing.

Monk: So you can just tell by the bio of a guy if he's going to fit. Is that it? Is that what you're really trying to find out?

Conner: No. I'd say not really "fit" at all. If anything I think people look for diversity and look for people who might shift the mold. I think what people really look for is perhaps this idea of, going to this service-to-humanity thing, unselfish interests, leadership potential, not just [interest in] turning a buck.

Monk: But it's okay if you have money and you're a capitalist pig and make a ton of dough.

Conner: It's happened, but the capitalist pigs that have gone here have donated a lot of money. People really take seriously the whole mission to educate the most dedicated and able young men toward a life of service to humanity. People take that really seriously and there's all kinds of discussion and personal reflection on what that means to you.

Monk: Did you grow up in suburbia? The city? Where did you grow up?

Conner: I grew up pretty much in middle Austin.

Monk: In growing up did you have any experiences remotely similar to this?

Conner: Boy Scout service projects. That was about it.

Monk: So this was kind of a wake-up call.

Conner: The point of it is not for us to know labor, but to really experience it. If I want to provide leadership to this country I should have an idea of what a farmer goes through. There are just a lot of lessons to learn out here. You learn what it is to screw up a job. Pretty much if you screw up out here you're hurting someone else. That's a pretty big responsibility. We're all pretty much workaholics out here. At Deep Springs responsibility is thrust upon you. I think that's pretty unique. The learning curve is pretty steep. The unofficial motto is "Don't Fuck Up."

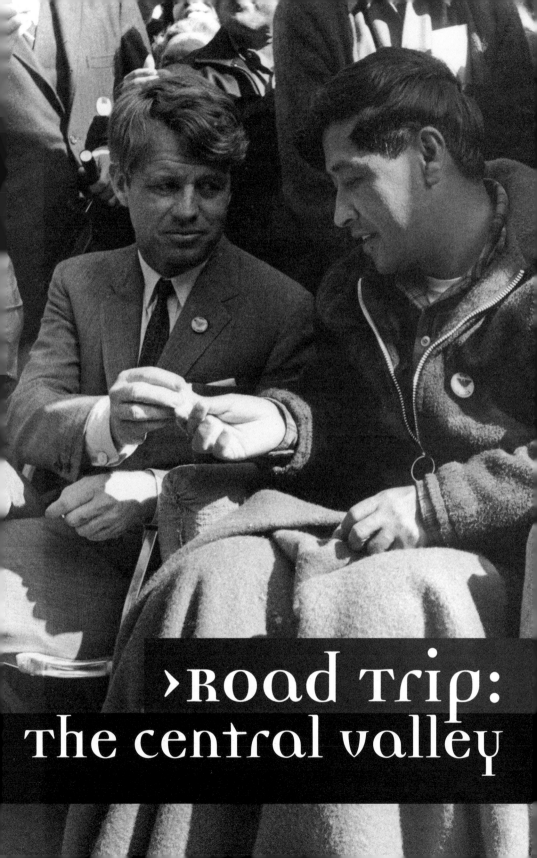

›road trip:
the central valley

The vast Central Valley is my favorite region in this grand and noble state. This is because it comes the closest in look and feel to the region of my birth, the Great Midwest. By "look and feel" I don't mean only that it is flat, agricultural, and largely Christian, but that, because many of the residents of this area originally came from the Midwest, here are still found those time-worn virtues of honesty, simplicity, and clearheaded practical earthiness that I find so gratifying back home on the Plains. We met the most sincere people in California in the Central Valley, folks with their hearts in the right place—in community, family, and the earth around them.

A Reflective Stop at the Abbey of New Clairvaux

As explained in our book *Mad Monks on the Road* (Simon & Schuster), 3 months after leaving San Francisco, and after a few months of gardening in neighboring Chico, in June 1986, the Monks loaded up their beloved 1972 Ford Econoline van and drove out of John Deming's driveway in Paradise, California, with two cats (Nurse and Nurse's Aide), a sole Macintosh 128 K computer, and sacks of brown rice in tow. Our first stop was a creek running the northern boundary of the Abbey of New Clairvaux, 7th and C streets, in Vina (☎ 530/839-2434). After getting stuck in the sand, nearly losing our cats, and having an abrupt awakening to life on the road, we took a swim in beautiful Deer Creek. With that baptism, our journey began in earnest. Half a million miles later, a world of experiences stored in our hearts, and one of the fruits of our travels the book you now hold in your hands, the journey never stopped and most likely never will.

The Grapevine

You know you've left Los Angeles when you hit this gorgeous, thrilling, winding steep incline on a section of Interstate 5 about 50 miles outside the city. It is a mystical patch of freeway leading to the promised land of pure desert valley down below. Everyone who drives 5 notices the transformation that occurs once you make it over these hills—you feel a sudden release of tension, a relaxing spaciousness, the defining moment of a great journey about to begin. As a tonic against the effects of severe urban congestion and smog, we routinely make the 1-hour trek over the Grapevine to the rest stop waiting on the other side. It clears the head and prepares one to return to the demands of urban life, especially if you can score some action on the outer fringes.

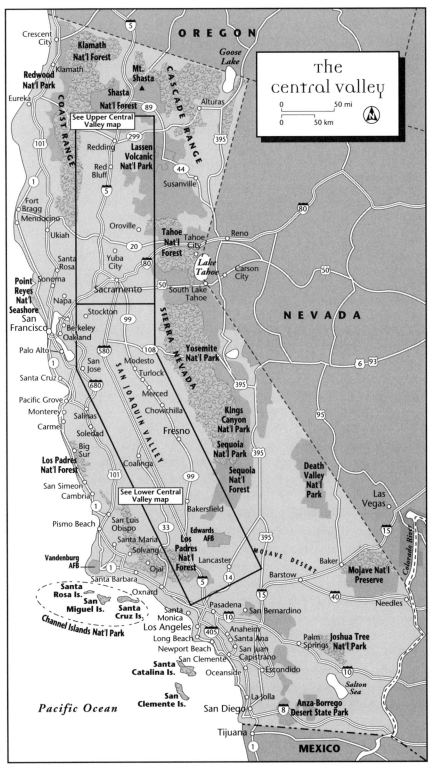

The Central Valley

Today, the monks at New Clairvaux abbey are still singing for afternoon Vespers, all twenty-eight of them, bless their souls. Their Central Valley monastery still sits on 580 acres of walnut and prune orchards (which they actively farm), not far from the Sacramento River. The grounds are bordered by Deer Creek, with a fair-size sandbar for off-road camping most of the year. Retreatants are invited to spend the night in simple guest cottages for a $30 donation that includes meals. We camped on the sandbar in sleeping bags under a starlit sky. Back in 1986, our stay was extended when a beautiful brother, a Carmelite hermit named Henry, came bearing a jar of fruit for our evening meal. We spent many nights together around a campfire, eating fresh peaches and baring our souls. We've lost touch with dear Henry, but perhaps some day our paths will cross again. In the meantime, pull off the road, savor the tranquillity, take a dip in the healing waters of Deer Creek, and listen for the melodic bells that once roused us from our slumber to morning prayers in this, the first sacred spot on a blessed thirteen-year pilgrimage.

Bakersfield

As Monks we are naturally drawn to cities like Bakersfield because they have that elusive small-city atmosphere that most California cities lack. Like the role of Irish culture as the hinge of European history, medium-size towns like Bakersfield serve as the steady, hardworking hinges of California consciousness—which, in the minds of most, is pretty much unhinged as it is.

In very literal terms, Bakersfield marks the beginning of the great agricultural land mass known as the Central Valley, where most of the country's lemons, grapes, and, yes, cotton, is grown, and where many immigrants arrive to scratch out a living in the New World. But the broad streets of Bakersfield offer much more. It's a place where L.A. film-industry people come to search for props in the city's excellent and large antique stores (try the **Central Park Antique Mall** at 701 19th St., ☎ 805/633-1143, across from the **Great American Antique Mall** at 625 19th St., ☎ 805/322-1776). It's where Manhattan Beach moms come to purchase inexpensive baby supplies. It's where California country-and-western aficionados settle in to enjoy probably the best country bar scene on the West Coast. Where all manner of folks come to experience the capital of **gourmet Basque cuisine** (there are seven different Basque restaurants here at last count). And, yes, like so much of Southern California, it's a fine place to **drill for oil.** A neighboring town is called Oildale. The nickname for Bakersfield High's sports teams is The Drillers. And you will see little oil wells almost everywhere you look. In residential areas. Near high-rises. Even in

the Stockdale West Mall, where a little oil pump goes at it at most hours, right next to the Discovery Shop, Split Ends Hair Salon, and right across the way from the Taj Mahal (the restaurant, that is).

The Bakersfield Sound

The oil drilling around here, which is as ubiquitous as slot machines in Vegas, is a familiar sight to the Oklahoma and Texas families that came to the Kern River area during the Dust Bowl of the 1930s, settling in encampments like Little Okie. Bakersfield is one of the places families like Steinbeck's Joads might have settled (in fact, the Sunset Labor Camp in neighboring Weedpatch is where *The Grapes of Wrath* was filmed), bringing with them many of the customs of home, most notably the music. Which is why in the 1940s and 1950s, Bakersfield, California, was a hotbed of honky-tonk country, with Texas transplants like **Buck Owens** and **Bill Woods** (who "taught Buck Owens how to sing"), and Bakersfield natives **Merle Haggard** and **Billy Mize** leading the way at a range of bars, including the late but legendary Blackboard. They and musical offspring like Bobby Durham still reside

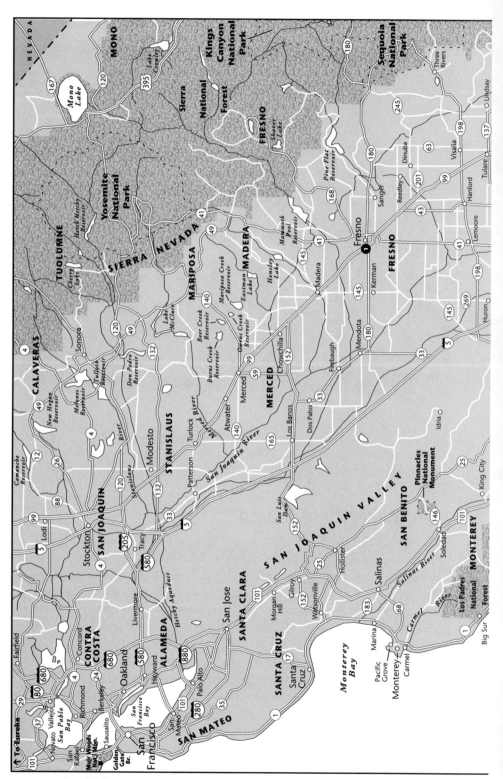

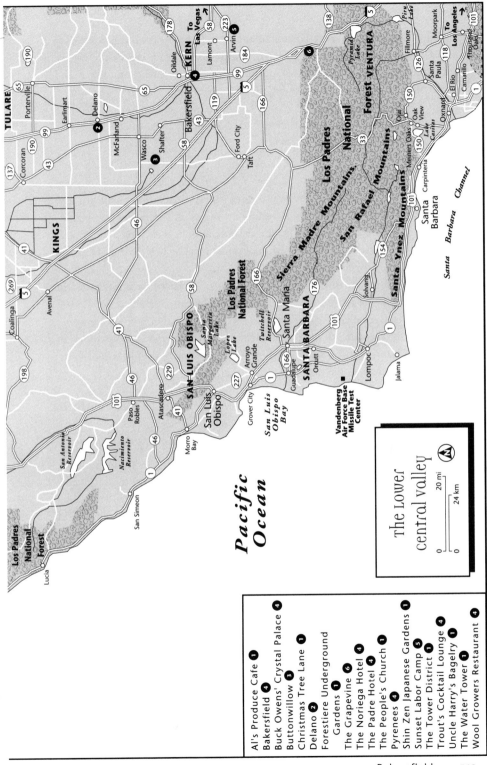

The Lower central valley

20 mi
24 km

Legend

Al's Produce Cafe ❶
Bakersfield ❹
Buck Owens' Crystal Palace ❹
Buttonwillow ❸
Christmas Tree Lane ❶
Delano ❷
Forestiere Underground
  Gardens ❶
The Grapevine ❻
The Noriega Hotel ❹
The Padre Hotel ❹
The People's Church ❶
Pyrenees ❹
Shin Zen Japanese Gardens ❶
Sunset Labor Camp ❺
The Tower District ❶
Trout's Cocktail Lounge ❹
Uncle Harry's Bagelry ❶
The Water Tower ❶
Wool Growers Restaurant ❹

here. Buck Owens is the most famous of the lot. He has a world-class recording studio across from the "River Thee-ate-er," and owns and runs the **Buck Owens' Crystal Palace,** a $6.7-million restaurant, museum, and store, where on Friday and Saturday nights Buck and his Buckaroos entertain locals and tourists alike.

> **Buck Owens' Crystal Palace.** 2800 Pierce Rd., at Hwy. 99 (Bakersfield).
☎ **805/328-7560.** www.buckowens.com.

"The Palace" is essentially the Hard Rock Cafe of Country Music; "honky-tonk without the smoke and fights." A la New York's All-Star Cafe, three giant video screens tower behind the stage and dance floor, showcasing country pop hits and occasionally a few of Buck's greatest, including the sweet, fun "Streets of Bakersfield" video he did with the charismatic Dwight Yoakam, a move that resuscitated Buck's reputation as an edgy honky-tonk performer after years as host of *Hee Haw* had reduced him to a corny joke.

Surprisingly, for such an obvious tourist ploy, the Crystal Palace serves decent country vittles, and has top-notch service to boot. The locals say Buck is worth $100 million. The clean, efficient Crystal Palace shows why. Now if only the place would let up on the predictable "country pop" (I mean, how many videos of women in wedding dresses can one Monk stand?!), and showcase some of the old-school country that put this town on the map.

> **Trout's Cocktail Lounge.** 805 North Chester, across from Taco Bell and next door to Karol's Friendly Cafe (Oildale). ☎ **661/399-6700.** Free admission.

Fortunately, you can still catch traces of the "Golden Age of the Bakersfield Sound" come Monday nights at the legendary Trout's, where, according to a former owner, "Merle Haggard drank his first legal drink." Situated on North Chester in Oildale, just down from Kakes by Karen and World Alive Ministries, you'll see the flashing red neon of the bar's leaping trout. Inside, behind the 1940s brick facade, you'll find Bakersfield's last authentic honky-tonk. On Sundays, Red Simpson, the Rush Springs, Oklahoma, native who wrote many of Buck and Merle's hits, including "Sam's Place" and "You Don't Have Very Far to Go," single-handedly entertains a crowded bar full of senior citizens two-stepping the night away. Thursday through Sunday, Bobby Durham ("My Past Is Present"), his lovely wife Theresa Spanke, and the Tex Pistols take the stage.

For all you new wave honky-tonkers from Seattle to Tokyo, Trout's is an absolutely essential rite of passage. Not only for the music, but for the hearty clientele, some of whom look like they were rode hard and put away wet but are still alive and kickin'. Vernon Hoover, who owned Trout's for thirty-six years (1956 to 1991) before his partner's legs gave out, still tends bar most nights. He's seen them all come and go. He notes that "Bobby Durham's been playing here since he was 12 years old." He also might have served Merle Haggard that "first legal drink."

Bedding Down in Bakersfield

› The Padre Hotel. 1813 H St., at 18th St. ☎ 805/322-1419. $25 a night 2 beds. Amenities: barber shop, shoe shine, plus the cafe serves a $2.22 breakfast (2 hotcakes, 2 sausages, 2 eggs) and 75¢ coffee.

When I told a managing editor at the late *Might Magazine* that we were doing a guidebook on California, he replied, "Go to Bakersfield. Everyone knows about San Francisco and L.A." Amen to that. Bakersfield is everything the two major cities of California are not—quieter, less eccentric, with less star power, but graspable, navigable, with a history and set of characters all its own. Take, for instance, the unparalleled Monk highlight in the entire town, the "Alamo Tombstone" (a.k.a. the Padre Hotel) and adjoining Town Casino Lounge, still owned by the colorful Milton "Spartacus" Miller, the kind of steadfast rebel that cities like Bakersfield produce and even tolerate, but who would get lost or quashed in the L.A. metro maze.

Milton took the Spartacus moniker himself because of his fights with City Hall to save his hotel—and save all of downtown Bakersfield for that matter, from what he sees as an evil cabal of developers bent on destroying the last vestiges of downtown diversity. Spartacus in Roman lore was a freer of slaves. To say that Spartacus Miller is freeing slaves would be a bit of a stretch. The Jewish hotelier's use of the term applies more to the figurative enslavement of the town's poor and marginalized, of which Miller is now one himself, having been kept from fully utilizing his hotel by what he regards as unfair city fire codes, though he does rent out several of the rooms to full-time residents, a few others to transients, and still others to regular businesses like private eyes and union locals. Situated next to the Greyhound Bus terminal, Miller's Tombstone gets loads of untouchables stumbling through its doors, panhandling anyone who happens to be straggling in the lobby. Late on an autumn Monday night there's a feeling of beautifully stark desperation around the area. Until one catches a couple of colorfully attired and overly perfumed art-school tourists from Cologne, Germany, marching back to their rooms, lodging at the Tombstone because of a mention in a Lonely Planet guide. As with many Germans in America, they are cold and standoffish, afraid that any and all friendly strangers are dangerous intruders. It gets one to thinking that either we sucked every last vestige of confidence out of the Germans by our thorough triumph in World War II or they are a people with a concern for security that borders on paranoia. Their ridiculous insularity was the only sad aspect of our visit to the Tombstone tableau, which in its faded, dusty, noirish way feels similar in mood to the hotel in *Barton Fink*.

Combined with the derelict charms of the **Town Casino Lounge** in the Padre's lobby (1813 H St., ☎ **805/324-2594**), you will be hard-pressed not to find seriously edgy real-life entertainment any night of the week.

We chatted with Spartacus as the kitchen prepared to close, and as the Lounge started to fill up. He is recovering from chemotherapy, but you can still catch glimpses of the feisty creative showman/provocateur who brought in exotic entertainment during the hotel's prime, and who put a giant ALAMO TOMBSTONE sign atop the building during his lengthy battle with Bakersfield City Hall. "Nobody is going to take my hotel from me," he says firmly, with almost tearful passion in his voice. Spartacus wants to sell his beloved building, but only on his own terms. He may die trying. (See the interview with Spartacus later in this chapter.)

Dining in Bakersfield

Late night on any weekday in Bakersfield leaves the Monkish gourmand three dining options: dining at Denny's next to the Motel 6 on White Lane, dining at Carrow's next to the Motel 6 on California, or Milt's Coffeeshop at the Olive Drive exit off the 99. We suggest you get here early in the evening, so you can partake of what really makes Bakersfield famous—the cuisine.

There are a variety of authentic places to eat in this town—the hamburgers, pies, and Hopperesque vibe at **Happy Jack's** (1800 20th at G St.), the genuine Mexican grub at the **Arizona Cafe** (809 Baker), the Friday-night fish-and-chips and mutant driller trash at **Westchester Bowls Coffee Shop** (1819 30th St. near F), but, let's face it, Bakersfield is Basque country. Sheepherders, that is. Family-style. Long wooden tables. We recommend choosing one of the following Basque restaurants, not necessarily for the food, but for ambiance you can taste.

> **The Noriega Hotel.** 525 Sumner St. (Bakersfield). ☎ **805/322-8419.** $9 lunch, $15 dinner.

This 1893 Basque landmark is the real deal in Basque aesthetics, culture, and cuisine, serving a single seating prix-fixe family-style lunch and dinner in the traditional Basque manner—that is, at noon and 7pm sharp. Which is why it pays to make reservations, not only to insure yourself a spot, but so the cooks know how much food to make. The night I was there the Junior League of Bakersfield was hosting their Christmas dinner. A room full of smiling, well-scrubbed white women in red Christmasy attire, dyed blonde hair, and the requisite wedding rings only added to the local charm. The Noriega is called a "hotel" because it still acts as a boarding house for visiting Basque sheepherders. How Old World can you get! There is nothing like the Noriega in all of Southern California. A definite must-stop.

> **Pyrenees.** 601 Summer St. (Bakersfield). ☎ **805/323-0053.**

Almost as cool as the Noriega in decor, with mounted buck on the wall and that logging-camp mess-house feel Basque restaurants often have. If you couldn't get into the Noriega, try here.

> **Wool Growers Restaurant.** 620 E. 19th near Baker St. (E. Bakersfield).
☎ **805/327-9584.**

Though Barbra Streisand is a regular, this Basque food stronghold will never score high on the old gourmand-a-meter. As a large red plastic bowl of hot cabbage soup, a mighty plate of red beans and ham, a giant bowl of iceberg salad with vinaigrette dressing, a plate of pork and another plate of beef tips are set down before you, with a basket of white bread to sop it all up, you realize this is peasant food, food for the hungry working man, meant to be eaten in large quantities to sustain long days in the fields. It is not subtle in the least. Which is pretty much the nature of most family-style eateries we've tried in our time. But the food at Wool Growers is hearty and satisfying in its way. Most importantly, the friendly waitresses speak Basque, and many of the patrons are Basque. No doubt some are descendants of those original Basque settlers who tended sheep on Colonel Thomas Baker's 136-square-mile Kern River oil field.

Everything Else in Bakersfield

Before you leave Bakersfield you must lunch at **Luigi's,** 725 E. 19th St. (☎ **805/ 322-0926**). Around since 1911, with checkered tablecloths, and walls covered with seven decades of photos of local athletes, Luigi's is a good, clean place to savor Old Bakersfield ambiance. Try the Luigi sandwich, and make sure you stop in next door at Luigi's grocery store, which carries an excellent selection of imported Italian foods. Luigi's is only open for lunch, so plan accordingly.

After Luigi's be sure to take a drive down old **Union Avenue,** the town's main drag before the 99 freeway came through. You'll pass the famed **Bakersfield sign,** dozens of sketchy motels with names like Sunland, Bakersfield Lodge, and Country Inn (none of which you should ever even think of staying in unless you want crackies and prostitutes for neighbors), the intriguing circular **Basque Chateau** (a building to stop and appreciate, but not a place to eat), and the **Golden West Jaussaud's Casino,** near Union Avenue and Main Street, with its $20-limit games of Omaha, Blackjack, Pai Gow, and Seven-Card Stud, and some good old Southern accents to complete the scene.

Spartacus of Bakersfield:
The Monk Interview

Is he nuts? Or just very determined? One thing's for certain, Bakersfield has definitely been effected by his presence. Born in Chicago, Milton "Spartacus" Miller moved to town in the fifties to run the Padre Hotel. He's managed it with incredible fanfare and guile, through thick and thin. Mostly thin. He's a stocky, intelligent, generous man (he paid for my dinner), who seems beloved by everyone who works for him. His assistant, Peggy Deaver, has been with Mr. Miller since the 1950s. He only has one problem: The city wants him out. And Spartacus Miller ain't budging.

Monk: How long have you owned this place?

SM: I've been the trustee of the place since 1954. Not the owner. It's a limited type of partnership where one gentleman stands out.

Monk: So this is kind of a trust but you were the de facto head of the building.

SM: Legal and de facto. De facto because I had two-thirds of it.

Monk: Obviously you still rent rooms here, right?

SM: One floor.

Monk: When you first bought this there were certain fire regulations. Then years later there became new fire regulations, which you were unable or unwilling to meet. What was the deal there?

SM: Unwilling. And if I had the money I still wouldn't do it. This building's solid concrete. It was an abuse of power by the authorities here.

Monk: So you ran into a snag in the early sixties.

SM: I ran into a snag because the town was not a democracy. The town had no mayor. The mayor of Bakersfield is in a situation where he has no authority.

Monk: He's just another member of the City Council?

SM: Yeah. The mayor never had authority and he was always put there as a good guy by the people in power. So it was a political power situation. The people were not being represented, only special interests.

Monk: So those special interests were opposed to you for some reason.

SM: They wanted the building.

Monk: Who in particular were those special interests who wanted the building?

SM: Well, Dean Gay for one. He was buying up all the properties downtown and putting them out of business.

Monk: And they were using fire regulations to make that happen.

SM: They were putting people out of business one way or another, whether it be fire regulations or structure [violations]. There was discrimination.

Monk: Against small business owners. But you managed to survive. The building is here and you are still the trustee of this building. How did you win?

SM: Well, you never win when you fight City Hall. Join 'em, that's what they say. I became a supervisor from '68 to '72 because I took on the city tooth and nail.

Monk: You got elected?

SM: With no money, to the Board of Supervisors. When I got in I said, "I'm going to represent my district." So I became sort of a martyr for the people. I wanted to reduce crime and all that kind of stuff.

Monk: You would have run for mayor if that had any power.

SM: It had no power. The county was not honest with the people. They were only taking care of their own special interests. I was running for Congress in '70 because I was so popular.

Monk: What brought you to Bakersfield?

SM: I was manufacturing radios called the Crest Radio in L.A.

Monk: What's the name of the company?

SM: Electrical Research and Manufacturing Company. And I was the president. I didn't know much about radios except to sell them. I was in Los Angeles. I got $1,000 a month and was living in the Piccadilly Hotel next to the Ambassador. I had a car. They owned 500 rooms in the Hayward Hotel. After Pearl Harbor all those hotels were being sold cheap because we thought the Japanese soldiers were coming in. I came to Bakersfield in '54. I had encouraged my friends in Chicago to buy this sleeper, The Padre, for $220,000 back in '46.

Monk: So it never was a four-star hotel with expensive rooms?

SM: No. But to get in with $220,000 was a pretty good deal. But the moment I got it I [supposedly] became Al Capone's lawyer. That was the story that the police vice squad was putting out. They said Al Capone shot off my missing fingers.

Monk: How did you lose the fingers?

SM: Hunting pheasant in Mitchell, South Dakota.

Monk: So they tried to brand you as some kind of Mafia guy and that's how they tried to take the building away from you.

SM: They would try to keep people from coming in here and keep me from being able to pay the mortgage.

Monk: They just wanted the building?

SM: There were about half a dozen people that came in and [ran the] El Cajon. It was the old type of Spanish building and that was my only competition.

Monk: For cheap overnight accommodations?

SM: Yeah. But I had nice rooms. Nothing has been done to them except for being refurnished. It's all reinforced solid concrete. Back in '28 they used the best kind of concrete.

Monk: Did you use all the floors?

SM: Yeah. I took all of the widows [in town] and rented them the rooms at about $75 dollars a month. There were a hundred of them so I would have money to pay the payroll and it went over real big at that point. I also gave them food from five o'clock until three in the morning.

Monk: So you had a lot of women living here and free food.

SM: They got free food. Then I [got involved in a restaurant/bar called the Mason] and put a girl in a swing and a girl in a bathtub. The girl would take a bath in a public place. The chief of police said, "I've got jurisdiction. I'm going to bury you. You can't let her expose body parts right on the floor." We ran a different ad every week advertising our different entertainers. All kinds of people came. Even Johnny Carson has been here before.

Monk: These people came to see the girls but you wanted them to stay at your hotel?

SM: That's about it. I got good business that way. We'd get four of them in a cab for a buck-and-a-quarter a piece and all they had to do was pay the admission for the Mason. The rooms went for $4, $3 for servicemen. They got a dollar off.

Monk: You got the servicemen! This place was loaded with servicemen, I hear. So there's a hundred widows and how many hundreds of servicemen staying here every night?

SM: And salesmen came here on Monday.

Monk: So there were a lot of things happening in the fifties. Bakersfield was a happening spot and good times were had by all.

SM: That's right. And the chief of police didn't like it.

Monk: This woman who did this act where she stepped out of a bathtub, is that why you have the bathtub in the bar?

SM: That's right. We brought in a card room in about '59. This was about the time an ordinance came through [that threatened to put me out of business].

Monk: Who was this chief of police who had it in for you?

SM: Grayson.

Monk: So you were having too good of a time so the police chief shut you down.

SM: That's right.

Monk: So you've managed to hang on to the hotel for all these years. They just have not succeeded in kicking you out of here.

SM: I fought City Hall and won.

A Bakersfield-area labor camp

Near Bakersfield

› **Sunset Labor Camp.** Weedpatch. Take Hwy. 223 east from 99 (on the way be sure to grab a bite at Beryl's Cafe, 16051 S. Union, where *Fearless,* starring Jeff Bridges, was filmed), then north on the Weed Patch Hwy. till the Sunset High School. The Labor Camp is just east.

Every visitor who seeks to apprehend the history of the Central Valley needs to visit the historic Sunset Labor Camp, famous as a place where the movie *The Grapes of Wrath* (starring Henry Fonda) was filmed. There's not much to it. But if one is to understand the migrant worker experience in California one needs to grasp the conditions under which migrant workers lived, and still live. While not as guarded as a prison, the Camp feels like a compound. The workers live in bland, brown, barely functional shacks, even to this day. Imagine what these shacks were like before Cesar Chavez campaigned for migrant laborer rights. Arrive between April and October, during the height of the farming season, when you can drive down the side roads off 99 and see men and women bent over in the fields, doing the hard physical picking that brings all manner of fruit to our tables. Lemons, peaches, grapes—they seem such benign sweet foods. Until we realize the bittersweet labor that goes into harvesting them. The Sunset Labor Camp and others like it remind us that the labor of migrant workers is something we should never take for granted. And for the sons and daughters of migrant workers, who have risen to a higher station in the New World, the Sunset Labor Camp is a stark reminder of their humble bare-knuckle roots.

Buttonwillow

Few people know that cotton is California's number-one agricultural product, and that Buttonwillow is the de facto "heart of cotton country." To get a sense of what the area is all about, visit the **Farmers Cooperative Gin.**

As you head into town from the east you'll see a large building to the south with "Farmers Cooperative Gin, Inc. Since 1937, Grower Owned," emblazoned on the side. Go on a Sunday or holiday, as you'll be free to walk the grounds without supervision. And the only sound you'll hear is the rattle and hum of a few machines, which aren't actually operating, but which must be kept on at all hours. Like other massive machinery I've seen, the machinery here is old, dark, and frighteningly efficient. Keep walking south across the property, past the bales of cotton, past the gin, past the small bunches of stray cotton scattered around the property (and throughout the town for that matter). At first, you'll think you're hearing another machine in the distance, and then a fan, and then giant sprinklers, then rushing water. You're sure it's rushing water, as you head towards the irrigation ditch. As you get up to it, you see that the ditch is completely dry. You look across the vast flat fields of the surrounding Central Valley. No sprinklers. Then you look up at the massive power lines connecting monstrous transformers as far as the eye can see. This is the sound you hear. The sound of rushing electric current. As loud as the loudest river rapids. You will never forget it.

Delano

Just as civil rights activists well remember the significance of towns like Selma and Birmingham, those helping the cause of the United Farm Workers well remember the battles waged at Salinas (1970), Coachella (1973), Calexico (1978) and, first and foremost, Delano (1965).

Cesar E. Chavez

Cesar E. Chavez was a Delano native and landowner who fought to create the United Farm Workers union. However, the legacy of Chavez seems almost forgotten in this town. Perhaps because he was so successful. Or perhaps, as some members contend, because the union he worked so hard to build has self-destructed in recent years, putting all its focus into organizing strawberry workers in Watsonville, while floods of undocumented workers are brought in to break strikes throughout the state.

While the glory that was Delano is gone, there is still a place you can go to capture the spirit of Chavez and his heroic struggle. Drive a few miles west on the Garcas highway till you see the giant radio towers of the Voice of America. As an apt metaphor that has never gone unnoticed by journalists covering the movement, across the highway from the Voice of America you will see a boarded-up adobe gas station that was part of the **UFW headquarters** in the late 1960s. Collectively known as "Forty Acres," the area included the gas station, a newspaper office, an administrative building, clinic, the first farm-worker credit union, and later the Agbayani Retirement Village, which is still there on the northeast corner of the 40 acres. The Retirement Village was named for an early Filipino UFW member, who,

Breadbasket to the World

Spending time in the Central Valley is absolutely crucial to getting a proper reading on the character of California. This is because after the gold rush, and long before the entertainment, defense, and computer industries took off, the big money in this state was in farming.

In many ways, it still is. For all the popular imagery about spoiled actresses, crass and decadent producers, and greedy agents, California is still a farming state. If you get outside the major cities, you will clearly see what we mean. Naturally, urban cultural trends have invaded the heart of the Central Valley. Downtown Delano—near where Cesar Chavez and the United Farm Workers got their start—now sports Streetwise Music, a house and hip-hop record store serving the new breed of Latino, black, and Filipino kids in the area, many of whom don't have a clue what Cesar stood for. And satellite television regularly brings in images from the dream factories to the south. But agriculture is still the predominant industry and culture in the Central Valley. Which doesn't mean it's dullsville, either.

The farmers of the Central Valley are among the most innovative in the world. At the turn of the century, growers here realized the importance of winning over the East Coast market. To compete with the massive horticultural industry in New York State and elsewhere, Central Valley growers pooled their resources and created a system that worked. As a result of the ingenuity of these California farmers, interstate produce transportation, refrigeration, and more were developed. All of which gave the California farmer a leg up on the East Coast competition. Central Valley farmers astutely realized that Eastern consumers would be enamored with having oranges in January, and pushed the envelope of scientific innovation to allow for year-round mono-crops. It was mono-agriculture that set Central Valley farming apart. Mono-agriculture is also what precipitated two huge developments that profoundly shaped the character of the region: (1) the increased use of pesticides to protect crops from predators; (2) the hiring of migrant of laborers to pick the produce. While California is a true state of immigrants, no one region has made it tougher on immigrants than the Central Valley.

like many brought over to work the fields, was barred by law from marrying Anglos, and, consequently, died a single man in a foreign land.

It was on these "Forty Acres" that Chavez fasted for twenty-five days in order to set an example of nonviolent sacrifice for the increasingly frustrated and harassed picketers in the long, troubled three-year general strike against the Delano table-grape growers. And it was here, on March 10, 1968, in the company of 10,000 United Farm Workers, that Senator Robert Kennedy came to share mass with Chavez as he ended his fast. If you stand in this place a little while, you can re-create the powerful scene in your own mind.

Father Garcas once called Delano, "the cradle of Christianity in the Valley." In another era, it was a notorious red-light district, until an expanded Highway 99 brought down most of the brothels and bars. But in its heyday, in the sixties and seventies, it was ground zero for a world-renowned movement to protect those who pick our food. All Monk travelers should go here to pay tribute to the men and women who laid down their lives for this noble cause.

Postscript: On April 23, 1993, after fasting for several days to "regain moral strength," Cesar Chavez died in his sleep. On April 29th, 35,000 people followed Cesar's funeral casket from Delano to Forty Acres. From a look around Delano today, you would never know it. No sign, no marker, no trace. Cesar E. Chavez is buried at La Paz, the current headquarters of the United Farm Workers, in Keene, California. For more information on Cesar Chavez and the farm-worker movement, contact the **Cesar E. Chavez Foundation,** P.O. Box 62, Keene, CA 93531 (☎ **805/822-5571,** ext. 230; www.ufw.org; E-mail: cecf@ufwmail.com).

Fresno:
The Raisin d'Etre

If I was asked to describe Fresno in one word, I would reply "Christians." Hispanic Catholics. Caucasian Protestants. In both cases, Christians, of the fundamentalist variety. Fresno mayor Jim Patterson is a Christian who regularly attends the largest Christian congregation in the city, the People's Church on North Cedar. On the radio dial, where you'd expect a rap or rock station in most cities, here you find Christian radio, with frequent quotations from scripture, lectures about the importance of "personal responsibility" (the Ken Kaye Show is big on that), and discussions about what distinguishes a "true Christian" from an "unbeliever." Not surprisingly, Bill McCartney's Promise Keepers have a strong foothold in this sports- and Christ-loving town.

Now, we don't necessarily disagree with Christians. In fact, on several issues we are in complete solidarity. For instance, fundamentalist Christianity is a necessary bulwark against the inevitable excesses in our increasingly libertarian democracy.

We single out "Christians" because their presence is far more palpable in Fresno than in any other major city in California. While San Francisco is defined by social tolerance and innovation, and Los Angeles by its mass entertainment machine, Fresno is defined by its family values. People choose to stay in Fresno because they do not relate to the values and lifestyles of the two big, glamorous, ambitious, money-driven, and seemingly Godless cities of the state. They feel more comfortable in a city whose best-known celebrities are Tom Seaver and Jerry Tarkanian. In fact, more locals probably know "Tark" than Fresno native son William Saroyan. It's a city where discussions you'd overhear at the Fig Garden bookstore are more likely to center around "church" matters than auditions, agents, or "growth boundaries." Fresno is a city where mass is "critical," but there's no "Critical Mass." While the

Tule Fog

Too-oo-lee, too-lee baby, too-oo-lee, too-lee baby, won't ya come and rescue me from the too-lee fog. Yeah, that's right. Tule fog is pronounced "too-lee." It is an Indian word, meaning . . . Ah heck, I don't remember what it means. But anyone who's lived in the Central Valley between December and February knows what it is. And it is *nasty.* Imagine the worst blizzard you've ever experienced, visibility down to the "I Brake for Dykes" bumper sticker on the Volvo in front of you—that's what tule-fog season feels like in the Central Valley.

It is a dense, low-lying fog that completely envelopes the city on some days, not only totally blocking visibility, but, more importantly, adding a sense of mysticism and melancholy normally missing

from these sunny plains. Makes for great realism too, though possibly depression. It was with the omnipresent tule fog in the foreground, and the memories of Chavez and Saroyan in the background, that I made my entry into Fresno.

Web is probably as popular here as in any other part of California, no Fresno Internet start-up is about to shake the stock market with an outrageously popular IPO. While Hollywood occasionally deigns to film here, outside of a 1986 four-part satirical takeoff on Dallas entitled *Fresno: The Power, the Passion, the Produce* (starring Carol Burnett and Charles Grodin as heirs of Kensington Raisins—"we will dry no vine before it's time"), broadcast media usually skips over the raisin capital.

Which, in a strange way, is why we say a visit to Fresno is essential to any thorough California experience. As with most of the Central Valley, Fresno's message takes awhile to reveal itself. On the surface, it seems like any other midsize American town, with its share of Kinkos, Starbucks, and endless cookie-cutter strip malls and housing developments. But then you realize that is precisely its point. Fresno's unremarkability is what makes it so glaringly different from the aesthetic extremes that characterize other major California cities (and, in fact, what makes it the fast-food restaurant test capital of America).

Though only an hour and a half from three of the nation's most astonishing national parks (Yosemite, Sequoia, and Death Valley), Fresno is confidently, serenely, even smugly *normal*. Sure, it has it's share of poverty, illiteracy, and crime, but, the prevailing mind set is suburban, not urban. In other words, "We are superior to those cesspools of degradation to the north and south." Of course, Fresno's suburban family-values mind set is why the city has had such a difficult time eliciting citizen interest in downtown revitalization. Despite the best laid plans of mayors and planners, Fresnoans keep gravitating to what is accessible, which means the northside malls. The concept of an exciting, revitalized, eye-catching downtown pedestrial walk is appealing to Fresnoans; there's just considerable doubt whether people would actually show up. There's even a voter-approved plan to build a downtown stadium for the local Triple A baseball team, the Fresno Grizzlies (one of only two farm teams in the country with games broadcast in Spanish and English), which continually gets scuttled in favor of north-side redevelopment. What Fresno most needs is a Portland-style urban growth boundary. Unfortunately, it's not likely to happen any time soon, as the city continues to expand outward, gobbling up more and more precious farmland.

Interestingly, Fresno's middle-of-the-road, middle-class normality springs from those very farms it's eating up. Agricultural areas, as a rule, tend to be more culturally conservative. And, let's face it, Fresno is almost entirely dependent on agriculture, for better and, lately, worse. The vagaries of the ag business have recently left 14.5% unemployment, the highest for any urban area in the state. What's more, the frost of late 1998 killed almost the entire lemon and orange crop. In a more diversified city and county, such a calamity would not be felt so severely. But in Fresno such a freeze has serious ripple effects throughout the entire local economy.

On the upside, Fresno's relative isolation, and agrarian base, also makes for a considerably lower cost of living. California is a state of dreamers. Filled with people from elsewhere who came here to start anew. Unfortunately, the cost of living in California's two major cities has become so prohibitively high that the American dream is proving unreachable for most residents. Not so in the city of Fresno, where one can still purchase a three-bedroom home for under $100,000.

In a city that strives so hard to preserve a mono-economy and morality, it's not surprising that various oddities should be buried (in one case, literally) beneath the comfortably conformist surface. As Monks, it is our sacred duty to uncover such oddities. Here then are:

The Monks' Top Ten Irrefutable Highlights of Fresno, California

1. **Forestiere Underground Gardens.** 5021 W. Shaw Ave., 2 blocks east of Hwy. 99. ☎ **559/271-0734.** From Hwy. 101, exit Shaw Ave. Head east a few blocks.

   The Forestiere family does not seek publicity. Nor, despite what old-time locals say, do they seek to make their namesake garden a popular tourist attraction. In fact, according to Fresno's city manager, Bob "Wolf" Quesada, the Forestiere family has done their darndest to prevent city financial support for their project. You might think they are shooting themselves in the foot until you actually visit the gardens and see why they so strenuously seek independence. As any local will tell you, this is the highlight of the Fresno area, mainly because it has remained so true to its—pah dum—roots.

   Baldasare Forestiere was the ultimate survivalist. After migrating from Sicily in the 1890s, he spent the better part of his life digging tunnels under Fresno. These aren't ordinary tunnels, but an impressive underground labyrinth that includes connecting rooms, patios, passageways, gardens, an aquarium, and even an auto tunnel for parking the car. Initially, Forestiere intended to cultivate citrus groves on his 70 acres, like any normal Fresno farmer might do. But when he discovered solid hardpan beneath his land, plans changed. He dug his first tunnel to avoid the stifling summer heat and never stopped digging. As you slowly descend into the Forestiere Underground Gardens, you're immediately struck by the ingenuity behind his work. Through arched passageways 14 feet below the earth, you reach cozy living quarters that include beds carved into walls, a functioning kitchen, a fish pond, a chapel, and living areas with two wood-burning stoves. This man, armed with nothing more than a pick, shovel, and wheelbarrow, hauled out tons of earth and developed an elaborate underground orchard that included oranges, lemons, olives, figs, avocados, and pears. The trees thrived beneath circular holes that let in the sunlight, the angles of the holes forcing rainwater toward the root systems. Mr. Forestiere was one hell of a hermit and would have fared quite well during the bomb-shelter mania of the 1950s had he survived that long (he died in 1946). In fact, you might say he was a forerunner of today's Y2K survivalists. He never married and was obsessed with privacy, developing an elaborate scheme of multiple peek-holes and sight-lines that allowed him to keep an eye on every corner of his estate, spying on potential intruders. Being a Roman Catholic, he borrowed heavily from Christian mysticism, with threes and sevens figuring prominently in his design and gardening. As our tour guide and hostess, Lorraine, was quick to point out, "the love of God shows up in all his work." That Fresno Christian mind set shows up even underground.

2. **Al's Produce Cafe.** 1456 G St. at Stanislaus. ☎ **209/233-9226.** 6am–3pm Mon–Sat, 7am–3pm Sun.

We visited other ethnic eateries in Fresno—George's Armenian restaurant (excellent kebabs), Irene's (good burgers)—but none can match the character and ambiance of Al's. Just don't go asking intelligent questions of the help. Two of the waitresses did not even know the name of the current city mayor. The other thought his name was Peterson, not Patterson. It's either a sad commentary on Mr. Patterson or clear evidence that the city needs to bridge a major-league cultural divide.

Al's is a bona fide Fresno-locals cafe. The morning I ate there I was accompanied by Daniel Crotty, the manager of the largest Spanish radio station (of ten) in the area, and by deputy city manager Bob "Wolf" Quesada, a.k.a. "Wolf Man Bob" or simply "Jess." Bob is an Al's regular and a magnet for the Fresno fringe, which I discovered a little while into my great $6 machaca breakfast.

Standing next to the seated Bob, I caught sight of a tall, agitated, 75-year-old man with a TKO'd face and a mind that had lost one too many split decisions. He had rushed into Al's to show off an old high-school photo, which allegedly contained the mug of an old prizefighter friend. He was eagerly showing the photo to the waitresses, who listened to his stories as if he was Gentleman Jim Corbett, and when I invited him to sit down at our table he immediately began to explain his connection to a boxer friend in the photo, a man named "Slaughterhouse." Just as I was about to probe further, Wolf Man Bob said what a great boxing name Slaughterhouse was, which did not meet with our friend's approval: He jumped up out of the booth and was out the door faster than Ali's left hook. The whole scene phased neither Bob nor the waitresses. Which is why I like Al's Produce Cafe. It's got a big heart, and a whole mess of tolerance.

Factoid: Al's is situated in the heart of the Fresno Produce Market, the largest produce market in America, where growers bring their hand-picked oranges and lemons to sell to distributors.

3. The Fresno Water Tower. SE Corner of Fresno and O St.

In the absence of an obvious Fresno city symbol, this combination water tower/public library in the shape of a Medieval Romanesque tower will have to suffice. Built in 1894 by the manic depressive George Maher, who, during one of his upswings, conceived this remarkable masterpiece.

4. The People's Church. 7172 North Cedar. ☎ **559/298-8001.**

This is the largest Christian congregation in a town rife with Christian congregations. It's essentially the Crystal Cathedral of Fresno, with 60-year-old women wearing too much cheap Parisian perfume and plenty of over-50 men in Buster Brown shoes using lots of grease in their hair.

The Fresno Water Tower

You must go, not only because a little Bible never did any harm, but because of a giant sculptural scroll that sits high on a wall near the stage. It reads "Till the Whole World Knows Jesus." Amen to that. The great thing about the People's Church is that once service is over, the parishioners get down to what's really on everybody's mind—the 49ers game, the Web, and golf. Whether you like it or not, going to the People's Church is essential to grasping the spirit of Fresno—the white spirit of Fresno, that is. Fresno is ethnically diverse, with sizable populations of Hmong, black, and Hispanic, but you wouldn't know it from a visit to the "People's" Church. Guess those aren't the "people" the name refers to.

5. **Shin Zen Japanese Gardens.** In Woodward Park, north side of Fresno at corner of Alluvial and Friant roads. ☎ 209/498-1551.

Set in 300-acre Woodward Park, a bird and wildlife sanctuary with 4 miles of hiking trails, this 3-acre Japanese garden focuses on the four seasons and has waterfalls, wooden bridges, a koi pond, and a moon bridge over the lake. It's open weekdays 5pm to dusk (May to Sept) and weekends 10am to dusk year-round.

6. **Christmas Tree Lane.** Going north on Van Ness, starts at Shields and continues for nearly 2 miles to just south of Shaw Ave.

If you're searching for the ideal California city to experience Christmas, try Fresno. At least it's an ideal city to see Christmas lights. From early December to early January, on a 2-mile stretch of Van Ness Avenue, neighbors have pooled resources to string a series of Christmas lights and decorations. Heartwarming and stunning.

7. **A press conference with Jerry Tarkanian.**

The scandal-plagued winningest basketball coach in NCAA history is back at his alma mater, pretty much carrying on where he left off at UNLV. Only one difference: While he still recruits athletes with troubled pasts, he's not winning as many games. You can see it in the Armenian warrior's face—the fire is gone. It almost feels like Tark is here as a figurehead, collecting a paycheck but letting the assistants take care of such pesky tasks as negotiating with probation and police officers, arranging paid tutors, and—oh yeah—coaching. Still, a postgame press conference with the Tark is a sight to be seen. Practically every reporter in town fills the room, as Tark puts a friendly nonchalant spin on the game and the status of his predictably unreliable minions.

8. **Uncle Harry's Bagelry.** 5789 North 1st St., at Herndon. ☎ 559/490-7450. Other locations are at Shaw and Cedar, Bullard and Palm, and one at Shaw and Palm in a former Noah's in Fig Garden Village. (How's that for adding insult to bagelry?)

On the surface, this is just another bagelry. But, wait a minute, this isn't a national chain like Noah's. This is a local chain that "noodged" out Noah's. Why? Because the folks at Harry's understood the fundamental principle of Fresno survival: Support the community, and the community will support you (most of the time). In larger cities like L.A., chains can survive quite well without bothering to integrate into a neighborhood. Not here. Come Sunday morning for bagels and latte, and maybe you'll catch a glimpse of Nancy "Thigpen" Glassberg, mother of The Artist Formerly Known as Kelsey.

9. **The Tower District.** As determined by the Tower District Specific Plan of 1991, the boundaries of the Tower District are as follows: The western boundary is Fruit, the northern boundary is Shields between Fruit and Maroa (as well as Clinton between Maroa and Blackstone), the eastern boundary is Blackstone, and the southern boundary is Freeway 180 and H St. For more information on the Tower District go to www.tower2000.com.

Fresno locals invariably told the Monk he should check out the many fine restaurants and cafes along the newly revitalized shopping and entertainment corridor known as the Central Tower District. The name of the area comes from the preserved streamline moderne movie palace The Tower, now anchoring a neighborhood that contains the requisite Starbucks and Blockbuster, several beauty salons, groovy cafes like Revue and Java Cafe, retro-clothing stores like Valentino (where Jim bought a cheap bowler), and upscale (and largely overpriced) gourmet eateries like Echo, the Daily Planet—with its hideaway booths and "Star Room"—and Vini Vidi Vici.

I chose Vini Vidi Vici over the more conceptual eateries that abound in the area. Remember those 1970s restaurants with exposed brick walls, an open kitchen, and a piano player performing classics like "Sentimental Journey"? Vini is keeping that retro yuppie tradition alive. California cuisine and its dicta of fresh, organic, and local seems to have passed this place by. It would have met the Monk man's standards had the prices been in keeping with a town sporting 14.5% unemployment, but at twenty-two bucks for a tower of squab and a heap of white basmati rice, and an additional eight buckaroos for an appetizer of small purple

Hmong/Hmonk

Fresno has the largest concentration of Hmongs outside Asia. Hmongs are Vietnamese mountain people who assisted the United States during the Vietnam War and in return were guaranteed citizenship.

cabbage crepes (advertised as duck and cabbage crepes, but no duck), I felt more fleeced than a sheep in 1940s Sumner. Usually at places that overcharge their customers, you expect a fanatically tight well-oiled machine. Not here. The chairs seemed weak and chintzy, the menu limited, and hey, guys, do something about the ring around the inside of the toilet bowl, will ya? I came. I ate. I was disappointed.

The highlight of the Tower District is Grandma Marie's Chicken Pie Shop. While the breakfast oatmeal comes recommended, the real reason one dines at Grandma's is the authentic lime-green Naugahyde booths and stools. In other cities, this would be turned into a campy concept. Not here. It remains, unlike a lot of the Tower District, the real deal.

10. Yosemite. 1 hr. up Hwy. 41 from Fresno.

The local joke goes that Fresno is a great place to live because there are so many great places to escape to. There's truth in that adage—though, in fact, it actually elevates Fresno's desirability. Fresno is only an easy 1-hour drive up Highway 41 to the Yosemite Park Gate. If anything will impact the cultural mix in the city in the years to come, it is surely the city's proximity to the most gorgeous nature in America.

The Northern Central Valley

> **The Delta King.** 1000 Front St. (Old Sacramento). ☎ 800/825-KING.

We're not going to endorse the Delta King for the reasons that every other guide-book in the world endorses this authentic paddle-wheeler-turned-floating-hotel permanently docked at the L Street landing in Old Town Sacto. We don't give a flying turkey buzzard about the brass-poster beds, stately rooms, mediocre Pilothouse restaurant, and cutesy charm. Overall it falls into the same category as covered bridges and hot-air balloons. And the position we take on such saccharine-sweet Hallmark card scenes is generally "thanks, but no thanks." What the Monks most like about this piece of floating real estate (that sunk a few times and was used as barracks during World War II) is the mere idea of fishing right outside your door. Not that they encourage it. And you probably wouldn't want to eat the fish anyhow. But it's a boat. It floats. You can spend the night, get really toasted, and cast a line. For an old Arkie like Michael Monk, winner of the annual Purdy Rod and Reel, that makes the Delta Queen a keeper.

Foster's Big Horn: heads, heads, heads.

> **Foster's Big Horn.** 143 Main St. (Rio Vista). ☎ 707/374-2511.

When Bill Foster went hunting he took no prisoners. Lacking a museum, Mr. Foster mounted his trophies in this unassuming Sacramento Delta restaurant and bar. Upon entering you are completely overpowered by the carnage. Hundreds of furry heads stare menacingly from all walls. An enormous, full-grown African elephant measuring 13 feet from the base to its extended trunk looms over the back of the room. A moose with an antler spread of over 76 inches is joined by hundreds of deer, antelope, lions, water buffalo, and leopards. A giraffe occupies the corner. Full-size rhinos are on adjacent walls. With over 252 heads hanging overhead, the Bighorn boasts one of the largest collections of big-game trophies *anywhere*—and 95% of these critters were shot by Foster himself.

Though Foster left this earthly plane in 1963, his spirit remains. You walk past a curved bar with a host of regulars hunched over their beer. In the back, green and white linoleum tiles cover the floor. Dinosaur tablecloths cover the tables. The food is a mistake. In fact, the lamb we ordered was so horrible we became suspect. But you don't come to Foster's Big Horn to eat, gosh darn it. You come to gawk. That's because, in the grand tradition of California roadhouses (Moss Beach Distillery near Half Moon Bay, Duarte's in Pescadero), Foster's DEFINITELY has the highest number of endangered species. Go visit to savor a time when a gambler and bootlegger like ole Bill Foster could proudly display his massive big-game kill without fear of attitude from the California PC police.

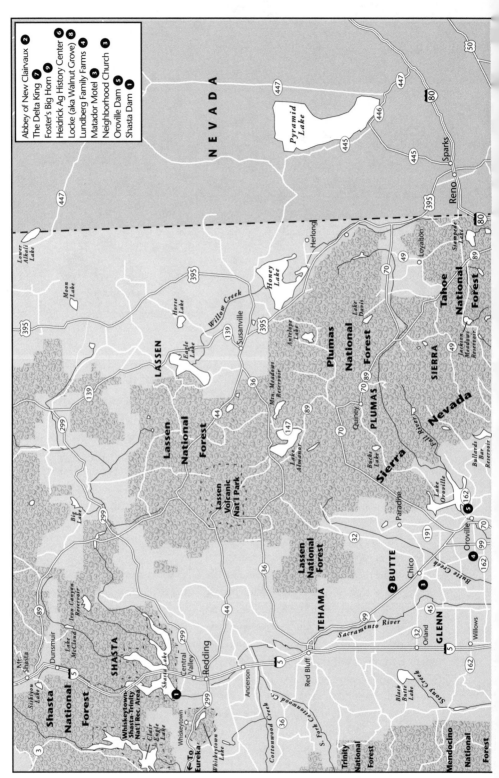

Abbey of New Clairvaux ❷
The Delta King ❼
Foster's Big Horn ❾
Heidrick Ag History Center ❻
Locke (aka Walnut Grove) ❽
Lundberg Family Farms ❹
Matador Motel ❸
Neighborhood Church ❸
Oroville Dam ❺
Shasta Dam ❶

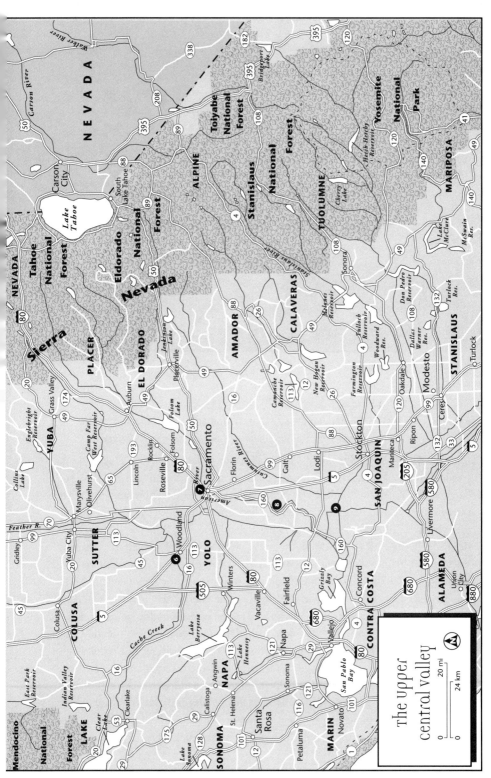

At the Heidrick Ag History Center

> **Heidrick Ag History Center.** 1962 Hays Lane (Woodland). From I-5, exit at Rd. 102. Hays Lane runs parallel on the east side of freeway. ☎ **530/666-9700.**

Old man Hays collected trucks. Old man Heidrick collected tractors. Hays is dead. Heidrick is not. Thanks to their mutual obsessions, what now stands in the heart of Sacramento Valley is a double-warehouse-size museum of tractors and trucks. It opened in 1998 and houses an amazing collection of antique vehicles and machinery, with over 130,000 square feet of interactive exhibits. For instance, you can wander through the Fred C. Heidrick Antique Ag Collection and see perfectly restored tractors and grain pullers, with pre-rubber tires. You can see combines the size of small houses. You'll learn that the Caterpillar was invented in Woodland, and that the combine hails from Stockton. And by the time you hit the exit, you will have expanded your ag vocabulary with terms like "sower, reaper, bundler, and separator."

Next door in an adjacent warehouse is the Hays Antique Truck Museum. Over 130 trucks spanning a period from 1903 to the 1950s are laid out in a chronological timeline. Old man Hays drove chicken trucks in the twenties and had his own trucking business through the Great Depression. On hand are trucks with names like Jumbo, Mack, Locomobile, Defiance, Oldsmobile, and Peterbilt. War trucks and ancient snow blowers are alongside lumber trucks and wharf-side drayage trucks. Recorded forest sounds play behind the forest trucks. There's a 1-ton 1957

GMC pickup built entirely from wood. There are chain drives, friction drives, internal drives, steam, gas, diesel, and electric engines. Get the picture? THERE'S A LOT OF TRUCKS. You leave with a vicarious thrill of what these turn-of-the-century farmers experienced as they rolled out their fabulous new machines and sent the mules to the glue factory.

› Locke (a.k.a. Walnut Grove)

Though weekend yuppies, families, and bikers make the trek down to drink and eat steak in the town's weirdly named bar/restaurant, **Al the Wops,** the highlight of this old Chinese settlement is the achingly authentic crooked wooden buildings, which sit below the highway and levee. Also worth noting is the **Dai Loy Museum,** an old gambling hall with relics of Locke's Chinese past. The drive here through the heart of the Sacramento Delta is half the fun. From Sacramento, take I-5 south, exit and turn right on Twin Cities Road, follow until it dead ends, turn left on Levee Road, and go approximately 1.5 miles to the town of Locke. Turn left into first road entering the settlement. Park and walk up main street. From San Francisco, take I-80 east, exiting on Highway 4 east. At Antioch, take Highway 160 north past the town of Ryde. Turn right at first available bridge, crossing over the canal, and then turn left on Levee Road. Drive through Walnut Grove. Go approximately 2 miles more to the town of Locke. Turn right into first road entering the settlement. Park and walk up main street.

› Lundberg Family Farms. 5370 Church St. (Richvale). ☎ 530/882-4551.

Monks eat brown rice. Lots of brown rice. Lundberg brown rice at that. Which is why we must pay homage to the Lundberg family, who grow the highest quality organic brown rice in the world. That's no small endorsement, as we've been connoisseurs of the stuff for over two decades. For the past sixty years the Lundberg family has been growing brown rice products in the fertile Sacramento Valley. When father Albert Lundberg left Nebraska during the dust bowl he arrived in Richvale committed to using farming techniques that cared for rather than ravaged the soil. Resisting the use of pesticides and herbicides all around him, Mr. Lundberg stuck to his guns and developed his land using the strictest organic farming principles. Needless to say, he was well ahead of his time. He passed on this legacy to his four sons, Wendell, Eldon, Homer, and Harlan. To this day, the large-scale organic farming practiced by the Lundberg brothers remains the industry standard. We like the Lundbergs. They run a feel-good corporate farm with a proper dose of ecologically correct attitude. And they operate according to good solid Christian values, without getting all preachy about it—one reason they've managed to remain popular in both the liberal natural-products industry and the mainstream marketplace. As many others no doubt agree, the Monks can say with confidence that the Lundberg brothers are "outstanding in their field." Call ahead. They give you a fascinating tour.

The Matador Hotel:
Satan Beware!

› **Matador Motel.** 1334 Esplanade (Chico). ☎ **530/342-7543.**

This classic fifties motel harbors a great deal of sentimental value to the Monks, because it is the site of the Great Breakdown of 1994. Back in the days when the Monks were driving the gas-guzzling, chronically broken Monkmobile, with groupies and angry girlfriends hot on our tails, we had the good sense to wait out a costly transmission repair by checking into room 31 of the Matador, across from the Chico Nut Factory. For well over a month we huddled inside from the pouring winter rains, writing a book and watching factory workers unload truckloads of nuts. As we soon learned, the Matador was not without its own nuts. Chief among them was a woman named Faith, who resided just a few doors down. Daughter of a late Washington D.C. insider, Faith was a wealthy widow who owned an enormous ranch and at least a half dozen dogs. Her room was lit like a Christmas tree with enough Jesus paraphernalia to make Mary Magdalene jealous. Each morning Faith would drive to the kennel, return with her dogs, and walk them around the motel for hours on end. Each evening she'd return them to the kennel. Rumor had it that unsavory conditions caused her husband's death, so she was a bit superstitious about returning to her sprawling ranch home. When she wasn't walking the dogs around the Matador she was walking one of her many personalities, one of whom took to shouting at Michael, "Satan Beware!!" This usually preceded a few hexes and crosses thrown up in his face.

The motel itself is pure Mission Revival, with arching porticos, red-tiled roofs, and faux bell towers. Near the street is a fair-size swimming pool surrounded by towering palms. The Holy Mother resides above an alcove. Velvet matador paintings hang in many rooms. On our return visit, Faith was still there. During a more recent unmedicated moment she apparently left her keys in the ignition and her car running for fear the engine would get cold. When a passerby helped himself to the car, she refused to call the police because "Jesus wouldn't have done that." Next door to the Matador is **Big Al's drive-in.** Big Al's has been serving up dirt-cheap hot dogs, hamburgers, fries, and malts for over forty years. It's red-and-white awning and bright yellow HAPPY BURGER sign were always a cheerful contrast to the winter gray skies. Big Al's was always busy. There were always lines. When we weren't hunkered down with the nuts at the Matador we were chowing down at Big friendly Al's, where nobody called us "Satan."

> **Neighborhood Church.** 2801 Notre Dame Blvd., at Hwy. 99 (Chico).
☎ 530/343-6006.

On the outskirts of Chico stands the wackiest church structure in California. This immense dome looks like either a UFO or a halved golf ball, depending on your perspective. Housing a nondenominational Christian congregation, the worshippers are anything but wacky. Get your picture taken, then hit the road.

The Neighborhood Church, Chico

> **Oroville Dam.** Kelly Ridge Rd. (Oroville). ☎ **530/534-2306.**

California boasts both the tallest dam in the United States and the largest earthen dam in the world, the latter located right here in "Horroville," home of obese geriatrics, macroneurotic hypochondriacs, and right-wing gun-totting rednecks. Though the Oroville Dam's earthen wall doesn't hold an architectural candle to such concrete wonders as the Hoover Dam, the sheer magnitude of water contained in its 15,500 acres is impressive. It also ranks as the number-one place to not be standing in case of an earthquake. It has more seismic monitors than anywhere on earth. And let me tell you, when The Big One rolls, that is gonna be one hell of a tidal wave crashing down the hill. Fed by three branches of the Feather River, water from this lake travels by aqueducts throughout central California. Climb the 47-foot viewing tower and pray to Ohsawa that those monitors are doing their job.

> **Shasta Dam.** 16349 Shasta Dam Blvd. (Redding). ☎ **530/275-4463.** North of Redding on I-5 take Shasta Dam exit. Head west 4 miles. Turn right on Lake Blvd. Follow to dam.

To get the full monty of Mount Shasta you simply go to Shasta Dam and behold the shimmering reflection of Mount Shasta across more than 35 miles of rippling water. Lake Shasta stands behind the second largest dam in the United States. Finished in 1945, the dam harnesses the Sacramento, McCloud, and Pit rivers, feeding the state's largest hydroelectric generating plant. Big, better, biggest! We love these big toys. You'll take a nifty tour down into the bowels of the dam, descending 43 stories on an elevator to visit the power plant. Most of the Sacramento Valley is irrigated from the canals that branch off this water. Bobbing in the lake are countless houseboats, pleasure craft, jet skis, and fishermen. It's crass. It's big. It's man-made and plentiful. How Californian can you get?

>index

Page numbers in *italics* refer to maps.

About the Authors

A mutant of Omaha, an adult child of Catholic Republicans, and two-time state debate champion, **Jim Crotty** is one of the most innovative talents Nebraska has ever produced (or at least he thinks so). For twelve years Jim has traveled America in the wildly painted Monkmobile, co-authoring *Monk* (the world's only mobile magazine), pioneering "dashboard publishing," selling thousands of ads from pay phones, revolutionizing the "perzine" or "personal zine" (where the editors are the prime subjects—a form otherwise known as narcissism), all while acting as the publicity machine for the mobile monastery. Jim authored the slanguistic classic *How to Talk American* (Houghton Mifflin, 1997), and co-authored the *USA Phrasebook* (Lonely Planet, 1995), *Mad Monks on the Road* (Simon & Schuster, 1993), *The Mad Monks' Guide to New York City* (Macmillan, 1999), and the *Monks' Guide to New York CD ROM* (Monk Media, 1998). He dreams of holding a steady, high-paying job in corporate America some day, but will invariably be kept from that goal by all those who deeply appreciate his seriously skewed approach to life, death, and real work.

Michael Lane grew up in trailer parks throughout the South, landed in the Haight-Ashbury scene at 17, rode the wave of the counterculture, and for the last several decades has chased life relentlessly down the road. As co-author of *Monk* magazine and the epic *Mad Monks on the Road* (Simon & Schuster, 1993) and *The Mad Monks' Guide to New York City* (Macmillan, 1999), Michael's past twelve years—including his inimitable encounters with cultural misfits, rebels, and ordinary folk—have been documented in excruciatingly honest detail. His book *Pink Highways* (Carol Publishing, 1995) chronicled his outlandish pre-Monk adventures, including a near-death experience before a Morroccan firing squad and a marathon evening held at gunpoint under the spell of Jimi Hendrix. Mike currently lives in Los Angeles with his muse and partner, Jim Crotty, though next year he may be living in your backyard.

Jim and Mike have been prominently featured in most national and international media, including *Time, Newsweek,* the *New York Times,* the *Los Angeles Times, Wired News, Rolling Stone, USA Today, Der Stern* (Germany), *Brutus* (Japan), and *Panorama* (Italy), and have appeared on ABC's *Good Morning America, MTV News, CBS News, the BBC, CNN, CBS Street Stories,* and NPR's *Morning Edition* and *Whadya' Know?*

GET MONKED

Let the journey continue! For the full-tilt Monk experience we encourage all Monks and Monkettes who have grand illusions about the great highway to order our other works.

How to Talk American, by Jim Crotty (Houghton Mifflin), $12

Pink Highways, by Michael Lane (Carol Publishing), $20

Mad Monks' Guide to New York City (Macmillan Travel), $16

Mad Monks' Guide to New York CD-ROM (A multimedia companion to the NYC guidebook), $10

You may order by calling 212-465-3231, or by mail to 101 West 23rd St., #2322, NY, NY 10011 (MC/Visa accepted; includes P&H; checks payable to Monk)

Visit us online at **www.monk.com**